Roger Concept Tailor Co.

Cavin Cheung
張 嘉 耀

Room 504, 5/F, Takshing House, 20 Des Voeux Road Central, Hong Kong.
香港中環德輔道中 20 號德成大廈 5 字樓 504 室
Tel: (852) 2537 8449   Fax: (852) 2537 2448   Mobile: (852) 6136 3661
E-mail: rogerconcept@yahoo.com.hk
www.rogerconcept.com

"All you've got to do is decide to go
and the hardest part is over.

So go!"

TONY WHEELER, COFOUNDER – LONELY PLANET

請送我到
Please Drive Me To

花園道
山頂纜車站

Garden Road Peak Tram
Station

Contents

Plan Your Trip   4

Explore Hong Kong   62

Understand Hong Kong   281

Survival Guide   315

Hong Kong Maps   360

Left: Tian Tan Buddha (p193)

Above: Grand Lisboa Casino (designed by Dennis Lau and Ng Chun Man; p250)

Right: Peak Tram (p84)

Welcome to Hong Kong

This enigmatic city of soaring towers, ancient rituals and action movies is safe, friendly and wonderfully well organised.

Neighbourhoods & Islands

The tantalising neighbourhoods and curious islands that make up Hong Kong are a sensory delight awaiting exploration. You can find yourself swaying along on a double-decker tramcar one moment, then cheering with the hordes at the city-centre horse races, or simply gazing out at the magnificent harbour. Over 70% of Hong Kong is mountains and sprawling country parks, some also home to geological gems. Escape the city limits on one of the world's best transport systems and spend your day wandering in a Song-dynasty village, hiking surf-beaten beaches or scouring for sea shards on a deserted island.

Cuisine

If there were a mosaic of all the smells and flavours of all the restaurants in Hong Kong, it would be close to a food nirvana. The city that lives to eat is home to many a demon in the kitchen, whether the deliciousness in the pot is Cantonese, Shanghainese, Vietnamese, French, Japanese or Italian. Whatever your preference, your gastronomic curiosities and desires will likely be sated in Hong Kong – over a bowl of noodles with beef brisket, a basket of vegetarian dim sum, your first-ever stinky tofu, a plate of freshly steamed prawns fragrant with garlic or the culinary creations of the latest celebrity chef.

Shopping

From ready-to-wear Chinese jackets to bespoke kitchen knives, the sheer range and variety of products on Hong Kong's shelves is mind-bending. Every whim, need and pocket is catered for in true enterprising spirit by an equally dazzling number of venues – swanky malls where the wealthy hang out, chic street-level boutiques, bazaars flaunting garments or gadgetry, warehouses chock full of furniture, and a colourful mix of markets where you can haggle to your heart's content. The city has no sales tax so prices are generally attractive to visitors.

Culture

Beyond the glass and steel of Hong Kong's commercial persona, the city also boasts a vibrant cultural scene that features the eclectic influences of its Chinese roots, colonial connections and a wondrous pool of homegrown talent. Here, you're just as likely to find yourself applauding at Asia's top film festival, as you are joining in dawn taichi or reading the couplets of a local poet to the drumbeat of a dragon boat. Culture could also mean indie music under the stars, an art walk, your first Cantonese opera – not to mention the exhibitions and events staged year-round at the many museums and concert halls.

Why I Love Hong Kong

By Piera Chen, Author

I love Hong Kong because it has a complexity that eludes definition, sometimes even by its own people. I can be soul-searching near the Chinese border, lunching with Sikhs at a Sikh temple, splurging on a set of kitchen knives, arguing with bohos about the merits of a dress – all within five hours – followed by a night of Cantonese opera, tango or karaoke, anywhere I choose. Hong Kong is so intense and so full of possibilities that I'm glad there's the Rule of Law (and an awesome transport system) to stop it from whirling into chaos. Though even then it might be a sweet chaos – who knows? But for me, Hong Kong's pretty darn perfect.

For more about our authors, see p384.

Top: Hong Kong Island skyline from Victoria Peak (p84)

Hong Kong's
Top 16

Star Ferry from Kowloon to Hong Kong Island (p69)

1 A floating piece of Hong Kong heritage and a sightseeing bargain, the legendary Star Ferry was founded in 1880 and plies the calm waters of Victoria Harbour in the service of families, students, office workers, boat buffs and tourists. At only $2.50, the 15-minute ride with views of skyscrapers marching up jungle-clad hills must be one of the world's best-value cruises. While the vista is more dramatic when you're Island-bound, the art deco Kowloon pier, resembling a finger pointing at the Island, is arguably more charming.

◉ *Hong Kong Island: Central*

The Peak (p84)

2 Rising above the financial heart of Hong Kong Island, Victoria Peak offers superlative views of the city and the mountainous countryside beyond. Ride the hair-raising Peak Tram (in operation since 1888) to the cooler climes at the top as a teeming mass of moneyed skyscrapers and choked apartment blocks unfolds below. At dusk Victoria Harbour glitters like the Milky Way in a sci-fi movie poster as the lights come on in this astonishing metropolis. A view to die for!

VIEWING PLATFORM, VICTORIA PEAK

◉ *Hong Kong Island: the Peak & the Northwest*

JOHN SONES SINGING BOWL MEDIA/GETTY IMAGES ©

Markets *(p148)*

3 Mong Kok with its eclectic mix of speciality markets is your best bet for a rewarding sprawl crawl. The Tung Choi St Market/Ladies' Market (p148) has a mile-long wardrobe of clothes which range from 'I Love HK' tees and football jerseys, to granny swimwear and sexy lingerie; the flower market sells exotic seeds and gardening tools alongside buckets of fragrant florals; and the goldfish market has stalls showcasing these exotic creatures in softly humming, UV-lit tanks. Complementing these are vertical markets such as a multistorey computer mall, and a mobile phone and gadget lover's heaven. JADE MARKET (P161)

🔒 *Kowloon*

Man Mo Temple *(p85)*

4 Ditch the Soho watering holes and experience Chinese folk religiosity in this atmospheric 19th-century institution. Forever wreathed in thick sandalwood smoke from the slow-burning incense coils, the popular temple is dedicated to Man and Mo, the gods of literature and war. Formerly a cultural and political focal point for the Chinese community, the dimly lit space now commands a much bigger following beyond obedient students and assorted street fighters, as the public come to perform age-old rites and have their fortunes told. HANGING INCENSE SPIRALS INSIDE MAN MO TEMPLE

👁 *Hong Kong Island: the Peak & the Northwest*

Wan Chai Dining *(p113)*

5 If you were to hurl yourself, eyes closed, into a random neighbourhood eatery and expect to emerge smacking your lips, you'd stand the best chance if you were in Wan Chai. The district is home to a great many restaurants suiting a range of pocket sizes. Regional Chinese cooking, European cuisines, Asian kitchens, East-West fusion, classy, midrange, hole in the wall... Just name your craving and head on down to the Wanch; you're certain to find it there. DIM SUM DINERS

🍴 *Hong Kong Island: Wan Chai & the Northeast*

Temple Street Night Market (p139)

6 Beneath the glare of naked bulbs, hundreds of stalls sell a vast array of booty, from bric-a-brac to clothes, luggage and even sex toys. You can browse for handy gadgets or quirky souvenirs, and test your bargaining skills. Nearby, fortune-tellers beckon in English from dimly lit tents, and Cantonese opera singers strike a pose *en plein air*. If you're hungry, the many open-air stalls offer snacks or a full seafood meal. Sure, it's touristy, but its mesmerising and impenetrable aura makes everyone – including locals – feel like a welcome visitor.

⊙ *Kowloon*

Hong Kong Wetland Park (p171)

7 Surreally nestled under an imposing arc of apartment towers, this 61-hectare ecological park in crowded Tin Shui Wai is a swampy haven of biodiversity. This is urban/nature juxtaposition at its best – and curiously most harmonious. Precious ecosystems in this far-flung yet easily accessible part of the New Territories provide tranquil habitats for a range of waterfowl and other wildlife. Forget the man-made world for a moment and delve into a landscape of mangroves, rivers and fish-filled ponds. WALKING TRAIL, HONG KONG WETLAND PARK

⊙ *New Territories*

Shopping *(p159)*

8 An afternoon's visit to Tsim Sha Tsui's shopping quarters should yield a few gems. If you're seeking Chinese-style gifts, comb the streets near the southern end of the area for that silk gown, teapot or trinket. If glamour is what you're after, join the uberwealthy mainland tourists for marathon card-swiping in the designer stores and luxury malls stretching for a kilometre along Canton Rd. Want something unique? Head over to Granville Rd for that supersized orange blazer or a micromall nearby for those asymmetrical earrings and thigh-high boots. SHOPPING CENTRE, KOWLOON TONG

🔒 *Kowloon*

Happy Valley Races (p111)

9 Every Wednesday night the city horseracing track in Happy Valley comes alive, with eight electrifying races and an accompanying carnival of food and beer. You can try your luck at betting or simply enjoy the collective exhilaration and the thunder of ironed hooves. Races were first held here in the 19th century by European merchants who imported stocky stallions from Mongolia, which they rode themselves. Now there are races every week except in the sweltering months of July and August, when the beasts and their jockeys retreat into air-conditioned comfort.

👁 *Hong Kong Island: Wan Chai & the Northeast*

Tian Tan Buddha (p193)

10 A favourite with local day trippers and foreign visitors alike, the biggest bronze outdoor seated Buddha in the world lords over the western hills of Lantau. Visit this serenely mammoth statue via the scenic Ngong Ping 360 cable-car ride. Tuck into some monk food at the popular vegetarian restaurant in the Po Lin Monastery below. Buddha's Birthday in May is a lively time to visit this important pilgrimage site.

👁 *Outlying Islands*

Riding the Trams (p321)

11 Nicknamed 'ding dings' by locals, trams have been sedately chugging back and forth between the Eastern and Western districts of the Island since 1904. A century later the world's largest fleet of still-operating double-decker tramcars continues to negotiate pathways through the city's heavy traffic. Board a 'ding ding' – Hong Kong's low-carbon transport option – and watch the city unfold like a carousel of images as you relax and ponder tomorrow's itinerary. It's the fun option, too: high fives between passengers on passing trams are not unheard of.

DOUBLE-DECKER TRAM ON QUEENS ROAD CENTRAL

🚶 *Transport*

Tsim Sha Tsui East Promenade *(p138)*

12 Gleaming skyscrapers lined up between emerald hills and a deep-blue harbour with criss-crossing boats – Hong Kong's best-known imagery is of the Island but, like a hologram, its beauty only shimmers into view when you're looking from the Tsim Sha Tsui East Promenade in Kowloon, especially after sundown. Home to windswept museums and a world-class concert venue, the promenade offers pockets of culture as you stroll its length, as intimate with one of the world's best views as you can get without falling into the water.

◉ *Kowloon*

Exploring Lamma (p194)

13 If there were a soundtrack for the island of Lamma, it would be reggae. The island has a laid-back vibe that attracts herb-growers, musicians and New Age therapists from a rainbow of cultures. Village stores stock Prosecco, and island mongrels respond to commands in French. Soak up the vibes in the village, and hike to the nearest beach, your unlikely compass three coal-fired plants against the skyline, looking more trippy than grim. Spend the afternoon chilling by the beach, and then, in the glow of the day's final rays, head back for steamed prawns, fried calamari and beer by the pier. BOATS AND SEAFOOD RESTAURANTS, SOK KWU WAN (P195)

🏃 *Outlying Islands*

Hiking the Hong Kong Trail (p60)

14 Right on the city's doorstep, the Hong Kong Trail transports you into emerald hills, secluded woodland and lofty paths that afford sumptuous views of the rugged south and (eventually) glimpses of its wavy shore once you've tackled the formidable Dragon's Back ridge. Starting from the Peak, the 50km route snakes across the entire length of Hong Kong Island, past picturesque reservoirs, WWII battlefields and cobalt bays. Spread over five country parks, this delightful trail invites both easy perambulations and harder hikes. HONG KONG TRAIL, SHEK O COUNTRY PARK

🏃 *Sports & Activities*

Walled Villages *(p166)*

15 Let Yuen Long's walled villages take you back over half a millennium ago, to a wild and windy time when piracy was rife along the South China coast. Isolated from China's administrative heart, Hong Kong, with its treacherous shores and mountainous terrain, was an excellent hideout for pirates. Its earliest inhabitants built villages with high walls, some guarded by cannons, to protect themselves. Inside these walls today you'll see ancestral halls, courtyards, pagodas, temples, wells and ancient farming implements – vestiges of Hong Kong's precolonial history, all carefully restored. ANCESTRAL HALL, PING SHAN HERITAGE TRAIL (P166)

⊙ *New Territories*

Ruins of the Church of St Paul, Macau *(p233)*

16 Macau's Eiffel Tower and Statue of Liberty is a dramatic gate perched on a hill 26m above sea level, in the middle of the city. A sweep of stairs with landings and balustrades lead you to it, and then to nowhere. Once part of a Jesuit church (c 17th century) that was destroyed in a fire, the facade, with fine carvings and detailed engravings featuring Christian, Chinese and Japanese influences, is a captivating historical fragment and a document in granite of Macau's unique Mediterrasian culture.

⊙ *Macau*

What's New

New Hipstervilles

Soaring rent has exiled artists and independents to the western and eastern ends of Hong Kong Island. Sheung Wan and Western District are fast gaining a reputation as a bohoville with the opening of new restaurants, coffee shops and art galleries (see p96). On Island East, Chai Wan's warehouses have been turned into art spaces, which are featured in the annual 'Art East Island' open-studio and exhibition event (see p113).

Rustic European Food

Sophisticated midrange eateries have sprung up in Central and districts further west, serving rustic French or Italian dishes (including bone marrow and sweetbread) to adventurous but discerning eaters. (p72)

Asia Society Hong Kong Centre

Hong Kong's oldest remaining explosives magazine morphed into this stunning centre, which houses an excellent gallery, restaurant, theatre and bookstore. (p107)

Yau Ma Tei Theatre

This historic theatre and old pumping station reopened in 2012 after extensive restoration works. It's now a performance and rehearsal venue for Cantonese opera. Take a peek even if nothing's on. (p146)

Heritage Hotels

A pirate-battling police station in Tai O fishing village has become a boutique hotel (p208); while the 96-year-old English rose, Helena May is now a hostel (p269).

Live Music

Hong Kong's live-music scene is thriving like never before; there's the annual festival of indie music, Clockenflap (www.clockenflap.com), and the proliferation of dives such as Hidden Agenda. (p159)

Dance

Tango, salsa and swing are big in Hong Kong, with socials happening at least once a week and anyone is welcome to join in. (p45)

Foo Tak Building

This tenement building in Wan Chai houses an underground bookstore, indie publishers and artist studios. It has been a happening place for the past few years. (p124)

Ritz-Carlton

Soaring 500m above ground level, the highest hotel on earth (at the time of writing) came into being in 2011, offering the lap of five-star luxury to those who can afford it. (p276)

Mandarin's House

In Macau, the elegant 19th-century ancestral home of a famous author-merchant reopened two years ago after a facelift; one of the most delightful labyrinths to lose your way in. (p239)

For more recommendations and reviews, see **lonelyplanet.com/ hongkong**

Need to Know

Currency

Hong Kong dollar ($) for Hong Kong and Pataca (MOP$) for Macau.

Language

Cantonese is spoken in Hong Kong and Macau. English is also widely used.

Visas

Not required for visitors from the US, Australia, New Zealand, Canada, the EU, Israel and South Africa for stays of up to 30 days.

Money

ATMs widely available. Credit cards accepted in most hotels and restaurants; some budget places only take cash.

Mobile Phones

Set your phone to roaming or buy a local SIM card.

Time

Hong Kong Time (GMT/UTC plus eight hours)

Tourist Information

Hong Kong Tourism Board (Map p378; Star Ferry Concourse, Tsim Sha Tsui; ☺8am-8pm) and Macau Government Tourist Office (Map p240; Largo do Senado; ☺9am-6pm).

Your Daily Budget

The following are average costs per day for Hong Kong; Macau is about 20% to 30% cheaper.

Budget less than $600

➡ Guesthouse $130–$350

➡ *Cha chaan tangs* (tea cafes) and *dai pai dongs* (food stalls) for food $60-$100

➡ Museum Wednesdays (free); night markets (free); horse races ($10)

➡ Bus, tram, Star Ferry for transport

Midrange $600–$1600

➡ Double room (hostel or budget hotel) $520–$880

➡ Chinese dinner with three dishes $300

➡ Drinks and live music $400

Top end over $1600

➡ Boutique or four-star hotel double room $2000

➡ Dinner at top Chinese restaurant from $800

➡ Cantonese opera ticket $400

Advance Planning

Two months before Check dates of Chinese festivals; book accommodation and tickets for major performances and concerts; book a table at a top restaurant.

One month before Check listings and book tickets for fringe festivals and live entertainment; research dining options and book a table at a popular restaurant.

Two weeks before Book harbour cruises, nature tours; sign up for email alerts from entertainment and events organisers.

One week before Check the weather forecast.

Useful Websites

➡ **Lonely Planet** (www.lonelyplanet.com/hong-kong, www.lonelyplanet.com/china/macau)

➡ **Discover Hong Kong** (www.discoverhongkong.com)

➡ **Urbtix** (www.urbtix.hk)

➡ **Time Out Hong Kong** (www.timeout.com.hk)

➡ **Hong Kong Observatory** (www.hko.gov.hk)

➡ **WOM Guide** (www.womguide.com)

WHEN TO GO

With moderate temperatures and clear skies, October to early December is the best time to visit. June to August is hot, humid and rainy. Beware of typhoons in September.

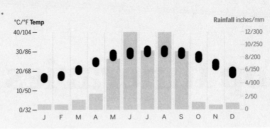

Arriving in Hong Kong

Hong Kong International Airport Airport Express MTR train to city centre from 5.50am to 1.15am, $90 to $100; buses to various parts of Hong Kong from 6am to midnight, $20 to $48; taxi to city centre $230 to $300.

Lo Wu and Lok Ma Chau MTR train to city centre from 6am to midnight, $30 to $45.

Macau Ferry Terminal MTR train to city centre from 6am to midnight, $4 to $11; taxi $20 to $60.

China Ferry Terminal MTR train to city centre from 6am to midnight, $4 to $11; taxi $20 to $70.

For much more on **arrival**, see p316.

Getting Around

A prepaid Octopus Card can be used on most forms of public transport in Hong Kong. For shorter stays, buy a one-day or three-day pass for unlimited rides on the MTR (available at any MTR station).

➡ **MTR** Hong Kong's subway and train system covers most of the city and is the easiest way to get around. Most lines run 6am to midnight.

➡ **Bus** Extensive network and ideal for short rides. Most bus lines run from 6am to midnight.

➡ **Tram** Runs on the northern strip of Hong Kong Island. Slow, but great views. Runs from 6am to midnight.

➡ **Ferry** Star Ferry connects Hong Kong Island and Kowloon through the scenic harbour. Runs from 7.30am to 10.20pm. More modern ferry fleets run between Central and outlying islands.

For much more on **getting around**, see p319.

Sleeping

Hong Kong offers a full range of accommodation, from closet-sized rooms to palatial suites. Rooms are relatively expensive by Asian standards, though generally still cheaper than in the US and Europe.

Most hotels are on Hong Kong Island between Central and Causeway Bay, and on either side of Nathan Rd in Kowloon, where you'll also find more budget places. During low seasons prices fall sharply, particularly the midrange and top-end options, when you can get discounts of up to 60% if you book online.

Useful Websites

➡ **Discover Hong Kong** (www.discoverhongkong.com) Provides hotel search based on location and facilities.

➡ **Asia Travel** (www.hongkonghotels.com) Has better deals than others.

➡ **Hotel.com** (www.hotels.com/Hong-Kong) Specialises in cheap lodging.

For more on **sleeping**, see p263

SMOKING

All indoor areas of eateries are now technically smoke-free. Smokers are seeking out restaurants with unsheltered outdoor spaces where the ban does not apply. In districts such as Soho, where restaurants tend to have open fronts, customers often step outside to get their fix.

Top Itineraries

Day One

The Peak & the Northwest (p82)

 Catch the legendary Peak Tram up to **Victoria Peak** for stunning views of the city. Then descend and walk to **Sheung Wan**, checking out the shopping options along the way. Stop at **Man Mo Temple** for a taste of history and explore the burgeoning community on **Tai Ping Shan Street**.

> **Lunch** Hollywood Rd (p90) is bursting at the seams with restaurants.

Kowloon (p135)

Take the **Star Ferry** to Kowloon. Enjoy the views along **Tsim Sha Tsui East Promenade** and savour your stroll to the **Museum of History** for some context to your day's impressions.

> **Dinner** Yè Shanghai (p154) serves modern, delicious Shanghainese cuisine.

The Peak & the Northwest (p82)

 After dinner in **Tsim Sha Tsui**, take the metro to **Soho** for drinks and dancing.

Day Two

Wan Chai & the Northeast (p104)

 Embrace (man-made) nature at the lovely **Hong Kong Park**, then head over to Queen's Rd East to explore the sights and streets of **old Wan Chai**. Tram it to Causeway Bay for homewares gift shopping at **G.O.D**.

> **Lunch** Irori (p116) is fabulously Japanese.

Kowloon (p135)

Browse for souvenirs at **Chinese Arts & Crafts**. Then relax and people-watch at **Middle Road Children's Playground**, before taking afternoon tea in style at the **Peninsula**. Bus it north to **Yau Ma Tei**, where you can check out the **Tin Hau Temple**, **Jade Market** and traditional shops along **Shanghai Street**.

> **Dinner** Temple Street Night Market (p142) for cheap food under the stars.

Kowloon (p135)

 Have your fortune told and catch some Cantonese opera at **Temple Street Night Market**.

Day Three

Aberdeen & the South (p127)

 Bus it to **Aberdeen** for a cruise on the charming **Aberdeen Harbour**, then head over to **Ap Lei Chau** to check out the indoor **wet market** in the old town. Follow with shopping (for bargain designer furniture and clothing) at **Horizon Plaza** and a late lunch inside a spacious and attractive furniture shop.

 Lunch Tree Cafe (p132) for salads, sandwiches and coffee.

Kowloon (p135)

Spend the rest of the afternoon and early evening admiring temples in New Kowloon: the Taoist **Sik Sik Yuen Wong Tai Sin Temple** and the Buddhist **Chi Lin Nunnery**.

Dinner Chi Lin Vegetarian (p156) for tasty Chinese vegetarian.

Kowloon (p135)

Still in New Kowloon, head to the Ritz Carlton for stellar drinks at **Ozone**, the world's highest bar, then, beset with the munchies, indulge in late-night dim sum at **One Dim Sum**.

Day Four

Kowloon (p135)

 Start your fourth day with a **taichi class** by the Tsim Sha Tsui waterfront. Boats to **Macau** are just around the corner at the **China Ferry Terminal** – why not hop aboard?

 Lunch Clube Militar de Macau (p246) for great Portuguese wining and dining.

Macau (p232)

Explore the sights around the **Largo do Senado**. Walk along Rua Central through much of the Unesco-listed **Historic Centre of Macau**, including the **ruins of the Church of St Paul**. Shop for souvenirs at **Macau Creations** at the foot of the steps. Then cab it to Northern Macau Peninsula to stroll among the designer shops and historic sites in the atmospheric **St Lazarus District**.

Dinner António (p258) dishes up sumptuous Portuguese classics.

Macau (p232)

Make your way back to the Macau Peninsula to play the tables or sip cocktails at **MGM Grand Macau** before catching the ferry back to Hong Kong.

If You Like...

Views

Victoria Peak Pilgrims the world over come here for unbeatable views of the city. (p84)

Tsim Sha Tsui Harbourfront Lap up Hong Kong's iconic skyline from the water's edge. (p138)

Bus 6 Jump on bus 6 (the most scenic bus route) for a white-knuckle ride around the beautiful southern bays. (p130)

High Island Reservoir Climb the dramatic East Dam to survey this engineering feat and the

polygonal rock formations below it. (p188)

Tung Ping Chau Mother Nature's flight of fancy brought 'layered cakes' of stunning sedimentary rocks to this remote island. (p187)

Lion Rock Visit the city's all-seeing guardian in Kowloon for its cross-harbour study of population density. (p183)

Tsing Ma Bridge Inspect this marvellous suspension bridge and the lush landscape surrounding it. (p156)

Pak Nai Drink in the sunset at this westernmost edge of Hong Kong. (p172)

Modern Architecture

HSBC Building The Norman Foster masterpiece commands a special place in the city's hearts and minds. (p68)

Bank of China Some scoff at IM Pei's ingenious design as a futuristic meat cleaver. (p70)

MICHAEL MCQUEEN/GETTY IMAGES ©

Skyscrapers including the Bank of China Tower (middle), Hong Kong Island Central

23

Old Bank of China Six decades on, this art deco gem still exudes terrific modernity. (p70)

Jardine House Hong Kong's first true skyscraper is otherwise known as the 'House of 1000 Arseholes'. (p71)

Asia Society Hong Kong Centre A beautiful roof garden grows out of an overgrown former military site. (p107)

Two International Finance Centre A wannabe Angkor Wat? Or the ultimate phallic temple to Mammon? What do you think? (p71)

Hong Kong Convention & Exhibition Centre A stingray washed up on an artificial island. (p107)

Hong Kong Cultural Centre Why are there no windows in the greatest location of all? (p142)

Parks & Gardens

Victoria Peak Garden The peak above the Peak. This landscaped haven of calm commands untrammelled views of the city. (p84)

Kowloon Walled City Park The former sin city par excellence reincarnated as a traditional Jiangnan (southern Yangtze) garden. (p147)

Nan Lian Garden A splendid Tang-style garden adorned with a pagoda, tea pavilion, koi pond, Buddhist pines and sedimentary cloudlike boulders. (p141)

Hong Kong Zoological & Botanical Gardens Enveloped by skyscrapers, this stronghold of nature has graced the city since 1871. (p70)

Hong Kong Park A rainforest-like aviary and the city's oldest colonial building lie in this heavily man-made leisure space. (p106)

Ocean Park The marine life is the best draw of this highly popular amusement park. (p129)

Astropark Fitted with Chinese and Western astronomical instruments, this little-known park is for the stargazer in you. (p188)

Kowloon Park The overworked urban lung throbs over the peninsula's artery that is Nathan Rd. (p144)

Unusual Eats

French toast, Hong Kong style Probably the best-loved indigenous comfort food. Heart attack on a plate! Liberally served in any *cha chaan tang*. (p133)

Snake soup A winter favourite trusted for its warming properties. (p92)

Ox Tongue Elastic and generously absorbent. A perfect match with tomato spaghetti. (p156)

Chiu Chow pig's blood with chives A timeless delicacy in the form of jiggly russet cubes. (p93)

Roast pigeon Flying rats have never tasted so crispy yet tender. A deep-flavoured local alternative to Peking duck. (p184)

Cow innards Cheap and nutritious, they simmer away in vats of glorious stock behind steamy noodle-shop windows. (p154)

Turtle jelly A bittersweet Chinese herbal triumph (turtle substances are spared these days). Ladies eat it for good skin. (p90)

Yin Yeung The quintessential Hong Kong concoction of tea mixed with coffee. (p91)

For more top Hong Kong spots, see:
➡ Eating (p34)
➡ Drinking & Nightlife (p43)
➡ Entertainment (p48)
➡ Shopping (p51)
➡ Sports & Activities (p57)

PLAN YOUR TRIP IF YOU LIKE...

Deer penis According to Chinese medicine, wine made from this ancient Viagra is an effective remedy for sports injuries. (p91)

Hiking

Sai Kung East Country Emerge from the luxuriant mountains to find the idyllic Tai Long Wan beach. (p186)

Dragon's Back A popular see-the-sea ramble that undulates to the somnolent village of Shek O. (p131)

Lamma Island Take a gentle 4km hike across the leafy island to the embrace of waterside seafood restaurants. (p194)

Hong Kong Cemetery Wander through this hilly, overgrown, deeply atmospheric resting place of Hong Kong's good and naughty. (p109)

Pok Fu Lam Reservoir to the Peak A picturesque ascent past dense forests, waterfalls and military ruins. (p84)

Ng Tung Chai Waterfalls Pack a picnic and aim for the waterfalls amid the lush greenery. (p174)

Tai Mo Shan Several hiking trails thread up and around Hong Kong's tallest mountain. (p169)

Colonial & East-meets-West Architecture

Former Legislative Council Building The most imposing colonial edifice left in town. (p71)

Government House Residence of Hong Kong's British governors between 1855 and 1997. An elegant, indubitably rare Georgian-Japanese hybrid. (p70)

Hong Kong City Hall Classic Bauhaus. An ode to modernism. The place to get married in Hong Kong. (p70)

Tai Fu Tai Mansion A valuable fusion of East-meets-West interior designs for the old scholar-gentry class. (p173)

King Yin Lei Clark Gable's *Solider of Fortune* was filmed in this magnificent Chinese Renaissance-style mansion in 1955. (p89)

Central Police Station & Central Magistracy The stern cousins trace the history of law enforcement in Hong Kong. (p86)

Kam Tong Hall The grand Edwardian mansion previously housed the Mormons and is now home to Dr Sun Yat-sen Museum. (p87)

St John's Cathedral Criticised for blighting the colony's landscape when it was first built, today it's an oft-forgotten reminder of dear old Blighty. (p71)

Béthanie Two octagonal cow sheds plus a neo-Gothic chapel equal a new performing-arts space. (p130)

Shek Lo This Eurasian mansion with a classy rounded balcony resembles a minifort. (p174)

Festivals

Tin Hau's Birthday Don't miss the colourful fishing boats procession to the 'Big Temple' in Joss House Bay. (p189)

Dragon Boat Festival Rock to the thumping drum beats as dragon boats roar down water courses in races around the city. (p26)

Hungry Ghost Festival Traditional Chinese theatre is performed in public playgrounds to entertain underworld visitors during their month-long holiday. (p26)

Mid-Autumn Festival An exhilarating fire dragon slithers through Tai Hang for three nights under the poetic full moon. (p112)

Cheung Chau Bun Festival Get up close and personal with the quirky islanders. (p211)

Chinese New Year The most significant occasion on the Chinese cultural calendar. Victoria Park in Causeway Bay erupts in a sea of colour and fragrance during the annual Chinese New Year flower market. (p109)

Hong Kong International Film Festival Action time for cinema buffs and casual moviegoers alike. (p25)

Hong Kong Arts Festival The city's premier cultural event showcases Asia's top talents alongside artists from all over the world. (p25)

Traditional Culture

Tai O Visit the stilt-houses in Hong Kong's southwestern corner for a glimpse of the city's fishing past. (p202)

Walled villages Dotted around the New Territories, they preserve traces of an old, agricultural way of life. (p174)

Folk voodoo In full swing every March after the first (mythological) thunder of the year rouses the animal world. (p109)

Morning taichi in a park Get out of bed and join the grannies for some meditative 'shadow boxing'. (p144)

Martial arts Learn from kung fu masters in Kowloon Park every Sunday afternoon. Gratis. (p144)

Cantonese opera The endangered art is conserved at Sunbeam Theatre and the restored Yau Ma Tei Theatre. (p123 and p146)

Lion dance Expect lots of it during Chinese New Year and at the bigger Tin Hau birthday celebrations. (p191)

Month by Month

February

The marquee of clammy clouds may seal up the city in perfect hibernation mode but nothing can dampen the spirits around the most important festival on the Chinese cultural calendar.

Chinese New Year

Vast flower markets herald the beginning of this best-loved traditional Chinese festival. Wear red and be blessed at Wong Tai Sin Temple. Find your spot by Victoria Harbour and savour the fireworks spectacle.

Spring Lantern Festival

Valentines will be busy this month as a colourful lantern festival coinciding with the first full moon marks the end of the New Year celebrations and a day for lovers.

Hong Kong Arts Festival

Lasting five to eight weeks, Hong Kong's premier cultural event (www.hk.artsfestival.org) scintillates with a feast of music, performing arts and popular entertainment, ranging from classical fare to innovative art forms, by hundreds of local and international talents.

Hong Kong Marathon

In 2012 a record-breaking 70,000 athletes competed in this top Asian marathon (www.hkmarathon.com). The annual event also includes a half-marathon, a 10km race and a wheelchair race.

March

Pleasant weather returns with steadily rising temperatures – though humidity levels can get very high – as spring blossoms glow across the city.

'Beat the Little Man'

Witness folk sorcery performed by literally slaphappy old ladies under Canal Rd Flyover in Wan Chai or at Yau Ma Tei's Tin Hau Temple. Armed with high heels, they dish out rhyming curses to petty villains in the world.

Hong Kong Artwalk

Sixty-plus art galleries in Central, Soho, Wan Chai, Happy Valley and Aberdeen throw open their doors for a one-night experience (www.hongkongartwalk.com). Viewers will be served drinks and nibbles as they raise money for charity.

Hong Kong International Film Festival

For two weeks every year, this four-decade-old staple in the local arts calendar (it sometimes runs into early April) features the latest Asian cinema among the 240 plus films it screens from around the world (www.hkiff.org.hk).

Hong Kong Flower Show

For approximately 10 days, Victoria Park turns into a

colourful sea of fragrant floral displays as horticulturalists from over 20 countries experiment with their green fingers.

🏃 Hong Kong Sevens

Hong Kong's most famous sporting event – and probably its most original, for the Rugby Sevens was invented here in 1975 – this eternally popular tournament promises fierce competition, as well as a reliable glut of carnivalesque partying from the fans (www.hksevens.com.hk).

May

The city steams up, especially in the urban areas, as the long summer months begin. The first heavy showers of the year purify as religious celebrations thrive.

🎎 Birthday of Tin Hau

A festival dedicated to the patroness of fisherfolk and one of the harbour city's most popular deities. Key celebrations include a colourful floats parade in Yuen Long and traditional rites at the 'Big Temple' in Joss House Bay.

🎎 Cheung Chau Bun Festival

This unique, week-long festival on Cheung Chau climaxes on Buddha's birthday when local children 'float' through the island's narrow lanes as characters from myth and modern politics while the more daring townsmen scramble up bun-studded towers as midnight strikes.

🎎 Buddha's Birthday

Devotees stream to Buddhist monasteries and temples all over the territory on the eighth day of the fourth lunar month to pray to the revered deity and ceremoniously bathe his statues with scented water.

☆ Le French May

Misleadingly named, this celebration of all things Gallic often starts in April and ends in June – so much the better, as it returns with a rich arts program of consistently high quality, plus the obligatory fine food and wine (www.frenchmay.com).

June

The heavens are truly open, the mercury spikes, strong air-conditioning switches on citywide to soothe the nerves of locals and visitors alike.

🎎 Dragon Boat Festival

This festival, also known as Tuen Ng (Double Fifth), commemorates the death of the 3rd-century BC poet-statesman Qu Yuan who drowned himself to protest government corruption. Dragon boat races are held and sticky rice dumplings eaten, to mark the occasion.

August

Seven million souls palpitate and perspire in the sweltering heat. Torrential downpours are common but there is always a sun-toasted beach near you in this sprawling archipelago of 260-plus islands.

🎎 Hungry Ghost Festival

Restless spirits take leave from hell during the seventh moon to roam the earth. Netherworld money, food and even whole (paper) apartments are burned to propitiate the visitors. Fascinating folk traditions come alive across the city.

September

Good old summer lingers but the humidity factor starts to recede. Continue to hug the ocean coastlines for free respite as school kids swap their buckets and spades for mighty dunes of homework.

🎎 Mid-Autumn Festival

Pick up a lantern and wax lyrical over a moonlit picnic on the 15th night of the eighth lunar month. This family occasion remembers a 14th-century anti-Mongol uprising with much cheerful munching of once-subversive round 'mooncakes'.

November

At long last Hong Kong mellows. Temperatures sensibly cool down to around 22°C and rainfall ceases significantly, much to the delight of ramblers and other countryside merrymakers.

🏃 Oxfam Trailwalker

What began as a fundraising exercise drill by local Ghurkha soldiers in 1981 is

(Top) Giant lanterns for the Mid-Autumn Festival
(Bottom) Flag-sellers at the Chinese New Year fair

MICHAEL COYNE/GETTY IMAGES ©

RICHARD I'ANSON/GETTY IMAGES ©

today a celebrated endurance test that challenges hikers in teams of four to complete the 100km MacLehose Trail in 48 hours (www.oxfamtrailwalker.org.hk).

🏃 Hong Kong Cricket Sixes

Sometimes staged on the last weekend of October, this three-day tournament pits Hong Kong's top cricketers against select teams from 12 nations at the historic Kowloon Cricket Club.

December

Arguably the best time of the year to visit the city. Sunny days and clear blue skies reign. The delightful weather is perfect for all outdoor activities, though brace for the Christmas shopping crowds.

✨ Hong Kong Winterfest

Rejoice as neon Yuletide murals appear on the Tsim Sha Tsui harbourfront. Ferry across to Statue Sq to see the illuminated Christmas trees and fake snow. Join teenage revellers around Times Sq to ring in the birth of the Holy Sprog.

🏃 Hong Kong International Races

Billed as the Turf World Championships, master horsemen and equine stars across the planet descend on the beautifully set Sha Tin Racecourse to do battle (http://racing.hkjc.com). Expect fanatical betting from the 60,000 plus who religiously pack the stands.

With Kids

Hong Kong is a great destination for kids, though the crowds, traffic and pollution might take a little getting used to. Food and sanitation are of a high standard. The city is jam-packed with things to entertain the young ones, often just a hop, skip and jump away from attractions for you.

Giant panda, Ocean Park (p129)

Child-Friendly Museums

Science Museum

The three storeys of action-packed displays at Hong Kong's liveliest museum are a huge attraction for youngsters from toddlers to teens. There's a theatre where staff in lab coats perform wacky experiments.

History Museum

This excellent museum brings the city's history to life in colourful ways. Kids will enjoy the 'Hong Kong Story' exhibition with its splendid replicas of local traditions, such as a Chinese wedding and a life-sized fishing junk.

Space Museum

Kids eager to test their motor skills will go berserk – there are buttons to push, telescopes to peer through, simulation rides and computer quizzes. Older kids will enjoy the Omnimax films shown in the theatre.

Railway Museum

Thomas and his friends jolt to life at this open-air museum converted from a historic railway station; it comes complete with old coaches and a train compartment.

Heritage Museum

Though some youngsters may appreciate the displays, the real gem is the hands-on children's discovery gallery where they can dress up, play puzzle games and enjoy an exhibition of vintage toys.

Parks Children Like

Ocean Park

Hong Kong's premier amusement park offers white-knuckle rides, a top-notch aquarium, real pandas and a cable-car ride overlooking the sea.

Hong Kong Park

Ducks, swans and turtles inhabit the ponds here, and the massive forestlike aviary has an elevated walkway that lets visitors move through the tree canopy to spy on the birds.

Hong Kong Zoological & Botanical Gardens

After a visit here, your offspring will have seen the American flamingo, the Burmese python, the two-toed sloth and may even be able to tell a buff-cheeked gibbon from a cheeky child.

Middle Road Children's Playground

This breezy playground, with swings and slides for all ages, is a utopia of sorts, where you'll see kids of different ethnicities and social classes united in the language of play.

HK Wetland Park

Patience may be required for appreciation of the wetland habitats, but not for the themed exhibition galleries, the theatre and 'Swamp Adventure' play facility.

Kowloon Park

This large verdant venue has plenty of running room, lakes with waterfowl, two playgrounds, swimming pools and an aviary.

Disneyland

The latest attraction at this famous theme park is Toy Story Land.

Twilight Disney

Disneyland takes on a special magic after dark though very few visitors ever notice. There are some fun things to do during the twilight hours (6pm to 9pm). The more imaginative kids might enjoy them and they'll let you make flexible use of your time and avoid the lines.

➧ Do the 'Jungle Cruise' ride after sunset; it becomes a 'night safari'.

➧ Climb Tarzan's Tree House, now looking romantic under the glow of period lamps.

➧ Wait for the 'It's a Small World' clock to chime the evening hour with the parade of dolls in front of its pastel-and-gold facade, now sparkling with thousands of colourful lights.

➧ Ride the Tomorrowland Orbitron flying saucers; they're lit up and the constellation globe and the planets will be twinkling with fibre-optic stars.

➧ Rather than staying for the fireworks, exit out to the Disney fountain piazza to listen to the coolest 'lounge jazz' instrumental versions of the Disney songs; great musical arrangements.

➧ Catch the five-minute dancing-fountain interlude at the Mickey Mouse Foundation, complete with the light show which you don't get to see during the day.

➧ For panoramic views, watch the fireworks from the platform level of the train station, above the park's entrance.

Boats & Trams

Peak Tram

Older children may be fascinated by the ride on the gravity-defying Peak Tram and the age-defying mannequins at Madame Tussauds, but the same may scare younger ones.

Star Ferry

Cruise liner, barge, hydrofoil, fishing junk... Your mini-mariner will have a blast naming passing vessels, as their own tugboat nimbly dodges the swipes of a gigantic dragon in tempestuous Victoria Harbour.

Trams

Looking out of the window on the top deck of a narrow vehicle that rattles, clanks and sways amid heavy traffic can be exhilarating.

Symphony of the Stars Lightshow

Children will be awestruck by the dance of laser beams projected from skyscrapers on both sides of the harbour, to accompanying music. Bring the Darth Vader costume.

Shopping with Kids

For dozens of outlets dedicated to children, head to:

➡ Ground floor, Ocean Terminal at Harbour City (p142)

➡ Level 2, Festival Walk (p162)

➡ Level 9, Times Sq (p126)

➡ Level 9, Mega Box (p162)

Horizon Plaza (p134) has megastores selling kids' books and clothing. Tai Yuen St is known for traditional toy shops (p125) catering to youngsters of all ages.

Ice Skating

These malls have indoor ice rinks:

➡ Elements (p162)

➡ Festival Walk (p162)

➡ Cityplaza (p126)

Check the websites for the latest rates and opening hours.

Dolphin-Watching

See the second-smartest animal on earth in the wild – and it's in bubble-gum pink! Hong Kong Dolphinwatch runs three four-hour tours a week to waters where Chinese White Dolphins may be sighted (see p205).

Play Pilot

If your children are over five, let them dress like a pilot and try flying a virtual Boeing 737 at Flight Experience (see p162). Sweaty palms guaranteed. Advance booking essential.

Like a Local

Some charming values and die-hard habits permeate everyday life in Hong Kong. From the right cultural etiquette to the city's unbridled love of food, money and the bulldozer, here are some quick-fire tips to help you tap the depths of this great metropolis.

cha chaan tang (tea cafe), Hong Kong Island Central

GREG ELMS/GETTY IMAGES ©

Cultural Etiquette

Greetings

Some find cheek kisses too spine-tingling. Others secretly wish for more. Generally speaking, a simple 'Hello, how are you?' and a light handshake will do. Remove your shoes before entering someone's home.

Face

The cornerstone of human relations in this part of the world. Think status and respect: be courteous and never lose your temper in public.

Gifts

If you want to give flowers, chocolates or wine as a gift to someone, they may appear reluctant for fear of seeming greedy, but insist and they'll give in. Don't be surprised if they don't open a gift-wrapped present in front of you, though; to do so would be impolite.

Colours

These are often symbolic. Red symbolises good luck, happiness and wealth (though writing in red can convey anger and unfriendliness). White symbolises death, so think twice before giving white flowers.

Table Manners

Healthy Eating

Dishes tend to be communal at Chinese meals. Ask for separate serving chopsticks or spoons with each dish if the restaurant does not already provide them. This close attention to food hygiene became the norm after the 2003 SARS outbreak.

Mind Your Chopsticks

Don't stand your chopsticks upright in the middle of a bowl – that resembles two incense sticks at a graveside offering. If you can't manage chopsticks, don't be afraid to ask for a fork. Nearly all restaurants have them.

Tea Language

When someone refills your dainty teacup (you'll soon lose count of how often this happens), you can tap two fingers (index and middle) gently on the table twice instead of saying thank you with a greasy mouth full of food. Mastering this (allegedly) centuries-old shibboleth is efficient endearment.

Bones & Tissue

Your plate is the preferred spot for bones, but at budget places diners put them on the table beside your plate or bowl. If you find that disconcerting, place a tissue under or over your rejects.

Food Obsessions

Swallow & Scribe

Legions of food critics, amateur or otherwise, file reports to the user-driven, bilingual restaurant-review website www.openrice.com every day.

Dim Sum – a Fact of Life

Morning dim sum is a daily ritual for many retirees and a family affair at weekends (though many pay more attention to their iPhone or games console than what's on the table – or to each other).

Tea Break

When mid-afternoon comes, pop into a *cha chaan tang* (tea cafe) for some snacks while the elderly folks sitting around you debate the morning's meat prices and stock-market fluctuations. These spaces function as community focal points for the aged and housewives to go to swap local gossip – and boltholes for many a stressed office worker.

Nectar in the Night

In the evening the fashionable postprandial activity is to go to a domestic dessert shop in a group for some anti-aging black sesame soup, silky smooth steamed egg pudding or exotica in the form of durian crepes and suchlike.

Steamy Winter

In winter hotpot at a *dai pai dong* (food stall) is a soul-warming, convivial experience. Poach slivers of meat, seafood and assorted vegetables in a cauldron of tasty stock and your night will be transformed.

Money Matters

Jockey Clubs

Step into any Jockey Club off-course betting centre (often found in public housing estates, near markets or transport terminals) on any race day/night and you'll be met with a maelstrom of emotions as punters literally try to defy the odds. Occasionally you'll hear a squeal of joy but more often than not, invectives pepper deep sighs of desperation as some numbers thunder past the live TV screens every 30 minutes. Outside, high rollers squat on the pavement en masse, heads buried in race cards, in search of the forever elusive winning formula.

Stocks & Shares

Similarly, look out for the hole-in-the-wall brokerage firms on any weekday and you'll find crowds of (not necessarily small-time) investors deeply engrossed by the live stock market updates on the wall-mounted panels.

Local 'hoods

Full-scale gentrification has yet to arrive in these areas but the dictates of urban development are already changing their character. Go and soak up their gritty, earthy, neighbourly vibes before it's too late.

Yau Ma Tei

Stroll Shanghai St for traditional barbers, Chinese wedding costume-makers and artisans of other time-honoured crafts.

Sham Shui Po

Find flea markets, 1930s shophouses, postwar housing estates and even an ancient tomb in this resilient working-class district.

Queen's Road West

The pungent smells of dried seafood and Chinese herbal medicine lead you into this meandering parade of industrious small traders.

For Free

Hong Kong is not a cheap place to visit and prices creep up at every opportunity, as any veritable local can testify. But with a bit of planning, you can still indulge yourself for very little money.

Cheap & Cheerful

Not quite free but near enough to warrant inclusion, for a couple of dollars you can rattle your way through the urban canyon of high-rises on a tram. Give up pocket change again for the voyage of a lifetime on the Star Ferry (p69).

Be seated by 11am and brunch on hearty dim sum – many Chinese restaurants offer discounted prices either side of the noon–2pm lunch hours. For more grassroots austerity, don't miss the sizeable mid-afternoon tea sets ($20 to $30) at the city's own fast-food chains.

At sundown, generous happy hours characterise many bars, and on Tuesdays, a movie ticket generally costs $10 to $25 less than usual. Experience a night at the races for only $10 entry – pick the right horse and you could recoup your travel budget (p111).

Museum Hopping

Wednesday is 'admission free' day at seven Hong Kong museums: Museum of Art (p142), Museum of History (p144), Heritage Museum (p182), Science Museum (p144), Space Museum (p143; excluding the Space Theatre), Museum of Coastal Defence (p113) and Dr Sun Yat-sen Museum (p87).

Liberal Views

Enjoy panoramic island views from the 43rd-floor viewing platform in the Bank of China building (p70). Or bring your own booze to the public terrace at International Finance Centre and watch sunset over Victoria Harbour (p71).

Taichi in Kowloon Park

Start your day with a free taichi lesson courtesy of the Hong Kong Tourist Board (p144).

Browse the Markets

No one's forcing you to buy the souvenir T-shirts and kitsch items on display (p148).

Dating Nature

Sixty per cent of Hong Kong is officially countryside. Gratis. To miss it is to sin.

Gallery Trail

Admire expensive art for free in Soho's galleries (p296).

Stock Exchange

See how they make money in Hong Kong's nerve centre (p70).

Dim sum preparation

Eating

One of the world's most delicious cities, Hong Kong offers culinary excitement whether you're spending $20 on a bowl of noodles or $2000 on a seafood feast. The best of China is well represented, be it Cantonese, Shanghainese, Northern or Sichuanese. Similarly, the smorgasbord of non-Chinese – French, Italian, Spanish, Japanese, Thai, Indian – is the most diverse in all of Asia.

Diners in a noodle bar

Cantonese Cuisine

The dominant cuisine in Hong Kong is Cantonese and it's easily the best in the world. Many of China's top chefs had fled to the territory around 1949; it was therefore here and not in its original home, Guǎngzhōu, that Cantonese cuisine flourished.

This style of cooking is characterised by an obsession with freshness. Seafood restaurants display tanks full of finned and shelled creatures enjoying their final moments on terra infirma. Flavours are delicate and balanced, obtained through re-strained use of seasoning and light-handed cooking techniques such as steaming and quick stir-frying.

REGIONAL VARIETIES

Cantonese cuisine refers to the culinary styles of Guǎngdōng province, as well as Chiu Chow (Cháozhōu) and Hakka cuisines. Chiu Chow dishes reflect a penchant for seafood and condiments. Deep-fried soft-boned fish comes with tangerine oil; braised goose, a vinegar and garlic dip. Hakka cuisine is known for its saltiness and use of preserved meat. Salt-baked chicken and pork stewed with preserved vegetables fed many hungry families and famished workers back in leaner times.

MODERNISATION

Hong Kong's chefs are also an innovative bunch who'll seize upon new ingredients and find wondrous ways of using them. For example, dim sum has expanded to include mango pudding, and shortbread

tarts stuffed with abalone and chicken. Black truffles – the kind you see on French or Italian menus – are sometimes sprinkled on rolled rice sheets and steamed. And it works.

NEED TO KNOW

Price Ranges

The price indicators below are based on Hong Kong dollars per person for a two-course meal with a drink.

$	less than $200
$$	$200 to $400
$$$	more than $400

Opening Hours

➡ Lunch 11am–3pm

➡ Dinner 6pm–11pm

Some restaurants are open through the afternoons, while others are also open for breakfast. Most restaurants open on Sunday and close for at least two days during the Lunar New Year.

Reservations

Most restaurants (midrange or above) take reservations. At very popular addresses, including many listed here, booking is crucial, especially for weekend dinners. Popular restaurants may serve two or even three seatings a night.

How Much?

Forty dollars will buy you noodles and some greens, or a set meal at fast-food chains such as Cafe de Coral (www.cafedecoralfastfood.com) or Fairwood (www.fairwood.com.hk). A proper sit-down lunch in a midrange restaurant costs at least $80 and dinner $120 per head. Dinner at upscale restaurants will set you back at least $600 per person.

Tipping

Tipping is not a must as every bill includes a 10% service charge, but this almost always goes into the owner's coffers, so if you're happy with the service, tip as you see fit. Most people leave behind the small change.

Eating out in Sai Kung (p187)

Pastéis de nata (egg tarts) at Lord Stow's Bakery (p258), Macau

EMMA WOOD/ALAMY ©

Dining Local
DIM SUM

Dim sum are Cantonese tidbits consumed with tea for breakfast or lunch. The term literally means 'to touch the heart' and the act of eating dim sum is referred to as yum cha, meaning 'to drink tea'.

In the postwar period, yum cha was largely an activity of single males, who met over their breakfast tea to socialise or exchange tips about job-seeking. Soon yum cha became a family activity.

Each dish, often containing two to four morsels steamed in a bamboo basket, is meant to be shared. In old-style dim sum places, just stop the waiter and choose something from the cart. Modern venues give you an order slip, but it's almost always in Chinese only. However, as dim sum dishes are often ready-made, the waiters should be able to show you samples to choose from.

SOY SAUCE WESTERN

'Soy sauce Western' (si yau sai chaan) features Western-style dishes prepared with a large dollop of wisdom from the Chinese kitchen. It's said to have emerged in the 1940s when the ingenious chef of Tai Ping Koon (see p117) decided to 'improve' on Western cooking by tweaking recipes, such as replacing dairy products with local seasoning – many Chinese back then were lactose-intolerant – and putting rice on the menu.

His invention met its soul mate when White Russians, who had fled to Shànghǎi after the Bolshevik Revolution, sought refuge in Hong Kong in 1949; they soon cooked up what's known as Shanghainese–Russian food (see p156).

The two schools of Western-inspired cuisine offered affordable and 'exotic' dining to locals at a time when authentic Western eateries catered almost exclusively to expatriates. Eventually the two styles mingled, spawning soy sauce Western as we know it today. Popular dishes include Russian borscht, baked pork chop over fried rice and beef stroganoff with rice.

CHA CHAAN TANG

Tea cafes (茶餐廳, *cha chaan tang*) are cheap and cheery neighbourhood eateries that appeared in the 1940s serving Western-style snacks and drinks to those who couldn't afford Earl Grey and cucumber sandwiches. Their menus have since grown to include more substantial Chinese and soy sauce Western dishes.

Some tea cafes have bakeries creating European pastries with Chinese characteristics, such as pineapple buns (菠蘿包, *bo law bao*), which don't contain a trace of the said fruit; and cocktail buns, which have coconut stuffing (雞尾包, *gai may bao*).

See the Drinking chapter (p44) to learn about the typical tea and coffee (and tea-coffee) beverages that *cha chaan tangs* are renowned for.

Dai Pai Dongs

A *dai pai dong* (大牌檔) is a food stall, hawker-style or built into a rickety hut crammed with tables and stools that sometimes spill out onto the pavement. After WWII the colonial government issued food-stall licenses to the families of injured or

---

HOW HONG KONGERS EAT

Many busy Hong Kongers take their breakfast and lunch at tea cafes. A full breakfast at these places consists of buttered toast, fried eggs and spam, instant noodles and a drink. The more health-conscious might opt for congee, with dim sums of rolled rice sheets (*chéung fán*) and steamed dumplings with pork and shrimp (*siù máai*).

Lunch for office workers can mean a bowl of wonton noodles, a plate of rice with Chinese barbecue or something more elaborate.

Afternoon tea is popular at the weekends. On weekdays it is the privilege of labourers and ladies of leisure (*tai-tais*). Workers are said to vanish, Cinderella fashion, at 3.15pm sharp for their daily fix of egg tarts and milk tea. For *tai-tais*, tea could mean scones with rose-petal jam with friends or a bowl of noodles at the hairdresser's.

Dinner is the biggest meal of the day. If prepared at home, what's on the table depends on the traditions of the family, but usually there's soup, rice, veggies and a meat or fish dish. Everyone has their own bowl of rice and/or soup, with the rest of the dishes placed in the middle of the table for sharing. Dining out is also extremely common, with many families eating out three to five times a week.

deceased civil servants. The licenses were big so the stalls came to be known as *'dai pai dongs'* (meaning 'big license stalls').

Dai pai dongs can spring up anywhere: by the side of a slope, in an alley or under a tree. That said, these vintage places for trillion-star dining are fast vanishing; most have now been relocated to government-run cooked-food centres.

The culinary repertoire of *dai pai dongs* varies from stall to stall. One operator may specialise in congee while its neighbour whips up seafood dishes that give restaurants a run for their money. In places where there's a cluster of *dai pai dongs*, you can order dishes from different operators.

Walled Village Cuisine

The modern history of Hong Kong begins with the First Opium War, but the roots of its cuisine go much further back. The local inhabitants who dwelled here ate what they could herd, grow or catch from the sea. Certain ancient food traditions from these peoples remain, most notably walled village cuisine, best known for the 'basin feast' (盆菜, *poon choy*; see p173). The story has it that the last emperor of the southern Song dynasty (AD 1127–1279), fleeing from the Mongols, retreated to a walled village in Hong Kong with his entourage. The villagers, lacking decent crockery, piled all kinds of food into a large basin to serve the royal guests. *Poon choy* has become a dish for festive occasions in the New Territories ever since.

International Cuisine

From monkfish liver sushi to French molecular cuisine, Hong Kong has no shortage

Sautéed garoupa fillet with vegetables, Tim's Kitchen (p92), Sheung Wan

of great restaurants specialising in the food of other cultures. The variety and quality of Asian cuisines is outstanding, surpassing even that of Tokyo. Then there's the exceptional array of Western options. Hong Kong's affluent and cosmopolitan population loves Western food, especially European. This is evidenced by the number of international celebrity chefs with restaurants here, such as Joël Robuchon and Pierre Gagnaire. Prices at these and other top addresses can be steep, but there's also a burgeoning number of excellent eateries specialising in rustic French or Italian that cater to food lovers with medium-sized pockets.

Self-Catering

The two major supermarket chains, **Park'N'Shop** (www.parknshop.com) and **Wellcome** (www.wellcome.com.hk), have megastores that offer groceries as well as takeaway cooked food.

Their gourmet counterparts include the following:

Great Food Hall (Map p370; ☎2918 9986; www.greatfoodhall.com; Basement, Two Pacific Place, Admiralty; ◷10am-10pm)

VEGGIES BEWARE

There are 101 ways to accidentally eat meat in Hong Kong. A plate of green is probably cooked in meat stock and served with oyster sauce. Broth made with chicken is a prevalent ingredient, even in dishes where no meat is visible. In budget restaurants, chicken powder is used liberally. The safe bet for veggies wanting to go Chinese is to patronise vegetarian eateries or upscale establishments. For more options besides the ones listed in this guide (denoted by the icon 🍴), see http://vegan.hk/Vegan -Rest.html.

Citysuper (Map p374; ☑2506 2888; www.city super.com.hk; Basement 1, Times Square, Causeway Bay; ⊙10.30am-10pm) There are also numerous other branches.

Oliver's, the Delicatessen (Map p362; ☑2810 7710; www.oliversthedeli.com.hk; 201-205, Prince's Bldg, 10 Chater Rd, Central; ⊙8.30am-8pm)

Taste (Festival Walk, Kowloon Tong; ⊙7am-midnight) A classy version of Park'N'Shop.

Three Sixty (Map p362; ☑2111 4480; www.threesixtyhk.com; 3rd & 4th fl, Landmark Bldg, 1 Pedder St; ⊙8am-9pm Mon-Sat, 9am-9pm Sun; ⓂCentral, exit C) Wellcome's upmarket version.

Wet markets for fresh produce (6am–7pm) can be found all over town, including the following places:

Graham St Market (Map p366; Graham St, Central; ◻5B)

Bowrington Rd (off Map p374; Bowrington Rd, Causeway Bay; ⓂCauseway Bay, exit A)

Chun Yeung St (Chun Yeung St, North Point; ⓂNorth Point, exit A2)

Canton Rd (Map p383; Canton Rd, Mong Kok; ⓂMong Kok, exit C3)

Cooking Courses

Hong Kong is a good place to hone your skills in the art of Chinese cookery.

Home Management Centre (香港家政中心; ☑2510 2828; www.hec.com.hk; 10th fl, Electric Centre, 28 City Garden Rd, North Point; per session $90; ⊙10:30am-12:30pm Wed;) Teaches three simple Chinese recipes in English; walk-ins allowed. On the website, navigate to Electric Living/Home Management Centre.

Peninsula Academy (Map p378; ☑2696 6693; www.peninsula.com; The Peninsula, Salisbury Rd, Tsim Sha Tsui; per class incl lunch $1300) Every one or two months one of the chefs from the five-star hotel teaches a different cuisine.

Towngas Cooking Centre (煤氣烹飪中心; Map p374; ☑2576 1535; www.towngascooking. com; Basement, Leighton Centre, 77 Leighton Rd, Causeway Bay; per class $300-350) Conducts classes in a range of Chinese cooking styles.

Publications & Blogs

The popular website **Open Rice** (www.open rice.com) has restaurant reviews penned by

PLAN YOUR TRIP EATING

Serving a noodle lunch

the city's armchair gourmands. Some dedicated foodies have their own blogs, such as the highly illuminating **Diary of a Growing Boy** (www.diarygrowingboy.com).

The best sources for travellers looking for up-to-the-minute restaurant recommendations include the following:

Good Eating (www.scmp.com)

HK Magazine Restaurant Guide (http://hk.asia-city.com/restaurants)

WOM Guide (www.womguide.com)

BC Magazine (www.bcmagazine.net)

Best of the Best Culinary Guide (www.discoverhongkong.com/eng/dining/best-culinary-award.html)

Top: Preparing tea
Middle: Dim sum
Bottom: Sushi plate

Lonely Planet's Top Choices

Yin Yang (p114) Delicious and wow-worthy dishes by the town's most creative chef.

Tim's Kitchen (p248) Healthy and refined Cantonese cooking with two Michelin stars.

Club Qing (p90) Modern Chinese a cut above the rest in a graceful dining room.

Dong Lai Shun (p149) Well-executed Northern Chinese and a plethora of other options by a versatile kitchen.

Lung King Heen (p72) Exquisite dim sum, pristine service and sweeping harbour views.

Cêpage (p114) The chef is a true artist when it comes to haute French cooking and minimalist plating.

Best by Budget

$
One Dim Sum (p154)

Ziafat (p151)

Linguini Fini (p72)

Yoga Interactive Vegetarian (p150)

Wang Fu (p92)

Ser Wong Fun (p92)

$$
Bistronomique (p93)

Posto Pubblico (p90)

Yardbird (p92)

Ammo (p114)

Irori (p116)

Sha Tin 18 (p183)

$$$
Manor Seafood Restaurant (p116)

Kimberley Chinese Restaurant (p150)

Caprice (p72)

Chairman (p92)

Island Tang (p74)

Yè Shanghai (p154)

Best for Dim Sum

West Villa (p117)

City Hall Maxim's Palace (p74)

Luk Yu Tea House (p90)

Lin Heung Kui (p93)

Tim Ho Wan (p156)

Fook Lam Moon (p154)

Best for Seafood

Aberdeen Fish Market Canteen (p132)

Lei Yue Mun (p156)

Chuen Kee Seafood Restaurant (p188)

Tai Hing Seafood Restaurant (p198)

Ap Lei Chau Market Cooked Food Centre (p132)

Best for Noodles

Yat Woon Min (p120)

Ho To Tai Noodle Shop (p173)

Tasty Congee and Noodle Wonton Shop (p74)

Mak's Noodle (p91)

Ho Hung Kee (p116)

Best Dai Pai Dongs

Tung Po Seafood Restaurant (p120)

Gi Kee Seafood Restaurant (p120)

Ap Lei Chau Market Cooked Food Centre (p132)

Best for Soy Sauce Western

Tai Ping Koon (p117)

Queen's Café (p156)

Best Cha Chaan Tang

Mido Café (p155)

China Cafe (p155)

Lan Fong Yuen (p91)

Best for Vegetarian

Yoga Interactive Vegetarian (p150)

Pure Veggie House (p113)

Chi Lin Vegetarian (Long Men Lou; p156)

Life Cafe (p90)

Gun Gei Healthy Vegetarian (p117)

Bookworm Cafe (p198)

Best for Meat

Piggy Grill (p155)

Kimberley Chinese Restaurant (p150)

Iroha (p117)

Ba Yi Restaurant (p93)

Robatayaki (p155)

Chan Kan Kee (p93)

Best for Italian

Posto Pubblico (p90)

Linguini Fini (p72)

Bella Vita (p117)

Grissini (p115)

Sabatini (p154)

Ammo (p114)

Best for French

Gaddi's (p150)

Bistronomique (p93)

Caprice (p72)

Amber (p75)

L'Atelier Joël de Robuchon (p74)

Chef Studio (p132)

Best for Japanese

Robatayaki (p155)

Zuma (p75)

Irori (p116)

Iroha (p117)

Sushi Fuku-suke (p116)

Inagiku (p74)

Best for Southeast Asian

Old Bazaar Kitchen (p115)

Golden Bull (p151)

Cheong Fat (p156)

DALAT (p114)

家嫂 (p151)

Good Satay (p150)

Best for East Asian

Din Tai Fung (p154)

Chicken HOF & Soju Korean (p150)

Irori (p116)

Yat Woon Min (p120)

Best for Spicy Food

San Xi Lou (p114)

Ziafat (p151)

Joon Ko Restaurant (p115)

Yu (p117)

Cheong Fat (p156)

Woodlands (p150)

Best for Sweets

Yuen Kee Dessert (p93)

Tai Cheong Bakery (p91)

Petite Amanda (p75)

Vero Chocolates (p114)

Sweet Dynasty (p154)

Honeymoon Dessert (p189)

Best for Ambience

Island Tang (p74)

Lock Cha Tea Shop (p114)

Stables Grill (p150)

Ammo (p114)

Madam Sixty Ate (p115)

Mido Café (p155)

Best for Lunch Specials

Caprice (p72)

Pierre (p75)

L'Atelier Joël de Robuchon (p74)

Heichinrou (p74)

Irori (p116)

Sushi Fuku-suke (p116)

Best for Unusual Food

Good Spring Co (p91)

Wo Mei (p155)

Ser Wong Fun (p92)

Chan Chun Kee (p93)

Ping Shan Traditional Poon Choi (p173)

Lan Kwai Fong

Drinking & Nightlife

Energetic Hong Kong knows how to party and does so visibly and noisily. Drinking venues run the gamut from British-style pubs through hotel bars and hipster hang-outs, to karaoke bolt-holes aimed at a young Chinese clientele. The last few years have seen a heartening surge in the number of wine bars and live-music venues, catering to a diverse, discerning and fun-loving population.

Lan Kwai Fong

Once synonymous with partying in Hong Kong, Lan Kwai Fong was undergoing a complete facelift at the time of writing, with buildings being torn down to make way for new, possibly even more upscale ones. For now, there are still bars and those remain lively.

Soho & Sheung Wan

Soho is, for now at least, the new Lan Kwai Fong. Geared more to dining than drinking,

it's just a short journey away from LKF on foot or via the Central Mid-levels Escalator up the hill. As rent rises in Central, the extent of the bar district is stretching ever further west towards the western end of Sheung Wan.

Wan Chai

While Wan Chai remains a byword for sleaze (and a long-standing port of call for American sailors and GIs since the Vietnam War), it has cleaned its act up of late. Much of the

NEED TO KNOW

Business Hours

➡ Bars open noon or 6pm and stay open until 2am to 6am; Wan Chai bars stay open the latest.

➡ Cafes usually open between 8am and 11am and close between 5pm and 11pm.

Happy Hour

➡ During certain hours of the day, most pubs, bars and even certain clubs give discounts on drinks (usually from a third to half off) or offer two-for-one deals.

➡ Happy hour is usually in the late afternoon or early evening – 4pm to 8pm, say – but times vary widely from place to place. Depending on the season, the day of the week and the location, some happy hours run from noon until as late as 10pm, and some start up again after midnight.

Prices

➡ Beer from $45/pint

➡ Wine from $50/glass

➡ Whisky from $50/shot

➡ Cocktail $80–$200

➡ Cover charge for dance clubs $200–$700 (including one drink)

Latest Information

➡ *Time Out* (www.timeout.com.hk)

➡ *HK Magazine* (http://hk.asia-city.com)

➡ *bc magazine* (www.bcmagazine.net)

Dress Code

Usually smart casual is good enough for most clubs, but patrons wearing shorts and flip-flops will not be admitted. Jeans are popular in Hong Kong and these are sometimes worn with heels or a blazer for a more put-together look. Hong Kong's clubbers can be style-conscious, so dress to impress!

western part of the district offers lively, respectable bars, although hostess bars still line Lockhart Rd. Old Wan Chai, further inland around Queen's Rd East behind the tram tracks, is becoming another little epicentre of fine dining and sophisticated drinking.

Tsim Sha Tsui

If you head back from the bustle of Nathan Rd there are some nifty little bar areas, such as the karaoke bar scene around Minden Rd and the food-and-drink ghetto along Knutsford Tce in the north of Tsim Sha Tsui.

How Much?

It's not cheap to drink in Hong Kong. An all-night boozy tour of the city's drinking landscape can set you back at least $800. That said, it's possible to cut corners while still soaking up the atmosphere – lots of youngsters do that. Buy your drinks from a convenience store and hang out with the revellers standing outside the bars. The alley near a convenience store in Soho is called 'Cougar Alley' for a reason.

Wine & Whisky Bars

An exciting development since the government removed all taxes on wine imports in 2008 is the arrival of new wine bars, including some that offer tastings of premium wines using new 'enomatic' technology that permits them to open a bottle and preserve the contents indefinitely. This means tasting a seriously rare (and expensive) wine is possible without completely bankrupting yourself.

Another recent trend is whisky-drinking, and a growing number of bars is devoted to the savouring of the amber liquid, including a couple of stylish Japanese whisky bars.

Cafes

Where soulless coffee chains used to dominate Hong Kong's coffee-drinking scene, a handful of hip cafes have sprung up that serve a good cuppa.

CHA CHAAN TANG

Tea cafes (茶餐廳; *cha chaan tang*) are perhaps best known for their Hong Kong–style 'pantyhose' milk tea (奶茶; *nai cha*) – a strong brew made from a blend of several types of black tea with crushed egg shells thrown in for silkiness. It's filtered through a fabric that hangs like a stocking, hence the name, and drunk with evaporated milk. 'Pantyhose' milk tea is sometimes mixed with three parts coffee to create the quintessential Hong Kong drink, tea-coffee or *yin yeung* (鴛鴦), meaning 'mandarin duck', a symbol of matrimonial harmony.

COFFEE, TEA OR TEA-COFFEE?

Tea fragrant and strong, made from

five different blends, in cotton bags or legendary

stockings – tender, all-encompassing, gathering –

brewed in hot water and poured into a teapot, its taste

varying subtly with the time in water steeped.

Can that fine art be maintained? Pour the tea

into a cup of coffee, will the aroma of one

interfere with, wash out the other? Or will the other

keep its flavour: roadside foodstalls

streetwise and worldly from its daily stoves

mixed with a dash of daily gossips and good sense,

hard-working, a little sloppy...an indescribable taste.

Leung Ping-kwan (translated by Martha Cheung)

Dance

TANGO

Hong Kong has a small but zealous community of tango dancers, usually white-collar workers, professionals and expats. **Tango Tang** (www.tangotang.com), the most prominent of all the schools, has all tango events, including those by other organisers, posted on its website. You can join any of the many *milongas* (dance parties) held every week at restaurants and dance studios all over town.

The **Hong Kong Tango Festival** (www.hktangofest.com), held at the end of the year, features classes, workshops and more parties. See the website for details on how to join.

SALSA

Hong Kong's vibrant salsa community holds weekly club nights that are open to anyone in need of a good time. Check out www.dancetrinity.com or www.hongkong-salsa.com. The annual **Hong Kong Salsa Festival** (http://hksalsafestival.com), held around February, features participants from the world over. The website has details of events including the after-parties.

SWING

If you like swing, there are socials with live jazz bands (and sometimes free beginners' class) at least six times a month. The calendar on www.hongkongswings.com has more.

Party with lovely drag hostesses every first and third Sunday of the month at gay-friendly bar Tivo (p98). There's a DJ, two-for-one cocktails, and food for the hungry. The frolicking starts at 7pm and heats up as the night wears on.

Karaoke

Karaoke clubs are as popular as ever with the city's young citizens, with a sprinkling of clubs in Causeway Bay and Wan Chai, and local dives in Mong Kok. The aural wallpaper at these clubs is most often Canto-pop covers, compositions that often blend Western rock or pop with Chinese melodies and lyrics, but there is usually a limited selection of 'golden oldies' and pop in English.

GAY & LESBIAN HONG KONG

While Hong Kong's gay scene may not have the vibrancy or visibility of cities like Sydney, it has made huge strides in recent years and now counts more than two dozen gay bars and clubs.

Bars & Clubs

DYMK (Map p362; ☑2868 0626; 16 Arbuthnot Rd, Central; ☺6pm-4am; ⓜCentral, exit D2) 'Does your mother know?' is an upmarket, gay-friendly bar catering to a discerning crowd of professionals who lounge in the dimly but stylishly lit booths.

Virus (Map p374; ☑2904 7207; 6/F, Pak Tak Centre, 468 Jaffe Rd) The local lesbian crowd that comes here for the cheap beer and karaoke is young; not a bad place to get a feel for the scene, but not to meet people, as the customers tend to hang out in tightly knit groups.

Propaganda (Map p362; ☑2868 1316; Lower Ground fl, 1 Hollywood Rd, Central; ☺9pm-4am Tue-Thu, to 6am Fri & Sat, happy hour 9pm-1.30am Tue-Thu; ⓜCentral, exit D2) Hong Kong's default gay dance club and meat market; cover charges ($120 to $160) apply on Friday and Saturday (which also get you into Works on Friday). Enter from Ezra's Lane.

T:me (Map p362; ☑2332 6565; www.time-bar.com; 65 Hollywood Rd; ☺6pm-2am Mon-Sat) A small and chic gay bar located in a back alley off Hollywood Rd, close to Club 71; drinks are a bit on the pricey side but it has happy hour throughout the week.

Volume (Map p362; ☑2857 7683; 83-85 Hollywood Rd, Central; ☺6pm-4am, happy hour 7.30-9.30pm; ☐26) A swanky, kitsch, mirror-lined, late-night cocktail bar that pumps out a range of sounds, from '80s hits to the latest dance genres, to a mixed crowd of gay and expat locals.

Works (Map p362; ☑2868 6102; 1st fl, 30-32 Wyndham St, Central; ☺7pm-2am, happy hour 7-10.30pm Mon-Fri; ⓜCentral, exit D2) The sister club to Propaganda is where most gay boyz out on the town start the evening, and sees some heavy FFFR (file-for-future-reference) cruising till it's time to move on to the P; a cover charge ($60 to $100) applies on the weekend.

Explode (Map p374; ☑2890 8882; 9th fl, Jardin Centre, 50 Jardine's Bazaar, Causeway Bay; ☺9pm-late; ⓜCauseway Bay, exit F) A local bar and karaoke lounge with space for some 100 hunks rubbing elbows; there are monthly theme nights such as beach boys contests and singing contests.

Boo (Map p382; ☑2736 6168; www.boobar.com.hk; 5th fl, Pearl Oriental Tower, 225 Nathan Rd, Jordan; ☺7pm-2am Sun-Thu, to 4am Fri, 9pm-4am Sat, happy hour 7-9pm; ⓜJordan, exit C1) This low-key gay bar on Nathan Rd with a karaoke jukebox seems to attract huggable 'bear' types in the local gay community; there's a DJ every Saturday from 9pm.

Other Resources

Dim Sum (http://dimsum-hk.com) A free, monthly gay magazine with listings.

Gay Home Stay HK (☑5100 6877; www.gayhomestayhk.com; 21 Hung Kwong St, To Kwa Wan; s/d/tw $460/560/560) Run by the enterprising Akis Tan, a seasoned traveller and certified masseur, this apartment inside a tenement building caters to the gay community; also operates gay-friendly tours within Hong Kong and to Shēnzhèn and Guǎngzhōu.

Les Peches (☑9101 8001; lespechesinfo@yahoo.com) Hong Kong's premier lesbian organisation has monthly events for lesbians, bisexual women and their friends.

One-Nil (onenilhk@gmail.com) A gay football network.

OUTconcorde (Map p362; ☑2526 3391; www.outconcorde.com; 1st fl, Galuxe Bldg, 8-10 On Lan St, Central) A gaycentric travel consultancy owned and operated by gay travel professionals.

Utopia Asia (www.utopia-asia.com/hkbars.htm) A website with listings of gay-friendly venues and events in town.

Lonely Planet's Top Choices

Globe (p96) Spacious but cosy with fine imported beers and the first cask-conditioned ale brewed in Hong Kong.

Gecko Lounge (p97) Great wines, French tunes and an artsy French vibe make for a cool and intimate drinking experience.

Executive Bar (p122) Exclusive whisky and cocktail bar where you can catch some serious Japanese mixology in action.

Club 71 (p97) Where all the activists, artists, musicians and the socially conscious go to rant and revel.

Pawn (p122) A gastropub housed in a historic pawn shop and three tenement houses overlooking the tram tracks.

8th Estate Winery (p129) Hong Kong's first ever winery in a factory building produces locally made wine from grapes sourced worldwide.

Best for Views

Sevva (p75)

Aqua Spirit (p157)

Ozone (p157)

Back Beach Bar (p134)

Sugar (p123)

Intercontinental Lobby Lounge (p158)

Best for a Cuppa

Peninsula Hong Kong (p274)

Teakha (p96)

Barista Jam (p96)

Lan Fong Yuen (p91)

Capo's Espresso (p96)

Mido Cafe (p155)

Best for Cocktails

Butler (p157)

Oriental Sake Bar Yu Zen (p122)

Yun Fu (p98)

Bar 42 (p97)

Sevva (p75)

Best for Whisky

Butler (p157)

Whiskey Priest (p98)

Macallan Whisky Bar & Lounge (p258)

Best for Wine

Amo Eno (p75)

Flying Winemaker (p97)

Central Wine Club (p98)

Best Pubs

Whiskey Priest (p98)

Smugglers Inn (p133)

Delaney's (p121)

Best for Clubbing

Dragon-i (p97)

Likuid (p98)

Club 97 (p98)

Beijing Club (p98)

Best for People-Watching

Peak Cafe Bar (p97)

Classified Mozzarella Bar (p121)

Quay West (p98)

Bit Point (p97)

1/5 (p121)

Staunton's Wine Bar & Cafe (p97)

Best for Unpretentious Drinking

Pier 7 (p75)

Quay West (p98)

Agave (p122)

Bit Point (p97)

Best for Watching Sports

Amici (p121)

Liberty Exchange (p75)

Whiskey Priest (p98)

Dickens (p122)

Delaney's (p121)

Best for Quirky Vibes

Ned Kelly's Last Stand (p157)

Snake King Yan (p158)

Fullcup Café (p158)

Best for Local Vibes

Utopia (p157)

Habitat (p121)

Fullcup Café (p158)

Vibes (p157)

Best for Bar Food

Dickens (p122)

Delaney's (p121)

Classified Mozzarella Bar (p121)

Agave (p122)

AMOY (p121)

Girls in Chinese opera costume

 # Entertainment

Hong Kong's arts and entertainment scene is healthier than ever. The increasingly busy cultural calendar includes music, drama and dance hailing from a plethora of traditions. The schedule of imported performances is nothing short of stellar. And every week, local arts companies and artists perform anything from Bach and stand-up to Cantonese opera and English versions of Chekhov plays.

The Arts

Local Western music ensembles and theatre troupes give weekly shows, while famous foreign groups are invited to perform often, particularly at the Hong Kong Arts Festival in March. The annual event attracts world-class names in all genres of music, theatre and dance, including the likes of the Bolshoi Ballet, Anne-Sophie Mutter and playwright Robert Wilson.

Cinema

Hong Kong is well served with cinema, screening both mainstream and art-house films. Cinemas usually show local productions and Hollywood blockbusters. The vast majority of films have both English and Chinese subtitles.

Cinema buffs from all over Asia make the pilgrimage to the **Hong Kong International Film Festival** (www.hkiff.com) held each year in March and April.

Concerts

Hong Kong is a stop on the big-name concert circuit, and a growing number of internationally celebrated bands and solo artists perform here. These include mainstream acts and those on the edge of the mainstream – from U2, Robbie Williams and Red Hot Chilli Peppers, to Kings of Convenience, Deerhoof and Mogwai.

Live Music

Hong Kong's live-music scene has been undergoing a renaissance of late with a growing number of venues hosting independent musicians (imported and local) at least several nights a week. The options range from a smooth evening of jazz to a raucous night of goth metal, not to mention dub step, post-rock drum 'n' bass and electronica.

The **Fringe Club** (☑2521 7251; www.hkfringe.com.hk; 2 Lower Albert Rd, Central; Ⓜ Central, exits D1, D2 & G), **Backstage Live** (☑2167 8985; www.backstagelive.hk; 1st fl, Somptueux Central, 52-54 Wellington St, Central; Ⓜ Central, exit D1) and Grappa's Cellar (p78) are popular venues. And don't miss the clandestine dive Hidden Agenda (p159).

The **Hong Kong International Jazz Festival** (www.hkjazz.org) caters to jazz lovers.

Clockenflap

The highlight in Hong Kong's live-music calendar is the excellent multi-act outdoor music festival known as **Clockenflap** (www.clockenflap.com). The two-day event has featured dozens of local, regional and international acts performing at the West Kowloon promenade.

Flamenco

A couple of flamenco bands perform regularly in Hong Kong – Sol Y Flamenco (usually on once a month at Backstage Live or the Fringe Club) and Reorientate (a fusion world-music band). Flamenco dancer and teacher **Ingrid Sera-Gillet** (http://hkflamenco.com) performs with both. For more on performances and drop-in classes, contact the following:

Clara Ramona Flamenco (www.hk-flamenco-dance-arts.com)

Felah Mengus (www.felah-mengus.com)

Flamenco Hong Kong (www.flamenco.hk)

Hong Kong Flamenco Arts Centre (www.fachk.com)

NEED TO KNOW

Tickets & Reservations

These main ticket providers have tickets to every major event in Hong Kong. You can book through the website, by phone or purchase tickets at the performance venues.

Urbtix (☑2734 9009; www.urbtix.hk/; ◷10am-8pm)

Cityline (☑2317 6666; www.cityline.com.hk; ◷10am-8pm)

Hong Kong Ticketing (☑3128 8288; www.hkticketing.com; ◷10am-8pm)

Prices

Expect to pay around $80 for a seat up the back for the Hong Kong Philharmonic and from about $600 for a performance by big-name international acts or an international musical such as *Chicago*.

Movie tickets cost between $65 and $100, but can be cheaper at matinees, at the last screening of the day on weekends and on holidays (usually 11.30pm), or on certain days of the week. Almost all non-English-language films have both Chinese and English subtitles.

What's On

Artmap (www.artmap.com.hk)

Artslink (www.hkac.org.hk; ◷10am-6pm)

bc magazine (www.bcmagazine.net)

HK Magazine (http://hk-magazine.com)

Time Out (www.timeout.com.hk; HK$18)

Cantonese Opera

Hong Kong is one of the best places on earth to watch Cantonese opera. The best time to watch it is during the Hong Kong Arts Festival in February/March and the Mid-Autumn Festival, when outdoor performances are staged in Victoria Park. You can also catch a performance at the Temple Street Night Market or during Chinese festivals.

There are daily performances at the Sunbeam Theatre (p123) and at the new Yau Ma Tei Theatre (p146). If you don't speak Cantonese, the best way to book tickets for the Sunbeam Theatre is through the Urbtix or CityLine systems.

Lonely Planet's Top Choices

Hong Kong International Film Festival (p48) Asia's top film festival features both esoteric titles and crowd pleasers.

Clockenflap (p49)

Hong Kong Arts Festival (p25) Hong Kong's most exciting outdoor music festival.

Hidden Agenda (p159) The city's most visible clandestine live-music venue.

Street Music Concert (p123) Free under-the-stars live music, from Bach to original jazz.

Best for Live Music

Peel Fresco (p99)

Backstage Live (p49)

Joyce Is Not Here (p99)

Grappa's Cellar (p78)

Fringe Club (p49)

Best Underground Vibe

xxx (p99)

Cattle Depot Artist Village (p149)

Grappa's Cellar (p78)

Makumba Africa Lounge (p99)

Best for Theatre

Hong Kong Arts Centre (p123)

Hong Kong Academy for the Performing Arts (p123)

Hong Kong Cultural Centre (p158)

Hong Kong City Hall (p70)

Fringe Club (p49)

Cattle Depot Artist Village (p149)

Cheongsams (tight-fitting Chinese dresses) for sale

Shopping

Everyone knows Hong Kong as a place of neon-lit retail pilgrimage. This city is positively stuffed with swanky shopping malls and brand-name boutiques. All international brands worth their logo have outlets here. These are supplemented by the city's own retail trailblazers and a few creative local designers. Together they are Hong Kong's shrines and temples to style and consumption.

Antiques

Hong Kong has a rich and colourful array of Asian (especially Chinese) antiques on offer, but serious buyers will restrict themselves to reputable antique shops and auction houses only. Forgeries and expert reproductions abound. Remember that most of the quality pieces are sold through auction houses such as Christie's, especially at its auctions in spring and autumn.

Most of Hong Kong's antique shops are bunched along Wyndham St and Hollywood Rd in Central and Sheung Wan. The shops at the western end of Hollywood Rd tend to carry cheaper paraphernalia, including magazines, Chinese propaganda posters and badges from the Cultural Revolution.

For old-style Chinese handicrafts, the main places to go are the large emporiums.

Clothing
DESIGNER BRANDS & BOUTIQUES
The best places to find global design brands and luxury stores are in m

NEED TO KNOW

Business Hours

➡ Central: generally 10am to 8pm

➡ Causeway Bay: 11am to 9.30pm or 10pm

➡ Tsim Sha Tsui: 11am to 8pm

➡ Most shops are open on Sunday

➡ Winter sales are in January; summer sales, late June and early July

Service

Service is attentive and credit cards are widely accepted.

Duty-Free

There's no sales tax in Hong Kong so ignore the 'Tax Free' signs in some stores. However, you will pay duty on tobacco, perfume, cosmetics and cars. In general, almost everything is cheaper when you buy it outside duty-free shops.

Warranties & Guarantees

Some imported goods have a Hong Kong–only guarantee. If it's a well-known brand, you can return the warranty card to the Hong Kong importer to get one for your country. Grey-market items imported by somebody other than the official agent may have a guarantee that's valid only in the country of manufacture, or none at all.

Refunds & Exchanges

Most shops won't give refunds, but they can be persuaded to exchange purchases if they haven't been tampered with and you have a detailed receipt.

Shipping Goods

Many shops will package and post large items for you, but check whether you'll have to clear the goods at the country of destination. Smaller items can be shipped from the post office or try **DHL** (⌨2400 3388).

Trouble?

➡ **HKTB's Quality Tourism Services** (QTS; ⌨2806 2823; www.qtshk.com)

➡ **Hong Kong Consumer Council** (⌨2929 2222; www.consumer.org.hk; ⊙9am-5.45pm Mon-Fri)

IFC and the Landmark in Central, Pacific Place in Admiralty and Festival Walk in Kowloon Tong. Some of these shops such as Prada have outlets at Horizon Plaza in Ap Lei Chau selling off-season items at discounted prices.

There's also an embarrassment of midrange malls showcasing second- or third-tier brands, fast fashion outlets like Mango and Zara and local retailers such as Giordano.

For something a little more unique, there are cool independents opened by local designers and retailers in Sheung Wan, Wan Chai and Tsim Sha Tsui. You'll see some brilliant pieces but the range of styles is limited, simply because these places are few and far between.

STREET MARKETS & MINI-MALLS

The best hunting grounds for low-cost garments are in Tsim Sha Tsui at the eastern end of Granville Rd, and Cheung Sha Wan Rd in Sham Shui Po. The street markets on Temple St in Yau Ma Tei and Tung Choi St in Mong Kok have the cheapest clothes. You may also try Li Yuen St East and Li Yuen St West, two narrow alleyways linking Des Voeux Rd Central with Queen's Rd Central. They are a jumble of inexpensive clothing, handbags, backpacks and costume jewellery.

For a truly local shopping experience, the mini-malls in Tsim Sha Tsui are teeming with all things young and trendy, both locally designed or imported from the mainland or Korea. Usually you can negotiate a lower price when you purchase more than one item. And if you have a good eye, you can end up looking chic for very little.

Handicrafts & Souvenirs

For old-school Chinese handicrafts and other goods such as hand-carved wooden pieces, ceramics, cloisonné, silk garments and place mats, head to the large Chinese emporiums, such as Chinese Arts & Crafts and Yue Hwa Chinese Products Emporium.

You'll also find a small range of similar items (but of a lesser quality) in the alleyways of Tsim Sha Tsui, but remember to check prices at different vendors and bargain.

If you prefer something in a modern Chinese style, Shanghai Tang (the fashion boutique with branches all over town) has a range of cushions, tableware, photo frames and other home accessories.

The furniture store G.O.D. has a wide range of homeware and contemporary office products but with a cheeky Hong Kong twist.

Art

An increasing number of art galleries in Hong Kong sell paintings, sculptures, ceramic works and installations – some very good – by local artists. Like antique and curio shops, most of the city's commercial art galleries are found along Wyndham St and Hollywood Rd in Central and Sheung Wan.

The annual Hong Kong Art Fair, Hong Kong Artwalk in March, Le French May and Fotanian in October offer great opportunities to acquire art or simply acquaint yourself with the city's interesting visual-arts scene.

Gems & Jewellery

The Chinese attribute various magical qualities to jade, including the power to prevent ageing and accidents. The Jade Market in Yau Ma Tei is diverting, but unless you're knowledgeable about jade, limit yourself to modest purchases.

Hong Kong also offers a great range of pearls – cultured and freshwater. Retail prices for other precious stones are only marginally lower than elsewhere. The more reputable jewellery-shop chains – and there are many in Tsim Sha Tsui and Mong Kok catering to tourists from the mainland – will issue a certificate that states exactly what you are buying and guarantees that the shop will buy it back at a fair market price.

Leather Goods & Luggage

All the brand names such as Louis Vuitton, Samsonite and Rimowa are sold at Hong Kong department stores, and you'll also find some local vendors in the luggage business. The popularity of hiking and travel has triggered a proliferation of outdoor-products shops that carry high-quality

THE LOW-DOWN ON HIGH-TECH SHOPPING

Hong Kong has a plethora of shops specialising in electronic and digital gadgets, but the product mix and prices may vary. Similarly, vendors' command of English can range from 'enough to close a deal' (Mong Kok, Sham Shui Po) to 'reasonable' (the rest). Shopkeepers are generally honest but some have been known to sell display or secondhand items as new ones. All things considered, Wan Chai is your safest bet, but if you're a bit of a geek, the malls and flea market in Sham Shui Po are worth exploring.

Wan Chai Computer Centre (p124) Everything you need, from iPhones and tablets to notebooks, laptops and custom-made white-box computers; some leeway for bargaining.

Star Computer City (p160; Tsim Sha Tsui) The most expensive of the lot; strong in Mac products; no custom-made white-box computers.

In Square (p126; Causeway Bay) Prices are high with more gadgets than hardware.

Ap Liu Street Flea Market (p162; Sham Shui Po) A poor man's gadget heaven – everything new and used, including tablets, speakers and satellite dishes, but with a leaning towards hard-to-find batteries, remotes that control five TV brands, remote-controlled toys, parallel-import mobile phones, headphones and Chinese-made android tablets (50% to 70% less than prices in the US).

Golden Computer Arcade & Golden Shopping Center (p162; Sham Shui Po) Everything you need at cheaper prices than in Wan Chai; prices drop on Saturday and Sunday; items are displayed with price tags – they don't expect you to bargain.

Mong Kok Computer Centre (p161) Cheap Chinese-made tablets selling for half to 70% of the price you'd pay for the same product in the US; custom-made white boxes; no computer parts for sale.

Sin Tat Plaza (p161; Mong Kok) *The* mobile-phone mall for iPhones, iPads, androids, Chinese-made replicas, knock-offs, parallel import phones (from Japan, Korea, the US and Europe), fake phones and phones that double up as a lighter. Beware: it's full of re-packaged secondhand phones sold as new.

Top: Cityplaza shopping centre (p126), Quarry Bay

Left: Shanghai Tang (p78), Central

backpacks. If you're looking for a casual bag or daypack, check out Li Yuen St East and Li Yuen St West in Central or Stanley Market.

Cameras

One of the best spots in Hong Kong to buy photographic equipment is Stanley St in Central. Everything carries price tags, though some low-level bargaining may be possible. Never buy a camera without a price tag. This will probably preclude many of the shops in Tsim Sha Tsui. That said, Tsim Sha Tsui has a couple of places on Kimberley Rd dealing in used cameras, and there are plenty of photo shops on Sai Yeung Choi St in Mong Kok.

Watches

Shops selling watches are ubiquitous in Hong Kong and you can find everything from a Rolex to Russian army timepieces and diving watches. Avoid the shops without price tags. The big department stores and City Chain are fine, but compare prices.

Local Brands & Designers

Hong Kong doesn't have a profusion of quirky, creative one-offs or unique vintage items as in London, New York or Copenhagen (have you seen the rent landlords charge here?). But the city has a small, passionate band of local designer boutiques offering value, character and style across a range of goods, especially in fashion and furniture.

Soho, Wan Chai, Causeway Bay and Tsim Sha Tsui are the best places to find them. Some stores like Homeless carry a smattering of chic, design-oriented goods (local and imported) while others, such as furniture store G.O.D. and fashion boutiques Shanghai Tang and Initial, have in-house design teams.

Defensive Shopping

Hong Kong is not a nest of thieves just waiting to rip you off, but pitfalls can strike the uninitiated.

Whatever you're in the market for, always check prices in a few shops before buying. The most common way for shopkeepers to cheat tourists is to simply overcharge. In some of the electronic stores in the tourist shopping district of Tsim Sha Tsui, many goods do not have price tags. Checking prices in several shops therefore becomes essential. Sometimes stores will quote a reasonable or even low price on a big-ticket item, only to get the money back by overcharging on accessories.

Spotting overcharging is the easy part, though. Sneakier (but rarer) tricks involve merchants removing vital components that should have been included for free (and demanding more money when you return to the shop to get them). Another tactic is to replace some of the good components with cheaper ones.

Bargaining

Sales assistants in department or chain stores rarely have any leeway to give discounts, but you can try bargaining in owner-operated stores and certainly in markets.

Some visitors believe that you can always get the goods for half of the price originally quoted. But if you can bargain something down that low, perhaps you shouldn't be buying it from that shop anyway. Remember you may be getting that DSLR cheap but paying high mark-ups for the memory card, or worse, it may have missing components or no international warranty.

Remember not to be too intent on getting the best deals. Really, what's HK$2 off a souvenir that's being sold for HK$20? Probably not much to you, but it may mean a lot to the old lady selling them.

Lonely Planet's Top Choices

G.O.D. (p124) Awesome lifestyle accessories, homewares and gifts – Hong Kong to the bone with a whiff of mischief.

Wattis Fine Art (p101) Antique maps and nostalgic photographs of Hong Kong and Macau.

Shanghai Tang (p78) Classy homeware and clothing in a modern chinoiserie style.

Pottery Workshop (p103) Excellent ceramic works by Hong Kong's home-grown artists.

Lane Crawford (p79) Luxury department store specialising in stylish clothing, homeware and accessories.

Daydream Nation (p123) Locally designed streetwear – edgy, wearable and with a touch of theatricality.

Best for Fashion

Joyce (p79)

Initial (p159)

Vivienne Tam (p162)

9th Muse (p101)

Horizon Plaza (p134)

Lu Lu Cheung (p102)

Best for Gifts

Yue Hwa Chinese Products Emporium (p161)

Chinese Arts & Crafts (p161)

Curio Alley (p160)

Picture This (p78)

Mountain Folkcraft (p102)

Lam Kie Yuen Tea Co (p103)

Best for Antiques

Arch Angel Antiques (p101)

Tai Sing Fine Antiques (p101)

David Chan Photo Shop (p162)

Honeychurch Antiques (p101)

Indosiam (p102)

Picture This (p78)

Best for Art

Karin Weber Gallery (p102)

Saamlung (p79)

C&G Artpartment (p147)

Pearl Lam Galleries (p79)

Chai Wan factory warehouse (p113)

Jockey Club Creative Arts Centre (p147)

Best for Books

Flow (p101)

Hong Kong Reader (p161)

ACO Books (p124)

MCCM Bookshop (p124)

Page One (p162)

Kelly & Walsh (p124)

Best for Gadgets

Wan Chai Computer Centre (p124)

Golden Computer Arcade (p162)

Golden Shopping Center (p162)

Ap Liu Street Flea Market (p162)

Sin Tat Plaza (p161)

Mong Kok Computer Centre (p161)

Best Malls

IFC Mall (p78)

Pacific Place (p124)

Elements (p162)

Festival Walk (p162)

Rise Shopping Arcade (p159)

Times Square (p126)

Best for Food & Beverages

Portrait Winemakers & Distillers (p102)

Tak Hing Dried Seafood (p161)

Yiu Fung Store (p125)

Citysuper (p80)

Three Sixty (p80)

Best Markets

Stanley Market (p134)

Ap Liu Street Flea Market (p162)

Temple Street Night Market (p146)

Cheung Sha Wan Road (p163)

Tung Choi St Market/Ladies' Market (p148)

Best for Quirky Items

Sino Centre (p161)

Chan Wah Kee Cutlery Store (p160)

Picture This (p78)

Tai Yuen Street Toy Shops (p125)

Bespoke swords by Antonio Cejunior (p254)

Ap Liu Street Flea Market (p162)

Dragon-boat racing (p58), Dragon Boat Festival

Sports & Activities

Hong Kong offers countless ways to have fun and keep fit. From golf and frisbee to cycling and windsurfing, you won't be stumped for something active to do. There are also gyms, yoga studios and spas offering everything from aromatherapy to foot massage. If you prefer watching people play, the world's most exciting dragon boat racing takes place right here!

Climbing

Hong Kong is peppered with excellent granite faces and volcanic rocks in some striking wilderness areas. The best place to climb is on Tung Lung Chau, which has a technical wall, a big wall and a sea gully. Follow the path to the fort on the island and when you see the Holiday Store, ask the folks there to show you where it is. All climbers stop there for noodles and supplies. A **ferry** (☎2560 9929) leaves Sai Wan Ho typhoon shelter for the island four to six times a day on Saturday

and Sunday. On weekdays you can probably just show up at the typhoon shelter and haggle with sampan operators. Tai Tau Chau, near Shek O beach, also has excellent granite, some with bolted routes.

The **Hong Kong Climbing** (www.hongkong climbing.com) website is a handy resource for climbers.

Cycling

Hong Kong's natural terrain makes for some fabulous cycling. The ambitious

NEED TO KNOW

Maps

The Map Publications Centre sells excellent maps detailing hiking and cycling trails; buy online (www.landsd.gov.hk/mapping/en/pro&ser/products.htm) or at major post offices (www.landsd.gov.hk/mapping/en/pro&ser/outlet.htm).

Information & Facilities

Environmental Protection Department (www.epd.gov.hk) Lists of country and marine parks.

Hong Kong Tourism Board (☑2508 1234; www.discoverhongkong.com) Website has a full list of what's on.

Leisure and Cultural Services Department (☑2414 5555; www.lcsd.gov.hk) Lists of fields, stadiums, beaches, swimming pools, water-sports centres etc, including equipment for hire.

South China Athletic Association (☑2577 6932; www.scaa.org.hk; Hong Kong Club House, 88 Caroline Hill Rd, Causeway Bay) Has sports facilities for hire.

Also check the sports sections of English-language newspapers.

More Ideas

➡ Birdwatching (www.hkbws.org.hk)

➡ Dolphin-watching (see p30)

➡ Hiking and kayaking trips, try **Natural Excursion Ideals** (☑9300 5197; www.kayak-and-hike.com)

➡ Outdoor sports (www.hkoutdoors.com)

New Territories Cycle Track Network Construction project is due for completion in 2013.

The longest bicycle track runs from Sha Tin through Tai Po to Tai Mei Tuk, taking you through parks, and past temples and the waterfront. The **Hong Kong Cycling Alliance** (http://hkcyclingalliance.org) website has road rules and safety for cyclists.

You need a (free) permit for mountain biking. Check with the **Mountain Biking Association** (www.hkmba.org) or www.crazyguyonabike.com/doc/Hongkong for permit details.

Dragon Boat Racing

Hong Kong is possibly the best place in the world to watch dragon boat racing because the traditions underlying the practice are still very much alive. The city has over 20 races a year with most taking place from May to July. The **Hong Kong Tourism Board** (www.discoverhongkong.com) website has information on the main events.

Football (Soccer)

Hong Kong has a fairly lively amateur soccer league. Games are played at the **Happy Valley Sports Ground** (☑2895 1523; Sports Rd, Happy Valley; 🚋Happy Valley), a group of pitches inside the Happy Valley Racecourse, and at **Mong Kok Stadium** (旺角大球場; ☑2380 0188; 37 Flower Market Rd, Mong Kok; Ⓜ Prince Edward, exit B1). For match schedules and venues, check the sports sections of the English-language newspapers or contact the **Hong Kong Football Association** (☑2712 9122; www.hkfa.com). For casual football matches, visit http://casualfootball.net.

Golf

Hong Kong has only one public golf course but some private clubs open their doors on weekdays for a green fee (HK$700 to HK$2000 for 18 holes).

The scenic Jockey Club Kau Sai Chau Public Golf Course (see p188), the territory's only public golf course, is open to non-Hong Kong residents on weekdays. A ferry departs for Kau Sai Chau every 20 minutes (from 6.40am to 7pm weekdays, to 9pm Friday to Sunday), from the pier near the Wai Man Rd car park.

The **Hong Kong Golf Club** (www.hkgolfclub.org) welcomes nonmembers on weekdays at its Fanling and Deep Water Bay (see p131) venues.

The **Hong Kong Golf Association** (☑2504 8659; www.hkga.com) has a list of driving ranges and tournaments held in the territory, including the Hong Kong Open Championships, one of Asia's leading professional golf tournaments (it's usually played in November or December).

Gyms & Yoga Studios

Yoga and fitness are big business here, with the largest slices of the pie shared out among a few big names. If you want a personal yoga teacher, try Gauranga Nityananda (p163). Pure Fitness (p81) has comprehensive gym facilities.

SNAKES ALIVE

Take care when bushwalking in the New Territories, particularly on Lamma and Lantau Islands. Poisonous snakes, the most common being the bamboo pit viper, are a hazard, although they will not attack unless surprised or provoked. Go straight to a public hospital if bitten; private doctors do not stock antivenene. Other fauna to be aware of in the New Territories are wild boars, which can be hugely dangerous if they choose to attack. Steer well clear if you spot one and back off slowly if you're already too close.

Hiking

Many visitors are surprised to learn that Hong Kong is an excellent place for hiking. Lengthy wilderness trails criss-cross the territory and its islands through striking mountain, coast and jungle trails. The four main ones are the MacLehose Trail, at 100km the longest in the territory; the 78km-long Wilson Trail, which runs on both sides of Victoria Harbour; the 70km-long Lantau Trail; and the Hong Kong Trail (see boxed text, p60), which is 50km long. Hong Kong's excellent public-transport network makes it feasible to tackle these trails a section at a time.

For full details and advice on routes and suggested itineraries, invest in one of the excellent hiking guides that are widely available in Hong Kong bookshops. Before heading out it's also a good idea to consult the official Hong Kong hiking website (www.hkwalkers.net) for updates on weather and the condition of the trails (landslides can sometimes mean route closures or diversions). Hikers can camp on remote beaches and most venues run by the following:

Country & Marine Parks Authority (☎2150 6868; www.parks.afcd.gov.hk)

Hong Kong Youth Hostels Association (HKYHA; ☎2788 1638; www.yha.org.hk)

Horse Racing

Horse racing is Hong Kong's biggest spectator sport. There are two racecourses: one in Happy Valley and one at Sha Tin. Attending one of the Wednesday race meetings (7.00pm, HK$10 entrance fee) at Happy Valley during the racing season (Sep to June) is a great way to experience racing in Hong Kong.

Martial Arts

Hong Kong has a glut of martial-arts programs, but only a few have special arrangements for English-speaking visitors.

Hong Kong Tourism Board (☎2508 1234; www.discoverhongkong.com) Runs free taichi lessons on the waterfront outside the Cultural Centre.

Shaolin Wushu Culture Centre (see p210) Offers overnight stays.

Wan Kei Ho International Martial Arts Association (see p103) Has a local and foreign following.

Parkour

The **Hong Kong Parkour Association** (香港飛躍道協會; www.parkour.hk) has training/practice sessions every Tuesday evening (from 7.30pm to 9.30pm) at one of 15 open spots in town. Beginners and veterans are welcome to join for free. Call **Gon** (☎6837 7068) or **Tim** (☎6198 2734). Check the website for training locations.

Rugby

The **Rugby World Cup Sevens** (www.hksevens.com.hk) sees teams from all over the world come together in Hong Kong in late March for three days of lightning-fast 15-minute matches at the 40,000-seat **Hong Kong Stadium** (☎2895 7926; www.lcsd.gov.hk/stadium; ⊟Happy Valley) in So Kon Po. Even nonrugby fans scramble to get tickets, because the Sevens is a giant, international, three-day party. For inquiries and tickets, contact the **Hong Kong Rugby Football Union** (☎2504 8311; www.hkrugby.com).

Running

The best places to run on Hong Kong Island include Harlech and Lugard Rds on the Peak, Bowen Rd above Wan Chai, the track in Victoria Park and the Happy Valley racecourse (as long as there aren't any horse races!). In Kowloon a popular place to run is the Tsim Sha Tsui East Promenade. Lamma makes an ideal place for trail runners, with plenty of paths and dirt trails, great views and, best of all, no cars.

Scuba Diving

Hong Kong has some surprisingly worthwhile diving spots, particularly in the far

...NG TRAIL

...without exerting yourself too much, the **Hong Kong Trail** (港島徑) ... is a great choice. The 50km route comprises eight sections of ...y, beginning on the Peak (take the Peak tram up to the Peak and follow ...e) and ending near Shek O, on Island South.

...e of the easiest and most scenic sections runs for about two hours along a mountain ridge called Dragon's Back. Voted by *Time* (Asia) as the best urban hike in Asia, it takes you past woods, then up to the windy spine of the dragon where there are views of sundrenched beaches and billowing hills streaked with cloud shadow. Then it's all the way down to Shek O Rd, where you can hoof it or bus it to Shek O's beach for a rewarding meal, a swim or a game of frisbee.

The hike is manageable by anyone remotely fit, including kids as young as four. If you want something more challenging, head to Sai Kung in the New Territories or Lantau Island.

northeast, and there is certainly no shortage of courses. One of the best sources of information for courses and excursions is Sai Kung–based **Splash Hong Kong** (☎2792 4495, 9047 9603; www.splashhk.com). The following outfits also give lessons and organise dives:

Bunn's Divers (p125) Organises dives in Sai Kung on Sunday for about $500 (less for members).

Ocean Sky Divers (p163) This dive shop runs PADI courses and organises local dives.

Spa Treatments & Therapies

Whether you want to be spoilt rotten with thousand-dollar caviar facials or have a simple foot rub, Hong Kong's extensive pampering sector can assist. Most of the top hotels operate their own spas. For less elaborate routines, you'll find plenty of places in Central and Kowloon offering spa treatments, massages and reflexology.

Ultimate Frisbee

Ultimate has a dedicated following among expats and visitors, and some locals in the 20s and 30s age group. Check the Hong

Kong Ultimate Frisbee Association website (www.hkupa.com/) for details, including the twice-a-week pick-ups. Around May each year, the HKUPA organises a Hat Tournament (accompanied by much partying) that visitors are welcome to register for and participate in.

Wakeboarding

Most operators of this popular sport are based in Sai Kung (New Territories) and Tai Tam (Hong Kong Island). Rates are about HK$700 per hour. Try **Tai Tam Wakeboarding Centre** (☎3120 4102; www.wakeboard.com. hk) or **Hong Kong Wakeboard** (☎9021 4221).

Windsurfing, Kayaking & Canoeing

The best time for windsurfing is October to December. Check the Leisure and Cultural Services Department website (www.lcsd. gov.hk) for government-run water-sports centres providing canoes, windsurfing boards, kayaks and other equipment for hire, some only to holders of the relevant certificates.

PLAN YOUR TRIP SPORTS & ACTIVITIES

Lonely Planet's Top Choices

Dragon boat racing (p58) Feel the heart-pounding excitement of these atmospheric races that evolved from an ancient ritual.

Horse racing in Happy Valley (p111) The thunderous action at this urban racecourse makes for an unforgettable experience.

Rugby Sevens (p59) Join rugby fans for three days of lightning matches and wild partying.

Kayaking in Sai Kung (p187) Paddle in clear waters surrounded by hills and geological wonders.

Walking Hong Kong's trails (p59) A palette of hills, history, grottoes and good food.

Morning taichi (p163) Learn the Chinese art of shadow boxing from a master.

Best for Socialising

Ultimate frisbee (p60)

Parkour (p59)

Football (playing it; p58)

Dragon boat races (p58)

Best for Swimming

Beaches on Lamma Island (p194)

Beaches on Lantau Island (p199)

Beaches on Cheung Chau Island (p210)

Beaches in Sai Kung (p184)

Beaches at Island South (p131)

Best for Scenery

Hoi Ha Wan Hiking Trail (p187)

Cycling at Plover Cove Reservoir (p177)

High Island Reservoir (p188)

Eastern Nature Trail (p126)

Tai Tam Waterworks Heritage Trail (p126)

Hiking on Tung Ping Chau (p187)

Best for Martial Arts

Hong Kong Shaolin Wushu Culture Centre (p210)

Wan Kei Ho International Martial Arts Association (p103)

Wing Chun Yip Man Martial Arts Athletic Association (p163)

Best for Toning Up

Spa at the Four Seasons (p81)

Ten Feet Tall (p81)

Happy Foot Reflexology Centre (p103)

Gauranga Nityananda (p163)

Best One-Stop Sports Facilities

South China Athletic Association (p126)

Victoria Park (p126)

Kowloon Park (p144)

Explore Hong Kong

HONG KONG'S TOP SIGHTS

Neighbourhoods at a Glance

❶ Hong Kong Island: Central (p66)

The financial heart of Asia's financial hub is replete with corporate citadels, colonial relics and massive monuments to consumerism. It's where you'll find the stock exchange, the Four Seasons, Gucci, Prada and celebrity chefs, all housed in a compelling mix of modernist architecture. Dynamic during the day, it retires soon after sundown.

❷ Hong Kong Island: the Peak & the Northwest (p82)

Victoria Peak, soaring above the residences in the Mid-Levels, offers a great vantage point from which to gaze back on Hong Kong. Down below, Sheung Wan and Western District

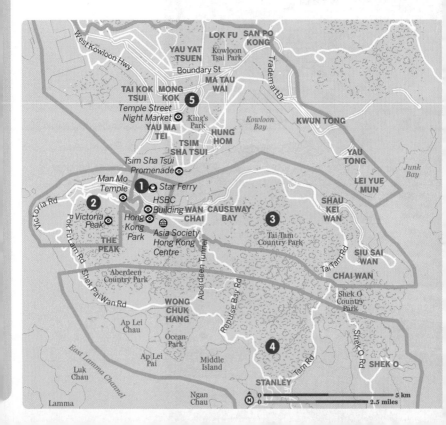

have, between them, something for everyone, whether it's historical jewels, antiques and fine art (Hollywood Rd), stylish hedonism (Lan Kwai Fong, Soho), boho havens, or life, simple and unadorned.

❸ Hong Kong Island: Wan Chai & the Northeast (p104)

Quiet Admiralty offers class and quality over quantity, whether it's shopping, lodging, sights or dining. To its east, prolific Wan Chai is a seat of culture, a showcase for folk traditions and a nightlife guru, not to mention Hong Kong's most versatile kitchen. In the shopping hub of Causeway Bay, restaurants, traffic and department stores jockey for space with a racecourse and a cemetery (both in Happy Valley).

❹ Hong Kong Island: Aberdeen & the South (p127)

The southern district is the island's backyard playground – from the beaches of Repulse Bay and Deep Water Bay to Stanley Market, the waterfront bazaar and Ocean Park, the amusement park. Aberdeen Harbour offers boat rides down memory lane to a bygone era when thousands lived on junks moored in the harbour, while sleepy Ap Lei Chau surprises with a shopping hot spot and top-notch seafood.

❺ Kowloon (p135)

Tsim Sha Tsui is endowed with four museums, an unbeatable harbour setting, and all the superlatives Central has to offer on a more human scale. Other assets include leafy parks, colonial gems and the most diverse ethnic mix in all of Hong Kong. Indigenous Yau Ma Tei is a mosaic of night markets, guesthouses, martial-arts dens and postwar cafes, while Mong Kok is a riot of sardine-packed commercialism. In New Kowloon a Buddhist nunnery and a Taoist temple await.

❻ New Territories (p164)

The New Territories offers much cultural and natural interest. Ancient walled villages (Sheung Shui, Fan Ling, Yuen Long), wetlands teeming with aquatic and bird life (Yuen Long), temple complexes (Tsuen Wan, Sha Tin, Fan Ling), a solid museum in Sha Tin, and generous expanses of unspoiled country are just some of its attractions. Notably, the Sai Kung Peninsula has breathtaking hiking trails, delicious seafood and romantic beaches.

❼ Outlying Islands (p192)

From the old-world streetscapes of Cheung Chau and Peng Chau, to the monasteries and hiking trails of Lantau, and the waterfront seafood restaurants of Lamma, Hong Kong's 'outlying islands' offer a host of sights and activities.

NEIGHBOURHOODS AT A GLANCE

Hong Kong Island: Central

Neighbourhood Top Five

1 Taking a cruise on the legendary **Star Ferry** (p69).

2 Getting personal with skyscrapers you've seen in *Batman* by venturing inside the **Bank of China Buildings** (p70) and the **HSBC Building** (p68), and zooming in from (what feels like) half a metre away on the rooftop terrace at **Sevva** (p75).

3 Enjoying top-notch dim sum at **Lung King Heen** (p72) followed by French desserts or artisanal cheeses at **Caprice** (p72).

4 Shopping with the wealthy (or watching the wealthy shop) at the **IFC Mall** (p71).

5 Taking your morning constitutional and paying the animals a visit at the **Zoological & Botanical Gardens** (p70).

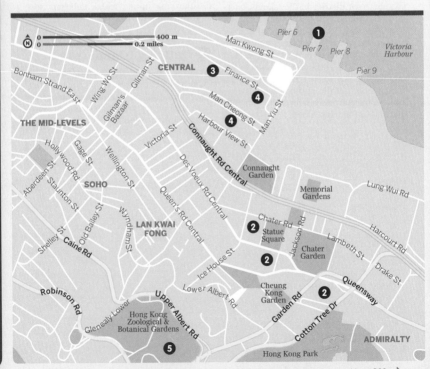

For more detail of this area, see Map p362 ➡

Explore Central

Whatever time of the day you plan on visiting Hong Kong's CBD, it's worth remembering that shops here close relatively early (6pm or 7pm), and by mid-evening, the dust has settled. It's also advisable to have lunch outside the noon-to-2pm insanity when hordes of hungry suits descend on every table in sight.

Travelling on the MTR, take the Statue Sq exit and spend an hour looking around the Former Legislative Council Building and other memorials to Hong Kong's past. In the next couple of hours, check out the architecture in the vicinity – glass-and-steel modernity like the HSBC Building and colonial-era survivors like the Gothic St John's Cathedral.

Head over to the Zoological and Botanical Gardens for some hobnobbing with the rhesus monkeys. Recharged after an hour, make a beeline for the harbour for some retail therapy at the IFC Mall. Take as long as you like, then hop on the Star Ferry to Kowloon.

Local Life

➡ **Lil' Manila** Every Sunday, Filipina maids take over Statue Sq and the nearby pavements to eat, sing, chat and read the Bible.

➡ **Hang-outs** On weekdays at 3pm, well-coiffed ladies of leisure congregate at Sevva (p75) for Marie Antoinette's Crave (it's a cake).

➡ **Shopping** Li Yuen St East and West, two alleyways that link Des Voeux Rd Central with Queen's Rd Central, have a jumble of inexpensive clothing, handbags and jewellery.

Getting There & Away

➡ **MTR** Central station on the Island and Tsuen Wan lines.

➡ **Airport Express** Hong Kong station below IFC Mall connects (by underground walkway) with Central MTR station on one side and Central Piers on the other.

➡ **Star Ferry** Ferries from Tsim Sha Tsui in Kowloon arrive at Central Pier 7.

➡ **Bus** Buses start and end their journeys at Central bus terminus below Exchange Sq.

➡ **Tram** Runs east and west along Des Voeux Rd Central.

➡ **Outlying Islands Ferry** Ferries to Discovery Bay, Lamma, Cheung Chau, Lantau and Peng Chau (Central Piers 3 to 6).

➡ **Central Escalator** Runs from the former Central Market to the Mid-Levels.

➡ **Peak Tram** Runs from the lower terminus (33 Garden Rd) to the Peak.

Lonely Planet's Top Tip

To enjoy Central's top-notch French and Italian restaurants without breaking the bank, go for the lunch specials. Most restaurants offer specials for the convenience of business lunchers and frugal foodies. Some may even serve breakfast and/or afternoon tea, weekend lunch buffets or sell gourmet sandwiches at a takeaway station. Remember to book in advance if you're dining in for lunch.

Best Places to Eat

➡ Lung King Heen (p72)
➡ Caprice (p72)
➡ Linguini Fini (p72)
➡ Island Tang (p74)
➡ Tasty Congee and Noodle Wonton Shop (p74)

For reviews, see p72

Best Places to Drink

➡ Sevva (p75)
➡ Amo Eno (p75)
➡ Red Bar (p78)

For reviews, see p75 ➡

Best Places to Shop

➡ Shanghai Tang (p78)
➡ Blanc de Chine (p78)
➡ Saamlung (p79)
➡ Lane Crawford (p79)

For reviews, see p78 ➡

TOP SIGHTS
HSBC BUILDING

The stunning HSBC headquarters, designed by British architect Sir Norman Foster in 1985, is a masterpiece of precision, sophistication and innovation. And so it should be. On completion in 1985 it was the world's most expensive building (costing over US$1 billion). The HSBC Building reflects the architect's wish to create areas of public and private space, and to break the mould of previous bank architecture. A lighting scheme fitted later enabled the building to stand out equally at night.

The two bronze lions guarding the main entrance were designed for the bank's previous headquarters in 1935; the lions are known as Stephen – the one roaring – and Stitt, after two bank employees of the time. The Japanese used the lions as target practice during the occupation; you can still see bullet holes on Stitt. Rub their mighty paws for luck.

The 52-storey glass and aluminium building is full of examples of good feng shui (Chinese geomancy). There's no structure blocking its view of Victoria Harbour because water is associated with prosperity. The escalators are believed to symbolise the whiskers of a dragon sucking wealth into its belly. They're built at an angle to the entrance, supposedly to disorient evil spirits which can only travel in a straight line.

The ground floor is public space, which people can traverse without entering the bank. From there, take the escalator to the 3rd floor to gaze at the cathedral-like atrium and the natural light filtering through its windows.

DON'T MISS...

➡ Lighting scheme at night
➡ Stephen & Stitt
➡ Feng shui features
➡ The atrium

PRACTICALITIES

➡ 滙豐銀行總行大廈
➡ Map p362
➡ www.hsbc.com. hk/1/2/about/home/ unique-headquarters
➡ 1 Queen's Rd, Central
➡ admission free
➡ ⊙escalator 9am-4.30pm Mon-Fri, to 12.30pm Sat
➡ Ⓜ Central, exit K

TOP SIGHTS
STAR FERRY

You can't say you've 'done' Hong Kong until you've taken a ride on a Star Ferry, that legendary fleet of electric-diesel vessels with names like *Morning Star* and *Twinkling Star*. At any time of the day the 30¢-ride, with its riveting views of skyscrapers and soaring mountains, must be one of the world's best-value cruises. At the end of the 10-minute journey, watch as a crew member casts a hemp rope to a colleague who catches it with a billhook, the way it was done in 1888 when the first boat docked.

The Star Ferry was a witness to major events in Hong Kong history, including on Christmas Day 1941, when the colonial governor, Sir Mark Aitchison Young, took the ferry to Tsim Sha Tsui, where he surrendered to the Japanese at the Peninsula. (For more ferry history, see p71.)

Take your first trip on a clear night from Tsim Sha Tsui to Central. It's less dramatic in the opposite direction. That said, you can turn to face the rear and bid adieu to the glorious view as it slips away from you. If you don't mind the noise and diesel fumes, the lower deck (only open on the Tsim Sha Tsui–Central route) is better for pictures.

The pier you see on Hong Kong Island is an uninspiring Edwardian replica that replaced the old pier (Streamline Moderne style and with a clock tower) at Edinburgh Pl that was demolished despite vehement opposition from Hong Kong people. The Kowloon pier remains untouched.

The Star Ferry operates on two routes – Tsim Sha Tsui–Central and Tsim Sha Tsui–Wan Chai. The first is more popular. The coin-operated turnstiles do not give change but you can get it from the ticket window.

DON'T MISS...

➡ The views
➡ Kowloon pier
➡ The hemp rope & billhook routine

PRACTICALITIES

➡ 天星小輪
➡ Map p362
➡ ☏ 2367 7065
➡ www.starferry.com.hk
➡ adult $2-3, child $1.40-1.80
➡ every 6-12min, 6.30am-11.30pm (Tsim Sha Tsui–Central)
➡ every 8-20min, 7.20am-11pm (Tsim Sha Tsui–Wan Chai)
➡ Ⓜ Central–Tsim Sha Tsui
➡ Ⓜ Wan Chai–Tsim Sha Tsui

◉ SIGHTS

STATUE SQUARE
SQUARE

Map p362 (皇后像廣場; Edinburgh Pl; MCentral, exit K) This leisurely square used to house effigies of British royalty. Now it pays tribute to a single sovereign – the founder of HSBC, the banking giant who owns the square. While it lacks statues, there's plenty to see. In the northern area of the square (reached via a pedestrian underpass) is the **Cenotaph** (和平紀念碑), built in 1923 as a memorial to Hong Kong residents killed during the two world wars. To the east the **Hong Kong Club Building** (香港會所大廈; 1 Jackson Rd), resembling a swimming stingray, houses a prestigious club of that name that was still not accepting Chinese members until well after WWII. On the south side of Chater Rd, Statue Sq has a pleasant collection of fountains and seating areas, although it's somewhat marred by tiling, which gives it the look of a 1980s municipal washroom.

FREE HONG KONG ZOOLOGICAL & BOTANICAL GARDENS
PARK

Map p362 (香港動植物公園; www.lcsd.gov.hk/parks; Albany Rd; ⊙terrace gardens 6am-10pm, zoo & aviaries to 7pm, greenhouse 9am-4.30pm; ▣3B, 12) Built in the Victorian era, this garden has a pleasant and expansive collection of fountains, sculptures and greenhouses, plus a playground, zoo and some fabulous aviaries. Along with exotic trees, plants and shrubs, some 160 species of bird reside here. The zoo is surprisingly comprehensive, with more than 70 mammals and 40 reptiles, and is also one of the world's leading centres for the captive breeding of endangered species. Albany Rd divides the gardens, with the plants and aviaries in the area to the east, close to Garden Rd, and most of the animals to the west.

HSBC BUILDING
BUILDING

See p68.

BANK OF CHINA BUILDINGS
BUILDING

Map p362 (MCentral, exit K) The awesome **Bank of China Tower** (中銀大廈; 1 Garden Rd), designed by architect Chinese-born American architect IM Pei, is Hong Kong's fourth-tallest structure. Rising from the ground like a cube, it is successively reduced, quarter by quarter, until the south-facing side is left to rise upward on its own. The **public viewing gallery** (⊙ 8am-6pm Mon-Fri) on the 43rd floor offers panoramic views of Hong Kong. The **old BOC building** (舊中國銀行大廈; 1 Bank St), though now one of the shortest buildings in Central, is majestic in its own right.

EXCHANGE SQUARE
BUILDING

Map p362 (交易廣場; 8 Connaught Pl; MCentral, exit A) This complex of office towers is home to the Hong Kong Stock Exchange and a number of corporate headquarters. The main draw is the attractive and relatively peaceful open-air space, featuring fountains and sculptures by Henry Moore and Taiwanese artist Ju Ming. Access is via a network of overhead pedestrian walkways stretching west to Sheung Wan and linked to buildings on the other side of Connaught Rd.

FORMER FRENCH MISSION BUILDING
HISTORIC BUILDING

Map p362 (前法國外方傳道會大樓; 1 Battery Path; MCentral, exit K) The **Court of Final Appeal**, the highest judicial body in Hong Kong, is now housed in the neoclassical former French Mission building, a charming structure built in 1868. It served as the Russian consulate until 1915 when the French Overseas Mission bought it and added a chapel and a dome. The building was the headquarters of the provisional colonial government after WWII. Just before the mission building is pretty **Cheung Kong Garden**, which developers were required to lay out when they built the 70-storey Cheung Kong Centre to the south.

GOVERNMENT HOUSE
HISTORIC BUILDING

Map p362 (禮賓府; ☑2530 2003; www.ceo.gov.hk/gh; Upper Albert Rd; MCentral, exit G) Parts of this erstwhile official residence of the Chief Executive of Hong Kong, and previously the colonial governors, date back to 1855. Other features were added by the Japanese, who used it as military headquarters during the occupation of Hong Kong in WWII. It's open to the public three or four times a year, notably one Sunday in March, when the azaleas in the gardens are in full bloom.

HONG KONG CITY HALL
BUILDING

Map p362 (香港大會堂; ☑2921 2840; 5 Edinburgh Pl; ⊙9am-11pm; MCentral, exit J3) The City Hall, built in 1962, is a major cultural venue in Hong Kong, with concert and recital halls, a theatre and exhibition

STAR FERRY'S STARS

The Star Ferry was founded in 1888 by Dorabjee Nowrojee, a Parsi from Bombay who had worked his way up from a cook to the owner of a hotel in Hong Kong. At the time, most locals were crossing the harbour on sampans. Nowrojee bought a steamboat for the use of his family and friends, and this later evolved into the first Star Ferry. Parsis believe in Zoroastrianism, a religion from Persia, and the five-pointed star on the Star Ferry logo is in fact an ancient Zoroastrian symbol.

The Star Ferry features in Hong Kong's history. In 1966 thousands gathered at the Tsim Sha Tsui pier to protest against a proposed 5¢ fare increase. It evolved into a riot as the protestors threw stones at buses and set vehicles on fire on Nathan Rd. The 1966 Riot is seen as the trailblazer of local social protests leading to colonial reforms.

No surprise then that, on an overcast day, the only stars you'll see over Victoria Harbour are those of the Star Ferry.

galleries. Within the Lower Block, entered to the east of City Hall's main entrance, the **Hong Kong Planning & Infrastructure Exhibition Gallery** (☎3102 1242; www.infrastructure.gallery.gov.hk; 2 Murray Rd; admission free; ⊙10am-6pm) may not sound like a crowd-pleaser, but may awaken the Meccano builder in more than a few visitors.

JARDINE HOUSE — BUILDING

Map p362 (怡和大廈; 1 Connaught Pl; MHong Kong, exit B2) This 52-storey silver monolith punctured with 1750 porthole-like windows was Hong Kong's first true 'skyscraper' when it opened in 1973. Inevitably the building has earned its own irreverent nickname: the 'House of 1000 Arseholes'. In the basement is the live-music venue and Italian restaurant, Grappa's Cellar (see p78).

FORMER LEGISLATIVE COUNCIL BUILDING — BUILDING

Map p362 (前立法會大樓; 8 Jackson Rd; MCentral, exit G) The colonnaded and domed building (c 1912) was built of granite quarried on Stonecutters Island, and served as the seat of the Legislative Council from 1985 to 2012. During WWII it was a headquarters of the Gendarmerie, the Japanese version of the Gestapo, and many people were executed here. Standing atop the pediment is a blindfolded statue of Themis, the Greek goddess of justice and natural law.

FREE ST JOHN'S CATHEDRAL — BUILDING

Map p362 (聖約翰座堂; ☎2523 4157; www.stjohnscathedral.org.hk; 4-8 Garden Rd; ⊙7am-6pm; MCentral, exit J2) Services have been held at this Anglican cathedral since it opened in 1849, except in 1944, when the Japanese army used it as a social club. It suffered heavy damage during WWII and after the war the front doors were remade using timber salvaged from HMS *Tamar*, a British warship that used to guard the entrance to Victoria Harbour. You walk on sacred ground in more ways than one at St John's: it is the only piece of freehold land in Hong Kong. Enter from Battery Path.

The cathedral's choir conducts evensong on the third Sunday of each month (from 6pm) from September to June. You can join them for practice (4.30pm) and worship. Call the cathedral and ask for the choirmaster, Alan Tsang.

STAR FERRY — FERRY

See p69.

ONE & TWO INTERNATIONAL FINANCE CENTRE — BUILDING

Map p362 (國際金融中心; 1 Harbour View St; Two IFC; 8 Finance St; MHong Kong, exit F) These tapering, pearl-coloured colossi (respectively 39 and 88 storeys), which some say resemble electric shavers, sit atop the International Finance Centre (IFC) Mall. Both were partly designed by Cesar Pelli, the architect responsible for the World Financial Center in downtown Manhattan. The highest you can get is to the **Hong Kong Monetary Authority Information Centre** (金管局資訊中心; ☎2878 1111; www.info.gov.hk/hkma; 55th fl, Two IFC; admission free; ⊙10am-6pm Mon-Fri, to 1pm Sat), which contains a library and exhibition areas related to Hong Kong's banking history. There are half-hour guided tours (at 2.30pm Monday to Friday and at 10.30am on Saturday).

WORLD WIDE HOUSE
BUILDING

Map p362 (環球大廈; 19 Des Voeux Rd; MCentral, exit G) Most of the tiny shops at this unspectacular arcade cater specifically to the needs of the Filipina domestic helpers working in Hong Kong, who congregate in the streets around this area every Sunday. The products and services being sold at these shops – many run by Filipinos – include food, clothing, cosmetics and phone cards.

CENTRAL MARKET
HISTORIC BUILDING

Map p362 (中環街市; between Jubilee St, Queen Victoria St, Queen's Rd Central & Des Voeux Rd; MCentral, exit C) Central Market is tight-lipped about its glorious past. Rebuilt in 1938 in the then fashionable Bauhaus style (with shuttered windows) from a humble structure, it was for a long time one of the premier food markets. Maids, housewives and cooks would come as far as Happy Valley to buy their chicken and cabbage. When pork was scarce after the war, there were long lines here whenever horsemeat was on sale. In 1967 the then governor, clearly impressed by what he saw during a visit, crowned it the 'biggest meat market in Southeast Asia'.

There's word Central Market will be turned into a shopping arcade with 'local flavour'. Ironically, its role now as a Sunday picnicking spot for overworked Filipina maids seems more in keeping with the utopian-socialism spirit of Bauhaus.

 EATING

TOP CHOICE LUNG KING HEEN
CANTONESE, DIM SUM $$$

Map p362 (龍景軒; 3196 8888; www.fourseasons.com/hongkong; Four Seasons Hotel, 8 Finance St; set lunch/dinner $450/1280; ☺lunch & dinner; MHong Kong, exit E1) The world's first Chinese restaurant to receive three stars from the Michelin people, still retains them. The Cantonese food, though by no means peerless in Hong Kong, is excellent in both taste and presentation, and when combined with the harbour views and the excellent service, provides a truly stellar dining experience. The signature steamed lobster and scallop dumplings sell out early.

TOP CHOICE CAPRICE
MODERN FRENCH $$$

Map p362 (3196 8888; www.fourseasons.com/hongkong; Four Seasons Hotel, 8 Finance St; set lunch/dinner from $480/980; ☺lunch & dinner; MHong Kong, exit E1) In contrast to its rather opulent appearance, this restaurant has a straightforward menu, and the meals are masterfully created from ingredients flown in daily from France. The selections change, but experience says anything with duck, langoustine or pork belly is out of this world. Their artisanal cheeses, imported weekly from France, are the best you can get in Hong Kong.

TOP CHOICE LINGUINI FINI
ITALIAN, ORGANIC $

Map p362 (2857 1333; www.linguinifini.com; ground fl & 1st fl, L Place, 139 Queen's Rd Central, Central; lunch/dinner from $120/200; ☺lunch & dinner; MCentral, exit D2) An awesome choice for casual Italian – the pasta is made fresh, sausages and meats are home-cured and produce is sourced from local organic farms. The 'nose-to-tail' approach to pork means you get rare delectables like fried testa and tripe cooked with tomatoes. Graffiti by local artist Start from Zero graces the walls. At the time of writing, the first floor is also open for breakfast (from 7am to 11am) and tea (from 2.30pm to 6pm).

WATERMARK
EUROPEAN $$

Map p362 (2167 7251; www.cafedecogroup.com; Shop L, Level P, Central Pier 7, Star Ferry, Central; lunch/brunch & dinner; lunch/brunch from $300, dinner from $500; Star Ferry) With its location on the Star Ferry Pier, Watermark commands almost panoramic views of Victoria Harbour. It's airy during the day and romantic at night, and some tables can actually feel the sway of the waves. Highlights of its solid European menu include the dry aged ribeye and seafood dishes.

LEI GARDEN
CANTONESE, DIM SUM $$$

Map p362 (利苑酒家; 2295 0238; Shop 3007-3011, Level 3, IFC Mall, 1 Harbour View St; meals $200-800; ☺lunch & dinner; MHong Kong, exit E1) Military-like quality control of the food has earned seven of nine Lei Garden branches, including this one, one or more Michelin stars. That said, this is the most contemporary of all the branches. Don't miss its award-winning creation: sweet

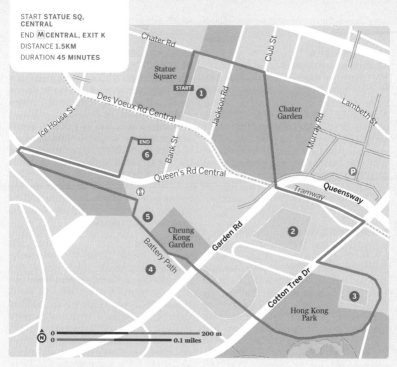

START **STATUE SQ, CENTRAL**
END M **CENTRAL, EXIT K**
DISTANCE **1.5KM**
DURATION **45 MINUTES**

HONG KONG ISLAND: CENTRAL NEIGHBOURHOOD WALK

Neighbourhood Walk
Exploring Hong Kong's Heart

➡ Begin the walk at Statue Sq and take in the handsome outline of the neoclassical ❶ **Legislative Council Building**, one of the few colonial-era survivors in the area and the seat of Hong Kong's modern legislature.

Walk southwest through Chater Garden park and cross over Garden Rd to the angular, modern lines of the ❷ **Bank of China Tower**, which has amazing views from the 43rd floor.

Duck into Hong Kong Park for the free ❸ **Flagstaff House Museum of Tea Ware**, displaying valuable pots, cups and other elegant tea ware. Sample some of China's finest teas in the serene cafe.

From here take elevated walkways west over Cotton Tree Dr, through Citybank Plaza, over Garden Rd and through Cheung Kong Garden to ❹ **St John's Cathedral**, dating from 1849. It is a modest building to earn the title of cathedral, especially with the towering corporate cathedrals now surrounding it, but it is an important historic Hong Kong monument all the same.

Follow Battery Path past the ❺ **Former French Mission Building** to Ice House St. Cross over and walk right (east) along Queen's Rd Central to the ❻ **HSBC building** and up the escalator (if it's open) to the large airy atrium. Walk through the ground-floor plaza to pat Stephen and Stitt, the two lions guarding the exit to Des Voeux Rd Central. The closest Central MTR station entrance is a short distance to the north along the pedestrian walkway between Statue Sq and Prince's Building.

sago soup with mango and pomelo ($30 a bowl).

TASTY CONGEE & NOODLE WONTON SHOP NOODLES $

Map p362 (正斗粥麵專家; www.tasty.com. hk; Shop 3016-3018, IFC Mall, 1 Harbour View St; meals $75-100; ☺11.30am-10.45pm; MHong Kong, exit E1) One of the more affordable places to dine in this luxury mall has a long line at lunch. So learn from the ladies of leisure – shop first, eat later. It'll be worth the wait – the hallmark shrimp wontons are so good even the loudish decor won't distract you. Other must-tries include the flat rice noodles stir-fried with beef and the prawn congee.

GREYHOUND CAFÉ THAI, FUSION $

Map p362 (☎2383 1133; www.greyhoundcafe. com.hk; Shop 1082, IFC Mall, 1 Harbour View St; meals from $175; ☺8am-10.30pm Mon-Sat, from 11am Sun; MHong Kong, exit E1) This favourite haunt of Asian tourists in Thailand has brought its modern Thai cafe food to Hong Kong. The long menu features both hits (signature chicken wings, iced tea) and misses (pasta with Thai anchovy), but the true winners are the desserts (both coconut- or mango-infused Thai and chocolaty Western).

CITY HALL MAXIM'S PALACE CANTONESE $

Map p362 (☎2521 1303; 3rd fl, Lower Block, Hong Kong City Hall, 1 Edinburgh Pl; meals from $120; ☺lunch & dinner; MCentral, exit K) This place offers a typically Hong Kong dim sum experience – noisy, cheerful, in a huge kitschy hall with hundreds of locals and many dim sum choices that are paraded on trolleys. A seat by the window will let you see land reclamation in progress where the old Queen's Pier used to be. There's breakfast dim sum on Sundays from 9am but people start queuing for a table at 8.30am.

ISLAND TANG CANTONESE, DIM SUM $$

Map p362 (港島廳; ☎2526 8798; www.is landtang.com; Shop 222, Galleria, 9 Queen's Rd Central, Central; set lunch from $308, dinner from $350; ☺lunch & dinner; MCentral, exit D1) With art deco interior à la 1930s Shànghǎi, Island Tang could have been a place where, as the Chinese say, one comes to 'devour the decor'. But we found you want to devour the food too! The Cantonese selections range from dim sum and fried milk to abalone,

which means a meal here can set you back $300 or $3000.

L'ATELIER JOËL DE ROBUCHON MODERN FRENCH $$$

Map p362 (☎2166 9000; www.joel-robuchon. com; Shop 401, Landmark, Queen's Rd Central, Central; set lunch/dinner from $398/980; ☺lunch & dinner; MCentral, exit G) This red-and-black workshop of the celebrity chef's three-part wonder in Hong Kong has a tantalising list of tapas (from $300) and a 70-page wine list. For the haute version, visit **Le Jardin** (☺7.30am-10pm Mon-Sat) next door, which also serves breakfast. **Le Salon de The** (☺8am-8pm), one floor down, has some of the best sandwiches, pastries and cakes in town for dine-in or takeaway.

HEICHINROU CANTONESE $$

Map p362 (聘珍樓; ☎2868 9229; www.heichin rou.com; G05 & 107-108, Nexxus Bldg, 41 Connaught Rd Central, Central; set lunch/dinner from $150/400; ☺lunch & dinner; MCentral, exit C) It's everything you'd expect from a modern Cantonese restaurant of this price range in Hong Kong – polished service, a somewhat formal ambience, refined cooking and good teas. This makes its self-touting as the 'oldest Chinese restaurant in Japan' seem baffling. Honestly, would old Chinese restaurants in Japan be this good? The set afternoon tea with six dim sum and a staple for $60 is a steal.

LUPA ITALIAN $$$

Map p362 (☎2796 6500; www.diningconcepts. com.hk/lupa; 3rd fl, LHT Tower, 31 Queen's Rd Central, Central; lunch from $300, dinner from $500; ☺lunch & dinner; MCentral, exit D2) Mario Batali is the latest celebrity chef to open an eatery in Hong Kong. More of a trattoria than a restaurant, Lupa serves rustic New York–style Italian food that includes fried whitebait, and pasta with rabbit ragu. The pizzas were our favourite. Despite reports that Lupa doesn't measure up to Batali's outlets in New York, our only complaint was his orange Crocs.

INAGIKU JAPANESE $$$

Map p362 (稻菊日本餐廳; ☎2805 0600; www.fourseasons.com/hongkong; Level 4, Four Seasons Hong Kong, 8 Finance St; set lunch/ dinner from $200/400; ☺lunch & dinner; MCentral, exit A) Inagiku is, in a word, perfection. It's one of the best (and priciest) Japanese restaurants in town, with tasteful interiors and harbour views to boot. The *kaiseki* (traditional multicourse meal) features seasonal ingredients (some flown in from Japan, ironically, but fresh nonetheless), impeccably prepared and artfully presented.

PIERRE
MODERN FRENCH **$$$**

Map p362 (📞2825 4001; www.mandarinoriental. com/hong kong; Mandarin Oriental, 5 Connaught Rd; set lunch/dinner from $448/1448; ⏰lunch Mon-Fri, dinner Mon-Sat; 🚇Central, exit F) The godfather of fusion, Pierre Gagnaire, has created a provocative menu that reflects his talented understanding of food and its flavours; dessert might be a caramelised rocket salad – and it works. The decor, with portholes and chandeliers, is reminiscent of a cruise liner, especially when adding the harbour view.

PETITE AMANDA
BAKERY **$**

Map p362 (www.petiteamanda.com; Shop 2096, Podium Level 2, IFC Mall, 1 Harbour View St, Central; bread/pastries from $21/40; ⏰9am-8pm Mon-Fri, from 10am Sat & Sun; 🚇Hong Kong, exit E1) The creations at this petite patisserie opened by model-turned-pastry chef Amanda Strang are beautiful, delicious and fattening. The Charlotte aux Poires and the Amarina are very popular.

ZUMA
MODERN JAPANESE **$$$**

Map p362 (📞3657 6388; www.zumarestaurant. com; Levels 5 & 6, Landmark, 15 Queen's Rd Central; set lunch/dinner from $290/970; ⏰lunch & dinner; 🚇Central, exit G) This uberchic import from London specialises in modern Japanese food and has miles of space in which to serve it. There is a robata counter, a sushi bar and a terrace. The Sunday brunch ($428), with free-flowing sake and champagne for an extra $122, is very popular. We've seen happy brunchers require assistance to leave the place.

AMBER
MODERN EUROPEAN **$$$**

Map p362 (📞2132 0066; www.mandarinoriental. com/landmark; 7th fl, Landmark Mandarin Oriental, 15 Queen's Rd Central; set lunch/dinner from $518/1288; ⏰lunch Mon-Sun, dinner Mon-Sat; 🚇Central, exit G) This elegant Michelin-starred restaurant with dusklike lighting and hanging organ pipes may feel a tad formal, but once you've sampled Chef Ekkebus' interpretations of traditional French cuisine, such as the Mieral Bresse pigeon,

you will warm to Amber. It's food thoughtfully cooked with a lot of heart.

DRINKING

⌈TOP⌋
CHOICE SEVVA
COCKTAIL BAR

Map p362 (📞2537 1388; www.sevva.hk; 25th fl, Prince's Bldg, 10 Chater Rd, Central; ⏰noon-midnight Mon-Thu, to 2am Fri & Sat; 🚇Central, exit H) If there was a million-dollar view in Hong Kong, it'd be the one from the balcony of stylish Sevva – skyscrapers so close you see their arteries of steel, with the harbour and Kowloon in the distance. At night it takes your breath away, and Sevva's cocktails are a wonderful excuse to let it. Book ahead if you want a table on the balcony, but even if you don't, you can go out to take pictures.

AMO ENO
WINE BAR

Map p362 (Shop 3027, Podium Level 3, IFC Mall, 1 Harbour View St; 🚇Hong Kong, exit E) 'Love wine' delivers a sophisticated wine experience, whether you're a debutant or a connoisseur. You can browse by colour, grape and price on a table with a touch-screen top, then pick your poison, and the size of pour from a total of 72 bottles kept in enomatic machines. Even the decor is inspired by wine and there are wine-themed knick-knacks for sale.

PIER 7
BAR

Map p362 (www.cafedecogroup.com; Shop M, Roof Viewing Deck, Central Pier 7, Star Ferry, Central; ⏰9am-midnight, happy hour 6-9pm; 🚇Hong Kong, exit A1) Located on the top floor of the Star Ferry terminal, Pier 7 has a large outdoor terrace from which you can see neighbouring skyscrapers and the hills of Kowloon (and a sliver of the harbour). It's an unpretentious place for quiet pre-movie or postdinner drinks and light refreshments. On random weekends there are themed parties and reggae DJs in the house, and the vibe turns shaggy.

LIBERTY EXCHANGE
SPORTS BAR

Map p362 (www.lex.hk; Two Exchange Sq, 8 Connaught Pl; happy hour 3-8pm; 🚇Hong Kong, exit A1) This American bar and bistro with an inviting open front is hugely popular with bankers and hedgies. On any given Friday evening, it's packed with people exchanging

KIMBERLEY COOLE/GETTY IMAGES ©

1. Tsim Sha Tsui East Promenade (p138)

The promenade offers resplendent views across Victoria Harbour to Hong Kong Island and the Star Ferry terminal.

2. Graham Street Market (p86)

Lined with seafood and produce stalls, this is one of Hong Kong's oldest and most colourful markets.

3. Hong Kong Zoological & Botanical Gardens (p70)

Hong Kongers practise taichi in the Victorian-era gardens, amid fountains, birds and sculptures.

4. Old and new architecture

The Bank of China Tower (p70) rises up behind the Former Legislative Council Building (p71).

RICHARD I'ANSON/GETTY IMAGES ©

industry gossip over cocktails, wine or beer, or watching sports on one of the big TV screens.

RED BAR
BAR

Map p362 (⛶8129 8882; L4, Two IFC, 8 Finance St; ⊙noon-midnight Mon-Thu, to 3am Fri & Sat, to 10pm Sun, happy hour 6-9pm; Ⓜ Hong Kong, exit E1) Red Bar's combination of alfresco drinking and harbour views is hard to beat on Hong Kong Island. DJs playing funk and jazz turn up the volume as the weekend approaches.

CAPTAIN'S BAR
BAR

Map p362 (Ground fl, Mandarin Oriental, 5 Connaught Rd Central, Central; ⊙11am-2am Mon-Sat, to 1am Sun; Ⓜ Central, exit F) This is a clubby, suited place that serves ice-cold draught beer in chilled silver mugs, as well as some of the best martinis in town. This is a good place to talk business, at least until the cover band strikes up at 9pm. Dress is smart casual (no shorts or sandals please).

MO BAR
BAR

Map p362 (Landmark, 15 Queen's Rd Central, Central; ⊙11am-2am Mon-Sat; Ⓜ Central, exit D1) If you want style and substance, the swish MO Bar, attached to the Mandarin's swanky outpost, offers a luxurious, softly lit setting, great service and first-rate wines and cocktails.

☆ ENTERTAINMENT

GRAPPA'S CELLAR
LIVE MUSIC

Map p362 (⛶2521 2322; www.elgrande.com.hk/outlets/HongKong/GrappasCellar; 1 Connaught Pl; Ⓜ Hong Kong, exit B2) For at least two weekends a month, this underground Italian restaurant morphs into a jazz or rock music venue – chequered tablecloths and all. Call or visit the website for event and ticketing details.

PALACE IFC CINEMA
CINEMA

Map p362 (⛶2388 6268; Podium L1, IFC Mall, 8 Finance St; Ⓜ Hong Kong, exit F) This eight-screen cinema complex in the IFC Mall is arguably the most advanced and comfortable in the territory. But you can't pull up the armrests if you're seated in the back row.

 ## SHOPPING

🅃🄾🄿 SHANGHAI TANG
CLOTHING, ACCESSORIES

Map p362 (上海灘; ⛶2525 7333; www.shanghaitang.com; The Shanghai Tang Mansion, 1 Duddell St; Ⓜ Central, exit D1) Shanghai Tang has reopened in a four-floor 'mansion' near its old address. If you fancy a cheongsam (a body-hugging Chinese dress for women) with a modern twist, a Chinese-style clutch or a lime-green mandarin jacket, this is the place to go. Custom tailoring is available; it takes two weeks to a month and requires a fitting. Shanghai Tang also stocks a range of lifestyle objects – cushions, picture frames, teapots, even mah-jong tile sets, designed in a modern chinoiserie style.

FOOK MING TONG TEA SHOP
FOOD, DRINK

Map p362 (福茗堂; ⛶2295 0368; Shop 3006, IFC Mall, 8 Finance St; Ⓜ Central, exit A) Tea-making accoutrements and carefully chosen teas of various ages and grades are available here, from gunpowder to Nanyan Ti Guan Yin Crown Grade – costing anything from $10 to $9000 per 100g.

PICTURE THIS
GIFTS

Map p362 (⛶2525 2803; www.picturethiscollection.com; Shop 212, Prince's Bldg, 10 Chater Rd; Ⓜ Central, exit H) The vintage posters, photographs, prints and antiques maps of Hong Kong and Asia on sale here will appeal to collectors or anyone seeking an unusual gift or souvenir. There's also an assortment of antiquarian books related to Hong Kong. Prices are not cheap but they guarantee all maps and prints to be originals. Sunday opening hours are noon to five.

IFC MALL
MALL

Map p362 (⛶2295 3308; www.ifc.com.hk; 8 Finance St; Ⓜ Hong Kong, exit F) Hong Kong's most luxurious shopping mall boasts 200 high-fashion boutiques linking the One and Two IFC towers and the Four Seasons Hotel. Outlets include Patrick Cox, Geiger, Longchamp, Kenzo, Vivienne Tam, Zegna... we could go on. The Hong Kong Airport Express Station is downstairs.

BLANC DE CHINE
CLOTHING, ACCESSORIES

Map p362 (源; ⛶2104 7934; www.blancdechine.com; Shop 123, Prince's Bldg; ⊙10.30am-7.30pm Mon-Sat, noon-6pm Sun; Ⓜ Central, exit H) This sumptuous store specialises in traditional Chinese men's jackets or silk dresses for women, off the rack or made to measure.

NEW ART GALLERIES IN CENTRAL

All brands from the West want to get their teeth into the mainland market. GAP has done it; Abercrombie & Fitch will do it. Why would the art world be any different? Art galleries have been setting up shop in Central at an almost unprecedented rate since late 2011. That said, not many present works by Hong Kong artists, and it remains to be seen whether the heat is sustainable. At the time of writing, most of the following were holding their inaugural exhibitions.

Saamlung (Map p362; ☑5181 5156; http://saamlung.com; 26b Two Chinachem Plaza, 68 Connaught Rd Central, Central; ⊙noon-6pm Tue-Fri, weekends by appointment only; Ⓜ Hong Kong, exit E1) Sitting on the top floor of a dreary-looking mall, Saamlung is arguably the most exciting new art space in town; it presents work by emerging local artists, as well as artists from China and around the world.

Pearl Lam Galleries (藝術門; Map p362; 601-605 Peddar Bldg, 12 Pedder St, Central; Ⓜ Central, exit H) Owned by the daughter of an entertainment mogul, this gallery was in the midst of holding its inaugural exhibition (on Chinese contemporary abstract art) and setting up a new website at the time of writing.

White Cube (Map p362; ☑2592 2000; http://whitecube.com; ground & 1st fl, 50 Connaught Rd Central, Central; ⊙11am-7pm Tue-Sat; Ⓜ Hong Kong, exit E1) The Londoner's first branch outside the UK; White Cube is known for showing edgy and confrontational works.

Galerie Perrotin (Map p362; ☑3758 2180; 17th fl, 50 Connaught Rd Central, Central; Tue-Sat; Ⓜ Hong Kong, exit E1) This place opened with an exhibition of new work by Brooklyn artist Kaws.

Gagosian (Map p362; ☑2151 0555; 7th fl, Pedder Bldg, 12 Pedder St; Tue-Sat; Ⓜ Central, exit H) This American-based heavyweight represents the estates of Andy Warhol and Jeff Koons.

Simon Lee (Map p362; ☑2801 6252; www.simonleegallery.com; 304 Pedder Bldg, 12 Pedder St; closed Sat in Aug; Ⓜ Central, exit H) A London-based gallery that's holding its debut exhibition of works by American artist Sherrie Levine.

Ben Brown (Map p362; ☑ 2522 9600; www.benbrownfinearts.com; 301 Pedder Bldg; 12 Pedder St; ⊙11am-7pm Tue-Sat, Mon by appointment only) Ben Brown is a London-based gallery with a focus on German photography and Italian painting.

The satin bed linens are exquisite (as are the old ship's cabinets in which they are displayed). The tailor-made sequined Chinese dresses are gorgeous but they take about four weeks (with one fitting) to make. So unless you're in Hong Kong after a month, the shop will ship it to you.

HONG KONG BOOK CENTRE BOOKS
Map p362 (☑2522 7064; www.hongkongbookcentre.com; Basement, On Lok Yuen Bldg, 25 Des Voeux Rd, Central; ⊙9am-6.30pm Mon-Fri, to 5.30pm Sat; Ⓜ Central, exit B) This basement shop has a vast selection of English-language books and magazines, particularly business titles.

JOYCE CLOTHING, ACCESSORIES
Map p362 (☑2810 1120; www.joyce.com; Ground fl, New World Tower, 16 Queen's Rd Central; ⊙10.30am-7.30pm; Ⓜ Central, exit D1) This multi-designer store is a good choice if you're short of time rather than money: Issey Miyake, Alexander McQueen, Marc Jacobs, Comme des Garçons, Chloé, Pucci, Yohji Yamamoto and several Hong Kong fashion names are just some of the designers whose wearable wares are on display. There's another branch in **Admiralty** (☑2523 5944; Shop 334, 3rd fl, Pacific Place, 88 Queensway). For the same duds at half the price, visit **Joyce Warehouse** (☑2814 8313; 21st fl, Horizon Plaza Arcade, 2 Lee Wing St, Ap Lei Chau; ⊙closed Mon) in Horizon Plaza in Ap Lei Chau.

LANE CRAWFORD DEPARTMENT STORE
Map p362 (連卡佛; ☑2118 3388; Level 3, IFC Mall, 8 Finance St; Ⓜ Central, exit A) This branch of Hong Kong's original Western-style department store, the territory's answer to

Harrods in London, is the flagship. Everything on sale here from fashion to crockery is very, very stylish. There are also branches in **Admiralty** (☑2118 3398; Level One, Pacific Place, 88 Queensway, Admiralty; ⏲10am to 9pm), **Causeway Bay** (☑2118 3638; Ground & 1st fl, Times Square, 1 Matheson St; ⏲10am-9pm Sun to Thu, to 10pm Fri & Sat) and **Tsim Sha Tsui** (☑2118 3428; 3 Canton Rd; ⏲10am-10pm).

CITYSUPER FOOD, DRINK

Map p362 (www.citysuper.com.hk; Shop 1041-1049, IFC Mall, 8 Finance St, Central; ⏲10.30am-9.30pm; Ⓜ Hong Kong, exit F) Citysuper sells a range of top-notch imports of hard-to-find ingredients from all over the world, as well as natural foods. The prices, of course, are high. There's a branch in **Causeway Bay** (☑2506 2888; Basement 1, Times Square, 1 Matheson St; ⏲10.30am-10pm).

HARVEY NICHOLS DEPARTMENT STORE

Map p362 (☑3695 3389; www.harveynichols.com; Landmark Bldg, 1 Pedder St; ⏲10am-9pm Mon-Sat, to 7pm Sat; Ⓜ Central, exit G) Britain's Harvey Nichols has brought its diverse, profuse and on-the-pulse range of couture and smart street fashions to Hong Kong, occupying four floors at the Landmark.

THREE SIXTY FOOD, DRINK

Map p362 (☑2111 4480; 3rd & 4th fl, Landmark Building, 1 Pedder St; ⏲8am-9pm Mon-Sat, 9am-9pm Sun; Ⓜ Central, exit G) This gourmet version of a regular supermarket features a large organic and natural-foods section, and produce from all over the world. There's also a terrific food court with a wide selection of cuisines on the upper floor. Three Sixty has another branch in **New Kowloon** (Shop 1090, Elements Mall, 1 Austin Rd West, Tsim Sha Tsui, above Kowloon Station).

LANDMARK MALL

Map p362 (置地廣場; ☑2525 4142; www.centralhk.com; 1 Pedder St; Ⓜ Central, exit G) The most central of all shopping centres, the Landmark has high fashion and good eating in a pleasant, open space. It has become a home almost exclusively to the very high-end fashion brands and boutiques (Gucci, Louis Vuitton, TODs etc).

PRINCE'S BUILDING MALL

Map p362 (太子大廈; ☑2504 0704; www.centralhk.com; 10 Chater Rd; Ⓜ Central, exit K) You may find the layout of Prince's Building disorienting, but it's worth a look for its speciality fashion, toy and kitchenware shops, and the latest art galleries. The selection is rather eclectic but invitingly so.

GIORDANO LADIES CLOTHING

Map p362 (☑2921 2955; www.giordanoladies.com; Ground fl & 1st fl, Lansing House, 43-45 Queen's Rd Central, Central; ⏲11am-9pm Mon-Sat, to 8pm Sun; Ⓜ Central, exit D1) Giordano Ladies offers elegant clothing for women that are signified by soft, flowing lines and a conservative palette. There is office attire, leisurewear and basic items, meant to mix and match well with most wardrobes.

DYMOCKS BOOKS

Map p362 (Shop 2007-2011, 2nd fl, IFC Mall, 1 Harbour View St, Central; ⏲9.30am-9pm; Ⓜ Hong Kong, exit F) Has a mainstream selection of books and magazines, mostly English-language, in several branches.

CITY CHAIN WATCHES

Map p362 (時間廊; ☑2259 9020; www.citychain.com; Shop 120, Man Yee Arcade, 60-68 Des Voeux Rd Central, Central; ⏲10am-8pm; Ⓜ Central, exit D2) With over 60 outlets in Hong Kong, City Chain has a wristwatch for almost every whim, look and occasion, ranging from the slightly dressy to the downright sporty. But look elsewhere if you're after diamond-studded time pieces and other pawn-shop favourites.

WING ON DEPARTMENT STORE DEPARTMENT STORE

Map p362 (永安百貨; ☑2852 1855; www.wingonet.com; 7th fl, Wing On Centre, 211 Des Voeux Rd Central, Central; ⏲Mon-Sat; Ⓜ Sheung Wan, exit E3) The last truly one-stop-shop department store in Hong Kong. Sure, it's a little old-fashioned but you can find almost everything you need there, from garden hoses to iPhone covers, baby pacifiers to Italian leather jackets. And there are super-friendly ladies to help you too!

🏃 SPORTS & ACTIVITIES

IMPAKT MARTIAL ARTS & FITNESS CENTRE MARTIAL ARTS

Map p362 (☑2167 7218, www.impakt.hk; 2nd fl Wing's Bldg, 110-116 Queen's Rd Central, Central; Ⓜ Central, exit D2) Impakt makes an impact by being one of the few martial arts centres with female trainers. They teach Muay Thai, kickboxing, Jiu Jitsu, karate etc to GI Jane wannabes and veterans alike. You can walk in for a one-off class or to use the gym facilities for $200. You can book personal private training for upwards of $300 per person per hour.

TOP **TEN FEET TALL** FOOT MASSAGE
CHOICE

Map p362 (☏2971 1010; www.tenfeettall.com.hk; 20th & 21st fl, L Place, 139 Queen's Rd Central; ☺11am-midnight Sun-Thu, to 1am Fri & Sat, last appointment). Opened by the owner of Dragon-i (p97), this sprawling comfort den (745 sq metres) offers a range of treatments from foot reflexology and shoulder massage, to hardcore pressure point massage and aromatic oil treatments. The interiors are created by French restaurant designers.

SPA AT THE FOUR SEASONS SPA

Map p362 (☏3196 8900; www.fourseasons.com/hongkong/spa.html; 8 Finance St, Central; ☺8am-11pm; ⓂHong Kong, exit F) A 1860-sq-metre, ultra-high-end spa with a comprehensive range of beauty, massage and health treatments, plus ice fountain, hot cups, moxibustion and even a 'herbal cocoon room'.

PURE FITNESS GYM

Map p362 (☏8129 8000; 3rd fl, Two IFC Mall, 8 Finance St; drop-in pass $300; ☺6am-midnight Mon-Sat, 8am-10pm Sun; ⓂHong Kong, exit F) A pleasant gym offering comprehensive facilities and/or classes for cardio-strength training, cycling, kickboxing, yoga, Pilates and dance fitness. It's a favourite among the professionals working in the area.

Hong Kong Island: the Peak & the Northwest

LAN KWAI FONG & SOHO | SHEUNG WAN | WESTERN DISTRICTS | THE MID-LEVELS | THE PEAK

Neighbourhood Top Five

1 Hopping aboard the **Peak Tram** (p86), enjoy the absurdly steep climbs to **Victoria Peak** (p86), and taking in the stunning night views from the top of the island.

2 Strolling the narrow streets of **Sheung Wan** (p86) to discover the history of 19th-century Hong Kong.

3 Bar-hopping your way through the gentle incline of the hedonistic **Lan Kwai Fong** (p96).

4 Stimulating your taste buds at one of the city's best private kitchens, **Club Qing** (p90).

5 Trawling through the **boutiques in Soho** (p101) or the treasure trove of **Cat Street** (p86).

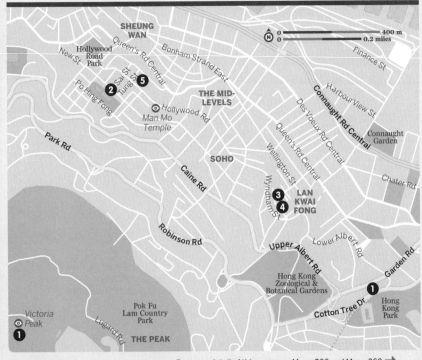

For more detail of this area, see Map p366 and Map p368 ➤

Explore: the Peak & the Northwest

Begin by exploring Sheung Wan's old neighbourhoods in the morning, which is when the temples and the odoriferous wholesale stores get into full swing. Sample some local fare during lunch in the area before heading to Hollywood Rd to browse the antique shops and galleries. If time allows, trek up to the Mid-Levels to check out the museums and religious monuments there. Then take the Peak Tram in Central to Victoria Peak; catch the sunset or stay for a little while for the breathtaking views of the city when it is lit up at night. Come back down to Soho for a nice dinner, and pub crawl in Lan Kwan Fong.

Local Life

➡ **Hang-outs** For a more intellectual chatter in Lan Kwai Fong or Soho, head to Club 71 (p97) or Gecko Lounge (p97), a magnet for creative types.

➡ **Galleries** Buying artworks on Hollywood Rd will probably bust a hole in your wallet while the galleries that showcase emerging artists in Tai Ping Shan St (p87) may offer a more-than-window-shopping experience.

Getting There & Away

➡ **Bus** For Lan Kwai Fong, Soho and Wan Chai bus 26 along Hollywood Rd links Sheung Wan with Central, Admiralty and Wan Chai. For the Western District bus 3B from Jardine House in Central, and buses 23, 40 and 40M from Admiralty stop along Bonham Rd. In the Mid-Levels bus 26 from Central goes along Hollywood Rd; bus 3B from Jardine House in Central and bus 23 from Admiralty have stops on Robinson Rd. For the Peak bus 15 from Central bus terminus below Exchange Sq runs along Queen's Rd East and terminates below the Peak Galleria.

➡ **MTR** Central station is on the Island and Tsuen Wan lines; Sheung Wan station on the Island line.

➡ **Macau ferry** The terminal is at Shun Tak Centre (for Sheung Wan).

➡ **Tram** Runs along Des Voeux Rd Central and Des Voeux Rd West (for Sheung Wan). The Peak Tram lower terminus is on Garden Rd, runs to the Peak Tower (for the Peak).

➡ **Central Escalator** For Caine Rd and Robinson Rd (for Mid-Levels).

➡ **Green Minibus** Bus 8 or 22 from Central pass Caine Rd (for Mid-Levels).

Lonely Planet's Top Tip

If you find Lan Kwai Fong and Soho are more for party animals, head to the neighbourhood around Tai Ping Shan St (p87) in Sheung Wan. The area used to be just about temples, but these days it's a burgeoning boho haven, with low-key but quality cafes, galleries and boutiques popping up alongside weather-beaten shrines.

 Best Places to Eat

➡ Club Qing (p90)
➡ Tim's Kitchen (p92)
➡ Yardbird (p92)

For reviews, see p89 ➡

 Best Places to Drink

➡ The Globe (p96)
➡ Club 71 (p97)
➡ Gecko Lounge (p97)

For reviews, see p96 ➡

Best Places to Shop

➡ Wattis Fine Art (p101)
➡ Ranee K (p102)
➡ The Pottery Workshop (p103)
➡ Flow (p101)

For reviews, see p101 ➡

LONELY PLANET/GETTY IMAGES ©

TOP SIGHTS
VICTORIA PEAK

High on the list of must-sees for all visitors to Hong Kong is Victoria Peak, the highest point (552m) on Hong Kong Island. It's one of the most touristy spots in town, and it's not hard to see why. Sweeping views of the vibrant metropolis, verdant woods, easy but spectacular walks around the Peak: these are all reachable in just eight minutes from Central by the legendary Peak Tram.

The best way to get to the Peak is by the 125-year-old **Peak Tram** (single/return $28/40; ⊙7am-midnight). The lower terminus in Central has an interesting **gallery** which houses a replica of the earliest carriage to run on this first funicular railway in Asia.

Some 500m to the northwest of the Peak Tram upper terminus, up steep Mt Austin Rd, is the site of the old governor's mountain lodge, which was burned to the ground by Japanese soldiers during WWII. The beautiful gardens still remain, however, and are open to the public. It's a vantage point less frequented by visitors, so you're likely to enjoy the views chaos-free.

You can walk around the Peak without exhausting yourself. Harlech Rd on the south side and Lugard Rd on the northern slope together form a 3.5km loop that takes about an hour to walk. You can also continue for a further 2km along Peak Rd to Pok Fu Lam Reservoir Rd. Another good walk leads down to the University of Hong Kong (p87). Walk to the west side of Victoria Peak by taking either Lugard or Harlech Rds. After reaching Hatton Rd, follow it down. The 50km-long Hong Kong Trail (p60) also starts on the Peak.

DON'T MISS

➡ Peak Tram
➡ Peak Trails
➡ Victoria Peak Garden

PRACTICALITIES

➡ Map p370
➡ ☏2522 0922
➡ www.thepeak.com.hk
➡ Victoria Peak, Hong Kong Island
➡ Admission free
➡ ⊙24hr (Peak Tram 7am-midnight)
➡ 🚋Peak Tram Lower Terminus, 33 Garden Rd, Central
➡ 🚌Bus 15 from Central, below Exchange Sq

WIBOWO RUSLI/GETTY IMAGES ©

TOP SIGHTS
MAN MO TEMPLE

You'll smell the incense and see wafting billows of smoke before you reach the temple. Built in the mid-19th century, Man Mo Temple is one of the oldest and most famous temples in Hong Kong. It is a favourite with parents who come to pray for good health and good grades for their kids. The temple is dedicated to two deities. Man Cheong, the civil deity, was a Chinese statesman of the 3rd century BC. He is now worshipped as the god of literature, and is represented holding a writing brush. Kwan Tai, a Han-dynasty soldier born in the 2nd century AD, is now venerated as the red-cheeked god of war. He is always seen holding a sword.

Outside the main entrance are four gilt plaques on poles that are carried at procession time. Two plaques describe the gods being worshipped inside, while the others request silence and respect within the temple grounds and warn menstruating women to keep out of the main hall. Inside the temple are two 19th-century sedan chairs shaped like houses, which are used to carry the two gods at festival time. The coils suspended from the roof are incense cones burned as offerings by worshippers.

Off to the side, the hall next to the temple is **Lit Shing Kung**, literally 'the saints' palace', which is for the worship of other Buddhist and Taoist deities.

Another hall, **Kung Sor** (meeting place), used to serve as a court of justice to settle disputes among the Chinese community before the modern judicial system was introduced. Now you'll find fortune-tellers who are ready and willing to tell you of your fate.

DON'T MISS

➡ The main temple
➡ Lit Shing Kung
➡ Fortune-tellers

PRACTICALITIES

➡ Map p368
➡ ☎2540 0350
➡ 124-126 Hollywood Rd
➡ admission free
➡ ⊗8am-6pm
➡ 🚌26

◉ SIGHTS

◉ Lan Kwai Fong & Soho

GRAHAM ST MARKET
MARKET

Map p366 (Graham St; Ⓜ Central, exit D2) Street markets are an undeniably pungent part of Hong Kong's heritage, and this 160-year-old open market along the steep, narrow Graham St is one of the oldest and the most colourful. Fish-chopping, vegetable-washing and ice-melting are the daily routines here. However, the green light has been given for redevelopment of this street over the next decade, so for now the future of the many family-run stalls here, as well as their ingeniously constructed sunshade from inverted umbrellas, is uncertain.

CENTRAL POLICE STATION
HISTORIC BUILDING

Map p366 (10 Hollywood Rd; 🚌 26) After years of uncertainty, this enormous colonial compound, built in various stages between 1841 and 1919, together with the adjacent former magistracy and Victoria Prison, will be preserved in full. There are plans to revitalise the buildings as an art gallery, cinema, museum and boutique shopping mall, all to be managed by an NGO. The renovation is expected to be completed in 2014. In the meantime it is opened occasionally for arts exhibitions.

◉ Sheung Wan

MAN MO TEMPLE
TEMPLE

See p85.

QUEEN'S ROAD WEST
INCENSE SHOPS
PAPER OFFERINGS

Map p368 (🚌 26) Head along Queen's Rd West, several hundred metres past the end of Hollywood Rd, and you'll find several shops selling incense and paper offerings. These are burned to propitiate the spirits of the dead. There's quite a choice of spirit-world combustibles to make a consumer heaven for the deceased, including complete mini-sets of kitchenware, dim sum, cars, gold and silver ingots, the popular hell banknotes, and even maids and chauffeurs. You may buy them as souvenirs, but if you're superstitiously minded, remember that hanging onto these offerings rather than burning them is seen as bad luck here.

CAT STREET
STREET

Map p368 (摩囉街; ⊘ 9am-6pm; 🚌 26) Located southwest of Sheung Wan MTR station and just north of (and parallel to) Hollywood Rd is **Upper Lascar Row**, the official name of 'Cat St', which is a pedestrians-only lane lined with antique and curio shops and stalls selling found objects, cheap jewellery, carvings and newly minted ancient coins. It's a fun place to trawl through for a trinket or two, but expect even the apparently recent memorabilia to be mass-produced fakes. There are proper shops on three floors of the **Cat Street Galleries** (Casey Bldg, 14/f 38 Lok Ku Rd; ⊘ 11am-7pm Mon-Sat), a small but interesting shopping centre that is entered from Upper Lascar Row. However, its days are numbered, with a residential high-rise soon to be erected over this prime plot of land.

WESTERN MARKET
HISTORIC BUILDING

Map p368 (西港城; 🕿 6029 2675; 323 Des Voeux Rd Central & New Market St; ⊘ 9am-7pm; Ⓜ Sheung Wan, exit B) When the textile vendors were driven out of the lanes linking Queen's Rd Central and Des Voeux Rd Central in the early 1990s, they moved to this renovated old market (1906) with its distinctive four-corner towers. Now bolts of cloth are laid out on the 1st floor of the building. The top floor is a restaurant (see p92).

MAN WA LANE
STREET

Map p368 (Ⓜ Sheung Wan, exit A1) This alley just east of the Sheung Wan MTR station is a good introduction to traditional Sheung Wan. Kiosks here specialise in name chops: a stone (or wood or jade) seal that has a name carved in Chinese on the base. When dipped in red Chinese ink, the name chop can be used as a stamp or even a 'signature'. The merchant will create a harmonious and auspicious Chinese name for you.

POSSESSION STREET
STREET

Map p368 (🚌 26) A short distance west of Cat St, next to Hollywood Road Park and before Hollywood Rd meets Queen's Rd West, is Possession St. This is where Commodore Gordon Bremmer and a contingent of British marines planted the Union flag on 26 January 1841 and claimed Hong Kong Island for the Crown (though no plaque marks this birthplace of colonial Hong Kong).

TAI PING SHAN STREET   STREET

Map p368 (□26) Shortly after the founding of the colony, the local residents in Central were relocated to this area. Traces of early Chinese settlements are long gone, but several temples founded in the 19th century are still clustered around where Tai Ping Shan St meets Pound Lane. **Kwun Yam Temple** (觀音堂; Map p368; 34 Tai Ping Shan St) honours the ever-popular goddess of mercy, Kwun Yam. Further to the northwest, the **Pak Sing Ancestral Hall** (百姓廟; Map p368; 42 Tai Ping Shan St) was originally a storeroom for bodies awaiting burial in China. It contains the ancestral tablets of around 3000 departed souls.

Near the southeast end of the street where it meets with Bridges St are a handful of up-and-coming galleries, cafes and lifestyle shops.

◉ Western Districts

UNIVERSITY OF HONG KONG   UNIVERSITY

(香港大學; ☑2859 2111; www.hku.hk; Pok Fu Lam Rd; □23 & 40 from Admiralty) Established in 1911, HKU is the oldest and most prestigious university in Hong Kong, and arguably in the whole of Asia. The **Main Building**, completed in the Edwardian style in 1912, is a declared monument. Several other early-20th-century buildings on the campus, including the **Hung Hing Ying** (1919) and **Tang Chi Ngong Buildings** (1929), are also protected.

The **University Museum & Art Gallery** (☑2241 5500; www.hku.hk/hkumag; Fung Ping Shan Bldg, 94 Bonham Rd; admission free; ◎9.30am-6pm Mon-Sat, 1-6pm Sun) houses collections of ceramics and bronzes spanning 5000 years, including some exquisite blue and white Ming porcelain. The museum is to the left of the university's Main Building and opposite the start of Hing Hon Rd.

◉ The Mid-Levels

DR SUN YAT-SEN MUSEUM   HISTORIC BUILDING, MUSEUM

Map p368 (孫中山紀念館; ☑2367 6373; http://hk.drsunyatsen.museum; 7 Castle Rd, Mid-Levels; adult/concession $10/5, Wed free; ◎10am-6pm Mon-Wed & Fri-Sat, 10am-7pm Sun; □3B, alight at the Hong Kong Baptist Church on Caine Rd) The museum, dedicated to the father of modern China, is housed in a marvellous Edwardian-style building, which itself is more interesting than the exhibitions. Originally named Kom Tong Hall and built in 1914, the mansion was the residence of Ho Komtong, a tycoon from an influential Eurasian family in the early colonial era. It was converted into a Mormon Church in 1960, and became the museum that it is today in 2006.

Dr Sun Yatsen was a key figure in modern Chinese history and he had many links with Hong Kong, but the dull displays here do not really do justice to his legendary life.

HONG KONG MUSEUM OF MEDICAL SCIENCES   MUSEUM

Map p368 (香港醫學博物館; ☑2549 5123; www.hkmms.org.hk; 2 Caine Lane; adult/concession $10/5; ◎10am-5pm Tue-Sat, 1-5pm Sun; □3B, alight at Ladder St bus stop on Caine Rd) This small museum houses medical implements and accoutrements (including an old dentistry chair, an autopsy table and herbal medicine vials and chests), and offers a rundown on how Hong Kong coped with the 1894 bubonic plague. The exhibits comparing Chinese and Western approaches to medicine are unusual and instructive, but the museum is less interesting for its exhibits than for its architecture: it's housed in what was once the Pathological Institute, a breezy Edwardian-style brick-and-tile structure built in 1905 and fronted by palms and bauhinia trees.

OHEL LEAH SYNAGOGUE   SYNAGOGUE

Map p368 (莉亞堂; ☑2589 2621, 2857 6095; 70 Robinson Rd; ◎10.30am-7pm Mon-Thu by appointment only, service times 7am Mon-Fri, 6pm Mon-Thu; □3B or 23) This Moorish Romantic temple, completed in 1902, is named after Leah Gubbay Sassoon, the matriarch of a wealthy and philanthropic Sephardic Jewish family that traces its roots back to the beginning of the colony. Be sure to bring ID if you plan to visit the sumptuous interior.

ROMAN CATHOLIC CATHEDRAL OF THE IMMACULATE CONCEPTION   CHURCH

Map p368 (香港聖母無原罪主教座; ☑2522 8212; 16 Caine Rd; ◎9.30am-5.30pm Mon-Fri, 9.30am-12.30pm Sat; □23, alight at Caritas Centre on Caine Rd) This Gothic revival cathedral was built in 1888 and financed largely by the Portuguese faithful from Macau.

START **KENNEDY TOWN TRAM (SUTHERLAND ST STOP)**

END **SHEUNG WAN MTR STATION (ENTRANCE/EXIT B)**

DISTANCE **1.9KM**

DURATION **ONE HOUR**

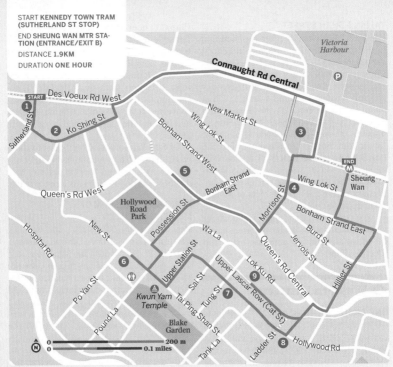

Neighbourhood Walk

Hong Kong's Wholesale District

Begin the tour at the Sutherland St stop of the Kennedy Town tram. Have a look at (and a sniff of) Des Voeux Rd West's many **①** **dried seafood shops** piled with all manner of desiccated sea life. Walk south on Sutherland St to Ko Shing St, to browse the positively medieval-sounding goods on offer from the **②** **herbal-medicine traders**.

At the end of Ko Shing St, re-enter Des Voeux Rd West and walk northeast. Continue along Connaught Rd West, where you'll find several floors of market stalls occupying the attractive colonial building housing the **③** **Western Market**.

At the corner of Morrison St, walk south past Wing Lok St and Bonham Strand, which are both lined with **④** **shops selling ginseng root and edible birds' nests**. Then turn right onto Queen's Rd Central to the shops selling paper funeral offerings for the dead.

Hungry? Walk forward to Queen's Rd West for a quick Chiu Chow fix at **⑤** **Chan Kan Kee**.

Retrace your steps, climb up Possession St, then take a left into Hollywood Rd, before turning right to ascend Pound Lane to where it meets Tai Ping Shan St, where you'll spot two **⑥** **temples**. Look to the right for Pak Sing Ancestral Hall and to the left for Kwun Yam Temple.

Turn left into Tai Ping Shan St, then left again to descend Upper Station St to the start of Hollywood Rd's **⑦** **antique shops**. There's a vast choice of curios and rare, mostly Chinese, treasures.

Continuing east on Hollywood Rd brings you to the **⑧** **Man Mo Temple**, one of the oldest temples in the territory and dedicated to the civil and martial gods Man Cheong and Kwan Tai.

Take a short hop to the left down Ladder St to Upper Lascar Row, home of the **⑨** **Cat Street Market**, which is well stocked with Chinese memorabilia and inexpensive curios and gift items. Ladder St brings you back to Queen's Rd Central. Cross the road and follow Hillier St to Bonham Strand. Due north is the Sheung Wan MTR station.

PIPPING THE PEAK

There's something just as brilliant to see on the scenic bus 15 route to the Peak as the summit itself: **King Yin Lei** (景賢里; 45 Stubbs Rd; 🚌15, alight at Evergreen Villa or Bradbury School), a splendid Chinese Renaissance-style mansion built in 1937, has appeared in various movies over the years, including Clark Gable's *Soldier of Fortune* (1955) and Bruce Lee's *Enter the Dragon* (1973). With green roof tiles and verandahs overlooking the courtyard, this 1580-sq-metre palace reflects the rising status of the Chinese community in the 1930s, given that only a few Chinese taipans were able to set up homes in the Peak area in the early 20th century. The property changed hands many times, and was partially demolished in 2007, but plans to bulldoze the site for redevelopment were halted by government intervention after public outcry. The government has since bought and restored the property. You won't have to scale the walls around the mansion to know what is meant by prewar splendour: the grand structure is clearly visible from street level and bus 15 stops right in front of it. Until it finds a new incarnation, the **Antiquities and Monuments Office** (www.amo.gov.hk) will continue to run occasional tours of the property.

JAMIA MOSQUE   MOSQUE
Map p368 (些利街清真寺; ☎2523 7743; 30 Shelley St) Erected in 1849 and also called the Lascar Mosque, this is the oldest mosque in Hong Kong. It's not open to non-Muslims, who can admire the facade from the terrace out front. The mosque is accessible by the Central Escalator.

◉ The Peak

VICTORIA PEAK   LANDMARK
See p84.

POLICE MUSEUM   MUSEUM
(警隊博物館; ☎2849 7019; www.police.gov.hk/hkp-home/english/museum; 27 Coombe Rd; admission free; ◷2-5pm Tue, 9am-5pm Wed-Sun; 🚌15, alight at the stop btwn Stubbs Rd & Peak Rd) So, you've seen stacks of Hong Kong crime flicks, and you're still obsessed by those mysterious gangsters? Then come to this seldom-visited museum in pretty Wan Chai Gap to satisfy your curiosity. The protagonist in this former police station is the local police force, which was formed in 1844, but the real star is the triads. The intriguing Triad Societies Gallery uncovers the beliefs and rituals they follow, and the very well-supplied Narcotics Gallery is worthwhile.

PEAK TOWER   NOTABLE BUILDING
(凌霄閣; ☎2849 0668; 128 Peak Rd; ◷10am-11pm Mon-Fri, 8am-11pm Sat, Sun & public holidays; 🚋Peak Tram) The anvil-shaped Peak Tower makes a good grandstand for many of the best views of the city and harbour.

On Level P1 there's an outpost of **Madame Tussauds** (☎2849 6966; adult/child $170/100; ◷10am-10pm), with eerie (and often creepy) wax likenesses of international stars, as well as local celebrities such as Jackie Chan and Michelle Yeoh. There is an open-air **viewing terrace** (adult/child $30/15) on Level 5.

PEAK GALLERIA   LOOKOUT
(山頂廣場; 118 Peak Rd; 🚌15, alight at the stop btwn Stubbs Rd & Peak Rd) The building is designed to withstand winds of up to 270km/h, theoretically more than the maximum velocity of a No 10 typhoon. The only attraction here is the admission-free viewing deck, which is larger than the one in the Peak Tower.

✖ EATING

Restaurants in Soho have a preclubbing vibe and most are midrange or top end. **I Love Soho** (www.ilovesoho.hk) is a complete online guide to the area.

Sheung Wan has more local flavour and is particularly well known for Chiu Chow cuisine, while Western Districts, especially the strip at the end of the Praya in Kennedy Town, are winning supporters with a new dining scene. Restaurants in the Mid-Levels cater mostly to local residents who don't feel like trekking down to sea level.

Quality choices on Victoria Peak are sparse, though many restaurants here offer gorgeous views of the island.

✕ Lan Kwai Fong & Soho

🔺TOP CHOICE CLUB QING MODERN CHINESE $$$

Map p366 (☑2536 9773; www.clubqing.com; 10th fl, Cosmos Bldg, 8-11 Lan Kwai Fong, Central; set lunch per person $260, dinner per person from $380; ⏰lunch & dinner; Ⓜ Central, exit D2) This private kitchen sits above the swirl of Lan Kwai Fong, and its Mandarin-style dining hall is filled with elegant wooden furniture and refined tea ware. Chef Andy has elevated steaming and frying to an art form, and creates innovative masterpieces. The Dan Chung tea, served at the end of the meal, is as memorable as the dishes. There are only four tables, so booking a week in advance is recommended. Menu and reservations available online. Cash only.

🔺TOP CHOICE LIFE CAFE VEGETARIAN, INTERNATIONAL $

Map p366 (☑2810 9777; 10 Shelley St; meals from $100; ⏰noon-10pm; 🔌) Right next to the Central Escalators, Life is a vegetarian's dream, serving organic vegan food and dishes free of gluten, wheat, onion and garlic. Housed in a three-storey prewar building, it is filled with intimate seating; some find it too intimate to converse, but we love the window-watching tables, and the roof terrace is a nice place to chill over a bottle of white during summer months.

BUTAO RAMEN JAPANESE $

Map p366 (豚王; ☑2530 0600; 8-13 Wo On Lane, Central; ramen from $75; ⏰11am-9pm Mon-Sat; Ⓜ Central, exit D2) From the line of customers waiting out front, you have to believe that this street-side joint serves the best ramen in town. Only 300 bowls of noodles are sold daily and there are four broth flavours. We love the signature rich Butao (pork) broth. You can customise how long the noodles should be cooked and the intensity of the broth. Just put a tick in the right boxes on the order sheet.

OLÉ SPANISH RESTAURANT & WINE BAR SPANISH $$$

Map p366 (☑2523 8624; 1st fl, Shun Ho Tower, 24-30 Ice House St; tapas $60-315; ⏰lunch & dinner Mon-Sat; Ⓜ Central, exit D1) Any Spaniard living in Hong Kong would point to this charismatic place as the best Spanish restaurant in town. The paella is just one dish showcasing the culinary authenticity here. All meals are elevated with a glass of *rioja, ribera* or other delicate vino from the extensive list.

SING KEE DAI PAI DONG $

Map p366 (盛記; ☑2541 5678; 9-10 Stanley St, Central; dishes from $50; ⏰lunch & dinner; Ⓜ Central, exit D2) In the fine-dining enclave of Soho, finding a good, unpretentious meal can be a tricky task. Sing Kee, one of the few surviving *dai pai dongs* (food stalls) on the island, has withstood the tide of gentrification, and still retains a working-class, laugh-out-loud character. There's no English signage; look for the crammed tables and steam billowing out from the cooking station at the end of Stanley St.

POSTO PUBBLICO ITALIAN, ORGANIC $$

Map p366 (☑2577 7160; 28 Elgin St, Soho; set lunch from $130, meals from $150, cocktails from $75; ⏰breakfast, lunch & dinner; 🚌26) A New York–style Italian bistro, the 'Public Place' has won the heart of eco-foodies in town with its delicious and sustainable seafood, all-natural meats, and hand-picked vegetables from local organic farms. The brown leather banquettes, high ceilings and wooden tables all ooze an elegant yet relaxed ambience. No service charge.

ROBATA ZAWAZAWA JAPANESE $$$

Map p366 (☑2536 9898; www.zawazawa.com. hk; Lower Ground fl, 41 Wyndham St, Central; meals from $128, dinner from $298; ⏰lunch & dinner Mon-Fri, dinner Sat; Ⓜ Central, exit D2) You eat with your eyes and mouth in this teeny-weeny grill eatery. The colourful paper umbrella lampshades and the kimono obi–inspired wall decor are a visual feast, which infuses the restaurant with an Edo-era charm. Washing down the juicy skewers with the homemade plum sake is truly something to relish.

LUK YU TEA HOUSE CANTONESE, DIM SUM $$

Map p366 (陸羽茶室; ☑2523 5464; 24-26 Stanley St; lunch/dinner from $180/350; ⏰breakfast, lunch & dinner; Ⓜ Central, exit D2) This elegant establishment is arguably the most famous teahouse in Hong Kong. With Eastern art deco interiors featuring ceiling fans and stained-glass windows, it could almost be the setting of a mystery novel. Dim sum is available till 5.30pm.

KUNG LEE JUICE $

Map p366 (公利真料竹蔗水; ☑2544 3571; 60 Hollywood Rd, Soho; juices from $10; ⏰11am-

11pm; 📓26) In the heart of Soho, this vintage stall has been quietly selling herbal teas and fresh sugarcane juice as if it is still 1948. It sells turtle jelly, too, for those who are curious to try – it's good for cooling down your body and for skin complexion.

GOOD SPRING CO
TEA $

Map p366 (春回堂; ☑2544 3518; Ground fl, 8 Cochrane St, Central; ⊘8.45am-8pm; MCentral, exit D2) You may just want to get some 24-flavour tea or the less sophisticated chrysanthemum tea, which all help clear heat and humidity in the body. Or, you might consult the English-speaking herbalist for some medicinal tea. This may be a simple herbal infusion, or contain ingredients not for the squeamish, such as powdered deer's horn, desiccated deer's penis or monkey's visceral organs. Whatever the ingredients, the resulting brew is invariably dark brown, sour in smell and bitter to taste. Drink up now.

PASTIS BISTRO FRANCAIS
FRENCH $$

Map p366 (☑2537 5702; Ground fl, Wyndham St; mains $145-288; ⊘noon-11.30pm Mon-Sat; MCentral, exit D2) The look of the place, and the food on your plate, are so French you may have to pinch yourself to remember you're in Hong Kong. And, if you are not French, it's likely that you are the only non-French diner there. The menu features homemade Provençal fare, best ordered with a glass of red.

WAGYU
STEAKHOUSE $$

Map p366 (☑2525 8805; Ground fl, 3 The Centrium, 60 Wyndham St, Central; set lunch/dinner from $78/169; ⊘breakfast, lunch & dinner; MCentral, exit D2) There are three Wagyus serving different fares in this neighbourhood, and this one has the most diverse clientele. The name already suggests quality steak, but you can also chill here anytime of the day, sip a coffee or beer at its open-front bar and people-watch.

YELLOW DOOR KITCHEN
SICHUANESE, SHANGHAINESE $$

Map p366 (黃色門廚房; ☑2858 6555; www.yellowdoorkitchen.com.hk; 6th fl, 37 Cochrane St; set lunch/dinner $90/298; ⊘lunch & dinner Mon-Fri, dinner Sat; MCentral, exit D1) This homely eatery that is recommended by the Michelin inspectors lets you enjoy variety even when you're dining solo. Dishes are served in taster-sized portions that add up to a lip-smacking whole. Gracing a wall is the calligraphic graffiti of Tsang Tsou-choi (1921–2007) aka the 'King of Kowloon'. Reservations a must.

YUNG KEE RESTAURANT
CANTONESE, DIM SUM $$

Map p366 (鏞記; ☑2522 1624; 32-40 Wellington St; lunch $80-300, dinner from $380; ⊘lunch & dinner; MCentral, exit D2) The goose roasting in the coal-fired ovens here has been the talk of the town since 1942. Celebrities and other well-to-dos are regular diners, but this establishment is welcoming even if you're not a who's who in town. During lunch hours, it's a popular dim sum place for the Central workforce.

TAI CHEONG BAKERY
BAKERY $

Map p366 (泰昌餅家; ☑2544 3475; 35 Lyndhurst Tce, Central; ⊘7.30am-9pm Mon-Sat, 8.30am-9pm Sun; 📓40M) Tai Cheong was most famous for its lighter-than-air profiteroles (sa yung) until former governor Chris Patten was photographed wolfing down its egg-custard tarts. Since then 'Fat Patten' egg tarts have hogged the limelight.

LAN FONG YUEN
CAFE $

Map p366 (蘭芳園; ☑2544 3895, 2854 0731; 2 & 4a Gage St; ⊘7am-6pm Mon-Sat; 📓5B) Don't be fooled by the rickety facade: it hides an entire cha chaan tang (tea cafe). Lan Fong Yuen (1952) is largely believed to be the inventor of 'pantyhose' milk tea. Over a thousand cups of the silky brew are sold per day. Watch staff work their magic while you wait for a table. The city's 'signature' yin yeung, a mixture of tea (70%) and coffee (30%), is said to be an invention from here, too. A cover charge ($20 per head) applies.

MAK'S NOODLE
NOODLES, CANTONESE $

Map p366 (麥奀雲吞麵世家; ☑2854 3810; 77 Wellington St; noodles $32-48; ⊘11am-8pm; 📓40M) At this legendary shop, noodles are made the traditional way with a bamboo pole and served perched on a spoon placed over the bowl so they won't go soggy. The beef brisket noodles are equally remarkable.

FLYING PAN
AMERICAN $

Map p366 (☑2140 6333; 9 Old Bailey St; breakfast sets $60-120; ⊘24hr; 📓26) If you feel a bit empty after an all-night pub crawl, and want something to comfort your belly, a full English breakfast at night sounds not a bad idea, no? Breakfast is served 24/7 in a 1950s-American-diner setting at the Flying

HONG KONG ISLAND: THE PEAK & THE NORTHWEST EATING

Pan. Other popular items on the menu include the fluffy Belgian waffles and eggs Benedict.

SER WONG FUN
CANTONESE $

Map p366 (蛇王芬; ☑2543 1032; 30 Cochrane St; meals from $70; ☉11am-10.30pm; ⓂCentral, exit D1) In the cooler months diners flock here for the snake soup, which is eaten with lemon leaves and fritters. Non-snake eaters come for the duck's liver sausage and chicken claypot rice, and a plethora of simple and tasty dishes.

JASHAN
INDIAN $

Map p366 (☑3105 5300; 1st fl, Amber Lodge, 23 Hollywood Rd, Central; lunch buffet $118, meals from $150; ☉lunch & dinner; ☐26) This institution is Michelin-listed but remains a very affordable Indian choice. The recent facelift has brought a modern design in gentle vermilion tone, and the comfy banquettes by the window offer views of the historic police station opposite. The meals give a taste of India from regional dishes to national staples. During lunch hours it's jam-packed with diners who come for its elaborate buffet.

WANG FU
DUMPLINGS, NORTHERN CHINESE $

Map p366 (王府; ☑2121 8089; 65 Wellington St; meals from $35; ☉lunch & dinner Mon-Sat; ☐40M) In expats-infested Soho, this humble eatery is where locals and visitors from northern China gobble down platefuls of dumplings or slurp noodles. Choices are sparse, but they are cheap and delicious.

ASSAF
LEBANESE $$

Map p366 (☑2851 6550; Shop B, Ground fl, Lyndhurst Bldg, 37 Lyndhurst Tce; set lunch $90, meals from $200; ☉11am-late; ☐40M) This cosy place specialises in meze and other tasty tidbits, including baklava soaked in rose syrup. The Assaf brothers also own **Beyrouth Cafe Central** (☑2854 1872; 39 Lyndhurst Tce) next door, which does takeaway sandwiches and kebabs.

VBEST TEA HOUSE
CANTONESE $

Map p366 (緻好茶館; ☑3104 0890; 17 Elgin St; lunch/dinner from $120/180; ☉lunch & dinner Mon-Sat) Tucked away on a steep street off Soho, this understated family-run restaurant serves MSG-free comfort food. The owners' children grew up on this, so you can't go too wrong.

✖ Sheung Wan, The Mid-Levels & Western Districts

TOP CHOICE TIM'S KITCHEN
CANTONESE $$$

Map p368 (桃花源; ☑2581 9098; 84-90 Bonham Strand, Sheung Wan; meals from $400; ☉lunch & dinner Mon-Sat; ⓂSheung Wan, exit A2) This winner of two Michelin stars had a substantial facelift and expansion after it relocated to Bonham Strand. Expect well-executed Cantonese dishes cooked in a healthy manner. Popular dishes, such as stir-fried prawn, crab claw poached with winter melon and braised pomelo skin, need to be pre-ordered.

CHAIRMAN
CANTONESE $$$

Map p368 (大班樓; ☑2555 2202; Ground fl, 18 Kau U Fong, Sheung Wan; lunch/dinner from $178/528; ☉lunch & dinner; ⓂSheung Wan, exit E2) Don't be put off by the kitschy name. The Chairman is indeed a high-fliers' dining hall, but in this convivial ambience the public are also welcome. Their health-conscious but authentic Cantonese dishes take your taste buds on an epicurean journey, but getting a table is a pain. Reservations essential.

YARDBIRD
JAPANESE $$

Map p368 (☑2547 9273; 33-35 Bridges St; meals from $300; ☉6pm-late Mon-Sat; ☐26) If you are in the mood for yakitori, this Japanese bistro with a New York touch is an ebullient place to partake. The bar table at centre stage ignites a festive, social space. No reservations are accepted, and getting a table is never easy, but diners here simply don't care. Have some cocktails at the bar, or sip their highbrow sake, chat with the entertaining staff, enjoy the music. This is the place to see and to be seen.

GRAND STAGE
DIM SUM $$

Map p368 (大舞臺飯店; ☑2815 2311; 2nd fl, Western Market, 323 Des Voeux Rd Central, Sheung Wan; dim sum from $25, dinner from $180; ☉dim sum 11.30am-3pm, dinner 7pm-midnight; ⓂSheung Wan, exit E2) Send your taste buds on a trip at this ballroom-turned-restaurant which serves some of the best dim sum in town. Atop the historical Western Market, the Grand Stage is also one of the few dining venues that occupies a heritage site yet manages not to be wallet-shatteringly expensive.

LIN HEUNG KUI
DIM SUM $

Map p368 (蓮香居; ☑2156 9328; 2nd & 3rd fl, 46-50 Des Voeux Rd West, Sheung Wan; dim sum $13-19, dinner from $120; ☉dim sum 6am-4pm, dinner 5-11pm; ☐5B from Central) This is one of the few old-school dim sum restaurants where you can pick dim sum from the strolling carts or the cooking stations. The grandfather-like waiters still wear their traditional white tunics and black trousers, and serve you tea from huge brass kettles. The place is no-frills, so service charges aren't expected. At dinnertime the restaurant offers old Cantonese classics (eg baked fish intestines with eggs and tangerine peels) that are rarely served in other restaurants these days. The signature 'eight treasure duck' has to be ordered a day in advance.

YUEN KEE DESSERT
DESSERTS, CANTONESE $

off Map p368 (源記; ☑2548 8687; Ground fl, 32 Centre St, Sai Ying Poon; ☉noon-11.30pm; ☐101 or 104 on Queen's Rd Central, Central) This old-timers' favourite (in operation since 1855), is renowned for its sweet Mulberry Mistletoe tea with lotus seeds and egg (桑寄蓮子雞蛋茶). It pairs well with the eggy sponge cake.

TOP CHOICE PICCOLO PIZZERIA & BAR
ITALIAN $$

(☑2824 3000; Shop 1e, Davis St, Kennedy Town; meals from $150; ☉dinner Mon, lunch & dinner Tue-Sat; ☐5B or 5X from Central) This was one of the first players behind the new dining scene in Kennedy Town. Piccolo's pizzas – thin, crispy and cheap – are among the best in town. The open kitchen design allows diners to view the giant gas oven through a glass wall at the back. There's a **branch** (☑2824 3001; Ground fl, 1 Wun Sha St, Tai Hang) in Tai Hang.

BISTRONOMIQUE
FRENCH $$

(☑2818 8266; Ground fl, 1b Davis St, Kennedy Town; lunch/dinner from $98/400; ☉lunch & dinner Tue-Sun; ☐5B or 5X from Central) The French love unusual ingredients as much as the Cantonese. Favourites like bone marrow, frogs legs and pork belly are cooked in a very homey, Gallic way in this high-ceilinged bistro. The incredibly good-value lunches allow you to sample fancy creations at pauper's prices.

GAIA RISTORANTE
ITALIAN $$$

Map p368 (☑2167 8200; www.gaiaristorante.com; Ground fl, Grand Millennium Plaza, 181 Queen's Rd Central; lunch/dinner from $350/500; ☉lunch & dinner; Ⓜ Sheung Wan, exit E2) Gaia is considered one of the best Italian restaurants in Hong Kong. The chef here finds endless ways to combine different vegetables, meat, fish and sauces, so you'll never know what's on the menu. It gets good crowds for its antipasto lunch buffet.

BA YI RESTAURANT
CHINESE $$

(巴依餐廳; ☑2484 9981; Ground fl, 43 Water St, Sai Ying Pun; ☉lunch & dinner; meals from $100; Ⓜ Central exit B, green minibus 55) This halal restaurant brings the meaty fare in northwest China to the island, and you can savour mutton in all its glory – grilled, braised, fried or boiled with lashings of spices and herbs – in a rustic setting. Take green minibus 55 outside the United Chinese Bank Building on Des Voeux Rd Central and get off at St Paul's College.

CHAN KAN KEE
CHIU CHOW $

Map p368 (陳勤記鹵鵝飯店; ☑2858 0033; Ground fl, 11 Queen's Rd West; meals from $50; ☉lunch & dinner; ☐5) For an authentic Chiu Chow (the northeastern part of Guǎngdōng) treat, this family-run eatery serves classic marinated goose, baby oyster omelette and salted vegetable duck soup. It's jam-packed during lunch hours.

CHAN CHUN KEE
CHIU CHOW $

Map p368 (陳春記; ☑3542 5793; Shop 5, 1 Queen St, Queen St Cooked Food Market, Sheung Wan; meals from $30; ☉8am-7pm; ☐5 or 5B from Central) Warning to vegetarians: different parts from a pig will confront you in every repast at this Chiu Chow eatery. The locals flock to this unpretentious kitchen for its pig's blood and innards soup (豬紅豬雜湯). For a less exotic adventure, try the fish skin dumplings or fish balls with noodles.

KAU KEE RESTAURANT
NOODLES $

Map p368 (九記牛腩; ☑2850 5967; 21 Gough St; noodles from $30; ☉12.30-7.15pm & 8.30-11.30pm Mon-Sat; Ⓜ Sheung Wan, exit E2) You can argue till the noodles go soggy about whether crowded Kau Kee has the best beef brisket in Hong Kong. Whatever the verdict, the meat – served with noodles in a beefy broth – is definitely hard to beat.

KWUN KEE RESTAURANT
CANTONESE $

off Map p368 (坤記煲仔小菜; ☑2803 7209; Wo Yick Mansion, 263 Queen's Rd W, Sai Ying Pun; meals from $100; ☉11am-12.30am Mon-Sat, 6-11.30pm Sun; ☐) Hong Kong's top brass make pilgrimages to this very local place

KARL JOHAENTGES /GETTY IMAGES ©

JAKE WYMAN/CORBIS ©

1. Nightlife in Lan Kwai Fong (p96)
Once synonymous with partying in Hong Kong, Lan Kwai Fong is still the place for bar-hopping and late nights.

2. Peak Tram (p84)
Take the 125-year-old Peak Tram to the top of Victoria Peak for sweeping views of the city.

3. Cat Street Market (p86)
A pedestrian-only lane full of stalls selling trinkets and curios.

4. Man Mo Temple (p85)
Visitors light incense offerings in this temple dedicated to the gods of literature and war.

GREG ELMS/GETTY IMAGES ©

THE PERFECT BREW

Cute little cafes are popping up in Sheung Wan, thanks to the soaring rentals in Central that have driven small businesses westward. Here are some quality venues where you can sip tea or coffee, and chill.

Teakha (茶家; Map p368; ☑2858 9185; Shop B, 18 Tai Ping Shan St, Sheung Wan; ◷11am-6pm Wed-Fri, noon-7pm Sat & Sun; ◻26) Organic milk teas, be it the Indian Chai or *Hojicha* Latte with Hokkaido black sugar, are best enjoyed with the homemade scone in this oasis just off the main street. The tea wares are so cute you can't help buying them as souvenirs.

Cafe Loisl (Map p368; ☑9179 0209; Tai On Tce, Sheung Wan; ◷8am-7pm Mon-Fri, 9am-8pm Sat & Sun; ◻26) An attempt to replicate a Viennese coffee house, this little spot has a laid-back boho vibe. The serene terrace setting makes it a perfect spot to relax, sip coffee and read novels.

Knockbox Coffee Company (Map p368; 14b Tai Ping Shan St, Sheung Wan; ◷8am-5pm Mon-Thu, 8am-10pm Fri, 12.30pm-6pm Sat & Sun; ◻26) Hardly big enough to swing a cat in, this cafe offers espresso-based coffees, and the baristas are ready to share their encyclopaedic knowledge of choosing, grinding and roasting beans.

Barista Jam (Map p368; ☑2854 2211; Shop D, Ground fl, 126-128 Jervois St, Sheung Wan; ◷8am-6pm Tue-Fri, 10am-6pm Sat & Sun; Ⓜ Sheung Wan, exit A2) Serious drinkers make the pilgrimage to this grey-walled institution. The chocolate pastries pair well with their freshly brewed coffee.

Capo's Espresso (Map p368; ☑2545 9128; Ground fl, 4 Gilman's Bazaar, Sheung Wan; ◷7.30am-10pm Mon-Fri, 11am-6pm Sat; Ⓜ Sheung Wan, exit E2) This mafia-themed coffee shop serves good-flavoured espresso, Aussie pies and cakes.

for its claypot rice (available only at dinner). Rice and toppings such as Chinese sausage and chicken are cooked in claypots over charcoal stoves until the grains are infused with the juices of the meat and a layer of rice crackle is formed at the bottom of the pot.

NGAU KEE FOOD CAFÉ CANTONESE $

Map p368 (牛記茶室; ☑2546 2584; 3 Gough St; ◷11am-12.30am; Ⓜ Sheung Wan, exit E2) The beef brisket with turnips and the stuffed eggplants are famed at this crowded eatery. The boss will be happy to recommend dishes when he's not doubling as the delivery boy.

✖ The Peak

PEAK LOOKOUT INTERNATIONAL, ASIAN $$

(太平山餐廳; ☑2849 1000; 121 Peak Rd; lunch/dinner from $250/350; ◷10.30am-11.30pm Mon-Thu, 10.30am-1am Fri, 8.30am-1am Sat, 8.30am-11.30pm Sun; ◻Peak Tram) You'll admit that this 60-year-old establishment, with seating in a glassed-in verandah and on an outside terrace, has more character than all other Peak eateries combined.

The food is excellent – especially the Indian and Western selections – as are the views.

DRINKING & NIGHTLIFE

Expect all-night street parties in Lan Kwai Fong, and occasionally in Soho. Bars come and go every month in these areas. Check the neighbourhood guide **I Love LKF** (www.ilovelkf.hk) for the most up-to-date information. Every Thursday night, **Hong Kong Pub Crawl** (www.hongkongpubcrawl.com; $100) organises a pub crawl and it's a great way to see Hong Kong's nightlife. For what you pay, you'll visit four bars and get free entry to a club.

🍷 Lan Kwai Fong & Soho

TOP CHOICE **GLOBE** PUB

Map p366 (45-53 Graham St, Soho; ◷10am-2am; Ⓜ Central, exit D1) Beer does matter in this bar: in addition to the impressive imported beer list, it's also one of the few bars that serves T8, the first cask-conditioned ale brewed in Hong Kong. Occupying an enviable 370-sq-metre space, the bar has a huge dining area with long wooden tables and comfy banquettes, where comfort food is served. Happy hour is from 9am to 8pm.

PEAK CAFE BAR
BAR

Map p366 (9-13 Shelley St, Soho; ☺happy hour 5-8pm; 🚇13, 26, 40M) The Peak Cafe Bar doesn't really crown the island, but cascades alongside the Central Escalator. The Victorian decor in this two-level bar is as impressive as the cocktails and the food. The open-front entrance makes it an excellent place to people-watch.

GECKO LOUNGE
LOUNGE, WINE BAR

Map p366 (☎2537 4680; Lower ground fl, 15-19 Hollywood Rd; ☺4pm-2am Mon-Thu, 4pm-4am Fri & Sat, happy hour 6-9pm; Ⓜ Central, exit D1) Entered from narrow Ezra's Lane off Cochrane or Pottinger Sts, Gecko is an intimate lounge and wine bar run by a friendly French sommelier and wine importer with a penchant for absinth. The well-hidden DJ mixes good sounds with kooky Parisian tunes. Great wine list, obviously.

BAR 42
BAR

Map p366 (42 Staunton St, Soho; ☺happy hour 4-8pm; Ⓜ Central, exit D2) The much-loved Barco is now Bar 42, but the change of name doesn't change its adorable nature. The staff are as great as ever and the cosy lounge with a small courtyard at the back still has a cool mix of locals and expats. The board games are at the ready to get your brain functioning.

BIT POINT
BAR

Map p366 (Ground fl, 31 D'Aguilar St; ☺happy hour 4-9pm; Ⓜ Central, exit D2) Bit Point is essentially a German-style bar where beer drinking is taken very seriously. Most beers here are draught pilsners that you can order in a glass boot if you have a thirst big enough to kick. Bit Point also serves some pretty solid Teutonic fare.

CLUB 71
BAR

Map p366 (Basement, 67 Hollywood Rd, Central; ☺happy hour 3-9pm; 🚇26) This friendly bar, named after the huge protest march held in 2003, is a haven for artists, activists and bohemians. In an uncanny historical coincidence, the garden in front of the bar

is the site where a group of Chinese revolutionaries used to hang out in the early 20th century to plot their campaign to overthrow the Qing dynasty. The socially conscious keep coming back. Find it by taking a sharp right down a narrow alley off Hollywood Rd or via a small footpath running west off Peel St.

ALHAMBRA
HOOKAH LOUNGE

Map p366 (4th fl, Ho Lee Commercial Bldg, 38-44 D'Aguilar St, Central; ☺closed Sun; Ⓜ Central, exit D2) Water-pipe devotees can puff all they want at this *shisha* lounge while cigar smokers are forced to light up outside. Named after the famous Moorish palace in Spain, this intimately lit space has a great covered terrace where you can also sip cocktails, Turkish coffee or peppermint tea.

FLYING WINEMAKER
WINE BAR

Map p366 (31 Wyndham St, Central; ☺happy hour 3-8pm; Ⓜ Central, exit D1) This tastefully appointed wine 'gallery' has a lounge (and a lab!) upstairs where you can sample wines made by the Hong Kong–born winemaker (also the owner) Eddie McDougall, alongside many other fine handcrafted wines. The big windows offer good views of the street and the Fringe Club.

STAUNTON'S WINE BAR & CAFE
WINE BAR, CAFE

Map p366 (10-12 Staunton St, Soho; ☺happy hour 5-9pm; 🚇26) Staunton's is swish, cool and on the ball with decent wine. It's right next to the Central Escalator and has a lovely terrace.

INSOMNIA
CLUB

Map p366 (Lower ground fl, Ho Lee Commercial Bldg, 38-44 D'Aguilar St, Central; ☺happy hour 5-9pm; Ⓜ Central, exit D2) Come here when you can't sleep, as it fills up only when other bars are starting to wind down. It's a people-watching place with a wide, open frontage, and there's a Filipino band doing covers out the back.

DRAGON-I
BAR, CLUB

Map p366 (Upper ground fl, the Centrium, 60 Wyndham St; ☺terrace happy hour 3-9pm Mon-Sat; 🚇26) The who's who in town and Kate Moss wannabes sway to this fabulous club to see and to be seen. The venue has an indoor bar and restaurant, with a terrace over Wyndham St filled with caged songbirds. DJs fill the dance floor with hip hop, R&B and jazz throughout the week.

ANGEL'S SHARE WHISKY BAR BAR
(2805 8388; www.angelsshare.hk; 2nd fl, Amber Lodge, 23 Hollywood Rd, Central; 3pm-2am Mon-Thur, to 3am Fri & Sat; Central, exit D1) One of Hong Kong's best whisky bars, this clubby place has over 100 whiskies from the world over – predominantly Irish, but also French, Japanese and English. One of these, a 23 year-old Macallan, comes straight out of a large 180-litre oak barrel placed in the centre of the room. If you're hungry, there's a selection of whisky-inspired dishes.

LA DOLCE VITA BAR
Map p366 (9-11 Lan Kwai Fong Lane; happy hour 5.30-8pm; Central, exit D2) This is a popular place for postwork brews, with room to prop on the heart-shaped bar or stand on the terrace and watch the preening mob crawl by.

TIVO BAR
Map p366 (43-55 Wyndham St, Central; closed Sun; Central, exit D2) One of the best of a lively string of bars along Wyndham St, Tivo is a cut above the peanuts and beer standard of the 'Fong just around the corner. Wine, *aperitivo* (Italian predinner drink) and an often glamorous crowd make a winning combination.

CENTRAL WINE CLUB WINE BAR
Map p366 (3rd fl, Sea Bird House, 22-28 Wyndham St, Central; happy hour 6-9pm, closed Sun; Central, exit D1) This ultraclassy bar is an excellent place to sample the fine old-world wines, with over 500 bottles on offer on its iPad wine list. Blues and jazz provide the soundtrack to your evening. Nonmembers are subject to a 15% service charge.

YUN FU BAR
Map p366 (Basement, 43-55 Wyndham St, Central; noon-2am Mon-Sat; Central, exit D2) This tiny but delightful circular bar with Imperial China decor is well worth stopping by for one of the fresh fruit cocktails and to soak up the sounds coming from the DJ's tiny cubbyhole.

BAR 1911 BAR
Map p366 (27 Staunton St, Soho; happy hour 5-9pm Mon-Sat; 26) This is a refined bar with fine details (stained glass, burl wood bar, ceiling fan) and a 1920s Chinese vibe. It's usually a tad less crowded than nearby

competitors, which makes it a great haven from the hubbub of the 'Fong.

WHISKEY PRIEST PUB
Map p366 (Ground & 1st fl, 12 Lan Kwai Fong; happy hour 4-9pm; Central, exit D2) This Irish pub has a sports bar setting, so enjoy Guinness, Kilkenny or Harp on tap, or any of the 60 types of whisky, while watching footy on the TV.

LIKUID CLUB
Map p366 (Ground fl, 58-62 D'Aguilar St, Central; happy hour 6-10pm Wed-Sun; Central, exit D2) When Likuid opened in 2011, it made headlines as the founder was just 18 years old. Now its bubbly, curvy design, equipped with ultra-high-tech lighting and sound system, has attracted high-class genre-hopping DJs to this latest hot spot in the 'Fong. The crowd's hip, the bouncers can be picky and the line-ups are often high profile.

CLUB 97 BAR, CLUB
Map p366 (Ground fl, Cosmos Bldg, 9-11 Lan Kwai Fong, Central; happy hour 3-8pm; Central, exit D2) This schmoozy lounge bar has a popular happy hour (it's a gay event on Friday night) and there's reggae on Sunday. It has a members-only policy to turn away the underdressed, so make an effort to get in.

BEIJING CLUB BAR, CLUB
Map p366 (2-8 Wellington St, Central; Central, exit D2) Often packed with hot and sweaty revellers attracted by the neon interior and the mix of R&B, hip hop and dance music. Dress up.

Sheung Wan & Western Districts

QUAY WEST BAR
(2816 6739; Shop 5, Ground fl, Ka Fu Bldg, 25 New Praya Kennedy Town, Kennedy Town; 5 or 5B) Tucked away towards the end of Kennedy Town, this new neighbourhood bar occupies a gorgeous location on the Praya, offering unbeatable views of the sunset and the harbour. The decor is minimalist, the vibe unpretentious. It's right next to Manhattan Heights.

OOLAA BAR
Map p368 (Ground fl, Centre Stage, Bridges St, Sheung Wan; 26) This cavernous bar knows how to attract the boozers even though it

is slightly off the action in Soho. The vast open-fronted lounge bar, the wooden alfresco terrace, and the strong wine and cocktail lists all make it a great predinner meeting spot for wine and appetisers.

CAGE BAR
Map p368 (3 Mee Lun St, NoHo; ⊙happy hour 7-9pm Mon-Sat; ⧉26) Escape the crowds at this endearingly decorated (be gentle with the antique birdcages) and intimate newcomer, which boasts two outdoor terraces overlooking quiet streets in a charming little corner of Sheung Wan.

 ENTERTAINMENT

☆ Lan Kwai Fong & Soho

TAKEOUT COMEDY CLUB COMEDY
Map p366 (⧉6220 4436; www.takeoutcomedy. com; Basement, 34 Elgin St, Soho; ⧉26) If your idea of a perfect evening involves laughing, Hong Kong's first comedy club will blow your socks off with consistent stand-up and improvised acts in English, Cantonese and Mandarin.

MAKUMBA AFRICA LOUNGE LIVE MUSIC
Map p366 (⧉2522 0544; http://makumbahk. com; Ground fl, Garley Bldg, 48 Peel St, Soho; ⊙5pm-late; ⧉26) This is the premier club for African and reggae music. During research we were told of its upcoming relocation, so check the address before dropping by.

PEEL FRESCO JAZZ
Map p366 (⧉2540 2046; www.peelfresco.com; 49 Peel St, Soho; ⊙5pm-late; ⧉26) A classy jazz venue with massive paintings taking centre stage. It's also famed for the pop stars that come in and out. Soul and reggae are also played here.

JOYCE IS NOT HERE LIVE MUSIC
Map p366 (⧉2851 2999; 38-44 Peel St, Soho; ⊙11am-late Tue-Fri, 10am-late Sat & Sun, happy hour 4.33-8.54pm; ⧉26) Cosy and friendly, this little cafe has something for everyone, from poetry readings and live music on Thursday to booze and Sunday brunch.

CULTURE CLUB LIVE MUSIC
Map p366 (⧉2127 7936; www.cultureclub. hk; 15 Elgin St, Soho; ⊙2.30-11.30pm; ⧉26)

In addition to the free Tango night which takes place every second or third Saturday of the month, this multipurpose venue is where amateur musicians hold their debut performances on Friday nights. It also features some intriguing music performances such as the blindman *nányīn* (a vanishing traditional form of Cantonese music).

HARD ROCK CAFÉ LIVE MUSIC
Map p366 (⧉2111 3777; www.hardrock.com; 55 D'Aguilar St, Central; ⊙11am-late Sun-Thu, to 4am Fri & Sat; Ⓜ Central, exit D1) This American chain may sound a knackered choice, but its enviable 380-sq-metre space, talented bands and rock classics keep the customers coming back for more.

☆ Sheung Wan

JAVA JAVA LIVE MUSIC
Map p368 (⧉2549 7739; 188 Hollywood Rd; ⊙8am-9pm Mon-Thu, 8am-midnight Fri & Sat, 9am-9pm Sun; ⧉26) A cool cafe during the day, Java Java holds an open-mic night every Thursday starting from 6pm, and does live music every Friday and Saturday night. A lot of local indie musicians play acoustic sets here.

XXX LIVE MUSIC
Map p368 (⧉9156 2330; www.xxxgallery. hk; Basement, Fui Nam Bldg, 212 Wing Lok St; Ⓜ Sheung Wan, exit A2) You'll feel like an insider once you successfully find this underground club. Accessible from the door next to the main entrance of the building, this bare concrete basement is raw, straightforward (it's also a gallery, by the way), and attracts electronic music lovers and general clubbers alike. Opening hours are irregular. Check the website for events.

SHEUNG WAN CIVIC CENTRE THEATRE, LIVE MUSIC
Map p368 (上環文娛中心; ⧉booking 2853 2678, enquiries 2853 2689; 5th fl, Sheung Wan Municipal Services Bld, 345 Queen's Rd Central, Sheung Wan; ⊙9am-11pm, box office 10am-6.30pm; Ⓜ Sheung Wan, exit A2) This government-run performance venue shares a building with a wet market and cooked food centre. Its year-round program leans towards drama by local theatre troupes, some engagingly experimental, and concerts by independent musicians and bands.

START **BIT POINT**
END **CLUB 71**
DISTANCE **800M**
DURATION **AS LONG AS YOU CAN LAST!**

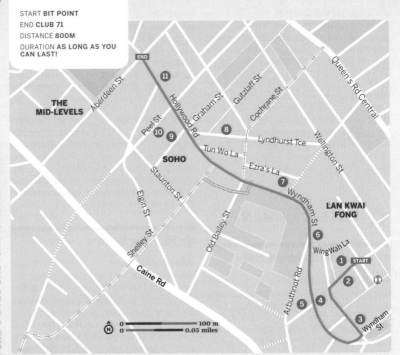

Neighbourhood Walk
Pub Crawl

➡ Order a schnapps in ① **Bit Point** to kick things off. Then smoke a hookah and chill on the terrace at ② **Alhambra**.

When you are ready to get moving again, climb uphill to ③ **Likuid** to soak up the sumptuous beats and cutting-edge funk. Then turn right onto Wyndham St, where ④ **Yun Fu** boasts scruffy surrounds and marvellous sounds. Opposite Yun Fu is ⑤ **Dragon-I** where supermodels await if you can get past the door police.

Retrace your steps back to Hollywood Rd, and grab some snacks to enjoy with a bottle of Prosecco in ⑥ **Tivo**, where you'll be mixing with the attractive crowd.

Want more wine? Slightly off Hollywood Rd is the famous ⑦ **Gecko Lounge**. It may be tiny, but it's fun and French. Afterwards, if you're feeling peckish, a good place to refuel is ⑧ **Assaf** on Lynhurst Tce which serves great kebabs, perfect for recharging the batteries.

Ready for still more? Then march on up to Graham St and sample some locally brewed beer at ⑨ **The Globe**, or head to ⑩ **Makumba Africa Lounge** on Peel St for some reggae vibes.

Wrap up the night in ⑪ **Club 71**, a relaxed and friendly watering hole off Hollywood Rd.

🛍 SHOPPING

The inexorably gentrifying Hollywood Rd, which stretches from Central to Sheung Wan, is home to some of Hong Kong's best galleries and antique shops. Stores on Cat St sell tack and curios, but beware of scams. Western Market is a good spot for buying fabrics.

🛍 Lan Kwai Fong & Soho

TOP CHOICE WATTIS FINE ART ANTIQUES
Map p366 (2nd fl, 20 Hollywood Rd; ⏰10.30am-6pm Mon-Sat; 🚌26) This upstairs gallery has the best collection of antique maps for sale. The selection of old photographs of Hong Kong and Macau is also very impressive. You enter the shop from Old Bailey St.

TOP CHOICE FLOW BOOKS
Map p366 (7th fl, 29 Hollywood Rd, Central; ⏰noon-7.30pm; 🚌26) Having moved further up along the Central Escalator and to a higher floor (from Lyndhurst Tce), Flow is still tiny, and still determined to nurture a love for reading. A sprawling jumble of secondhand English titles covers almost every inch of the shop. You'll need some patience to uncover the gem you're seeking; alternatively, let the friendly owner Lam Sum guide you to the right shelf.

TAI SING FINE ANTIQUES ANTIQUES
Map p366 (大成古玩有限公司; 3rd fl, 12 Wyndham St; ⏰10.30am-5.30pm Mon-Sat; Ⓜ️Central, exit D2) Tai Sing has been selling quality Chinese antiques for more than half a century, with a special focus on porcelain.

ARCH ANGEL ANTIQUES ANTIQUES
Map p366 (53-55 Hollywood Rd; ⏰9.30am-6.30pm; 🚌26) Though the specialities are ancient porcelain and tombware, Arch Angel packs a lot more into its three floors: it has everything from mah-jong sets and terracotta horses to palatial furniture.

HONEYCHURCH ANTIQUES ANTIQUES
Map p366 (29 Hollywood Rd; ⏰9am-6.30pm Mon-Sat; 🚌26) This fine shop, run by an American couple for more than four decades, specialises in antique Chinese furniture, jewellery and English silver. There's a wide range of stock, with items from the early Chinese dynasties right up to the 20th century.

LINVA TAILOR CLOTHING, ACCESSORIES
Map p366 (年華時裝公司; 38 Cochrane St; ⏰9.30am-6.30pm Mon-Sat; 🚌26) Fancy a cheongsam (tight-fitting Chinese dress)? Bring your own silk or choose from Miss Tong's selection. If you're pushed for time, the bespoke tailors are happy to mail the completed items to you.

CHOCOLATE RAIN JEWELLERY, ACCESSORIES
Map p366 (Ground fl, 67a, Chung Hing Court, Peel St, Soho; ⏰noon-9pm; 🚌26) The whimsical frontage of this Peel St favourite is an accurate introduction to the (work)shop of Prudence Mak, one of Hong Kong's favourite DIY crafters. The necklaces, bracelets and bags are handmade from recycled materials by the designer, and they all have the signature Fatima Doll imprinted or crafted on them. Every piece sold here is unique.

9TH MUSE JEWELLERY, ACCESSORIES
Map p366 (Unit 1204, One Lyndhurst Tower, 1 Lyndhurst Tce, Central; ⏰10.30am-7.30pm; Ⓜ️Central, exit D2) This secret treasure trove in Lyndhurst Tce has sucked legions of fashionistas to its provocative selection of refined jewellery and handcrafted handbags. The great news is that you don't need to break the bank to own them. The shop also has a growing line of home accessories.

CARPET CENTRE CARPETS
Map p366 (Lower ground fl, Shop A, 29 Hollywood Rd, Central; 🚌26) Apart from rugs, kilims and tapestries, this carpet boutique also sells a wide range of high-quality Pashmina scarfs, wraps and shawls. Enter from Cochrane St.

BOOK ATTIC BOOKS
Map p366 (Cockloft, 2 Elgin St, Soho; ⏰noon-6pm Mon-Sat; 🚌26) Another great secondhand bookshop, Book Attic is an oasis of calm amid the hustle and bustle of Soho. The tiny tea corner makes this place a nice retreat when browsing through the wide-ranging titles, which include an interesting selection of spiritual books. As if this is not enough, the tea is free. Say thanks to friendly owner/book lover Jennifer.

OLYMPIA GRAECO-EGYPTIAN COFFEE FOOD, DRINK
Map p366 (奧林比亞接臣咖啡; Ground fl, 24 Old Bailey St; ⏰11am-7pm; 🚌26) This place has been around since the year dot and it still grinds the best beans in town.

FACES OF HONG KONG FASHION

Designers, both established and emerging, are popping up everywhere in the heart of Lan Kwai Fong and Soho. The following are the hot crop of local heroes.

Lu Lu Cheung (Map p366; 50 Wellington St, Central; ⊙10.30am-8pm Sun-Thu, to 10pm Fri & Sat; ⓂCentral, exit D2) Bold yet sophisticated, Lu Lu's casual wear and evening dresses use natural fabrics, such as wool, cotton, silk and linen, in muted tones. She works with layers and textures that employ mesh or floral embroidery.

Ranee K (Map p368; 25 Aberdeen St, Central; ⊙11.30am-8pm; ⓺26) Young local designer Ranee K is a rising star for her combinations of dramatic prints and textures, as well as for her deft adoption of cuts and styles from both East and West in her evening and ready-to-wear lines.

Pursue by Joel (Map p366; 2nd fl, 13 Lan Kwai Fong; ⊙2-9pm; ⓂCentral, exit D2) Joel Chan is associated with high-quality materials and playful tailor-made designs. His shop, which doubles as a bar and gallery, has a fine collection of stylish menswear and women's evening gowns.

Nude is Rude (Map p366; 7 Lan Kwai Fong; ⊙11am-8pm Mon-Fri, 1-6pm Sat; ⓂCentral, exit D2) Emerging designer Marisa Zeman creates body-flattering resort and casual wear with soft materials such as modal jersey and silk. Her kaftans and flowing dresses are versatile enough to be worn in multiple ways.

Fang Fong Projects (Map p366; 69 Peel St, Central; ⊙11am-8pm Sun-Thu, noon-9pm Fri & Sat; ⓺26) Wu Lai-fan's very wearable dresses are a clever mix of vintage fabric and modern 1980s silhouette. The shop also has her own collection of designs that are hardly available elsewhere in Hong Kong.

L Plus H (Map p366; 17th fl, Stanley 11, 11 Stanley St, Central; ⊙10am-7pm Mon-Sat; ⓂCentral, exit D2) Founded by a group of socially driven entrepreneurs, L Plus H teams up with local designers and is proud of its 100% 'Designed and Made in Hong Kong' label. Fine knitwear is its forte.

PORTRAIT WINEMAKERS & DISTILLERS   WINE

Map p366 (31 Staunton St, Soho; ⊙closed Sun; ⓺26) Homegrown wines are still a novelty here, but this Hong Kong–based wine and spirit maker already has quite a few award-winning wines, and you can sample and buy them in the outlet in Soho. Distilling demonstrations are held every Thursday, Friday and Saturday night.

MOUNTAIN FOLKCRAFT   GIFTS, SOUVENIRS

Map p366 (高山民藝; 12 Wo On Lane; ⊙closed Sun; ⓂCentral) This is one of the nicest shops in the city for folk craft. It's piled with bolts of batik and sarongs, clothing, wood carvings, lacquerware and papercuts made by ethnic minorities in China and other Asian countries. Prices, while not cheap, are not outrageous either.

PHOTO SCIENTIFIC   PHOTOGRAPHY

Map p366 (攝影科學; 6 Stanley St; ⊙9am-7pm Mon-Sat; ⓂCentral, exit D2) This is the favourite of Hong Kong's pro photographers. You'll almost certainly find equipment elsewhere for less, but Photo Scientific has a rock-solid reputation with labelled prices, no bargaining, no arguing and no cheating.

Sheung Wan

KARIN WEBER GALLERY   ANTIQUES, ARTS & CRAFTS

Map p368 (20 Aberdeen St; ⊙11am-7pm Mon-Sat, 2-6pm Sun; ⓺26) Karin Weber has an enjoyable mix of Chinese country antiques and contemporary Asian artworks. She is able to arrange antique-buying trips to Guǎngdōng for serious buyers.

INDOSIAM   BOOKS, ANTIQUES

Map p368 (1st fl, 89 Hollywood Rd; ⊙2-7pm; ⓺26) Hong Kong's first truly antiquarian bookshop deals in rare titles relating to Asian countries. It's particularly strong on Thailand, China and the former French colonies. It also sells vintage newspapers and old Chinese prints.

LAM KIE YUEN TEA CO FOOD, DRINK

Map p368 (林奇苑茶行; Ground fl, 105-107 Bonham Strand East; ⊙9am-6.30pm Mon-Sat; ⓂSheung Wan, exit A2) For tea lovers, Lam Kie Yuen, which has been selling tea since 1955, is testament to just how much tea there is in China. From unfermented, slightly to fully fermented and everything in between, there's simply too much choice. Can't make a decision? The owner will invite you to sit down for a taste beforehand. The *Dàhóng-páo* tea from Fújiàn is exceptional.

POTTERY WORKSHOP HOMEWARES

Map p368 (樂天陶社; ☑9842 5889; 24 Upper Station St, Sheung Wan; ⊙noon-6pm Sat & Sun, by appointment Mon-Fri; ⓠ26) This much-loved pottery workshop has continued to showcase funky crockery made by local and mainland artisans after its move from the Fringe to Sheung Wan. The ceramic teaspoons are so cute you simply don't want to put them back. Access from Tai Ping Shan St.

HAJI GALLERY GIFTS

Map p368 (24c Tai Ping Shan St; ⊙2-7pm Tue-Sun; ⓠ26) This 7-Eleven-store sized gallery focuses on artwork by emerging local artists, and the prices are more affordable than you might think. Other than the rows of paintings on one side of the wall, the shop has an interesting collection of CDs, bags and T-shirts, all locally designed.

SELECT-18 VINTAGE

Map p368 (Ground fl, Grandview Garden, 18 Bridges St; ⊙2-7pm Tue-Sun; ⓠ26) Run by a stylist-turned-vintage collector, this den of sartorial pleasures has been keeping local celebrities stylishly clad in vintage frocks. Other than clothes, boots, jackets and purses for young women, the store also has a curious collection of vintage furniture and suitcases.

LOMOGRAPHY PHOTOGRAPHY

Map p368 (2 Po Yan St; ⊙11am-7pm; ⓠ26) Even if you're not a Lomographer, it's hard not to like this shop, what with its cute collection of cameras, flash units and Lomo-inspired accessories. The upstairs gallery regularly exhibits Lomo artworks.

HOMELESS HOMEWARES, GIFTS

Map p368 (28 Gough St, Central; ⓂSheung Wan, exit A2) This flagship of a growing contemporary interiors retail chain is packed full of good ideas and portable gifts to take home, from smart gadgets such as laser clocks to quirky, practical and ornamental mugs, chairs and decorative items.

LA CABANE A VIN WINE

Map p368 (Basement fl, 97 Hollywood Rd; ⊙5-9pm Mon-Tue, noon-9pm Wed-Sat; ⓠ26) This is the city's first natural wine shop and it specialises in organic and biodynamic wines. The staff are more than willing to discuss the non-interventionist production of these small-quantity wines with you. Entrance on Shin Hing St.

WING ON DEPARTMENT STORE

Map p368 (永安; ☑2852 1888; 211 Des Voeux Rd Central; ⓂSheung Wan, exit E3) 'Forever Peaceful' is notable for being locally owned. It carries a range of goods but is especially well known for inexpensive electronics and household appliances.

SPORTS & ACTIVITIES

HAPPY FOOT REFLEXOLOGY CENTRE SPA

Map p366 (知足樂; ☑2544 1010; 6th, 11th & 13th fl, Jade Centre, 98-102 Wellington St, Central; ⊙10am-midnight; ⓂCentral, exit D2) Foot/body massage starts at $198/250 for 50 minutes.

WAN KEI HO INTERNATIONAL MARTIAL ARTS ASSOCIATION MARTIAL ARTS

Map p368 (尹圻灝國際武術總會; ☑2544 1368; www.kungfuwan.com; 3rd fl, Yue's House, 304 Des Voeux Rd Central, Sheung Wan; ⓂSheung Wan, exit A) Master Wan teaches northern Shaolin kung fu to a wide following of locals and foreigners alike. Classes are offered in the evenings from Monday to Thursday. Depending on how many classes you take, the monthly fees vary from $300 to $1400.

Hong Kong Island: Wan Chai & the Northeast

ADMIRALTY | WAN CHAI | CAUSEWAY BAY | HAPPY VALLEY | ISLAND EAST

Neighbourhood Top Five

1 Combing the rows of **narrow streets** (p110) sandwiched between Queen's Rd East and Johnston Rd for old houses, Taoist temples, traditional shops, open-air bazaars and screaming wet markets.

2 Feeling your adrenalin soar at the **Happy Valley Racecourse** (p111) on a Wednesday night, beer in hand.

3 Experiencing sublime taste in Admiralty: aesthetic at the **Asia Society Hong Kong Centre** (p107) and culinary at **AMMO** (p114).

4 Shopping for Hong Kong–style, retro-with-a-twist souvenirs at **G.O.D.** (p124) in Causeway Bay.

5 Having a night of debauchery on **Lockhart Road** (p121) in Wan Chai.

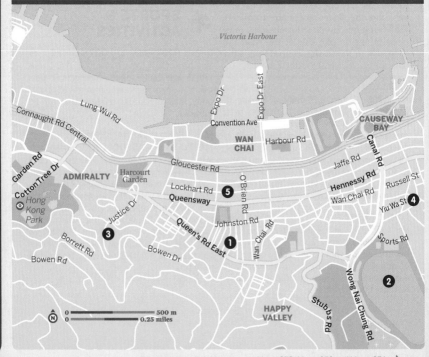

For more detail of this area, see Map p370, Map p372 and Map p374 →

Explore Wan Chai & the Northeast

Stroll through the Pacific Place mall connected to Admiralty MRT station and pay a leisurely two-and-a-half hour visit to Hong Kong Park and the Asia Society Hong Kong Centre. Head downhill and over to Queen's Rd East nearby. Spend two hours exploring the 'old' Wan Chai area. Have some ethnic food; choices are plenty. Continue your journey to 'new' Wan Chai, closer to the harbour, to the Wan Chai Computer Centre or further north to the Hong Kong Convention & Exhibition Centre. Tram it to Causeway Bay, arriving after the lunch hour to avoid the crowds. Spend some time shopping or head east to Victoria Park to people-watch under a tree. Enjoy happy-hour drinks here or hop on an eastbound 'ding ding' and play it by ear.

Local Life

➡ **Lil' Jakarta** Indonesian maids gather at Victoria Park (p109) on Sundays to eat, sing and pray.

➡ **Toy shops** Gen-Xers bring their kids to the Tai Yuen St toy shops (p125) to relive childhood innocence, and buy lanterns during the Mid-Autumn Festival.

➡ **Hipsterville** The atmospheric area around Star, Moon and St Francis Sts (p121) is where hipsters and tastemakers hang out.

➡ **Fujian Town** North Point is the stronghold of Hong Kong's Fujianese community (p111).

Getting There & Away

➡ **Bus** Buses operate from Admiralty bus station below Queensway Plaza. To get to Causeway Bay and Happy Valley from Admiralty and Central, buses 5, 5B and 26 stop along Yee Wo St. Green Minibus 40 from Stanley calls along Tang Lung St and Yee Woo St.

➡ **MTR** Admiralty station is on the Island and Tsuen Wan lines. Wan Chai station is on the Island line. Get to Causeway Bay and Happy Valley from the Causeway Bay and Tin Hau stations on the Central line. Take the Island line from Causeway Bay to get to Island East.

➡ **Tram** Trams run east along Queensway, Johnston Rd and Hennessy Rd to Causeway Bay, and west to Central and Sheung Wan. To get to Causeway Bay and Happy Valley trams run along Hennessy Rd and Yee Wo St to Central and Shau Kei Wan; along Percival St to Happy Valley, and along Wong Nai Chung Rd to Causeway Bay, Central, Kennedy Town and Shau Kei Wan. For Island East, trams run all the way to Chai Wan.

➡ **Star Ferry** Wan Chai ferry pier to Tsim Sha Tsui, Kowloon.

Lonely Planet's Top Tip

Viewing the Island's east districts from a moving tram imparts a charming cinematic quality to your impressions, as these primarily residential areas can underwhelm on foot. Add speed to the uniformity of housing blocks and you get rhythm and pattern. The bonus is that you can hop off when something tickles your fancy. The district is served by some 30 stops on the eastbound tramline.

 ### Best Places to Eat

➡ Yin Yang (p114)

➡ Tung Po Seafood Restaurant (p120)

➡ Cēpage (p114)

➡ Pure Veggie House (p113)

➡ AMMO (p114)

For reviews, see p113 ➡

 ### Best Places to Drink

➡ Executive Bar (p122)

➡ Pawn (p122)

➡ Classifieds Mozzarella Bar (p121)

For reviews, see p121 ➡

 ### Best Places to Shop

➡ G.O.D. (p124)

➡ Daydream Nation (p123)

➡ Wan Chai Computer Centre (p124)

For reviews, see p123 ➡

HONG KONG ISLAND: WAN CHAI & THE NORTHEAST

MANFRED GOTTSCHALK/GETTY IMAGES ©

TOP SIGHTS
HONG KONG PARK

Designed to look anything but natural, Hong Kong Park emphasises artificial creations such as its fountain plaza, conservatory, waterfall, playground, taichi garden and viewing tower. Yet the eight-hectare park is beautiful and, with a wall of skyscrapers on one side and mountains on the other, makes for dramatic photographs.

The best feature is the **Edward Youde Aviary** (尤德觀鳥園; Map p370; ☺9am-5pm). Home to more than 600 birds representing some 90 species, it's like a rainforest planted in the middle of the city. Visitors walk along a wooden bridge suspended some 10m above the ground and at eye level with tree branches. The **Forsgate Conservatory** (☺9am-5pm) overlooking the park is the largest in Southeast Asia.

At the park's northernmost tip is **Flagstaff House Museum of Tea Ware** (茶具文物館; Map p370; ☑2869 0690; www.lcsd.gov.hk/ce/museum/arts/english/tea/intro/eintro.html; 10 Cotton Tree Dr; admission free; ☺10am-5pm Wed-Mon). Built in 1846, it now houses a collection of antique Chinese tea ware. The ground-floor cafe is a great place to recharge over a pot of fine tea.

The **KS Lo Gallery** (羅桂祥茶藝館; Map p370; ☑2869 0690; 10 Cotton Tree Dr; admission free; ☺10am-5pm Wed-Mon) contains rare Chinese ceramics and stone seals.

On the eastern edge of the park, the **Hong Kong Visual Arts Centre** (香港視覺藝術中心; Map p370; ☑2521 3008; www.lcsd.gov.hk/ce/Museum/Apo/en/vac.html; 7A Kennedy Rd; admission free; ☺10am-9pm Wed-Mon), housed in beautiful former Victoria Barracks, supports local artists and stages exhibitions.

DON'T MISS...

➡ Edward Youde Aviary

➡ Flagstaff House Museum of Tea Ware

➡ KS Lo Gallery

➡ Hong Kong Visual Arts Centre

PRACTICALITIES

➡ 香港公園

➡ Map p370

➡ ☑2521 5041

➡ www.lcsd.gov.hk/ parks/hkp/en/index. php

➡ 19 Cotton Tree Dr, Admiralty

➡ admission free

➡ ☺park 6am-11pm

➡ Ⓜ Admiralty, exit C1

◉ SIGHTS

◉ Admiralty

HELENA MAY   HISTORIC BUILDING

Map p370 (梅夫人婦女會主樓; ☑2522 6766; www.helenamay.com; 35 Garden Rd, Central; MAdmiralty, then ☐12A) The Helena May was opened in 1916 by the wife of a governor as a social club for working, single European women, for whom the colony had little to offer by way of 'respectable' entertainment like ballet lessons and tea parties. The colonial building with features of the Palladian and beaux arts styles was used to stable horses during the Japanese Occupation. Currently a private club and hostel (see p269), it runs 20-minute tours in English and Chinese once every two months on a Saturday (10am to noon; see the website for dates). Reservations are compulsory and accepted a month in advance.

HONG KONG PARK   PARK

See p106.

TOP CHOICE **ASIA SOCIETY HONG KONG CENTRE**   HISTORIC BUILDING, GALLERY

Map p370 (亞洲協會香港中心; Hong Kong Jockey Club Former Explosives Magazine; ☑2103 9511; http://asiasociety.org/hong-kong; 9 Justice Dr, Admiralty; ◷gallery 11am-5pm Tue-Sun, to 8pm last Thu of the month; MAdmiralty, exit F) An architectural feat, this magnificent site integrates 19th-century British military buildings, including a couple of explosives magazines, and transforms them into an exhibition gallery, a multipurpose theatre, an excellent restaurant (p114) and a bookstore, all open to the public. The architects Tod Williams and Billie Tsien eschewed bold statements for a subdued design that deferred to history and the natural shape of the land. The result is a horizontally oriented site that offers an uplifting contrast to the skyscrapers nearby. The centre is an easy walk from the hotels in Admiralty.

TAMAR PARK   PARK

Map p370 (添馬公園; Tamar St, Admiralty; MAdmiralty, exit A) This harbour-front park on the site of the New Central Government Offices is an inviting collection of verdant lawns where you can soak up the rays. It's part of a 4km promenade running along the northern shoreline of Hong Kong Island, from Central Piers, outside the IFC mall, past the Hong Kong Convention and Exhibition Centre, and all the way to North Point. Much of the walkway, though, is heavily under construction.

NEW CENTRAL GOVERNMENT OFFICES   BUILDING

Map p370 (添馬艦新政府總部; Tamar St, Admiralty; MAdmiralty, exit A) A contemporary building at the picturesque Tamar Site (*HMS Tamar* was a British naval vessel) now houses the headquarters of the HKSAR government, the legislature and the Chief Executive's Office.

◉ Wan Chai

HONG KONG CONVENTION & EXHIBITION CENTRE   BUILDING

Map p372 (香港會議展覽中心; ☑2582 8888; www.hkcec.com.hk; 1 Expo Dr; ☐18) Due north of the Wan Chai MTR station, the massive Convention & Exhibition Centre, which was built in 1988 and extended onto an artificial island in the harbour for the official ceremony of the return of sovereignty to China in 1997, has been compared with a bird's wing, a banana leaf and a lotus petal. It's a leading venue for large trade fairs, exhibitions and conventions.

CENTRAL PLAZA   BUILDING

Map p372 (中環廣場; 18 Harbour Rd; ☐18) Central Plaza, Hong Kong's third-tallest building, looks garish with its glass skin of three colours – gold, silver and terracotta. But it provides direct connection to Hong Kong Convention & Exhibition Centre and Wan Chai MTR station through an elevated pedestrian footbridge.

GOLDEN BAUHINIA SQUARE   MONUMENT

Map p372 (金紫荊廣場; Golden Bauhinia Sq, 1 Expo Dr; MWan Chai, exit A5, ☐18) A 6m-tall statue of Hong Kong's symbol stands on the waterfront just in front of the Hong Kong Convention & Exhibition Centre to mark the establishment of the Hong Kong SAR in 1997. The flag-raising ceremony, held daily at 8am and conducted by the Hong Kong police, is a must-see for mainland tourist groups. There's a pipe band on the 1st, 11th and 21st of each month at 7.45am.

LOCAL KNOWLEDGE

CLOCK OF COLOURS

Central Plaza in Wan Chai, the lanky skyscraper sticking out from behind the Hong Kong Convention & Exhibition Centre when you're looking from Kowloon, is one of the world's biggest clocks. Between 6pm and midnight daily, there are four illuminated lines shining through the glass pyramid at the top of the building.

The bottom level indicates the hour: red is 6pm, white 7pm, purple 8pm, yellow 9pm, pink 10pm and green 11pm. When all four lights are the same colour, it's right on the hour. When the top light is different from the bottom ones, it's 15 minutes past the hour. If the top two and bottom two are different, it's half-past the hour. If the top three match, it's 45 minutes past the hour.

So what time is it now?

HONG KONG ARTS CENTRE   CULTURAL BUILDING
Map p372 (香港藝術中心; www.hkac.org.hk; 2 Harbour Rd; ⓂAdmiralty, exit E2) Due east of the Academy for the Performing Arts is the Hong Kong Arts Centre. Along with theatres, including the **Agnès B Cinema**, you'll also find here the two-floor **Pao Sui Loong & Pao Yue Kong Galleries** (包玉剛及包兆龍畫廊（包氏畫廊）; admission free; ☺10am-6pm, to 8pm during exhibitions), which hosts retrospectives and group shows in all visual media. The new Daydream Nation (p123) shop is also here.

HONG KONG ACADEMY FOR THE PERFORMING ARTS   CULTURAL BUILDING
Map p372 (香港演藝學院; www.hkapa.edu; 1 Gloucester Rd; ⓂAdmiralty, exit E2) With its striking triangular atrium and an exterior Meccano-like frame (a work of art in itself), the academy building (1985) is a Wan Chai landmark and an important venue for music, dance and scholarship.

SOUTHORN PLAYGROUND   PARK
Map p372 (修頓球場; ☺6am-11.30pm; ⓂWan Chai, exit A3) This unspectacular-looking sportsground is in fact the social hub of old Wan Chai, offering up a cross-section of life in the 'hood at any time of the day. Seniors come to play chess, students and amateur athletes to shoot hoops and kick ball. There are hip-hop dance-offs, housewives shaking a leg, outreach social workers, cruising gays and a daily trickle of lunchers from the banks and construction sites. Southorn is bound by Hennessy, Luard and Johnston Rds, and the Wan Chai Computer Centre.

PAK TAI TEMPLE   TEMPLE
off Map p372 (北帝廟; 2 Lung On St; ☺8am-5pm; ⓂWan Chai, exit A3) A short stroll up Stone Nullah Lane takes you to a majestic Taoist temple built in 1863 to honour a god of the sea, Pak Tai. The temple – the largest on Hong Kong Island – is impressive. The main hall contains a 3m-tall copper likeness of Pak Tai cast in the Ming dynasty.

HUNG SHING TEMPLE   TEMPLE
Map p372 (洪聖古廟; 129-131 Queen's Rd East; ☺8am-5.30pm; ⌨6 or 6A, ⓂWan Chai, exit A3) Nestled in a nook on the southern side of Queen's Rd East, this narrow, dark and rather forbidding temple is built atop huge boulders. It was erected in honour of a deified Tang-dynasty official who was known for his virtue (important) and ability to make predictions of great value to traders (ultra-important).

OLD WAN CHAI POST OFFICE   BUILDING
Map p372 (舊灣仔郵政局; 221 Queen's Rd East; ☺10am-5pm Wed-Mon; ⌨6 or 6A) A short distance to the east of Wan Chai Market is this tiny colonial-style building erected in 1913 and now serving as a resource centre operated by the **Environmental Protection Department** (☏2893 2856; ☺10am-5pm Mon-Tue & Thu-Sat, 10am-1pm Wed, 1-5pm Sun).

HONG KONG HOUSE OF STORIES   MUSEUM
Map p372 (香港故事館; ☏enquiries 2117 5850, Suki Chau for tour enrolment 2835 4376; http://houseofstories.sjs.org.hk; 74 Stone Nullah Lane; ☺11am-5pm; ⌨6 or 6A) Opened by local residents and fans of Wan Chai, this tiny museum is in the historic **Blue House**, a prewar building with cast-iron Spanish balconies reminiscent of New Orleans. The not-for-profit museum sells local handicrafts and runs private tours in English. Email a month in advance to arrange. A two-hour tour is $600 so the more of you, the cheaper.

LOVER'S ROCK
LANDMARK

(姻緣石; off Bowen Rd; green minibus 24A) Lover's Rock or Destiny's Rock (Yan Yuen Sek) is a phallus-shaped boulder on a bluff at the end of a track above Bowen Rd. It's a favourite pilgrimage site for women with relationship or fertility problems. It's busy during the **Maidens' Festival**, held on the seventh day of the seventh moon (mid-August). The easiest way to reach here is to take green minibus 24A from the Admiralty bus station. Get off at the terminus (Shiu Fai Tce) and walk up the path behind the housing complex.

KHALSA DIWAN SIKH TEMPLE
TEMPLE

Map p372 (☎2572 4459; www.khalsadiwan.com; 371 Queen's Rd East; ⊗4am-9pm; ⊡) Sitting quietly between a busy road and a cemetery is Hong Kong's largest Sikh temple, a descendant of a small original built in 1901 by Sikh members of the British army. The temple welcomes people of any faith, caste or colour to join in their services. Sunday prayer (9am to 1pm) sees some 1000 believers and nonbelievers in collective worship (fewer at the daily prayers, 4am to 8am and 6pm to 8pm). More famous are its free vegetarian meals (11.30am to 8.30pm), a simple dal or *sabzi* (vegetable stew) handed to anyone walking through the blue-and-white gates. You could return the favour by helping to wash the dishes.

HONG KONG CEMETERY
CEMETERY

(香港墳場; www.fehd.gov.hk/english/cc/introduction.html; ⊗7am-6pm or 7pm; Causeway Bay, exit A, ⊡1, 8X, 117) Crowded and cosmopolitan, dead Hong Kong is no different from the breathing city. Tombstones jostle for space at this Christian cemetery (c 1845) located on Wong Nai Chung Rd alongside the Jewish, Hindu, Parsee and Muslim Cemeteries, and St Michael's Catholic Cemetery. Burial plots date to the mid-1800s and include colonialists, tycoons and silver-screen divas.

After exiting the MTR, follow Russell St, turn left into Wong Nai Chung Rd, and walk south for 15 minutes. The entrances of the cemeteries are scattered close to each other, opposite the public entrance of the Happy Valley Racecourse.

◉ Causeway Bay

NOONDAY GUN
HISTORIC SITE

Map p374 (香港怡和午炮; 221 Gloucester Rd; ⊗7am-midnight; Causeway Bay, exit D1) Built in 1901, this recoil-mounted 3lb cannon is one of the few vestiges of the colonial past in Causeway Bay. The gun stands in a small garden opposite the Excelsior Hotel on Gloucester Rd and is fired at noon every day.

The Noonday Gun is accessible via a tunnel through the basement car park in the World Trade Centre, just west of the Excelsior Hotel. From the taxi rank in front of the hotel, look west for the door marked 'Car Park Shroff, Marina Club & Noon Gun'.

VICTORIA PARK
PARK

Map p374 (維多利亞公園; www.lcsd.gov.hk/en/ls_park.php; Causeway Rd; admission free; ⊗6am or 7am-11pm; Tin Hau, exit B) Victoria Park is the biggest patch of public greenery on Hong Kong Island. The best time to go is on a weekday morning, when it becomes a forest of people practising the slow-motion choreography of taichi. The park becomes a flower market a few days before the Chinese New Year. It's also worth a visit during

LOCAL KNOWLEDGE

RENT-A-CURSE GRANNIES

Under the **Canal Road Flyover** (Map p374) between Wan Chai and Causeway Bay, you can hire little old ladies to beat up your enemy. From their perch on plastic stools, these rent-a-curse grannies will pound paper cut-outs of your romantic rival, office bully or whiny celeb with a shoe (their orthopaedic flat or your stilettos – your call) while rapping rhythmic curses. All for only $50. Hung Shing Temple (p108) has a 'master' who performs the same with a symbolic 'precious' sword for the exorbitant sum of $100.

Villain hitting or villain exorcism (打小人; *da siu yan*) is a practice related to folk sorcery. It's performed throughout the year but the most popular date is the Day of the Awakening of Insects when the sun is at an exact celestial longitude of 345° (usually between 5 and 20 March on the Gregorian calendar). It's believed to bring reconciliation or resolution, though that too could be symbolic.

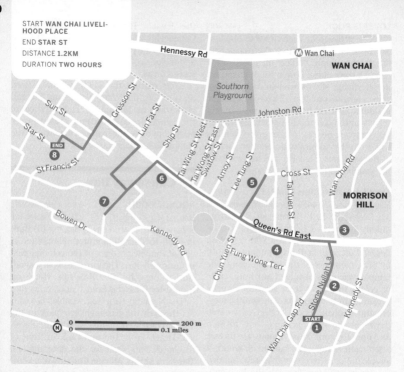

START **WAN CHAI LIVELI-HOOD PLACE**
END **STAR ST**
DISTANCE **1.2KM**
DURATION **TWO HOURS**

Neighbourhood Walk
Old Wan Chai's Forgotten Streets

A short stroll from the main bus routes and Wan Chai metro (exit A3), you'll start to get a feel for the neighbourhood as it was in the 19th century at ❶ **Pak Tai Temple**, a stunning temple built 150 years ago by local residents. Further down the slope, the ❷ **House of Stories** will show you what life was like in Wan Chai in the last century.

The Streamline Moderne exterior of the historic ❸ **Wan Chai Market** is all that remains of the place now fronting a shopping centre. Once the hub of the neighbourhood, the market was used as a mortuary by Japanese forces in WWII. Just to the west, the pocket-sized ❹ **Old Wan Chai Post Office** is Hong Kong's oldest post office.

Take a quick look at ❺ **Spring Garden Lane**, one of the first areas developed by the British, and imagine what it was like when prostitutes hawked their wares there in the 1900s. Then head along Queen's Rd East to peep inside the mysterious ❻ **Hung**

Shing Temple (c 1847), once a seaside shrine.

Just west of the temple turn up the hill along Ship St and stand before the now derelict ❼ **Ghost House** at 55 Nam Koo Tce. Its history is a wretched one: it was used by Japanese soldiers as a brothel housing 'comfort women' in WWII.

The ❽ **Star Street neighbourhood** is a quiet little corner of town that manages to contain the old, including a family-run *dai pai dong* (food stall) on St Francis St, and the new, in the form of quaint boutiques and restaurants. On 31 Wing Fung St, just above Classifieds Mozzarella Bar, is a six-storey balconied building in art deco style. Admiralty MTR can be reached by an escalator and underground travelator entered at the bottom of Wing Fung St.

VICKIE'S ANGRY UNCLES

Victoria Park has always been associated with freedom of expression, a reputation owed mainly to the candlelight vigil which takes place here on 4 June, but also to the current affairs debate 'City Forum' which turns it into a mini Hyde Park every Sunday.

Spanning two MTR stations and with multiple entrances, the park provides a leafy detour and short cut for many locals. Among the regulars are a group of retired, pro-Communist old men who during 'City Forum' on Sundays (noon to 1pm), would hang out near the venue and holler against speechifying pro-democracy politicians to drown them out.

These men came to be known as the 'Uncles of Victoria Park' (維園阿伯), but the term has since evolved to include any politically minded old man with a gripe. And Hong Kong certainly has no shortage of these.

the **Mid-Autumn Festival**, when people turn out en masse carrying lanterns.

CAUSEWAY BAY TYPHOON SHELTER
TYPHOON SHELTER

Map p374 (銅鑼灣避風塘; off Hung Hing Rd, Causeway Bay; MCauseway Bay, exit D1) Not so long ago the waterfront in Causeway Bay was a mass of junks and sampans huddling in the typhoon shelter for protection, but these days it's nearly all yachts. The land jutting out to the west is Kellett Island. It is home to the **Royal Hong Kong Yacht Club** (香港遊艇會; 2832 2817).

TIN HAU TEMPLE
TEMPLE

Map p374 (天后廟; 10 Tin Hau Temple Rd; 7am-5pm; MTin Hau, exit B) Southeast of Victoria Park, Hong Kong Island's most famous Tin Hau temple is dwarfed by surrounding high-rises. This temple dedicated to the patroness of seafarers has been a place of worship for three centuries, though the current structure is only about 200 years old. The central shrine contains an effigy of Tin Hau with a blackened face.

LIN FA TEMPLE
TEMPLE

Map p374 (蓮花宮; Lin Fa Kung St W, Tai Hang; 8am-5pm; MTin Hau, exit B) 'Lotus' is a pretty Buddhist temple with an octagonal front, a boulder jutting into its rear, and elaborate frescos (see boxed text, p112).

Happy Valley

TOP CHOICE **HAPPY VALLEY RACECOURSE**
HORSE RACING

Map p374 (跑馬地馬場; www.hkjc.com/home/english/index.asp; 2 Sports Rd, Happy Valley; admission $10; 7pm-10.30pm Wed Sep-Jun; Happy Valley) An outing at the races is one of the quintessential Hong Kong things to do, especially if you happen to be around during one of the weekly Wednesday evening races here. The punters pack into the stands and trackside, cheering, drinking and eating, and the atmosphere is electric.

The first horse races were held here in 1846. Now meetings are held both here and at the newer and larger (but less atmospheric) Sha Tin Racecourse (see p183) in the New Territories. Check the website for details on betting and tourist packages.

Racing buffs can also visit the **Hong Kong Racing Museum** (off Map p374; 2nd fl, Happy Valley Stand, Wong Nai Chung Rd; admission free; 10am-5pm Tue-Sun, to 12.30pm race days).

Island East: North Point & Quarry Bay

CHUN YEUNG STREET MARKET
MARKET

(春秧街街市; Chun Yeung St, North Point; MNorth Point, exit A4) Hop on an eastbound tram, and past Fortress Hill you'll turn into an old narrow street teeming with market stalls and old tenement buildings. This is the famous Chun Yeung St Market, and at 5pm it's so busy you wonder why no one ever got hit by the tram.

Flanking the tram tracks are vegetable stalls, meat vendors, and stores selling foodstuff from Fújiàn, such as pig intestines stuffed with egg and all kinds of meat balls. North Point has a huge Fujianese community, and you'll hear their dialect spoken on Chun Yeung St.

As the tram turns the corner into King's Rd, you'll pass the nondescript **Wah Fung Chinese Department Store** (華豐國貨; 395 King's Rd). Once Hong Kong's largest Chinese department store, its rooftop served as a hideout for underground Communists during the 1967 Riots.

WORTH A DETOUR

THE SOUND & SCENT OF TAI HANG *MADELEINE SLAVICK*

To get to Tai Hang, take bus 26 from Central. The single- or double-decker lets you off on a slope under a *bak lan* tree, a white orchid that stands about eight storeys high. Alight into scent, then descend the stairs, thousands of leaves overhanging, and more scent: incense from a neighbourhood temple. Just ahead is Tai Hang, a quiet, low-rise pocket of Hong Kong tucked in a valley.

Many of the residents have grown up in Tai Hang. Friendliness prevails. Children are doted on. Whole families take walks. Many elders like to sit in plastic chairs along the main road to watch the days continue, one after another, a thermos of tea at hand. Mornings are calmest.

At mealtimes and especially in the evenings, Tai Hang bursts with many happy people eating: homemade congee 19 hours a day, gourmet cheese, late-night sweets, Vietnamese and Japanese and Thai, pasta and pizzerias, wine bars, beer bars, coffee bars, an oyster bar and more.

The congee shop (p120) is a centre of the community open from 6am until 1.30am the following day. At least eight members of the family work here together. The youngest have slept in a crib alongside the shop, then used stools as desks, and now help serve a customer or two. The teenagers help after school. It's the grandparents and parents and an uncle or two who run the shop.

But there is more to Tai Hang than food. Small-scale walk-ups, an art deco building from the 1930s, a clay-tile roofed home (one of the oldest remaining single-family homes of its kind on Hong Kong Island), sidewalk furniture, three picturesque temples, a public garden full of flowering trees, several rooftop gardens, and at least one skyscraper in the making, probably green-skirted with scaffolding nets.

And birdsong in Tai Hang is plentiful. The first round starts at about 3.30am. Raptors loop from time to time, cockatoos may perch on aerials, screeching, and the family who runs the fruit shop keep a huge turtle on their rooftop. Plus there are the cats and dogs, many for the lap.

Lin Fa Temple (p111) was named for the lotus, for the purity and shape of the blossom. Step inside to find a huge and holy stone, a goddess who used to be male, and 60 divinities of time. A corner window stays open during the day for passersby to have direct access to the Goddess of Mercy, and many people bow, hands in prayer, from 50m away.

Flowers. *Bak lan. Lin fa.* One of the best places for flowers is a tiny alley off Tung Lo Wan Rd near the Metropark Hotel. A family has been selling flowers there for about 55 years, and a generous bunch goes for far less than $55. If you arrive or leave Tai Hang by MTR (nearest station: Tin Hau), you will pass the alley with blooms and buckets.

Tai Hang is recognised by Unesco for its **Mid-Autumn Festival**, when residents lead a handmade dragon measuring 68m and stuck with thousands of incense sticks through their streets to cleanse the neighbourhood of all that may be unwell. For three nights, scent and smoke enter each street, lane, home, all to the sound of drum and dance and gong. The tradition has been happening annually since 1880, when it was conducted to control the plague. Nowadays a lion dance might also happen on Buddha's Birthday, closer to springtime.

Tai Hang: a community at any time of day and season.

Madeleine Slavick is a former Tai Hang resident and author of Fifty Stories Fifty Images.

⊙ Island East: Sai Wan Ho

HONG KONG FILM ARCHIVE MUSEUM
(香港電影資料館; ☑2739 2139, bookings 2734 9009, 2119 7383; www.filmarchive.gov.hk; 50 Lei King Rd, Sai Wan Ho; admission free; ⊙box office noon-8pm, resource centre 10am-7pm Mon-Wed & Fri, to 5pm Sat, 1-5pm Sun; MSai Wan Ho, exit A) The archive is worth a visit, even if you know little about Hong Kong film. It has over 6300 reels and tapes, as well as magazines, posters and scripts. There's a small **exhibition hall** (opening hours vary) and a **cinema**. Check online for exhibitions and screenings. From the MTR station, walk north on Tai On St and west on Lei King Rd.

⊙ Island East: Shau Kei Wan

**HONG KONG MUSEUM OF
COASTAL DEFENCE** MUSEUM
(香港海防博物館; ☑2569 1500; http://hk.coastaldefence.museum; 175 Tung Hei Rd, Shau Kei Wan; adult/concession $10/5; ⊙10am-5pm Fri-Wed; MShau Kei Wan, exit B2) This museum occupies a knockout location in the Lei Yue Mun Fort (1887), which has sweeping views down to the Lei Yue Mun Channel and southeastern Kowloon. Exhibitions in the old redoubt cover Hong Kong's coastal defence over six centuries. There's a historical trail through the casemates, tunnels and observation posts almost down to the coast.

As you leave the MTR, follow the museum signs on Tung Hei Rd for about 15 minutes. Bus 85, which is accessible via exit A3 and runs along Shau Kei Wan Rd between North Point and Siu Sai Wan, stops on Tung Hei Rd outside the museum.

⊙ Island East: Chai Wan

ART IN CHAI WAN ART VILLAGE
The old, industrial town of Chai Wan is fast gaining a reputation as a hipsterville, with artists and nonprofits setting up shop in its warehouses and the opening of the cafe Chaiwanese in an airy factory space. Happening annually in May, **Art East Island** (www.arteastisland.wordpress.com; Chai Wan Industrial City Phase 1, 60 Wing Tai Rd, Chai Wan; MChai Wan, exit A) is an

open-studio-cum-art-walk event showcasing the galleries and artist studios in Chai Wan. It's organised by **10 Chancery Lane** (www.10chancerylanegallery.com), which has a gallery in Soho.

Some names that caught our eye include **Platform China** (站台中国; www.platformchina.com; ☑Claudia Albertini 9768-8093; hk.platformchina@gmail.com; ⊙by appointment only), a Běijīng-based gallery showcasing the works of promising young Chinese artists, and **Tangram Design Studio** (www.tngrm.net), set up by former Zara designer Paola Sinisterra who moved to Hong Kong and launched her womenswear label in 2012 – the contemporary and comfortable clothes feature an exciting mix of prints and can be ordered on Tangram's website.

LAW UK FOLK MUSEUM MUSEUM
(羅屋民俗館; ☑2896 7006; www.lcsd.gov.hk/en/ce/museum/history/en/luf.php; 14 Kut Shing St, Chai Wan; admission free; ⊙10am-6pm Mon-Wed, Fri & Sat, 1-6pm Sun; MChai Wan, exit B) This small museum occupies two restored Hakka village houses that have stood in a district of office buildings, warehouses and workers' flats for over two centuries. The courtyard and bamboo groves are peaceful, and the displays – furniture, household items and farming implements – simple but charming.

✕ EATING

Admiralty has a few exceptional restaurants. Wan Chai, with its wealth of cuisines in all price ranges, is Hong Kong's food capital; while Causeway Bay is an eclectic amalgam of eateries, many upscale, many Japanese. Down-at-heel North Point is home to a number of old Chinese restaurants and *dai pai dongs* (food stalls).

✕ Admiralty

TOP CHOICE PURE VEGGIE HOUSE VEGETARIAN, CHINESE $$
Map p370 (☑2525 0556; 3rd fl, Coda Plaza, 51 Garden Rd; meals $200-400; ⊙11am-10pm; MAdmiralty, then bus 12A; ✍) The Buddhist restaurant cooks up some of the best vegetarian fare in town. Delicious and MSG-free dim sum and an assortment of

innovative Chinese dishes are served by well-mannered staff in a setting resembling a rustic inn. There are great Sichuanese offerings too – vegetarian, of course.

TOP CHOICE AMMO
EUROPEAN **$$**

Map p370 (☎2537 9888; Asia Society Hong Kong Centre, 9 Justice Dr; lunch set from $188, dinner from $400; ⊙11.30am-11.30pm Sun-Thu, to 12.30pm Fri & Sat) Awash in a coppery light the colour of bullets, this sleek cafe at the Asia Society Hong Kong Centre features chandeliers and copper panels evoking the site's past as an explosives magazine. The excellent menu is well thought out and pricey, with a selection of mostly Italian mains, preceded by tapas available at cocktail hour (from $58). Bookings essential.

CÉPAGE
MODERN FRENCH **$$$**

Map p370 (☎2861 3130; 23 Wing Fung St; set lunch/dinner from $370/680; ⊙lunch & dinner, closed Sun; �M Admiralty, exit F) At this elegant address, the multitalented chef Sebastian Lepinoy creates excellent French dishes that he presents like works of art. The menu includes classics such as pork belly, but magically transformed *sous vide* and topped with caviar. Also available is a wine list cataloguing over 2000 labels.

SAN XI LOU
SICHUANESE **$$**

Map p370 (三希樓; ☎2838 8811; 7th fl Coda Plaza, 51 Garden Rd; meals $200-450; ⊙11am-10.30pm; 🚍12A from M Admiralty) If the fresh ingredients, the range of dishes and the complexity of the spices don't tell you this is Hong Kong's finest Sichuanese kitchen, the large numbers of Sichuanese expats who keep coming back for its feisty creations should.

LOCK CHA TEA SHOP
VEGETARIAN, CHINESE **$$**

Map p370 (樂茶軒; ☎2801 7177; www.lockcha.com; Ground fl, KS Lo Gallery, Hong Kong Park; dim sum $15-28, tea from $25; ⊙10am-10pm; M Admiralty, exit C1; ⊘) Set in the lush environs of Hong Kong Park, Lock Cha offers a dozen teas and 20 varieties of tiny but tasty vegetarian dim sum in a replica of an ancient scholar's study. On most Sunday afternoons (4pm to 6pm), there are Chinese music performances or tea talks for $100 per person (see website for details). Do reserve a seat. The music is popular; the tea shop is dainty.

VERO CHOCOLATES
DESSERT **$**

Map p370 (☎2559 5882; www.verochocolates.com; 1st fl, Fenwick Pier, 1 Lung King St; ⊙10am-8pm Tue-Sun; M Admiralty, exit E2) Bright and airy Vero serves chocolate thick and dark ($48 for a cup of Signature Chocolate made with 71% cocoa) as well as pastries stuffed, garnished or drizzled with chocolate made on site. It has an upscale **chocolate shop** (Map p362; Shop 236, 2nd fl, Landmark Atrium, 15 Queen's Rd Central) at the Landmark.

DALAT
VIETNAMESE **$**

Map p370 (大叻越南牛肉粉餐廳; ☎2527 6788; 10 Anton St; meals $40-90; ⊙11.30am-midnight; M Admiralty, exit F) In terms of price performance, this modest eatery makes some of the best *pho* (soup; bowl small/medium/large $32/$36/$42) in town, with tender beef in broth fragrant with herbs, and a bottomless side of chilli peppers. The Vietnamese curries come with buttered baguette straight out of the oven.

✕ Wan Chai

TOP CHOICE YIN YANG
CHINESE **$$**

Map p372 (鴛鴦飯店; ☎2866 0868; www.yin yang.hk; 18 Ship St; lunch $180-280, dinner from $680; ⊙lunch & dinner Mon-Sat; M Wan Chai, exit B2) Margaret Xu, the chef of Yin Yang, calls her cooking New Hong Kong. A former ad-agency owner who taught herself how to cook, Margaret grows her own organic vegetables and uses old-fashioned tools, such as stone-grinds and terracotta ovens, to create Hong Kong classics with a clean, contemporary twist. Yin Yang is housed in a three-storey 1930s heritage building. Dinner is a tasting menu, but you'll have to book at least five days in advance. The website mentions a deposit, but that's negotiable. There are takeaway options as well.

BO INNOVATION
CHINESE **$$$**

Map p372 (廚魔; ☎2850 8371; www.boinnovation.com; 60 Johnston Rd; lunch $200-1080, dinner $680-1080; ⊙noon-2pm Mon-Fri, 7-10pm Mon-Sat) Innovative Bo takes classic Chinese dishes apart and reassembles them in surprising ways, using molecular gastronomy. The pork dumpling is a wobbly blob of ginger-infused pork soup encased in a transparent wrapper that explodes in the mouth. The Chinese sausage and rice ice cream is nothing like you'd ever imagine.

Worth a try if you've never had molecular cuisine.

GRISSINI
ITALIAN $$$

Map p372 (☑2588 1234; http://hongkong.grand. hyatt.com; Grand Hyatt Hong Kong, 1 Harbour Rd; set lunch/dinner from $350/700; ⊗lunch & dinner, closed Sat lunch; ⋈Wan Chai, exit A1; ☑) Fluffy, chewy and addictive, the foot-long grissini here are – appropriately – the best in town. But leave room for the Milanese specialities and pair them with a bottle from the 1000-strong cellar. This stylish restaurant has floor-to-ceiling windows commanding views of the harbour (and construction in progress). The Sunday champagne brunch ($545) is our favourite buffet in town.

MADAM SIXTY ATE
MODERN EUROPEAN $$$

Map p372 (☑2527 2558; www.madamsixtyate. com.hk; Shop 8, 1st fl, The Podium, J Senses, 60 Johnston Rd; set lunch/dinner from $148/680; ⊗noon-11pm; ⋈Wan Chai) There are chic eats aplenty, yet few are fun like Madame. The modern European dishes here may not be the best in town, but they're evocatively named and playfully plated, and when served against the restaurant's surrealist paintings, makes dinner (or lunch) a very pleasant experience.

LA CREPERIE
CREPERIE $

Map p372 (☑2529 9280; 1st fl, 100 Queen's Rd E; meals $70-200; ⊗11am-11pm Mon-Sun; ⋈Wan Chai, exit A3) Decorated like a seaside town in Brittany, this quaint 20-seat creperie whips out sumptuous galettes and airy crepes, which are best savoured with some imported cider served in bowls. If you fancy French andouille sausage, La Creperie is one of the only places in town where you'll find that pungent delicacy.

OLD BAZAAR KITCHEN
SINGAPOREAN, MALAYSIAN $

off Map p372 (老巴刹廚房; ☑2893 3998; 207 Wan Chai Rd; lunch/dinner from $50/150; ⊗lunch & dinner Mon-Sat; ⋈Wan Chai, exit A2) The short menu of tasty Singaporean, Malaysian and Chinese dishes at this unpretentious eatery are executed with more flair than authenticity, but it's convincing. The chef's knack for working magic with culinary influences has won him a huge following among foodies. Try the ox tongue dishes and the noodles.

CHE'S CANTONESE RESTAURANT
CANTONESE $$

Map p372 (車氏粵菜軒; ☑2528 1123; 4th fl, The Broadway, 54-62 Lockhart Rd; meals $180-800; ⊗lunch & dinner; ⋈Wan Cha, exit C) This Cantonese restaurant, favoured by suits, serves home-style dishes and a small but delectable selection of dim sum. The crispy barbecued pork bun is a clever take on the *char siu bao*. The decor is simple but tables are a tad too close for comfort.

HANG ZHOU RESTAURANT
CHINESE $$

Map p372 (杭州酒家; ☑2591 1898; 1st fl, Chinachem Johnston Plaza, 178-188 Johnston Rd; lunch $80-200, dinner $250-1800; ⊗11.30am-2.30pm & 5.30-10.30pm; ⋈Wan Chai, exit A5) A food critics' favourite, this establishment with one Michelin star excels at Hángzhōu cooking, the delicate sister of Shanghainese cuisine. Dishes such as shrimps stir-fried with tea leaves show how the best culinary creations should engage all your senses.

LIU YUAN PAVILION
SHANGHAINESE $$

Map p372 (留園雅敍; ☑2804 2000; 3rd fl, The Broadway, 54-62 Lockhart Rd; meals $200-600; ⊗lunch & dinner; ⋈Wan Chai, exit C) This pretty restaurant in airy yellows makes superb Shanghainese classics, including tasty Shanghainese pastries. It has a loyal following among the local Shanghainese community, so do book ahead.

NINO'S COZINHA
PORTUGUESE, MACANESE $$

Map p372 (☑2866 1868; http://ninosgroup. com; 5th fl, 202 QRE Plaza, 202 Queen's Rd East; meals $400-800; ⋈Wan Chai, exit B2) The Portuguese-Chinese couple here whip up solid Macanese and Portuguese classics that would give most restaurants in Macau a run for their money. Favourites such as the oxtail stew and baked duck rice evolved from heirloom recipes of the owners. Ask for a table on the rooftop if you smoke. Book early.

JOON KO RESTAURANT
KOREAN $$

Map p372 (純子餐廳; 209 Jaffe Rd; lunch from $11, dinner from $200; ⊗lunch & dinner; ⋈Wan Chai, exit A1; ☑) This small family-run shop comes recommended by Korean friends. Carnivores must try the beef ribs and ox tongue, while vegetarians shouldn't miss the cold noodles. The side dishes are equally well made and they're generous about refilling. Speak slowly when ordering; the nice Korean owners and their Nepalese staff understand little English.

CAPITAL CAFE
TEA CAFE $

Map p372 (華星冰室; ☑2666 7766; Shop B1, Ground fl, Kwong Sang Hong Bldg, 6 Heard St; meals $35-50; ◷7am-11pm; ⓂWan Chai, exit A2) Designed to resemble a vintage *cha chaan tang* (tea cafe), but cleaner and more gimmicky than the real thing, this joint is the pet project of the owner of an eponymous Canto-pop record label that was famous in the '70s and '80s. It serves good old classics like toast with fluffy scrambled eggs and iced red bean drink, as well as fancier laced-with-black-truffle versions.

JOI HING FOOD SHOP
CANTONESE $

Map p372 (再興燒臘飯店; ☑2519 6639; 1c Stewart Rd; meals $25-45; ◷10am-10pm; ⓂWan Chai, exit A4) This basic stall is one of your best bets for Cantonese barbecue – succulent slivers of barbecued pork, goose, chicken and liver over freshly steamed rice. The menu is simply cards stuck on the wall. Just see what your neighbours are having and point.

MANG AMBO'S FILIPINO RESTAURANT
FILIPINO $

Map p372 (☑2143 6877; 120 Jaffe Rd; meals $25-40; ◷11am-10pm; ⓂWan Chai, exit A1) Pinoy domestic workers, musicians and businessmen come to this hole in the wall for its skewers, crispy pan-roasted pork and pork-blood stew. A full meal will set you back a hefty $30.

✕ Causeway Bay

ᴛᴏᴘCHOICE MANOR SEAFOOD RESTAURANT
CANTONESE $$$

Map p374 (富瑤酒家; ☑2836 9999; Shop F-G, 440 Jaffe Rd; meals $300-2000; ◷lunch & dinner; ⓂCauseway Bay, exit B) Upscale Manor does most Cantonese dishes well, but is best known for a now-rare classic. *Gum chin gai* (金錢雞; literally 'gold coin chicken', though it has no chicken) is a succulent 'cholesterol sandwich' of chicken liver, barbecued pork and lard – all marinaded in Chinese wine, roasted to perfection and eaten between pancakes. It's guilt-laden, melt-in-your-mouth goodness.

ᴛᴏᴘCHOICE IRORI
JAPANESE $$

Map p374 (酒處; ☑2838 5939; 2nd fl, Bartlock Centre, Yiu Wa St; lunch/dinner from $150/300; ◷lunch & dinner; ⓂCauseway Bay, exit A) Irori's versatile kitchen turns out raw and cooked delicacies of an equally impressive standard. Seasonal fish is flown in regularly from Japan, and carefully crafted into sushi and sashimi. To warm the stomach between cold dishes, there's a creative selection of tasty tidbits, such as fried beef roll and yakitori (grilled skewers).

FORUM
CANTONESE, DIM SUM $$$

Map p374 (富臨飯店; ☑2891 2555; 485 Lockhart Rd; $500-1600; ◷lunch & dinner; ⓂCauseway Bay, exit C) The abalone dishes at this expensive eatery have fans from across the world. What restaurant owner Yeung Koon-yat does with these molluscs has earned him membership of Le Club des Chefs des Chefs and the moniker 'King of Abalone'. If on a budget, you can make a meal of dim sum for under $350.

FARM HOUSE
CANTONESE $$

Map p374 (農圃飯店; ☑2881 1331; www.farmhouse.com.hk; meals $200-1300; ◷lunch & dinner; ⓂCauseway Bay, exit F) Families from the expensive residences nearby come for dinner when their maids are on leave. And it's not hard to see why. The masterful takes on home cooking, such as the steamed pork patty with duck egg and squid, are so well executed it would be hard for any maid or housewife to beat. The ambience is relaxing and it's in a relatively quiet corner of Causeway Bay. Lunch sets start at $268, dinner sets at $198.

HO HUNG KEE
NOODLES $

Map p374 (何洪記; ☑2577 6558; 2 Sharp St; meals $35-180; ◷11.30am-11.30pm; ⓂCauseway Bay, exit A) The tasty noodles, wontons and congee at this bright little shop are cooked according to the ancient recipes of the Ho family, and clearly they still work. Ho Hung Kee is always packed during lunch, even before it was awarded one Michelin star.

SUSHI FUKU-SUKE
JAPANESE $$$

Map p374 (鮨福助; ☑2955 0005; 11th fl, Macau Yat Yuen Centre, 525 Hennessy Rd; meals $260-1000; ◷lunch & dinner; ⓂCauseway Bay, exit D4) An elegant sushi bar with clean lines and pine wood like you'd find in Tokyo, which is where the chef/owner used to work. If you're not too hungry, there's a fairly reasonable lunch set for under $200. The two chef's menus (from $800) at dinner comprise sushi or sashimi and some hot side dishes.

IROHA
JAPANESE $$

Map p374 (伊呂波燒肉; ☑2882 9877; www.iroha.com.hk; 2nd fl, 50 Jardine's Bazaar; lunch/dinner from $150/500; ☺lunch & dinner; Ⓜ Causeway Bay, exit E) Bright and noisy, Iroha specialises in *yakiniku*, the Japanese style of grilling meat or vegetables over a burner. Among the dizzying range of Wagyu cuts on offer, the beef rib finger *(nakaochi karubi)* with its perfect fat-to-meat ratio and just-right chewiness comes highly recommended. If you love steak, be prepared to spend.

IR 1968
INDONESIAN $$

Map p374 (印尼餐廳1968; ☑2577 9981; www.ir1968.com; 28 Leighton Rd; meals from $180; ☺noon-11pm; Ⓜ Causeway Bay, exit A) Despite the year of its establishment (1968), this restaurant is all teak chic and Bali cool. It's rumoured that the handsome brothers manning the restaurant have almost as much pull as the beef rendang and the gado gado. There are lunch sets for $68 to $88.

FIAT CAFFE
ITALIAN $

Map p374 (www.fiat.com.hk; Shop G5-G6, Leighton Centre, 77 Leighton Rd; meals from $100; ☺11am-10pm; Ⓜ Causeway Bay, exit A) This new cafe belonging to the Italian automotive brand offers one of the best deals in town for a casual bite and a decent espresso. Perhaps after munching on grilled sardines, customers will be in the mood to hop over to the Fiat showroom and buy a Panda.

BELLA VITA
ITALIAN $$$

Map p374 (☑2577 0699; www.bellavita.com.hk; 11th fl, Cubus, 1 Hoi Ping Rd; lunch/dinner from $300/500; ☺lunch & dinner; Ⓜ Causeway Bay, exit A) Excellent modern Tuscan fare prepared by a chef from the region, and served in a cosy setting with dark woods and heavy drapes. Signature dishes such as the Fiorentina steak and grilled octopus are flawless, but pricey. The Sunday brunch includes an antipasti buffet, a main and dessert for $500.

TAI PING KOON
SOY SAUCE WESTERN, CHINESE $$

Map p374 (太平館餐廳; ☑2576 9161; www.taipingkoon.com; 6 Pak Sha Rd; meals $80-350; ☺11am-11.20pm; Ⓜ Causeway Bay, exit F) Soy sauce Western is believed to have been invented by the first Tai Ping Koon in Guǎngzhōu. Today tasty classics such as smoked pomfret and ox tongue with rice are still served in neat, if slightly worn, surrounds by the waiters who have been here for decades. There are branches in **Yau Ma Tei** (Map p382; ☑2384 3385; 19-21 Mau Lam St, Yau Ma Tei; Ⓜ Jordan, exit B2) and **Tsim Sha Tsui** (Map p380; ☑2721 3559; 40 Granville Rd; Ⓜ Tsim Sha Tsui, exit B1).

WEST VILLA
CANTONESE, DIM SUM $$$

Map p374 (西苑酒家; ☑2882 2110; Shops 101-102, 1st fl, Lee Gardens Two, 28 Yun Ping Rd; meals from $350; ☺lunch & dinner; Ⓜ Causeway Bay, exit E) West Villa does the *char siu* (barbecued pork) job well – just slightly charred at the edges and with a golden lean-to-fat ratio. It also makes some of the best soy-sauce chicken in town, and a soup (pre-ordering required) comprising chicken, conch meat, honeydew melon and a dozen other ingredients its competitors would kill to know.

GUN GEI HEALTHY VEGETARIAN
CHINESE, VEGETARIAN $

off Map p374 (根記健康素食; ☑2575 7595; No 6 Bowrington Rd Market & Cooked Food Centre, 21 Bowrington Rd, Wan Chai; meals $32-70; ☺lunch & dinner; Ⓜ Causeway Bay, exit A; ☑) Pronounced 'gun gei geen hong so sic' (literally, 'Gun Gei Healthy Vegetarian'), this *dai pai dong* makes simple but delicious vegetarian dishes. There are more choices at dinner, but you'll need a Chinese-speaker to help you book a table and pre-order dishes. The lunch special has three dishes, one soup and as much rice as you need. Just go to the food cart and point.

YU
SICHUANESE, NOODLES $

Map p374 (渝酸辣粉; ☑2838 8198; 4 Yiu Wa St; ☺noon-5pm & 6-11pm; Ⓜ Causeway Bay, exit A) Addicts of the Sichuanese peppercorn flock to this guileless little shop for that tingling and numbing feeling, which only happens when the Sichuanese fare is done right. From tame to full-blown, you can choose the level of spiciness for your noodles; there are some nonspicy offerings too. Yu doesn't take reservations for Friday and Saturday.

PUMPERNICKEL
BAKERY, EUROPEAN $

Map p374 (黑麥; ☑2576 1302; Shop B, 13 Cleveland St, Fashion Walk; meals $80-150; ☺11am-11pm; Ⓜ Causeway Bay, exit E) This laid-back cafe treats its bread with as much reverence

CHARLES BRISCOE-KNIGHT/GETTY IMAGES ©

1. Shopping in Causeway Bay (p123)
Malls, department stores and smaller outlets selling fashion, electronics and homewares fill the streets of Causeway Bay.

2. Wan Chai Markets (p125)
Vendors offer a variety of fresh produce at Wan Chai's markets, including vegetables and spices.

3. Hong Kong Park (p106)
These 8 hectares of beautiful parkland are bordered by skyscrapers on one side and mountains on the other.

4. Happy Valley Racecourse (p111)
A night at the races is a quintessential Hong Kong outing.

JOHN SONES/SINGING BOWL MEDIA/GETTY IMAGES ©

as its salads and pastas, which makes it a refreshing choice for a light meal.

HONG KEE CONGEE SHOP
CHINESE $

Map p374 (康記粥店; ☑2808 4518; 11 King St, Tai Hang; congee from $13; ⓢ6am-midnight; Ⓜ Tin Hau, exit B) Family-run Hong Kee has been sitting quietly in this corner of Tai Hang for 30 years. The food is fresh, homemade and inexpensive – a generous bowl of congee for as little as $13. Try the rice dumpling, fried bread stick and congee with liver, frog or tripe, fish or chicken, or maybe thousand-year-old egg. (See also p112.)

🍴 Happy Valley

GI KEE SEAFOOD RESTAURANT
DAI PAI DONG, CANTONESE $

(鉄記海鮮飯店; ☑2574 9937; Shop 4, 2nd fl, Wong Nai Chung Municipal Services Bldg, 2 Yuk Sau St; meals $60-300; ⓢdinner; ➡1 from Des Voeux Rd Central, ⓐ) Reserve a table or expect to queue for a plastic stool at this *dai pai dong* perched above a wet market. Chan Chung-fai, the man in the kitchen who turns out tantalising dishes such as chicken with fried garlic, is an award-winning cordon bleu chef with a huge fan following that includes the likes of Zhang Ziyi and Jacky Chan.

🍴 Island East: North Point & Quarry Bay

⬛TOP CHOICE YAT WOON MIN
TAIWANESE, NOODLES $

(壹碗麵; ☑2578 0092; Ground fl, Ngan Fai Bldg, 93 Wharf Rd, North Point; meals $50-100; ⓢnoon-9pm; Ⓜ North Point, exit A1) A refreshing contrast to most noodle shops in town, this place offers a variety of handmade strands of varying widths and textures that are more Taiwanese or Northern Chinese than Cantonese. Its hallmark ribbons, thick and close to an inch wide, are tossed al dente with flavourful ingredients such as stewed beef brisket.

THAI SOM TUM
THAI $

off Map p374 (泰爽甜; ☑3622 1795; Shop C1, 2/F, Electric Road Municipal Services Bldg, 229 Electric Rd, North Point; meals $50-100; ⓢlunch Mon-Fri, dinner Mon-Sun; Ⓜ Fortress Hill, exit B; 🚇) Feisty Thai *dai pai dong* that has perfected the

demonic art of frying and grilling. The 'neck of pork', sliced into luscious slivers, is grilled à la minute; down a Singha while you wait. The Thai-style fried fish, presented like a tribal headdress, is a wonder to taste and behold.

FUNG SHING RESTAURANT
CANTONESE $$

(鳳城酒家; ☑2578 4898; 62-28 Java Rd, North Point; meals $80-300; ⓢ9am-3pm & 6-11pm; Ⓜ North Point, exit A2) Fung Shing is a traditional Cantonese restaurant that specialises in the cuisine of the Shùndé district, formerly known as 'Fung Shing' or Phoenix City (check out the gilt phoenix with green eyes). It's a little rough around the edges but the food is good. Must-tries include fried prawn on toast and minced quail meat wrapped in lettuce.

KIN'S KITCHEN
CANTONESE $$

Map p374 (留家廚房; ☑2571 0913; 9 Tsing Fung St, Tin Hau; meals $180-450; ⓢlunch & dinner; Ⓜ Tin Hau, exit A2) Opened by art critic-turned-restaurateur Lau Kin-wai, this understated restaurant touts its Cantonese classics with a modern spin. The owner, looking quite the *bon vivant* with silver hair and rosy cheeks, is sometimes seen discussing the delicious smoked chicken with customers. Lunch sets available from $88.

HUNG'S DELICACIES
CHIU CHOW, CANTONESE $

(阿鴻小吃; ☑2570 1108; Shop 4, Ground fl, Ngan Fai Bldg, 84-94 Wharf Rd, North Point) Ever since it plucked a Michelin star, there's always a line outside this humble shop. Go outside peak meal times and you'll land a seat (tables are shared), or buy takeout from the missus. The signature Chiu Chow dishes such as marinaded goose lend themselves well to consumption anywhere.

TUNG PO SEAFOOD RESTAURANT
DAI PAI DONG, CANTONESE $

(東寶小館; ☑2880 9399; 2nd fl, Municipal Services Bldg, 99 Java Rd, North Point; meals $80-180; ⓢdinner; Ⓜ North Point, exit A1) Tung Po has revolutionised *dai pai dong* cooking, and it's easy to see why. Beer is served in chilled porcelain bowls, to be downed bandit style. The young staff strut around in rubber boots, serving Cantonese dishes with a twist. Book ahead (reservations 2.30pm to 5.30pm) or go before 7pm.

✖ Island East: Chai Wan

CHAIWANESE
CAFE **$**

(柴灣人; ☑3698 0935; www.chaiwanese.com; Unit 1307, Phase 1, Chai Wan Industrial City, 60 Wing Tai Rd, Chai Wan; meals $35-80; ⏱9am-8.30pm Mon-Sat; Ⓜ Chai Wan, exit A, 🚌788; ✈) This warehouse-turned restaurant is a welcome addition to an area known for its factories. The utilitarian feel of counter service and concrete flooring is tempered by soaring ceilings and whitewashed walls decorated with plants. The tasty salads and sandwiches are served in generous portions.

🍷 DRINKING & 🍸 NIGHTLIFE

🍷 Admiralty

CLASSIFIED MOZZARELLA BAR
BAR

Map p370 (31 Wing Fung St; Ⓜ Admiralty, exit F) We love the scrubbed wooden table, the designer lamp and the open frontage of this quiet and stylish bar. Take a seat near the pavement and people-watch as you enjoy your pick from 150 bottles and some quality tapas.

1/5
CLUB

Map p370 (1st fl, Starcrest Bldg, 9 Star St; ⏱happy hour 6-9pm Mon-Fri; Ⓜ Admiralty, exit F) Pronounced 'one-fifth', this sophisticated lounge bar and club has a broad bar backed by a two-storey drinks selection from which bar staff concoct some wonderful cocktails. It gets packed on the weekend with a dressy professional crowd, but it's still a good place to chill. 1/5 stays open till the wee hours.

🍷 Wan Chai

MES AMIS
BAR

Map p372 (81-85 Lockhart Rd; ⏱happy hour 4-9pm; Ⓜ Wan Chai, exit C) A slightly more stylish place in the lap of girly club land, Mes Amis has a good range of wines and a Mediterranean-style snacks list. There's a DJ from 11pm on Friday and Saturday. Mes Amis stays open till 6am Friday and Saturday.

CHAMPAGNE BAR
BAR

Map p372 (Ground fl, Grand Hyatt Hotel, 1 Harbour Rd; ⏱5pm-2am; Ⓜ Wan Chai, exit A1) Take your fizz in the sumptuous surrounds of the Grand Hyatt's Champagne Room, kitted out in art deco furnishings to evoke Paris of the 1920s. Live blues or jazz happens most evenings and the circular main bar is always busy.

AMOY
BAR

Map p372 (廈門餐廳酒吧; Shop D2, 1 Amoy St; Ⓜ Wan Chai, exit A3) This tiny bar on a quiet street between Queen's Rd East and Johnston Rd has reasonably priced wine, beer, cocktails and sake, and to go with that, oysters and cherry clams on ice and a range of warm canapés.

COYOTE'S BAR AND GRILL
BAR

Map p372 (www.coyotebarandgrill.com; 114-120 Lockhart Rd; ⏱happy hour 3-8pm; Ⓜ Wan Chai, exit C2) Coyote's has some 70 margaritas made from a choice of 35 tequilas. If that's not enough, go for the 'dentist chair' challenge. The said piece of furniture is usually hidden in the back of the bar and brought out only on request. For $50, you can lie back and have the bartender pour a deluge of spirits direct from the bottles into your throat.

DELANEY'S
BAR, PUB

Map p372 (Ground & 1st fl, One Capital Place, 18 Luard Rd, Wan Chai; ⏱happy hour noon-9pm; Ⓜ Wan Chai, exit C) At this immensely popular Irish watering hole you can choose between the black-and-white-tiled pub on the ground floor and a sports bar and restaurant on the 1st floor. The food is good and plentiful; the kitchen allegedly goes through 400kg of potatoes a week.

HABITAT
LOUNGE

Map p372 (29th fl, QRE Plaza, 202 Queen's Rd East; ⏱6pm-3am, happy hour 6-9pm; Ⓜ Wan Chai, exit A3) Young professionals come to this relaxing space for after-dinner drinks and to celebrate special occasions. There are slouchy couches and cane tables, and the views across Wan Chai are stunning. In need of a quiet tête-à-tête? Head up to the roof.

AMICI
SPORTS BAR

Map p372 (www.amicihongkong.com; 1st fl, Empire Land Commercial Centre, 81-85 Lockhart Rd; ⏱happy hour noon-9pm; Ⓜ Wan Chai, exit C) The champion of Wan Chai sports bars features ample screens, five beers on tap, decent American-Italian food and a long happy hour. A few local football supporters' clubs have made Amici their base, and it's easy to see why. The atmosphere during live broadcasts of big sporting events is contagious.

AGAVE
BAR

Map p372 (Shop C & D, 93 Lockhart Rd; ☺happy hour 3-9pm; ⓂWan Chai, exit C) Fans of tequila will be ecstatic here – there are 170 brands of the spirit, and the bartenders are heavy-handed with it. Interiors are brightly coloured with cactus-themed adornments and jovial atmosphere.

PAWN
BAR

Map p372 (www.thepawn.com.hk; 62 Johnston Rd; ⓂWan Chai, exit A3) This handsome three-storey establishment used to be a row of tenement houses and the century-old Woo Cheong pawn shop. Now it's occupied by a restaurant and a bar. The slouchy sofas with space to sprawl, shabby chic interiors designed by a filmmaker, plus great little terrace spaces overlooking the tram tracks, make this an ideal location to sample a great selection of lagers, bitters and wine.

CARNEGIE'S
PUB

Map p372 (Ground fl, 53-55 Lockhart Rd; ☺happy hour 11am-9pm Mon-Sat; ⓂWan Chai, exit C) The rock memorabilia festooning the walls makes it all seem a bit Hard Rock Café-ish, but this place is worth a look all the same. From 9pm on Friday and Saturday, Carnegie's fills up with young revellers, many of whom will end up dancing on the bar which has brass railings in case they fall.

🍷 Causeway Bay

TOP CHOICE EXECUTIVE BAR
LOUNGE BAR

Map p374 (✆2893 2080; 7th fl, Bartlock Centre, 3 Yiu Wa St; ☺5pm-1am Mon-Sat; ⓂCauseway Bay, exit A) You won't be served if you just turn up at this clubby, masculine bar high above Causeway Bay – it's by appointment only. Odd perhaps, but worth the trip if you are serious about whisky and bourbon. Several dozen varieties are served here, in large brandy balloons with large orbs of ice hand-chipped by the Japanese proprietor to maximise the tasting experience.

CHAPEL BAR
BAR

(27 Yik Yam St, Happy Valley; ☺happy hour 4.30-8.30pm; 🚌) A low-key neighbourhood bar, the Chapel has beers on tap, the sports channel and British-Indian food. What more can one ask for? Thursday is quiz night (from 9.30pm), but book if you want to go because it's popular.

DICKENS BAR
BAR

Map p374 (www.mandarinoriental.com/excelsior/dining/dickens_bar; Basement, Excelsior Hong Kong, 281 Gloucester Rd; ☺happy hour 5-8pm; ⓂCauseway Bay, exit D1) Dickens has been popular with expats and locals for decades. Recently renovated, it has a longer beer list that includes rare selections like Black Sheep Ale, and improved modern British pub grub. The big-screen sports coverage is still there, and so is the still-popular curry buffet at lunch.

EAST END BREWERY & INN SIDE OUT
PUB

Map p374 (Ground fl, Sunning Plaza, 10 Hysan Ave; ☺happy hour 2.30-8.30pm; ⓂCauseway Bay, exit F) These two related pubs flank a central covered terrace where you can while away the hours on a warm evening, sipping beers and throwing peanut shells on the ground. East End has imported microbrews.

ORIENTAL SAKE BAR YU-ZEN
LOUNGE

Map p374 (http://hk-yuzen.com; 21st fl, Circle Plaza, 499 Hennessy Rd; cover charge per person $150; ☺7pm-4am Mon-Sat, to 1am Sun; ⓂCauseway Bay, exit B2) Sleek with just a hint of decadence, this sake den offers a range of premium sakes and creative cocktails. You can sip your drink sitting at the bar or reclining, like some modern opium-smoker, on cushions in a curtained dais. There's no happy hour.

BUBBLE LA VILLA 37
BAR

off Map p374 (37th fl, Times Tower, 393 Jaffe Rd; ⓂCauseway Bay, exit C) The rationale at this place is that as long as the views are mind-blowing, a bar can run amok with decor. And we almost agree. Sure, the mix of clubby sofas, futuristic bulbs and a super-long TV screen was wacky, but throw in the panoramic views and the Enomatic wine machines, and the wine, and things start to feel kind of cool.

Island East: North Point & Quarry Bay

SUGAR LOUNGE

(32nd fl, East Hotel, 29 Taikoo Sing Rd, Quarry Bay; ⊙5pm-2am Mon-Sat, noon-11.30pm Sun; MTai Koo, exit D1) This new bar inside a new business hotel has a lounge with illuminated floors, and an open deck which maximises the impact of the superb East Island views – silvery high-rises on one side and the old Kai Tak airport runway on the other. On a clear night, it's a stunning backdrop to your rendezvous, so understandably, tables fill up fast. Go at 6pm.

☆ ENTERTAINMENT

TOP CHOICE STREET MUSIC CONCERT LIVE MUSIC

(☑2582 0280; www.kungmusic.hk, www.hkac. org.hk; ⊙6.30-9pm Sat, once a month) Don't miss one of the free outdoor gigs thrown by eclectic musician Kung Chi-sing. One Saturday a month, the musician holds a concert outside the Hong Kong Arts Centre (p123). The exciting line-ups have included anything from indie rock, punk and jazz to Cantonese opera and Mozart. It's excellent, professional-quality music performed in an electrifying atmosphere. Check the website for dates.

SUNBEAM THEATRE THEATRE

(新光戲院; ☑2856 0161, 2563 2959; Kiu Fai Mansion, 423 King's Rd, North Point; MNorth Point, exit B1) Cantonese opera is performed at this vintage theatre throughout the year. Performances generally run for about a week, and are usually held five days a week at 7.30pm, with occasional matinees at 1pm or 1.30pm.

HONG KONG ARTS CENTRE DANCE, THEATRE

Map p372 (香港藝術中心; ☑2582 0200; www. hkac.org.hk; 2 Harbour Rd, Wan Chai; MWan Chai, exit C) The Hong Kong Arts Centre is a popular venue for dance, theatre and music performances. See also p123.

PUNCHLINE COMEDY CLUB COMEDY

Map p372 (☑2598 1222; www.punchlinecom edy.com/hongkong; Duetto, 2nd fl, Sun Hung Kai Centre, 30 Harbour Rd, Wan Chai; ☐18, alight at Wan Chai Sports Ground) A veteran on the scene, the Punchline hosts local and imported acts every third Thursday, Friday and Saturday from 9pm to 11pm. Entry costs around $300. Book tickets online or call.

WANCH LIVE MUSIC

Map p372 (☑2861 1621; 54 Jaffe Rd, Wan Chai; MWan Chai, exit C) This place, which derives its name from what everyone calls the district, has live music (mostly rock and folk with the occasional solo guitarist thrown in) seven nights a week from 9pm. Jam night is Monday from 8pm.

AMC PACIFIC PLACE CINEMA

Map p370 (☑2869 0322; 1st fl, 1 Pacific Pl, Admiralty; MAdmiralty, exit F) This cinema inside the Pacific Place mall in Admiralty screens some of the more interesting current releases.

HONG KONG ACADEMY FOR THE PERFORMING ARTS DANCE, THEATRE

Map p370 (香港演藝學院; ☑2584 8500; www. hkapa.edu; 1 Gloucester Rd, Wan Chai; MAdmiralty, exit E2) The APA is a major performance venue for dance, music and theatre. See also p108.

WINDSOR CINEMA CINEMA

Map p374 (皇室戲院; ☑3516 8811; 4th fl, Windsor House, 311 Gloucester Rd, Causeway Bay; Causeway Bay, exit E) Part of the 12-strong UA circuit, this comfortable cineplex is just west of Victoria Park.

SHOPPING

Admiralty's sleek shopping mall, Pacific Place, can be accessed via Admiralty MTR station. Wan Chai is a good spot for medium- and low-priced clothing, sporting goods and footwear. Causeway Bay is a crush of shopping malls, department stores and smaller outlets selling designer and street fashion, electronics, sporting goods and household items.

TOP CHOICE DAYDREAM NATION CLOTHING

Map p372 (☑3741 0758; www.daydream-nation. com; 2nd fl, Hong Kong Arts Centre, 2 Harbour Rd, Wan Chai; MWan Chai, exit C) Soaring rent has exiled this dreamy nation from its home near Star St to the Hong Kong Arts Centre.

WAN CHAI'S UPRIGHT ARTISTS' VILLAGE

Foo Tak Building (富德樓), overlooking the tram tracks, looks no different from any old tenement block in Wan Chai, but tucked away in its 14 storeys are the studios and/or living quarters of artists, activists, indie film groups, publishers and musicians.

Foo Tak was built in 1968 as a residential building, but in the 2000s, its landlady turned the property into an art village. Now young, 'starving' artists can rent the units within the premises for a small sum of money.

The best way to experience Foo Tak is to pay a visit to Art and Culture Outreach (ACO) Books (藝鵠) on the 1st floor, where there is an updated directory of the entire block. Then proceed to the 14th floor and check out each level from top down. The building itself is interesting to walk around in. Despite a major renovation in 2003, it still retains some of the features of late 1960s local architecture.

You can check out the websites of the following for the latest events. **Ying e Chi** (☑2836 6383; www.yec.com), on the 4th floor, is an indie film group that hosts regular free screenings. **Visible Record** (www.visiblerecord.com), on the 3rd floor, promotes documentary films.

A 'Vogue Talent 2010' brand founded by two of most creative local designers around (Kay Wong and her brother Jing, who's also a musician), DN is known for its highly wearable fashion and accessories that come with a touch of theatricality. Check their website for the latest opening hours.

G.O.D. `TOP CHOICE`   HOMEWARES, GIFTS

Map p374 (www.god.com.hk; Leighton Centre, Sharp St East, Causeway Bay; Ⓜ Causeway Bay, exit A) If you only have time for one souvenir place, make it G.O.D. This cheeky lifestyle store named with an acronym that, they say, means 'goods of desire' and nothing else, gives a witty take on an older and less affluent Hong Kong. If you're into retro with a twist, you'll dig it here. G.O.D. has five branches, including one at JCCAC (p147).

WAN CHAI COMPUTER CENTRE   ELECTRONICS

Map p372 (灣仔電腦城; 1st fl, Southorn Centre, 130-138 Hennessy Rd, Wan Chai; ☉10am-8pm Mon-Sat; Ⓜ Wan Chai, exit B2) A safe bet for anything digital and electronic.

MCCM BOOKSHOP BOOKS   BOOKS

Map p372 (http://mccmbookshop.wordpress. com; Ground fl, Hong Kong Arts Centre, 2 Harbour Rd, Wan Chai; Ⓜ Wan Chai, exit C) This tiny bookstore in the lobby of the Hong Kong Arts Centre has a strong focus on the performing and visual arts, as well as literature, architecture and cultural studies. It's run by **MCCM Creations** (www.mccm creations.com), one of the city's more active small presses.

ART AND CULTURE OUTREACH (ACO) BOOKS   BOOKS

off Map p372 (藝鵠; ☑2893 4808; www.aco.hk; 1st fl, Foo Tak Bldg, 365 Hennessey Rd, Wan Chai; ☉Mon-Sat; Ⓜ Causeway Bay, exit B) Bookstore, art gallery and event space, ACO (富德樓) is the hub of Foo Tak Building, a residential block-turned-artists' village in the heart of Wan Chai. It has an esoteric collection of over 3000 books in Chinese and English, with an artistic and intellectual bent. There are also CDs and DVDs; and it holds cultural events.

KELLY & WALSH   BOOKS

Map p370 (☑2522 5743; Glass House, L2, Pacific Place, 88 Queensway, Admiralty; Ⓜ Admiralty, exit C1) A good selection of art, design and culinary books plus a handy kids' reading lounge.

ANTEPRIMA CLOTHES   CLOTHING

Map p370 (☑2918 0886; www.anteprima.com; Shop 223, 2nd fl, Pacific Place, 88 Queensway, Admiralty; ☉11am-8pm Sun-Thu, 11.30am-8.30pm Fri & Sat; Ⓜ Admiralty, exit F, ☒) The sophisticated womenswear by a Milan-based Japanese designer, in silk, wool and fine cotton, comes with hefty price tags that belie its ethereality. That said, most of the pieces are made to outlast fashion fads. Bestsellers include the knitwear and signature 'wire bag'.

PACIFIC PLACE   MALL

Map p370 (太古廣場; ☑2844 8988; www.pa cificplace.com.hk; 88 Queensway, Admiralty; Ⓜ Admiralty, exit F) Pacific Place has a couple of hundred outlets, dominated by higher-end men's and women's fashion and accessories. There's also a **Lane Crawford** (Level 1) department store and a **Joyce** (Shop 334) boutique.

COSMOS BOOKS   BOOKS

Map p372 (天地圖書; ☎2866 1677; www.cosmosbooks.com.hk; Basement & 1st fl, 30 Johnston Rd, Wan Chai; ☐6, 6A or 6X) This chain-store branch has a good selection of China-related books in the basement. Upstairs are English-language books (nonfiction is strong). Enter the Wan Chai store from Lun Fat St and the Tsim Sha Tsui branch from Granville Rd.

KUNG FU SUPPLIES   SPORTS

Map p372 (功夫用品公司; ☎2891 1912; Room 6a, 6th fl, Chuen Fung House, 188-192 Johnston Rd, Wan Chai; ☺Mon-Sat; ☐6, 6A or 6X) If you need to stock up on martial-arts accessories, including uniforms, nunchakus and safety weapons for practice, or just want to thumb through a decent collection of books and DVDs, this is the place to go. The staff here is very helpful.

BUNN'S DIVERS   SPORTS

Map p372 (賓氏潛水學院; ☎3422 3322; www.bunnsdivers.com; Mezzanine, Chuen Fung House, 188-192 Johnston Rd, Wan Chai; Ⓜ Wan Chai, exit A3) Masks, snorkels, fins, regulators, tanks – Hong Kong's longest-established dive shop also runs dive tours and training courses.

SONJIA   CLOTHING, HOMEWARES

Map p370 (www.sonjiaonline.com; 2 Sun St, Wan Chai; ☺9.30am-7.30pm Mon-Sat; Ⓜ Admiralty, exit F) Anglo-Korean Hong Kong designer Sonjia Norman creates sumptuous womenswear in silk, velvet and cotton, much of it hand-finished with embroidery, in her atelier here. The adjoining store stocks a select bunch of homeware to suit every taste.

D-MOP   CLOTHING, ACCESSORIES

Map p374 (www.d-mop.com.hk; 8 Kingston St, Causeway Bay; Ⓜ Causeway Bay, exit E) Decked out in wood and steel, D-mop has a diverse selection ranging from edgy dressy to chic street, and brands from all over the world. It's one of the sole retailers of Y-3 and Nike White Label.

PEOPLES' RECREATION
COMMUNITY   BOOKS

Map p374 (人民公社; www.peoplebookcafe.com; 1st fl, 18 Russell St, Causeway Bay; ☺9am-midnight; Ⓜ Causeway Bay, exit A) Located across Causeway Bay's monument to consumerism is this specialist bookstore with a leftist bent. Its tomes, mostly on Chinese politics and society, are snapped up by locals and mainland tourists keen on reading about topics censored back home. There's a limited collection in English and a small cafe.

YIU FUNG STORE   FOOD

Map p374 (么鳳; 3 Foo Ming St, Causeway Bay; Ⓜ Causeway Bay, exit A) Hong Kong's most famous store (c 1960s) for Chinese pickles and preserved fruit features sour plum, liquorice-flavoured lemon, tangerine peel, pickled papaya and dried longan. Just before the Lunar New Year, it's crammed with shoppers.

ISLAND BEVERLEY MALL   MALL

Map p374 (金百利商場; 1 Great George St, Causeway Bay; Ⓜ Causeway Bay) Crammed into buildings, up escalators and in back lanes are Hong Kong's malls of microshops selling local designer threads, garments from other parts of Asia and a kaleidoscope of kooky accessories.

WAN CHAI'S MARKETS

The area sandwiched by Queen's Rd East and Johnston Rd in Wan Chai is a lively outdoor bazaar thronged with vendors, shoppers and parked cars. Cross St (Map p372) and the northern section of Stone Nullah Lane feature **wet markets** (Map p372; ☺7.30 am-7pm) in all their screaming splendour. **Tai Yuen Street**, aka 'toy street' (玩具街; woon gui kaai) to locals, has hawkers selling goldfish, plastic flowers and granny underwear, but it's best known for its traditional **toy shops** (14-19 Tai Yuen St) where you'll find not only kiddies' playthings, but clockwork tin and other kidult collectibles. Spring Garden Lane and Wan Chai Rd are a treasure trove of quirky shops selling everything from Indian and Southeast Asian spices to funerary offerings and gadgets.

TIMES SQUARE
MALL

Map p374 (時代廣場; www.timessquare.com.hk; 1 Matheson St, Causeway Bay; MCauseway Bay, exit A) The 10 floors of retail organised by type are slightly less high-end than in Central, but with selections of electronics. There are restaurants on the 10th to 13th floors, and snack bars, cafes and a super-market in the basement.

IN SQUARE
ELECTRONICS

Map p374 (10th-11th fl, Windsor House, 311 Gloucester Rd, Causeway Bay; MCauseway Bay, exit D1) This building in Causeway Bay hous-es dozens of reliable but pricey computer shops.

MOUNTAIN SERVICES
OUTDOOR EQUIPMENT

(名峰行; Shop 1, 52–56 King's Rd, North Point; ⊘Mon-Sat; MFortress Hill, exit A) This excellent shop sells climbing and hiking gear and pretty much everything you need for tack-ling Hong Kong's hills and country parks. Turn left when you exit the MTR station and walk for three minutes.

CITYPLAZA
SHOPPING MALL

(太古城; ☑2568 8665; www.cityplaza.com.hk; 18 Tai Koo Shing Rd, Tai Koo Shing, Quarry Bay; MTai Koo, exit D2) The largest shopping centre in eastern Hong Kong Island, with 180 shops, Cityplaza is directly linked to the MTR.

SPORTS & ACTIVITIES

EASTERN NATURE TRAIL
HIKING

(東區自然步道) Belonging to Stage 5 of the Hong Kong Trail, this 9km, three-hour nature trail, so called because of the indig-enous trees and birds you'll meet along it, starts on Mount Parker Rd in Quarry Bay and ends on Wong Nai Chung Gap Rd in Tai Tam. The trail features historic sites includ-ing WWII military relics and a house in red brick that belonged to a sugar refinery. You'll pass beautiful Tai Tam Country Park as you descend to Tai Tam Reservoir. Fol-lowing Tai Tam Reservoir Rd, you'll reach Wong Nai Chung Gap Rd.

Take exit B from Tai Koo MTR station, head 600m west and turn into Quarry St. The start of the trail is near the Quarry Bay Municipal Services Building at 38 Quarry St.

TAI TAM WATERWORKS HERITAGE TRAIL
HIKING

(大潭水務文物徑) This scenic trail will take you past reservoirs and a handsome collection of some 20 historic waterworks structures. These bridges, aqueducts, valve houses, pumping stations and dams, many still working, are feats of Victorian utilitarian engineering.

The 5km trail, which ends at Tai Tam Tuk Raw Water Pumping Station, takes about two hours. Enter at Wong Nai Chung Gap near the luxury flats of **Hong Kong Parkview** (陽明山莊; 88 Tai Tam Reservoir Rd), or at the junction of Tai Tam Rd and Tai Tam Reservoir Rd. On weekends you'll see residents taking a walk with their dogs, kids, maids, chauffeurs and nannies.

From Admiralty MTR station, bus 6 takes you to Wong Nai Chung Reservoir. Walk east along Tai Tam Reservoir Rd.

HONG KONG TENNIS CENTRE
TENNIS

(香港網球中心; ☑2574 9122; 133 Wong Nai Chung Gap Rd, Happy Valley; per hr day/evening $42/57; ⊘7am-11pm) The Hong Kong Tennis Centre, with 17 courts, is on a spectacular hill pass between Happy Valley and Deep Water Bay on Hong Kong Island. It's usually easy to get a court during working hours.

ROYAL HONG KONG YACHT CLUB
BOATING

Map p374 (香港遊艇會; ☑2832 2817; www.rhkyc.org.hk; Hung Hing Rd, Kellett Island, Cause-way Bay; MCauseway Bay, exit D1) It's private but you can try to get visiting membership if you belong to a reciprocal club. Subscrip-tion fees are waived for the first two weeks for visitors.

SOUTH CHINA ATHLETIC ASSOCIATION
GYM

Map p374 (南華體育會; ☑2577 6932; www.scaa.org.hk; 5th fl, South China Sports Complex, 88 Caroline Hill Rd, Causeway Bay; visitor member-ship HK$50) The SCAA has a 1000-sq-metre gym, with modern exercise machinery and an aerobics room, as well as a sauna, a steam room and massage room.

VICTORIA PARK
TENNIS

Map p374 (Hing Fat St, Causeway Bay; ⊘6am or 7am-11pm; MCauseway Bay, exit E) The park has 13 standard tennis courts, two lawn bowls greens, swimming pools, as well as foot-ball pitches, basketball courts and jogging trails.

Hong Kong Island: Aberdeen & the South

ABERDEEN | POK FU LAM | STANLEY | SHEK O | REPULSE BAY | DEEP WATER BAY

Aberdeen & the South Top Five

1 Lounging around the beaches in **Shek O** (p131) or **Stanley** (p131), or people-watching in famous **Repulse Bay** (p131).

2 Having hair-raising fun in **Ocean Park** (p129) and befriending the resident pandas.

3 Sampling Hong Kong's best seafood at **Aberdeen** (p132).

4 Catching a glimpse into the lives of seafarers by hopping on a **sampan** (p129) at Aberdeen.

5 Shopping till you drop in Hong Kong's **largest outlet mall** (p134) in Ap Lei Chau.

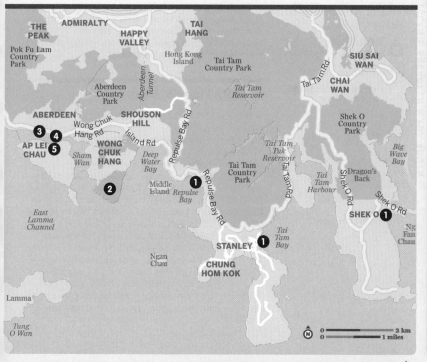

For more detail of this area, see Map p376 and Map p377 ➡

Lonely Planet's Top Tip

The beaches on the south side of Hong Kong are best enjoyed on weekdays when you can have them to yourself. The discreet St Stephen's Beach boasts fine water quality and near-perfect sunset views.

Best Places to Eat

➡ Verandah (p133)

➡ Crown Wine Cellars (p132)

➡ Aberdeen Fish Market Canteen (p132)

For reviews, see p132 ➡

Best Place to Drink

➡ Smugglers Inn (p133)

For reviews, see p133 ➡

Best Place to Shop

➡ Horizon Plaza (p134)

For reviews, see p134 ➡

Explore: Aberdeen & the South

The long coastline along the south of the island means you'll need a half to a full day to explore each of the areas listed below. Beach hopping is doable. Start with famous Repulse Bay and then escape to the quieter South Bay. Alternatively, head to popular Shek O and slink your way up further to discreet Big Wave Bay.

Aberdeen's theme park, Ocean Park, is a store of fun for kids and adults alike. Expect a full day there. More sedentary travellers can opt for a boozy brunch or a hearty seafood lunch in Aberdeen. If you need a walk to help digest all that food afterwards, make a stop in nearby Pok Fu Lam to see the gorgeous Béthanie Chapel as well as Pok Fu Lam Village, one of the oldest settlements in Hong Kong. Treasure hunters can find designer bargains in Ap Lei Chau in Aberdeen.

Stanley, with a lively market, friendly beaches, plus a fascinating mix of museums and heritage sites, certainly deserves another full day of exploration.

Local Life

➡ **Shopping** When shopping in the mammoth Horizon Plaza (p134), wear sensible shoes like the locals, and have a taxi call-centre number ready (☎2368 1318).

➡ **Seafood** It's common for foodies to buy their own seafood in a wet market and have it cooked in a *dai pai dong* (food stall) of their choice. Ap Lei Chau Market and its associated Cooked Food Centre (p132) offer seafood lovers that winning formula.

Getting There & Away

➡ **Bus** For Shek O, take bus 9 from Shau Kei Wan MTR station (exit A3). For Stanley from Shau Kei Wan, take bus 14 from Shau Kei Wan Rd, a short walk from the MTR station (exit A3). Buses 6, 6A, 6X, 66 and 260 come here via Repulse Bay. These routes all begin in Central, below Exchange Sq. For Aberdeen, Buses 73 and 973 from Stanley call at Repulse Bay and Aberdeen Main St. Green minibus 40 runs from Tang Lung St in Causeway Bay to Stanley via Ocean Park. Buses 40 and 40M leave for Pok Fu Lam from Wan Chai Ferry Pier via Admiralty. Buses 7, 90B and 91 link Pok Fu Lam with Aberdeen Praya Rd in Aberdeen. To get to Repulse Bay from Central, below Exchange Sq, take bus 6, 6A, 6X, 66 or 260. To get here from Aberdeen take bus 73 or 973 – both stop on Aberdeen Main Rd. To get to Deep Water Bay from Central, below Exchange Sq, take bus 6A, 6X or 260. To get here from Aberdeen take bus 73 or 973.

👁 SIGHTS

👁 Aberdeen

OCEAN PARK

AMUSEMENT PARK

off Map p376 (☑3923 2323; www.oceanpark.com. hk; Ocean Park Rd; adult/child 3-11yr $280/140; ☺10am-7.30pm; ☐6A, 6X, 70 & 75 from Central, 629 from Admiralty, 72, 72A & 92 from Causeway Bay or 973 from Tsim Sha Tsui) It may have to compete with the natural crowd-pulling powers of Disneyland on Lantau, but for many Ocean Park remains the top theme park in Hong Kong. The accolade is in no small part thanks to a successful revamp of this local institution, which has seen new rides and attractions added to the constantly expanding site as well as consistently record-breaking visitor numbers. The presence of four giant pandas plus four very cute, rare red pandas – all gifts from the mainland – has also contributed to the dramatic turnaround in the park's fortunes.

The park is divided into two main sections. The main entrance is on the Waterfront (lowland) side and is linked to the main section on the Summit (headland) via a scenic cable car ride and a marine-themed funicular train called the Ocean Express.

The major attractions at the **Waterfront** are Amazing Asian Animals and Aqua City, where animals and sea creatures come with some worthwhile educational content. The newest addition is the Grand Aquarium which boasts the world's largest aquarium dome with a 5.5m diameter and is home to 5000 fish (400 species). Another brand-new zone, Old Hong Kong, is a replica of the old buildings and communities that once graced Wan Chai and older parts of Kowloon. To the north is Whiskers Harbour, which thrives on an assortment of kids-oriented rides.

On the **Summit**, the Thrill Mountain has plenty of white-knuckle rides, such as the celebrated roller coaster, Hair Raiser. In Marine World you'll find sea lions and seals plus daily dolphin and killer-whale shows. Meanwhile, the Chinese Sturgeon Aquarium showcases another living gift from the mainland.

SAMPAN TOURS

BOAT TRIPS

Map p376 (Aberdeen Promenade) Sampan tours are a fun way to see parts of the island's south coast, and you can easily find sampan operators milling around the eastern end of the Aberdeen Promenade. Usually they charge around $68 per person for a 30-minute ride (about $120 to Sok Kwu Wan and $150 to Yung Shue Wan on Lamma). If you want just a glimpse of the harbour, you can take a small ferry across to Ap Lei Chau Island (adult/child under 12 $1.80/1), which is also a destination for bargain hunters drawn to its outlet stores (p134). Alternatively, just hop on the free ferry to Jumbo Kingdom Floating Restaurant (p132) and come back.

If you fancy more luxury, **Island Junk** (Map p376; ☑2877 5222; www.islandjunks. hk; Shum Wan Rd, Aberdeen) runs a daily boat tour ($550) that leaves Aberdeen at 11am and arrives in Stanley, via Sok Kwu Wan on Lamma, four hours later. The price includes a seafood lunch. A minimum of eight people is required.

The promenade can be easily accessed from Aberdeen bus terminus. To get to it just take the pedestrian subway under Aberdeen Praya Rd.

8TH ESTATE WINERY

WINERY

off Map p376 (☑2518 0922; www.the8estatewin ery.com; Room 306, 3/F, Harbour Industrial Center, 10 Lee Hing St, Ap Lei Chau; admission $100; ☺2-5pm Sat, by appointment Mon-Fri; ☐90 from Exchange Sq in Central) Hong Kong boasts the highest per capita wine consumption in Asia, but winemaking was almost unheard of until 2008, the year this lovely winery was born. Hidden in a factory building behind the shopping complex of Horizon Plaza on Ap Lei Chau, the winery has no chateaux or vineyards, but you can enjoy the gorgeous ocean views on its terrace or in the elegantly decorated barrel rooms while tasting the 'Made in Hong Kong' wines. The winery is also famous for sourcing grapes worldwide to make its own wines. Admission includes a 30-minute tour of the winery, wine tasting and a gift voucher. To get there from Ap Lei Chau bus terminus, either take a taxi ($20) or wait for the free shuttle bus to Horizon Plaza. From there, walk south to Lee Hing St (five minutes).

TEMPLES & SHRINES

TEMPLES

Map p376 (Aberdeen Main Rd) If you have time to spare, a short walk through Aberdeen will bring you to a **Tin Hau temple** (天后廟; Map p376; 182 Aberdeen Main Rd; ☺8am-5pm) from 1851. Once you're in the vicinity, check out the series of quirky **shrines** that are dedicated to local deities; you'll see them on the slope behind the rest area on Old Main St.

◉ Pok Fu Lam

BÉTHANIE HISTORIC BUILDING

(伯大尼; ☎2854 8918; www.hkapa.edu/asp/general/general_visitors.asp; 139 Pok Fu Lam Rd; admission $30; ◑11am-5pm; ☒7, 40, 40M, 90B or 91) Perched on hilly Pok Fu Lam (off Map p376), a college and residential area northwest of Aberdeen, this beautiful restoration is a highlight in this part of town. The complex, which now houses a film school, was built by the French Mission in 1875 as a sanatorium for priests from all over Asia to rest and recover from tropical diseases before they returned to their missions. The guided tour will include a visit to the neo-Gothic **Béthanie Chapel**, a new theatre in the two octagonal **Dairy Farm cowsheds**, and the wine cellar-converted **museum** which displays the history of the mission. Tours are run hourly and it's wise to call ahead, as some venues may not be accessible when they're being hired. The nearest bus stop is at the junction of Pok Fu Lam Reservoir and Pok Fu Lam Rd.

POK FU LAM VILLAGE VILLAGE

off Map p376 (薄扶林村; www.pokfulamvillage.org; ☒7, 40, 40M, 90B, or 91) Lying 200m south across the road from Béthanie, Pok Fu Lam Village, a settlement full of shacks and makeshift huts, is quite a contrast to the condos behind. You can catch a glimpse of the Hong Kong of yesteryear when refugees from China built their temporary-turned-permanent homes here. There's a 200-year-old pagoda on the northern side of the village, and a spectacular fire dragon dance takes place here during the Mid-Autumn Festival.

◉ Stanley

MURRAY HOUSE HISTORIC BUILDING

Map p377 (美利樓; Stanley Bay; ☒6, 6A, 6X or 260) Across the bay from Stanley Main St stands this three-storey colonnaded affair. Built in 1848 as officers' quarters, it took pride of place in Central, on the spot where the Bank of China Tower now stands, for almost 150 years until 1982. It was re-erected here stone by stone and opened in 2001.

HONG KONG CORRECTIONAL SERVICES MUSEUM MUSEUM

Map p377 (香港懲教博物館; ☎2147 3199; www.csd.gov.hk/english/hkcsm/hkcsm.html; 45 Tung Tau Wan Rd; admission free; ◑10am-5pm Tue-Sun; ☒6, 6A, 6X or 260) Mock cells, gallows and flogging stands are the gruesome draws at this museum, about 500m southeast of Stanley Village Rd, which traces the history of jails, prisons and other forms of incarceration in Hong Kong.

ST STEPHEN'S COLLEGE'S HERITAGE TRAIL HERITAGE WALK

Map p377 (聖士提反書院文物徑; ☎2813 0360; www.ssc.edu.hk/ssctrail/eng; 22 Tung Tau Wan Rd; admission free; ☒6, 6A, 6X or 260) WWII history buffs can visit the beautiful campus of St Stephen's College which sits right next to Stanley Military Cemetery. Founded in 1903, the school was turned into an emergency military hospital on the eve of the Japanese invasion of Hong Kong in 1941 and became an internment camp after the city fell. The 1½-hour guided tour by students takes you to eight sites in the campus. Poignant reminders of the war include the colonial-style **School House**, which witnessed what has become known as the St Stephen's College Massacre when Japanese soldiers stormed into the building and killed 56 British and Canadian soldiers who were still wounded in their beds, on Christmas Eve in 1941. The austere **Chapel** was built in 1950 on the highest point of the campus in memory of the war victims. There's also a **museum** showing the school's interesting history as the Eton of the East. Admission to the trail is by guided tour on Saturdays, Sundays and public holidays only. Reserve in advance.

STANLEY MILITARY CEMETERY CEMETERY

off Map p377 (赤柱軍人墳場; ☎2557 3498; Wong Ma Kok Rd; ◑8am-5pm; ☒14 or 6A) South of Stanley Market, this cemetery for armed forces personnel and their families is also a highlight in Stanley. The oldest graves date back to 1843 and are an intriguing document of the colonial era. The earlier graves show just how great a toll disease took on European settlers, while the number of graves from the early 1940s serves as a reminder of the many who died during the fight for Hong Kong and subsequent internment at the hands of occupying Japanese forces. To reach the cemetery, walk south along Wong Ma Kok Rd for 15 minutes.

ST STEPHEN'S BEACH
BEACH

off Map p377 (🚌6A or 14) Just a stone's throw from Stanley Military Cemetery is this great little bolthole, St Stephen's Beach, which comes handily with a cafe, showers and changing rooms. In summer you can hire windsurfing boards and kayaks from the water-sports centre.

OLD STANLEY POLICE STATION
HISTORIC BUILDING

Map p377 (舊赤柱警署; 88 Stanley Village Rd; 🚌6, 6A, 6X or 260) The most interesting building in the village itself is this two-storey structure from 1859. It now contains, less interestingly, a Wellcome supermarket.

TEMPLES & SHRINES
TEMPLES

Map p377 (🚌6, 6A, 6X or 260) At the western end of Stanley Main St, past a tiny **Tai Wong shrine** (大王廟) and through the Stanley Plaza shopping complex, is a **Tin Hau temple** (天后廟; 119 Stanley Main St), built in 1767. Its appearance has completely changed over the years, however, and it's now a concrete pile. A sign explains that the tiger skin hanging on the wall came from an animal that 'weighed 240 pounds, was 73 inches long, and three feet high [and] shot by an Indian policeman, Mr Rur Singh, in front of Stanley Police Station in the year 1942'.

◉ Shek O

SHEK O
BEACH

(🚌9 from Shau Kei Wan MTR station, exit A3) Thirteen kilometres northeast of Stanley, Shek O is a laid-back village that still oozes an old-world charm and has one of the best (and quieter) beaches on the island.

Shek O has enough activities to keep you amused plus several passable dining and drinking options. **Shek O beach** has a large expanse of sand, shady trees to the rear, showers, changing facilities and lockers for rent. From **Dragon's Back** (龍脊), the 280m-high ridge to the west of the village, there's both paragliding and abseiling. Cycling around Shek O Peninsula is possible. **Tung Lok Barbecue Store** (同樂沙灘士多; ☑2809 4692; ☺Apr-Sep), in the centre of the village, rents bicycles (from $20 a day). The fine and often deserted **Big Wave Bay** (🚌9 or 309, Sun only) beach is 2km to the north of Shek O. To get to Big Wave Bay follow the road north out of town, travel past the 18-hole Shek O Golf & Country Club (see p134), then turn east at the roundabout and keep going until the road ends. One of eight **prehistoric rock carvings** discovered in Hong Kong is on the headland above Big Wave Bay.

◉ Repulse Bay

REPULSE BAY
BEACH

off Map p377 (淺水灣; 🚌6, 6A, 6X or 260) A posh beach suburb, Repulse Bay is Hong Kong's most famous beach and home to some of its richest residents. The hills around the beach are strewn with luxury apartment blocks, and more are on their way.

The long beach with tawny sand at Repulse Bay is visited by Chinese tourist groups year-round and, needless to say, packed on weekends in summer. It's a good place if you like people-watching. The beach has showers and changing rooms and shade trees at the roadside, but the water is pretty murky.

Towards the southeast end of Repulse Bay beach is **Kwun Yam Shrine** (觀音廟), an unusual shrine to Kwun Yam. The surrounding area has an amazing assembly of deities and figures – goldfish, rams, the money god and other southern Chinese icons, as well as statues of Tin Hau. Most of the statues were funded by local personalities and businesspeople during the 1970s. In front of the shrine to the left as you face the sea is **Longevity Bridge** (長壽橋); crossing it is supposed to add three days to your life.

Middle Bay and **South Bay**, about 10 and 30 minutes to the south respectively, have beaches that are usually much less crowded.

◉ Deep Water Bay

DEEP WATER BAY
BEACH

A quiet little inlet with a beach flanked by shade trees, Deep Water Bay is a few kilometres northwest of Repulse Bay. There are a handful of places to eat and have a drink, and some barbecue pits at the southern end of the beach. If you want a dip in the water, this spot is usually less crowded than Repulse Bay. Deep Water Bay beach is a centre for wakeboarding.

EATING

Choices in Shek O and Repulse Bay are sparse, but you'll still manage to eat decently, and enjoy the views on the coast. Stanley boasts the largest number of midrange restaurants, with a few standing out. Aberdeen and Ap Lei Chau are home to a few hidden gems if you dig beneath the kitsch.

Aberdeen

TOP CHOICE ABERDEEN FISH MARKET CANTEEN
CANTONESE, SEAFOOD $$

Map p376 (香港仔魚市場海鮮餐廳; ☎2552 7555; 102 Shek Pai Wan Rd; meals from $350; ⊙11.30am-2pm) Who knows seafood better than the fisherfolk? Hidden in the fish market, this understated eatery run by local fishermen is truly an in-the-know place for ultrafresh seafood. There's no menu here, and you will need a Cantonese-speaking friend to help you book a table at least two days in advance (two weeks for weekends). Tell the owner Ah Lo your budget and he'll source the best sea creatures available and apply his Midas touch to them. Walk-in visitors can try the excellent Hong Kong–style French toast and other *cha chaan tang* (tea cafe) staples. Only open during lunch hours. There's no English signage; look for the nondescript one-storey yellow building with a green roof at end of the fish market.

CROWN WINE CELLARS
EUROPEAN $$$

(☎2580 6287; www.crownwinecellars.com; 18 Deep Water Bay Dr, Shouson Hill; meals from $400; ⊙dinner Mon-Fri, lunch & dinner Sat & Sun; ☐minibus 6) The WWII bunkers on the hill have been transformed into a top-notch wine cellar, with a colonial-style glasshouse restaurant surrounded by towering trees. You can tour the site and have a meal there by subscribing to the one-time 'silver' membership free of charge. Take minibus 5 on Lockhart Rd, right behind Sogo department store in Causeway Bay, and make a stop at the top of Deep Water Bay Dr.

TOP DECK
INTERNATIONAL $$$

Map p376 (珍之寶; ☎2552 3331; www.cafe decogroup.com; Top fl, Jumbo Kingdom, Shum Wan Pier Dr, Wong Chuk Hang; weekend brunch Sat/Sun $338/418; ⊙5pm-midnight Tue-Fri, 11am-late Sat, Sun & public holidays) The weekend brunch with free-flowing champagne is the drawcard at Top Deck. The theatrical decor, resort-style awnings, and the garish Chinese pagoda on the rooftop may not be everyone's cup of tea, but it has a sun-kissed deck and the harbour views are gorgeous.

JUMBO KINGDOM FLOATING RESTAURANT
CANTONESE $$

Map p376 (珍寶海鮮舫; ☎2553 9111; www. jumbo.com.hk; Shum Wan Pier Dr, Wong Chuk Hang; lunch $60-200; ⊙lunch & dinner Mon-Sat, breakfast, lunch & dinner Sun) The larger of two floating restaurants moored in Aberdeen Harbour, the Jumbo has interiors that look like Běijīng's Imperial Palace crossbred with Macau's Casino Lisboa – a flamboyant spectacle so kitsch it's fun. Eschew the overpriced Dragon Court on the 2nd floor and head to the 3rd floor for dim sum. There's free transport for diners from the pier on Aberdeen Promenade.

TREE CAFE
CAFE $

(☎2870 1582; www.tree.com.hk/cafe/; 28/F, Horizon Plaza, 2 Lee Wing St, Ap Lei Chau; meals from $60; ⊙10.30am-7pm) The Horizon Plaza shopping mall is quite out of the way, so if you're feeling peckish after a shopping spree, why not rest your legs in this glam cafe hidden in the eponymous furniture shop on the very top floor of the building? The coffee is arguably among the best on the island. Thoughtfully, there is also a play area for the little ones.

AP LEI CHAU MARKET COOKED FOOD CENTRE
DAI PAI DONG, SEAFOOD $

Map p376 (鴨利洲市政大廈; 1st fl, Ap Lei Chau Municipal Services Bldg, 8 Hung Shing St; ☐minibus 36X from Lee Garden Rd, Causeway Bay, or from Aberdeen Promenade by sampan) Sharing a building with a market, six *dai pai dong* operators cook up a storm in sleepy Ap Lei Chau. **Pak Kee** (栢記; ☎2555 2984; ⊙dinner) and **Chu Kee** (珠記; ☎2555 2052; ⊙dinner) both offer simple but tasty dishes in the $40 to $60 range, and affordable seafood selections. You can also buy seafood from the wet market downstairs and pay them to cook it for you the way you want. Every evening fishermen and dragon boaters come here for the cheap beer and the food.

CHEF STUDIO
FRENCH $$$

Map p376 (☎3104 4664; Kwai Bo Industrial Bldg, 40 Wong Chuk Hang Rd; 5-course tasting menu for 2 $1100; ⊙ dinner Mon-Sat; ☐70 from Exchange

Sq in Central) You may not be sure what you're walking into (the factory building housing the restaurant is yet to be revitalised), but once you enter the cavernous finedining venue, you'll be in a far better world. This high-end speakeasy flaunts minimalist chic, and there's a mini organic farm on the balcony. The open kitchen allows you to chit chat with the chef and see how the ingredients are carefully prepared. Eddy Leung, the mastermind here and a lauded practitioner of eco-foodism, wows diners with his French-inspired dishes. Reservation a must. No corkage fee.

✕ Stanley

LUCY'S   INTERNATIONAL $$
Map p377 (☎2813 9055; 64 Stanley Main St; meals from $180; ⊘lunch & dinner) If the waterfront restaurants are too formulaic for you, seek out this cosy restaurant in Stanley Market. Lucy's has earned a loyal local following for its tasty French-inspired recipes, friendly service and relatively reasonable prices.

SEI YIK   CANTONESE, DAI PAI DONG $
Map p377 (泗益; ☎2813 0503; 2 Stanley Market St; meals from $30; ⊘6am-7pm Wed-Mon) Weekenders flock to this small tin-roofed *dai pai dong,* right opposite the Stanley Municipal Building, for its fluffy Hong Kong–style French toast with *kaya* (coconut jam) spread. No English signage; look for the long queue of pilgrims and the piles of fruits that hide the entrance.

SAFFRON BAKERY CAFÉ   CAFE, BAKERY $
(breakfast from $50, meals from $125) Stanley (Map p377; ☎2813 0270; http://saffronbakery.com; Shop G04 Ground fl, Stanley Plaza; ⊘11.30am-11pm); Repulse Bay (☎2812 2016; Shop G120, Repulse Bay Shopping Arcade, 109 Repulse Bay Rd; ⊘8.30am-6pm) Yummy mummies love the truly artisanal organic bread and the kids-friendly atmosphere in the recently renovated cafe in Stanley.

✕ Shek O

HAPPY GARDEN   THAI $
(石澳樂園; ☎2809 4165; 786 Shek O Village; lunch/dinner from $50/80; ⊘11am-11pm; ☐9 from Shau Kei Wan MTR station, exit A3) This humble mum-and-dad operation makes everyone happy with fresh seafood, authentic Thai

fare and decent prices. Upstairs, the terrace offers some views of the ocean. The restaurant is in front of the car park by the beach.

BLACK SHEEP   INTERNATIONAL $$
(黑羊餐廳; ☎2809 2021; 330 Shek O Village; meals from $180; ⊘dinner Mon-Fri, lunch & dinner Sat & Sun; ☐9 from Shau Kei Wan MTR station, exit A3) This whimsically decorated spot is famous for its pizza and fresh mint lemonade. The menu is written on the blackboard and is updated regularly.

✕ Repulse Bay

⬚TOP CHOICE VERANDAH   INTERNATIONAL $$$
(露台餐廳; ☎2292 2822; www.therepulsebay.com; 1st fl, The Repulse Bay, 109 Repulse Bay Rd; ⊘lunch, tea & dinner Tue-Sat, brunch, tea & dinner Sun) A meal in the grand Verandah, run by the prestigious Peninsula, is a special occasion indeed. The large restaurant features a recently restored and refurbished interior that is literally dripping with colonial nostalgia, what with the grand piano at the entrance, the wooden fans dangling from the ceiling, and the marble staircases with wooden banisters. The Sunday brunch is famous (book ahead), and the afternoon tea the best this side of Hong Kong Island.

SPICES RESTAURANT   SOUTHEAST ASIAN $$$
(香辣軒; ☎2292 2821; www.therepulsebay.com; The Repulse Bay, 109 Repulse Bay Rd; ⊘lunch & dinner Mon-Fri, lunch, tea & dinner Sat, Sun & public holidays) The high ceilings, rattan chairs and sparkling wooden flooring evoke the romantic vibes that you'd expect from a beachfront hang-out in Bali. The interior is oriental minimalism, and the open terrace is the best spot for a sundowner. The menu runs the gamut of seafood, satay and curry.

⬚ DRINKING & NIGHTLIFE

SMUGGLERS INN   PUB
Map p377 (Ground fl, 90A Stanley Main St, Stanley; ⊘happy hour 6-9pm; ☐6, 6A, 6X or 260) This is arguably the most popular pub on the Stanley waterfront, offering perhaps the closest thing to an English pub in Hong Kong.

BACK BEACH BAR
BAR

(273 Shek O Village, Shek O Back Beach, Shek O; ☉7pm-midnight Mon-Fri, 2pm-midnight Sat; ➡9 from Shau Kei Wan MTR station, exit A3) Hidden on the quiet Shek O Back Beach is this very rustic beach bar which consists of no more than two narrow brick tables, some stools and benches made from discarded wood. A sea-facing shrine stands right next to this rugged ensemble. Enjoy reggae beats and the sound of the lapping waves while sipping beer. From Shek O bus terminal, turn right into the path that leads to an abandoned school and a health centre. The beach is at the end of the path.

SHOPPING

HORIZON PLAZA
OUTLETS

off Map p376 (新海怡廣場; 2 Lee Wing St, Ap Lei Chau, Aberdeen; ☉10am-7pm; ➡90 from Exchange Sq in Central) Tucked away on the southern coast of Ap Lei Chau, this enormous outlet, in a converted factory building, boasts more than 150 shops over 28 storeys. Most locals come here to buy furniture, but you'll also find Alexander McQueens on offer and Jimmy Choos at knock-down prices. Our favourites are **Tree** (28/F), a chic wooden furniture shop on the top floor; **Lane Crawford** (25/F), which has a high-end footwear section that you shouldn't miss; and **Bluebell Fashion Warehouse** (19/F), another multibrand outlet that carries a number of designer labels that won't bust a hole in your wallet. (A heads-up: waiting for the lifts is a frustrating exercise here, it's wise to start from the top floor and work your way down.)

To get there, take bus 90 and alight at Ap Lei Chau Estate Terminus. Then take the free shuttle minibus that operates (irregularly) between 7.45am and 7.30pm. There's no bus stop for the shuttles. Wait at the bus station's staff booth near the taxi stand, or it's a 20-minute walk to the outlet.

STANLEY MARKET
MARKET

Map p377 (赤柱市集; Stanley Village Rd; ☉9am-6pm; ➡6, 6A, 6X or 260) No big bargains or big stings, just reasonably priced casual clothes, bric-a-brac and formulaic art, all in a nicely confusing maze of alleys running down to Stanley Bay. It's best to go during the week; on the weekend the market is bursting at the seams with tourists and locals alike.

SPORTS & ACTIVITIES

ABERDEEN BOAT CLUB
BOATING

Map p376 (香港仔遊艇會; ☎2552 8182; www.abclubhk.com; 20 Shum Wan Rd, Aberdeen; ➡70, 73 & 793) This boat club offers sailing and windsurfing courses to both members and nonmembers.

ABERDEEN MARINA CLUB
BOATING

Map p376 (深灣遊艇俱樂部; ☎2555 8321; www.aberdeenmarinaclub.com; 8 Shum Wan Rd, Aberdeen; ➡70, 73 & 793) Nonmembers must be accompanied by a member in this swish clubhouse.

SHEK O GOLF & COUNTRY CLUB
GOLF

(石澳高爾夫球會; ☎2809 4458; 5 Shek O Rd, Shek O; greens fees $300-500; ➡3, 309) An 18-hole course located on the southeastern edge of Hong Kong Island. Nonmembers must be accompanied by a member.

Kowloon

TSIM SHA TSUI | YAU MA TEI | MONG KOK | NEW KOWLOON

Neighbourhood Top Five

1 Strolling the **Tsim Sha Tsui East Promenade** (p138) against the backdrop of Victoria Harbour.

2 Enjoying scones and Earl Grey at the **Peninsula** (p143) lobby, as a string quartet saws away.

3 Savouring the sounds, smells and flavours of the **Temple Street Night Market** (p139).

4 Experiencing a Taoist ceremony or having your fortune told at the **Sik Sik Yuen Wong Tai Sin Temple** (p140).

5 Browsing with gadget geeks and comb-over uncles at **Ap Liu Street Flea Market** (p162).

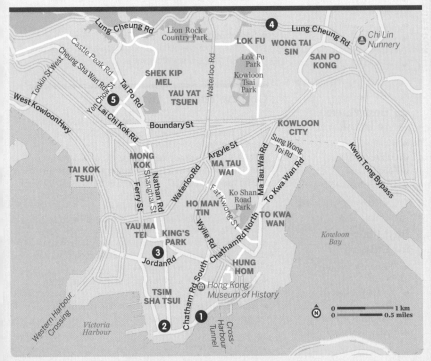

For more detail of this area, see Map p378, Map p382, Map p383 and Map p380 ➡

Lonely Planet's Top Tip

Ethnic pockets abound in Kowloon, especially in Tsim Sha Tsui. Indians, Pakistanis and Africans live and hang out in and around Chungking Mansions where you can find the best Indian grocery stores in town; Korean eateries and minimarts proliferate on Kimberley St and Austin Avenida; Nepalese (former Gurkhas) congregate near the Temple Street Night Market in Yau Ma Tei; and Kowloon City lays claim to an elephant's share of Hong Kong's Thai stores and restaurants.

Best Places to Eat

➡ Dong Lai Shun (p149)
➡ Kimberley Chinese Restaurant (p150)
➡ One Dim Sum (p154)
➡ Yoga Interactive Vegetarian (p150)
➡ Piggy Grill (p155)

For reviews, see p149 ➡

 Best Places to Drink

➡ Butler (p157)
➡ Ozone (p157)
➡ Fullcup Café (p158)
➡ Aqua Spirit (p157)

For reviews, see p157 ➡

Best Places for Culture

➡ St Andrew's Church (p144)
➡ Yau Ma Tei Theatre (p146)
➡ Museum of Art (p142)
➡ Hidden Agenda (see p159)

Explore Kowloon

Start your day by spending an hour or two at the Museum of History, then take a leisurely half-hour stroll to the Star Ferry Concourse via the scenic Tsim Sha Tsui East Promenade. Check out the sights along the way, such as the Cultural Centre and the clock tower, and follow up with lunch at an Indian or Shanghainese restaurant.

Walk to Yau Ma Tei, stopping at St Andrew's Church and Kowloon British School along the way. Spend 90 minutes exploring: Tin Hau Temple, the Jade Market and Shanghai St. Then do any one or two of the following: take the MTR to Prince Edward for the Yuen Po St Flower and Bird Market followed by a visit to Mong Kok; visit Sham Shui Po and the Ap Liu Street flea market; or go to Diamond Hill to immerse yourself in the tranquillity of Chi Lin Nunnery.

Have dinner at one of the roadside stalls in Yau Ma Tei, then it's on to the Temple Street Night Market. Wrap up your day with drinks at a bar in Tsim Sha Tsui.

Local Life

➡ **Hang-out** Local artists and writers like to chill on the upper floor of Mido Café (p155).

➡ **Shopping** Fashionistas seek affordable additions to their wardrobes at the Rise Shopping Arcade (p159) and street-level shops at Granville Circuit.

➡ **Street performance** Musicians and performance artists take over the pedestrianised stretch of Sai Yeung Choi St in Mong Kok every evening.

Getting There & Away

➡ **Bus** Buses 2, 6, 6A and 9 run up Nathan Rd to Yau Ma Tei. Buses 5 and 26 leave from Tsim Sha Tsui to Ma Tau Chung Rd in New Kowloon.

➡ **MTR** For Tsim Sha Tsui, go to the Tsim Sha Tsui, Tsim Sha Tsui East and Hung Hong stations. For Yau Ma Tei use the Yau Ma Tei station. For Mong Kok, there are the Mong Kok and Prince Edward stations. To get to New Kowloon use the Sham Shui Po and Cheung Sha Wan stations on the Tsuen Wan line; Kowloon Tong, Lok Fu, Wong Tai Sin, Diamond Hill and Kowloon Bay stations on the Kwun Tong line; Kowloon Tong station on the East Rail line; and Kowloon Station on the Tung Chung line and Airport Express line.

➡ **Macau Ferries** For Tsim Sha Tsui, the China ferry terminal is on Canton Rd.

➡ **Star Ferry** The Tsim Sha Tsui station is at the western end of Salisbury Rd.

TOP SIGHTS
HONG KONG MUSEUM OF HISTORY

If you only have time to visit one museum, consider making it the Hong Kong Museum of History. Its whistle-stop overview of the territory's archaeology, natural history, ethnography and local cultures will help to give context to your experience of Hong Kong.

The eight galleries of the museum's permanent exhibition, 'The Hong Kong Story', take you on a fascinating walk through the territory's history, starting with the natural environment and prehistoric Hong Kong – about 6000 years ago – and ending with the territory's return to China in 1997 (interestingly, there's hardly anything on life post-1997).

You'll encounter colourful replicas of the dwellings of early inhabitants, such as the Tanka boat people and the Puntay who resided in walled villages, as well as a Chinese marriage procession. You'll see traditional costumes and beds; a re-creation of an arcaded Central street from 1881, including a Chinese herbal medicine shop that tells its own story through the taped voice of its owner; a tram from 1913; and WWII film footage, including interviews with Chinese and foreigners taken prisoner by the Japanese.

One section is devoted to the formation of Hong Kong's urban culture, featuring replicas of a retro grocery store, soda fountain and the interiors of a poor man's home. There's a cinema decorated in '60s style, with three screenings daily (11am, 2pm, 4pm) of old Cantonese films – an attraction for seniors who come here for the movies, the memories and the free air-conditioning.

The museum's gallery for special exhibitions features topics of significance in Hong Kong and Chinese history, such as 'Centenary of China's 1911 Revolution' and 'Dockyards of Hong Kong'.

DON'T MISS

➡ 'The Hong Kong Story'
➡ Special exhibitions

PRACTICALITIES

➡ 香港歷史博物館
➡ Map p380
➡ ☑2724 9042
➡ http://hk.history.museum
➡ 100 Chatham Rd South
➡ adult/concession $10/5, Wed free
➡ ⊙10am-6pm Mon & Wed-Sat, to 7pm Sun
➡ free guided tours in English (10.30am & 2.30pm Sat & Sun)
➡ Ⓜ Tsim Sha Tsui, exit B2

TOP SIGHTS
TSIM SHA TSUI EAST PROMENADE

The resplendent views of Victoria Harbour make this walkway one of the best strolls in Hong Kong. Go during the day to take pictures, visit the museums and watch boats and people going about their business. Then on your way to dinner or the Star Ferry Pier after sundown, revisit the views, now magically transformed with the skyscrapers of Central and Wan Chai decked out in their neon robes.

A good place to begin your journey is at the old Kowloon-Canton Railway Clock Tower, a landmark of the age of steam, near the Star Ferry Concourse. In 1966 thousands gathered here to protest against a fare increase. The protest erupted into the 1966 Riot, the first in a series of social protests leading to colonial reform.

Passing the Cultural Centre and the Museum of Art, you'll arrive at the **Avenue of the Stars** (星光大道), Hong Kong's lacklustre tribute to its once-brilliant film industry. The highlight here is a 2.5m tall bronze statue of kung fu icon Bruce Lee.

From here, every evening, you can watch the **Symphony of Lights** (⊙8-8.20pm), the world's largest permanent laser light show projected from atop 40 skyscrapers.

The walk takes you past the hotels of the reclaimed area known as Tsim Sha Tsui East, and past that to the Hong Kong Coliseum and the Hung Hom train station. The further north you go, the quieter it gets, and tourists and pleasure boats are replaced by container barges, lovers and quiet men angling for fish.

The promenade is packed during the **Chinese New Year** fireworks displays in late January/early February and in June during the **Dragon Boat Festival**.

DON'T MISS

➡ The views
➡ Clock tower
➡ Bruce Lee statue
➡ Symphony of Lights

PRACTICALITIES

➡ 尖沙咀東部海濱花園
➡ Map p380
➡ 🚢Star Ferry
➡ ⓂTsim Sha Tsui, exit E

TOP SIGHTS
TEMPLE STREET NIGHT MARKET

The liveliest night market in Hong Kong, Temple St extends from Man Ming Lane in the north to Nanking St in the south and is cut in two by the historic Tin Hau temple complex. It's a great place to go for the bustling atmosphere, the smells and tastes on offer from the *dai pai dongs* (see p37), the random free Cantonese opera performances and some fortune-telling. The market is at its best from about 7pm to 10pm, when it's clogged with stalls and people.

While you may find better bargains over the border in Shēnzhèn, people still shop here for cheap clothes, watches, pirated CDs, fake labels, footwear, cookware and everyday items. Any marked prices should be considered suggestions – this is definitely a place to bargain.

For alfresco dining, head for Woo Sung St, running parallel to the east, or to the section of Temple St north of the temple. You can get anything from a bowl of noodles to Chiu Chow–style oyster omelettes and Nepalese curries, costing anywhere from $30 to $300. There are quite a few seafood and hotpot restaurants in the area.

Every evening a gaggle of fortune-tellers sets up tents in the middle of the market where they'll make predictions (consultation from $100) about your life by reading your face, palm or date of birth. Some keep birds that have been trained to pick out 'fortune' cards. Accuracy aside, it's all quite entertaining. Most operators speak some English.

If you're in luck, you'll catch an extract of a Cantonese opera performed under the stars. Some of the most famous divas and maestros of the opera stage began their careers in this humble fashion. Or so they say.

If you want to carry on, visit the charming Yau Ma Tei Wholesale Fruit Market (p146) which comes alive from 4am.

DON'T MISS

➡ Shopping
➡ Street food
➡ Fortune-tellers
➡ Cantonese opera performance
➡ Yau Ma Tei Wholesale Fruit Market

PRACTICALITIES

➡ 廟街夜市
➡ Map p382
➡ ⊘6-11pm
➡ Ⓜ Yau Ma Tei, exit C; follow Man Ming Lane

TOP SIGHTS
SIK SIK YUEN WONG TAI SIN TEMPLE

An explosion of colourful pillars, roofs, lattice work, flowers and incense, this busy Taoist temple is a destination for all walks of Hong Kong society, from pensioners and businesspeople to parents and young professionals. Some come simply to pray, others to divine the future with *chim* (bamboo 'fortune sticks') which are shaken out of a box onto the ground and then interpreted by a fortune-teller.

The complex, built in 1973, is dedicated to a deified healer named Wong Tai Sin who, as a shepherd in Zhèjiāng province, was said to have transformed boulders into sheep. In fact, the district (an MTR station and a housing estate) is named after him – ironic given he was said to have been a hermit. When he was 15 an immortal taught Wong how to make a herbal potion that could cure all illnesses. He is thus worshipped both by the sick and those trying to avoid illness. The term 'Wong Tai Sin' is sometimes used to describe people who are generous to a fault.

Taoist ceremonies and rituals take place at the main altar. The image of the deity was brought to Hong Kong from Guǎngdōng province in 1915. Behind the main altar and to the right are the **Good Wish Gardens** (admission by donation $2; ⊙9am-4pm), replete with pavilions (the hexagonal Unicorn Hall, with carved doors and windows, is the most beautiful), zigzag bridges and carp ponds.

To the left as you enter the complex is an arcade of fortune-tellers (consultation from $100), some of whom speak English. The busiest times at the temple are around Chinese New Year, Wong Tai Sin's birthday (23rd day of the eighth month – usually in September) and on weekends.

DON'T MISS

➡ The architecture
➡ Bamboo fortune sticks
➡ The main altar
➡ Ceremonies
➡ Good Wish Gardens
➡ Unicorn Hall

PRACTICALITIES

➡ 嗇色園黃大仙祠
➡ ☑2327 8141/2351 5640
➡ www.siksikyuen. org.hk
➡ 2, Chuk Yuen Village, Wong Tai Sin, Kowloon
➡ donation $2
➡ ⊙7am-5.30pm
➡ Ⓜ Wong Tai Sin, exit B2

TOP SIGHTS
CHI LIN NUNNERY

One of the most beautiful and arrestingly built environments in Hong Kong, this large Buddhist complex, originally dating from the 1930s, was rebuilt completely of wood (and not a single nail) in the style of a Tang-dynasty monastery in 1998. It's a serene place with lotus ponds, bonsai tea plants, bougainvillea and silent nuns delivering offerings of fruit and rice to Buddha or chanting behind intricately carved screens.

Built to last a thousand years, Chi Lin Nunnery is the world's largest cluster of handcrafted timber buildings, one exhibiting a level of artistry rarely found in faux-ancient architecture. The design, involving intricately interlocking sections of wood joined without a single nail, is intended to demonstrate the harmony of humans with nature.

You enter through the Sam Mun, a series of 'three gates' representing the Buddhist precepts of compassion, wisdom and 'skilful means'. The first courtyard, which contains the delightful Lotus Pond Garden, gives way to the Hall of Celestial Kings, with a large statue of the seated Buddha surrounded by deities. Behind that is the main hall, containing a statue of the Sakyamuni Buddha.

Connected to the nunnery is **Nan Lian Garden** (南蓮園池; ☎3658 9311; www.nanliangarden.org; ⊘10am-6pm), a Tang-style garden featuring a golden pagoda, a koi pond and a collection of bizarre rocks sourced from all over China.

Also here is the small but excellent Chi Lin Vegetarian (Long Men Lou; see p156) and the elegant **Pavilion of Pine and Tea** (Song Cha Xie; ☎3658 9390; tea leaves from $150; ⊘noon-7.30pm).

DON'T MISS

➡ Faux-Tang architecture
➡ Sam Mun
➡ Lotus Pond Garden
➡ Hall of Celestial Kings
➡ The main hall
➡ Nan Lian Garden

PRACTICALITIES

➡ 志蓮淨苑
➡ ☎2354 1888
➡ www.chilin.org
➡ 5 Chi Lin Dr
➡ admission free
➡ ⊘nunnery 9am-4.30pm, garden 6.30am-7pm
➡ Ⓜ Diamond Hill, exit C2; go through Hollywood Plaza and turn east on to Fung Tak Rd

👁 SIGHTS

👁 Tsim Sha Tsui

HONG KONG MUSEUM OF ART MUSEUM
Map p378 (香港藝術館; www.lcsd.gov.hk; 10 Salisbury Rd; adult/concession $10/5, Wed free; ⏱10am-6pm Fri-Wed, to 8pm Sat; ⛴Star Ferry, MTsim Sha Tsui, exit E) The excellent Hong Kong Museum of Art is a must for lovers of the fine as well as the applied arts. It has seven galleries spread over six floors, exhibiting Chinese antiquities, Chinese fine art, historical pictures and contemporary Hong Kong art; it also hosts temporary international exhibitions.

The seventh gallery houses the Xubaizhi collection of painting and calligraphy. Highlights include some exquisite ceramics in the **Chinese Antiques Gallery**; the **Historical Pictures Gallery**, with its 18th- and 19th-century Western-style paintings of Macau, Hong Kong and Guǎngzhōu; and the **Gallery of Chinese Fine Art**, which combines contemporary Chinese art and 20th-century collections of painting and calligraphy from Guǎngdōng. Audio guides are available for $10 and there are free English-language tours at 11am Tuesday to Sunday.

FORMER KCR CLOCK TOWER HISTORIC BUILDING
Map p378 (前九廣鐵路鐘樓; Tsim Sha Tsui Star Ferry Concourse, southern tip of Salisbury Rd; ⛴Star Ferry) This 44m-high clock tower (1915) was once part of the southern terminus of the Kowloon–Canton Railway (KCR). Operations moved to the modern train station at Hung Hom in late 1975. The station was demolished in 1978, though you can see a scale model of what it looked like at the Hong Kong Railway Museum (p175) in Tai Po in the New Territories.

HONG KONG CULTURAL CENTRE CULTURAL BUILDING
Map p378 (香港文化中心; www.lcsd.gov.hk; 10 Salisbury Rd; ⏱9am-11pm; ⛴Star Ferry) Overlooking the most beautiful part of the harbour, the aesthetically challenged and windowless Cultural Centre is a world-class venue containing a 2085-seat concert hall, a Grand Theatre that seats 1750, a studio theatre for up to 535, rehearsal studios and a decent foyer. On the building's south side

is the beginning of a viewing platform from where you can gain access to the Tsim Sha Tsui East Promenade (p138).

NATHAN ROAD STREET
Map p378 (彌敦道; MTsim Sha Tsui) Kowloon's main drag is a bit of a traffic- and pedestrian-choked scrum of electronics shops and jewellery stores. It's nonetheless an iconic Hong Kong scene stacked with seedy guesthouses rubbing shoulders with top-end hotels, and tenement blocks separated by patches of green. And it's completely safe – which is just as well since you won't be able to avoid criss-crossing it if you spend any time in the area.

FORMER MARINE POLICE HEADQUARTERS HISTORIC BUILDING
Map p378 (前水警總部; www.1881heritage.com; 2a Canton Rd, Tsim Sha Tsui; exhibition hall admission free; ⏱10am-10pm; ⛴Star Ferry) Built in 1884, this gorgeous Victorian-style complex is one of Hong Kong's four oldest government buildings. It was used continuously by the Hong Kong Marine Police except during WWII, when it was taken over by the Japanese navy.

In 2009 the complex was converted into a very glamorous and nakedly commercial property called 'Heritage 1881'. The developer removed some of the structures and turned the rest, including the stables, the pigeon houses and a bomb shelter into shops, restaurants and a small hotel. Why 1881? Because the real date contains the number '4' which has a similar pronunciation to 'death' in Chinese, and the property tycoon is superstitious.

OCEAN TERMINAL BUILDING
Map p378 (⬚www.oceanterminal.com.hk; Salisbury Rd, Tsim Sha Tsui; ⏱10am-9pm; ⛴Star Ferry) The building you see jutting 381m into the harbour is a major cruise terminal in Hong Kong, and a shopping mall. You enter it at the western end of the clock tower.

Originally Kowloon Wharf Pier (c 1886), the largest pier on this side of the harbour, it was later rebuilt into a cruise terminal and a multistorey shopping centre. In 1966 it reopened as the Ocean Terminal, which with its 112 shops and the $70 million that went into its expansion, was the largest shopping centre in all of Hong Kong. Today it's part of the massive Harbour City shopping complex that stretches for half a kilometre north along Canton Rd and offers

TST, BREEZE FOR THE FEET

The crowds and the traffic might obscure it, but Tsim Sha Tsui (TST) is one of the most walkable urban areas in Hong Kong. Architect Freddie Hai once put a ruler on the area's pavements and found most to be 250m to 300m long. Metro stations have a catchment radius of 500m, the rough equivalent of an eight-minute stroll. At half the length, streets in TST take only four minutes.

What's more, linking most of TST's meandering avenues are T-junctions (where one road joins another at right angles but does not cross it). The very layout of the T-junction creates a sense of neighbourly enclosure while dangling the promise of fresh horizons at every corner. So reaching Canton Rd from Peking Rd, would it be right to the Macau Ferry Terminal or left to the Space Museum?

Compare this to the sprawling, criss-crossing grid that is Yau Ma Tei – a fascinating area buzzing with life that could also alienate or disorient if you're new to it.

And good old Nathan Rd is never more than four blocks away no matter where you're at in TST. Born just shy of the harbour, Kowloon's earliest strip of asphalt runs past Yau Ma Tei to end in Mong Kok, offering the reassurance of a linear narrative in a labyrinthine plot, and a choice of many, many endings.

priceless views of Tsim Sha Tsui's western waterfront.

PENINSULA HONG KONG   HISTORIC BUILDING
Map p378 (香港半島酒店; www.peninsula.com; cnr Salisbury & Nathan Rds, Tsim Sha Tsui; MEast Tsim Sha Tsui, exit L3) The Peninsula (c 1928), in a thronelike building, is one of the world's great hotels. Though it was once called 'the finest hotel east of Suez', the Peninsula was in fact one of several prestigious hotels across Asia where everybody who was anybody stayed, lining up with (but not behind) the likes of the Raffles in Singapore and the Peace (then the Cathay) in Shànghǎi. Taking afternoon tea here is one of the best experiences in town – dress neatly and be prepared to queue for a table.

HONG KONG SPACE MUSEUM & THEATRE   MUSEUM
Map p378 (香港太空館; www.lcsd.gov.hk; 10 Salisbury Rd, Tsim Sha Tsui; adult/concession $10/5, Wed free; ⊙1-9pm Mon & Wed-Fri, 10am-9pm Sat, Sun & public holidays; MEast Tsim Sha Tsui, exit J) This golf-ball-shaped building on the waterfront houses two exhibition halls and a planetarium with a large concave screen. Films are mostly narrated in Cantonese but translations by headsets are available (☑2734 2722 for show times and prices). The museum has a dated feel, but kids and kidults should have a blast with the virtual paraglider and 'moon-walking'. The museum shop sells dehydrated 'astronaut' ice cream in three flavours.

TOP CHOICE MIDDLE ROAD CHILDREN'S PLAYGROUND   PARK
Map p380 (中間道兒童遊樂場; Middle Rd, Tsim Sha Tsui; ⊙7am-11pm; MEast Tsim Sha Tsui, exit K) Accessible via a sweep of stairs from Chatham Rd South, this hidden gem atop the Tsim Sha Tsui East MTR station has play facilities, shaded seating and views of the waterfront. On weekdays it's the quiet backyard playground of the ethnic minorities living nearby, but on weekends it's filled with children and picnickers of as many ethnicities as there are ways to go down a slide.

The park's eastern exit is connected to the handsome **Tsim Sha Tsui East Waterfront Podium Garden** (尖沙咀東海濱平台花園; Map p380) with its tasteful granite structures and white sail canopies. On weekends skateboarders and traceurs come here to practise. The podium sits on top of the Tsim Sha Tsui East (Mody Rd) Bus Terminus.

SIGNAL HILL GARDEN & BLACKHEAD POINT TOWER   PARK
Map p380 (訊號山公園和訊號塔; Minden Row, Tsim Sha Tsui; ⊙tower 9-11am & 4-6pm; MEast Tsim Sha Tsui, exit K) The views from the top of this knoll are quite spectacular, and if it were the 1900s the ships in the harbour would probably be returning your gaze – a copper ball in the handsome Edwardian-style tower was dropped at 1pm daily so seafarers could adjust their chronometers. The garden is perched above the Middle Rd Children's Playground. Enter from Minden Row (off Mody Rd).

PARK PARK

九龍公園; www.lcsd.gov.hk; Nathan ...s, Tsim Sha Tsui; ☺6am-midnight; ...Tsui, exit C2) Built on the site ...cks for Indian soldiers in the colonial army, Kowloon Park is an oasis of greenery and a refreshing escape from the hustle and bustle of Tsim Sha Tsui. Pathways and walls criss-cross the grass, birds hop around in cages, and towers and ancient banyan trees dot the landscape. In the morning the older set practise taichi amid the serene surrounds, and on Sunday afternoon Kung Fu Corner stages martial arts displays, with 'play-in' sessions for visitors.

FOOK TAK ANCIENT TEMPLE TEMPLE

Map p378 (福德古廟; 30 Haiphong Rd, Tsim Sha Tsui; ☺6am-8pm; MTsim Sha Tsui, exit C2) Tsim Sha Tsui's only temple is a smoky hole in the wall with a hot tin roof. Little is known about its ancestry except that it was a built in the Qing dynasty and renovated in 1900. Before the war worshippers of its Earth God were the coolies from Kowloon Wharf nearby, where the Ocean Terminal now stands. Today most incense offerers are white-haired octogenarians – the temple specialises in longevity.

HAIPHONG RD TEMPORARY MARKET MARKET

Next door to Fook Tak Ancient Temple is a 'temporary' wet market that's been temping there for the last three decades. It looks sleepy from the outside, but as you venture past the florists, vegetable vendors and halal meat stalls catering to the Muslim community, you'll see a cacophonous sprawl of *dai pai dongs* (see p37), including Tak Fat Beef Balls (p154).

KOWLOON MOSQUE & ISLAMIC CENTRE MOSQUE

Map p378 (九龍清真寺; 105 Nathan Rd; Tsim Sha Tsui; ☺5am-10pm; MTsim Sha Tsui, exit C2) This mosque, with its dome and carved marble, is the largest Islamic house of worship in Hong Kong. It serves the territory's 70,000-odd Muslims, more than half of whom are Chinese, and can accommodate 2000 worshippers. Muslims are welcome to attend services here, but non-Muslims should ask permission to enter. Remember to remove your footwear.

FORMER KOWLOON BRITISH SCHOOL HISTORIC BUILDING

Map p378 (前九龍英童學校; www.amo.gov.hk; 136 Nathan Rd, Tsim Sha Tsui; MTsim Sha Tsui, exit B1) The oldest surviving school building for the children of Hong Kong's expatriate community is a listed Victorian-style building that now houses the **Antiquities and Monuments Office** (古物古蹟辦事處). Constructed in 1902, it was subsequently modified to incorporate breezy verandahs and high ceilings, prompted possibly by the frequent fainting spells suffered by its young occupants.

TOP CHOICE ST ANDREW'S ANGLICAN CHURCH CHURCH

Map p378 (聖安德烈堂; www.standrews.org.hk; 138 Nathan Rd, Tsim Sha Tsui; ☺7.30am-10.30pm; MTsim Sha Tsui, exit B1) Hidden on the top of a knoll between the Former Kowloon British School and the Hong Kong Observatory, is a charming building in English Gothic style – it's Kowloon's oldest Protestant church and it's dedicated to the patron saint of Scotland. Built in 1905 in granite and red brick, the church was turned into a Shinto shrine during the Japanese occupation. Nearby you'll see the handsome former vicarage with its columned balconies (c 1909). The church is accessed from the eastern side of Nathan Rd via steps or the slope encircling a semicircular space fronted by an old stone wall.

HONG KONG OBSERVATORY HISTORIC SITE

Map p378 (香港天文台; ☎2926 8200; www.hko. gov.hk; 134a Nathan Rd, Tsim Sha Tsui; MTsim Sha Tsui, exit B1) This historic monument, built in 1883, is sadly not open to the public, except for two days in March every year (see website for dates). It continues to monitor Hong Kong's weather and sends out those frightening signals when a typhoon is heading for the territory.

HONG KONG MUSEUM OF HISTORY MUSEUM

See p137.

HONG KONG SCIENCE MUSEUM MUSEUM

Map p380 (香港科學館; ☎2732 3232; http:// hk.science.museum/eindex.php; 2 Science Museum Rd; adult/concession $25/12.50, Wed free; ☺1-9pm Mon-Wed & Fri, 10am-9pm Sat, Sun & public holidays; MTsim Sha Tsui, exit B2) Illustrating the fundamental workings of technology, such as computers and telecommunications, and practical demonstrations of

START **KOWLOON BRITISH SCHOOL**
END **KOWLOON UNION CHURCH**
DISTANCE **2.5KM**
DURATION **TWO HOURS**

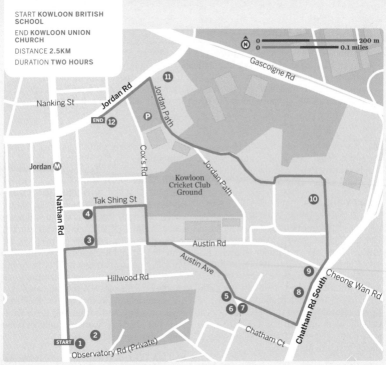

Neighbourhood Walk
Vestiges of Local & Colonial Life in Tsim Sha Tsui

Tsim Sha Tsui's lesser-known northern end is a treasure trove of postwar buildings and colonial relics. Start your journey at ❶ **Kowloon British School** and ❷ **St Andrew's Church**, respectively Kowloon's oldest 'international' school and Anglican church.

Further north on Nathan Rd, turn right into Austin Rd, a former stronghold of middle-class Shanghainese. Check out ❸ **Pak On Building** (百安大廈, 105 Austin Rd), with its lobby littered with shops, including, at the far end near ❹ **Tak Shing St**, a liquor store that stocks absinth.

Further down, Austin Rd branches out into Austin Ave. At the corner, you'll see a late-1960s building with rounded balconies spiralling skyward. Exploring Austin Ave, you'll find ❺ **Carnival Mansion** (嘉華大廈, 15B Austin Ave) has a courtyard where you can stare up at a vortex of rickety postwar homes. If you enter a building, you'll see yellow terrazzo stairs with green balustrades made by Shanghainese craftsmen half a century ago.

Next door, the chaotic ❻ **Success** (成功文具行) is possibly the oldest surviving stationery shop in TST. Here you'll also spot the curious ❼ **'triangular public toilet'** (三角公廁), junction of Kimberley Rd and Austin Ave) which is also a power substation.

Continue down Austin Ave. Making a left on Chatham Rd South, you'll see ❽ **Rosary Church** (玫瑰堂), Kowloon's oldest Catholic church, then ❾ **St Mary's Canossian College** (嘉諾撒聖瑪利書院), built around 1900. At the canon-guarded gate of ❿ **Gun Club Hill Barracks** (槍會山軍營, 127 Austin Rd), now occupied by the People's Liberation Army (PLA), turn right into leafy Jordan Path.

Note how functional buildings loom up on your right, while the manicured lawns of the colonial recreation clubs unfurl on your left. Nearing Jordan Rd, you'll see the ⓫ **PLA hospital** (解放軍駐軍醫院) with its darkened windows. Crossing Cox's Rd takes you to a Victorian-style Anglican church, ⓬ **Kowloon Union Church** (九龍佑寧堂, 4 Jordan Rd), built in 1927.

BEWARE: FAKE MONKS

Real monks never solicit money. But during your stay, you may be approached in temples, on streets, even in bars and shopping malls by conartists in monk outfits toting stone chimes or other props, who'll try to make you part with your money. The more aggressive ones may offer fake Buddhist amulets for sale, or force 'blessings' on you then pester you for a donation. When accosted, tell them 'no' firmly and ignore them.

the laws of energy, physics and chemistry, the Hong Kong Science Museum is a great hands-on experience capable of entertaining adults as well as children.

ROSARY CHURCH   CHURCH

Map p380 (玫瑰堂; ☑2368 0980; http://rosarychurch.catholic.org.hk; 125 Chatham Rd South, Tsim Sha Tsui; ☺7:30am-7:30pm; ⓂJordan, exit D) Kowloon's oldest Catholic church, Rosary Church was built in 1905 with money donated by a Portuguese doctor in Hong Kong, initially for the benefit of the Catholics in an Indian battalion stationed in Kowloon, and later for the burgeoning local Catholic community. It has a classic Gothic style with a yellowish facade reminiscent of the churches in Macau.

⊙ Yau Ma Tei

TEMPLE STREET NIGHT MARKET   MARKET
See p139.

TIN HAU TEMPLE   TEMPLE

Map p382 (cnr Temple St & Public Square St, Yau Ma Tei; ☺8am-5pm; ⓂYau Ma Tei, exit C) This large, incense-filled sanctuary built in the 19th century is one of Hong Kong's most famous temples dedicated to the goddess of the sea. The public square before it is Yau Ma Tei's communal heart where fishermen once laid out their hemp ropes to sun next to Chinese banyans that today shade chess players and elderly men. **Yau Ma Tei Police Station** (油麻地警署; 627 Canton Rd) is a listed blue and white structure one block to the east along Public Square St.

HONG KONG INTERNATIONAL
HOBBY & TOY MUSEUM   MUSEUM

Map p382 (香港國際玩具博物館; www.hktoymuseum.org; 330 Shanghai St, Yau Ma Tei; ☺2-7pm, closed Tue; ⓂYau Ma Tei station, exit C) The collection here is by no means overwhelming but there are quite a number of Gundam robots.

WHOLESALE FRUIT MARKET   MARKET

Map p382 (油麻地果欄; cnr Shek Lung St & Reclamation St, Yau Ma Tei; ☺2-6am; ⓂYau Ma Tei, exit B2, turn right) The historic and still operating Yau Ma Tei Wholesale Fruit Market, founded in 1913, is bounded by Ferry St, Waterloo Rd and Reclamation St with Shek Lung St running through it. This charming cluster of one- or two-storey brick and stone buildings with pre-WWII signboards is a hive of activity from 4am to 6am. You'll see trucks loading and offloading fresh fruit, and bare-backed workers manoeuvring piles of boxes under the moon.

YAU MA TEI THEATRE   BUILDING

Map p382 (油麻地戲院; ☑2264 8108; www.lcsd.gov.hk/ymtt; ⓂYau Ma Tei, exit B2) Two gorgeous historic buildings have been converted into a performance and training centre for Cantonese opera. Yau Ma Tei Theatre, adjacent to the Wholesale Fruit Market, was built in the late 1920s. For decades, its art deco interiors kept many a coolie and rickshaw driver entertained, but losing business to modern cinemas in the '80s, it began showing erotic films and selling porn videos to stay afloat. The neoclassical **Red Brick House** (紅磚屋) was the Engineer's Office of the Former Pumping Station (前水務署抽水站工程師辦公室, 8 Waterloo Rd) built in 1895. The new venue has a 300-seat auditorium, a dressing room and rehearsal facilities. To book tickets call ☑2374 2598.

BRUCE LEE CLUB   MUSEUM

Map p382 (李小龍會; ☑2771 7093; www.bruceleeclub.com; Shop 160-161, In's Point, 530 Nathan Rd, Mong Kok; ☺1-9pm; ⓂYau Ma Tei, exit A1) Founded by Bruce Lee's fans, this mini-museum/souvenir shop has action figures, film publications and other memorabilia related to the kung fu icon.

⊙ Mong Kok

YUEN PO STREET BIRD
GARDEN & FLOWER MARKET   PARK, MARKET

Map p383 (園圃街雀鳥花園 & 花墟; Yuen Po St/Boundary St; ⊙7am-8pm; ⓂPrince Edward, exit B1) In this enchanting corner of Mong Kok, you will find a handful of old men out 'walking' their caged songbirds. Stick around long enough and you should see birds being fed squirming caterpillars with chopsticks. There are also feathered creatures for sale, along with elaborate cages carved from teak and bamboo. Adjacent to the garden is the flower market on Flower Market Rd, which theoretically keeps the same hours but only gets busy after 10am, especially on Sunday.

C&G ARTPARTMENT   GALLERY

Map p383 (☏2390 9332; www.candg-artpartment.com; 3rd fl, 222 Sai Yeung Choi St South, Mong Kok; ⊙2-7.30pm Thu-Mon; ⓂPrince Edward, exit B2) This exciting new space behind the Pioneer Centre (始創中心) in Mong Kok is very much involved in nurturing the local art scene and representing artists who are politically and socially minded. It's opened by artists Gum and Clara, who also work as a social worker and an art teacher. The gallery has erratic opening hours so call before you go.

⊙ New Kowloon

FREE LEI CHENG UK HAN TOMB
MUSEUM   MUSEUM

(李鄭屋漢墓博物館; www.lcsd.gov.hk; 41 Tonkin St; ⊙10am-6pm Mon-Wed, Fri & Sat, 1-6pm Sun; ⓂCheung Sha Wan, exit A3) Don't expect a terracotta army, but for those interested in the area's ancient history, this is a significant burial vault dating from the Eastern Han dynasty (AD 25–220). The tomb consists of four barrel-vaulted brick chambers set around a domed central chamber. It's encased in a concrete shell for protection and visitors can only peep through a plastic window.

JOCKEY CLUB CREATIVE
ARTS CENTRE   ARTS CENTRE

(賽馬會創意藝術中心; www.jccac.org.hk; 30 Pak Tin St, Shek Kip Mei; ⊙10am-10pm; ⓂShek Kip Mei, exit C) Over 150 artists have moved into these factory premises that used to churn out shoes and watches. Many studios are closed on weekdays, but you can visit the breezy communal areas and **G.O.D. Street Culture Museum & Store** (Unit L2-09; ⊙12.30-6.30pm, closed Mon & Tue), which has an attractive 'old Hong Kong' display and regular opening hours.

KOWLOON WALLED CITY PARK   PARK

(九龍寨城公園; www.lcsd.gov.hk/parks/wcp/en/index.php; Tung Tau Tsuen, Tung Tsing, Carpenter & Junction Rds; ⊙park 6.30am-11pm,

KOWLOON SIGHTS

HONG KONG'S WORKING ARTISTS

It's romantic to visit an artists' village but unless you go during the annual open-studio events, you may not bump into any artists. The majority of them have day jobs. In an expensive city with bills to pay or families to support, they return to their studios only at night or at the weekends.

While some artists don't mind visitors, many prefer to work in solitude, even if they leave their doors ajar for the breeze or a friendly cat. Some artists may even live in the studios, so respect their privacy. However, your visit to these places can still be very rewarding. Spaces that open year-round include commercial galleries (some stocking the works of the artists), bookstores, cafes and workshops running classes for the public.

Some studios open by appointment only, so check the websites and make contact before you go. All of these art hubs are in interesting buildings – abandoned factories and cavernous warehouses (Jockey Club Creative Arts Centre and Chai Wan, p113), a former abattoir (Cattle Depot Artist Village, p149) and a '60s tenement building (Foo Tak Building, p124). And if you chance upon an open door during your rambles, you can always ask if you're welcome.

START Ⓜ PRINCE EDWARD, EXIT A

END Ⓜ JORDAN, EXIT A

DISTANCE **4.5KM**

DURATION **TWO HOURS**

Neighbourhood Walk

Kowloon's Teeming Market Streets

➡ A 10-minute walk away from Ⓜ Prince Edward (exit A), **① Yuen Po Street Bird Garden** is the gathering place for mostly old men who air their caged birds here and feed them grasshoppers with chopsticks. A little further along, Flower Market Rd is lined with fragrant and exotic blooms and plants.

At the end of the street, take a left turn onto Sai Yee St, then right onto Prince Edward Rd West and then a left turn onto Tung Choi St: the first couple of blocks are dominated by bicycle shops, but they then give way to the **② Goldfish Market**, a dozen or so shops trading in these extravagantly hued fish. You'll see an amazing variety, with the real rarities commanding high prices.

Sharpen your elbows. The **③ Tung Choi St market**, also known as the Ladies' Market, is crammed with shoppers and stalls selling mostly inexpensive clothing. Refuel on Taiwanese at Tai Pak before continuing south.

Beneath the naked light bulbs, hundreds of stalls at the **④ Temple Street Night Market** sell a vast array of booty from bric-a-brac to clothes, shoes, luggage and accessories. Turn right at Shanghai St, cut down Hi Lung Lane to Temple St and turn right. The market runs right down to Jordan Rd.

Fragrant smoke curls from incense spirals at **⑤ Tin Hau Temple**. Fortune-tellers nearby use everything from tarot cards, palmistry and even tame sparrows to deliver their predictions. Chinese opera singers sometimes also practice in the area.

A great place to pick up an inexpensive trinket, the large covered **⑥ Jade Market** contains dozens of stalls selling jade, the much-valued precious stone. At Jordan Rd turn east, then south into Nathan Rd to find Jordan MTR station.

ABCS OF TAO

Taoism is an indigenous Chinese religion that thrived from the Tang to the Ming dynasties. Though never declared a national religion, its influence has been ubiquitous in all aspects of Chinese life. In contemporary Hong Kong, construction projects are preceded by a ritual performed to appease the deities of nature – in short, for good feng shui, a Taoist-influenced belief. During the first two weeks of the Lunar New Year, millions pay their respects at Taoist temples. The majority of funeral rites in Hong Kong are presided over by Taoist priests, and Cheung Chau's famous Bun Festival has roots in Taoist ceremonies. Unlike evangelical religions stressing crusading and personal conversion, Taoism addresses the needs of daily life such as cures for illnesses, protection from evil spirits and funerary requirements. It does not attempt to sublimate the mundane, which is why Taoist temples tend to be more decorative and colourful than Buddhist places of worship.

exhibition room 10am-6pm closed Wed; 🚋1 from Star Ferry pier, alight opposite the park at Tung Tau Tsuen Rd) This attractive park was the site of a Chinese garrison in the 19th century. Excluded from the lease of the New Territories, the 3-acre enclave became a lawless slum that technically remained part of China throughout British rule. It was infamous for its gangs, prostitution and drug dens. The British eventually relocated the 30,000 residents and built a park in its place. There's a model of the walled city on display at the park.

SIK SIK YUEN WONG TAI SIN TEMPLE
TEMPLE
See p140.

CHI LIN NUNNERY
BUDDHIST
See p141.

CATTLE DEPOT ARTIST VILLAGE
VILLAGE
(牛棚藝術村; 63 Ma Tau Kok Rd, To Kwa Wan; 🚋106, 12A or 5C to Ma Tau Kok Rd) A century-old slaughterhouse deep in the entrails of Kowloon has reincarnated into an artists' village, its red-brick buildings housing studios and exhibition halls. Though many are closed during the day, the depot is an interesting place to explore. To ensure the doorman lets you in, call a tenant ahead of time to let them know you're coming. Friendly **1a Space** (📞2529 0087; www.oneaspace.org.hk; Unit 14, ⏰noon-8pm Tue-Sun) keeps regular opening times. And so does **Artist Commune** (藝術公社; 📞2104 3322; www.artist-commune.com; Unit 12; ⏰noon-8pm Tue-Sun). The village is in the northern part of To Kwa Wan, an area on the east coast of Kowloon. You'll see a Town Gas storage facility close to the village.

SAM KA TSUEN SEAFOOD PRECINCT
NEIGHBOURHOOD
(三家村避風塘; Ⓜ Yau Tong, exit A2) The 'village' of Lei Yue Mun is one of Hong Kong's prime seafood venues; around two-dozen fish restaurants line winding Lei Yue Mun Praya Rd overlooking the typhoon shelter. The area is a lively place to dine by the water at night and is always busy. After leaving the MTR, follow Cha Kwo Ling Rd and Shung Shun St south for 15 minutes or catch green minibus 24M from outside the station. Bus 14C links the Yau Tong Centre halfway down the hill with the Kwun Tong MTR station.

EATING

Kowloon doesn't have quite as many upmarket restaurants as Hong Kong Island but there's a riveting assortment of ethnic eateries to fit all budgets in Tsim Sha Tsui. For hearty local fare, head for Yau Ma Tei or Mong Kok. Kowloon City is renowned for its solid Thai and Chiu Chow eateries.

Tsim Sha Tsui

TOP CHOICE **DONG LAI SHUN**
CHINESE $$$
Map p380 (東來順; 📞2733 2020; www.rghk.com.hk; B2, The Royal Garden, 69 Mody Rd, Tsim Sha Tsui; set lunch $200-400, set dinner $300-450; ⏰lunch & dinner; Ⓜ East Tsim Sha Tsui, exit P2) While the mainland outlets of this Běijīng chain are of varying quality, this Hong Kong branch is excellent. Besides Northern Chinese dishes which are superbly executed, its

phonebook of a menu also has Shanghainese and Sichuanese favourites, and even Cantonese seafood. Dong Lai Shun is famous for its mutton hotpot – this involves dunking paper-thin slices of mutton into boiling water and eating it with sesame sauce and other condiments. The atmosphere is a little formal but the service is warm.

TYPHOON SHELTER HING KEE RESTAURANT
CANTONESE $$$

Map p378 (避風塘興記; ☑2722 0022; 1st fl Bowa House, 180 Nathan Rd, Tsim Sha Tsui; meals $300-1000; ◎6pm-5am; Ⓜ Jordan, exit D) This celebrity haunt is run by a feisty fisherman's daughter who's known for her brilliant dishes prepared the way they were on sampans. The signature crabs smothered in a mountain of fried garlic are a wonder to behold. If you take the garlic home, it goes well with congee or noodles the next day. The service can be a little edgy. Be sure you know the price of every dish before you order.

WOODLANDS
INDIAN, VEGETARIAN $

Map p380 (活蘭印度素食; ☑2369 3718; Upper Ground fl, 16 & 17 Wing On Plaza, 62 Mody Rd; meals $55-130; ◎noon-3.30pm & 6.30-10.30pm; Ⓜ East Tsim Sha Tsui, exit P1; ☑) Located above a department store, good old Woodlands offers excellent-value Indian vegetarian food to compatriots and the odd local. Dithering gluttons should order the thali meals, which are served on a round metal plate with 10 tiny dishes, a dessert and bread.

CHICKEN HOF & SOJU KOREAN
KOREAN $

Map p380 (李家 Chicken; ☑2375 8080; Ground fl, 84 Kam Kok Mansion, Kimberley Rd, Tsim Sha Tsui; meals from $150; ◎5pm-4am; Ⓜ Jordan, exit D) This place with darkened windows may look dodgy from the outside, but in fact it's a Korean gastropub with a friendly owner who'll holler a greeting when customers enter. The excellent fried chicken, made with a light and crispy batter, comes in five versions. Traditional fare like Korean barbecue is also available. Whatever you order, steer clear of the pupa soup. Ours tasted so musty, we thought we were eating a library.

KIMBERLEY CHINESE RESTAURANT
CHINESE $$$

Map p380 (君怡閣中菜廳; ☑2369 8212; M fl, Kimberley Hotel, 28 Kimberley Rd, Tsim Sha Tsui; meals $300-600; Ⓜ Tsim Sha Tsui, exit B1) This restaurant is famous for the Kimberley Pig – a 30-day piglet stuffed with sticky rice that's

been cooked with shallots and garlic, then roasted whole. Each piglet ($900) will feed at least five hungry people. You need to order it two days in advance, and pay a (negotiable) deposit of $200 the day before. Still hungry? Try the beef ribs.

STABLES GRILL
EUROPEAN $$$

Map p378 (☑3988 0104; www.hulletthouse.com; 1881 Heritage, Hullett House, 2a Canton Rd, Tsim Sha Tsui; meals from $400; ◎noon-10.30pm; 🚢 Star Ferry) The home of horses of the Former Marine Police Headquarters is now an atmospheric restaurant with tables spilling out on to a beautiful garden. Welcoming visitors are the two original stable doors, which are thoughtfully matched by vintage woods inside the restaurant, including panels salvaged from an old boat. The menu features grilled foods and a variety of tapas and pastas. The grilled scallops were very good. Service was mediocre but the setting more than made up for it.

GOOD SATAY
SOUTHEAST ASIAN $

Map p380 (好時沙嗲; ☑2739 9808; Shop 144-148, 1st fl, Houston Centre, 63 Mody Rd, Tsim Sha Tsui; meals from $70; ◎noon-10pm; Ⓜ Tsim Sha Tsui, exit G) This place on the 1st floor of a dowdy shopping and office complex doesn't look promising but its Southeast Asian cooking is great value for money. We loved the Hainan chicken rice, stir-fried turnip cake, and satays. It's packed at lunch.

GADDI'S
FRENCH $$$

Map p378 (☑2315 3171; www.peninsula.com/Hong_Kong; 1st fl, The Peninsula, 19-21 Salisbury Rd, Tsim Sha Tsui; set lunch/dinner from $450/1500; ◎lunch & dinner; Ⓜ East Tsim Sha Tsui, exit L3) Gaddi's, which opened just after WWII, was one of those restaurants where wealthy families celebrated their special occasions. Today the classical decor may be a tad stuffy, the live Filipino band gratuitous, but the food – traditional French with contemporary touches – is without a doubt still among the best in town.

TOP CHOICE YOGA INTERACTIVE VEGETARIAN
VEGETARIAN, ASIAN $

Map p380 (互動瑜伽素食; ☑9327 7275, 3422 1195; www.yogafitnesshk.com; 15B, Hillview Ct, 30 Hillwood Rd, Tsim Sha Tsui; meals $160; Ⓜ Jordan, exit D; ☑) This place only opens two or three nights a week and usually you're required to book a week in advance. That said, if you're lucky enough to catch them

151

when they already have a large booking and there's only one or two of you, they might be able to fit you in sooner. The Asian vegetarian dishes, cooked by an experienced yoga instructor, are among the best in town and portions are very generous. Call for details. Take the lift to the 14th floor and ascend one flight of stairs.

家嫂 SOUTHEAST ASIAN $

(4C, Ground fl, Windsor Mansion, 17 Austin Ave, Tsim Sha Tsui; meals from $35; [M]Jordan, exit D; [✆]) The name of this little green shop is 'ga sou', meaning, 'sister-in-law' (wife of one's elder brothers), and its Singaporean laksa noodles are among the better ones in town. The Thai Tom Yum version isn't too shabby either. In fact, most of its noodle dishes are tasty, though the level of authenticity may vary. Service can be less than attentive.

CHING YAN LEE CHIU CHOW RESTAURANT
CHIU CHOW $$

Map p380 (正仁利潮州菜館; [✆]2366 6556; 10a Hau Fook St, Tsim Sha Tsui; meals from $250; [◷]11:30am-midnight; [M]Tsim Sha Tsui, exit B1) Resist the upsell hard sell at this family-run establishment. If staff can't sell you the shark's fin and the cold crab, they'll suggest adding conch meat to your veggies, which will inflate your bill by $500. So be firm. Stick with the menu or agree on the price beforehand. All said, the Chiu Chow food here is excellent.

GOLDEN BULL
VIETNAMESE $$

Map p378 (金牛苑越南菜館; [✆]2730 4866; Shop 101, 1st fl, Ocean Centre, Harbour City, 3-9 Canton Rd, Tsim Sha Tsui; set lunch from $150, dinner from $220; [◷]noon-11.30pm; [M]Tsim Sha Tsui, exit C1) The families who descend on this place are coming for harbour views and the tasty Vietnamese and fusion food. The beef *pho* (soup) is excellent; there's a Wagyu version too.

MANDARIN CHICKEN RICE
ASIAN $

Map p380 (文華雞飯; Ground fl, Leader Commercial Bldg, 54 Hillwood Rd, Tsim Sha Tsui; meals $50-80; [◷]noon-9.30pm; [M]Jordan, exit D) This basic eatery sells only one thing – Hainan-style chicken rice – and its variations, and they're done well. The chicken is succulent, the rice aromatic and the condiments add the right kick.

STEAK HOUSE
INTERNATIONAL $$$

Map p380 ([✆]2313 2323; http://hongkong-ic.din ing.intercontinental.com; InterContinental Hong Kong, 18 Salisbury Rd; meals from $400; [◷]6-11pm

Mon-Sat, noon-2.30pm Sun; [M]East Tsim Sha Tsui, exit J) At this first-rate steakhouse, imported beef exhilarates even without the trimmings (exotic salts and mustards, gourmet steak knives), and the salad bar ($300 per person) is a garden of delight. **Harbourside** ([✆]2313 2495; [◷]6am-midnight), in the same hotel, has great pizzas, Western and Asian dishes and a popular Sunday brunch (noon to 2.30pm).

ZIAFAT
MIDDLE EASTERN, INDIAN $

Map p378 ([✆]2312 1015, 6th fl, Harilela Mansion; 81 Nathan Rd, Tsim Sha Tsui; [◷]11am-midnight; [M]Tsim Sha Tsui, exit R; [✆]) This halal restaurant serves up decent Arabic and Indian food such as falafel, lentil soup, kebabs and curries. It's in an oldish building along with budget hostels and guesthouses but the restaurant is clean, quiet and humbly furnished with Arabic art and calligraphy.

AL MOLO
ITALIAN $$$

Map p378 ([✆]2730 7900; www.diningconcepts. com.hk; Shop G63, Ground fl, Ocean Terminal, Harbour City, 7-23 Canton Rd, Tsim Sha Tsui; meals $350-900; [◷]noon-11pm; [⛴]Star Ferry) The first Hong Kong venture of New York–based chef and restaurateur Michael White has brick walls, iron fittings and an alfresco area where you can savour homemade semolina pasta with seafood to the delicious views of the Tsim Sha Tsui harbourfront.

PARAMITA VEGETARIAN HOUSE
VEGETARIAN, CHINESE $

Map p378 (波羅密素食; [✆]2736 3939; 3rd fl, Daily House, 35-37 Haiphong Rd, Tsim Sha Tsui; set lunch $38-55; [◷]11am-11pm; [M]Tsim Sha Tsui, exit A1; [✆]) Paramita is creative with mock meat which comes stewed, fried, stir-fried, in salads and skewered. There are abundant other choices too. Set lunches are not available on the first and 15th day of each lunar month when many omnivores go vegetarian for religious or personal reasons.

TANDOORI NIGHTS
INDIAN $

Map p380 ([✆]2971 0009; www.tandoorinightshk. com; 2nd fl, 22-24 Cameron Rd, Tsim Sha Tsui; meals from $160; [◷]lunch & dinner; [M]Tsim Sha Tsui, exit B1; [✆]) Tandoori Nights (formerly Bombay Dreams) serves tasty Indian fare in clean, upmarket surrounds. The daily lunch buffet at $90 is very popular and you can order Cobra or Kingfisher to go with it. There's live music by Ghazal singers from 8pm that can drown out your conversation if you're seated close to the stage.

KOWLOON EATING

DOUGLAS KEISTER/CORBIS ©

1. Avenue of the Stars (p138)
This tribute to Hong Kong's film industry, once known as the 'Hollywood of the Far East', is part of the Tsim Sha Tsui East Promenade.

2. Peninsula Hong Kong (p143)
Take afternoon tea in the Peninsula (c 1928), one of the world's great hotels.

3. Yuen Po Street Bird Garden (p147)
Watch locals 'walking' their caged songbirds amid stalls selling birds and elaborate wooden cages.

ANDREW J LOTERTON/THE PENINSULA HONG KONG ©

T'ANG COURT
CANTONESE, DIM SUM **$$$**

Map p378 (唐閣; ☎2375 1133; http://hongkong.langhamhotels.com; Langham Hotel, 8 Peking Rd, Tsim Sha Tsui; lunch $200-2000, dinner $500-2000; ⊙lunch & dinner; ⓂTsim Sha Tsui, exit L4; ✍) As befitting a restaurant named after China's greatest dynasty, T'ang Court has mastered the art of Cantonese cooking, from baked oysters on the half-shell to an honest plate of greens. The atmosphere is hushed and the decor includes deep-pile carpets and heavy silks. If that seems too formal, rest assured, the polished service will make you feel right at home, like an emperor in his palace. T'ang Court has one Michelin star.

YÈ SHANGHAI
SHANGHAINESE, DIM SUM **$$$**

Map p378 (夜上海; ☎2376 3322; www.elite-concepts.com; 6th fl, Marco Polo Hotel, Harbour City, Canton Rd, Tsim Sha Tsui; meals $300-600; ⊙lunch & dinner; ⓂEast Tsim Sha Tsui, exit L4) The name means 'Shànghǎi Nights'. Dark woods and subtle lighting inspired by 1920s Shànghǎi fill the air with romance. The modern Shanghainese dishes are also exquisite. The only exception to this Jiangnan harmony is the Cantonese dim sum being served at lunch, though that too is wonderful. Ye Shanghai has two Michelin stars.

BRANTO
VEGETARIAN, INDIAN **$**

Map p378 (印度素食餐廳; ☎2366 8171; 1st fl, 9-11 Lock Rd, Tsim Sha Tsui; meals $50-120; ⊙lunch & dinner; ⓂTsim Sha Tsui, exit E) Branto offers great vegetarian Indian food, basic service, basic surroundings and nonstop Indian music videos.

DIN TAI FUNG
TAIWANESE, NOODLES **$$**

Map p378 (鼎泰豐; www.dintaifung.com.tw; Shop 130, 3rd fl, 30 Canton Rd, Tsim Sha Tsui; meals $120-300; ⊙11.30am-10.30pm; ⓂTsim Sha Tsui, exit C1; ✍) Whether it's comfort food or a carb fix you're craving, the dumplings and noodles at this Michelin-starred Taiwanese chain will do the trick. Queues are the norm and it doesn't take reservations.

TAK FAT BEEF BALLS
NOODLES **$**

Map p378 (德發牛肉丸; Haiphong Rd Temporary Market, Haiphong Rd, Tsim Sha Tsui; ⊙9am-8pm; ⓂTsim Sha Tsui, exit A1) This famous *dai pai dong* (see p37) is one of a handful operating in this market. Pick a seat in the sprawl and order the beef ball noodles ($22), which are famed for their bounce and their hint of dried mandarin peel. There's a version with beef innards too.

SWEET DYNASTY
CANTONESE, DESSERTS **$$**

Map p378 (糖朝; ☎2199 7799; 100 Canton Rd, Tsim Sha Tsui; meals $70-$300; ⊙8am-midnight, to 11pm Fri; ⓂTsim Sha Tsui, exit A1; ✍) From a dessert-and-congee shop, the Sweet Dynasty has evolved into a mini empire with locations all over Asia, its extensive menu encompassing all popular Cantonese dishes. But some say its desserts, noodles and congee are still the best. It's clean and modern but gets crowded when busy.

FOOK LAM MOON
CANTONESE, DIM SUM **$$$**

Map p380 (福臨門; ☎2366 0286; www.fooklammoon-grp.com; Shop 8, 1st fl, 53-59 Kimberley Rd, Tsim Sha Tsui; meals $400-2000; ⊙lunch & dinner; ⓂTsim Sha Tsui, exit B1) FLM is dubbed 'celeb canteen' by locals. But even if you're not rich and famous, FLM will treat you as if you were. The huge menu contains costly items such as abalone which would shoot your bill up to at least $1000 per head. But no one will snub you if you stick to the dim sum (from $60 a basket), which is heavenly and available only at lunch. There's a branch in **Wan Chai** (☎2866 0663; Shop 3, Newman House, 35-45 Johnston Rd; ⓂWan Chai, exit B2).

SABATINI
ITALIAN **$$$**

Map p380 (☎2733 2000; www.rghk.com.hk; 3rd fl, Royal Garden Hotel, 69 Mody Rd, Tsim Sha Tsui; lunch $200-800, dinner $600-900; ⊙lunch & dinner; ⓂEast Tsim Sha Tsui, exit P2) One of two branches of Sabatini of Rome, this place serves up excellent Italian favourites in a jovial, faux-rustic setting. Want romance with your risotto? An avuncular Filipino trio will serenade you at your table till you're weak at the knees. Booking advised.

SPRING DEER
NORTHERN CHINESE **$$$**

Map p380 (鹿鳴春飯店; ☎2366 4012; 1st fl, 42 Mody Rd, Tsim Sha Tsui; meals $80-550; ⊙lunch & dinner; ⓂTsim Sha Tsui, exit N2) Hong Kong's most authentic northern-style roasted lamb is served here. The Peking duck is decent, but the service can be about as welcoming as a Běijīng winter, c 1967. Booking is essential.

✖ Yau Ma Tei & Mong Kok

ONE DIM SUM
DIM SUM **$**

Map p383 (一點心; Ground fl, Kenwood Mansion, 15 Playing Field Rd, Mong Kok; meals $30-50; ⊙11-1am; ⓂPrince Edward, exit A) One of two cheap and cheery dim sum places in town with a Michelin star. Customers place orders by ticking their selections of 45 items that also include soup, congee and rice steamed with chicken or spare ribs. There's always a line at the door but the wait is usually under 30 minutes.

GOOD HOPE NOODLE
NOODLES **$**

Map p383 (好旺角麵家; ☎2393 9036; 146 Sai Yeung Choi St, Mong Kok; meals $25-80; ⏰11am-3am; Ⓜ Mong Kok (exit B3) This old noodle shop (recently commended by the Michelin people) may look a little shabby but its noodles and congee, whipped up the way they have been for decades, have kept fans coming back for more.

MIDO CAFÉ
TEA CAFE **$**

Map p382 (美都餐室; 63 Temple St; meals $25-80; ⏰9am-10pm; Ⓜ Yau Ma Tei, exit B2) Opened in 1950, this vintage *cha chaan tang* (see p37) is arguably the most famous tea cafe in Hong Kong. With its mosaic tiles and metal latticework, it stands astride a street corner that comes to life at sundown. Ascend to the spacious upper floor and take a seat next to a wall of iron-framed windows overlooking Tin Hau Temple. The food is passable; the retro 1950s tiles more noteworthy – take a photo of them to use as a novel wallpaper for your mobile phone or computer, or to send to your hipster friends back home.

CHINA CAFE
TEA CAFE **$**

Map p383 (中國冰室; 1077a Canton Rd, Mong Kok; meals $30-50; ⏰7am-7pm; Ⓜ Mong Kok, exit A2) An old, two-floor *cha chaan tang* (see p37) oozing with retro charm. The drinks and pastries are decent. Like Mido, this place also has nice Hong Kong–style tiles.

✖ New Kowloon

⬛TOP CHOICE PIGGY GRILL
CHINESE **$$**

(賣豬仔特式燒烤坊; www.piggygrill.com; ☎2194 8180; Ground fl, 17 Shun Ning Rd, Sham Shui Po; meals $80-300; ⏰noon-11pm; Ⓜ Sham Shui Po, exit D2) This hidden gem serves the best roast suckling pig ($490 each) in town, trotters down. But you'll need to place your order a day in advance (call ☎2194 8188). This is so they can partially precook the two-week old swine from Vietnam. Then when you arrive for your meal, they'll crackle the skin just prior to serving – a 10-minute process the chef is happy to let you capture on camera. The

grilled dishes are excellent too. Piggy Grill delivers too for about $600 a pig but you'll need to order a day in advance and have a Chinese friend tell them your address.

WO MEI RESTAURANT
CHINESE **$$**

(和味館; ☎2748 0002; Ground fl, 29-33 Shun Ning Rd, Cheung Sha Wan; meals $100-400; ⏰lunch & dinner; Ⓜ Cheung Sha Wan, exit A2; ⬦) Wo Mei treats food with passion. Ingredients are carefully sourced, cooked à la minute and served piping hot. No surprise it's well loved by food critics. But there's another reason people come – the restaurant is known for its creepy-crawlies such as bamboo worms, honeybee pupae, scorpions and aquatic beetles, which are fried and sprinkled with salt and pepper. Some say they taste like French fries but better.

ROBATAYAKI
JAPANESE **$$$**

(爐端燒日本餐廳; ☎2996 8438; Ground fl, Harbour Grand Kowloon Hotel, 2 Harbour Front, Whampoa Gardens, Hung Hom; lunch/dinner from $300/450; ⏰noon-10.30pm) We love this farmhouse-style restaurant where excellent Japanese skewers are cooked before your eyes by chefs seated on a wooden deck surrounded by fresh ingredients on display. To order, just point at what you want and the chef will scoop it up on a wooden paddle, cook it and serve it back to you on the same device. Take minibus 5 from Hankow Rd in Tsim Sha Tsui all the way to the final stop at the Whampoa bus terminus. The hotel is three minutes' walk away.

KOWLOON TANG
CHINESE **$$$**

Map p382 (九龍廳; ☎2811 9398; www.kowloon tang.com; Shop R002-003, Civic Square, 3rd fl, Elements Mall, 1 Austin Rd, West Kowloon; meals $300-2000; ⏰noon-10.30pm; Ⓜ Kowloon, exit U3) Located on the rooftop of the Elements Mall, Kowloon Tang, the cousin of Island Tang across the harbour, serves excellent Cantonese classics, a convincing Peking duck and sumptuous Western-style desserts in a fashionably retro setting. It has great cocktails too!

TIN LUNG HEEN
CANTONESE **$$$**

Map p382 (天龍軒; ☎2263 2270; www.ritzcarl ton.com/hongkong; 102nd fl, Ritz-Carlton Hong Kong, International Commerce Centre, 1 Austin Rd West, West Kowloon; meals $300-1800; ⏰lunch & dinner; Ⓜ Kowloon, exit U3) The decor here is formal and imposing – you expect Hu Jin Tao to walk in any minute for his fried rice. But the service is smooth and personable and we were floored by the sweeping views of West Kowloon. The famous *char siu*, at $218, is the most expensive plate of barbecued pork in town but it's made from Spanish Iberico pork and you can taste the difference. When you book, do not ask for a window seat if you suffer from vertigo.

CHI LIN VEGETARIAN (LONG MEN LOU)
VEGETARIAN, CHINESE $

(添好運點心專門店; ☏3658 9388; Nan Lian Garden, 60 Fung Tak Rd; lunch/dinner $100/200; ☺11.30am-9pm; Ⓜ Diamond Hill, exit C2; 🖉) The location behind a waterfall and tasty vegetarian food make dining here a superb way to begin or end your visit to Chi Lin Nunnery and Nan Lian Garden. The elegant **Song Cha Xie** (松茶榭; Pavilion of Pine & Tea; ☺noon-7.30pm) nearby specialises in the art of Chinese tea drinking.

TIM HO WAN
DIM SUM $

off Map p383 (添好運; 9-11 Fuk wing St, Sham Shui Po; meals $40-200; ☺8am-10pm; Ⓜ Sham Shui Po, exit B1) A former Four Seasons dimsum chef re-creates his magic in the first budget dim sum eatery to receive a Michelin star. Get a ticket when you arrive and a table should be available in under than 30 minutes.

QUEEN'S CAFÉ
SOY SAUCE WESTERN $

(皇后飯店; ☏2265 8288; www.queenscafe.com; Shop 18, L1/F, Festival Walk, 80 Tat Chee Ave, Kowloon Tong; lunch/dinner from $80/150; ☺11am-11pm; Ⓜ Festival Walk. exit C) Queen's is a veteran of soy sauce Western cuisine (see p37), which accounts for its subdued yet assured atmosphere and its hearty baked dishes.

CHEONG FAT
THAI, NOODLES $

(昌發泰國粉麵屋; 27 South Wall Rd, Kowloon City; noodles from $30; ☺11.30am-11.30pm) Blasting music videos in this hole-in-the-wall eatery set the rhythm as you slurp up the tasty Chiang Mai noodles. The open kitchen has appetising cooked dishes on display, such as pork trotters with preserved vegetables. To get to Kowloon City, take minibus 25M from Kowloon Tong station (exit B2).

LEI YUE MUN
SEAFOOD, CHINESE $$$

One of Hong Kong's most popular seafood venues, the village of Lei Yue Mun has over a dozen seafood restaurants and seafood stalls lining a winding road overlooking the typhoon shelter. Once you've settled down in a restaurant, go outside and pick your dinner from one of the stalls with live seafood tanks, making sure you know how much you're paying and for what. The restaurant will take care of the rest.

KOWLOON EATING

WORTH A DETOUR

TSING MA BRIDGE
....

Ma Wan island was once an important gateway to Kowloon, where foreign vessels would drop anchor before entering Chinese waters. Today the reason to come here is to see **Tsing Ma Bridge**, the world's seventh-longest span suspension bridge at 1377m for the main span (the bridge's total length is 2160m), to the east and, to a lesser extent, Kap Shui Mun Bridge to the west. Together they form the rail and road link connecting Lantau with the New Territories via **Tsing Yi** island.

Looking like it has beached itself beneath the Tsing Ma Bridge is **Noah's Ark** (☏3411 8888; www.noahsark.com.hk; 33 Pak Yan Rd, Ma Wan; adult/child $130/100; ☺10am-6pm; Central-Park Island ferry), a peculiar mini–theme park loosely dedicated to the biblical story of Noah, with interactive games and distractions for younger kids as well as plenty of refreshment options. There is a direct bus service (one way/round trip $20/38) shuttling visitors between the park and Grand Century Place in Mong Kok.

On neighbouring Tsing Yi is the **Lantau Link Visitors Centre** (青嶼幹線訪客中心; ☏2495 5825, 2495 7583; admission free; ☺10am-5pm Mon-Fri, to 6.30pm Sat & Sun; MTR Tsing Yi, 🚌 green minibus 308M) and its **viewing platform** (admission free; ☺7am-10.30pm Sun-Fri, to 1.30am Sat), where you can get a close-up of the enormity of Tsing Ma Bridge and the Lantau Link. The centre contains models, photographs and videos of the construction process – very much a crowd-pleaser for trainspotters and the hard-hat brigade.

The more popular restaurants include **Lung Mun Seafood Restaurant** (龍門海鮮酒家; ☎2717 9886; 20 Hoi Pong Rd C), **Lung Yue Restaurant** (龍如海鮮酒樓; ☎2348 6332; 41 Hoi Pong Rd C) and **Sea King Garden Restaurant** (海皇園林酒家; ☎2348 1408; 39 Hoi Pong Rd C). They open for lunch and dinner.

To get to Lei Yue Mun from Yau Tong MTR station, use exit A2 and follow Cha Kwo Ling Rd and Shung Shun St south for 15 minutes or catch green minibus 24M from outside the station. Bus 14C links the Yau Tong Centre halfway down the hill with the Kwun Tong MTR station.

DRINKING & NIGHTLIFE

Tsim Sha Tsui

BUTLER
BAR

Map p380 (5th fl, Mody House, 30 Mody Rd, Tsim Sha Tsui; cover charge $200; MEast Tsim Sha Tsui, exit N2) A cocktail and whisky heaven hidden in the residential part of TST. You can flip through its whisky magazines as you watch the bartender (Uchida) create his magical concoctions with the flair and precision of a master mixologist in Ginza. We loved the fruit cocktails made from fresh citruses. A discreet and welcome addition to the TST drinking scene.

OZONE
BAR

Map p382 (☎2263 2263; 118th fl, ICC, 1 Austin Rd, West Kowloon; ☻5pm-2am; MKowloon, exit U3) Ozone is the highest bar in Asia. The imaginative interiors, created to evoke a cyberesque Garden of Eden, have pillars resembling chocolate fountains in a hurricane, myriads of refracted glass and colour-changing illumination. Equally dizzying is the wine list, with the most expensive bottle selling for over $150,000. Definitely a once-in-a-lifetime experience, in more ways than one.

AQUA SPIRIT
BAR

Map p378 (www.aqua.com.hk; 30th fl, 1 Peking Rd, Tsim Sha Tsui; ☻5pm-2am; MTsm Sha Tsui, exit L5) This uberfashionable bar with two-storey, floor-to-ceiling windows, commands dramatic views of the Hong Kong Island skyline. It's an awesome place for after-dinner

drinks with a date. The tables by the windows have a cover charge of $2000 each. There are DJs on weekends.

UTOPIA
BAR

Map p378 (26th fl, Hon Kwok Jordon Centre, 7 Hillwood Rd, Tsim Sha Tsui; ☻4.30pm-late; MJordan, exit D) Utopia is a wonderful place with premium views and a balcony but it forgets to charge you for them. The wine list of some 50 Old and New World bottles is reasonably priced for Tsim Sha Tsui and so are the draught beers, cocktails and fine finger foods. The vibe is tasteful-local and it has a dart board, too. There's happy hour all day Sunday and from 4.30pm to 9pm and midnight to close from Monday to Thursday.

TAPAS BAR
BAR

Map p380 (www.shangri-la.com; Lobby, Kowloon Shangri-La, 64 Mody Rd, Tsim Sha Tsui East; ☻3.30pm-1am; MEast Tsim Sha Tsui, exit P1) An intimate vibe and bistro-style decor make this a good place to unwind over champagne and tapas after a day of sightseeing.

NED KELLY'S LAST STAND
PUB

Map p378 (☎2376 0562; 11a Ashley Rd, Tsim Sha Tsui; ☻happy hour 11.30am-9pm; Tsim Sha Tsui, exit L5) Named after a gun-toting Australian convict, Ned's is one of Hong Kong's oldest pubs. Most of the expats and tourists who come here are attracted by the laid-back atmosphere and the Dixieland jazz band that plays and cracks jokes between songs. The bar is filled with old posters, rugby shirts and Oz-related paraphernalia. Sure, Ned's is tacky but they're damned proud of it.

VIBES
LOUNGE

Map p378 (☎2315 5999; www.themirahotel.com; 5th fl, The Mira Hong Kong, 118 Nathan Rd, Tsim Sha Tsui; ☻3pm-midnight; MTsim Sha Tsui, exit B1) A cross between Bali and Kowloon Park, this pleasant alfresco bar comes with resident DJ, cabanas and random tropical greenery. Try its 'molecular' cocktails which involve liberal uses of liquid nitrogen and foam.

KING LUDWIG BEER HALL
BEER HALL

Map p380 (☎2369 8328; www.kingparrot.com; 32 Salisbury Rd, Tsim Sha Tsui; ☻noon-1am Sun-Thu, to 2am Fri & Sat; MEast Tsim Sha Tsui, exit J1) This busy place with antler lighting fixtures is popular with visiting Germans and others hankering after fried pork knuckle and German beer on tap, including

Maisel's Weiss. It's just under Middle Road Children's Playground.

INTERCONTINENTAL LOBBY LOUNGE BAR

Map p380 (Hotel InterContinental Hong Kong, 18 Salisbury Rd, Tsim Sha Tsui; ⊙24hr; MEast Tsim Sha Tsui, exit J) Soaring plate glass and an unbeatable waterfront location make this one of the best spots to soak up that Hong Kong Island skyline and take in the busy harbour, although you pay for the privilege. It's an ideal venue from which to watch the evening lightshow at 8pm.

BAHAMA MAMA'S CLUB

Map p380 (4-5 Knutsford Tce, Tsim Sha Tsui; ⊙happy hour 5-9pm; MTsim Sha Tsui, exit B1) Bahama Mama's goes for a 'Caribbean island' feel, complete with palm trees and surfboards. It's a friendly spot and stands apart from most of the other late-night watering holes in this part of town. It's also the place to come for a foosball showdown. On Friday and Saturday nights there's a DJ spinning and a young crowd (similar to that at Carnegie's in Wan Chai) out on the bonsai-sized dance floor.

🍴 Yau Ma Tei

SNAKE KING YAN BAR

Map p382 (蛇王恩; 80a, Woo Sung St, Yau Ma Tei; MJordan, exit A) For something really badass, challenge yourself to a shot of rice wine mixed with snake bile at this specialty shop near the Temple Street Night Market. If that reviles you, there are bottles of other exotic infusions on display that you might prefer. Snake bile is believed to increase virility.

🍴 Mong Kok

FULLCUP CAFÉ CAFE

Map p382 (呼吸咖啡茶館; 4-6th fl, Hanwai Commercial Centre, 36 Dundas St, Mong Kok; ⊙noon-3am; MYau Ma Tei, exit A1) 'Full cup' sounds similar to the Chinese characters for 'breath', which is what this quirky three-storey cafe does – offer a breather in the midst of Mong Kok. With an eclectic collection of retro furniture and an alfresco space, it attracts a young Kowloon crowd that's artsy, edgy and nonexpat. Fullcup serves decent coffee, smoothies, beer and snacks. Some weekends feature live music performances.

⭐ ENTERTAINMENT

TOP CHOICE BROADWAY CINEMATHEQUE CINEMA

Map p382 (百老匯電影中心; ☎2388 3188; Ground fl, Prosperous Gardens, 3 Public Square St, Yau Ma Tei; MYau Ma Tei, exit C) The place for new art-house releases and rerun screenings. The Kubrick Bookshop Café next door serves good coffee.

DADA LIVE MUSIC

Map p380 (2nd fl, Luxe Manor, 39 Kimberley Rd, Tsim Sha Tsui; ⊙11am-2am Mon-Sat, to 1am Sun; MTsim Sha Tsui, exit X) Upstairs in the quirky hotel, Dada is an intimate cocktail bar decked out with florid wallpaper, bold purple and silver, and a couple of Dalí paintings. The crowd is creative, professional mid-30s. Live jazz Thursday, R&B Friday and Saturday.

HONG KONG CULTURAL CENTRE THEATRE, MUSIC

Map p378 (香港文化中心; www.lcsd.gov.hk; 10 Salisbury Rd; ⊙9am-11pm; ⛴Star Ferry) Hong Kong's premier arts performance venue, the world-class Cultural Centre venue contains a 2000-seat concert hall with an impressive Rieger pipe organ, two theatres and rehearsal studios.

AMC FESTIVAL WALK CINEMA

(又一城 AMC; ☎2265 8545; www.amccinemas. com.hk; Upper Ground fl & Levels 1 & 2, Festival Walk, 80-88 Tat Chee Ave, Kowloon Tong; MKowloon Tong, exit C2) This complex with 11 screens shows a mix of Chinese and Western films. Check ahead as the latter are sometimes dubbed, rather than subtitled in Cantonese.

GRAND OCEAN CINEMA CINEMA

Map p378 (☎2377 2100; www.goldenharvest. com; Marco Polo Hong Kong Hotel Shopping Arcade, Zone D, Harbour City, 3 Canton Rd, Tsim Sha Tsui; ⛴Star Ferry) The Grand Ocean Cinema screens the usual blockbusters.

UA ISQUARE CINEMA

Map p378 (☎3516 8811; 7th fl, iSquare, 63 Nathan Rd, Tsim Sha Tsui; MTsim Sha Tsui, exit J) Belonging to the UA circuit, this cinema at the iSquare mall screens mainly blockbusters.

ONE BROADWAY CINEMA

Map p378 (☎2388 3188; www.cinema.com.hk; L6–L11 The One, 100 Nathan Rd, Tsim Sha Tsui; MTsim Sha Tsui, exit D) This cinema at The One shows box-office hits from Hollywood and Hong

HONG KONG'S HIDDEN AGENDA

Founded in a clandestine band room in the gritty industrial hub of Kwun Tong, **Hidden Agenda** (☑9170 6073; www.hiddenagendahk.com; 2A, Wing Fu Industrial Bldg, 15-17 Tai Yip St, Kwun Tong; Ⓜ Ngau Tau Kok, exit B6) has risen to synonymity with underground music in Hong Kong. Its future, however, remains uncertain.

As Hong Kong sheds its role as a manufacturing hub, artists and musicians have been setting up shop in abandoned factories where the rent is cheap and space is abundant. However, complications often arise with the lease of these premises, neighbours complaining about the noise and landlords hoping to develop their property into something more lucrative.

No stranger to these problems, Hidden Agenda is now living it up, albeit precariously, at its third location – a relatively spacious warehouse-turned-venue accommodating 300 people, a bar and a CD shop. And while the music started out with a raucous, head-banging focus, the mix of performers has evolved to include a range of genres including post-rock, reggae, jazz, folk, techno, rock and punk.

Bands both local (My Little Airport, Chochukmo, Hungry Ghosts) and foreign (Tahiti 80, The Chariot, Anti-Flag, Bane, Da Bang, Two Gallants, Alcest, Pitchtuner) have performed here. There's usually one to five shows a week. Check the website for the latest.

Kong, and occasionally some of the more popular titles on the edge of the mainstream.

SHOPPING

Tsim Sha Tsui has the greatest range of goods on offer, from $20 trinkets to $12,000 leather boots, but they are mainly upmarket. To the north of Tsim Sha Tsui, Yau Ma Tei and Mong Kok cater mostly to local shoppers and offer good prices on clothing, sporting goods, camping gear, computers and other daily necessities. Shopping venues in New Kowloon run the gamut from glittering shopping malls to the cut-price computer centres of Sham Shui Po.

Tsim Sha Tsui

TOP CHOICE DAVID CHAN
PHOTO SHOP   PHOTOGRAPHY
Map p378 (陳烘相機; ☑2723 3886; Shop 15, Ground fl, Champagne Court, 16 Kimberley Rd, Tsim Sha Tsui; ⊘ Mon-Sat; Ⓜ Tsim Sha Tsui, exit B1) If you've decided to give the digital age a miss altogether, or at least still use film cameras, this dealer is the most reputable used-camera shop in town. The owner David Chan been working in the business since the 1960s and has some precious equipment in his collection. It's the place to buy expensive collectibles.

INITIAL   CLOTHING
Map p380 (www.initialfashion.com; Shop 2, 48 Cameron Rd, Tsim Sha Tsui; ⊘11.30am-11.30pm; Ⓜ Tsim Sha Tsui, exit B2) This attractive shop and cafe carries stylish, multifunctional urbanwear with European and Japanese influences. The clothes created by local designers are complemented by imported shoes, bags and costume jewellery.

RISE SHOPPING ARCADE   CLOTHING
Map p380 (利時商場; www.rise-hk.com; 5-11 Granville Circuit, Tsim Sha Tsui; Ⓜ Tsim Sha Tsui, exit B2) Bursting the seams of this minimall is cheap streetwear from Hong Kong, Korea and Japan, with a few knock-offs chucked in for good measure. Patience and a good eye could land you purchases fit for a Vogue photo shoot. It's best visited between 4pm and 8.30pm when most of the shops are open.

VENILLA SUITE   SHOES
Map p378 (www.venillasuite.com; L210 The One, 100 Nathan Rd, Tsim Sha Tsui; Ⓜ Tsim Sha Tsui, exit B2) This shoe shop belonging to the I.T. group has a great selection of fine-looking women's footwear inspired by the styles of top brands such as Manolo Blahnik and Jimmy Choo. Not as well made of course, but at a fraction of the price. It has a few branches including in **Mong Kok** (Map p383; ☑3514 4578; Shop 10 & 11, B1 Langham Pl, 8 Argyle St; ⊘11am-11pm).

CHINESE ARTS & CRAFTS DEPARTMENT STORE

Map p378 (中藝; www.cachk.com; Star House, 3 Salisbury Rd, Tsim Sha Tsui; ⓂTsim Sha Tsui, exit L5) From silk cushions to jade earrings, the pricey traditional-style gifts show you can keep your head and your poise while swimming in tourist clichés. On Hong Kong Island there are branches in **Admiralty** (Map p370; Shop 220, Pacific Place, 88 Queensway, Admiralty; ⓂAdmiralty, exit F) and a huge one in **Wan Chai** (Map p372; 2nd Causeway Centre; 28 Harbour Rd, Wan Chai; ⓂWan Chai, exit A5).

SWINDON BOOKS BOOKS

Map p378 (www.swindonbooks.com; 13-15 Lock Rd, Tsim Sha Tsui; ⓂTsim Sha Tsui, exit A1) This is one of the best 'real' (as opposed to 'supermarket') bookshops. An excellent range and knowledgable staff. Strong on local books and history in particular. Its sister is Central's Hong Kong Book Centre (p79).

K11 MALL

Map p380 (18 Hanoi Rd, Tsim Sha Tsui; ⓂEast Tsim Sha Tsui, exit D2) A new shopping mall catering to the young, middle-class market, K11 is known for its exhibition spaces for local artists. It's linked to the East Tsim Sha Tsui MTR station.

ONE MALL

Map p378 (www.the-one.hk; 100 Nathan Rd, Tsim Sha Tsui; ⓂTsim Sha Tsui, exit D) This mall has a collection of trendy fashion and accessory shops, and dining and drinking options with spectacular views of Kowloon.

ISQUARE MALL

Map p378 (國際廣場;www.isquare.hk; 63 Nathan Rd, Tsim Sha Tsui; ⓂTsim Sha Tsui, exits R & H) This medium-sized mall features shops and eateries that are young, trendy and relatively affordable, but is lacking in character.

GRANVILLE RD CLOTHING, ACCESSORIES

Map p380 (加連威老道出口店; Granville Rd; ⓂTsim Sha Tsui, exit B2) If you want to hunt for bargains and have the time and inclination to riffle through racks and piles of factory seconds, the dozen or so factory outlet stores along Granville Rd should reward you with items at a fraction of store prices.

I.T. CLOTHING, ACCESSORIES

Map p378 (www.ithk.com; Shop LG01 & LG16-17, Basement, Silvercord, 30 Canton Rd, Tsim Sha Tsui; ⓂTsim Sha Tsui, exit A1) This trendy shop carries an impressive selection of first- to third-

tier designer brands from Europe and Japan. It's similar to D-mop (p125) but less edgy and with more Japanese options. Prices are high but not outrageous. The I.T. group has shops in all the major shopping areas.

STAR COMPUTER CITY ELECTRONICS

Map p378 (星光電腦城; 2nd fl, Star House, 3 Salisbury Rd, Tsim Sha Tsui; ⓈStar Ferry) A large, handy and pricey computer mall (see p53).

CURIO ALLEY GIFTS, SOUVENIRS

Map p378 (⏰10am-8pm; ⓂTsim Sha Tsui, exit C1) This is a fun place to shop for name chops, soapstone carvings, fans and other Chinese bric-a-brac. It's found in an alleyway between Lock and Hankow Rds, just south of Haiphong Rd.

PREMIER JEWELLERY JEWELLERY

Map p378 (愛寶珠寶有限公司; ☎2368 0003; Shop G14-15, Ground fl, Holiday Inn Golden Mile Shopping Mall, 50 Nathan Rd, Tsim Sha Tsui; ⏰10am-7.30pm Mon-Sat, to 4pm Sun; ⓂTsim Sha Tsui, exit G) This third-generation family firm is directed by a qualified gemmologist and is one of our favourite places to shop. The range isn't huge but if you're looking for something particular, give Premier Jewellery a day's notice and a selection will be ready in time for your arrival. Staff can also help you design your own piece.

HARBOUR CITY MALL

Map p378 (www.harbourcity.com.hk; 3-9 Canton Rd; ⓂTsim Sha Tsui, exit C1) This is an enormous place, with 700 shops, 50 food and beverage outlets and five cinemas. Outlets are arrayed in four separate zones: for kids, sport, fashion, and cosmetics and beauty. There's also a large Lane Crawford department store. Every major brand is represented.

🏠 Yau Ma Tei & Mong Kok

TOP CHOICE **CHAN WAH KEE**

CUTLERY STORE HOMEWARES

Map p382 (陳華記刀莊; ☎2730 4091; 278d, Temple St, close to Bowring St, Yau Ma Tei; ⏰11am-6pm, closed Wed; ⓂJordan, exit C2) Eighty-year-old Mr Chan is one of the few remaining master knife-sharpeners in Asia, and he's still going strong. At this humble shop, he uses nine different stones to grind each blade, and alternates between water and oil. Mr Chan's clients have included chefs, butchers, tailors and homemakers from all over the world. He's had clients send him Japanese willow knives for his magic touch. Choppers, cleavers, slicers, paring knives, even scissors – he's done them all.

If you bring him your blade, he charges anything from $100 to $600 and the wait is three months. But if you buy from him, and he has quite a good selection (Japanese cleavers are a bargain at $600), he'll do it there and then. Prices range from $200 for a small paring knife to around $2000 for a Shun knife, depending on size.

JADE MARKET
MARKET

Map p382 (玉器市場; Battery St, Yau Ma Tei; ⊙10am-5pm; MYau Ma Tei, exit C) The Jade Market, near the Gascoigne Rd overpass just west of Nathan Rd, has some 400 stalls selling all varieties and grades of jade from inside two covered markets. Unless you really know your nephrite from your jadeite, it's probably not wise to buy any expensive pieces here, but there are plenty of cheap and cheerful trinkets on offer as well. **Shanghai Street** on the other side of Kansu St will take you back to a time long past. Once Kowloon's main drag before Nathan Rd, Shanghai St is still flanked by stores selling embroidered Chinese wedding gowns, sandalwood incense, professional kitchenware and Buddha statues. There's also a pawn shop at the junction of Saigon St, and mah-jong parlours (you can go inside but you can't take photos).

SINO CENTRE
MALL

Map p382 (信和中心; 582-592 Nathan Rd, Mong Kok; MYau Ma Tei, exit A2) This shabby go-to place for anything related to Asian animation and comics will give you a taste of another side of local culture. Its tiny shops selling new and back issues of Japanese manga, action figures, computer games, old-fashioned video games and other kidult bait attract everyone (well, mostly men) from students to teachers, writers to office workers.

HONG KONG READER
BOOKS

Map p383 (☏2395 0031; www.hkreaders.com; 7th fl, 68 Sai Yeung Choi St South, Mong Kok; ⊙2pm-midnight; MMong Kok, exit D3) Run by a handful of young people, this is a bilingual bookstore-cafe with an intellectual bent. If you're looking for the likes of Derrida or Milosz, here's the place to go. Check its website for the latest literary readings, though most are conducted in Cantonese.

Hong Kong Reader is above a 1010 telecommunications shop.

TAK HING DRIED SEAFOOD
FOOD

Map p382 (德興海味; ☏2780 2129; 1 Woosung St, Yau Ma Tei; ⊙9am-7.30pm; MYau Ma Tei, exit C) One of very few honest dried-seafood stores, this delightful corner establishment has glass jars stuffed with dried scallops, crocodile meat bird's nest, and oysters, though you might prefer the figs, cashews, candied lotus seeds and ginseng.

SIN TAT PLAZA
MALL

Map p380 (83 Argyle St, Mong Kok; MMong Kok, exit D2) Popular with locals, Sin Tat Plaza on busy Argyle St is dedicated to mobile phones of all persuasions, including a Chinese-made phone that doubles up as a lighter! It's also where to go to get your phone fixed and unlocked (see p53).

MONG KOK COMPUTER CENTRE
MALL

Map p383 (8-8a Nelson St, Mong Kok; ⊙1-10pm; MMong Kok, exit D3) Cheap but language can be a barrier, and you'll see more finished products than computer components (p53).

BRUCE LEE CLUB
SOUVENIRS

Map p382 (李小龍會; www.bruceleeclub.com; Shop 160-161, In's Point, 530 Nathan Rd, Mong Kok; ⊙1-9pm; MYau Ma Tei, exit A1) A small Bruce Lee museum and souvenir shop; see also p161.

PROTREK
OUTDOOR EQUIPMENT

Map p382 (www.protrek.com.hk; 522 Nathan Rd, Yau Ma Tei; ⊙noon-8pm Mon-Sat, 11.30am-9.30pm; MYau Ma Tei, exit C) This reliable shop with branches all over town is arguably your best bet for outdoor gear that will see you through from sea to summit. It runs training courses on outdoor activities as well. The English-speaking staff are very helpful.

YUE HWA CHINESE PRODUCTS EMPORIUM
DEPARTMENT STORE

Map p378 (裕華國貨; ☏2384 0084; 301-309 Nathan Rd, Yau Ma Tei; MYau Ma Tei, exit D) This enormous place, with seven floors of ceramics, furniture, souvenirs and clothing, has absolutely everything the souvenir-hunting tourist could possibly want, as well as bolts of silk, herbs, clothes, porcelain, luggage, umbrellas and kitchenware. There's also a branch in Tsim Sha Tsui on **Kowloon Park**

Dr (Map p378; ☑2317 5333; 1 Kowloon Park Dr) that's entered from Peking Rd.

LANGHAM PLACE MALL
MALL

Map p383 (朗豪坊; ☑3520 2800; 8 Argyle St, Mong Kok; Ⓜ Mong Kok, exit C3) This 15-storey supermall has some 300 shops that stay open till as late as 11pm. The focal point of the mall is the high-tech Digital Sky, where special events take place.

New Kowloon

PAGE ONE
BOOKS

Map p378 (Shop LG1 30, Lower Ground fl, Festival Walk, 80-88 Tat Chee Ave, Kowloon Tong; Ⓜ Kowloon Tong, exit C2). A chain, yes, but a good one. Page One has Hong Kong's best selection of art and design magazines and books; it's also strong on photography, literature, film and children's books. There's a smaller branch in **Tsim Sha Tsui** (☑2730 6080; Shop 3202, 3rd fl, Gateway Arcade, Harbour City, 25-27 Canton Rd; Ⓜ Tsim Sha Tsui, exit A1).

ELEMENTS
MALL

Map p382 (圓方; www.elementshk.com; 1 Austin Rd West, West Kowloon; Ⓜ Kowloon, exit U3) Kowloon's most upmarket shopping mall comprises five pleasant sections corresponding to the five elements of nature, each decorated with artwork reflecting the themes. Other thoughtful touches include good nursing facilities. Brands are the usual upmarket suspects, with a few design-oriented establishments. Austin Rd West is a new area built on reclaimed land that's connected to Austin Rd in Tsim Sha Tsui at its eastern end.

VIVIENNE TAM
CLOTHING, ACCESSORIES

(www.viviennetam.com; LG1 Shop 05, Festival Walk, Kowloon Tong; ◷11am-8.30pm Sun-Thu, to 9pm Fri & Sat; Ⓜ Kowloon Tong, exit C2) This enduring brand from New York–based designer Tam, who was trained in Hong Kong, sells eminently wearable, feminine but also streetwise women's foundation pieces, light gossamer dresses and slinky tops, plus a range of accessories.

AP LIU STREET FLEA MARKET
MARKET

(鴨寮街; Apliu St, btwn Nam Cheong St & Yen Chow St, Sham Shui Po; ◷noon-midnight; Ⓜ Sham Shui Po, exit A1) A geek's heaven, this flea market specialises in all things digital and

UPSTAIRS MONG KOK

Mong Kok can be intense. After all, it *is* the most densely populated spot on the face of the earth. But you don't have to shun it. To experience MK without the insanity, make a beeline for its upstairs spaces. Above-the-ground oases include C&G Artpartment (p147), Hong Kong Reader (p161), Fullcup Café (p158) and the Bruce Lee Club (p161).

electronic. The market spills over into Pei Ho St, also see p53.

TOP CHOICE GOLDEN COMPUTER ARCADE & GOLDEN SHOPPING CENTER
ELECTRONICS

(黃金電腦商場, 高登電腦中心; www.goldenarcade.org; 146-152 Fuk Wa St, Sham Shui Po; ◷11am-9pm; Ⓜ Sham Shui Po, exit D2) Occupying different floors of the same building opposite Sham Shui Po MTR station, these are *the* places to go for low-cost computers and peripherals. Golden Computer Arcade consists of the basement and ground floor. Golden Shopping Centre is on the 1st floor. The 3Cs are generally considered the 'best' in the building. In Golden Shopping Centre you'll find **Centralfield** (www.centralfield.com; Shop 10-11) and **Comdex** (匯訊; Shop 49) and in Golden Computer Arcade there's **Capital** (正都; www.cap.com.hk; Shops 49,51,53,55, basement) and another branch of **Comdex** (www.comdex.com.hk; Shops 57B, 61). See also p53.

FESTIVAL WALK
MALL

(又一城; www.festivalwalk.com.hk 80-88 Tat Chee Ave, Kowloon Tong; ◷11am-10pm; Ⓜ Kowloon Tong, exit C) Though not as big as most other malls, Festival Walk's design lends it an airiness that makes it nice to walk around. As well as some 200 shops, it has a cinema and an ice-skating rink.

MEGA BOX
MALL

(38 Wang Chiu Rd; Kowloon Bay; Ⓜ Kowloon Bay, exit A) For a mall this size, Mega Box is lacklustre compared to other options in town, but it has a cinema, an ice rink and a whole floor devoted to kids. There are shuttle buses to the mall. After exiting the Kowloon

Bay station, go through Telford Plaza and you'll see the shuttle bus stop.

CHEUNG SHA WAN ROAD
MARKET

(⏰10am-6.30pm Mon-Fri, to 4pm Sat, closed Sun; Ⓜ Sham Shui Po, exit C1) A riot of shops selling fabrics, trimmings, buttons, ribbons and other raw materials, as well as prét-à-porter clothing. You'll bump into fashion designers here.

SPORTS & ACTIVITIES

FREE TAICHI
TAICHI

Map p378 (☎2508 1234; www.discoverhongkong.com; Tsim Sha Tsui East Promenade; ⏰8-9am Mon, Wed & Fri; Ⓜ Tsim Sha Tsui, exit J). Let a sprightly master show you how to 'Wave hands like clouds' against the stunning views of Victoria Harbour, just outside the Museum of Art. Taichi or shadow boxing is supposed to give you a sharper mind and a fitter heart. Pre-registration required.

SOUTH CHINA SEA COLLECTIVE
TATTOO PARLOUR

Map p383 (南海合作社; ☎6333 5352; kowlooninink@gmail.com; 2nd fl, 234 Sai Yeung Choi St South, Mong Kok; per hr $1000) Tattoo artist and avid traveller Nic Tse is Chinese but speaks perfect English and he's well-versed in both cultures. We were impressed by his repertoire, which includes abstract contemporary designs, lines of poetry, interpretations of childhood dreams and minimalist armscapes. Interested parties should email Nic as early as possible to discuss specifics and book. Payment is in cash or via PayPal.

GAURANGA NITYANANDA
YOGA

Map p380 (☎3422 1195/9740 9846; www.yogafitnesshk.com; 15B, Hillview Ct, 30 Hillwood Rd,

Tsim Sha Tsui; Ⓜ Jordan, exit D) Brian Chan, chairman of the Society for Hong Kong Yoga Instructors who also teaches at The Peninsula, gives private yoga lessons. He's also the chef at Interactive Yoga Vegetarian (p150). Call for details.

WING CHUN YIP MAN MARTIAL ARTS ATHLETIC ASSOCIATION
MARTIAL ARTS

Map p378 (葉問國術總會; ☎2723 2306; Unit A, 5th fl, Alpha House, 27-33 Nathan Rd, Tsim Sha Tsui; Ⓜ Tsim Sha Tsui, exit E) The cost for three lessons a week (two or three hours each) for a month is $500. A six-month intensive course (six hours a day, six days a week) is around $5000, depending on the student.

OCEAN SKY DIVERS
DIVING

Map p378 (海天潛水訓練中心; ☎2366 3738; www.oceanskydiver.com; 1st fl, 17-19 Lock Rd; Ⓜ Tsim Sha Tsui, exit C1) Along with a full range of diving and snorkelling gear, this place is also worth consulting about dive courses and ideal dive sites all around the Hong Kong's coastline and islands.

KOWLOON PARK SWIMMING COMPLEX
SWIMMING

Map p378 (九龍公園游泳池; ☎2724 3577; Nathan & Austin Rds, Tsim Sha Tsui; adult/concession $19/9; ⏰6.30am-10pm, 1hr close at noon & 5pm; Ⓜ Tsim Sha Tsui, exit C2) This complex comes complete with four pools and waterfalls. Visit on a weekday; on weekends there are so many bathers it's difficult to find the water.

KING'S PARK TENNIS COURTS
TENNIS

Map p382 (☎2385 8985; 23 King's Park Rise, Yau Ma Tei; ⏰7am-11pm; Ⓜ Yau Ma Tei, exit D) There are six tennis courts here at the King's Park Recreation Ground – not to be confused with the King's Park, home of the Hong Kong Rugby Football Union.

KOWLOON SPORTS & ACTIVITIES

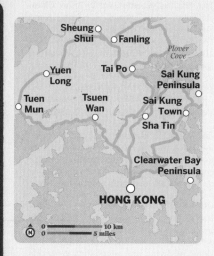

New Territories

Tsuen Wan p167
Has some of Hong Kong's most important Buddhist and Taoist monasteries.

Tuen Mun p169
Visit at leisure the temples and monasteries that dot the landscape.

Yuen Long p171
Hong Kong Wetland Park, laid-back Pak Nai and old walled villages.

Fanling & Sheung Shui p173
A heaven for history buffs, with fortified villages and historic ruins.

Tai Po p174
Lively markets and temples, plus an encyclopaedia of flora and fauna.

Plover Cove p177
Plover Cove is where you go to hike, hike, hike or bike, bike, bike!

Sha Tin p181
A New Town with a historical feel, temples and a heritage museum.

Sai Kung Peninsula p184
Pristine beaches and deserted coves grace this dramatic coastline.

Clearwater Bay Peninsula p189
The name says it all – beaches with crystal-clear water.

TOP SIGHTS
MAI PO MARSHES

You'll witness the magic of migration in Mai Po Marshes, one of the world's most significant wetlands and a major pit stop for the tens of thousands of migratory waterfowl travelling from Siberia to Australasia every winter. These months are the best time to visit this Hong Kong treasure as you're likely to spot a number of rare birds; in other months, nature lovers and urbanites alike come here for the sheer beauty and biodiversity of Mother Nature.

Mai Po Nature Reserve

Mai Po Marshes comprise some 1500 hectares of wetlands at the centre of which is a nature reserve jointly managed by the World Wide Fund for Nature Hong Kong (WWFHK) and the government's Agriculture, Fisheries & Conservation Department. Here, the fragile ecosystem abutting Deep Bay simply teems with life. It is a protected network of mudflats, *gei wai* (shallow shrimp ponds), reed beds and dwarf mangroves, offering a rich habitat of up to 380 species of migratory and resident birds, more than a third of them rarely seen elsewhere in the territory. The area attracts birds in every season but especially winter, when an average of 54,000 migratory birds – including such endangered species as the Dalmatian pelican, black-faced spoonbill, spotted and imperial eagle and black vulture – pass through the marshes.

The nature reserve includes the **Mai Po Visitor Centre** (☑2471 8272) at the northeastern end, where you must register; the **Mai Po Education Centre** (☑2482 0369) to the south, with displays on the history and ecology of the wetland and Deep Bay; floating boardwalks and trails through the mangroves and mudflats; and a dozen hides from where you can watch birds up close without being observed.

The **WWFHK** (世界自然基金會香港辦事處; ☑24hr hotline 2526 1011; www.wwf.org.hk; 1 Tramway Path, Central) can arrange guided visits to the marsh. Three-hour English **tours** ($70) leave the visitor centre at 9.30am, 10am, 2pm and 2.30pm on Saturdays, Sundays and public holidays. The tours can be booked online, but you still need to reserve well in advance, especially during the winter months. Visitors are advised to bring binoculars (these may be available for rent at the visitor centre for $20) and cameras, and to wear comfortable walking shoes but not bright clothing.

Visiting the nature reserve unaccompanied (for foreign visitors only) is possible but numbers are very limited. Going solo is in any case not recommended since you'll miss out on a lot of fun without a professional guide. Call well in advance to book a time. Pay the $100 entrance fee and $200 deposit at the visitor centre; the latter will be returned when you leave the reserve.

Bus 76K or red minibus 17 will drop you off at Mai Po Lo Wai, a village along the main road just east of the marsh. The WWFHK car park is about a 20-minute walk from there. Alternatively, a taxi from Sheung Shui will cost $70.

DON'T MISS

➡ Guided tours to the Reserve
➡ Floating boardwalks

PRACTICALITIES

➡ ☑2471 3480
➡ www.wwf.org.hk
➡ Mai Po, Sin Tin, Yuen Long
➡ admission $70
➡ ⊘9am-5pm
➡ ▢Take bus 76K from Sheung Shui East Rail or Yuen Long West Rail stations

TOP SIGHTS
PING SHAN HERITAGE TRAIL

This meandering 1km trail through three old but lively (partially walled) villages in northwestern New Territories will lead you down the memory lane of pre-colonial Hong Kong, including the spectacular Ping Shan Village. The trail boasts 12 well-restored historic buildings and a museum at Ping Shan dedicated to the powerful Tang clan, the protagonist of this 500-year-old village and considered the first immigrants to settle in Hong Kong.

Start with the **Ping Shan Tang Clan Gallery** (屏山鄧族文物館; ℝPing Shan) at the eastern end of the trail. Housed in a beautifully restored former police station, the gallery show-cases the history of the Tang clan and its relation to Ping Shan. The colourful collections include a traditional sedan chair, ritual wares and a giant wooden bed. The building it-self, by the way, was built in 1899 and was a colonial outpost to monitor 'untoward' villagers.

Retrace your steps to Ping Ha Rd and turn right. The small **Hung Shing Temple** is on your right-hand side, fol-lowed by **Ching Shu Hin Chamber** and **Kun Ting Study Hall** when you turn right again. North of them are the **Tang Ancestral Hall** and **Yu Kiu Ancestral Hall**, two of the larg-est ancestral halls in Hong Kong. The Tangs justifiably brag about them, especially the hall that bears their name, since it follows a unique three-halls-two-courtyards structure which shows the clan's prestigious status inside the imperial court.

Further on are some more temples and an old well. At the end of the trail is the three-storey **Tsui Sing Lau** (聚星樓; ℝTin Shui Wai), the only surviving ancient pagoda in Hong Kong.

DON'T MISS

➡ Ping Shan Tang Clan Gallery

➡ Tang Ancestral Hall

➡ Yu Kiu Ancestral Hall

PRACTICALITIES

➡ ☎2617 1959

➡ www.amo.gov.hk

➡ Ping Shan Tsuen, Yuen Long

➡ admission free

➡ ◷10am-5pm Tue-Sun

➡ ℝPing Shan Light Rail station and Tin Shui Wai on West Rail line serve two ends of the trail

Tsuen Wan

Explore

The industrial and residential New Town of Tsuen Wan is nothing special, but its outskirts can be rewarding, especially if you are an early bird.

Eating yum cha in the morning at one of the Chuen Lung Village teahouses is an experience. After breakfast hikers usually continue up to Tai Mo Shan Country Park. If you want to see vibrant temples, head back to the town centre and take a minibus bound for the serene Western Monastery and colourful Yuen Yuen Institute, the latter stuffed with all manner of deities; or make a pilgrimage to Chuk Lam Sim Monastery.

Do not miss the Hakka-themed Sam Tung Uk Museum before you head back to the MTR station.

The Best...

→ **Sight** Yuen Yuen Institute

→ **Place to Eat** Duen Kee Restaurant (p169)

Top Tip

Tak Wah Park in the centre of town, with ancient trees and footbridges over ponds, is an ideal spot to take a break from the hustle and bustle of Tsuen Wan.

Getting There & Away

The Tsuen Wan MTR station is on Sai Lau Kok Rd, with the Luk Yeung Galleria shopping centre above it. The main bus station is opposite the MTR on Castle Peak Rd (exit A2), but buses and green minibuses pick up and disgorge passengers throughout the New Town.

Bus Many buses from around the New Territories arrive at Tsuen Wan's central bus station, including bus 60M from Tuen Mun and 68M from Yuen Long. Bus 51 from Tai Mo Shan and Kam Tin stops along Tai Ho Rd.

MTR Tsuen Wan MTR station is on the Tsuen Wan line. Tsuen Wan West station is on the West Rail line.

Need to Know

→ **Area code** ☑852

→ **Location** 11km northwest of Kowloon Peninsula

→ **Last train to Kowloon** 12.30am from Tsuen Wan station; 12.24am from Tsuen Wan West station

SIGHTS

YUEN YUEN INSTITUTE TAOIST

off Map p168 (☑2492 2220; Lo Wai Rd; ☺8.30am-5pm; ☐green minibus 81) Stuffed with vivid statuary of Taoist and Buddhist deities plus Confucian saints, the Yuen Yuen Institute, in the hills northeast of Tsuen Wan, is very much on the tourist trail but well worth a visit nonetheless. The main building is a replica of the Temple of Heaven in Běijīng. On the upper ground floor are three Taoist immortals seated in a quiet hall; walk down to the lower level to watch as crowds of the faithful pray and burn offerings to the 60 incarnations of Taoist saints lining the walls.

To reach the institute, take minibus 81 from Shiu Wo St, two blocks due south of Tsuen Wan MTR station (exit B1). A taxi from the MTR station will cost around $40.

WESTERN MONASTERY MONASTERY

Map p168 (西方寺; ☑2411 5111; Lo Wai Rd; ☺8.30am-5.30pm; ☐green minibus 81) A short distance down from the Yuen Yuen Institute, the Buddhist Western Monastery offers a sharp contrast to what's going on up the hill. This is a tranquil complex in which to pass the time, observing points of interest both architectural and spiritual. After being greeted by a Bodhisattva statue in the entrance, the main building lies behind, styled as a classical Chinese palace. This comprises the Hall of Maitreya and the Great Buddha's Hall above it. Further behind is another two-storey building where, depending on what time of day you visit, you may witness scores of monks chanting mantras. This building is topped by a spectacular nine-storey pagoda.

To reach the monastery, take minibus 81 from Shiu Wo St, two blocks due south of Tsuen Wan MTR station (exit B1). A taxi from the MTR station will cost around $40.

Tsuen Wan

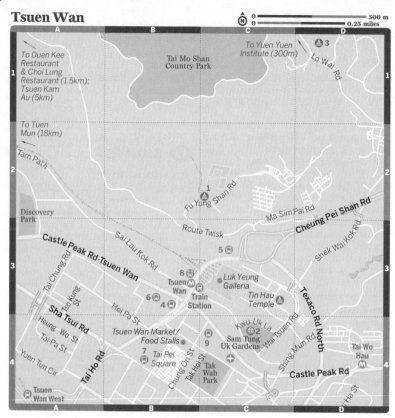

Tsuen Wan

CHUK LAM SIM
MONASTERY
MONASTERY, TEMPLE

Map p168 (竹林禪苑; ☎2490 3392; Fu Yung Shan Rd; ☺9am-4.30pm; ☐green minibus 85) In a lovely bucolic setting, Chuk Lam Sim (Bamboo Forest) Monastery is one of the most impressive temple complexes in Hong Kong.

The temple was completed in 1932 when (legend has it) Tou Tei, the earth god, told an elderly monk to build it. Ascend the flight of steps to the first temple, walk to the back and enter the second. This second temple contains three of the largest golden Buddhas in the territory. Flanking the trio on either side is an equally impressive line-up of 12 Bodhisattvas. The third temple contains another large image of Lord Gautama.

The monastery is northeast of Tsuen Wan MTR station. To reach it, take green minibus 85 from Shiu Wo St, which is two blocks due south of the MTR station (exit B1).

SAM TUNG UK MUSEUM
MUSEUM

Map p168 (三棟屋博物館; ☎2411 2001; 2 Kwu Uk Lane; admission free; ☺9am-5pm Wed-Mon; ⓜT-suen Wan) This imaginative and well-tended museum aims to portray traditional rural life as it was lived in this late-18th-century

TAI MO SHAN

Hong Kong's tallest mountain is Tai Mo Shan (957m). Several hiking trails thread up and around it, but you'll need to bring your own food and water. The Countryside Series *North-east & Central New Territories* map is the one you want for this area.

The **Tai Mo Shan Country Park Visitor Centre** (大帽山郊野公園遊客中心; ☑2498 9326; ☺9.30am-4.30pm Sat, Sun & holidays) is at the junction of Route Twisk (the name is derived from 'Tsuen Wan into Shek Kong') and Tai Mo Shan Rd, which is crossed by the MacLehose Trail.

The nearest MTR station is Tsuen Wan (Map p168). From there, catch bus 51 on Tai Ho Rd North, alighting at the junction of Route Twisk and Tai Mo Shan Rd in Tsuen Kam Au. Follow Tai Mo Rd, which forms part of stage No 9 of the MacLehose Trail, east to the summit. On the right-hand side, about 45 minutes from the bus stop, a fork in the road leads south along a concrete path to the Sze Lok Yuen Hostel. Bus 64 also links Tai Mo Shan with Yuen Long and Tai Po Market, and bus 25K runs between Tai Po Market and Tai Mo Shan.

Hakka walled village, the former residents of which (the Chan clan) were resettled in 1980. Within the complex a dozen three-beamed houses contain traditional Hakka furnishings, kitchenware, wedding items and agricultural implements, most of which came from two 17th-century Hakka villages in Bao'an county in Guǎngdōng province. Behind the restored assembly and ancestral halls is the old village school, with interactive displays and videos on such topics as Hakka women, traditional crafts and traditional food.

At the Tsuen Wan MTR station, take exit E and walk five minutes southeast along Sai Lau Kok Rd to Kwu Uk Lane and the museum.

✖️ EATING

The two old-style Cantonese teahouses in the village of Chuen Lung to the west of Tai Mo Shan and 5km northeast of Tsuen Wan are favourite breakfast joints for hikers bound for Tai Mo Shan Country Park. Catch minibus 80 that leaves from Chuen Lung St in Tsuen Wan (MTR exit B1) and get off at the last stop.

CHOI LUNG
RESTAURANT   CANTONESE, TEAHOUSE $
off Map p168 (彩龍茶樓; ☑2415 5041; 2 Chuen Lung Village, Route Twisk; dim sum from $10; ☺5.30am-3pm) In a two-storey house near the village entrance, this 40-year old establishment is renowned for using the mountain spring water from Tai Mo Shan

to make sweet bean curds. The teahouse is self-service – you pick your dim sum from the kitchen and make your own tea. The best dim sum time is between 8am and 10am when the widest choices are served. There is no English signage but it's identifiable by the stools in its open area.

DUEN KEE
RESTAURANT   CANTONESE, TEAHOUSE $
off Map p168 (端記茶樓; ☑2490 5246; 57-58 Chuen Lung Village, Route Twisk; ☺6am-2pm) Not far from Choi Lung and located closer to the fields is this equally popular – and similarly no-frills – yum cha joint. You can have dim sum under one of the parasols on the ground floor; but the true attraction lies upstairs where older villagers show off their caged birds while sipping tea. The home-grown watercress is the signature vegetable here.

Tuen Mun

Explore

As always in New Towns, the centre of Tuen Mun is mundane, but its neighbouring areas are a spiritual stronghold of yesteryear and still boast several attractive temples today, making a trip to this part of the New Territories more delightful. If you want to stretch your legs, walk uphill to Tsing Shan Monastery and enjoy the sweeping views of Tuen Mun Valley; lazybones can head to

Miu Fat Monastery and Ching Chung Temple, both of which are conveniently served by Light Rail.

Foodwise, try the local speciality, roast goose, in the neighbourhood of Shem Tseng; alternatively, healthy country fare is to be had in Lam Tei.

The Best...

➡ **Sight** Miu Fat Monastery (below)

➡ **Place to Eat** Farmer Restaurant (p171)

Top Tip

If you're travelling to Tuen Mun from Tsuen Wan, Kowloon or Hong Kong Island by bus, sit on the upper deck on the left side for spectacular views of the Tsing Ma Bridge.

Getting There & Away

Bus Bus 60M from Tsuen Wan MTR station (exit A3) travels along the coast to Tuen Mun.

Ferry Services to Tuen Mun ferry pier arrive from Tung Chung, Sha Lo Wan and Tai O (all on Lantau). Ferries to the airport, Tung Chung and Tai O on Lantau depart from the pier to the southwest of the town centre.

Light Rail Tuen Mun is towards the southern end of the useful Light Rail network. Other major points include Tin Shui Wai, Yuen Long and Siu Hong. The station is linked to the MTR station.

MTR Tuen Mun is on the West Rail line.

Need to Know

➡ **Area code** ☑852

➡ **Location** 30km northwest of Kowloon Peninsula

➡ **Last train to Kowloon** 12.15am from Tuen Mun West Rail station

 SIGHTS

MIU FAT MONASTERY　　　　BUDDHIST
(妙法寺; ☑2461 8567; 18 Castle Peak Rd; ◷9am-5pm; ⍟line 751) Miu Fat Monastery in Lam Tei, due north of Tuen Mun town centre, resembles a Thai-style temple and is one of the most eye-catching Buddhist complexes in the territory. Guarding the entrance to

the main temple are two stone lions and two stone elephants, and there are attractive gardens outside.

You'll find a golden likeness of Buddha and three larger statues of Lord Gautama in the temple. Also, you won't miss the soaring new extension, a 45m tower with a top storey resembling a huge crystal lotus blossom. Unsurprisingly, the structure glows at night.

This is an active monastery; you'll see brown-robed nuns in droves.

To get there take Light Rail line 751 from the Tuen Mun or Town Centre stops to Lam Tei station. The complex is on the opposite side of Castle Peak Rd; cross over the walkway and walk north 150m. Bus 63X, from the Mong Kok MTR station, also stops in front of the monastery.

TSING SHAN MONASTERY　　　BUDDHIST
(青山禪院; ☑2461 8050; Tsing Shan Monastery Path; ◷24hr; ⍟line 610, 615, 615P) Also known as Castle Peak Monastery, this temple complex is perched on the hill of Castle Peak, and is the oldest temple in Hong Kong. Founded by Reverend Pui To (literally, 'travelling in a cup') 1500 years ago, the complex you see today was rebuilt in 1926. You'll see a cluster of shrines and temples for different saints and Bodhisattvas, including one to Pui To in a grotto, as you ascend the hill. Some of these have slid into dilapidation; nonetheless they're imbued with a spooky charm.

The temple was also one of the shooting locations for the Bruce Lee classic *Enter the Dragon*.

To reach there, board Light Rail line 610, 615 or 615P and alight at Tsing Shan Tsuen. From there follow the sign to Tsing Shan Monastery Path, which is due west of the station. The steep path to the entrance of the monastery is a 30-minute walk.

CHING CHUNG TEMPLE　　　TAOIST
(青松觀; ☑2370 8870; Tsing Lun Rd; ◷7am-6pm; ⍟line 505) Green Pine Temple is a peaceful Taoist temple complex northwest of Tuen Mun town centre. Walk through the rows of bonsai trees, bamboo and ponds and you'll reach the main temple which is dedicated to Lu Sun Young, one of the eight immortals of Taoism who lived in the 8th century. An annual **Bonsai Festival** is held here in April.

Ching Chung Temple is directly opposite Ching Ching Light Rail station. To reach it from the Tuen Mun or Town Centre stations, catch line 505.

EATING

You'll find plenty of Chinese restaurants and noodle shops in Tuen Mun town centre, but it's best to travel out a bit further for something unusual and delicious.

FARMER RESTAURANT CANTONESE $
(農家菜館; ☑2461 2381; Block C, Lam Tei Mei Ling Court, Castle Peak Rd; dishes from $48; ☉lunch & dinner; ☒line 751) This Michelin-recommended restaurant has some honest country fare for health-conscious folks. Most of the produce is sourced from the nearby villages and the cooking principle here is less salt and less oil. Try its silky steamed tofu in lotus leaf.

**NANG KEE GOOSE
RESTAURANT** CANTONESE $
(能記; ☑2491 0392; 13 Sham Hong Rd, Sun Tsuen, Sham Tseng; roast goose per plate from $90; ☉10.30am-11pm; ☒234A or 234B from Tsuen Wan town centre) Sham Tseng has long been famous for roast goose, and this 50-year-old place is the most-visited restaurant in the area. Savour the crispy skin and succulent meat with some beer.

Yuen Long

Explore

Yuen Long is an important transport hub and a gateway to the Mai Po Marshes and the nearby walled villages.

Bring your binoculars and set off early for Mai Po. Morning hours are the best time to go birdwatching. If you didn't manage to book a guided tour to Mai Po, Hong Kong Wetland Park is a more than worthy substitute.

Then head back to town, enjoy lunch in Dai Wing Wah, sampling some walled-village dishes, before you visit one or two of those fortified hamlets in Kat Hing Wai and Shui Tau Tsuen.

An even better place to spend an hour or two in the afternoon is along the popular Ping Shan Heritage Trail.

Watching the sunset in Pak Nai at the westernmost edge of Hong Kong is an unforgettable experience. Afterwards, a seafood dinner in Lau Fau Shan is the best way to end the day.

The Best...
➡ **Sight** Mai Po Marshes (p165)
➡ **Place to Eat** Dai Wing Wah (p173)

Top Tip
There are several bird hides in Hong Kong Wetland Park. The mudflat hide at the end of the mangrove boardwalk is where you can see the greatest variety of birds.

Getting There & Away

Bus From Yuen Long West Bus Terminal on Kik Yeung Rd, bus 968 leaves for Tin Hau on Hong Kong Island; bus 76K calls at Mai Po, Pak Wo Rd in Fanling and Choi Yun Rd in Sheung Shui.

Green Minibus Buses 35 and 33 from Tai Fung St travel respectively to Lau Fau Shan and Pak Nai via Ping Shan.

MTR Yuen Long, Long Ping and Tin Shui Wai stations are on the West Rail line; Ping Shan station is on the Light Rail line.

Need to Know
➡ **Area Code** ☑852
➡ **Location** 30km northwest of Kowloon Peninsula
➡ **Last Train to Kowloon** 12.26am from Yuen Long West Rail station

SIGHTS

MAI PO MARSHES WILDLIFE RESERVE
See p165.

PING SHAN HERITAGE TRAIL HERITAGE WALK
See p166.

HONG KONG WETLAND PARK PARK
(☑2708 8885; www.wetlandpark.com/en/index.asp; Wetland Park Rd, Tin Shui Wai; adult/child $30/15; ☉10am-5pm Wed-Mon; ☒line 705 or 706)

This 60-hectare ecological park is a window on the wetland ecosystems of northwest New Territories. The natural trails, bird hides and viewing platforms make it a handy and excellent spot for bird-watching. The futuristic grass-covered headquarters houses interesting galleries (including one on tropical swamps), a film theatre, a cafe and a viewing gallery. If you have binoculars then bring them; otherwise be prepared to wait to use the fixed points in the viewing galleries and hides.

To reach the Hong Kong Wetland Park, take the MTR West Rail to Tin Shui Wai and board Light Rail line 705 or 706, alighting at the Wetland Park stop. It can also be reached directly from Hong Kong Island: jump on a 967 bus at Admiralty MTR bus station.

LAU FAU SHAN & PAK NAI VILLAGE

Towards the northwestern edge of Hong Kong waters is **Lau Fau Shan** (流浮山; green minibus 35), a rural fishing village that hosts the only oyster farm in the territory. Today most people come here for the seafood restaurants, but the small oyster market is interesting enough to merit a peep. You'll see oyster farmers shucking the shelled creatures on the waterfront. Sweeping Deep Bay and Shékǒu in Shēnzhèn lie just across the waters. To get to the shore, walk through the paved path (next to the public toilet) that's lined with restaurants and fish tanks.

Four kilometres southwest of Lau Fau Shan, **Pak Nai** (白泥; green minibus 33) is quite deserted on weekdays, but you're likely to see hordes of snap-happy locals here on late weekend afternoons, and you can't blame them. Literally 'white mud', Pak Nai is one of the best places to see the sunset in Hong Kong. This 6km stretch of coastline is dotted with mangroves, fish ponds, farms, shacks and muddy beaches sprinkled with oyster shells. Sunset can be watched from most parts of Deep Bay Rd (it continues as Nim Wan Rd after Upper Pak Nai), the only road meandering along the coastline. Just get off the minibus when you see a spot you like. Green minibus 33 goes from Yuen Long via Lau Fau Shan. Check the website of **Hong Kong Observatory** (www.hko.gov.hk) for the sunset times.

KAT HING WAI VILLAGE

(吉慶圍; 64K) This tiny village is 500 years old and was walled during the early years of the Ming dynasty (1368–1644). It contains just one main street, off which a host of dark and narrow alleyways lead. There are quite a few new buildings and retiled older ones in the village. A small temple stands at the end of the street.

Visitors are asked to make a donation when they enter the village; put the money in the coin slot by the entrance. You can take photographs of the old Hakka women in their traditional black trousers, tunics and distinctive bamboo hats with black cloth fringes, but they'll expect you to pay (around $10).

To get there from Yuen Long, get off at the first bus stop on Kam Tin Rd, cross the road and walk east for 10 minutes. Alternatively, take a taxi from Kam Sheung Rd West Rail station for less than $20.

SHUI TAU TSUEN VILLAGE

(水頭村; 64K) This 17th-century village, a 15-minute walk north of Kam Tin Rd, is famous for its prow-shaped roofs decorated with dragons and fish along the ridges.

The **Tang Kwong U Ancestral Hall** (9am-1pm & 2-5pm Sat, Sun & public holidays) and the nearby **Tang Ching Lok Ancestral Hall** (9am-1pm & 2-5pm Wed, Sat & Sun) were built in the early 19th century for ancestor worship. The sculpted fish on the roof of the entrance hall symbolises luck. Between these two buildings is the small **Hung Shing Temple**. South of them is the village's most impressive sight **Yi Tai Study Hall** (9am-1pm & 2-5pm Wed, Sat & Sun), built in the 19th century and named after the gods of literature and martial arts. The **Tin Hau temple** (天后廟) on the outskirts of the village to the north was built in 1722 and contains an iron bell weighing 106kg.

There's been a lot of building in and around the village – the old sits rather uncomfortably with the new. But the further north you walk, the calmer and more tranquil it becomes.

To reach Shui Tau Tsuen, which is signposted from Kam Tin Rd, walk north, go through the subway below the Kam Tin Bypass, pass Kam Tai Rd and cross over the river to Chi Ho Rd. Go over the small bridge spanning a stream, turn right and then left to enter the village from the east. The first thing you'll pass is the Yi Tai Study Hall.

EATING

DAI WING WAH
HAKKA $

(大榮華酒樓; 2nd fl, Koon Wong Mansion, 2-6 On Ning Rd; dim sum $14, dishes from $70; ⊙6am-midnight; ⊠Tai Tong Rd Light Rail station) The brainchild of celebrated chef Leung Man-to, Dai Wing Wah is most famous for its walled-village dishes. Leung sources local ingredients from small farms and food producers whenever possible, and complements them with his innovations in cooking. Must-eats include lemon-steamed grey mullet, smoked oysters and Malay sponge cake. From Tai Tong Rd Light Rail station, walk north along Kuk Ting St then turn left on to Sai Tai St. You'll see the restaurant sitting 30m away.

HO TO TAI NOODLE SHOP
CANTONESE $

(好到底麵家; ☑2476 2495; 67 Fau Tsoi St; ⊙8am-8pm; ⊠Tai Tong Rd Light Rail station) This 60-year-old Yuen Long institution is one of the world's cheapest Michelin restaurants. It is best known for the fresh Cantonese egg noodles and shrimp roe noodles that it churns out daily. Foodies from all corners come to slurp the delightful wonton noodles. An English menu is available at the cashier. The haunt is a three-minute walk south of Tai Tong Rd Light Rail station.

PING SHAN TRADITIONAL POON CHOI
BASIN FOOD $

(屏山傳統盆菜; ☑2617 8000; 36 Tong Fong Tsuen, Ping Ha Rd; per basin for 6 $380, for 8-10 $680, for 10-12 $800; ⊙11am-9pm; ⊠Hang Mei Tsuen Light Rail station) It's a group activity to have *poon choy* (or basin feast), a form of traditional village banquet in the New Territories. There are three tiers of food, with the most expensive ingredients spread out on top. Expect piles of meat, seafood and root vegetables. Reservations are a must. The two-storey restaurant is in the 'hood of the Ping Shan Heritage Trail.

HAPPY SEAFOOD RESTAURANT
SEAFOOD $$

(歡樂海鮮酒家; ☑2472 3450; 12 Shan Ting St, Lau Fau Shan; meals $250-800; ⊙lunch & dinner; ⊠minibus 35 from Tai Fung St) The world's youngest cordon bleu chef, Lau Ka-lun, dishes out innovative seafood in this rural restaurant. Try the signature fried rice with crab roe, scallops and ostrich meat.

Fanling & Sheung Shui

Explore

Begin with a visit to the Fung Ying Sin Temple, which is just a stone's throw from Fanling East Rail station. After a vegetarian lunch in the temple, head to Lung Yeuk Tau Heritage Trail for some village immersion.

For the more adventurous, off-the-beaten-path options include the seldom-visited walled village of Ping Kong, or Sha Tau Kok, where Japanese pillboxes from the WWII lie intact in the (still) unspoilt countryside.

The Best...

➡ **Sight** Lung Yeuk Tau Heritage Trail (p174)

Top Tip

Some walled villages along the Lung Yeuk Tau Heritage Trail are private properties; be discreet and show common sense when you visit.

Getting There & Away

Bus Most onward travel connections depart from the East Rail stations. Bus 76K to Yuen Long and Mai Po Marshes departs from Pak Wo Rd in Fanling and Choi Yun Rd in Sheung Shui. Bus 77K to Ping Kong stops at Yuen Long Jockey Club Rd in Fanling and Po Shek Wu Rd in Sheung Shui.

Green Minibus Bus 58K heads to Ping Kong from San Wan Rd in Sheung Shui.

MTR Take the MTR to Fanling and Sheung Shui East Rail stations.

Need to Know

➡ **Area Code** ☑852

➡ **Location** Fanling and Sheung Shui are in north-central New Territories, much closer to the mainland (5km) than to Tsim Sha Tsui (20km)

➡ **Last Train to Kowloon** 12.35am from Sheung Shui East Rail station; 12.37am from Fanling East Rail station

👁 SIGHTS

LUNG YEUK TAU
HERITAGE TRAIL
HERITAGE WALK

(龍躍頭文物徑; 🚌54K) This 4.5km-long trail northeast of Fanling meanders through five relatively well-preserved walled villages and, like the village of Ping Shan, they are home to the Tang clan. The most attractive of the lot is the oldest (800 years) but most intact **Lo Wai**, identifiable by its 1m-thick fortified wall. Unfortunately, it's not open to the public. Admire the exterior, before carrying on to the more welcoming villages of **Tung Kok Wai** to the northeast and **Sun Wai** towards the northern end of the trail.

Other attractions here include the **Tang Chung Ling Ancestral Hall** (松嶺鄧公祠; ⊘9am-5pm Wed-Mon) and the adjacent **Tin Hau Temple**. The ancestral hall was built during the Ming dynasty and the dragon motif that you'll see on some of the spirit tablets inside the building was a symbol of the clan's royal status. The temple houses two bronze bells; one is from 1695, the other, 1700. **Shek Lo**, literally 'stone cottage' and built in 1925, is an eclectic mix of colonial and traditional Chinese architectural styles. The cottage appears to be permanently locked, but it can be seen clearly from the east of Tsung Kyam Church, the start of the trail.

To get there from Fanling East Rail station (Exit C), take the green minibus 54K and ask to be dropped at Tsung Kyam Church (Shun Him Tong in Cantonese).

FUNG YING SIN TEMPLE
TEMPLE

(蓬瀛仙館; ☎2669 9186; 66 Pak Wo Rd, Fanling; ⊘8am-6pm; 🚇Fanling) This huge Taoist temple complex opposite the Fanling East Rail station has wonderful exterior murals of Taoist immortals and the Chinese zodiac, an orchard terrace, a herbal clinic and a **vegetarian restaurant** (Ground & 1st fl, Bldg A7; ⊘10am-5pm). Most important are the dozen ancestral halls behind the main temple, where the ashes of the departed are deposited in niche urns.

TAI FU TAI MANSION
HISTORIC BUILDING

(大夫第; San Tin, Yuen Long; ⊘9am-1pm & 2-5pm Wed-Mon; 🚌76K) Located between Yuen Long and Sheung Shui, this splendid Mandarin-style building complex from 1865 is eclectically fused with Western design. Members of the Man clan, another powerful family in the New Territories, lived here for well over a century until they moved out in 1980. The courtyard is encircled by stone walls with a guarded checkpoint. Inside, auspicious Chinese symbols are found in the woodcarvings along with art nouveau glass panels, and there is a European fountain.

Board bus 76K in Sheung Shui and get off at the San Tin stop.

PING KONG
VILLAGE

(🚌77K) This sleepy walled village in the hills south of Sheung Shui is seldom visited by outsiders. Like other walled villages still inhabited in Hong Kong, it is a mix of old and new, and has a lovely little **Tin Hau temple** (天后廟) in the centre.

To get to Ping Kong from Sheung Shui East Rail station (exit A), catch green minibus 58K from the huge minibus station south of Landmark North shopping centre on San Wan Rd. A taxi from the Sheung Shui East Rail station to Ping Kong costs $30.

Tai Po

Explore

Tai Po is perhaps the most interesting New Town in the New Territories since it attracts many visitors for reasons beyond the fact that it is a useful transport hub. Start early, and spend 30 minutes to an hour in the Railway Museum before proceeding to the charming Tai Po Market. If you come on Sunday, don't miss the Farmer's Market.

Make a wish to Lam Tsuen Wishing Tree if you have time, or head to Ng Tung Chai Waterfalls and the Kadoorie Farm nearby. If you're after more local flora and fauna, then don't go home without visiting the beautiful Fung Yuen Butterfly Reserve.

Tai Ming Sq in the town centre will have enough eateries to satisfy your grazing needs.

The Best...

➡ **Sight** Tai Po Market (p175)
➡ **Place to Eat** Yak Lok Barbecue Restaurant (p177)

WORTH A DETOUR

SHA TAU KOK

An off-limit frontier area for over 60 years, **Sha Tau Kok** (沙頭角), which lies 11km northeast of Fanling, was sealed off from the rest of Hong Kong in 1951 following the Communist takeover of China. While access to the border town itself is still restricted to local residents, the 400 hectares of land – and the patchwork of time-warped villages that it contains – to the west and southwest were partially reopened in February 2012.

Tam Shui Hang Village (担水坑村), the village right next to the frontier checkpoint, is worth a wee wander. It has a cluster of old and new village houses and several intact ancestral halls. To the northeast, WWII buffs may want to venture out to the rolling hills behind Shan Tsui Village to look for a group of **Japanese pillboxes** (日軍碉堡). From Tam Shui Hang Village, walk north (200m) to the antiquated **Kwan Ah School** (群雅學校), identifiable by a basketball court in front of it. Pass the Pak Kung shrine and descend to Shan Tsui Village. From here, take the path to your left and walk uphill for five minutes, and you'll see some trenches that will lead you to the pillboxes.

There are at least six pillboxes hidden in the mountains but the trails are not well marked. If you want to go further off the beaten path, the villagers may have some interesting pointers.

Bus 78K or green minibus 55K from Landmark North shopping centre in Sheung Shui take you to Sha Tau Kok. When you arrive at the frontier checkpoint, the friendly police will signal you to get off.

➡ **Place to Ride** Tai Po to Plover Cove Reservoir (p177)

Top Tip

Tai Po has a number of markets and nature sanctuaries that are more than worth a visit, so wake up early!

Getting There & Away

Bus Bus 71K runs between the Tai Wo and Tai Po Market East Rail stations.

Green Minibus For onward travel, start at Tai Po Market East Rail station or from Heung Sze Wui St, take bus 20K for San Mun Tsai; catch bus 25K at Tsing Yuen St to get to Ng Tung Chai (Tai Mo Shan).

MTR Take the MTR to Tai Po Market or Tai Wo East Rail stations.

Need to Know

➡ **Area Code** ☎852
➡ **Location** 13km to the Hong Kong–China border at Lo Wu; 18km north of Kowloon Peninsula
➡ **Last Train to Kowloon** 12.42am from Tai Wo East Rail station; 12.45am from Tai Po Market East Rail station

◉ SIGHTS

TAI PO MARKET MARKET

Map p176 (大埔街市; Fu Shin St; ☺6am-8pm; ▣Tai Wo) Not to be confused with the East Rail station of the same name, this street-long outdoor wet market is a stone's throw from the Hong Kong Railway Museum and is one of the most interesting markets in the New Territories.

MAN MO TEMPLE TEMPLE

Map p176 (文武廟; Fu Shin St; ☺8am-6pm; ▣Tai Wo) Towards the northern end of Fu Shin St, the double-hall Man Mo Temple from the late 19th century is a centre of worship for the Tai Po area. Like the Man Mo Temple in Sheung Wan, it's dedicated to the gods of literature and war.

HONG KONG RAILWAY MUSEUM MUSEUM

Map p176 (香港鐵路博物館; ☎2653 3455; 13 Shung Tak St; admission free; ☺9am-5pm Wed-Mon; ▣Tai Wo) Housed in the former Tai Po Market train station (built in 1913 in traditional Chinese style), this interesting museum has a narrow-gauge steam locomotive dating back to 1911 which, together with all the other valuable exhibits, charts the history of rail transport development in the territory.

Tai Po

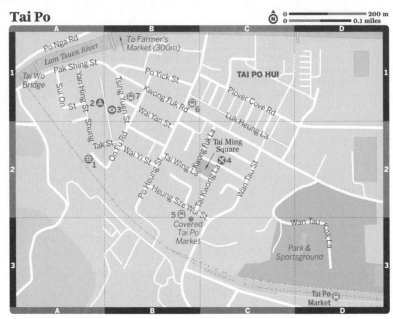

Tai Po

◎ Sights	(p175)
1 Hong Kong Railway Museum	A2
2 Man Mo Temple	A1
3 Tai Po Market	B1

✖ Eating	(p177)
4 Yak Lok Barbecue Restaurant	C2

ℹ Transport	(p175)
5 Bus & Minibus Stop	B2
6 Bus Stop 70,72,72A & 74	B1
7 Minibus 25K	B1

You can get to the museum most easily by alighting at Tai Wo East Rail station. From there, walk south through the Tai Wo Shopping Centre and housing estate, then cross the Lam Tsuen River via Tai Wo Bridge (the small one with the Chinese roof) leading from Po Nga Rd. The museum is just southeast.

FARMER'S MARKET
MARKET

off Map p176 (大埔農墟; http://hongkongfarmersmarket.org; Tai Wo St; ⊙9am-5pm Sun; ⮂Tai Wo) Every Sunday, dozens of local farmers showcase their produce and wares, from fruits to vegetables to natural cosmetics, right in the heart of Tai Po. The earlier you

come, the greater the buzz. From Tai Wo East Rail station, take exit B, walk through Tai Wo Plaza and follow the signpost to Oi Wo House. From there, you'll see an electric substation across the road. The entrance to the market is right next to it.

FUNG YUEN BUTTERFLY RESERVE
WILDLIFE RESERVE

(鳳園蝴蝶保育區; ☑3111 7344; www.fungyuen.org; 150 Fung Yuen Rd; admission $20; ⊙9am-5pm; ⮂green minibus 20A) Less than 4km northeast of Tai Po town lies this sprawling 42-hectare Special Site of Scientific Interest where more than 180 butterfly species will dazzle your eyeballs. A third of them are rare breeds, including the common birdwing and white dragontail. The best time to spot them is before 10am. Green minibus 20A leaves every half hour from Tai Po Market East Rail station. Ask to be dropped off at Fung Yuen Chun Kung Sor (鳳園村公所).

LAM TSUEN WISHING TREE
TEMPLE

(林村許願樹; Lam Kam Rd, Fong Ma Po; ⮂64K) Until a short time ago Tai Po was the springboard for this large banyan tree, laden with coloured streamers of paper tied to oranges, in the village of Fong Ma Po to the west. The idea was to write your wish on a piece of paper, tie it to the citrus

TWO-WHEELERS' TAI PO

One cycling route not to miss is the ride to Plover Cove Reservoir on the northeastern side of Tolo Harbour. Another is to the Chinese University of Hong Kong in Ma Liu Shui, on the southwestern side of the harbour. Allow half a day for either trip. There is also an inland route that goes to the university, but the coastal route linking the university with Tai Mei Tuk has the better views. Another option is to follow Ting Kok Rd east to the fishing village of San Mun Tsai.

Bicycles can be rented in season from several stalls around Tai Po Market East Rail station, but try to arrive early – they often run out during the busiest times. A number of bicycle shops line Kwong Fuk Rd northwest of the station.

fruit and then throw it as high as you could up into the tree. If your fruit lodged in the branches, you were in luck – and the higher it went, the more chance there was of your wish coming true. But in 2005 a large branch of the tree came crashing to the ground, dashing most punters' wishes once and for all.

Now the tree is being left alone to recover and, in the name of conservation, wish makers can only tie their wishing papers to Chinese-style wooden racks, or throw plastic fruits (available from the on-site vendors) onto a plastic tree. There's a small **Tin Hau temple** nearby, replete with fortune-tellers, to compensate for your curtailed wish making.

To reach the tree catch bus 64K from the Tai Po Market East Rail station and alight at Fong Ma Po.

NG TUNG CHAI WATERFALL & KADOORIE FARM & BOTANIC GARDEN   WATERFALL, GARDEN
(梧桐寨瀑布 & 嘉道理農場暨植物園; ☑2483 7200; www.kfbg.org.hk; Lam Kam Rd; admission free; ☉9.30am-5pm; ☐64K) The scenic area around the **Ng Tung Chai Waterfall** is a retreat from the hustle and bustle of downtown Tai Po. Reach the series of streams and waterfalls by bus 64K from Tai Po Market East Rail station, and get off at Ng Tung Chai stop. Enter the eponymous village and hike through the bamboo groves towards the **Man Tak Monastery** (萬德苑), which can be reached in 30 minutes. From the monastery, hike uphill for 20 more minutes and you'll see one of the waterfalls sliding down.

Kadoorie Farm & Botanic Garden, southwest of Ng Tung Chai, is primarily a conservation and teaching centre, but the gardens are especially lovely, with many indigenous birds, animals, insects and plants

in residence. You can reach the farm most easily on bus 64K.

EATING

Tai Ming Sq in Tai Po town centre has decent street food and many Chinese eateries serving old-style Hakka snacks.

YAK LOK BARBECUE RESTAURANT   CANTONESE $
Map p176 (一樂燒臘飯店; ☑2656 4732; 5 Tai Ming Lane; ☉11am-11pm; ☒Tai Po Market) Celebrity chef Anthony Bourdain counts among the many pilgrims who have made it to this family-run eatery to try the mouthwatering barbecued pork and roast goose. Chinese menu only, but the owner speaks decent English.

Plover Cove

Explore

Plover Cove has only two themes: hiking and cycling. Large parts of it are designated Geopark areas, so you'll see rugged rocks and mineral marvels, especially around Plover Cove Reservoir. Plan a full day here. For an easy walk, the 4.4km Pat Sing Leng Nature Trail is a good alternative.

The Best...

➡ **Sight** Plover Cove Reservoir (p180)
➡ **Place to Eat** Cafe de Country Art (p181)

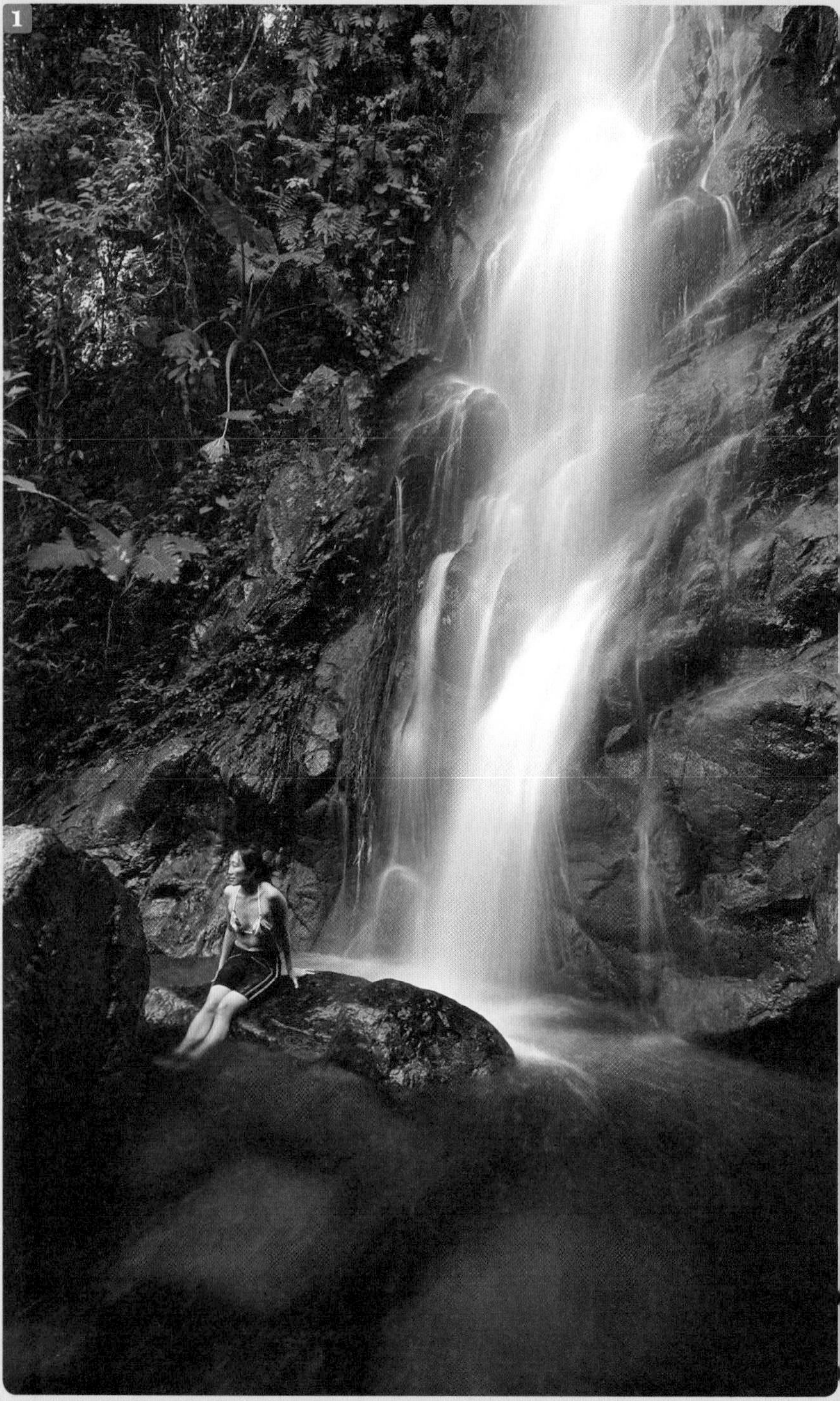
1

1. Hiking Trails

Hiking trails in the New Territories lead past waterfalls and parks.

2. Yuen Yuen Institute (p167)

Crowds come here to burn offerings to Taoist and Buddhist deities, represented by vivid statues.

3. Hong Kong Heritage Museum (p182)

Home to a rich collections of arts, the musuem also houses innovative temporary exhibits.

4. Hong Kong Wetland Park (p171)

These 61-hectares of swampy biodiversity are nestled beneath an arc of skyscrapers.

Top Tip

The challenging (uphill) but also scenic route to cycle is to begin in Tai Mei Tuk and go all the way north to the border at Sha Tau Kok.

Getting There & Away

Bus Take bus 75K (and additionally 74K or 275R on Sundays and holidays) from Tai Po Market East Rail station in Tai Po.

Green Minibus Bus 20C passes Tai Po Market East Rail station and Heung Sze Wui St in Tai Po on its way to Plover Cove.

Need to Know

➡ **Area Code** ☑852

➡ **Location** 12km northeast of Tai Po

➡ **Last Train to Kowloon** 12.45am from Tai Po Market East Rail station

SIGHTS

PAT SIN LENG NATURE TRAIL   OUTDOORS

(☐75K) This excellent 4.4km-long trail, which should take from two to 2½ hours, leads from the Plover Cove Country Park Visitor Centre at Tai Mei Tuk and heads northeast for 4km to Bride's Pool; there are signboards numbered 1 to 22, so there is little danger of getting lost. The scenery is excellent and the two waterfalls at Bride's Pool are delightful, but the place gets packed on the weekend. You can either return to Tai Mei Tuk via Bride's Pool Rd on foot or catch green minibus 20C, which stops at Tai Mei Tuk before carrying on to Tai Po Market East Rail station.

Those looking for a more strenuous hike can join stage No 9 of the **Wilson Trail** at Tai Mei Tuk on the Plover Cove Reservoir and head west into the steep Pat Sin Leng range of hills to Wong Leng Shan (639m). The trail then carries on westward to Hok Tau Reservoir and Hok Tau Wai (12km, four hours).

PLOVER COVE RESERVOIR   OUTDOORS

(☐75K) Now part of the Hong Kong Geopark, Plover Cove Reservoir was completed in 1968 and holds 230 million cubic metres of water. The reservoir was built in a very unusual way. Rather than build a dam across a river, of which Hong Kong has very few, a barrier was erected across the mouth of a great bay. The sea water was siphoned out and fresh water – mostly piped in from the mainland – was pumped in.

The area around Plover Cove Reservoir is good hiking and cycling country, and well worth at least a full day's exploring. The village of **Tai Mei Tuk**, the springboard for most of the activities in the Plover Cove area, is about 6km northeast of Tai Po Market East Rail station.

It may be worthwhile getting a copy of Universal Publications' *Tseung Kwan O, Sai Kung, Clearwater Bay,* or else the Countryside Series map *North-east & Central New Territories.*

UNIVERSITY SIGHTS

Chinese University of Hong Kong (香港中文大學; ☑2609 7000; www.cuhk.edu.hk; ☒University) has its main campus in Sha Tin. If you are in this neck of the woods, it's worth making time to see the university's **art museum** (香港中文大學文物館; ☑3943 7416; www.cuhk.edu.hk/ics/amm; Institute of Chinese Studies, Central Campus, admission free; ☉10am-5pm, closed public holidays). The four-floor East Wing Galleries house a permanent collection of Chinese paintings and calligraphy, but it is the ceramics and jade objets d'art that are especially worth inspecting, including 2000-year-old bronze seals and a large collection of jade flower carvings. The West Wing Galleries stage five to six special exhibitions each year.

Other than that, the **lotus pond** in Chung Chi Campus (you'll see it when you step out of the train station) is a photogenic spot, especially when the lotuses are blooming in spring; and the **Pavilion of Harmony** (合一亭) in hilly New Asia Campus offers panoramic views of Tolo Harbour.

A shuttle bus from University station travels through the campuses. The bus runs every 20 to 30 minutes daily and is free.

WORTH A DETOUR

TAI PO KAU NATURE RESERVE

The **Tai Po Kau Nature Reserve** (大埔滘自然護理區; Tai Po Rd; 🚌70 or 72) is a thickly forested 460-hectare 'special area' and is Hong Kong's most extensive woodlands. It is home to many species of butterflies, amphibians, birds, dragonflies and trees, and is a superb place in which to enjoy a quiet walk. The reserve is criss-crossed with four main tracks ranging in length from 3km (red trail) to 10km (yellow trail), plus a short nature trail of less than 1km. The reserve is supposed to emphasise conservation and education rather than recreation.

About 1km northwest of the reserve entrance and down steep Hung Lam Dr is the **Kerry Lake Egret Nature Park** and the overpriced **Museum of Ethnology** (🖉2657 6657; www.taipokau.org; 2 Hung Lam Dr; adult/concession $18/12; ⊙2-3pm & 5-6pm Sun & public holidays).

Tai Po Kau Nature Reserve lies south of Tai Po, less than 1km inland from Tolo Harbour. The main entrance and the information centre are at the village of Tsung Tsai Yuen in the northernmost part of the reserve along Tai Po Rd. The reserve is well served by buses. Bus 70 passes through Jordan and Mong Kok on its way here. Bus 72 can be used to get here from nearby the Sha Tin and Tai Po Market East Rail stations. A taxi from Tai Po Market East Rail station will cost around $25, and from the University East Rail station about $40.

Bicycles can be rented at several locations in Tai Mei Tuk, including **Lung Kee Bikes** (🖉2662 5266; bicycle rental per day $30; ⊙9.30am-6pm). A bicycle track along the coast runs from Tai Mei Tuk to Chinese University at Ma Liu Shui. Ting Kok Rd in Lung Mei Village is also where you'll find a row of popular restaurants. **Cafe de Country Art** (藝程雅聚; 🖉2824 1812; 64b Lung Mei Village; ⊙11am-10pm), set in a colourfully painted village house, wins points for its excellent (Western) food, cosy ambience and righteous prices.

The **Plover Cove Country Park Visitor Centre** (船灣郊野公園遊客中心; 🖉2665 3413; ⊙9.30am-4pm Sat, Sun & public holidays), a short distance further east from the car park on Ting Kok Rd, is where the Pat Sin Leng Nature Trail to Bride's Pool starts.

Sha Tin

Explore

You're likely to arrive in New Town Plaza, a claustrophobic shopping mall connected to Sha Tin station on the East Rail line, if you visit this busy part of the New Territories. There are a couple of noteworthy religious establishments in the area – 10,000 Bud-

dhas Monastery on Po Fook Shan Hill and Che Kung Temple by Shing Mun River.

The town's other key drawcard is the Hong Kong Heritage Museum, where you can relive Hong Kong's past in a range of thoughtfully constructed exhibitions.

If you'd rather have some raw outdoor action, then time your visit with one of the rip-roaring weekend race days at the beautifully set Sha Tin Racecourse.

Try the local speciality, roast pigeon, in the nostalgia-inducing Lung Wah Hotel Restaurant. If you want a bigger bird, the Peking duck at Sha Tin 18 will demand your total attention.

The Best...

➡ **Sight** Hong Kong Heritage Museum (p182)

➡ **Place to Eat** Lung Wah Hotel Restaurant (p184)

Top Tip

On race days, entry to the Sha Tin Racecourse is free from around 3pm (roughly halfway through the afternoon program).

Getting There & Away

Bus Buses into and out of Sha Tin leave from/terminate at City One Plaza Sha Tin bus station. Bus 182 links Sha Tin with Wan Chai, Admiralty and Central. Bus

Sha Tin

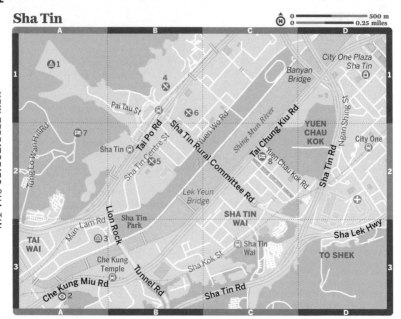

Sha Tin

170 connects Sha Tin East Rail bus station with Causeway Bay and Aberdeen. Bus 299 shuttles between Sha Tin and Sai Kung.

MTR Sha Tin, Tai Wai and Racecourse stations are on the East Rail line; Che Kung Temple station is on Ma On Shan line.

Need to Know

➡ **Area Code** ☑852

➡ **Location** 12km north of Kowloon Peninsula

➡ **Last Train to Kowloon** 12.57am from Sha Tin East Rail station

⦿ SIGHTS

HONG KONG HERITAGE MUSEUM MUSEUM
Map p182 (香港文化博物館; ☑2180 8188; www.heritagemuseum.gov.hk; 1 Man Lam Rd; adult/concession $10/5, Wed admission free; ⦿10am-6pm Mon & Wed-Sat, to 7pm Sun; ☒Che Kung Temple) Located southwest of Sha Tin town centre, this worthwhile museum boasts both rich permanent collections and innovative temporary exhibits in a dozen galleries.

The ground floor contains a book and gift shop, the wonderful **Children's Discovery Gallery**, with eight learning and play zones (including 'Life in a Village', 'Undersea Garden' and 'Mai Po Marsh') for kids aged four to 10, a **Hong Kong Toy Story** hands-on area for tots and an **Orientation Theatre**, with a 12-minute introductory video in English on the hour.

The 1st floor contains the best of the museum's permanent collection: the **New Territories Heritage Hall**, with mock-ups of traditional shops, a Hakka fishing village and scenes showing the history of the New Towns; the **Cantonese Opera Heritage Hall**, where you can watch old operas on video with English subtitles and 'virtually' make yourself up as a Cantonese opera character on computer or just enjoy the costumes and sets; and the **Chao Shao-an**

Gallery, devoted to the works of the eponymous water-colourist (1905–98) and founder of the Lingnan School of painting.

The 2nd floor contains another thematic gallery and the **TT Tsui Gallery of Chinese Art**, an Aladdin's cave of fine ceramics, pottery, bronze, jade and lacquerware, stone carvings and furniture.

To reach the Hong Kong Heritage Museum from Che Kung Temple MTR station, walk east along Che Kung Miu Rd, go through the subway and cross the footbridge over the channel. The museum is 200m to the east.

10,000 BUDDHAS MONASTERY   BUDDHIST

Map p182 (萬佛寺; ☑2691 1067; admission free; ⊘10am-5pm; ⓇSha Tin) This quirky temple about 500m northwest of Sha Tin station is worth the uphill hike to visit. Built in the 1950s, the complex actually contains more than 10,000 Buddhas. Some 12,800 miniature statues line the walls of the main temple and dozens of life-sized golden statues of Buddha's followers flank the steep steps leading to the monastery complex. There are several temples and pavilions split over two levels, as well as a nine-storey pagoda.

To reach the monastery, take exit B at Sha Tin station and walk down the ramp, passing a series of traditional houses at Pai Tau Village on the left. Take the left onto Pai Tau St, and turn right onto Sheung Wo Che St. At the end of this road, a series of signs in English will direct you to the left along a concrete path and through bamboo groves to the first of some 400 steps leading up to the monastery.

AMAH ROCK   LANDMARK

(望夫石) This oddly shaped boulder southwest of Sha Tin, like many local landmarks in Hong Kong, carries a legend. It seems that for many years a fisherman's wife would stand on this spot in the hills above **Lion Rock Country Park**, watching for her husband to return from the sea while carrying her baby on her back. One day he didn't come back – and she waited and waited. The gods apparently took pity on her and transported her to heaven on a lightning bolt, leaving her form in stone. The name of the rock in Cantonese is Mong Fu Shek, or 'Gazing Out for Husband Stone'.

As you take the MTR south from Sha Tin to Kowloon, Amah Rock is visible to the east (ie on the left-hand side) up on the hillside after Tai Wai East Rail station, but before the train enters the tunnel.

CHE KUNG TEMPLE   TAOIST

Map p182 (車公廟; ☑2691 1733; Che Kung Miu Rd; admission free; ⊘7am-6pm; ⓇChe Kung Temple) This large Taoist temple complex, rebuilt in 1993, is on the opposite bank of the Shing Mun River channel. It's dedicated to Che Kung, a Song-dynasty general credited with ridding Sha Tin of the plague. The best time to visit the temple is on the third day of Chinese New Year, when hordes of worshippers come here to rotate the sails of the copper windmill inside the temple for good luck.

SHA TIN RACECOURSE   RACECOURSE

(沙田賽馬場; ☑hotline 1817; www.hkjc.com; Penfold Park; admission on race days public stands $10, members enclosures $100-150; ⓇRacecourse) Northeast of Sha Tin town centre is Hong Kong's second racecourse, which can accommodate up to 80,000 punters. Races are usually held on Sunday afternoon (and sometimes on Saturday and public holidays) from September to early July; a list of race meetings is available from the Hong Kong Jockey Club website.

The Racecourse East Rail station, just west of the track, opens on race days only.

✖ EATING

SHATIN NEW TOWN PLAZA   FAST FOOD $

Map p182 (新城市廣場; ☑2684 9175; www.new townplaza.com.hk; 18 Sha Tin Centre St; ⊘10am-10pm; ⓇSha Tin) This multilevel shopping complex, connected to the Sha Tin station, has a large number of (mostly chain) eateries to fit everyone's taste and budget.

SHA TIN 18   CANTONESE, NORTHERN CHINESE $$

(沙田18; ☑3723 1234; www.hongkong.shatin.hyatt.com; Hyatt Regency Hong Kong, 18 Chak Cheung St; ⊘11.30am-3pm & 5.30-10.30pm; ⓇUniversity) The Peking duck (whole $498, half $268) here has put this hotel restaurant, adjacent to the campus of the Chinese University, in the gastronomic spotlight since its opening in 2009. Book your prized fowl 24 hours in advance. Tantalise your taste buds in two ways – pancakes with the crispy skin, and wok-fried mince duck with iceberg lettuce. The restaurant also boasts a tempting dessert counter.

SHING KEE DAI PAI DONG, CANTONESE $

Map p182 (盛記; ☎2692 6611; Shop 5, Lek Yuen Estate Market; ⊙6am-4pm & 7-11pm; ☐83k from Sha Tin New Town Plaza) Tucked in the oldest public housing estate in Sha Tin, this 30-year-old establishment is no ordinary *dai pai dong* (food stall). It resembles a gallery, with black-and-white photos stuck on the wall, CDs, toys, and potted plants in other corners. All, including the chairs, were picked up from public wheelie bins and arty-craftily recycled by the owner. Noodles are served in the daytime. In the evening, it turns into a popular hotpot joint, with several dozens of broths on offer. To get there, take bus 83K, or it's a 15-minute walk northeast from Sha Tin station.

LUNG WAH HOTEL
RESTAURANT CANTONESE $

Map p182 (龍華酒店; ☎2691 1828; www.lung wahhotel.hk; 22 Ha Wo Che; ⊙11am-11pm; ℝSha Tin, exit B) This is where Bruce Lee is said to have stayed during the filming of *The Big Boss*. It's now a restaurant, frequented by nostalgic adults. You'll find a small playground out front where peacocks are kept in cages, and an outdoor area where old men come to play mahjong. Foodwise, stick with the roast pigeon. To reach the hotel, walk north for 10 minutes along the railway line after exiting the train station.

Sai Kung Peninsula

Explore

The rugged and massive Sai Kung Peninsula is an outdoor pursuits paradise. The hiking is excellent here – the MacLehose Trail runs right across it. Sai Kung Town is a good base for exploring the easily accessible countryside here.

Hire a *kaido* (small, open-sea ferry), pack a picnic and drop anchor off one of the remote beaches. Long Ke and Tai Long Wan are among the most beautiful (and popular) beaches to loll around.

For a shoal of seafood possibilities, Sai Kung Town has a variety of fish menus to drool over.

The Sai Kung District Council's website www.travelinsaikung.org.hk is a useful planning resource.

The Best...

➤ **Sight** Tai Long Wan Hiking Trail (p186)
➤ **Place to Eat** Loaf On (p187)
➤ **Place to Drink** Steamers (p189)

Top Tip

Near the pier, you'll find one of the liveliest fish markets in Hong Kong, where fishermen sell their catch directly from their boats.

Getting There & Away

Sai Kung Town – Bus From Sai Kung Town, bus 299 heads to Sha Tin East Rail station, bus 92 runs to Diamond Hill and Choi Hung, bus 96R (Sunday and public holidays) heads to Wong Shek, Hebe Haven, and Choi Hung and Diamond Hill MTR stations, while bus 792M calls at Tseung Kwan O and Tiu Keng Leng MTR stations. Bus 94 goes to Wong Shek.

Sai Kung Town – Green Minibus From Sai Kung Town, buses 1A, 1M and 1S (12.30am to 6.10am) go to Hebe Haven and Choi Hung MTR station.

Pak Tam Chung – Bus Take bus 94 from Sai Kung Town.

Hoi Ha – Green minibus Minibus 7 makes the run from Sai Kung Town daily, with the first departure at 8.25am and the last at 6.45pm. A taxi from there will cost around $120.

Need to Know

➤ **Area Code** ☎852
➤ **Location** 21km northeast of Kowloon
➤ **Last Train to Kowloon** 12.20am from Tseung Kwan O station, 12.22am from Tiu Keng Leng MTR station

◉ SIGHTS

◉ Sai Kung Town

This small waterfront town has a cluster of restaurants and is also a stopping point and transport hub to and from the surrounding

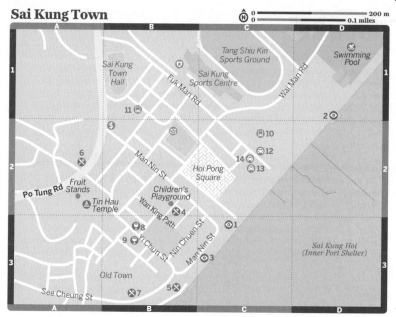

Sai Kung Town

countryside. A *kaido* trip to one or more of the little offshore islands and their secluded beaches is recommended. Windsurfing equipment can be hired from the **Windsurfing Centre** (☏2792 5605; ☺9.30am-6pm Sat & Sun, call ahead on weekdays) at Sha Ha, just north of Sai Kung Town. Bus 94, heading for the pier at Wong Shek and the springboard for Tap Mun Chau, will drop you off, or you could walk there from town in about 15 minutes.

◉ Hebe Haven

Cantonese speakers call this cove Pak Sha Wan (White Sand Bay), which is home to the **Hebe Haven Yacht Club** (白沙灣遊艇會; ☏2719 9682; www.hhyc.org.hk). It has a large fleet of yachts and other pleasure craft all but choking Marina Cove.

To swim at Trio beach, opposite the marina, catch a sampan from Hebe Haven (白沙灣) to the long, narrow peninsula called Ma Lam Wat; along the way you'll pass a small **Tin Hau temple** on a spit of land jutting out to the south. The beach is excellent and the sampan trip should only cost a few dollars. You can also walk to the peninsula from Sai Kung Town; it's about 4km.

LIONS NATURE EDUCATION CENTRE
OUTDOOR

(獅子會自然教育中心; ☏2792 2234; www.lnec. gov.hk; Pak Kong; admission free; ☺9am-5pm Wed-Mon; ☒92) One of the best kid-pleasing destinations around, this 34-hectare attraction,

WORTH A DETOUR

TAP MUN CHAU

The very isolated Tap Mun Chau, also known as 'Grass Island', is definitely worth the trip, and you will be rewarded with a something that's hard to come by in Hong Kong: isolation and an otherworldly feel. The sailing is particularly scenic from Wong Shek, as the boat cruises through the fjord Tai Tan Hoi Hap.

Tap Mun Village is noted for its **Tin Hau temple**, which was built in the early 18th century and is northeast from where the boat docks. The Birthday of Tin Hau festival, celebrated in late April/early May, is big here. Part of the temple is devoted to the god of war Kwan Tai.

Other attractions include seafood drying on racks in the sun, dragon boats bobbing in the harbour and, strangely, a herd of cows. It's an easy (and signposted) walk northward to **Mau Ping Shan** (125m), the island's highest point; a windy pebble **beach** on the southeastern shore; and an odd stone formation called **Balanced Rock**, 200m south of the beach.

If you want to stay here, the only option is to pitch a tent. There are shops selling snacks and drinks, and **New Hon Kee** (新漢記; ☑2328 2428; 4 Tap Mun Hoi Pong St; meals from $100; ☺lunch Mon-Fri, 11am-4.30pm Sat & Sun), a seafood restaurant popular with islanders and visitors alike, is a short walk northeast of the ferry pier on the way to Tin Hau temple.

The island is off the northeast coast of the New Territories, where the Tolo Channel empties into Mirs Bay (Tai Pang Wan in Cantonese). Ferries depart from Wong Shek in Sai Kung and Ma Liu Shui near University East Rail station.

2km northwest of Hebe Haven, is Hong Kong's first nature education centre. It comprises everything from an arboretum, a medicinal plants garden and an insectarium to a mineral and rocks corner and a shell house. The Dragonfly Pond, which boasts up to a quarter of the more than 100 dragonfly species found in Hong Kong, is the star of the show.

You can reach the centre on bus 92 from Diamond Hill MTR and Choi Hung, bus 96R on Sunday and holidays from Diamond Hill, and green minibus 1A from Choi Hung.

⊙ Pak Tam Chung

Pak Tam Chung (北潭涌) is the start of the MacLehose Trail (see p59).

SAI KUNG COUNTRY PARK VISITOR CENTRE   OUTDOORS

(西貢郊野公園遊客中心; ☑2792 7365; Tai Mong Tsai Rd; ☺9.30am-4.30pm Wed-Mon; ☐94) While you're in Pak Tam Chung, visit the Sai Kung Country Park Visitor Centre, which is to the south of the village, just by the road from Sai Kung. It has excellent maps, photographs and displays of the area's geology, fauna and flora, as well as useful information on the traditional villages nearby and Hoi Ha Wan Marine Park.

SHEUNG YIU FOLK MUSEUM   MUSEUM

(上窰民俗文物館; ☑2792 6365; admission free; ☺9am-4pm Wed-Mon; ☐94) This museum is a leisurely 20-minute walk south of Pak Tam Chung along the 1km-long **Pak Tam Chung Nature Trail**. The museum is part of a restored Hakka village typical of those found here in the 19th century. The village was founded about 150 years ago by the Wong clan, which built a kiln to make bricks. In the whitewashed dwellings, pigpens and cattle sheds – all surrounded by a high wall and watchtower to guard against pirate raids – there are farm implements, objects of daily use, furnishings and Hakka clothing.

⊙ Hoi Ha, Wong Shek, Chek Keng & Tai Long Wan

TAI LONG WAN HIKING TRAIL   OUTDOORS

(☐village bus 29R) The northern end of Sai Kung Peninsula boasts several rewarding hikes that will take you through some of the most pristine scenery in Hong Kong. The breathtaking 12km Tai Long Wan Hiking

Trail, which starts from the end of Sai Wan Rd and passes through beautiful coves like Sai Wan, Tai Long Wan and Chek Keng, is a perennially popular option. On weekdays you're likely to have the trail to yourself. The walk takes five to six hours; be sure to take along a copy of the *Sai Kung & Clearwater Bay Countryside Series* map.

Take the village bus 29R at Chan Man Rd (the stop is in front of McDonald's), get off at the last stop (Sai Wan Ting) and start the hike there. Departures are more frequent on Sundays and public holidays. A taxi ride will be under $100. The trail ends at Pak Tam Au, from where you can catch a minibus back to Sai Kung Town.

HOI HA WAN MARINE PARK OUTDOORS
(hotline 1823; Hoi Ha; green minibus 7) A rewarding 6km walk in the area starts from the village of Hoi Ha (literally 'Under the Sea'), now part of the Hoi Ha Wan Marine Park, a 260-hectare protected area blocked off by concrete booms from the Tolo Channel and closed to fishing vessels. It's one of the few places in Hong Kong waters where coral still grows in abundance and is a favourite with snorkellers and kayakers. Snorkels, masks and kayaks can be rented from **Wan Hoi Store** (雲海士多; 2328 2169) on the beach. You can visit anytime,

but 1½-hour tours of the marine park are available in English at 10.30am and 2.15pm on Sunday and public holidays. You must register with the **Agriculture, Fisheries & Conservation Department** (AFCD; 1823) in advance.

EATING

Food is the raison d'être for the flocks who descend on Sai Kung Town every weekend. It's reachable by bus 92 from Diamond Hill MTR bus terminus (exit C2). To get to Pak Sha Wan, take minibus 1A or 1M from Sai Kung Town.

TOP CHOICE LOAF ON CANTONESE, SEAFOOD $$
Map p185 (六福菜館; 2792 9966; 49 Market St; dishes $80-200; lunch & dinner) The motto here is: eat what they hunt. This three-storey Michelin-star restaurant is where fish freshly caught from the Sai Kung waters in the morning lands on customers' plates by midday. The signature fish soup and steamed fish sell out fast. There is no English signage, but it's identifiable by a lone dining table set outside. Reservations recommended.

WORTH A DETOUR

TUNG PING CHAU

The easternmost point of Hong Kong, kidney-shaped Tung Ping Chau (東平洲) sits in splendid isolation in Mirs Bay in the far northeast of the New Territories. The distance from Ma Liu Shui to the southwest, from where the ferry serving the island departs, is around 25km.

The island is part of Hong Kong Geopark. Together with the waters around it – which teem with sea life (especially corals) – it forms Hong Kong's fourth marine park.

Tung Ping Chau's highest point is only about 40m, but it has unusual rock layers in its cliffs, which glitter after the rain. The eastern coast hosts some of the best coral communities in Hong Kong and is good for snorkelling. There is a small **Tin Hau temple** on the southwestern coast of the island, and some small **caves** dotting the cliffs. A good 6km **walking trail** encircles the whole island.

At one time the island, which is called Tung Ping Chau (East Peace Island) to distinguish it from Peng Chau (same pronunciation in Cantonese) near Lantau, supported a population of 3000, but now it is virtually deserted. There are several food stalls in Sha Tau, a village east of the pier. All provide simple lodging (ie bunk beds) if you have a burning desire to stay here. One of them is **Ping Chau Store** (平洲士多; 2661 6941). Book ahead (a must); or pitch your tent in the campground at the eastern tip of the island.

Tsui Wah Ferry Services (2272 2022; www.traway.com.hk; round trip $90) runs ferries here on Saturdays, Sundays and public holidays. Boats depart from Ma Liu Shui near University East Rail station.

CHEZ LES COPAINS FRENCH $$$
(☎2243 1918; www.chezlescopains.com; 117 Pak Sha Wan; set lunch $120-190, set dinner $390-490, tea $90; ⏱dinner Mon-Fri, lunch & dinner Sat & Sun) Prices for this home-style French eatery are high, but the food is well reviewed and the dining room is warm and welcoming. Must-try includes the homemade goose liver terrine, duck leg confit and French *andouillette* (a rustic tripe sausage) prepared by the colourful cordon bleu chef Bonnie. The restaurant is located 2.5km southwest of the town centre. Take green minibus 1S and get off at Pak Sha Wan.

CHUEN KEE SEAFOOD RESTAURANT CANTONESE, SEAFOOD $$
Map p185 (全記海鮮菜館; ☎2792 6938; 87-89 Man Nin St; set meals for 2 $348; ⏱7am-11pm) Chuen Kee has two locations in Sai Kung. This is the plush branch of the **flagship** (☎2791 1195; 53 Hoi Pong St; ⏱11am-11pm) on the promenade. The elaborate display of fish

---

ISLAND-HOPPING IN SAI KUNG

Exploring the islands that encircle the peninsula is a delightful way to see Sai Kung. Most *kaido* (small, open-sea ferries) leave from the piers on the waterfront, just in front of Hoi Pong Sq.

The first island to the east of Sai Kung Town is **Yeung Chau** (Sheep Island). You'll be able to spot a horseshoe-shaped burial plot up on the slope; it's so designed for reasons dictated by feng shui. Southeast of Yeung Chau, **Pak Sha Chau** (White Sand Island) has a popular beach on its northern shore.

Just beyond Pak Sha Chau is the northern tip of the much larger **Kiu Tsui Chau** (Sharp Island), arguably the most popular island destination. Kiu Tsui Chau has several fine beaches: Kiu Tsui and, connected to it by a sand spit, Kiu Tau on the western shore; and Hap Mun on the island's southern tip. Both can be reached by *kaido* ($40) directly from Sai Kung Town.

The charming island of **Yim Tin Tsai** is accessible by 'scheduled' *kaido* (return $35, 15 minutes, departs hourly 10am to 3pm Saturday to Sunday). Literally 'little salt field', the island is so-called because the original fisherfolk who lived here augmented their income by salt-panning. A few minutes' walk from the jetty up a small flight of steps to the left is St Joseph's Chapel, the focal point of the island. The villagers, who all belong to the same clan, converted to Catholicism 150 years ago after St Peter appeared on the island to chase away pirates who had been harassing them. There's also a modest cafe open daily.

Yim Tin Tsai is connected to the much larger island of **Kau Sai Chau** by a narrow spit of land that becomes submerged at high tide. Kau Sai Chau is the site of the 36-hole **Jockey Club Kau Sai Chau Public Golf Course** (賽馬會滘西洲公眾高爾夫球場; Map p185), a public links course that can be reached by the course's direct ferry from Sai Kung (adult/concession $60/35 return, departs every 20 minutes daily from 6.40am to 7pm). Boats dock in Sai Kung Town at the long pier opposite the new Sai Kung Waterfront Park. The 19th-century Hung Shing Temple at the southern tip of Kau Sai Chau won a Unesco restoration award in 2000.

Beyond Kau Sai Chau is **Leung Shuen Wan** (糧船灣; High Island), a long trip from Sai Kung Town, and the **High Island Reservoir** (萬宜水庫; Map p185), which is now part of the Hong Kong Geopark. This largest reservoir of Hong Kong was built in 1978 by damming what was once a large bay with dolooses (huge cement barriers shaped like jacks); sea water was then siphoned out and fresh water pumped in. To the west of the dam is the newly opened **Astropark** (天文公園; ☎2792 6810; http://astropark .hk.space.museum; ⏱24hr), located in a water-sports centre, where you can stargaze from the naked-eye observation area. The park also has a replica of a 17th-century Chinese celestial globe and a campground. Reservations a must.

If you want to be out on the water for a longer period or have greater flexibility as to where you go, you can hire your own boat. *Kaido* owners can usually be found trawling for fares. Explain where you want to go, how long you want to spend there and which way you wish to return. The usual price for this kind of trip is about $300 on weekdays, more on the weekend.

and crustaceans at the door may make you cringe, but cringe will turn to crave once you've had a bite of the cooked versions.

ALI OLI BAKERY CAFE EUROPEAN, BAKERY $
Map p185 (☑2792 2655; 11 Sha Tsui Path; meals from $70; ☺8am-7.30pm Mon-Fri, to 9pm Sat & Sun) This much-loved bakery is a hiker's best friend, with simple sandwiches on European-style homemade bread, pies and preserves. Breakfast and set lunches are also offered here and best enjoyed at its outdoor tables.

HONEYMOON DESSERT DESSERTS $
Map p185 (滿記甜品; ☑2792 4991; 9, 10A, B&C Po Tung Rd; per person $30; ☺1pm-2.45am) This shop specialising in Chinese desserts such as sweet walnut soup and durian pudding is so successful that it has branches all over China and in Indonesia, not to mention some 20 locations in Hong Kong.

 DRINKING & NIGHTLIFE

STEAMERS BAR
Map p185 (66 Yi Chun St; ☺happy hour 2-8pm Mon-Fri; ☐92, 299) Steamers is graced by a blissful alfresco bar area where you can chill with some excellently blended cocktails and bar grub.

POETS PUB
Map p185 (55 Yi Chun St; ☺happy hour noon-9pm Mon-Fri; ☐92, 299) This down-to-earth pub opposite Steamers is a pleasant place for a pint and serves typical pub meals, such as pies, chips and beans.

Clearwater Bay Peninsula

Explore

Tseung Kwan O, accessible via the MTR station of the same name, is the springboard to the peninsula. There are several wonderful beaches for whiling away an afternoon. The most beautiful and popular are Clearwater Bay First Beach and Clearwater Bay Second Beach. They are often packed with local weekenders during the warmer months.

The Clearwater Bay Country Park offers some easy but exceptional walks with sweeping views of the bay.

The secluded Tai Miu Temple, dedicated to the goddess of heaven, is best visited during Tin Hau's Birthday Festival in April or May.

Seafood lovers will not want to miss Po Toi O Village: this is where you can enjoy sumptuous seafood and home-style cooking at its best.

The Best...

➡ **Sight** Tai Miu Temple (p190)
➡ **Place to Eat** Seafood Island (p191)
➡ **Place to Swim** Clearwater Bay Second Beach (p189)

Top Tip

Early birds shouldn't miss the breathtaking sunrise that can be watched in Clearwater Bay Second Beach. The first minibus starts at 6am.

Getting There & Away

Bus Bus 91 runs between Diamond Hill and Choi Hung MTR stations to Tai Au Mun.

Green Minibus Bus 103M runs between Tseung Kwan O MTR station and Clearwater Bay. Bus 103 runs to Kwun Tong ferry pier, and bus 16 to Po Lam MTR station.

Need to Know

➡ **Area code** ☑852
➡ **Location** 15km east of Tsim Sha Tsui, Kowloon. Junk Bay (Tseung Kwan O) is to the west of the peninsula and Clearwater Bay (Tsing Sui Wan) sits to the east; Joss House Bay (Tai Miu Wan) lies to the south.
➡ **Last train to Kowloon** 12.16am from Po Lam MTR station.

◉ SIGHTS

BEACHES BEACH
Bus 91 passes **Silverstrand beach** (銀線灣; Ngan Sin Wan) north of Hang Hau before reaching Tai Au Mun; if you wish, you can

get off at Silverstrand and go for a dip. If you're heading for Lung Ha Wan, get off the bus at Tai Au Mun Village and start walking. From Sai Kung, take bus 92 to where Hiram's Hwy and Clearwater Bay Rd meet and change there to bus 91.

From Tai Au Mun, Tai Au Mun Rd leads south to two fine, sandy beaches: **Clearwater Bay First Beach** (清水灣一灘) and, a bit further southwest, **Clearwater Bay Second Beach** (清水灣二灘). In summer try to go during the week, as both beaches get very crowded on the weekend.

CLEARWATER BAY COUNTRY PARK
OUTDOORS

The heart of the country park is Tai Au Mun, from where trails go in various directions, through the **Clearwater Bay Country Park Visitor Centre** (☑2719 0032; ☉9.30am-4.30pm Wed-Mon) to the southeast in Tai Hang Tun. Take Lung Ha Wan Rd north from Tai Au Mun to the beach at **Lung Ha Wan** (Lobster Bay) and return via the 2.3km **Lung Ha Wan Country Trail**.

TAI MIU TEMPLE
TEMPLE

(大廟; ☑2519 9155; ☉8am-5pm) This far-flung temple further south along Tai Au

---

SLEEPING IN THE NEW TERRITORIES

Good-value accommodation is in short supply in the New Territories. There are four official HI-affiliated hostels, all in the remote parts of the region. Walkers and hikers can pitch a tent at any one of 40 New Territories campsites managed by the **Country & Marine Parks Authority** (郊野公園及海岸公園管理局; ☑1823; www.afcd.gov.hk).

Bradbury Jockey Club Youth Hostel (☑2662 5123; www.yha.org.hk; 66 Tai Mei Tuk Rd; dm members under/over 18yr $65/95, d/q members $290/420; ☐75K) This is the HKYHA's flagship hostel in the New Territories and is open daily year-round. Bradbury is next to the northern tip of the Plover Cove Reservoir dam wall, a few hundred metres south of Tai Mei Tuk. To get here take bus 75K (or 275R on Sundays and public holidays) from Tai Po Market KCR East station to the Tai Mei Tuk bus terminus. The hostel is on the road leading to the reservoir.

Bradbury Hall Youth Hostel (☑2328 2458; www.yha.org.hk; Chek Keng, Sai Kung; dm members under/over 18yr $45/65; ☐94, 96R, 698R) Open only from Friday to Monday, this hostel is in the beautiful cove of Chek Keng, where some unspoilt beaches are just a flip-flop's throw away. The dorms are slightly dated but clean. To get there, take bus 94 from Sai Kung bus terminal to Pak Tam Au. Walk along stage 2 of the MacLehose Trail towards Chek Keng Village. The walk takes about 40 minutes. A faster way to the hostel is to take bus 96R or 698R to Wong Shek Pier, and then take a scheduled ferry to Chek Keng Pier. The boat journey is about 10 minutes.

Hyatt Regency Hong Kong (☑3723 1234; www.hongkong.shatin.hyatt.com; 18 Chak Cheung St, Sha Tin; r $2500-3000, ste $3500-12,500; @☎☰; ☐University) This is the plushest sleeping option as you head out towards the border with China. Views of Tolo Harbour or the rolling hills of Sha Tin can be seen in most rooms. It's a five-minute walk from University East Rail station.

Regal Riverside Hotel (Map p182; ☑2649 7878; www.regalriverside.com; 34-36 Tai Chung Kiu Rd; r $1300-1700, ste from $3800; ☐284, @☎☰; ☐Sha Tin Wai, exit A) Don't judge this hotel from the outside: a handsome and cavernous lobby will lead you to the well-decorated and spacious rooms. Those overlooking Shing Mun River have excellent views.

Pilgrim's Hall (Map p182; ☑2691 2739; www.tfssu.org/pilgrim.html; 33 Tao Fong Shan Rd; s/d with shared bathroom $260/400; @; ☐Sha Tin, exit B) This Lutheran Church–affiliated hostel provides a nice escape from the city as it's set on a peaceful hillside above the town. To get here, take the MTR East Rail to Sha Tin station, leave via exit B and walk down the ramp, passing a series of old village houses on the left. To the left of these houses is a set of steps signposted 'To Fung Shan'. Follow the path all the way to the top and you'll see Pilgrim's Hall. The walk should take around 20 minutes. A taxi from the nearest East Rail station in Tai Wai will cost around $24. The canteen serves simple and healthy meals (advance booking required).

TIN HAU BIRTHDAY FESTIVAL

Like the Taoist god Pak Tai, Tin Hau, the queen of heaven, is the protector of sea-farers and is widely worshipped along the South China coast. Her birthday, which will fall on 4 May in 2013 and 22 April in 2014, is a key saintly festivity for the older generations and swaggering businessmen alike. There will be a parade in Yuen Long featuring lion dances and Cantonese opera, and Tin Hau temples throughout the city will swell with visitors. But Tai Miu Temple is *the* place to go to as elaborate rites will be performed starting four days before Tin Hau's birthday.

You can take a minibus to go there, but you are totally missing the point if you don't take the **special ferry** (round trip $60) from North Point Pier (北角碼頭), which only operates on Tin Hau's birthday and the day before. About 50 boats will be carrying the faithful to and from the temple.

The 40-minute journey itself is quite a spectacle. Once the voyage begins, the ferry transforms into a floating temple, with grannies praying, preparing joss sticks and paper offerings, and burning them in the furnace on the deck. Hell money is thrown into the sea along the journey to appease the water deities. If you set off at around noon on the red-letter day, you'll see a flotilla of colourful fishing boats parading through Victoria Harbour. Finally the sea procession will arrive in Joss House Bay to pay homage to their protector.

Mun Rd is one of the most important Tin Hau temples in the territory. Built in the 13th century by two Fujianese in gratitude to the goddess for saving them during a sea storm, the temple was restored in 2009 and is the prime celebration venue during the Tin Hau Birthday Festival (see boxed text, above).

Just behind the temple is a **Song-dynasty rock carving** dating from 1274 and recording both the visit of a superintendent of the Salt Administration and the history of two temples in Joss House Bay. It is the oldest inscription extant in Hong Kong.

From Tai Miu, hikers can follow the 6.6km-long **High Junk Peak Country Trail** up to **Tin Ha Shan** (273m) and then continue on to **High Junk Peak** (Tiu Yu Yung; 344m) before heading eastward back to Tai Au Mun.

 EATING

Po Toi O is a small fishing village southeast of Clearwater Bay. The two seafood restaurants there draw in gourmands from all over Hong Kong.

SEAFOOD ISLAND CANTONESE, SEAFOOD **$$**
(海鮮島海鮮酒家; 2719 5730; Shop B, 7 Po Toi O Chuen Rd; meals from $180; ⊙lunch & dinner) Crustaceans of every kind are on full display at this energetic restaurant hidden in discreet Po Toi O Village. A totally non-luxe setting but with no-nonsense fare, Seafood Island is famed for its cuttlefish sashimi and razor clams. It's more a group activity to dine here. Grab a couple of friends and enjoy all the treats on offer.

🏃 SPORTS & ACTIVITIES

CLEARWATER BAY GOLF & COUNTRY CLUB GOLF
(清水灣高爾夫球鄉村俱樂部; ☑2335 3700; www.cwbgolf.org; 139 Tau Au Mun Rd, Clearwater Bay; greens fees $1800-2000; ☐91) A 27-hole course at the tip of Clearwater Bay in the New Territories.

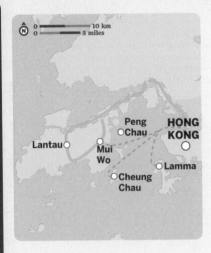

Outlying Islands

Lamma p194

The quickest island escape from downtown Hong Kong, laid-back Lamma exudes a bohemian charm and is home to many a commuter who prefers more space and greenery.

Lantau p199

The largest of the islands boasts bountiful sights and recreational possibilities: country parks, hiking trails, fishing villages, beaches, monasteries and the unmissable Big Buddha.

Cheung Chau p210

Think seafood and seafaring culture on this bustling isle of great windsurfing beaches and temples dedicated to water deities. The annual Bun Festival is a highlight.

Worth a Detour

At Peng Chau (p197), glimpse the last echoes of traditional village life in Hong Kong.

Po Toi (p209) is the southernmost island of Hong Kong, and offers scenic walks and delicious seafood.

Camping, rock climbing and stargazing are the drawcards of 'East Dragon Island', Tung Lung Chau (p214).

TOP SIGHTS
NGONG PING PLATEAU

No trip to Hong Kong is complete without visiting Ngong Ping Plateau for the seated Tian Tan Buddha statue, the biggest of its kind in the world. It can be seen aerially as you fly into Hong Kong, or on a clear day from Macau, but nothing beats coming up close and personal with this much-loved spiritual icon at over 500m up in the western hills of Lantau.

Commonly known as the 'Big Buddha', the **Tian Tan Buddha** (天壇大佛; admission free; ⊙10am-6pm) is a representation of Lord Gautama some 23m high (or 26.4m with the lotus), or just under 34m if you include the podium. It was unveiled in 1993, and today it still holds the honour as the tallest seated bronze Buddha statue in the world. It weighs 202 tonnes, by the way. It's well worth climbing the 268 steps for a closer look at the statue and the surrounding views. The Buddha's birthday, a public holiday in April or May, is a lively time to visit when thousands make the pilgrimage. Visitors are requested to observe some decorum in dress and behaviour. It is forbidden to bring meat or alcohol into the grounds.

The large bell within the Buddha is controlled by computer and rings 108 times during the day to symbolise escape from what Buddhism terms the '108 troubles of mankind'. On the second level of the podium is a small **museum** (☑2985 5248; ⊙10am-6pm) containing oil paintings and ceramic plaques of the Buddha's life and teachings.

Po Lin Monastery (寶蓮寺; Precious Lotus; ☑2985 5248; ⊙9am-6pm), a huge Buddhist complex built in 1924, is more of a tourist honeypot than a religious retreat today, attracting hundreds of thousands of visitors a year and it's still being expanded. Most of the buildings you'll see on arrival are new, with the older, simpler ones tucked away behind them. **Po Lin Vegetarian Restaurant** (寶蓮禪寺齋堂; ☑2985 5248; Ngong Ping; set meals regular/deluxe $60/100; ⊙11.30am-4.30pm) in the monastery is famed for its inexpensive but filling vegetarian food.

The most spectacular way to get to the plateau is by the 5.7km **Ngong Ping 360** (昂坪360; www.np360.com.hk; adult/child one way $86/44, return $125/62; ⊙10am-6pm Mon-Fri, 9am-6.30pm Sat, Sun & public holidays), a cable car linking Ngong Ping with the centre of Tung Chung (downhill and to the north). The journey over the bay and the mountains takes 25 minutes, with each glassed-in gondola carrying 17 passengers. The upper station is at the skippable theme-park-like **Ngong Ping Village** just west of the monastery.

DON'T MISS

- ⇒ Tian Tan Buddha
- ⇒ Po Lin Monastery
- ⇒ Ngong Ping 360

PRACTICALITIES

- ⇒ Map p200
- ⇒ ☑3666 0606
- ⇒ 11 Tat Tung Rd
- ⇒ admission free
- ⇒ ☐2 from Mui Wo, 21 from Tai O, 23 from Tung Chung or cable car

Lamma

Explore

Gentle walks, lounging on the beach and pootling through the seafood restaurants and bars are the things to do here. Begin your journey in Yung Shue Wan and enjoy brunch in one of the eclectic cafes on the main street.

The most interesting way to see a good portion of the island is to amble along the 4km-long Family Trail that runs between Yung Shue Wan and Sok Kwu Wan via Hung Shing Yeh beach. Those happy to be out in the hot sun should carry on to Tung O Wan, an idyllic bay some 30 minutes further south, and perhaps return to Sok Kwu Wan via Mo Tat Wan.

In the evening enjoy succulent seafood in one of the waterfront restaurants in Sok Kwu Wan.

The Best...

➡ **Sight** Lamma Family Trail (p195)
➡ **Place to Eat** Bookworm Cafe (p198)
➡ **Place to Drink** Diesel's Bar (p198)

Top Tip

Want huge swaths of the island all to yourself? Visit on a weekday to avoid the weekend crowds.

Getting There & Away

Ferry Ferries run from Yung Shue Wan pier to pier 4 of Central's Outlying Islands ferry terminal, Pak Kok Tsuen (Lamma) and Aberdeen; also from Sok Kwu Wan

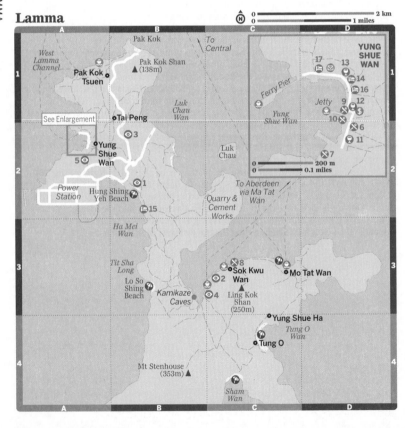

Lamma

pier to pier 4 of Central's Outlying Islands ferry terminal, Man Tat Wan (Lamma) and Aberdeen.

....

Need to Know

➡ **Area Code** ☑852

➡ **Location** 3km across the East Lamma Channel from Aberdeen. There are two main settlements on the island: Yung Shue Wan to the northwest and Sok Kwu Wan on the east coast of the island.

➡ **Last Ferry to Central** 11.30pm from Yung Shue Wan; 10.40pm from Sok Kwu Wan

⊙ SIGHTS

YUNG SHUE WAN   VILLAGE

Map p194 (🚢Yung Shue Wan ferry) Yung Shue Wan (Banyan Tree Bay) may be the largest settlement on the island but it remains a small village with little more than a car-free main street following the curve of the bay. In recent years the former hippy haven has

had to battle with rent hikes and population increases as developers foist their version of luxury on Lamma. A process of gentrification has inevitably set in, but Banyan Tree Bay has somehow managed to retain more than a whiff of rustic charm despite – or because of – the flowering of cafes, bars, New Age shops and other tourism-related businesses on the local scene. There is a small **Tin Hau temple** (天后廟) dating from the late 19th century at the southern end of the bay, where a pair of eccentric Western lion statues guard the entrance to the site.

SOK KWU WAN   VILLAGE

Map p194 (🚢Sok Kwu Wan ferry) If you continue on the **Family Trail** you'll see the socking great coal-fired power station that looms behind the hill near Yung Shue Wan. You'll also encounter a pavilion on a ridge, this time looking down onto Sok Kwu Wan, with its many fine restaurants, and fishing boats and rafts bobbing in the bay. Though still a small settlement, Sok Kwu Wan supports at least a dozen waterfront seafood restaurants that are popular with boaters. The small harbour is filled with rafts from which cages are suspended and fish are farmed. If entering Sok Kwu Wan from the south (ie from the Family Trail linking it with Yung Shue Wan), you'll pass three so-called **kamikaze caves** (神風洞): grottoes measuring 10m wide and 30m deep and built by the occupying Japanese forces to house motorboats wired with explosives to disrupt Allied shipping during WWII. They were never used. Further on and near the entrance to Sok Kwu Wan is a totally renovated **Tin Hau temple** (天后廟) dating back to 1826. Right on the water is **Lamma Fisherfolk's Village** (漁民文化村; ☑2982 8585; lammafisherfolks.com.hk; adult/child $60/$50; ⊙10am-7pm Mon-Fri), a floating museum and theme park on a raft that showcases the fishing culture and history of Hong Kong. Fishing tools and model vessels are on display, including a real 60-year-old junk. The admission includes a shuttle boat pick-up from Sok Kwu Wan ferry pier.

LAMMA WINDS   LANDMARK

Map p194 (南丫風采發電站) Standing in elegant contrast to that CO_2-belching, coal-fired power station, Lamma's giant wind turbine, close to the top of the ridge just southeast of Tai Peng village, makes a stirring sight (although in reality it is

LAMMA'S ENDANGERED TURTLES

Sham Wan has traditionally been the one beach in the whole of Hong Kong where endangered green turtles *(Chelonia mydas)*, one of three species of sea turtle found in Hong Kong waters, still struggle onto the sand to lay their eggs from early June to the end of August.

Female green turtles, which can grow to a metre in length and weigh 140kg, take between 20 and 30 years to reach sexual maturity and always head back to the same beach where they were born to lay their eggs, which takes place every two to six years. Fearing that Sham Wan would catch the eye of housing-estate developers and that the turtles would swim away forever, the area was declared a Site of Special Scientific Interest and closed. It is patrolled by the Agriculture, Fisheries & Conservation Department (AFCD) from June to October. Some eight turtles are known to have nested here since 1997 and some are now being tracked by satellite.

As well as developers, a major hurdle faced by the long-suffering turtles is the appetite of Lamma locals for their eggs. In 1994 three turtles laid about 200 eggs, which were promptly harvested and consumed by villagers. Several years later villagers sold eggs to Japanese tourists for $100 each. There is now a $50,000 fine levied on anyone caught on the beach during the nesting season. Anyone taking, possessing or attempting to sell one of the eggs faces a fine of $100,000 and one year in prison.

something of a white elephant generating far less power than was hoped for). There's a small information board on wind power and an electronic read-out at its base showing the power output of the turbine, but there's not much else to do here but admire its feathered blades scything the breeze and to take in the dramatic backdrop of freighters setting sail far below, with Hong Kong Island looming in the background. To reach it, follow the paths from Yung Shue Wan up to Tai Peng old village and turn right once you hit the concrete roadway linking the power station with Pak Kok.

HUNG SHING YEH BEACH   BEACH

Map p194 (⊜Yung Shue Wan ferry) About a 25-minute walk southeast from the Yung Shue Wan ferry pier, Hung Shing Yeh beach is the most popular beach on Lamma. Arrive early in the morning or on a weekday and you'll probably find it deserted, though you may find the view of the power station across the bay takes some getting used to. The beach is protected by a shark net and has toilets, showers and changing rooms. There are a few restaurants and drinks stands nearby – the latter open on the weekend only, except in summer.

Nestled in the leafy fringes of the beach is **Herboland** (香草原; ⊘10am-6pm), the first organic herb farm in the territory. With over 40 types of herbal tea to choose from, it'll take some mental power to decline a

cuppa in the farm's blissful tea garden before or after your exertions along the Family Trial.

LO SO SHING BEACH   BEACH

Map p194 (⊜Yung Shue Wan ferry) If you continue south from Hung Shing Yeh beach, the path climbs steeply until it reaches a **Chinese-style pavilion** near the top of the hill. From this vantage point, it becomes obvious that the island is mostly hilly grassland and large boulders, though more and more trees are being planted.

You will pass a second pavilion that offers splendid views out to the sea; from here a path leads from the Family Trail down to Lo So Shing beach, the most beautiful on Lamma.

MO TAT WAN   BEACH

The clean and relatively uncrowded beach at Mo Tat Wan (map p194) is a mere 20-minute coastal path walk east of Sok Kwu Wan. Mo Tat Wan is OK for swimming, but has no lifeguards. You can also reach it by *kaido* (small open-sea ferry) from Aberdeen, which continues on to Sok Kwu Wan.

SHAM WAN   BEACH

Map p194 (Deep Bay) Sham Wan is another beautiful bay to the southwest that can be reached from Tung O Wan by clambering over the hills. A trail on the left about 200m up the hill from Tung O Wan leads south to a small and sandy beach. Don't come here from June to October, when Hong Kong's endangered green turtles nest.

TUNG O WAN   BEACH

Long coveted by developers as a prime location for new condos and marina facilities, unspoiled Tung O Wan is still holding out against the might of the property dollar thanks to the combined resistance of local residents and environmentalists from other shores. Ringed by a long sandy beach, this small and secluded bay makes a rewarding detour while walking to Sok Kwu Wan from Yung Shue Wan or from Sok Kwu Wan itself. Just before the Tin Hau temple at the entrance to Sok Kwu Wan, follow the signposted path to the right southward,

up and over the hill to the tiny village of **Tung O**. The walk takes about 30 minutes over a rugged landscape, and the first half is a fairly strenuous climb up steps and along a path. Don't do this walk at night unless it's a full moon, as there are only a few street lights at the start in Sok Kwu Wan.

If coming from Mo Tat Wan, take the trail immediately to the west of the pavilion above the beach and follow the signposted path up the hill and through bamboo groves and fields. It takes about 25 minutes to reach the sleepy village of **Yung Shue Ha** on the fringes of the bay. All of the Chinese who live there are from the same clan and have the surname of Chow. A member of this clan, Chow Yun Fat, star of *Crouching Tiger, Hidden Dragon,* was born and raised in Tung O.

WORTH A DETOUR

PENG CHAU

Backwater Peng Chau does not possess much wow factor but it is perhaps the most traditionally Chinese of the Outlying Islands, with narrow alleyways, crowded housing, a covered wet **market** (坪洲街市) near the ferry pier, a couple of small but important temples, and interesting shops selling everything from humble household goods to religious paraphernalia. Come any day and you can count on the clatter of mah-jong tiles and Cantonese opera tunes leaking from old transistors to act as a soundtrack to this sleepy getaway.

The island's economy was traditionally supported by fishing and some cottage industries, now all but dead (having moved to mainland China), though you will find a couple of porcelain and gift shops on Wing Hing and Wing On Sts. There's a branch of **HSBC** (滙豐銀行; ☑2233 3000; 1 Wing Hing St; ◷Mon, Wed & Fri) nearby.

There are no cars on Peng Chau, and you can walk around it easily in an hour. Climbing the steps up to **Finger Hill** (95m), the island's highest point, and topped with the winged Chinese-style **Fung Ping Pavilion**, offers some light exercise and excellent views. To get to it from the ferry pier, walk up Lo Peng St, turn right at the **Tin Hau temple** (天后廟), containing a century-old 2.5m-long whale bone blackened by incense smoke, and walk south along Wing On St. This gives way to Shing Ka Rd, and Nam Shan Rd leads from here east up to Finger Hill. The water at otherwise-pleasant **Tung Wan beach**, a five-minute walk from the ferry pier, is too dirty for swimming and is not served by lifeguards.

There are a couple of local Chinese stores selling noodles and sandwiches near the waterfront, but your true anchor is **Les Copains d'abord** (☑3483 0692; ◷11am-9pm Tue-Sun), a French-owned wine bar and cafe where epicureans can affordably enjoy some well-selected vino by glass, along with gourmet smoked meats, olives, imported cheeses and other tasty accompaniments under the parasols. Or you can watch the ferry dock over a sunset libation. It's on the island's main square straight up from the pier.

Ferry services from Central leave from pier 6 of the Outlying Islands ferry terminal. Ferries also depart from Mui Wo and Chi Ma Wan on Lantau and from Cheung Chau. Additionally, regular *kaido* (small, open-sea ferries) operate to Peng Chau from the Trappist Monastery and Discovery Bay on Lantau.

EATING

While seafood dominates Lamma's culinary palate, the island offers the greatest choice of eateries and cuisines of any of the Outlying Islands. Most people head directly to Sok Kwu Wan where fish rule the menus. The restaurants crowd the waterfront on either side of the ferry pier and they'll be chock-full on weekend nights of locals and expats who have arrived by ferry, private yachts or on boats laid on by the restaurants themselves.

Yung Shue Wan, the most populated village, has a vast and eclectic range of inviting restaurants, mostly spread along its main street. There are a couple of good spots in the remote Mo Tat Wan and Hung Shing Yeh beaches for refreshment.

BOOKWORM CAFE
CAFE, VEGETARIAN $

Map p194 (南島書蟲; ☑2982 4838; 79 Main St, Yung Shue Wan; meals from $80; ◷10am-9pm Mon-Fri, 9am-10pm Sat, 9am-9pm Sun; ☻) Veggie foodies are in heaven in Bookworm, the granddaddy of healthy and eco-conscious eating in the Hong Kong dining scene. Tasty dishes include the dal and salad combo, goats' cheese *sanga* and shepherdess pie, and they pair well with the carefully selected organic wines. The cafe is also a secondhand bookshop.

TAI HING SEAFOOD RESTAURANT
CANTONESE, SEAFOOD $$

Map p194 (大興海鮮酒家; ☑2982 0339; 53 Main St, Yung Shue Wan; meals from $250; ◷lunch & dinner) The unassuming Tai Hing enjoys a stream of return customers for its honest home cooking. Lamma native Cheong Gor is the heart and soul of this semiprivate kitchen. Tell him your budget and he will pick the best seasonal seafood for you. Four hundred dollars (per head) will get you a

veritable seafood extravaganza. Reservations recommended.

WATERFRONT
INTERNATIONAL $

Map p194 (☑2982 1168; 58 Main St, Yung Shue Wan; meals from $90; ◷9am-2am) With great views and lapping waves a few steps from the terrace, this restaurant is both a popular breakfast joint and sundowner spot. Traditional British and Italian fare is served here, so is straightforward Indian grub.

RAINBOW SEAFOOD RESTAURANT
CHINESE, SEAFOOD $$

Map p194 (天虹海鮮酒家; ☑2982 8100; www.rainbowrest.com.hk; Shops 1a-1b, Ground fl, 23-25 First St, Sok Kwu Wan; meals from $180; ◷10am-10.30pm) Gigantic Rainbow may boast 800 seats but you still need to book ahead. Steamed grouper, lobster and abalone are the specialities in this waterfront restaurant. You have the option of being transported by its own ferries from Central Pier 9 or Tsim Sha Tsui Public Pier. Call or check its website for sailings.

BEST KEBAB & PIZZA
TURKISH $

Map p194 (☑2982 0902; 4 Yung Shue Wan Back St, Yung Shue Wan; meals from $80; ◷2-10pm Mon-Fri, noon-10pm Sat) This small, unpretentious Turkish-run eatery serves exactly what it says on the tin. The pizza, lamb chops and sizzling shish kebab are what the local residents rave about. Wash them down with the freshly brewed Turkish coffee and fruit teas.

DRINKING & NIGHTLIFE

Lamma is no party island, but there are several cosy bars in Yung Shue Wan where you can converse and watch the sun set over a cold one. Most bars serve what is very much a local crowd, consisting mostly of expats, in the evenings. You may be asked to sign a members' book, as some operate on club licences.

DIESEL'S BAR
BAR

Map p194 (51 Main St, Yung Shue Wan; ◷happy hour 6-9pm Mon-Fri; ⬓Lamma, Yung Shue Wan) Set inside the oldest building on the main street, Diesel's is the raunchiest but also fun and the most well-known drinking den

---

KAIDO SERVICES

Kaido are small ferries that serve more remote islands or destinations, with less frequent services than regular ferries and schedules that change from time to time. Check the Transport Department website (www.td.gov.hk) for the most up-to-date timetables before you set off.

SLEEPING IN LAMMA

There are holiday flats aplenty in Yung Shue Wan.

Jackson Property Agency (☎2982 0606; 15 Main St, Yung Shue Wan; 🚢Lamma, Yung Shue Wan) This agency has studios and apartments for rent on Lamma and all of them have a TV, private bathroom, microwave and fridge. Rooms usually start at $380 per night for two people from Sunday to Friday and go up to between $780 and $880 on Saturday.

Concerto Inn (☎2982 1668; www.concertoinn.com.hk; 28 Hung Shing Yeh beach, Hung Shing Yeh; r Sun-Fri $700-900, r Sat & eve of public holidays $800-1280; 🛜; 🚢Lamma, Yung Shue Wan) A lovely boutique inn on the beachfront, Concerto has some tastefully appointed rooms but it's quite some distance from the action. Stay here only if you want to get away from it all. Rooms for three or four people are actually doubles with a sofa bed or pull-out bed. The afternoon tea in the restaurant comes recommended by travellers.

Man Lai Wah Hotel (☎2982 0220; manlaiwahhotel@yahoo.com; 2 Po Wah Garden, Yung Shue Wan; r Mon-Fri $400-450, Sat & Sun $550-600; 🚢Lamma, Yung Shue Wan) Set ahead from the ferry pier, this guesthouse has tiny but spotless double-bed rooms with harbour views. Some have balconies.

Bali Holiday Resort (☎2982 4580; fax 2982 1044; 8 Main St, Yung Shue Wan; s/d Sun-Fri $350/400, Sat $700/800; 🚢Lamma, Yung Shue Wan) An agency rather than a resort as such, Bali Holiday Resort has about 30 studios and apartments sprinkled around the island. All have a TV, fridge and air-con and some have sea views.

on the island. The sun-kissed courtyard is a good spot to catch up on the latest island gossip.

FOUNTAINHEAD DRINKING BAR · BAR

Map p194 (17 Main St, Yung Shue Wan; ⊙happy hour all day Mon-Fri; 🚢Lamma, Yung Shue Wan) The cheerfully no-frills Fountainhead has a good mix of Chinese and expats in regular attendance, decent music and beer at affordable prices.

ISLAND SOCIETY BAR · BAR

Map p194 (6 Main St, Yung Shue Wan; ⊙happy hour 4-8pm; 🚢Lamma, Yung Shue Wan) The closest bar to the ferry pier, it is a favourite with older expats and hosts the best jam sessions on the island.

7TH AVENUE · BAR

Map p194 (7 Main St, Yung Shue Wan; ⊙noon-late; 🚢Lamma, Yung Shue Wan) Though the name doesn't match Lamma's ambience, this new kid on the block has a welcoming atmosphere with hookahs and outdoor seating, thanks to the 20-year-old entrepreneur who runs it. All food and booze are reasonably priced.

Lantau

Explore

The sheer size of Lantau makes it ideal for a multiday excursion. Begin either in Mui Wo or Tung Chung, the transport hubs on this largest island of Hong Kong. Head to the island's landmark, the Tian Tan Buddha on Ngon Ping Plateau, as early as possible to avoid the tourist hordes and enjoy the rugged beauty of the terrain. Then make a beeline to Tai O on the west coast, a charming fishing village and one of the few still surviving in Hong Kong.

For vigorous travellers, the mountain trails, including the 70km Lantau Trail which scales both Lantau Peak (the highest point on Lantau) and Sunset Peak (869m), will blow your socks off; or prepare to get wet at some of the island's best beaches along South Lantau Rd.

The Best...

➡ **Sight** Tian Tan Buddha (p193)
➡ **Place to Eat** Solo (p209)
➡ **Place to Sleep** Espace Elastique (p208)

Lantau

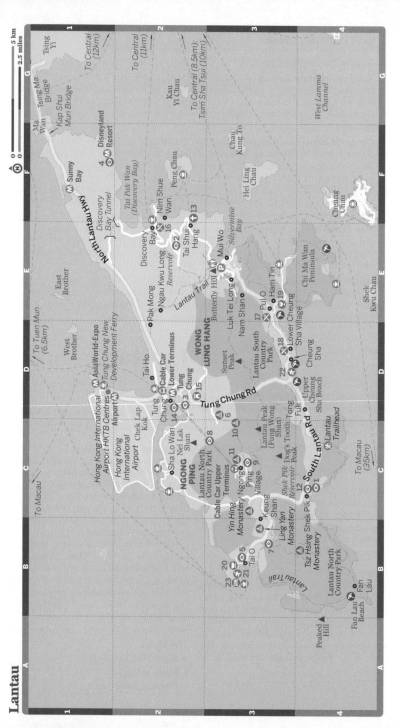

Top Tip

There are only 50 taxis serving the whole island. Have the call-service numbers ready, especially after hours.

Getting There & Away

Airport Express Takes you to Airport station at Chek Lap Kok.

Bus Mui Wo: served by bus 1 from Tai O, bus 2 from Ngong Ping and bus 3M from Tung Chung (main bus terminus by the MTR station).

Ngong Ping: other than the cable car, the best way to get here is on bus 2 from Mui Wo or bus 23 from Tung Chung.

Lantau

Tai O: reached on bus 1 from Mui Wo, bus 11 from Tung Chung or bus 21 from Ngong Ping.

Tung Chung: served by bus 3M from Mui Wo, bus 11 from Tai O and bus 23 from Ngong Ping.

All buses listed here run along some of, or all of, South Lantau Rd, the junction with Tung Chung Rd being the point at which the bus will join or leave the route.

Ferry Mui Wo: major services from Central leave from pier 6 at the Outlying Islands ferry terminal. Ferries also depart from Chi Ma Wan (also on Lantau), Cheung Chau and Peng Chau.

Chi Ma Wan: served by the interisland ferry from Mui Wo, Cheung Chau and Peng Chau.

MTR Tung Chung station is at the end of the line of the same name.

Taxi Telephone the call service on ☎2984 1328 or 2984 1368. Sample fares to Ngong Ping and the Tian Tan Buddha from Mui Wo and Tung Chung/Tai O/Hong Kong International Airport are $140/50/160.

Need to Know

➡ **Area Code** ☎852

➡ **Location** 8km west of Hong Kong Island. The most inhabited town Tung Chung is on the northern coast, while Mui Wo, the second-largest settlement, is on the eastern coast. The airport is right north of Tung Chung.

➡ **Last Ferry to Central** 11.30pm from Mui Wo

◉ SIGHTS

NGONG PING PLATEAU
See p193.

LANTAU PEAK   HILL
Known as Fung Wong Shan (Phoenix Mountain) in Cantonese, this 934m-high peak is the second-highest in Hong Kong after Tai Mo Shan (957m) in the New Territories. The view from the summit is absolutely stunning, and on a clear day it is possible to see Macau 65km to the west.

If you're hiking the length or the first several stages of **Lantau Trail** to Ngong Ping, you'll cross the peak. If you want to just climb up from Ngong Ping, the easiest and most comfortable way to make the climb is to spend the night at the Ngong Ping SG Davis Hostel, get up at the crack of dawn and pick up the signposted trail at the hostel that runs southeast to the peak. Many climbers get up earlier to reach the summit for sunrise; take a flashlight and wear an extra layer of clothes, as it can get pretty chilly at the top in the early hours, even in summer.

Another signposted trail leading east from the hostel will take you along the northern slopes of Lantau Peak to **Po Lam Monastery** (寶林寺) at Tei Tong Tsai and then south through a valley leading to Tung Chung, from where you can catch the MTR back to Kowloon or Hong Kong or bus 3M to Mui Wo. This charming walk – if you ignore the airport to the north – also takes you past **Lo Hon Monastery** (羅漢寺) as well as **Tung Chung Fort** (東涌炮台/東涌堡) and **Tung Chung Battery** (東涌小炮台).

MUI WO VILLAGE

Map p203 (☒Lantau) Mui Wo (Plum Nest) was Lantau's largest settlement before Tung Chung was born. Today a third of Lantau's population still lives in this sleepy town and its surrounding hamlets.

Silvermine Bay beach (銀礦灣), to the northwest of Mui Wo, is a decent beach with scenic views and opportunities for walking in the hills above. There's a complex with toilets, showers and changing rooms open from April to October.

Hike out to **Silvermine Waterfall** (銀礦瀑布) near the old **Silvermine Cave** northwest of the town if time allows. The waterfall is quite a spectacle when it gushes during the rainy season; the cave was mined for silver in the 19th century but has now been sealed off.

En route to the waterfall you'll pass the **Man Mo temple** (文武廟), originally built during the reign of Emperor Shen Zong (1573–1620) and renovated a couple of times in the last century.

The walk to the temple, cave and waterfall from Mui Wo is about 3km. Walk westward along Mui Wo Rural Committee Rd and then following the marked path north.

There are several old granite watchtowers in the area, including **Luk Tei Tong Watchtower** (鹿地塘更樓) on the Silver River and **Butterfly Hill Watchtower** (蝴蝶山更樓) further north. They were built in the late 19th century as safe houses and as coastal defences against pirates.

There are several decent places to stay and eat in Mui Wo. Bikes can be hired from **Friendly Bicycle Shop** (老友記單車專門店; ☎2984 2278; 13 Mui Wo Ferry Pier Rd; ◷10am-6pm Wed-Mon) near the Park 'n' Shop supermarket.

TOP CHOICE TAI O VILLAGE

Map p200 (☒1 from Mui Wo, 11 from Tung Chung, 21 from Ngong Ping) This village on the far-flung west coast of Lantau was once home to the Tanka people and an important trading and fishing port to China a century ago. Salt and fish are the major exports. Today Tai O is in decline, except perhaps as a tourist destination offering an intriguing glimpse of the life of a traditional fishing village.

A few of the salt pans still exist, but most have been filled in to build houses. Older people still make their living from duck farming, fishing, making the village's celebrated shrimp paste and processing salt fish, which you'll see (and smell) everywhere. It remains a popular place for locals to buy seafood – both fresh and dried.

As recently as the 1980s, Tai O also traded in IIs (illegal immigrants) brought from China under cover of darkness by 'snakeheads' (smugglers in human cargo) in long narrow boats, sending back contraband such as refrigerators, radios and TVs to the mainland.

Tai O is built partly on Lantau and partly on a tiny island about 15m from the shore. Until the mid-1990s the only way to cross was via a rope-tow ferry pulled by elderly Hakka women. That and the large number of sampans in the small harbour earned Tai O the nickname 'the Venice of Hong Kong'. Though the narrow iron Tai Chung footbridge now spans the canal, the rope-tow ferry is resurrected on some weekends and holidays: drop $1 in the box as you disembark.

Some of the tiny, traditional-style village houses still stand in the centre, including a handful of Tai O's famed **stilt houses** on the waterfront. There are a few houses that escaped a fire in 2000, plus a number of shanties, their corrugated-iron walls held in place by rope, and houseboats that haven't set sail for years.

The stilt houses and the local **Kwan Tai temple** (關帝廟), dedicated to the god of

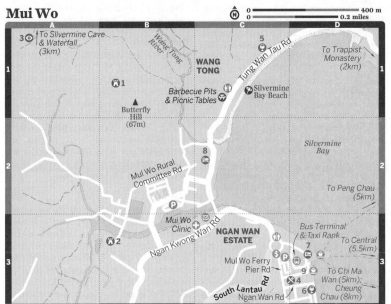

Mui Wo

To Silvermine Cave & Waterfall (3km)

Wong Tong River

WANG TONG

Tung Wan Tau Rd

To Trappist Monastery (2km)

Barbecue Pits & Picnic Tables

Silvermine Bay Beach

Butterfly Hill (67m)

Silvermine Bay

Mui Wo Rural Committee Rd

To Peng Chau (5km)

Mui Wo Clinic

Ngan Kwong Wan Rd

NGAN WAN ESTATE

Bus Terminal & Taxi Rank

To Central (5.5km)

Mul Wo Ferry Pier Rd

South Lantau Rd

Ngan Wan Rd

To Chi Ma Wan (5km); Cheung Chau (8km)

---

war, are on Kat Hing St. To reach them, cross the bridge from the mainland to the island, walk up Tai O Market St and go right at the Fook Moon Lam restaurant. There's a couple of other **temples** here, including an 18th-century one erected in honour of Hung Shing, patron of fisherfolk; it's on Shek Tsai Po St, about 600m west of the Fook Lam Moon restaurant.

At the end of Shek Tsai Po St stands the beautifully restored **Old Tai O Police Station** (舊大澳警署). Built in 1902, the former marine police station was originally set up to protect the surrounding waters from pirate activity. Sea raiders gradually became a thing of the past as the 20th century wore on but a new problem surfaced in the 1980s when a new wave of illegal immigrants and smugglers from China tried to sneak into the territory via Tai O. When that also became history, the station continued to serve as a patrol post until it was retired in 2002. The complex has undergone a delicate restoration since and in 2012, it re-opened as the charming Tai O Heritage Hotel (p208). Even if you aren't staying here, it's worth joining the free guided tour, which starts at 3pm daily. Online reservation is a must.

There are also brief **river boat tours** (☏9629 4581, 9645 6652; per 30min $20) departing from the footbridge.

LUNG TSAI NG GARDEN   GARDENS

Map p200 (龍仔悟園; ☒1 from Mui Wo, 11 from Tung Chung, 21 from Ngong Ping) This magical garden southwest of Ngong Ping, with a lotus pond crossed by a rickety zigzag bridge, was built by a wealthy merchant in the 1930s in a small valley near where the village of Lung Tsai once stood. The site is rather derelict, but atmospheric nonetheless, and the gardens are in excellent condition. You can get here via a water catchment path and trail from the Tai O Rd, a continuation of South Lantau Rd just west of Keung Shan. Alight from the bus after the Kwun Yam temple on Tai O Rd, which is about 2km past the turn-off for the Tian Tan Buddha. You'll see a country park sign and the start of the water catchment.

SOUTH LANTAU RD BEACHES

Map p200 (🚌1 from Mui Wo & Tai O, 2 from Ngong Ping, 3 from Tung Chung) Along South Lantau Rd is a succession of beaches that attract surfers, beachgoers and retirees alike. Just 5km southwest of Mui Wo, **Pui O** has a decent beach, but as it's the closest one to Mui Wo it can get very crowded. The village has several restaurants, holiday flats galore and, in season, stalls renting bicycles.

Hong Kong's longest beach, **Cheung Sha** (Long Sand), stretching over 3km on the southern coast of Lantau, is divided into 'upper' and 'lower' sections; a trail over a hillock links the two. **Upper Cheung Sha**, with occasional good surf, is the prettier and longer stretch and boasts a modern complex with changing rooms, toilets, showers and a snack bar. **Lower Cheung Sha** village has a beachfront restaurant and a water-sports centre. Some claim that the Venturi effect on the wind from Tung Chung makes this the best windsurfing beach in Hong Kong, especially from November to March.

The beach at **Tong Fuk**, the next village over from Cheung Sha, is not as nice, but the village has holiday flats, several shops and restaurants. To the northwest is the not-so-scenic sprawl of **Ma Po Ping Prison**.

West of Tong Fuk, South Lantau Rd begins to climb the hills inland before crossing an enormous dam holding back the **Shek Pik Reservoir**, completed in 1963, which provides Lantau, Cheung Chau and parts of Hong Kong Island with drinking water. Just below the dam is the granddaddy of Lantau's trio of jails, **Shek Pik Prison** (石壁監獄). Below the dam to the south but before the prison is a **Bronze Age rock carving** (銅器時代石刻), which is unusual in that it is so far from the coastline.

The trail along the water-catchment area east of Shek Pik Reservoir, with picnic tables and barbecue pits, offers some of the easiest and most peaceful walking on Lantau. From here you can also pick up the switchback trail to **Dog's Tooth Peak**

(539m), from where another trail heads north to Lantau Peak.

CHI MA WAN BEACH

Map p200 (🚢Interisland service from Mui Wo & Cheung Chau) Chi Ma Wan can be reached via the interisland ferry from Mui Wo and offers some excellent hiking opportunities; just be sure to get a map as the trails are not always clearly defined or well marked.

The Chi Ma Wan **ferry pier** is on the northeast coast; the large complex just south of the pier is the **Chi Ma Wan Correctional Institution**. There's a decent beach to the south at **Tai Long Wan**.

FAN LAU BEACH

Fan Lau (Divided Flow), on the southwestern tip of Lantau, has a couple of good beaches and the remains of **Fan Lau Fort**, built in 1729 to protect the channel between Lantau and the Pearl River estuary from pirates. It remained in operation until the end of the 19th century and was restored in 1985. The sea views from here are stunning.

The ancient **stone circle** is to the southeast of the fort. The circle probably dates from the Neolithic or early Bronze Age and may have been used in rituals.

The only way to reach Fan Lau is on foot. To get here from Tai O, walk south from the bus station for 250m and pick up stage No 7 (ie along the island's southwestern coast) of **Lantau Trail**, a distance of about 8km. The trail then carries on to the northeast and Shek Pik for another 12km, where you can catch bus 1 back to Mui Wo.

TRAPPIST MONASTERY MONASTERY

Map p200 (神樂院; ☎2987 6292; Tai Shui Hang; 🚢kaido from Peng Chau) Northeast of Mui Wo and south of Discovery Bay at Tai Shui Hang is the Roman Catholic Lady of Joy Abbey – better known as the Trappist Monastery. The monastery is known throughout Hong Kong for its cream-rich milk, sold in half-pint bottles everywhere, but the cows have been moved to the New Territories and Trappist Dairy Milk is now produced in Yuen Long.

The Trappists gained a reputation as one of the most austere religious communities in the Roman Catholic Church and the Lantau congregation was established at Peking in the 19th century. All of the monks here now are local Hong Kongers.

Trappist monks take a vow of absolute silence, and there are signs reminding visitors to keep radios and music players turned off and to speak in low tones.

You can reach the monastery on foot by following a well-marked coastal trail from the northern end of Tung Wan Tau Rd in Mui Wo, but it's much easier to get here by *kaido* from Peng Chau, a little island east of Lantau.

HONG KONG DISNEYLAND   AMUSEMENT PARK
Map p200 (香港迪士尼樂園; ☑1830 830; http://park.hongkongdisneyland.com; adult/child $399/285; Ⓜ Disney Resort Station) Ever since it claimed Hong Kong in 2005, this franchised theme park has served as a rite of passage for the flocks of Chinese tourists who come daily to steal a glimpse of one of America's most famous cultural exports. It's divided into five main areas – Main Street USA, Fantasyland, Adventureland, Toy Story Land and Tomorrowland – but don't expect too much. The overall scale is rather small, with only one real adrenalin-inducing roller-coaster ride (Space Mountain). The rest of the park is made up of tamer attractions and rammed with outlets selling Disney merchandise and fast food.

Disneyland is linked by rail with the MTR at Sunny Bay station on the Tung Chung line; passengers just cross the platform to board the dedicated train for Disneyland Resort station and the theme park. Journey times from Central/Kowloon/Tsing Yi stations are 24/21/10 minutes respectively.

TUNG CHUNG   HISTORIC SITE
Map p200 (ⓂTung Chung; ☐3M from Mui Wo, 11 from Tai O, 23 from Ngong Ping) Before 1994 Tung Chung, on Lantau's northern coast, was still an inaccessible farming village. Less than four years later, it was transformed into a new town and a new airport was added to nearby Chek Lap Kok. Today Tung Chung has the largest population on the island with a 760-hectare residential estate served by the MTR.

Annals record a settlement at Tung Chung as early as the Ming dynasty. There are several Buddhist establishments in the upper reaches of the valley, but the main attraction here is **Tung Chung Fort** (Tung Chung Rd; admission free; ☉10am-5pm Wed-Mon), which dates back to 1832, when Chinese troops were garrisoned on Lantau. The Japanese briefly occupied the fort during WWII. Measuring 70m by 80m and enclosed by granite-block walls, it retains

OUTLYING ISLANDS LANTAU

THE PINK DOLPHINS OF THE PEARL RIVER

Between 100 and 200 misnamed Chinese white dolphins *(Sousa chinensis)* – they are actually bubble-gum pink – inhabit the coastal waters around Hong Kong, finding the brackish waters of the Pearl River estuary to be the perfect habitat. Unfortunately these glorious mammals, which are also called Indo-Pacific humpback dolphins, are being threatened by environmental pollution, and their numbers are dwindling.

The threat comes in many forms, but the most prevalent – and direct – dangers are sewage, chemicals, overfishing and boat traffic. Some 200,000 cubic metres of untreated sewage are dumped into the western harbour every day, and high concentrations of chemicals such as DDT have been found in tissue samples taken from some of the dolphins. Several dolphins have been entangled in fishing nets and, despite the dolphins' skill at sensing and avoiding surface vessels, some have collided with boats. Pleasure boats buzzing around the Tai O area are a particular menace.

The dolphins' habitat has also been diminished by the destruction of the natural coastline of Lantau Island. The North Lantau Hwy consumed about 10km of the natural coastline. The Hong Kong Disneyland theme park required large amounts of reclamation in Penny's Bay.

Hong Kong Dolphinwatch (香港海豚觀察; ☑2984 1414; www.hkdolphinwatch. com; 15th fl, Middle Block, 1528a Star House, 3 Salisbury Rd, Tsim Sha Tsui) was founded in 1995 to raise awareness of these wonderful creatures and promote responsible ecotourism. It offers 2½-hour **cruises** (adult/child $380/190) to see the pink dolphins in their natural habitat every Wednesday, Friday and Sunday year-round. Guides assemble in the lobby of the Kowloon Hotel Hong Kong in Tsim Sha Tsui at 9am for the bus to Tung Chung via the Tsing Ma Bridge, from where the boat departs; the tours return at 1pm.

1

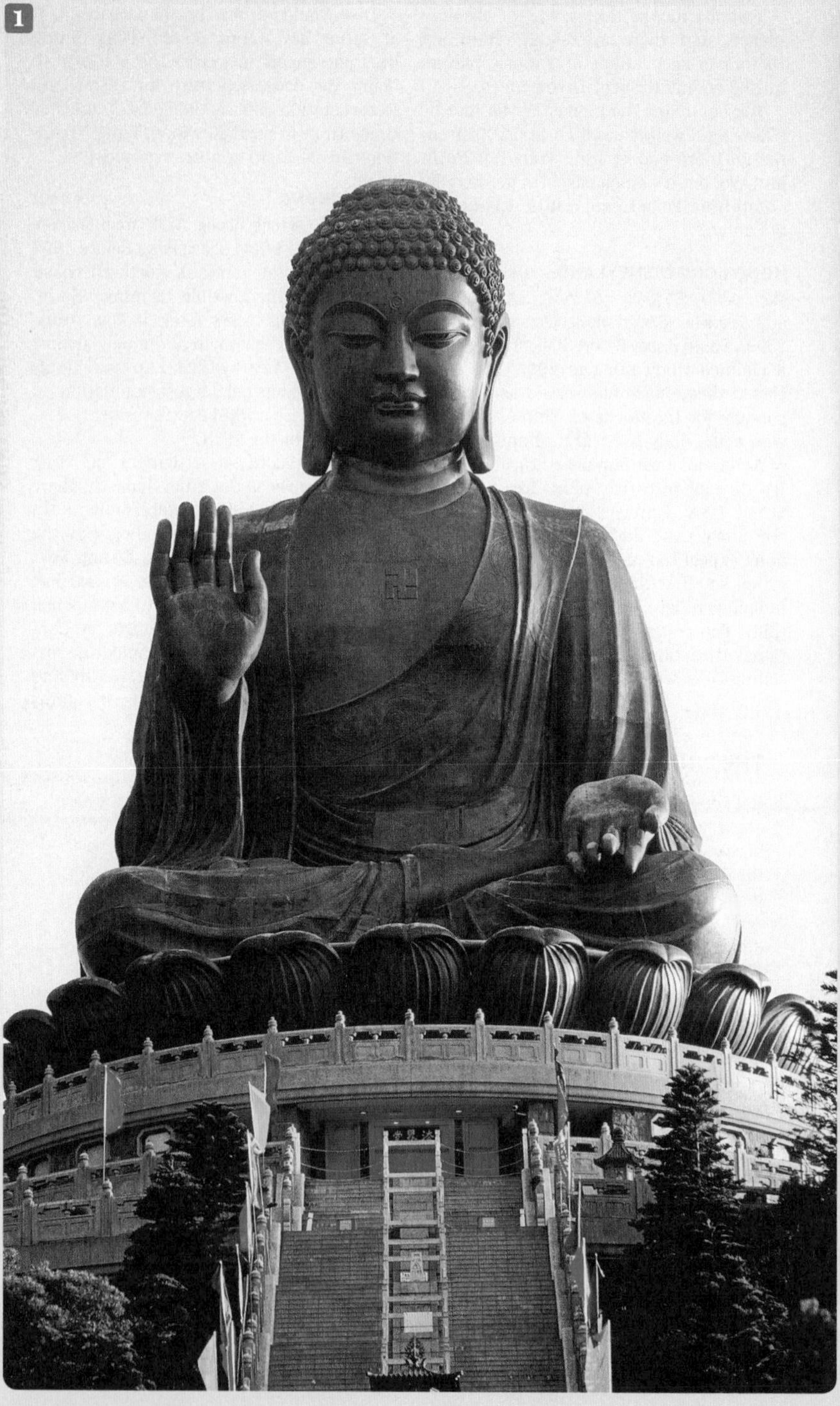

1. Tian Tan Buddha (p193)
The world's biggest bronze outdoor seated Buddha lords over the hills of Lantau.

2. Seafood in Yung Shue Wan (p195)
Lamma's largest settlement, Yung Shue Wan retains more than a whiff of rustic charm.

3. Cycling on Cheung Chau (p210)
This island is home to temples, beaches and an annual Bun Festival.

4. Tung Wan Beach (p211)
Cheung Chau's longest and most popular beach is a great spot for windsurfing.

six of its muzzle-loading cannons pointing out to sea.

About 1km to the north are the ruins of **Tung Chung Battery**, which is a much smaller fort built in 1817. All that remains is an L-shaped wall facing the sea, with a gun emplacement in the corner. The ruins were discovered only in 1980, having been hidden for about a century by scrub.

Facing Tung Chung Bay to the southwest in the village of Sha Tsui Tau is double-roofed **Hau Wong Temple** (侯王廟), founded at the end of the Song dynasty. The temple contains a bell dating from 1765 and inscribed by the Qing-dynasty emperor Qian Long.

DISCOVERY BAY   BEACH, GOLF
Map p200 (⬚Discovery Bay) With a fine stretch of sandy beach ringed by luxurious condominiums, 'DB' is a dormitory suburb on Lantau's northeastern coast for professionals who commute to Central. There

is no pressing need to visit except to ogle at residents in their converted golf carts, which cost $200,000 a pop.

There is a handful of decent restaurants in **Discovery Bay Plaza** (愉景灣廣場), just up from the ferry pier and the central plaza, and the 27-hole **Discovery Bay Golf Club** perched in the hills to the southwest.

Buses make the run to and from Tung Chung and the airport at Chek Lap Kok via the **Discovery Bay Tunnel** and the North Lantau Hwy. A **trail** leading from the golf course will take you down to Silvermine Bay and the rest of Lantau in a couple of hours.

 EATING

Lantau might not be able to compete with Lamma or Cheung Chau in the cuisine stakes, but there are enough decent eateries

---

SLEEPING IN LANTAU

You can rent holiday flats from kiosks set up at the Mui Wo ferry pier. Expect to pay $250 on weekdays and $350 on the weekend for a double room or studio. Not all the places are within walking distance of the ferry pier. The airport, needless to say, has enough hotels that are well geared for the tourist dollar.

Espace Elastique (歸田園居; ☑2985 7002; www.espaceelastique.com.hk; 57 Kat Hing St, Tai O; r Sun-Thu $600-1400, Fri & Sat $800-2230; @🛜🌊; ⬚Lantau) This cosy four-room B&B is one of the best-kept gems on Lantau. All rooms are tastefully decorated; the 2nd-floor double room with a balcony overlooking the main Tai O waterway gets booked up quickly. The friendly owner Veronica provides multilingual travel advice, plus a hearty breakfast in the cafe. The jacuzzi on the rooftop is a delight.

Tai O Heritage Hotel (大澳文物酒店; www.taioheritagehotel.com; Shek Tsai Po St, Tai O; r $1380-2500; @🛜🌊; ⬚Lantau) Housed in a century-old former police station, this is Lantau's newest hotel. All nine rooms are handsomely furnished in a contemporary style, offering top-of-the-line comfort. Our favourite is the inspector-office-turned–Sea Tiger Room, the smallest digs (24 sq metres) but with picture windows ushering in the sea breeze. It's a 20-minute walk from Kat Hing St. Alternatively, boats departing from the bridge near Kat Hing St can take you to the hotel ($10).

Silvermine Beach Resort (銀鑛灣渡假酒店; ☑6810 0111; www.silvermineresort.com; Silvermine Bay beach, Mui Wo; r $1180-1880, monthly packages from $13,800; @🛜🌊; ⬚Lantau) The north wing of the hotel got a facelift in 2011 but the entire property still wears a dated, 1980s ambience. Rooms are basic but clean, and the ones with sea views (in both wings) are particularly popular. It's less than 10 minutes' walk from the pier.

Ngong Ping SG Davis Hostel (☑2985 5610; www.yha.org.hk; Ngong Ping; dm members under/over 18 yr $55/80, nonmembers from $110; 🚌2, 21 or 23) This hostel is near the Tian Tan Buddha statue and is an ideal place to stay if you want to watch the sunrise at Lantau Peak. From the Ngong Ping bus terminus, take the paved path to your left as you face the Tian Tan Buddha, pass the public toilets on your right and follow the signs. The hostel is only open to HKYHA/HI cardholders or the guests of a cardholder and is only in service Friday to Monday.

WORTH A DETOUR

PO TOI

A solid favourite of weekend holidaymakers with their own seagoing transport, Po Toi is the largest of a group of five islands – one is little more than a huge rock. Hong Kong's territorial border lies just 2km to the south. Visitors frequent the seafood restaurants beyond the jetty at **Tai Wan**, the main settlement, in the island's southwest.

There's some decent walking on Po Toi, a tiny **Tin Hau temple** across the bay from the pier, and, on the southern coast, rock formations that (supposedly) look like a palm tree, a tortoise and a monk, and some mysterious **rock carvings** resembling stylised animals and fish. You can see everything here in an hour.

Ming Kee Seafood Restaurant (明記海鮮酒家; ☎2849 7038; ⏱11am-11pm) is one of a handful of restaurants in the main village of Po Toi Island, south of Hong Kong Island, and is by far the most popular with day trippers. Make sure you book ahead on the weekend.

Kaido (small, open-sea ferries) run to the ferry pier from Aberdeen and Stanley on Tuesdays, Thursdays, weekends and public holidays.

---

to soothe your belly. Tung Chung and Mui Wo have the island's largest concentration of restaurants, while Discovery Bay has its own line-up of dining venues around Discovery Bay Plaza. There are also some good choices further afield in Ngong Ping Plateau and Tai O, as well as the villages scattered along South Lantau Rd.

TOP CHOICE SOLO
CAFE $

(☎9153 7453; 86 Kat Hing St, Tai O; meals from $40; ⏱11am-6pm Mon-Sat; 🚌1 from Mui Wo) Framed by a backdrop of stilt houses and lush mountains, this sunny terrace right on the water invites lazy afternoons spent enjoying coffee. The tiramisu and the apple crumble with ice cream are as tempting as its fresh roasted coffee.

BAHÇE
TURKISH $

Map p203 (☎2984 0222; Shop 19, Ground fl, Mui Wo Centre, 3 Ngan Wan Rd, Mui Wo; mains from $95; ⏱11am-10.30pm Mon-Fri, 9.30am-10.30pm Sat & Sun) Near the ferry pier is this small, busy place where many locals and expats alike opt for its outdoor tables in the warmer months. The lamb and the kebabs are mouth-watering, and they pair well with the Typhoon, an English-style cask ale freshly brewed from the microbrewery next door.

TAI O LOOKOUT
FUSION $

Map p200 (☎2985 8383; Shek Tsai Po St, Tai O Heritage Hotel, Tai O; dishes from $70; ⏱11.30am-4.30pm; 🚌1 from Mui Wo) The appeal of this rooftop glasshouse restaurant lies probably more in the atmospheric period decor than in the food. The rotating ceiling fans, wooden booths and tiled floor ooze old-world charm, and the sweeping views of the South China Sea would make no one blame you if you came to just sip coffee and chill. The restaurant was trialing its menu at the time of writing but the fried rice is no run-of-the-mill house special as it's tossed with Tai O's famous shrimp paste. The same ingredient is applied to the pork chop bun, which is also worth a try.

SICHUAN BACK GARDEN
SICHUANESE $$

Map p200 (cecilie@happyjellyfish.com; www.happyjellyfish.com; Lo Uk Tsuen, Pui O; meal with beer per person $300; 🚌1 or 2 from Mui Wo) A Cantonese-speaking Norwegian firebrand dishing out tongue-lashing Sichuanese food? It may sound like a meal that's gone all horribly wrong but this dining speakeasy in backwater Pui O is no joke when it comes to authenticity. Cecilie, a self-proclaimed Cantonese fundamentalist, is the mastermind behind this private kitchen-cum-language school and homestay. Her culinary prowess and quirky sense of humour has earned her a staunch following from locals and expats alike. The back garden is also her home, perched on a slope overlooking Pui O cove and the outlying islands. Reserve three days in advance. A minimum of six people required.

STOEP RESTAURANT
MEDITERRANEAN $$

Map p200 (☎2980 2699; 32 Lower Cheung Sha Village; meals from $180; ⏱11am-10pm Tue-Sun; 🚌1 or 2 from Mui Wo) This Mediterranean-style restaurant with a huge terrace on Lower

Cheung Sha beach has acceptable meat and fish dishes and a South African *braai* (barbecue). Be sure to book on the weekend.

 DRINKING & NIGHTLIFE

CHINA BEACH CLUB   BAR
Map p203 (18 Tung Wan Tau Rd; ⊙noon-10pm Thu & Fri, 11.30am-10pm Sat & Sun, happy hour all day Fri-Sun; ⊠Lantau) This cheerful restaurant has an airy rooftop and a balcony overlooking Silvermine Bay Beach for those who want to chill over their home-style Greek moussaka or just kick back with a cocktail or beer. The two-for-one cocktail 'hour' can go on well into the night.

OOH LA LA   BAR
Map p200 (☑2984 8710; Pui O beach, Pui O; ☑1, 2, 3M, 4 or A35) Enjoy the soft sands and gently lapping waves while sipping the perfectly mixed sangria or mojitos in this beach bar. A treat for your taste buds is the Mediterranean barbecue. The bar has eccentric opening hours, so it's best to call ahead. It closes during the winter months.

CHINA BEAR   PUB
Map p203 (Ground fl, Mui Wo Centre, Ngan Wan Rd; ⊙10am-2am, happy hour 5-9pm Mon-Fri, 5-8pm Sat & Sun; ⊠Lantau) The most popular expat pub-restaurant in Mui Wo, China Bear boasts a wonderful open bar facing the water. It's right by the ferry terminal, making it the perfect spot for your first and last beer in Mui Wo, and for those in between perhaps.

🏃 SPORTS & ACTIVITIES

LONG COAST SEASPORTS   SURFING
Map p200 (☑8104 6222; www.longcoast.hk; 29 Lower Cheung Sha Village; ⊙10am-sunset Mon-Fri, 9am-sunset Sat & Sun) If sun, surf and sand are what you are after, then you need look no further. This water-sports centre has its own lodge and campground and offers windsurfing, sea kayaking and wakeboarding. Basic windsurfing costs from $120/300/500 for an hour/half-day/day, while a single kayak rents for $70/210 for an hour/half-day.

DISCOVERY BAY GOLF CLUB   GOLF
Map p200 (愉景灣高爾夫球會; ☑2987 7273; Valley Rd, Discovery Bay, Lantau; greens fees $1700; ⊠Discovery Bay) Perched high on a hill, this 27-hole course has impressive views of the Outlying Islands. Nonmembers Monday, Tuesday and Friday only.

HONG KONG SHAOLIN WUSHU CULTURE CENTRE   MARTIAL ARTS
Map p200 (香港少林武術文化中心; ☑2985 8898; Shek Tsai Po St, Tai O; http://shaolincc.org.hk; 2-day/3-day course weekday $400/700, weekend $460/760) Located outside the centre of action in Tai O is this low-key martial arts school, one of the few in Hong Kong that runs intensive short courses for curious first-timers. However, classes are offered on an irregular basis. It's wise to call ahead. On-site accommodation is available. It's next to the Hung Shing Temple.

Cheung Chau

Explore

The island boasts several interesting temples, with the most important being Pak Tai Temple. Visit here during the annual Bun Festival to indulge yourself and join in the hoopla.

The island has a few worthwhile beaches. Kwun Yam Wan and Nam Tam Wan beaches are two of those you want to loll around in the afternoon.

Visit Cheung Po Tsai cave if time allows. It's a reminder that the island was once a refuge for pirates in the 18th century and the cave is where booty was supposedly stashed.

Food is positively relished here. Munch on the island's renowned street snacks as you saunter through Cheung Chau Village, and savour the seafood alfresco at a harbourside restaurant in the evening.

The Best...

➡ **Sight** Pak Tai Temple (p211)

➡ **Place to Eat** Kam Wing Tai Fish Ball Shop (p214)

➡ **Place to Drink** Windsurfing Water Sports Centre & Café (opposite)

LOCAL KNOWLEDGE

CHEUNG CHAU'S BUN FESTIVAL

The annual **Bun Festival** (*Tai ping ching jiu* in Cantonese; www.cheungchau.org) honours the Taoist god Pak Tai and is unique to the island. It takes place over eight days in late April or early May, traditionally starting on the sixth day of the fourth moon. There are four days of religious observances.

The festival is best known for its bun towers: bamboo scaffolding up to 20m high that is covered with sacred rolls. If you visit Cheung Chau a week or so before the festival, you'll see the towers being built in front of Pak Tai Temple.

Hundreds of people scramble up the towers at midnight on the designated day to snatch the buns for good luck. The higher the bun, the greater the luck, so everyone tries to reach the top. In 1978 a tower collapsed under the weight of the climbers, injuring two dozen people. The race didn't take place again for over two decades until it was revived – with strict safety controls – in 2005.

The third day of the festival features a procession of floats, stilt walkers and people dressed as characters from Chinese legends and opera. Most interesting are the colourfully dressed 'floating children' who are carried through the streets on long poles, cleverly wired to metal supports hidden under their clothing. The supports include footrests and a padded seat.

Offerings are made to the spirits of all the fish and livestock killed and consumed over the previous year. During the four-day festival, the whole island goes vegetarian.

Top Tip

During the Bun Festival, it's wise to take a ferry to Mui Wo, and then take the inter-island ferry to Cheung Chau to avoid the long wait on Central ferry pier.

Getting There & Away

Ferry Services from Central leave from pier 5 of the Outlying Islands ferry terminal. Ferries can also be taken from Mui Wo and Chi Ma Wan on Lantau and from Peng Chau. Additionally, regular *kaido* operate between Cheung Chau village (sampan pier) and Sai Wan in the south of the island.

Need to Know

➡ **Area code** ☑852

➡ **Location** 10km southwest of Hong Kong Island

➡ **Last ferry to Central** 11.45pm Monday–Saturday, 11.30 Sunday & public holidays

⊙ SIGHTS

PAK TAI TEMPLE   TAOIST
Map p212 (北帝廟; ☑2981 0663; Pak She Fourth Lane; ⊙7am-5pm; ⊡Cheung Chau) This

colourfully restored temple from 1783 is the epicentre of the annual Cheung Chau Bun Festival (see boxed text above) in late April or early May. The most important and oldest temple on the island, it is dedicated to the Taoist deity Pak Tai, the 'Supreme Emperor of the Dark Heaven', military protector of the state, guardian of peace and order, and protector of fisherfolk. Legend tells that early settlers from Canton province brought an image of Pak Tai with them to Cheung Chau and, when the statue was carried through the village, Cheung Chau was spared the plague that had decimated the populations of nearby islands. A temple dedicated to the saviour was built six years later.

BEACHES   BEACH
Map p212 (⊡Cheung Chau) **Tung Wan beach**, east of the ferry pier, is not Cheung Chau's prettiest beach but it's the longest and most popular. The far southern end of Tung Wan is a great area for windsurfing; so is **Kwun Yam Wan**, a beach just south of Tung Wan beach.

Windsurfing has always been a popular pastime on Cheung Chau, and Hong Kong's only Olympic gold medallist to date, Lee Lai-shan, who took the top prize in windsurfing at the 1996 Atlanta Olympics, grew up here. At the northern end of Kwun Yam Wan, the **Cheung Chau Windsurfing Water Sports Centre** (☑2981 2772;

Cheung Chau

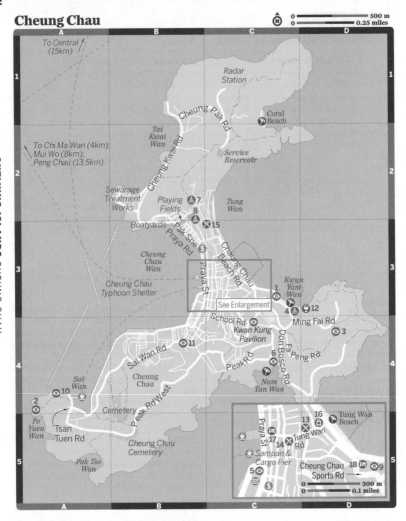

www.ccwindc.com.hk; 1 Hak Pai Rd; ⊙10am-7pm) rents sailboards for between $90 and $150 per hour, as well as single/double kayaks for $80/120. There are also windsurfing courses available for $1100 per day. The best time for windsurfing here is between October and December.

At the southeastern end of Kwun Yam Wan a footpath leads uphill past a **Kwun Yam temple** (觀音廟), which is dedicated to the goddess of mercy. Continue up the footpath and look for the sign to the **Fa Peng Knoll**. The concrete footpath takes you past quiet, tree-shrouded villas.

From the knoll you can walk down to signposted Don Bosco Rd; it leads due south to rocky **Nam Tam Wan**, where swimming is possible.

Peak Rd is the main route to the island's cemetery in the southwestern part of the island; you'll pass several pavilions along the way built for coffin bearers making the hilly climb. Once at the cemetery it's worth dropping down to **Pak Tso Wan**, a sandy, isolated spot that is good for swimming.

CHEUNG CHAU VILLAGE   VILLAGE
Map p212 (⛴Cheung Chau) The island's main settlement lies along the narrow strip of

Cheung Chau

land connecting the headlands to the north and the south. The waterfront is a bustling place and the maze of streets and alleyways that make up the village are filled with old Chinese-style houses and tumbledown shops selling everything from plastic buckets to hell money and other combustible grave offerings. The streets close to the waterfront are pungent with the smell of incense and fish hung out to dry in the sun.

SAMPAN RIDES
BOAT TRIP

Map p212 (⊜Cheung Chau) A great way to see the harbour and soak up the fishing-village atmosphere is to charter a sampan for half an hour (expect to pay $70 to $120 depending on the day, the season and the demand). Most sampans congregate around the cargo pier, but virtually any small boat you see in the harbour can be hired as a water taxi. Just wave and two or three will come forward. Be sure to agree on the fare first.

CHEUNG PO TSAI CAVE
CAVE

Map p212 (張保仔洞; ⊜Cheung Chau) This 'cave' – in truth not much more than a hole in some rocks – on the southwestern peninsula of the island is said to have been the favourite hideout of the notorious pirate Cheung Po Tsai, who once commanded a flotilla of 600 junks and had a private army of 4000 men. He surrendered to the Qing government in 1810 and became an official himself, but his treasure is said to remain hidden here.

It's a 2km walk from Cheung Chau village along Sai Wan Rd, or take a *kaido* (adult/child from $3/2) from the cargo ferry

pier to the pier at Sai Wan. From here the walk is less than 200m (uphill).

TIN HAU TEMPLES
TEMPLE

(⊜Cheung Chau) Cheung Chau has four temples dedicated to Tin Hau, the empress of heaven and patroness of seafarers. **Pak She Tin Hau temple** (北社天后廟) lies 100m northwest of the Pak Tai Temple. **Nam Tam Wan Tin Hau temple** (南氹灣天后廟) is just north of Nam Tam Wan; **Tai Shek Hau Tin Hau temple** (大石口天后廟) is to the west on Sai Wan Rd. **Sai Wan Tin Hau temple** (西灣天后廟) is west of Sai Wan, on the southwestern tip of the island. You can walk there or catch a *kaido* from the cargo pier.

✖ EATING

There are seafood restaurants galore on Pak She Praya Rd. They all have very similar à la carte and table d'hôte menus that are competitively priced. Expect to pay $140 for a three-course meal. Alternatively, around the south of the pier and at the start of Tai Hing Tai Rd, you can pick your fish or other seafood from the food stalls with fish tanks, and then pay the stallholders to cook them the way you like. The night market on Praya St right down the ferry pier starts bustling from 10pm every evening, with myriad food carts offering snacks and desserts for the insomniac. To get off the well-trodden waterfront, we recommend the following places.

KAM WING TAI FISH BALL SHOP CHINESE $

Map p212 (甘永泰魚蛋; ☑2981 3050; 106 San Hing St; balls $10; ☉10am-8pm) The long line snaking along the alley should tell you something about this celebrated pit stop. Hakka-style snack balls of minced fish and meat are served piping hot. A stick of chewy assorted balls is highly recommended.

HOMETOWN TEAHOUSE JAPANESE $

Map p212 (故鄉茶寮; ☑2981 5038; 12 Tung Wan Rd; sushi from $13; ☉11.30am-9pm, closed days vary between 1 per week & 1 per fortnight) Run by an amiable Japanese couple, this tiny backstreet eatery is positively flooded with both locals and tourists who come for its sushi and red-bean pastries ($5).

KWOK KAM KEE CAKE SHOP BAKERY $

Map p212 (郭錦記餅店; ☑2986 9717; 46 Pak She St; buns from $4; ☉6am-7pm) Not far from Pak Tai Temple, this 40-year-old bakery is the supplier of *Ping On Bao* (peace and prosperity buns), the round white buns with a lucky red stamp, for the Bun Festival. In fact you can get the fresh-from-the-steamer buns at 2pm everyday and they are tra-ditionally filled with sesame paste, lotus-seed paste or red-bean paste. The bakery has no English sign and is easy to miss. Look for the long line out front.

WINDSURFING WATER SPORTS CENTRE & CAFÉ INTERNATIONAL $$

Map p212 (長洲滑浪風帆中心露天茶座; ☑2981 8316; www.ccwindc.com.hk; 1 Hak Pai Rd; meals from $150; ☉10am-6pm) A favourite hang-out of windsurfers and divers, this place is owned by Lai Gun, uncle of the champion windsurfer Lee Lai-shan who won Olympic gold for Hong Kong in Atlanta. On a balmy afternoon, this cafe is a great spot to relax over fries, fish steak and a bottle of wine.

HING KEE BEACH BAR BAR $

Map p212 (興記士多; ☑2981 3478; Kwun Yam Wan Beach; ☉10am-8pm) This hole-in-the-wall drinking spot in quiet Kwun Yam Wan beach is a store and bar combo, and a popular hang-out for villagers and those in the know. Auntie Hing (the owner) does really good grub with her home-grown herbs.

WORTH A DETOUR

TUNG LUNG CHAU

Left alone at the eastern entrance to Victoria Harbour, uninhabited 'East Dragon Island' is Hong Kong's premier spot for rock climbing and stargazing.

Tung Lung Fort (東龍洲炮台; ⛴Tung Lung Chau), on the northeastern corner of the island, is evidence that the island was once considered strategic enough for protection. Built in the late 17th or early 18th century, it was attacked a number of times by pirate bands before being abandoned in 1810. The fort once consisted of 15 guardhouses and was armed with eight cannons, but little of it remains today except the outline of the exterior walls. There's an **information centre** (☉9am-4pm Wed-Mon) with pictures illustrating the history of the fort.

On the northern coast of the island is one of the earliest and largest in-situ **rock carvings** in the territory. The tortuous lines of the dragon-shaped carving (measuring 2.4m by 1.8m) are still clearly visible, and the walk down to the cliff is a leisurely one.

Tung Lung Chau lies to the south of the Clearwater Bay Peninsula across the narrow Fat Tong Mun channel. To the west is Shek O and Big Wave Bay on Hong Kong Island's east coast.

There are a couple of stores on the way to the fort that sell sandwiches, instant noodles and herbal tea on the weekends. You can pitch your tent in the campground below the fort or in the area near the lighthouse (access via the Holiday Store) which overlooks the stunning South China Sea. Camping facilities are primitive though.

Kaido (ferries) run from Sai Wan Ho on Hong Kong Island via Joss House Bay on the Clearwater Bay Peninsula in the New Territories. There is a single sailing each way on Thursdays (round trip $40), with more regular services only on weekends and public holidays. A weekend and holiday service also operates from Sam Ka Tsuen near Yau Tong MTR.

SLEEPING IN CHEUNG CHAU

Depending on the day of the week and the season, up to half a dozen kiosks opposite the ferry pier rent studios and apartments.

Warwick Hotel (☑2981 0081; www.warwickhotel.com.hk; Cheung Chau Sports Rd, Tung Wan beach; s/d Mon-Fri $1090/1290, Sat & Sun $1490/1690, ste from $1600, weekly/monthly packages from $5500/20,000; @; ⬆Cheung Chau) Don't be disappointed by the dated lobby and the outdoor area of this one and only hotel on the island. Some of its 66 rooms, especially the rooms with panoramic ocean views, are recently repainted and renovated. Hefty discounts are available on weekdays.

Cheung Chau B&B (☑2986 9990; www.bbcheungchau.com.hk; 12-14 Tung Wan Rd; r Sun-Thu from $520, Fri/Sat from $650/850; 🛜; ⬆Cheung Chau) This B&B is an alternative to the island's only hotel and the rooms offered by kiosks. The 22 likeable rooms and suites are near Pak Tai Temple and by Tung Wan. All are cheerfully appointed but some are little more than cubicles, so you might want to check first. The roof terrace at Tung Wan is a perfect spot to watch sunset and sunrise.

 # SHOPPING

YUANDME TEA

Map p212 (漁雁軒; ☑2981 8432; 2 Tung Wan Rd; ☺10am-8pm) A true heaven for tea lovers, this quaint tea shop specialising in quality Pu'er tea is a must-go before catching the ferry back. The elegant selection of tea-wares is as dazzling as the Asian and Western antiques acquired by the owners Lily and her husband. These two tea aficionados are ready to give you an inspirational lesson in tea ceremony.

Guǎngzhōu

0   40 km
0   20 miles

Shēnzhèn

HONG KONG

Day Trips from Hong Kong

Shēnzhèn p217

For most day visitors, Shēnzhèn is mostly about bargain shopping (followed by a cheap massage or good dim sum). Although the bargains are Shēnzhèn's main draws, some interesting cultural spaces have emerged that are gradually picking up steam. There are also a few theme parks worth checking out. You can buy a five-day, Shēnzhèn-only visa at the Lo Wu border crossing (Americans, and sometimes British, excluded).

Guǎngzhōu p223

Known to many as Canton, Guǎngzhōu, the capital of Guǎngdōng province, is a sprawling city with 12 million people that may seem chaotic to the uninitiated. But with patience, you'll discover charming old streets, ancient temples, elegant churches, majestic villas and sites of uprisings that changed the history of China. What's more, to prepare for the Asian Games in 2010, the city underwent a makeover that resulted in tougher traffic-law enforcement and greener roadsides. And fittingly enough, in Canton, you'll find Cantonese cuisine cooked at its best.

Shēnzhèn

Explore

On arriving at Shēnzhèn train station, take bus 101 or 204 for an hour's ride west to Window of the World in the Nánshān District. Spend about two hours there, before taking the metro to the next two stops east, respectively Huáqiáochéng station and Qiáochéngdōng station, to visit art galleries and the OCT-LOFT Art Terminal. If you're hungry, have something at the end of two hours, before heading east to Chēgōngmiào station to shop for knock-off designer furniture and a proper lunch. After lunch go further east to the Shēnzhèn Museum near Shìmín Zhōngxīn station to provide some context for your impressions. Spend an hour or so there. If you're up for more shopping, check out the Luóhú Commercial Centre, and enjoy dinner in the Luóhú District, before catching the train to Hong Kong.

The Best...

➡ **Sights** Window of the World (p219), OCT-LOFT Art Terminal (p218), Dàfēn Village (p221)

➡ **Places to eat** Phoenix House (p220), Jīn Yuè Xuān (p220), Máojiā Restaurant (p220)

Top Tip

At Dōngmén Market, you can have clothes, drapes or bedcovers custom-made for same-day pick-up. Place your order in the morning, do your sightseeing and pick up your goods before dinner. With clothes, stick to straightforward designs, and preferably provide an image of what you want.

Getting There & Away

Train MTR's Lo Wu-bound or Lok Ma Chau-bound trains (1st/2nd class HK$67/35 if you start from Hung Hom) are the most convenient transport to Shēnzhèn from Hong Kong. The first train to Lo Wu/Lok Ma Chau leaves Hung Hom station at 5.30/5.35am, the last at 11.07/9.35pm, and the trip takes about 43/48 minutes. Both connect with the metro in Shēnzhèn once across the border.

Bus China Travel Tours Transportation Services (CTS; ☑2764 9803; http://ctsbus. hkcts.com) has frequent buses to the Huánggǎng border crossing (near Lok Ma Chau) and Shēnzhèn Bay (深圳湾) at Shékǒu from multiple departure points including Metropark Hotel in Causeway Bay, CTS branches in Wan Chai, Sheung Wan, Mong Kok and Prince Edward. Fares range from HK$20 to HK$50 (one way). Check http://ctsbus.hkcts.com/routes/hk/hk_shenzhen.html for the most convenient departure point. Shēnzhèn has a cheap and efficient network of buses and minibuses (tickets ¥1.50 to ¥4).

Boat Chu Kong Passenger Transportation Company (☑2858 3876; www.cksp.com.hk) has seven jet-cat departures (economy/1st class HK$110/145, one hour) daily from **Macau Ferry Terminal** (Map p236; 200 Connaught Rd, Sheung Wan) to **Shékǒu port** (☑2669 1213) from 7.45am to 8.30pm. Fourteen ferries depart from Hong Kong airport (HK$220, 30 minutes one way) between 9am and 9.45pm.

Metro At present, Shēnzhèn has five metro lines (www.szmc.net). Fares start from ¥2 for the first 4km. Line 1 stretches from the Luóhú border crossing to the airport, passing through the Window of the World theme park. Line 4 starts at Fútián Check Point station, where passengers can interchange from Lok Ma Chau station across the border in Hong Kong.

Taxi In Shēnzhèn, taxis cost ¥10 for the first 2km, with each additional kilometre ¥2.40.

Need to Know

➡ **Area Code** ☑86 (0)755

➡ **Location** 35km from Hung Hom station

➡ **Tourist Office** (Shēnzhèn Tourist Consultation Centre, 深圳旅遊咨詢中心; ☑8232 3045; Ground fl, Shēnzhèn train station, east exit; ☉9am-6pm) Free and reasonably detailed maps available on request. There's another branch at Fútián Port that keeps the same hours.

Shēnzhèn

◉ SIGHTS

SHĒNZHÈN MUSEUM   MUSEUM

(深圳博物馆新馆; Shēnzhèn Bówùguǎn Xīnguǎn; ☎0755-8201 3036; www.shenzhen museum.com.cn; East Gate, Citizens' Centre, Fuzhong Sanlu, Fútián; admission free; ◷10am-5.30pm Tue-Sun; Ⓜ Shìmín Zhōngxīn, exit B) A good introduction to this incredible city is the new, hulking complex of Shēnzhèn Museum. It showcases the city's short yet dynamic history of social transformation before and after Deng Xiaoping's policies of *gǎigé kāifàng* (reform and opening) through spectacular life-sized dioramas and massive interactive multimedia presentations. The most interesting exhibits include the collections of propaganda art popular in the 1940s and the colourful scale models in the folk culture hall.

OLD SHĒNZHÈN MUSEUM   MUSEUM

(深圳博物馆老馆; Shēnzhèn Bówùguǎn Lǎoguǎn; www.shenzhenmuseum.com.cn; ☎8210 1036;

Tóngxīn Lù, Fútián; ◷10am-5.30pm; Ⓜ Kēxué Guǎn, exit A, ❑3, 12, 101, 102 or 104) The old Shēnzhèn Museum in Litchi Park (Lìzhī Gōngyuán) has been converted into a museum of ancient arts that has less interesting displays of some 20,000 jade, porcelain and bronze artefacts.

OCT-LOFT ART TERMINAL   MUSEUM, ARTS CENTRE

(华侨城创意文化园; Huáqiáochéng Chuàngyì Wénhuàyuán; ☎2691 1976; Enping jie, Overseas Chinese Town; ◷10am-5.30pm Tue-Sun; Ⓜ Qiáochéngdōng, exit A) The OCT-LOFT Art Terminal is an ambitious project intended to attract artists to gather and explore, discuss and consume. The excellent museum complex exhibits works of international and local contemporary Chinese artists. Some communist-era warehouses have been converted into artists' studios, bars and cafes.

For a complete list of museums, arts and cultural events, pick up a copy of

Shēnzhèn

the bi-monthly *Life Art* map, available at museums.

HÉ XIĀNGNÍNG ART GALLERY   GALLERY

(何香凝美術館; Héxiāngníng Měishùguǎn; ⌕2660 4540; www.hxnart.com; 9013 Shennan Lu; admission ¥20, Fri free; ⊙10am-5.30pm Tue-Sun; Ⓜ Huáqiáochéng, exit C, ⌕245 from Shēnzhèn Bay Port) Just one metro stop from the Art Terminal is Hé Xiāngníng Art Gallery. It has an esoteric collection of hybrid Japanese/Chinese water paintings by the legendary late master of modern Chinese art, He Xiangning. Pick up a pamphlet in English at the ticket office, as there are no English descriptions by the displays.

OCT ART & DESIGN GALLERY   GALLERY

(华美术馆; Huá Měishùguǎn; ⌕3399 3111; www.oct-and.com; 9009 Shennan Lu; adult/student ¥18/8; ⊙10am-5.30pm Tue-Sun; Ⓜ Huáqiáochéng, exit C) Adjacent to Hé Xiāngníng Art Gallery is the Běijīng Water Cube–like OCT Art & Design Gallery. The focus of this new gallery is on fresh, mainland avant-garde designers. A marvellous collection of inno-

vative design pieces in various art forms is on display. Exhibits change frequently.

WINDOW OF THE WORLD   THEME PARK

(世界之窗; Shìjiè Zhīchuāng; ⌕2660 8000; www.szwwco.com; adult/child under 12yr ¥120/60; ⊙9am-10.30pm; Ⓜ Shìjiè Zhīchuāng, exit J, ⌕90 or 245 from Shēnzhèn Bay Port) Just a few minutes' walk from the OCT Art & Design Gallery is a series of dated theme parks that are always packed with snap-happy Chinese tourists. They're fun destinations for a family day out. Window of the World hosts a collection of scale replicas of famous world monuments. Foreigners being misidentified as part of the exhibits is not unheard of.

SPLENDID CHINA   AMUSEMENT PARK

(锦绣中华; Jǐnxiù Zhōnghuá; ⌕2660 0626; www.cn5000.com.cn; adult/child under 12yr incl entry to China Folk Culture Village ¥130/60; ⊙9am-6pm; Ⓜ Huáqiáochéng, exit B, ⌕245 from Shēnzhèn Bay Port) Reverse roles at the adjacent Splendid China, home to miniature replicas of China's own famous sights. Included in the admission is **China Folk Culture Village** (中国民俗文化村; Zhōngguó Mínsú Wénhuà Cūn; ⌕2660 0626; www.cn5000.com.cn; adult/child under 12yr incl entry to Splendid China ¥120/60; ⊙9am-10pm; Ⓜ Huáqiáochéng, exit B), which has two-dozen faux minority villages complete with minority-culture demonstrations. A mini-monorail run by the Shēnzhèn Happy Line Tour Co links the three parks, along with several other sights.

OCT EAST   AMUSEMENT PARK, RESORT

(东部华侨城; Dōngbù Huáqiáochéng; ⌕2503 1837; www.octeast.com; Dàméishā, Yán Tián District; admission ¥150-280; ⊙9.30am-6pm) A whopping ¥3.5 billion went into the making of OCT East, an upmarket and beautiful theme park-cum-resort some 20km east of Shēnzhèn city. It feels like a supersized Universal Studios plus Disneyland, with a mock Swiss village, a golf complex, a tea valley and luxurious hotels to keep you pampered and entertained.

The park offers some stunning views that make it worth a couple of days to explore. You can rent a car from inside the park to tour around. To get here, an express bus (¥65, one hour) leaves hourly at exit E, Kowloon Tong MTR station in Hong Kong, between 8.15am and 5.15pm. In Shēnzhèn, Sightseeing Bus 1, which leaves from Window of the World, with stops at Dìwáng

DAY TRIPS FROM HONG KONG SHĒNZHÈN

Dàxià on Shennan Lu, goes to the park; get off at the last stop. A taxi from Luóhú train station is about ¥70.

DÀPÉNG FORTRESS
FORTRESS

(大鹏所城; Dàpéng Shǔochéng; ☎8431 9269; Péngchéng Village, Dàpéng Town, Lónggǎng District; adult/student & senior ¥20/10; ⊙10am-6pm) Further to the east is Dàpéng Fortress. This preserved walled town, still a lively village, was built 600 years ago and was a key battle site in the Opium Wars in the 19th century. To get here, board bus 360 at Yínhú bus station; the bus also stops near China Regency Hotel on Sungang Lu. The journey takes about 90 minutes. Alight at Dàpéng bus station (Dàpéng zǒngzhàn; 大鹏总站) and change to bus 966. Faster and easier is the Sha Tau Kok Express (HK$60, 90 minutes, hourly departure between 7am and 6.30pm) from Suffolk Rd (metro Kowloon Tong, exit C). At the Dàpéng bus station change to minibus 966.

 EATING

Being a city of immigrants, Shēnzhèn offers some excellent regional Chinese cooking, such as Hunanese and Sichuanese, in addition to Cantonese cuisine. The food courts in shopping malls like **The MixC** (MDàjùyuàn, exit C3) and **Coco Park** (MGòuwù Gōngyuán, exit C) have some decent options for budget travellers.

GRAND PRINCE
CHINESE $

(王子国宴; Wángzǐ Guóyàn; ☎8269 0666; Shop 45, 5th fl, The MixC, Bao'an Nanlu; lunch ¥38-50, dinner ¥80-150; ⊙lunch & dinner; MDàjùyuàn, exit C3) This classy restaurant serves up a wide variety of surprisingly affordable dishes from all over China in an impressive, spacious dining hall.

MÁOJIĀ RESTAURANT
HÚNÁN $

(毛家飯店; Máojiāfàndiàn; ☎8221 6569; 2nd fl, Yúnjǐng Háoyuán, 2033 Chunfeng Lu, Luóhú; meals ¥50-110; ⊙10am-10pm; ☐387 from Luóhú train station) This decent Húnán restaurant honours Mao Zedong, who was a native of Húnán. It's decked out with Mao paraphernalia, including a copper bust of the Chinese leader and a few poems he penned. Nonspicy options include sliced pumpkin with dates and 'Mao family' roast pork.

Disembark at Chūnfēngwànjiā bus stop and walk for five minutes.

JĪN YUÈ XUĀN
DIM SUM $

(金悦轩; ☎8886 8880; 1st-4th fl, Yǒusè Bldg, 6013 Shēnnán Dàdào; meal per person from ¥80; ⊙lunch & dinner; MChēgōngmiào, exit C or D) The meticulous 200-item dim sum menu is amazing, as is Jīn Yuè Xuān's impressive interior.

LAUREL
DIM SUM, CANTONESE $

(丹桂轩; Dānguìxuān; ⊙7am-11pm) Century Plaza Hotel (☎8232 1888; 2nd fl, Century Plaza Hotel, 1 Chunfeng Lu; meals per person ¥50-180) Luóhú branch (☎8232 3668; Shop 5010, 5th fl, Luóhú Commercial City) The main branch at the Century Plaza Hotel serves better dim sum, but the Luóhú branch is a handy choice if you are shopping at Luóhú Commercial City.

MADE IN KITCHEN
ASIAN, FUSION $

(厨房制造; Chúfáng Zhìzào; ☎8261 1639; 7th fl, Kingglory Plaza, 2028 Renmin Lu; lunch set from ¥40; ⊙9.30am-11.30pm; MGúomào, exit A) The menu in this attractive, stylish fusion spot is a feast for the eyes and palate, with over 400 diverse choices, from pad thai noodles to sashimi to steak. However, some items may not always be available.

MUSLIM HOTEL RESTAURANT
HALAL $

(穆斯林宾馆大餐馆; Músīlín Bīnguǎn Dàcānguǎn; ☎8225 9664; 2nd fl, Muslim Hotel, 2013 Wenjing Nanlu; dishes ¥38-68; ⊙10am-11pm; ☐minibus 430) If you fancy *huí* (Chinese Muslim) food, head for this halal restaurant, where there's a decent selection of beef and mutton dishes.

PHOENIX HOUSE
DIM SUM, CANTONESE $$

(凤凰楼; Fènghuánglóu; ☎8207 6688, 8207 6338; East Wing, Pavilion Hotel, 4002 Huaqiang Beilu; lunch ¥60-80, dinner ¥100-350; ⊙7.30am-11pm; MHuáqiánglù, exit A) The best Cantonese restaurant in town, but expect noisy waits for 30 minutes or more after 11.30am. Certain dim sum can be ordered piece by piece – good when you're dining alone. Given how busy it is, service is attentive.

SUMMER TEA HOUSE
VEGETARIAN, DIM SUM $

(静颐茶馆; Jìngyí Cháguǎn; ☎2557 4555; 7th & 8th fl, Jīntáng Dàxià, 3038 Bao'an Nanlu; meals ¥50-80; ⊙10am-1am; ⊙☑; M Dàjùyuàn, exit D) Tucked away in an office building near Xīhú Bīnguǎn is this veggies' favourite in Shēnzhèn, with good-for-you ingredients, a relaxing tea-tasting area and a smoke-free dining hall (hurrah!). No English menu, but colourful pictures illustrate the dishes. Vegetarian dim sum is available even for dinner. There are more filling dishes too, if you're hungry.

WEST LAKE SPRING HANGZHOU $

(西湖春天; Xīhú Chūntiān; ☎8211 6988; 2nd-3rd fl, Parkway Tower, 3019 Sungang Lu; dishes ¥21-180; ◷lunch & dinner; 🚍18, get off at Xīhú Bīnguǎn) This Hángzhōu restaurant gets the thumbs up from locals. There's an English-less menu with pictures. The signature dishes such as stir-fried freshwater shrimp with Lóngjǐng tea leaves (龙井虾仁; *lóngjǐng xiārén*; ¥138) deserve savouring.

 DRINKING

Finding a venue in Shēnzhèn for anything from a quiet drink to a raucous knees-up after a hard day of bargaining is easy. There are upmarket bars galore below Citic City Plaza (中信城市广场; Zhōngxìn Chéngshì Guǎngchǎng), at Coco Park in Fútián and SeaWorld (Hǎishàng Shìjiè; 海上世界) in Shékǒu.

YĪDÙTÁNG BAR

(一渡堂; Block F3, OCT-LOFT Art Terminal, Enping Lu, Huáqiáochéng; ◷10am-2am; Ⓜ Qiáochéngdōng, exit A) This warehouse-turned-bohemian-haunt in the OCT Contemporary Art Terminal is where local bands jam every night after 10pm. It has a good mix of blues and punk rock, and is absolutely pop-music-free.

TRUE COLOUR CLUB

(本色酒吧; Běnsè; ☎8230 1833; 4th fl, Golden World, 2001 Jiefang Lu; ◷9am-1am; Ⓜ Lǎojiē, exit A) Clubbers should check out this nighttime playground of young Shenzhenians. Its watering-hole-plus-dance-floor formula attracts city slickers and trendy young adults alike.

BEFORE SUNSET LOUNGE

(日落之前; Rìluòzhīqián; ☎8393 3936; City Citic Plaza, 1095 Shennan Zhonglu, Fútián; ◷4pm-2am; Ⓜ Kēxuéguǎn, exit D) Named after the Hollywood film, this bar at the upmarket City Citic Plaza features vinyl records and movie stills on its walls, a vintage movie projector and techno music. The owner is a filmmaker.

 ENTERTAINMENT

QUEEN'S SPA & DINING SPA

(皇室假期; Huángshì Jiàqī; ☎8225 3888; B1-5th fl, Golden Metropolis Bldg, Chunfeng Lu; ◷24hr; Ⓜ Gúomào, exit B) Shēnzhèn offers all sorts of body-perfecting services, from massage to manicure. Try the Queen's Spa & Dining near Gúomào metro. This spa wonderland offers aromatherapy and different types of massages (¥168 to ¥218; a minimum tip of ¥30 is mandatory). The pools, fruit bar and sleeping capsules allow you to lose days inside.

 **SHOPPING**

Shopping is the sole reason many people visit Shēnzhèn. An invaluable book to guide you is *Shop in Shenzhen: An Insider's Guide* by Ellen McNally, available in bookshops throughout Hong Kong and online from Amazon.

Interior designers and shrewd homeowners in Hong Kong are increasingly turning to Shēnzhèn to hunt for furniture and furnishings, including knock-off designer furniture. Unless you want a genuine Eames chair or Artemide lamp, most replicas in Hong Kong and overseas were made in Shēnzhèn anyway. Many places will pack and ship overseas, and if customers are prepared to haggle, vendors may lower the marked price by 30% to 50%.

Shoppers won't leave Shēnzhèn empty-handed, though the quality can vary. Some shops have been known to be cavalier about following specs and maintaining quality for larger items such as a set of cabinets on order. Shop around, and shop hard.

DÀFĒN VILLAGE ART

(大芬村; Dàfēncūn; ☎8473 2633; www.dafen villageonline.com; Dàfēn, Bùjí, Lónggǎng District) This art village is an eye-opener: with 600 studios-cum-stores, churning out thousands of copies of Rembrandts, Renoirs and Picassos every week (the website actually lets you browse by artist, style or painting size). Prices start from ¥300. Mind you, there are original works too – it's been estimated that there are about 50 original artists in Dàfēn Village, and thousands of copy artists. But, in an environment like this, even original works tend to be

SLEEPING IN SHĒNZHÈN

Hotels in Shēnzhèn discount deeply during the week, slicing as much as 60% off the regular rack rate, though you should ask for a discount no matter when you go.

➡ **Shangri-La Hotel** (香格里拉大酒店; Xiānggélǐlā Dàjiǔdiàn; ☑8233 0888; www.shangri-la.com/shenzhen; 1002 Jianshe Lu; d ¥1598-1950, ste ¥2500; 🛜) This classic, luxurious hotel, about 150m from Luóhú train station, is one of the best places to stay in Luóhú District, and offers free wi-fi. Its new branch, **Fútián Shangri-La** (Shēnzhèn Fútián Xiānggélǐlā Dàjiǔdiàn; 福田香格里拉大酒店; ☑0755-8828 4088; 4088 Yitian Lu; r ¥1340-1988, ste ¥2500; 🛜; Ⓜ Shìjiè Zhīchuāng), in Fútián District, also has spacious and sparkling rooms.

➡ **Shēnzhèn Loft Youth Hostel** (深圳侨城旅友国际青年旅舍; Shēnzhèn Qiáochéng Lüyǒu Guójì Qíngnián Lüshè; ☑2694 9443; http://weibo.com/loftyha; 3 Enping Lu, Huáqiáochéng; dm ¥60, d without bathroom ¥138, r ¥158; Ⓜ Qiáochéngdōng, exit A) This excellent hostel is in a tranquil residential area behind the OCT-LOFT Art Terminal. Rooms are spotless and the staff are helpful.

➡ **Vision Fashion Hotel** (深圳视界风尚酒店; Shēnzhèn Shìjiè Fēngshàng Jiǔdiàn; ☑2558 2888; www.visionfashionhotel.com; 5018 Shennan Donglu; r ¥386-798; Ⓜ Dàjùyuàn, exit B) Inside a theatre complex is this new boutique hotel with many different interior designs in its range of rooms. Some are chic, some bizarre. Its prime location and quiet environment make it a very good choice.

market-driven. That said, there are some nice pieces.

Dàfēn Village is also a great place to stock up on art supplies, with prices about half of those you'd find downtown. Bus 306 from Luóhú station takes you to the village in about an hour. A taxi ride costs around ¥70.

DŌNGMÉN MARKET
MARKET

(东门市场; Dōngmén Shìchǎng; Ⓜ Lǎojiē, Exit A) This chaotic market is popular for tailored suits, skirts, curtains and bedding. Prices are competitive. Most shops open from 10am to 10pm. Be extremely careful of pickpockets.

HUÁQIÁNG BĚI COMMERCIAL ST
ELECTRONICS

(Huáqiángběi Shāngyèjiē; Ⓜ Huáqiánglù, exit A) For electronics, Huáqiáng Běi is a living, breathing eBay, with shops and malls for blocks on end selling the latest tech gadgets, audiovisual equipment, android tablets, Bluetooth headsets, nonbranded laptops and accessories at rock-bottom prices.

KINGGLORY PLAZA
CLOTHING, ACCESSORIES

(金光华广场; Jīnguānghuà Guǎngchǎng; ☑8261 1100; www.kingglory.com.cn; 2028 Renmin Nanlu, Luóhú District; Ⓜ Gúomào, exit A) Sitting on top of the Gúomào metro station, this modern shopping mall is where many Hong Kong day trippers hang out. It's more upscale

than the much older Luóhú Commercial City one station away, featuring local and imported clothing and lifestyle brands, and a handful of decent restaurants.

LUÓHÚ COMMERCIAL CITY
CLOTHING, ACCESSORIES

(罗湖商业城; Luóhú Shāngyè Chéng; ☑8233 8178; www.tosz.com; Renmin Nanlu; ☺6.30am-midnight) An old favourite of Hong Kong day trippers, this multistorey mall, right next to the Luóhú train station, has 1000 stalls selling handbags, household fabric, clothing, accessories, knick-knacks and DVDs, as well as massage parlours, salons for manicures and acrylic nails, even dental clinics. Most shops are open 10.30am to 10pm.

CENTURY FURNISHINGS CENTRAL MALL
HOMEWARES

(世纪中心家居广场; Shìjìzhōngxīn Jiājūguǎngchǎng; ☑8371 0111; www.sz-sjzx.com; Shen Nan Da Dao, west of Xiāngmì Hú Water Park, Fútián District; ☺9.30am-8pm, to 8.30 Sat & Sun; Ⓜ Chēgōngmiào, exit A, 🚌101, 215 from Luóhú station) This mall has a whopping 30,000 sq metres of retail space for homewares and lifestyle products. There are three main zones. A and B are mainly tiles, sinks, showers, toilets and mirrors, while C consists mainly of lamps. It's also the most popular zone among leisure shoppers. Unless you're here for the whole day, you can skip A and

B. If you take a cab from Luóhú station, it's about ¥30.

GALAXY & TOP LIVING HOMEWARES
(星河第三空间; Xīnghédìsān Kōngjiān; www. topliving.cn; Galaxy Century Bldg, 3069 Caitian Lu, Fútián District; MGǎngshà, exit B) A one-stop mall for mid-to-upper-range furnishings that features some imported brands such as Simmons, Markor Furnishings and Ligne Roset. If you take a cab from Luóhú station, it's about ¥40.

Guǎngzhōu

Explore

If you're arriving in the morning, beat the crowds to the impressive New Guǎngdōng Museum (it closes at 5pm and is closed on Monday) in the southeastern district of Zhūjiāng New Town. Don't forget to take a peek at the fabulous Guǎngzhōu Opera House close by. That should take at least two hours. Hop on the metro and head west to the Chén Clan Ancestral Hall to spend an hour or two. If pressed for time, skip that and make a beeline for the stunning Mausoleum of the Nányuè King (it closes at 5.30pm) in the Yuèxiù District. Follow this with a leisurely stroll among the famous landmarks inside Yuèxiù Park. Depending on time available and interest, you can reverse the order, or replace Chén Clan Ancestral Hall with a trip to Shāmiàn Island in the southwest.

The Best...

➡ **Sights** Mausoleum of the Nányuè King (p224), New Guǎngdōng Museum (p225), Shāmiàn Island (p224)

➡ **Places to Eat** Bǐngshèng Restaurant (p228), Táo Táo Jū Restaurant (p229), Nánxìn (p229)

Top Tip

Most taxi drivers in Guǎngzhōu are migrant workers who don't know the city well. If possible, flag down the rare yellow or red cabs, which are driven by local drivers.

Getting There & Away

Train The most hassle-free transport to Guǎngzhōu is to take the high-speed intercity trains from Hung Hom station to Guǎngzhōu East train station (1¾ hours). It has 12 departures between 7.25am and 7.24pm, returning from Guǎngzhōu the same number of times from 8.19am to 9.32pm. One-way tickets cost $230/190 in 1st/2nd class for adults and $115/95 for children aged five to nine.

MTR One-way and return tickets for Guǎngzhōu can be booked in advance at MTR stations in Hung Hom, Mong Kok, Kowloon Tong and Sha Tin, and at MTR Travel at Admiralty station, or with a credit card on the MTR website (www. it3.mtr.com.hk) or via the Tele-Ticketing Hotline (☏2947 7888).

Bullet train A cheaper way to get from Hong Kong to Guǎngzhōu is to board a bullet train once you go across the Lo Wu border to Shēnzhèn. They run frequently between Shēnzhèn and Guǎngzhōu East train station (¥75 to ¥95, 52 minutes to 1¼ hours) from 5.35am to 10.50pm.

Bus CTS has frequent buses from Metropark Hotel in Causeway Bay and many CTS branches in Hong Kong to Guǎngzhōu (¥110). Check http://ctsbus. hkcts.com/routes/hk/hk_guangzhou.html for departure times and locations. The trip takes 2½ hours.

Metro Guǎngzhōu metro (www.gzmtr.com) has eight metro lines in full service and covers most of the sights in this chapter. Depending on the line, the metro runs from about 6.20am to 11pm. Fares start from ¥2 for the first 4km.

Taxi The flagfall is ¥10 for the first 2.3km, and ¥2.60 for every additional kilometre. A trip from the main train station to Shāmiàn Island should cost between ¥25 and ¥35. A taxi to/from the airport will cost about ¥160.

Need to Know

➡ **Area Code** ☏86 (0)20
➡ **Location** 185km from Hung Hom station
➡ **Tourist Office** (China Travel Service, CTS; 广州中国旅行社; Zhōngguó Lüxíngshè; ☏020-8333 6888; 8 Qiaoguang Lu; ⏰8.30am-6pm Mon-Fri, 9am-5pm Sat & Sun; MHǎizhū)

Guǎngchǎng, exit A) Located next to Hotel Landmark Canton, it offers various tours and books tickets.

➡ **Visa** Get it in advance in Hong Kong or Macau.

SIGHTS

MAUSOLEUM OF THE NÁNYUÈ KING
TOP CHOICE

MAUSOLEUM

(南越王墓; Nányuèwáng Mù; ☎8666 4920; 867 Jiefang Beilu; admission ¥15, audioguide ¥10; ◷9am-5.30pm; ⓜYuèxiù Gōngyuán) Lose your sense of time in the Mausoleum of the Nányuè King, a superb mausoleum from the 2000-year-old Nányuè kingdom now turned into one of China's best museums. A highlight is the burial suit of Zhao Mo (second king of Nányuè), which is made up of thousands of tiny jade tiles, gold jewellery and trinkets.

YUÈXIÙ PARK
PARK

(越秀公園; Yuèxiù Gōngyuán; ☎8666 1950; www.yuexiupark-gz.com; 13 Jiefang Beilu; admission ¥5; ◷6am-9pm; ⓜYuèxiù Gōngyuán) Near the mausoleum is this park, within which you'll find Guǎngzhōu's **Five Rams Statue** (五羊石像), a statue of the five immortals attributed to Guǎngzhōu's founding.

On top of a hill in the park is the redwalled, five-storey **Zhènhǎi Tower** (镇海楼; Zhènhǎi Lóu), which houses the **Guǎngzhōu City Museum** (广州市博物馆; Guǎngzhōushì Bówùguǎn; ☎020-8355 0627; admission ¥10; ◷9am-5.30pm; ⓜYuèxiù Gōngyuán).

The museum has an excellent collection that traces the city's history from the Neolithic period. On the east side of the tower is the **Guǎngzhōu Art Gallery** (广州美术馆; Guǎngzhōu Měishùguǎn), showcasing Cantonese embroidery, carved ivory decorations, and (oddly) displays outlining Guǎngzhōu's trading history with the West.

CHÉN CLAN ANCESTRAL HALL
HISTORIC BUILDING

(陈家祠; Chénjiā Cí; ☎020-8181 4559; 34 Enlongji Lu; admission ¥10; ◷8.30am-5.30pm; ⓜChénjiācí) Chén Clan Ancestral Hall is a spectacular ancestral shrine built in 1894 by the residents of 72 villages in Guǎngdōng, where the Chén lineage is the predominant family. The complex encompasses 19 buildings with exquisite carvings, statues and

paintings. Throughout, ornate scrolls depict stories from Chinese folklore and literature.

TEMPLE OF THE SIX BANYAN TREES
TEMPLE

(六榕寺; Liùróng Sì; 87-89 Liurong Lu; admission ¥15; ◷8am-5pm; ⓐ56) This temple was built in AD 1097 to enshrine Buddhist relics brought over from India. Located about 400m west is the **Temple of Bright, Filial and Piety** (光孝寺; Guāngxiào Chánsì; 109 Jinghui Lu; admission ¥5; ◷6am-5pm; ⓜXīmén Kǒu), the oldest temple in Guǎngzhōu, dating back to the 4th century. Many prominent monks came to teach here, including Bodhidharma, the founder of Zen Buddhism.

MOSQUE DEDICATED TO THE PROPHET
MOSQUE

(怀圣寺; Huáishèng Sì; ☎020-8333 3593; 56 Guangta Lu; ⓜXīmén Kǒu) The mosque dates from the Qing dynasty, but the original building on the site is thought to have been established in AD 627 by Abu Waqas, one of the Prophet Mohammed's uncles, making it the first of its kind in China.

CATHEDRAL OF THE SACRED HEART
CATHEDRAL

(石室教堂; Shíshí Jiàotáng; Yide Xilu; ⓜHǎizhū Guǎngchǎng) Cathedral of the Sacred Heart is an impressive twin-spired Roman Catholic cathedral built between 1863 and 1888. It was designed by a French architect in the neo-Gothic style and built entirely of granite.

SHĀMIÀN ISLAND
ISLAND

(Shāmiàn Dǎo; ⓜHuángshā) To the southwest of the city is the leafy oasis of Shāmiàn Island. It was acquired as a foreign concession in 1859 after the two Opium Wars and now offers peaceful respite from the city. Shamian Dajie, the main boulevard, is a gentle stretch of gardens, trees and old men playing Chinese checkers. The Roman Catholic **Church of Our Lady of Lourdes** (天主教露德圣母堂; Tiānzhǔjiào Lùdé Shèngmǔ Táng; Shamian Dajie; ◷8am-6pm), built by the French in 1892, is on the eastern end of the thoroughfare. Travellers recommend **Shāmiàn Traditional Chinese Medical Centre** (沙面国医馆; Shāmiàn Guóyīguǎn; ☎020-8121 8383; 85-87 Shamian Beijie; ◷11am-2am), at the western end of the island, for its massage (¥68 per hour).

FREE **MEMORIAL MUSEUM OF GENERALISSIMO SUN YAT-SEN'S MANSION** MUSEUM, HISTORIC SITE

(孙中山大元帅府纪念馆; Sūnzhōngshān Dàyuánshuàifǔ Jìniànguǎn; ☑020-8900 2276; www.dyshf.com; 18 Dongsha Jie Fangzhi Lu, Hǎizhū District; admission free; ☺9am-5pm Tue-Sun; Ⓜ Shì Èrgōng) Guǎngzhōu has several significant 'revolutionary sights'. The recently restored Memorial Museum of Generalissimo Sun Yat-sen's Mansion, on the other side of the river, was where Sun Yat-sen lived when he established governments in Guǎngzhōu in 1917 and 1923.

This beautiful complex consists of two Victorian-style buildings housing exhibits on the history of Guǎngzhōu during the revolutionary era and Sun's office and living room. A cab from Shāmiàn Island costs about ¥25, and from Shì Èrgōng station, about ¥10.

FREE **WHAMPOA MILITARY ACADEMY** HISTORIC BUILDING

(黄埔军校; Huángpǔ Jūnxiào; ☑020-8820 3564; ☺9am-5pm Tue-Sun) Much more interesting than the Memorial Museum is Whampoa Military Academy on Chángzhōu Island (Chángzhōu Dǎo; 长洲岛). Established in 1924 by Kuomintang, the academy trained a number of military elites for both Kuomintang and the Communist Party, who went on to fight in many subsequent conflicts and civil wars.

The present structure houses a museum dedicated to the revolutionary history of modern China. Take metro line 2 to Chìgǎng station, then exit C1. Then board bus 262 on Xingang Zhonglu to Xīnzhōu Pier (新洲码头; Xīnzhōu Mǎtou). Ferries (¥1.50) to the academy depart every 40 minutes past the hour from between 6.40am and 8.40pm.

FREE **XĪNHÀI REVOLUTION MUSEUM** MUSEUM

(辛亥革命纪念馆; Xīnhàigémìng Jìniànguǎn; ☑8252 5897; Junxiaolu, Changzhoujie, Huángpǔ District; ☑8820 3564; admission free; ☺9am-5pm Tue-Sun) The Xīnhài Revolution Museum was opened in October 2011 to commemorate the centenary of the Xīnhài Revolution aka 1911 Revolution. Led by Dr Sun Yat-sen, it overthrew the Qing dynasty (1644–1911). It is aptly placed on Chángzhōu Island which is also home to the Whampoa Military Academy, the Monument of the Northern Expedition and the Chángzhōu Gun Emplacement.

The 18,000-sq-metre museum, costing some ¥320 million, is housed in a modern structure resembling a slab of granite. There are 6600 items on display, belonging to themes, respectively: the revolution, famous Cantonese personalities during the revolution, and the life of Sun Wan, Sun Yat-sen's daughter by his first wife Lu Muzhen.

Take bus 383 or 430 and disembark at Chángzhōujie, or take line 4 of the metro and get off at Dàxuéchéng Běi, then take bus 383 to Chángzhōujie and walk for five minutes.

PEASANT MOVEMENT INSTITUTE HISTORIC SITE

(农民运动讲习所; Nóngmín Yùndòng Jiǎngxísuǒ; ☑020-8333 3936; 42 Zhongshan Silu; admission free; ☺9am-4.30pm Tue-Sun; Ⓜ Nóngjiǎng Suǒ) The communists had a stronghold here once. The Peasant Movement Institute was established in 1924 by the Communist Party. Mao Zedong and Zhou Enlai both taught here, before the school closed in 1926. You can see Mao Zedong's re-created personal quarters.

MEMORIAL GARDEN TO THE MARTYRS MEMORIAL

(烈士陵园; Lièshì Língyuán; admission ¥3; ☺8am-7pm) East of the Peasant Movement Institute, on Zhongshan Sanlu, is the Memorial Garden to the Martyrs, dedicated to those killed on 13 December 1927 under the orders of Chiang Kaishek. The massacre occurred when a small group of workers, led by the Communist Party, were gunned down by Kuomintang forces; over 5000 lives were lost.

GUǍNGZHŌU MUSEUM OF ART MUSEUM

(广州艺术博物院; Guǎngzhōu Yìshù Bówùguǎn; ☑8365 9337; 3 Luhu Lu; admission ¥20; ☺9am-5pm Tue-Fri, 9.30am-4.30pm Sat & Sun; ☐10 or 63) The museum has an extensive collection of works, ranging from ancient to contemporary Chinese art. There's a fantastic room on the top floor with displays of rare Tibetan tapestries.

TOP CHOICE **NEW GUǍNGDŌNG MUSEUM** MUSEUM

(广东省博物馆新馆; Guǎngdōngshěng Bówùguǎn; ☑3804 6886; 2 Zhujiang Donglu; ☺9am-5pm Tue-Sun; Ⓜ Zhūjiāng Xīnchéng, exit B1) This ultramodern museum designed by Hong Kong architect Rocco Yim occupies almost the entire block by

Guăngzhōu

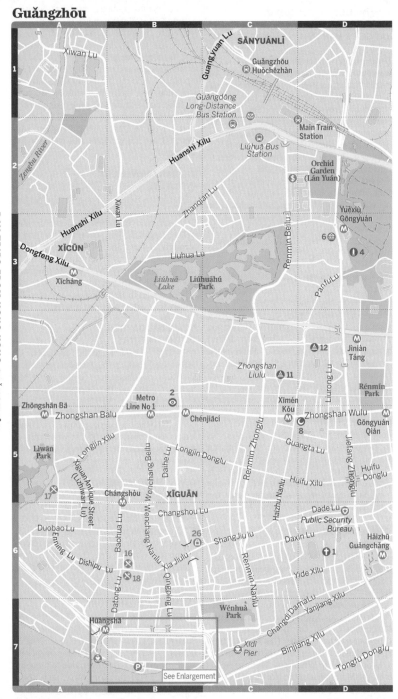

SĀNYUÁNLĬ

Guang Yuan Lu

Xiwan Lu

Guăngzhōu
Huŏchēzhàn

Guăngdōng
Long-Distance
Bus Station

Huanshi Xilu

Main Train
Station

Liúhuā Bus
Station

Zhanqian Lu

Orchid
Garden
(Lán Yuán)

Huanshi Xilu

Xiwan Lu

Yuèxiù
Gōngyuán

Renmin Beilu

Dongfeng Xilu

XĪCŪN

6 🏛

4

Xĭcháng

Liuhua Lù

Panfu Lu

Zengbu River

Liúhuā
Lake

Liúhuāhú
Park

12

Jiniàn
Táng

Zhongshan
Liulu

11

Liurong Lu

Rénmín
Park

Zhōngshān Bā

Metro
Line No 1

2

Xīmén
Kŏu

Zhongshan Wulu

Zhongshan Balu

Chénjiācí

8

Gōngyuán
Qián

Liwān
Park

Guangta Lu

Huifu
Donglu

Longjīn Xilu

Longjin Donglu

Renmin Zhonglu

Daihe Lu

Huifu Xilu

Haizhu Nanlu

Jiefang Zhonglu

17

Chángshòu

XĪGUĀN

Xiguan Antique Street
(Lìzhīwān Lù)

Changshou Lu

Dade Lu

Public Security
Bureau

Hăizhū
Guăngchăng

Duobao Lu

Baohua Lu

Wenchang Nanlu

26

ShangJiu lu

Daxin Lu

1

Enning Lu

Dishipu Lu

16

18

Xia Jiulu

Renmin Nanlu

Yide Xilu

Datong Lu

Qingping Lu

Wénhuà
Park

Changdi Damalu

Yanjiang Xilu

Huángshā

Xīdī
Pier

Binjiang Xilu

Tongfu Donglu

P

See Enlargement

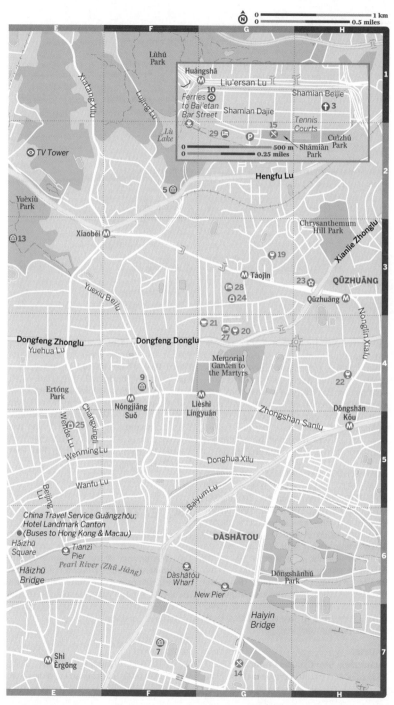

Inset (top right):

Huángshā

Liu'ersan Lu

10

Shamian Beijie

Ferries to Bai'etan Bar Street

Shamian Dajie

3

15

Tennis Courts

29

P

Cuìzhú Park

Shāmiàn Park

0 — 500 m
0 — 0.25 miles

Main map labels:

Lùhú Park

Lùjìng Lu

Xiàtáng Xīlù

Lù Lake

TV Tower

Yuèxiù Park

13

Hengfu Lu

5

Xiǎoběi

Chrysanthemum Hill Park

Xiānliè Zhōnglù

Yuexiu Beilu

19

Táojīn

23

QŪZHUĀNG

28

24

Qūzhuāng

Nónglín Xiàlù

21

27

20

Dongfeng Zhonglu

Yuehua Lu

Dongfeng Donglu

Memorial Garden to the Martyrs

4

22

Ertóng Park

9

Nóngjiǎng Suó

Lièshì Língyuán

Zhongshan Sanlu

Dōngshān Kǒu

Chángxīnglù

Wende Lu

25

Wenming Lu

Donghua Xilu

Wanfu Lu

Bǎiyúm Lu

Beijing Lu

China Travel Service Guǎngzhōu; Hotel Landmark Canton (Buses to Hong Kong & Macau)

Hǎizhū Square

Tiānzì Pier

DÀSHÀTOU

Pearl River (Zhū Jiāng)

Hǎizhū Bridge

Dàshàtóu Wharf

Dōngshānhú Park

New Pier

Haiyin Bridge

7

Shì Èrgōng

14

Guǎngzhōu

the waterfront. Its extensive collection illuminates the human and natural history of Guǎngdōng, as well as Chinese and Cantonese art, literature, and architecture. Inspired by the Chinese lacquer box, the museum's appearance is a striking contrast with the curvilinear design of the Guǎngzhōu Opera House further to the west, which was designed by celebrated Iraq-born British architect Zaha Hadid.

GUǍNGZHŌU OPERA HOUSE OPERA HOUSE
(广州大剧院; Guǎngzhōu dà jù yuàn; ☑3839 2888, 3839 2666; www.chgoh.org; 1 Zhujiang Xilu; ⓜZhūjiāng Xīnchéng, exit B1) Standing on the edge of a park, the biggest performance venue in southern China is stunning, with its futuristic panels knit together to form an other-worldly structure with subtle curves. A sweeping staircase and a ramp lead to its entrance. The Opera House has transformed the whole area with its surreal appearance, yet the ¥1300 million structure, constructed in five short years, is already suffering some disrepair.

CRUISES RIVER CRUISE
Guǎngzhōu Star Cruises Company (☑020-8333 2222) has evening cruises on the Pearl

River (¥48 to ¥88, two hours) between 6.30pm and 10pm. Boats leave from the **Tiānzǐ Pier** (Tiānzǐ Mǎtou; Beijing Lu), just east of Hǎizhū Bridge (Hǎizhū Qiáo; catch metro line 2 from Hǎizhū Guǎngchǎng metro), and head downriver as far as Èrshā Island (Èrshā Dǎo). **Guǎngzhōu Passenger Ship Company** (☑020-8101 3912) also has evening cruises (¥23 to ¥38, 1½ hours) from 7.30pm to 9.50pm leaving from **Xīdī Pier** (Xīdī Mǎtou; Yanjiang Xilu).

EATING

Guǎngzhōu is especially famous for its dim sum. In Xīguān District there are many tiny restaurants featuring some locally well-known *xīguān xiǎochī* (snacks and dessert), where you can bump elbows with the locals. A large expat population means there are also many restaurants serving international cuisines.

BǏNGSHÈNG RESTAURANT CANTONESE $$
(炳胜海鲜酒家; Bǐngshàng Hǎixiān Jiǔjiā; ☑020-3428 6910; 33 Dongxiao Lu; dishes from

¥48; ⏱11am-midnight; 🚇293, 886) Bīngshèng has a handful of branches in Guǎngzhōu, but the mammoth flagship beneath Hǎiyìn Bridge remains the best. Its sea bass sashimi with Shùndé flavour (海鲈刺身; hǎilú cìshēn) and bean curd with crab roe (豆腐花蒸蟹羔; dòufuhuā zhēngxiègāo) are outstandingly tasty. There is no English menu, so try to grab a Chinese friend to communicate. Reservations are impossible.

CHUĀNGUÓ YǍNYÌ   SICHUANESE $$

(川国演义; ☎020-3887 9878; Nánfāng Securities Bldg, 140-148 Tiyu Donglu; dishes from ¥35; ⏱10am-2pm & 5-9pm; 🚇 Tǐyù Zhōngxīn, exit B) This restaurant will fire up your taste buds with its authentic Sìchuān dishes. The Sìchuān hotpot is considered the best in Guǎngzhōu. Turn right as you exit the metro station, and walk for about 300m.

LUCY'S   AMERICAN $$

(露丝酒吧餐厅; Lùsī Jiǔbā Cāntīng; ☎8121 5106; 3 Shamian Nanjie; dishes ¥28-40; ⏱11am-2am; 🚇Huángshā) Western carnivores seeking comfort food should try this favourite on Shāmiàn Island. Enjoy decent burgers, buffalo wings, and beer for ¥16 a pint (happy hour is 4pm to 6pm).

PĀNXĪ RESTAURANT   DIM SUM $$

(泮溪酒家; Pānxī Jiǔjiā; ☎8172 1328; 151 Longjin Xilu; dishes from ¥40; ⏱7.30am-midnight; 🚇Chángshòu Lù) The majestic garden in this restaurant is as impressive as its dim sum and dishes like sauteéd clam and fish with vegetables. If you're lucky, you'll catch impromptu Cantonese opera singing by some of the customers here.

NÁNXÌN   DESSERTS $

(南信; ☎8138 9904; 47 Dishipu Lu; desserts ¥5-12, dishes ¥8-15; ⏱10am-midnight; 🚇Huángshā) A specialist in *xīguān xiǎochī*, this busy restaurant is a popular pit stop for Cantonese desserts and is near the Xia Jiulu/Shang Jiulu shopping quarter. Try the steamed egg whites with milk (双皮奶; shuāngpínǎi;).

TÁO TÁO JŪ RESTAURANT   DIM SUM, CANTONESE $$

(陶陶居; Táotáojū Jiǔjiā; ☎020-8139 6111; 20 Dishipu Lu; dishes from ¥36; ⏱6.45am-midnight) This restaurant is housed in an academy dating back to the 17th century. It's a bit more expensive than other Cantonese diners, but the fabulous 200-item dim sum menu makes up for it. Getting a table here is impossible after 11am.

DRINKING

Guǎngzhōu has a number of international-style bars where, in addition to sinking chilled Tsingtao and imported beers, you can scoff pizza, burgers, rice or noodles.

PEOPLE'S CAFÉ   CAFE

(☎8376 6677; 35 Jianshe Wumalu; coffee from ¥22, sandwiches from ¥30; ⏱7.30am-2.30pm; 🚇Táojīn) This popular cafe run by two Korean sisters serves homemade pastries and tasty sandwiches. At night it turns into a cheerful drinking spot.

C UNION   BAR, LIVE MUSIC

(喜窝城市会; Xǐwō; ☎3584 0144; Ground fl, Chéngshì Huì, 115 Shuiyin Lu; ⏱7pm-2am) Live music is the principal attraction at this unpretentious boozer. It hosts a good mix of local bands, from R&B to reggae. It's behind the Chéngshìhuì (城市会) building, in the Yuèxiù District. Only accessible by taxi.

PADDY FIELD   PUB

(☎8360 1379; 2nd fl, Central Plaza, 38 Hua Le Lu; ⏱11.30am-2.30pm & 4.30pm-2am Mon-Fri, 11.30am-2am Sat & Sun; 🚇Táojīn, exit A) This famous (and pricey) Irish pub is one of the expats' favourite drinking haunts for top-notch beer. It cranks up on Saturdays for the salsa party.

PING PONG   BAR

(乒乓空间; ☎2829 6306; Starhouse 60, 60 Xianlie Donghenglu; ⏱6pm-2am) This bohemian den hosts live music from time to time and offers a mix of theatre and exhibitions. It's a bit tricky to get here, though. Flag down a yellow taxi and ask the driver to drop you behind Xīnghǎi Conservatory (Xīnghǎi Yīnyuè Xuéyuàn Hòumiàn; 星海音乐学院后面).

WILBER'S   BAR

(☎3761 1101; 62 Zhusigang Ermalu; ⏱5pm-midnight Sun-Thu, to 2am Fri & Sat; 🚇Qūzhuāng) A gem that is tucked away in a historical villa, Wilber's has something for everyone: the patio is popular with ladies looking for a quiet natter, indoors is a gay-friendly drinking den, and a fine-dining restaurant occupies the upper floor. It serves the best martinis and margaritas in town.

ENTERTAINMENT

The free monthly entertainment guide, **That's PRD** (http://guangzhou.urbanatomy.com), available at most top-end hotels and Westernised bars and restaurants, and the comprehensive events-listings website **Guangzhou Stuff** (www.gzstuff.com) are invaluable resources for what's going on in town.

VELVET   CLUB
(Sīróngbā; ☑8732 1139; Ground fl, International Electronic Tower, 403 Huanshi Donglu; beer ¥55, cocktails ¥50; ☺7.30pm-3am; ⓂXiǎoběi) Guǎngzhōu's most famous club, popular with local and international DJs. With a full range of tunes to suit everybody, it's one of the best bets for a good night out.

GUĀNGZHŌU OPERA HOUSE   OPERA
(广州大剧院; Guǎngzhōu dà jù yuàn; ☑3839 2888, 3839 2666; www.chgoh.org; 1 Zhujiang Xilu; ⓂZhūjiāng Xīnchéng, exit B1) Check out the offerings at this world-class opera house designed by celebrated Zaha Hadid.

SHOPPING

Guǎngzhōu is a terrific place for cheap and cheerful shopping. Prices are reasonably cheap, and there are gems in its haystack of goods.

FĀNGCŪN TEA MARKET   TEA
(Fāngcūn Cháyè Shìchǎng; Fangcun Dadao; ⓂFāngcūn) A sprawling block-after-block market with tea shops and malls selling tea and teapots. Most target wholesale traders but retail is often possible.

XĪGUĀN ANTIQUE STREET   ANTIQUES
(Xīguān Gǔwán Chéng; Lizhiwan Lu; ⓂZhōngshān Bālù) If it's antiques you're after, there's no

---

SLEEPING IN GUĂNGZHŌU

Hotels in Guǎngzhōu are expensive. Prices rise even higher during the Canton Trade Fair in spring and autumn. Do not be put off by the posted rates though. Most hotels offer discounts from 30% to 60%, depending on the season. Top-end places add a 15% service charge to the quoted room rates. Most hotels have in-room broadband internet access.

➔ **7 Days Inn** (7天连锁酒店; Qītiān Liánsuǒ Jiǔdiàn; ☑020-8364 4488; fax 020-8364 4477; 32 Huale Lu; r ¥199-329; ⓂTáojīn) This chain hotel is the cheapest (but very decent) option in the five-star enclave in Yuèxiù District.

➔ **Westin Guǎngzhōu** (广州天誉威斯汀酒店; Guǎngzhōu Tiānyú Wēisītīng Jiǔdiàn; ☑020-2886 6868; www.starwoodhotels.com; 6 Linhe Zhonglu; s & d from ¥1260, ste from ¥2076) The luxurious Westin is the best place to stay in Tiānhé, if not in Guǎngzhōu. Staff are very welcoming and efficient, rooms are spacious and sparkling, and the location near the east train station is terrific.

➔ **Garden Hotel** (花园酒店; Huāyuán Jiǔdiàn; ☑8333 8989; www.thegardenhotel.com.cn; 368 Huanshi Donglu; r/ste from Y3200/5200; ⓂTáojīn) This lavish five-star hotel will impress you with its grand lobby, spiralling staircases, garden, elegant rooms and the impeccable service.

➔ **Guǎngzhōu Riverside International Youth Hostel** (广州江畔国际青年旅舍; Guǎngzhōu Jiāngpàn Guójì Qīngnián Lǚguǎn; ☑2239 2500; fax 2239 2548; 15 Changdi Lu; dm ¥50, s ¥108-138, d ¥148-198, ste ¥268; ⓂFāngcūn, exit B) Located in Fāngcūn next to a bar street, this emerging backpacker hub has spotless rooms. Ferries depart frequently from Huángshā pier on Shāmiàn Island to Fāngcūn pier right in front of the hostel.

➔ **White Swan Hotel** (白天鹅宾馆; Báitiān'é Bīnguǎn; ☑8188 6968; www.whiteswanhotel.com; 1 Shamian Nanjie; r ¥1600-1800, ste from ¥4100; ⓂHuángshā) With 843 rooms, this hotel is considered the most prestigious of Guǎngzhōu's hotels, complete with a waterfall and fish pond in the lobby, plus an excellent range of rooms and outlets.

better place to head than the Xīguān area, which has shops selling everything from ceramic teapots to Tibetan rugs.

TIĀNHÉ COMPUTER MARKETS ELECTRONICS
(天河电脑城; Tiānhé Diànnǎochéng; east end of Tianhe Lu; Ⓜ Shípáiqiáo or Gāngdǐng) A super-sized version of Huáqiáng Běi Commercial St in Shēnzhèn. Tonnes and tonnes of electronics and gadgets are sold in shops and malls straddling a few kilometres of the east end of Tianhe Lu.

WENDE LU ARTS & CRAFTS
Wende Lu, east of Beijing Lu, is a less touristy area that hosts an array of Chinese fine-art shops and galleries selling calligraphy, paintings and antique books.

XIA JIULU/SHANG JIULU CLOTHING
Xia Jiulu/Shang Jiulu ('Up Down Nine Street') is another pedestrian shopping street that has a bit more character. It's in one of the oldest parts of the city, where the buildings retain elements of both Western and Chinese architecture. It's a good place to look for discounted clothing.

HUALE LU & LIÙYÙN XIǍOQŪ CLOTHING
Huale Lu, behind the Garden Hotel, and Liùyùn Xiǎoqū, a leafy residential area clustered with trendy boutiques and cafes off Tianhe Nanyilu, are fashion destinations with the hottest looks at a fraction of the cost. To get to Liùyùn Xiǎoqū, enter from the alley next to the 7-Eleven store on Tianhe Nanyilu.

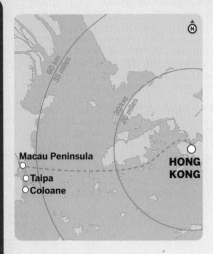

Macau Peninsula
Taipa
Coloane
HONG KONG

Macau

Macau Peninsula p234

Lying 65km to the west of Hong Kong, Macau is a city of duality. Its fortresses, churches and the food of its former Portuguese colonial masters speak to a uniquely Mediterranean style on the China coast, intermixed with alleys, temples and shrines. On the other hand, it's also the 'Vegas of the East' – the Special Administrative Region of Macau is the only place in China where gambling is legal.

The Islands: Taipa & Coloane p254

Taipa was once two islands that became joined together by silt from the Pearl River. Reclamation has succeeded in doing the same thing to Taipa and Coloane. Taipa has rapidly urbanised and it's hard to imagine that just a few decades ago it was an island of duck farms and boat yards. The small island of Coloane was a haven for pirates until 1910. Today it retains Macau's old way of life, though luxurious villas are finding their way onto the island.

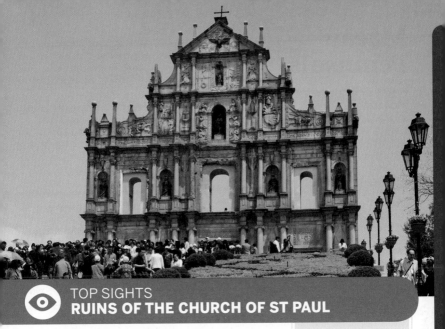

MANFRED GOTTSCHALK/GETTY IMAGES ©

TOP SIGHTS
RUINS OF THE CHURCH OF ST PAUL

The gate to nowhere is the most treasured icon in Macau. Once a Jesuit church in the early 17th century, all that remains of it now are the facade and the stairway. However, with its statues, portals and engravings that effectively make up a sermon in stone, it's one of the greatest monuments to Christianity in Asia.

The church was designed by an Italian Jesuit and built in 1602 by Japanese Christian exiles and Chinese craftsmen. After the expulsion of the Jesuits, a military battalion was stationed here. In 1835 a fire erupted in the kitchen of the barracks, destroying everything, except what you see today.

The facade has five tiers. At the top is a dove, representing the Holy Spirit, surrounded by stone carvings of the sun, moon and stars. Beneath that is a statue of the infant Jesus accompanied by the implements of the Crucifixion. In the centre of the third tier stands the Virgin Mary being assumed bodily into heaven along with angels and two flowers: the peony, representing China, and the chrysanthemum, a symbol of Japan. There are also gargoyles of Chinese lions at the edge of the pediment, similar to those that guard entrances to Chinese temples. And just below the pediment, on the right side of the facade, there is a dragon surmounted by the Holy Virgin.

DON'T MISS

➡ Facade details
➡ The stairway
➡ Museum of Sacred Art
➡ Crypt & Ossuary

PRACTICALITIES

➡ Ruinas de Igreja de São Paulo (大三巴牌坊)
➡ Map p236
➡ Travessa de São Paulo
➡ admission free
➡ 🚌8A, 17, 26, disembark at Luis de Camoes Garden

The facade is approached by six flights of 11 stairs each, divided by landings with an attractive balustrade running up each side, and a pretty floral display running up the right-hand side.

The small **Museum of Sacred Art** (天主教藝術博物館; Museu de Arte Sacra; Map p236; Rua de São Paulo; ⊘9am-6pm) contains polychrome carved wooden statues, silver chalices, monstrances and oil paintings. The **crypt** and **ossuary** (墓室; Museu de Arte Sacra e Cripta; Map p236; Travessa de São Paolo; admission free; ⊘9am-6pm) house the remains of Vietnamese and Japanese Christians martyred in the 17th century.

Macau Peninsula

Explore

Take bus 3 from the Macau–Hong Kong Ferry Terminal to the Largo do Senado and visit the Church of St Dominic, Lou Kau Mansion and other sights around the square. Wander up to the Ruins of the Church of St Paul, and then Mont Forte and the Macau Museum above it. Spend 90 minutes there. Before leaving the ruins, check out Nga Cha Temple to its right, and browse for souvenirs at the shops near the steps. Wander southwest through the tiny streets towards the Inner Harbour, stopping for an hour or two at the Mandarin's House and St Joseph's Seminary Church. After lunch head over to the A-Ma Temple and the Moorish Barracks for a quick look, before catching a cab north to the lovely St Lazarus district for the latest on the art scene.

The Best...

➡ **Sight** Ruins of the Church of St Paul (p233)

➡ **Place to Eat** Alfonso III (p248)

➡ **Place to Drink** Macau Soul (p249)

Top Tip

All the big-name casinos have free shuttle services to and from the ferry terminals, the Border Gate and the airport. Anyone can use these buses – no questions asked. You'll see them outside the ferry terminals and the casinos. For Border Gate and airport routes, enquire at the casinos.

Getting There & Away

Air For details of airlines, check the website of Macau International Airport (☑2886 1111; www.macau-airport.gov. mo), on Taipa. Sky Shuttle in Hong Kong (☑852-2108 9898; www.skyshuttlehk.com; HK$2600 Mon-Thu; HK$2800 Fri-Sun; ☺9am to 11pm) runs a 15-minute helicopter shuttle between Macau and Hong Kong.

Boat to China Yuet Tung Shipping Co (☑2877 4478; MOP$129) has a daily ferry from pier 11a, just off Rua das Lorchas, to

Shékǒu in Shēnzhèn. It takes 80 minutes and leaves at 10am, 12.30pm, 6.15pm and 8.15pm; returning at 8.15am, 9.45am, 11.45am and 6.30pm. Tickets can be bought up to three days in advance from pier 11a.

Sampans & ferries (MOP$12.50, MOP$20 departure tax; ☺hourly 8am-4pm) From a small pier near where Rua das Lorchas meets Rua do Dr Lourenço Pereira Marques to Wānzǎi.

Boats to Hong Kong TurboJet (☑in Hong Kong 790 7039, information 852-2859 3333, bookings 852-2921 6688; www.turbojet.com.hk; economy/super-class Mon-Fri HK$142/244, Sat & Sun HK$154/260, night crossing HK$176/275) has the most sailings. The 55-minute trip departs from Hong Kong–Macau Ferry Terminal (☑2547 4386; 200 Connaught Rd, Sheung Wan) and from Macau's Macau Ferry Terminal (Map p236; ☑8790 7039); see website for services to Hong Kong International Airport.

CotaiJet (☑2885 0595, in Hong Kong 852-2359 9990; www.cotaijet.com.mo; econ-omy/superclass Mon-Fri MOP$142/244, Sat & Sun MOP$154/260, night crossing MOP$176/275) departs every half-hour, from 7am to 1am; runs between Taipa Ferry Terminal and Hong Kong's Hong Kong–Macau Ferry Terminal; a feeder shuttle-bus service drops off at destinations on Cotai Strip; check website for services to Hong Kong International Airport.

New World First Ferry (☑2872 7676, in Hong Kong 852-2131 8181; www.nwff.com. hk; economy/deluxe Mon-Fri HK$140/245, Sat & Sun HK$155/260, night crossing MOP$175/275) departs every half-hour, from 7am to 10.30pm; 60- to 75-minute trip; runs between Macau Ferry Terminal and Hong Kong's China Ferry Terminal (33 Canton Rd, Tsim Sha Tsui).

Need to Know

➡ **Area code** ☑853

➡ **Location** 60km southwest of Hong Kong

➡ **Tourist Office** (☑2831 5566, tourism hotline 2833 3000; www.macautourism. gov.mo; 335-341 Alameda Dr Carlos d'Assumpcao, Edificio 'Hot Line', 12o andar; ☺9am-1pm & 2.30- 5.35pm Mon-Fri)

◉ SIGHTS

You'll find the lion's share of Macau's museums, churches, gardens, old cemeteries and important colonial buildings on the peninsula. In 2005 Unesco recognised this wealth by adding the Historic Centre of Macau, comprising eight squares and 22 historic buildings, to its World Heritage list. At many of the heritage sites, seniors over 60 and children under 11 are admitted free – just ask. The Macau Museums Pass (MOP$25) allows entry to a half-dozen museums over a five-day period.

◉ Central Macau Peninsula

LEAL SENADO   HISTORIC BUILDING

Map p240 (民政總署大樓; 163 Avenida de Almeida Ribeiro; 🚌 3, 6, 26 A, 18A, 33, disembark at Almeida Ribeiro) Facing Largo do Senado to the west is Macau's most important historical building, the 18th-century 'Loyal Senate', which now houses the Instituto para os Assuntos Cívicos e Municipais (IACM; Civic and Municipal Affairs Bureau). It is so named because the body sitting here refused to recognise Spain's sovereignty during the 60 years that it occupied Portugal. In 1654, a dozen years after Portuguese sovereignty was re-established, King João IV ordered a heraldic inscription to be placed inside the senate's entrance hall, and this can still be seen today. To the right of the entrance hall is the **IACM Gallery** (民政總署展覽廳; admission free; ⊙9am-9pm Tue-Sun), which features changing exhibits. On the 1st floor is the **Senate Library** (民政總署圖書館; ☑2857 2233; admission free; ⊙1-7pm Mon-Sat), which has a collection of some 18,500 books, and wonderful carved wooden furnishings and panelled walls.

RUINS OF THE CHURCH OF ST PAUL   RUIN

See p233.

MONTE FORT   FORTRESS

Map p240 (大炮台; Fortaleza do Monte; ⊙7am-7pm; 🚌7, 8) Just east of the ruins of the Church of St Paul, Monte Fort was built by the Jesuits between 1617 and 1626 as part of the College of the Mother of God. Barracks and storehouses were designed to allow the fort to survive a two-year siege, but the cannons were fired only once: during the aborted attempt by the Dutch to invade Macau in 1622. Disembark at Social Welfare Bureau.

MACAU MUSEUM   MUSEUM

Map p240 (澳門博物館; Museu de Macau; ☑2835 7911; www.macaumuseum.gov.mo; MOP$15, 15th of month free; ⊙10am-5.30pm Tue-Sun; 🚌7, 8) To capture the essence of Macau's history, head to this excellent museum housed in the Monte Fort. On the 1st level, 'Genesis of Macau' takes you through the early history of the territory, with parallel developments in the East and the West compared and contrasted. The highlight is the elaborate section devoted to the territory's religions. On the 2nd level (Popular Arts & Traditions of Macau), you'll see and hear everything from a re-created firecracker factory to the recorded cries of street vendors selling items such as brooms and scrap metal. Do not miss the recording of the Macanese poet José dos Santos Ferreira (1919–93), reading from his work in the local dialect. The top-floor Contemporary Macau exhibit focuses on the latest architecture and urban-development plans. Disembark at Social Welfare Bureau.

MACAU CATHEDRAL   CHURCH

Map p240 (大堂(主教座堂); A Sé Catedral; Largo da Sé; ⊙8am-6pm; 🚌3, 6, 26A, 18A) East of Largo do Senado is the cathedral. It's not a particularly attractive structure, consecrated in 1850 and completely rebuilt in 1937 in concrete. It has some notable stained-glass windows and is very active during major Christian festivals and holy days in Macau.

MUSEUM OF THE HOLY
HOUSE OF MERCY   MUSEUM

Map p240 (仁慈堂博物館; Núcleo Museológico da Santa Casa da Misericórdia; ☑2857 3938; 2 Travessa da Misericórdia; adult/student & senior over 65 MOP$5/free; ⊙10am-5.30pm Mon-Sat; 🚌3, 6, 26A) In the heart of Largo do Senado is the oldest social institution in Macau (established in 1569) and it served as a home to orphans and prostitutes in the 18th century. Today it's a museum containing items related to the holy house, including religious artefacts; Chinese, Japanese and European porcelain; the skull of its founder and Macau's first bishop, Dom Belchior Carneiro; and a portrait of Martha Merop, an orphan who became a tycoon and a patron of the house.

Macau Peninsula

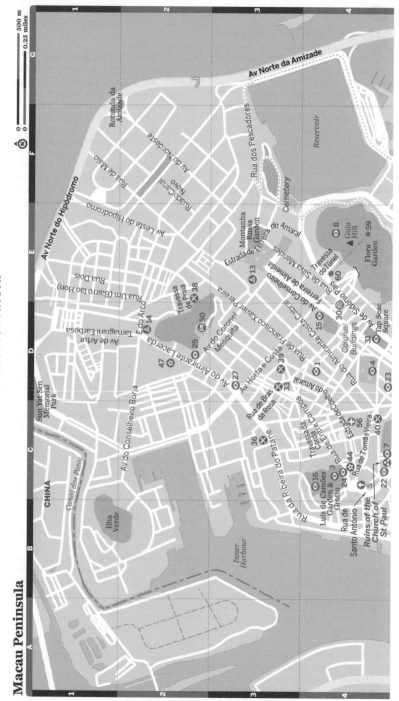

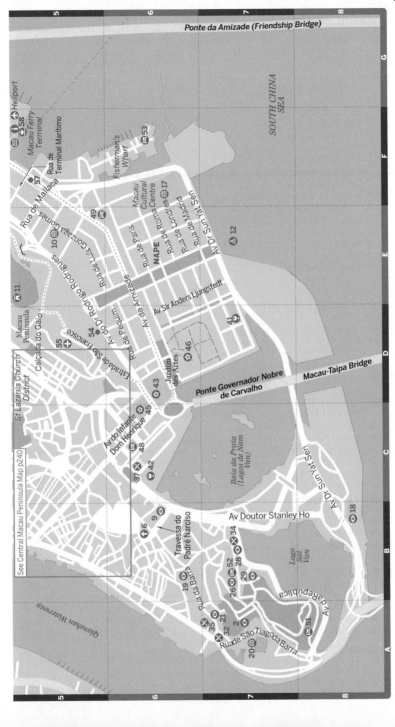

Ponte da Amizade (Friendship Bridge)

SOUTH CHINA SEA

Heliport

Macau Ferry Terminal

Rua de Terminal Marítimo

Fisherman's Wharf

Macau Cultural Centre

NAPE

Rua de Paris

Rua de Roma

Rua de Londres

Rua de Madrid

Av Dr Sun Yat Sen

Rua de Malaca

Rua de Luís Gonzaga Gomes

Macau Peninsula

St Lazarus Church District

See Central Macau Peninsula Map p240

Calçada do Gato

Estrada de São Francisco

Av do Dr Rodrigo Rodrigues

Av da Amizade

Rua de Peduim

Av Sir Anders Ljungstedt

Jardim des Artes

Ponte Governador Nobre de Carvalho

Macau-Taipa Bridge

Av do Infante Dom Henrique

Baia da Praia (Lagos de Nam Van)

Av Doutor Stanley Ho

Av Dr Sun Yat Sen

Lago Sái Van

Travessa do Padré Narciso

Rua da Barra

Av da República

Qianshan Waterway

Rua de São Tiago da Barra

Macau Peninsula

CHURCH OF ST DOMINIC   CHURCH

Map p240 (玫瑰堂; Igreja de São Domingos; Largo de São Domingos; ☉10am-6pm; 🚌3, 6, 26A) Northeast of Largo do Senado, this 17th-century baroque church with a beautiful altar and a timber roof contains the **Treasury of Sacred Art** (聖物寶庫; Tresouro de Arte Sacra; admission free; ☉10am-6pm), an Aladdin's cave of ecclesiastical art and liturgical objects exhibited on three floors.

FREE LOU KAU MANSION   HISTORIC BUILDING

Map p240 (盧家大屋; Casa de Lou Kau; ☎8399 6699; 7 Travessa da Sé; ☉9am-7pm Tue-Sun; 🚌2, 3, 3A, 4) Built in 1889, this Cantonese-style mansion with southern European elements belonged to merchant Lou Wa Sio (aka Lou Kau), who also commissioned the **Lou Lim Ioc Garden**. Behind the grey facade, an intriguing maze of open and semi-enclosed spaces blurs the line between inside and outside. The flower and bird motif on the roof can also be found in the **Mandarin House** and **A-ma Temple**. Free guided tours on weekends (from 10am to 7pm).

TOP CHOICE ST JOSEPH'S
SEMINARY CHURCH   CHURCH

Map p240 (聖若瑟修院及聖堂; Capela do Seminario Sao Jose; Rua do Seminario; ☉10am-5pm; 🚌9, 16, 18) St Joseph's, which falls outside the tourist circuit, is one of Macau's most beautiful models of tropicalised baroque architecture. Consecrated in 1758 as part of the Jesuit seminary, it features a white and yellow facade, a scalloped entrance canopy (European) and the oldest dome, albeit a shallow one, ever built in China. The most interesting feature, however, is the roof which features Chinese materials and building styles.

DOM PEDRO V THEATRE   CULTURAL BUILDING

Map p240 (崗頂劇院; Teatro Dom Pedro V; ☎2893 9646; Calçada do Teatro; 🚌9, 16, 18) Opposite the Church of St Augustine, Dom Pedro V is a colonnaded, neoclassical theatre built in 1858 and it's the oldest European theatre in China. It only opens for cultural performances.

TOP CHOICE SIR ROBERT
HO TUNG LIBRARY   LIBRARY

Map p240 (何東圖書館; 3 Largo de St Agostinho; ☉10am-7pm Mon-Sat, 11am-7pm Sun; @; 🚌9, 16, 18) Originally a country retreat of the late tycoon, this 19th-century colonial building

features an arcaded facade, Ionic columns, a dome and Chinese-style gardens. It was given an extension by architect Joy Choi Tin Tin, and the new airy four-storey building in glass and steel has Piranesi-inspired bridges connecting to the old house and a glass roof straddling the transitional space.

TOP CHOICE MANDARIN'S HOUSE   HISTORIC BUILDING

Map p236 (鄭家大屋; Caso do Mandarim; ☎2896 8820; www.wh.mo/mandarinhouse; 10 Travessa de Antonio da Silva; admission free; ☉10am-6pm Fri-Tue; 🚌28B, 16) Built in 1869, Mandarin's House has over 60 rooms and was the ancestral home of Zheng Guanying, an influential author-merchant whose readers included emperors, Dr Sun Yatsen and Chairman Mao. The compound features a moon gate, a passageway for sedans, delightful courtyards, exquisite rooms and a main hall with French windows, all arranged in that labyrinthine style typical of certain Chinese architecture.

CHURCH OF ST LAWRENCE   CHURCH

off Map p236 (聖老楞佐教堂; Igreja de São Lourenço; Rua de São Lourenço; ☉10am-6pm Tue-Sun, 1-2pm Mon; 🚌3, 6, 26A) The original church was built of wood in the 1560s but was rebuilt in stone in the early 19th century. It has a magnificent painted ceiling and one of the towers once served as an ecclesiastical prison. Enter from Rua da Imprensa Nacional.

CHURCH OF ST AUGUSTINE   CHURCH

Map p240 (聖奧斯定教堂; Igreja de Santo Agostinho; Largo de São Agostinho; ☉10am-6pm; 🚌3, 6, 26A) Southwest of Largo do Senado via Rua Central is the Church of St Augustine. Its foundations date from 1586, but the present church was built in 1814. The high altar has a statue of Christ bearing the cross, which is carried through the streets during the Procession of the Passion of Our Lord on the first Saturday of Lent.

SAM KAI VUI KUN TEMPLE   TAOIST, TEMPLE

Map p240 (三街會館; Sam Kai Vui Kun; Rua Sui do Mercado de São Domingos; ☉8am-6pm; 🚌3, 6, 26A) Literally 'a community hall for three streets', this temple was a meeting place for merchants and then an adjudication court before the Chinese Chamber of Commerce came into existence in 1912. The temple is dedicated to Kwan Yu, the god of war and justice. It gets particularly busy in May,

Central Macau Peninsula

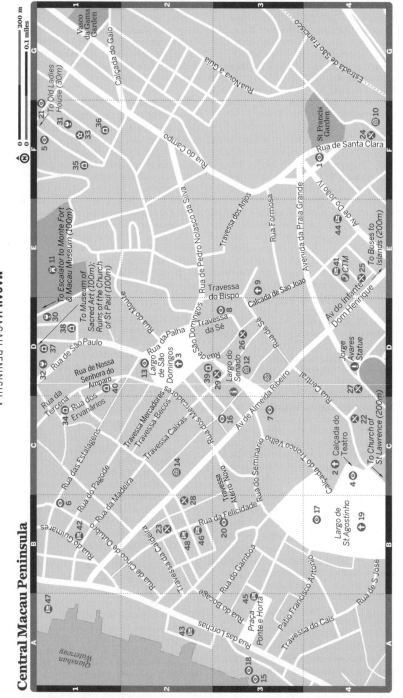

MACAU MACAU PENINSULA

0   0.1 miles
0   200 m

Qianshan Waterway

Vasco da Gama Garden

Calçada do Galo

Estrada de São Francisco

To Old Ladies 31 House (30m)

St Francis Garden

Rua de Santa Clara

Rua Nova a Guia

Rua do Campo

Rua de Pedro Nolasco da Silva

Travessa dos Anjos

Rua Formosa

Avenida da Praia Grande

Calçada de São João

To Escalator to Monte Fort & Macau Museum (100m)

To Museum of Sacred Art (100m); Ruins of the Church of St Paul (100m)

Rua do Monte

Travessa do Bispo

Rua da Sé

Av do João IV

Av do Infante Dom Henrique

CTM

To Buses to Islands (200m)

Jorge Alvares Statue

Rua de São Paulo

Rua da Palha

São Domingos

Travessa da Sé

Rua Central

Largo de São Domingos

Largo do Senado

Rua de Nossa Senhora do Amparo

Rua da Tercena

Rua dos Ervanários

Travessa Mercadores

Travessa Becos

Travessa Caixas

Rua das Mercadores & Lopes

Av de Almeida Ribeiro

Calçada de Tronco Velho

Calçada do Teatro

To Church of St Lawrence (200m)

Rua das Estalagens

Rua do Pagode

Rua da Madeira

Rua do Seminário

Largo de St Agostinho

Rua de Guimarães

Rua de Cinco de Outubro

Travessa da Caldeira

Travessa Ateiro Nov

Rua da Felicidade

Patio Francisco Antonio

Rua de S-Jose

Rua do Gamboa

Rua do Bocage

Rua das Lorchas

Praça Ponte e Horta

Travessa do Cais

Central Macau Peninsula

MACAU MACAU PENINSULA

June and July when locals celebrate three festivals in the god's honour.

TEMPLES TAOIST, TEMPLE

Macau has some interesting Chinese temples dedicated to important but lesser-worshipped deities. There's no better symbol of Macau's cultural diversity than **Na Tcha Temple** (Map p236; 哪吒廟; Templo de Na Tcha; Rua de Sao Paulo; admission free; ◎8am-5pm; ◙8A, 17, 26), sitting quietly beside the Ruins of the Church of St Paul. Built around 1888, it's dedicated to the child god of war to halt the plague occurring at that time. The wall outside the temple, often said to be a section of the old city walls, in fact belonged to the former St Paul's College located at the ruins. The **Nu Wa Temple** (Map p240; 女媧廟; Nui Wo Miu; cnr Rua das Estalagens & Travessa Dos Algibebes; admission free; ◎9am-5pm; ◙3, 6, 26A), a shrinelike temple in a faded yellow building also built in 1888, was consecrated to the Chinese equivalent of Gaia. The 200-year-old **Hong Kung Temple** (Map p240; 康公廟; Hong Kung Miu; cnr Rua das Estalagens & Rua de Cinco de Outubro; ◎8am-6pm; ◙3, 6, 26A) is dedicated to Li Lie, a Han-dynasty general. The boat-shaped sculpture in the middle of the main hall is for offering wine to the deities during religious festivities.

GOVERNMENT HOUSE BUILDING

Map p236 (特區政府總部; Sede do Governo; cnr Avenida da Praia Grande & Travessa do Padré Narciso) South of the Church of St Lawrence is the headquarters of the Macau SAR government. This pillared, rose-coloured building was built in 1849 for a Portuguese noble. It's open to the public for one day a year, usually in September or October.

CHINESE READING ROOM — HISTORIC BUILDING

Map p240 (八角亭圖書館; Rua de Santa Clara; ⊙9am-noon & 7pm-midnight; 🚍6) This former drinks booth (c 1926), known as the 'Octagonal Pavilion' in Chinese, has red windows and a slip of a staircase linking two floors.

PAWNSHOP MUSEUM — HISTORIC BUILDING

Map p240 (典當業展示館; Espaço Patrimonial – Uma Casa de Penhores Tradicional; ☑2892 1811; 396 Avenida de Almeida Ribeiro; admission MOP$5; ⊙10.30am-7pm, closed 1st Mon of month; 🚍3, 6, 26A) Housed in the former Tak Seng On (meaning 'virtue and success') pawnshop built in 1917, the Pawnshop Heritage Exhibition incorporates the fortress-like eight-storey granite tower with slotted windows where goods were stored on racks or in safes.

STREET OF HAPPINESS — STREET

Map p240 (福隆新街; Rua da Felicidade; 🚍3, 6, 26A) Not far west of Largo do Senado is Rua da Felicidade (Street of Happiness). Its red-shuttered terraces were once Macau's main red-light district. You may recognise it from *Indiana Jones and the Temple of Doom*, as several scenes were shot here. It's fun to wander west from here towards the Inner Harbour.

⭐ ST LAZARUS CHURCH DISTRICT — NEIGHBOURHOOD

Map p240 (瘋堂斜巷; Calcada da Igreja de Sao Lazaro; 🚍7, 8) A lovely neighbourhood with quiet houses and cobbled streets. Artists, designers and independents have been setting up shop here over the last few years. The new **St Lazarus Church District Creative Industries Promotion Association** (望德堂區創意產業促進會; www.cipa.org.mo) lines up tenants and organises cultural events, such as the weekly Sun Never Left – Public Art Performance (p250). Check the website for updates. G17, a new exhibition space for pottery artists, and Jabber Cafe, by fashion designer Venessa Cheah, are also in this neighbourhood.

OLD LADIES' HOUSE — HISTORIC BUILDING

Map p236 (仁慈堂婆仔屋; www.albcreativelab.com; 8 Calcada da Igreja de Sao Lazaro; ⊙noon-7pm Wed-Mon) The Old Ladies' House sheltered Portuguese refugees from Shànghǎi in WWII and later, homeless elderly women. It's now run by an art group. Out front, there's a poetic courtyard with an old well and magnificent old trees. The fashion boutique Lines Lab and new Portuguese grocery shop Mercearia Portuguesa are here.

G32 — HISTORIC BUILDING

Map p240 (☑2834 6626; 32 Rua de Sao Miguel; free guided tours 3-5pm Sat & Sun) G32 is a tenement building that's been restored and refurbished as a Macanese home from the 1960s and '70s. The three-story structure with a narrow staircase features wooden floorboards, apple-green floral wallpaper and retro furniture. The view from the roof will let you see how Macau's old Chinese buildings rub shoulders with Unesco-protected heritage and casino kitsch.

TAI FUNG TONG ART HOUSE — HISTORIC BUILDING

Map p240 (大瘋堂藝舍; ☑2835 3537; 7 Calcada de Sao Lazaro; ⊙2-6pm, closed Mon) Featuring a mix of Chinese and European architectural styles, this gorgeous historical building was built almost a century ago by a philanthropist. It was used as a Catholic school and subsequently as a youth amenities centre. It's now occupied by a group that promotes the area's Chinese heritage. The house has displays of traditional Chinese artefacts. And calligrapher Carlos Choi is here to demonstrate his calligraphy.

TAP SEAC SQUARE — SQUARE

Map p236 (塔石廣場; Praca do Tap Seac; 🚍7, 8) This new square lined with important historic buildings (Cultural Affairs Bureau, Central Library of Macau, Library for Macau's Historical Archives) was designed by Macanese architect Carlos Marreiros, who also created the Tap Seac Health Centre (adjacent to Cultural Affairs Bureau), a contemporary interpretation of Macau's neoclassical buildings.

OX WAREHOUSE — ARTS CENTRE

Map p236 (牛房倉庫; Armazem de Boi; ☑2853 0026; http://oxwarehouse.blogspot.com; cnr Avenida Coronel Mesquita & Avenida do Almirante Lacerda; ⊙noon-7pm Wed-Mon; 🚍1A, 12) One of the most happening nongovernment arts venues in Macau, this atmospheric former slaughterhouse hosts contemporary installations, exhibitions, workshops and performances by local and visiting artists. Much of the work is engagingly experiential in nature.

TOP CHOICE AFA (ART FOR ALL SOCIETY) GALLERY

Map p236 (全藝社; ☎2836 6064; www.afamacau. com; 10th fl, Edificio da Fabrica de Baterias N E National, 52 Estrada da Areia Preta; ⏰noon-7pm Mon-Sat) Macau's best contemporary art can be seen at this nonprofit gallery, founded in 2007 by local artist James Chu. AFA has held some 60 exhibitions of works by Macau's artists in Europe, Asia, China and Macau. There are also monthly solo exhibitions by Macau's artists. It's near the Mong Ha Multisport Pavilion (望廈體育館). AFA also has a branch in Běijīng.

Take bus 8, 8A, 18A or 7 and get off at Rua Da Barca or Rua De Francisco Xavier Pereira. Alternatively, it's a 20-minute walk from Largo do Senado.

◉ Southern Macau Peninsula

MACAU CULTURAL CENTRE CULTURAL BUILDING

Map p236 (澳門文化中心; Centro Cultural de Macau; ☎2855 5555, in Hong Kong 852 2380 5083; www.ccm.gov.mo; Avenida Xian Xing Hai; ⏰9am-7pm Tue-Sun; 🚌1A, 8, 12, 23) This US$100 million centre is the territory's prime venue for theatre, opera and other cultural performances. It's beside the wonderful Macau Museum of Art.

TOP CHOICE MACAU MUSEUM OF ART MUSEUM

Map p236 (澳門藝術博物館; Museu de Arte de Macau; ☎8791 9814; www.mam.gov.mo; Macau Cultural Centre, Avenida Xian Xing Hai; adult/student MOP$5/2, Sun free; ⏰10am-6:30pm Tue-Sun; 🚌1A, 8, 12, 23) Macau Museum of Art is a five-storey complex next to the Macau Cultural Centre. It is a well-curated museum featuring excellent exhibits by Chinese artists in Macau and China, as well as paintings by important Western artists who have lived in Macau, such as George Chinnery. Highlights include ceramics and stoneware excavated from Heisha in Macau, Ming- and Qing-dynasty paintings and calligraphy from Guǎngdōng province, precious ceramic statues from Shíwān in Guǎngdōng and seal carvings by Guǎngdōng masters. There are also 19th-century Western historical paintings from all over Asia, contemporary Macanese art and photographic works.

Creative Macau (☎ 875 3282; www.creative macau.org.mo; ⏰2-7pm Mon-Sat), an art space

that runs exhibitions, poetry readings and workshops, is also in the museum building.

KUN IAM STATUE & ECUMENICAL CENTRE MONUMENT

Map p236 (觀音像; Estátua de Kun Iam; Avenida Dr Sun Yat Sen; 🚌10A, 17) This 20m-high bronze figure, emerging Virgin Mary–like from a 7m-high lotus in the outer harbour, is probably the only statue in the world of the goddess of mercy that is not facing the sea.

A-MA TEMPLE TEMPLE

Map p236 (媽閣廟; Templo de A-Ma; Rua de São Tiago da Barra; ⏰7am-6pm; 🚌1, 1A, 5) Opposite the Maritime Museum, the A-Ma Temple was probably already standing when the Portuguese arrived, although the present one may only date from the 16th century. The temple is dedicated to A-Ma aka Tin Hau, the goddess of the sea, from which the name Macau is derived. Many believe that when the Portuguese asked the name of the place, they were told 'A-Ma Gau' (bay of A-Ma). In modern Cantonese, 'Macau' is Ou Mun, meaning 'gateway of the bay'.

MOORISH BARRACKS HISTORIC BUILDING

Map p236 (Calcada da Barra; 🚌2, 5, 7) These former barracks (c 1874) on Barra Hill were designed by an Italian in a neoclassical style inspired by Moorish architecture, to accommodate 200 Muslim Indian policemen from Goa. The confusion of Muslims with Moors is unfortunate, but it's also interesting because of its connection to dated Cantonese which refers to Indians as 'moh loh cha' ('moh loh' being a transliteration of 'Moorish'). The barracks now house the Macau Maritime Administration (澳門港務局大樓). Turn right as you leave A-Ma Temple; a 10-minute walk uphill will take you here.

PENHA HILL NEIGHBOURHOOD

Map p236 (西望洋山; Colina da Penha; 🚌6, 9, 16) Towering above the colonial villas along Avenida da República is Penha Hill, the most tranquil and least-visited area of the peninsula. From here you'll get excellent views of the central area of Macau. Atop the hill is the Bishop's Palace (主教府), built in 1837, and the **Chapel of Our Lady of Penha** (主教山小教堂; Capela de Nost-ra Señora da Penha; ⏰9am-5.30pm), once a place of pilgrimage for sailors.

MARITIME MUSEUM
MUSEUM

Map p236 (海事博物館; Museu Marítimo; 1 Largo do Pagode da Barra; adult/child Mon & Wed-Sat MOP$10/5, Sun MOP$5/3; ⏱10am-5.30pm Wed-Mon; ⏲2, 5, 7) The Maritime Museum has interesting boats and artefacts from Macau's seafaring past, a mock-up of a Hakka fishing village, and displays of the long narrow boats raced during the Dragon Boat Festival in June.

GRAND PRIX MUSEUM
MUSEUM

Map p236 (大賽車博物館; Museu do Grande Prémio; Basement, CAT, 431 Rua de Luís Gonzaga Gomes; adult/child MOP$10/free, adult incl Macau Wine Museum MOP$20; ⏱10am-6pm Wed-Mon; ⏲1A, 3, 10) Cars from the Macau Formula 3 Grand Prix, including the bright-red Triumph TR2 driven by Eduardo de Carvalho that won the first Grand Prix in 1954, are on display, while simulators let you test your racing skills.

FREE MACAU SECURITY FORCES MUSEUM
MUSEUM

Map p240 (澳門保安部隊博物館; Museu das Forças de Segurança de Macau; Calçada dos Quartéis; ⏱9am-5.45pm Mon-Fri, to 5pm Sat & Sun; ⏲6, 28A) Housed in the 17th-century **St Francis Barracks** (加思欄炮台; Quartéis de São Francisco), this museum has two rooms of exhibits relating to the police and their work. The building is set in the lovely **St Francis Garden** (加思欄花園; Jardim de São Francisco).

AVENIDA DA REPÚBLICA
NEIGHBOURHOOD

(⏲6, 9, 16) Avenida da República, along the northwest shore of Sai Van Lake, is the oldest Portuguese section of Macau. Here are several grand colonial villas not open to the public. The former Bela Vista Hotel, one of the most-storied hotels in Asia, is now the residence of the Portuguese consul general (葡國領事官邸). Nearby is the ornate **Santa Sancha Palace** (禮賓府; Palacete de

---

MACAU'S INNER BEAUTIES

Between the historic and the flashy, Macau has a lot to offer architecturally to those with patience and a good eye.

Lovely Libraries

Macau's libraries show by the way they relate to their surroundings how tiny proportions can be beautiful.

Sir Robert Ho Tung Library A 19th-century villa and its glass-and-steel extension rising above a garden, with Piranesi-like bridges between the two.

Chinese Reading Room Retirees and students come here to 'Octagonal Pavilion', built in 1926, to read the news and to study.

Sr Wong Ieng Kuan Library An oasis of calm between a boulder (which juts into the interior) and a banyan tree (which frames the entrance) in the Luís de Camões Garden.

Coloane Library Grotesque but cute, this mini Grecian temple c 1917 has a pediment containing the word 'library' in Chinese and Portuguese, and too-fat columns.

Modernist Marvels

Macau has an important heritage of modernism that is little known outside the city, especially in the Inner Harbour area.

Pier 8 (8號碼頭; Map p240; Rua do Dr Lourenco Pereira Marquez; ⏲5, 7) A stunner in grey 50 paces south of Macau Masters Hotel; best views from the **South Sampan Pier** next door.

East Asia Hotel (東亞酒店; Map p240; cnr Rua do Guimares & Rua da Madeira; ⏲5, 7) Chinese art deco in mint green; a little shabby, very chic.

Penha Hill 'Bishop's Hill' is littered with the stylish villas of the wealthy.

Almirante Lacerda (Red Market) This art deco market houses a bustling wet market.

Santa Sancha; Estrada de Santa Sancha), once the residence of Macau's Portuguese governors and now used to accommodate state guests.

MACAU TOWER
LANDMARK

Map p236 (澳門旅遊塔; Torre de Macau; www. macautower.com.mo; Largo da Torre de Macau; ⏰10am-9pm Mon-Fri, 9am-9pm Sat & Sun; 🚍9A, 18, 23) At 338m, Macau Tower towers over the narrow isthmus of land southeast of Avenida da República. You can stay put on the **observation decks** (MOP$80) or challenge yourself to a bungee jump organised by extreme-sports company **AJ Hackett** (🕿988 8656).

Northern Macau Peninsula

TOP CHOICE GUIA FORT
FORTRESS, CHURCH

Map p236 (東望洋炮台/東望洋山堡壘; Fortaleza de Guia; ⏰9am-5.30pm; 🚍2, 17, 25 Flora Garden stop) As the highest point on the Macau Peninsula, this fort affords panoramic views of the city and, when the air is clear, across to the islands and China. At the top you'll find a 15m-tall lighthouse, built in 1865 and the oldest on the China coast, and the stunning **Chapel of Our Lady of Guia** (聖母雪地殿教堂; Capela de Nossa Señora da Guia; ⏰10am-5pm Tue-Sun), built in 1622 and retaining almost 100% of its original features, including some of Asia's most valuable mural paintings.

You could walk up, but it's easier to take the **Guia Cable Car** (Teleférico da Guia; 1 way/return MOP$3/5; ⏰8am-6pm Tue-Sun) that runs from the entrance to **Flora Gardens** (Jardim da Flora; Travessa do Túnel; ⏰7.30am-8.30pm), Macau's largest public park.

LOU LIM IOC GARDEN
GARDENS

Map p236 (盧廉若公園; Jardim Lou Lim Ioc; 10 Estrada de Adolfo de Loureiro; ⏰6am-9pm; 🚍12, 16) People come to this Suzhou-style garden to relax, practise taichi or play Chinese musical instruments among shady trees, lotus ponds, bamboo groves and a bridge with nine turns (to escape from evil spirits who can only move in straight lines). The Victorian-style **Lou Lim Ioc Garden Pavilion** (盧廉若公園; Pavilhão do Jardim de Lou Lim Ioc; 🕿8988 4128; admission free; ⏰9am-9pm Tue-Sun) was where the Lou family received guests, including Dr Sun Yatsen, and is now used for exhibits and

recitals during the Macau International Music Festival in late October/November. Adjacent to the garden is the **Macao Tea Culture House** (澳門茶文化館; Caultura do Chá em Macau; ⏰9am-7pm Tue-Sun), displaying the local tea culture with exhibits of various teapots.

TOP CHOICE KUN IAM TEMPLE
TEMPLE

Map p236 (觀音廟; Templo de Kun Iam; Avenida do Coronel Mesquita; admission free; ⏰10am-6pm; 🚍1A, 10, 18A, stop Travessa De Venceslau De Morais) Dating back four centuries, Kun Iam Temple is Macau's oldest and most interesting temple. The likeness of Kun Iam, the Goddess of Mercy, is in the main hall; to the left of the altar and behind glass is a statue of a bearded arhat rumoured to represent Marco Polo. The first treaty of trade and friendship between the USA and China was signed at round stone table in the temple's terraced gardens in 1844.

FREE LUÍS DE CAMÕES GARDEN & GROTTO
GARDENS

Map p236 (白鴿巢公園; Jardim e Gruta de Luís de Camões; ⏰6am-10pm; 🚍8A, 17, 26) This relaxing garden is dedicated to the one-eyed poet Luís de Camões (1524–80), who is said to have written part of his epic *Os Lusíadas* in Macau, though there is little evidence that he ever reached the city. The **Sr Wong Ieng Kuan Library** is inside the garden.

CASA GARDEN
HISTORIC BUILDING

Map p236 (東方基金會會址; 13 Praça de Luís de Camões; 🚍8A, 17, 26) Quietly sitting east of the Luís de Camões Garden is this beautiful colonial villa, once the headquarters of the British East India Company when it was based in Macau in the early 19th century. Today the villa houses the sleek **Museu do Oriente** (東方基金會博物館; 🕿8398 1126; www.foriente.pt; 13 Praça de Luís de Camões; ⏰10am-5.30pm Mon-Fri, to 7pm during special exhibitions), which features exhibits of Chinese antiques, porcelain and contemporary art.

CHURCH OF ST ANTHONY
CHURCH

Map p236 (聖安多尼教堂; Igreja de Santo António; cnr Rua de Santo António & Rua do Tarrafeiro; ⏰7.30am-5.30pm; 🚍8A, 17, 26) Outside Casa Garden and next to the roundabout, this church, built from 1558 to 1608, was the Jesuit's earliest headquarters. The local Portuguese used to hold wedding ceremonies here, hence the church's name in Cantonese: Fa Vong Tong (Church of Flowers).

OLD PROTESTANT CEMETERY CEMETERY
Map p236 (基督教墳場; Antigo Cemitério Protestante; 15 Praça de Luís de Camões; ⏲8.30am-5.30pm; 🚌8A, 17, 26) As church law forbade the burial of non-Catholics on hallowed ground, this cemetery was established in 1821 as the last resting place of (mostly Anglophone) Protestants. Among those interred here are Irish-born artist George Chinnery (1774–1852), and Robert Morrison (1782–1834), the first Protestant missionary to China and author of the first Chinese-English dictionary.

CEMETERY OF ST MICHAEL THE ARCHANGEL CEMETERY
Map p236 (西洋墳場; Cemitério de São Miguel Arcanjo; 2a Estrada do Cemitério; ⏲8am-6pm; 🚌7, 8) This cemetery, northeast of Monte Fort, contains tombs and sepulchres that can only be described as baroque ecclesiastical works of art. Near the main entrance is the **Chapel of St Michael** (聖彌額爾小堂; Capela de São Miguel; ⏲10am-6pm), a doll-sized, pea-green church with a tiny choir loft and pretty porticoes.

FREE **SUN YAT SEN MEMORIAL HOUSE** MUSEUM
Map p236 (國父紀念館; Casa Memorativa de Doutor Sun Yat Sen; ☎2857 4064; 1 Rua de Silva Mendes; ⏲10am-5pm Wed-Mon; 🚌2, 9, 22, Victory Garden stop) This mock-Moorish house (c 1910) commemorates Dr Sun Yatsen (1866–1925), founder of the Chinese republic. Dr Sun's brother funded its construction, Dr Sun's son built it and his first wife Lu Muzhen lived there until she died in 1952. Yet Dr Sun himself, who married his well-known second wife Madame Song Qingling in 1915, never lived in it.

RED MARKET MARKET
Map p236 (紅街市大樓; Mercado Almirante Lacerda; cnr Avenida Almirante Lacerda & Avenida Horta e Costa; ⏲7am-7pm; 🚌23, 32) Designed by a Macanese architect, this three-storey art deco building houses a lively market selling dried foods, fresh flowers, live poultry, meat and seafood.

LIN FUNG TEMPLE TEMPLE
Map p236 (蓮峰廟; Lin Fung Miu; Avenida do Almirante Lacerda; ⏲10am-6.30pm; 🚌8, 28B) Once Taoist but now dedicated to Kun Iam, this temple (c 1592) was where people from Guǎngdōng province stayed when they visited Macau, including Lin Zexu, the commissioner charged with stamping out the opium trade. There's a **Lin Zexu Memorial Hall** (林則徐紀念館; Museu de Lin Zexu; ☎2855 0166; tourist/local adult MOP$10/5; ⏲9am-5pm Tue-Sun).

EATING

While Macau's Chinese cuisine is good, most people come here for Macanese or Portuguese food. Whatever cuisine you're after, making reservations is a must in midrange and fine-dining places. Most restaurants open from noon to around 3pm, and 6pm till 1pm.

Central Macau Peninsula

TOP CHOICE **ROBUCHON AU DÔME** FRENCH $$$
Map p236 (☎8803 7878; 43rd fl, Grand Lisboa, Avenida de Lisboa; lunch/dinner set from MOP$400/1588; ⏲lunch & dinner; 🚌3, 10) Relocated to the Grand Lisboa Hotel, Robuchon Au Dôme, formerly Robuchon A Galera, is encased in a glass dome, hence the name. Arguably the most tastefully decorated of the casino restaurants, it's also Macau's only restaurant with three Michelin stars and has everything you'd associate with the Robuchon name: elegant decor, fine Gallic creations and impeccable service. The wine cellar with 8000 bottles is one of best in Asia.

CLUBE MILITAR DE MACAU PORTUGUESE $$
Map p240 (陸軍俱樂部; ☎2871 4000; www.clubemilitardemacau.net; 975 Avenida da Praia

MEAL PRICES

This price guide is for the approximate cost of a two-course meal with drinks.

$	under MOP$200
$$	MOP$200–400
$$$	over MOP$400

MACAU CHOW

A typical Macanese menu is an enticing stew of influences from Chinese and South Asian cuisines, as well as those of former Portuguese colonies in Africa, India and Latin America. Coconut, tamarind, chilli, jaggery (palm sugar) and shrimp paste can all feature.

A famous Macanese speciality is *galinha africana* (African chicken), made with coconut, garlic and chillies. Other favourites include *casquinha* (stuffed crab), *minchi* (minced meat cooked with potatoes, onions and spices) and *serradura* (a milk pudding).

You'll find Portuguese dishes here too, such as *arroz de pato* (rice with duck confit) and *leitão assado no forno* (roasted suckling pig).

The historic 'Three Lamps' (Sam Jan Dung) district in the Northern Macau Peninsula is known for its Burmese and Indonesian eateries. The neighbourhood begins at Rotunda de Caros da Maia, with the three street lamps (actually there are four) that give it its name, and sprawls over several square blocks.

Grande; meals MOP$250-400; ⊙lunch & dinner; ▣6, 28C) Housed in Macau's most distinguished colonial building, with ceiling fans spinning lazily above, the Military Club is for those who romanticise about days gone by. There are some excellent Portuguese wines. The set lunch for MOP$128 is a steal.

LITORAL
MACANESE, PORTUGUESE $$
Map p236 (海灣餐廳; ☑2896 7878; http://restaurante-litoral.com; 261a Rua do Almirante Sérgio; meals from MOP$250; ⊙lunch & dinner; ▣1, 5, 7) This two-storey restaurant serves solid Macanese and Portuguese fare, including delicious stews and baked-rice dishes – many spun from the heirloom recipes of the matron Manuela, who runs the place.

CHAT YIN
BURMESE $
Map p236 (1 Rua de Bras da Rosa, San Kiu; noodles MOP$16-34; ⊙7.30am-6.30pm; ▣23, 32) Located in the 'three-lamp' district known for its Burmese cuisine, this joint with minty-green stuccoed walls whips up a sumptuous Burmese fish soup with noodles and the hearts of banana trees.

TOUNG KING
BURMESE, CHINESE $
Map p236 (東京小食館; 1c Rotunda da Carlos Da Maia, Santo Antonio; meals MOP$15-40; ⊙10am-10pm; ▣23, 32) The Burmese-style snacks here are much raved about by foodies, many of whom make a trip from Hong Kong just for the noodles with pig's brain (tastes just like tofu, the Chinese-Burmese owner assures) and pig's innards. If that's too heady, you might like the dry tossed egg noodles with dried shrimp, garlic, chilli and peanuts. We know someone who downed five plates!

LA PALOMA
SPANISH, MEDITERRANEAN $$$
Map p236 (芭朗瑪餐廳; ☑2837 8111; www.saotiago.com.ma; 2nd fl, Pousada de São Tiago, Avenida da República; set lunch from MOP$200, set dinner MOP$700; ⊙lunch & dinner; ▣9) This classy restaurant sitting on the foundations of a 17th-century fortress is a welcome change from the glitz of the casino restaurants. You might go inside just for a cup of coffee on its terrace, and no one could blame you. Its romantic ambience is unbeatable (and so are its tapas and paella).

TOU TOU KOI
CANTONESE $$
Map p240 (陶陶居酒家; ☑2857 2629; 6-8 Travessa do Mastro; lunch MOP$150, dinner from MOP$250; ⊙lunch & dinner; ▣3, 6, 26A) Located down an alley just opposite the Pawnshop Museum, this granny of a Chinese restaurant has been serving sumptuous dim sum and traditional Cantonese cuisine, including some old, hard-to-find dishes, for the last 80 years. It has a huge following among foodies in Hong Kong and Macau.

EIGHT
CANTONESE $$$
Map p236 (8餐廳; ☑8803 7788; www.grandlisboahotel.com; 2nd fl, Grand Lisboa, Avenida de Lisboa; lunch/dinner from MOP$200/450; ⊙lunch & dinner; ▣3, 10, 28B) With water (a symbol for money) cascading down the wall, opulent chandeliers dripping crystals and an auspicious numeral for a name, The Eight can only belong to a casino. Granted, it's an excellent restaurant set apart from other similar places by the solid dim sum, the chef's creativity and two Michelin stars. Getting a table is almost impossible without a reservation.

XINA CAFE
MEDITERRANEAN $

Map p236 (☏2835 0489; 72b Rua Tomas Vieira; lunch dishes MOP$25-60, dinner per person MOP$250; ⏰11.30am-6.30pm Tue-Sun; ✐; 🚌7, 8) 'China' serves simple salads and tapas during the day. In the evening its owner Pedro cooks superb, Mediterranean-style dinners for the lucky few who manage to land a seat at his table (you'll need to book in groups of six or more, two days in advance).

O PORTO
MACANESE $

Map p236 (☏2859 4643; 17 Travessa da Praia; mains MOP$70-110; ⏰12.30-2pm & 6.30-10.30pm, closed Wed; 🚌2, 10, 12) Not to be confused with O Porto Interior on Rua do Almirante Sérgio, this modest place serves affordable Macanese dishes, with a few luxuries: checkered tablecloths, football paraphernalia and warm service. It's near the steps leading to Mong Ha Hill.

TOP CHOICE LUNG WAH TEA HOUSE
CANTONESE $

Map p236 (龍華茶樓; http://lungwahteahouse. com; Avenida do Almirante Lacerda; dim sum from MOP$14, tea MOP$10; ⏰7am-2pm; ✐; 🚌23, 32) There's grace in the retro furniture and the casual way it's thrown together in this airy Cantonese teahouse (c 1963). Take a booth by the windows overlooking the Red Market where the teahouse buys its produce everyday. There's no English menu; just point and take. Lung Wah sells an excellent array of Chinese teas.

ALFONSO III
PORTUGUESE $$

Map p240 (亞豐素三世餐廳; ☏2858 6272; 11a Rua Central; starters MOP$70-200, mains MOP$98-210; ⏰lunch & dinner; 🚌3, 6, 26A) A short stroll southwest of the Leal Senado is this tiny restaurant that has won a well-deserved reputation among the Portuguese community in Macau. Tables are often in short supply, so phone ahead.

A LORCHA
MACANESE, PORTUGUESE $$

Map p236 (船屋葡國餐廳; ☏2831 3193; 289a Rua do Almirante Sérgio; lunch/dinner from MOP$150/200; ⏰lunch & dinner Wed-Mon; 🚌1, 5, 10) 'The Sailboat' is listed in every guidebook and has been extremely popular with visitors from Hong Kong for decades. One reason for its popularity is that it's within walking distance of the A-Ma Temple. If you go not expecting creative surprises, you'll enjoy its solid Macanese fare, such as oxtail stew. Portions are generous.

HENRI'S GALLEY
MACANESE $$

Map p236 (美心亨利餐廳; ☏2855 6251; www. henrisgalley.com.mo; 4G-H Avenida da República; meals MOP$130-350; ⏰11am-10pm; 🚌6, 9, 16) The wonderful Macanese chef Henri Wong is the soul of this 34-year-old institution. Mr Wong expertly prepares Macanese specialities like African chicken and Macau sole with unique recipes containing secret ingredients. The Sai Van Lake setting, though a little out of the way, is superb.

OU MUN CAFÉ
CAFE $

Map p240 (澳門咖啡; 12 Travessa de São Domingos; sandwiches from MOP$22, lunch set MOP$80; ⏰9am-10pm Tue-Sun) This much-loved cafe has a full menu but you see more Macanese and Portuguese customers coming in for its freshly made Portuguese-style pastries, chocolates and coffee than for its savoury dishes.

TOP CHOICE TIM'S KITCHEN
CHINESE $$$

Map p236 (桃花源小廚; ☏8803 3682; Shop F25, East Wing, Hotel Lisboa, Avenida de Lisboa, Praia Grande; lunch/dinner from MOP$200/400; ⏰lunch & dinner; 🚌3, 6, 26A) Tim's (with one Michelin star) captures some of the best moments of Cantonese cooking. Fresh ingredients are meticulously prepared using methods that preserve or highlight their original flavours, resulting in dishes that look simple but taste divine – a giant 'glass' prawn shares a plate with a sliver of Chinese ham; a crab claw lounges on a cushion of winter melon surrounded by broth.

WONG CHI KEI
CANTONESE $

Map p240 (黃枝記; 17 Largo do Senado; dishes MOP$25-53; ⏰8am-midnight; 🚌3, 6, 26A) Decked out in traditional Chinese hardwood furniture, this eatery serves up similar dishes to those in the humbler noodle shops on the side streets but prices are higher and the environment is cleaner and less crowded. It attracts a lot of tourists and locals due to its convenient location right in the Largo do Senado.

CHEONG KEI
CANTONESE $

Map p240 (祥記麵家; 68 Rua da Felicidade; noodles MOP$18-50; ⏰noon-1am; 🚌3, 6, 26A) Peak-time queues at the door are a clue that this long-standing noodle joint on the 'street of happiness' has a loyal following. Try the noodles tossed with shrimp roe. There are just a few communal tables; be prepared to trade elbows with the locals.

MARGARET'S CAFÉ E NATA
CAFE **$**

Map p240 (瑪嘉烈蛋撻店; 17a Rua Alm Costa Cabral, Avenida de Almeida Ribeiro; cakes & sandwiches MOP$10-35; ⊙6.30am-8pm Mon-Sat, 9am-7pm Sun; 🚍3) If you want to try the legendary Macanese egg tarts but don't want to go all the way to Lord Stow's in Coloane, this busy cafe (supposedly founded by Stow's ex-wife) does an equally sweet and melty version. At least we can't tell the difference. It also has good-value sandwiches.

PAVILIONS SUPERMERCADO
SUPERMARKET

Map p240 (百利來超級市場; 421 Avenida da Praia Grande; 🚍18, 23, 32) In the centre of the Macau Peninsula, Pavilions has a wide selection of imported food and drinks, including a Portuguese section in the basement.

NEW YAOHAN
SUPERMARKET

(新八佰伴; Avenida Comercial de Macau; ⊙10.30am-10pm; 🚍18, 23, 32) This supermarket on the 7th floor of the department store has imported Japanese and international food.

HYPER GOURMET
SUPERMARKET

(Ground fl, Magnolia Ct, Ocean Gardens, Avenida dos Jardins do Oceano, Taipa; ⊙10am-10pm) In Taipa, Hyper Gourmet carries European foodstuffs.

DRINKING & NIGHTLIFE

CORNER'S WINE BAR & TAPAS CAFÉ
BAR, CAFE

Map p240 (三巴角落; 3 Travessa de São Paulo, Macau Peninsula; ⊙cafe noon-5pm, bar 5pm-mid-

---

night Sun-Thu, to 1am Fri & Sat; 🚍8A, 17, 26) This popular rooftop bar and tapas joint attracts a cool, arty crowd. It's in a great location across from the cathedral ruins. A close-to-perfect evening can be spent lounging on its plush pink couches, sipping wine amid soft lighting and soothing music.

MACAU SOUL
BAR

Map p240 (澳感廊; ☑2836 5182; www.macau soul.com; 31a Rua de Sao Paulo; 🚍8A, 17, 26) Huddled in the shadows of the ruins of St Paul, Macau Soul is elegantly decked out in woods and stained-glass windows. Run by two English retirees, it has a basement where blues bands perform to packed audiences. Opening hours vary so phone ahead.

CINNEBAR
BAR

Map p236 (霞酒廊; ground fl, Wynn Macau, Rua Cidade de Sintra, NAPE, Macau Peninsula; ⊙3pm-midnight; 🚍8, 10A, 23) Cinnebar is a good place to go for a quiet natter. It has a fantastic combination of swish and casual: upmarket and classy surroundings indoors and a relaxed, amicable atmosphere in its outdoor seating area around the swimming pool and the garden. Some exotically blended cocktails and homemade snacks are served in this lobby bar.

MGM GRAND MACAU
BAR

Map p236 (Grande Praça, Avenida Dr Sun Yat Sen, Macau Peninsula; 🚍8, 3A, 12) If you can't make up your mind where to sip in the city, MGM Grand has several excellent bars that offer a bit of something for everyone. The sleek, high-up **Aba Bar** (⊙5pm-2am) has a beautiful glass cellar stocked with a variety of wines that attracts beautiful urbanities at all times. Next door is the **Russian Room** (魚子屋; ⊙5pm-2am), a sparkling and splendidly designed pub for the high-heeled types to wash down caviar with the expertly selected vodka. The spirited **Lion's Bar** (⊙7pm-5am Tue-Sun), in the middle of the casino, has live bands playing pop, funk and R&B on most nights of the week.

SKY 21 LOUNGE
LOUNGE

Map p236 (www.sky21macau.com; 21st-23rd fl, AIA Tower, 215a-301 Avenida Comercial de Macau, Avenida de Almeida Ribeiro; 🚍18, 23, 32) Zen and cyber come together in this new lounge bar with alfresco seating commanding panoramic views of Macau. It often has live jazz on Sundays and special parties on Saturdays.

EVENTS & TICKETS

The bimonthly events calendar *CCM+* and its monthly counterpart for up-market entertainment *Destination Macau* are available for free at Macau Government Tourist Office outlets and larger hotels. You can book tickets to most events through these websites:

Macau Ticket (www.macauticket.com)

Cotai Ticketing (www.cotaiticketing.com)

JABBER CAFE

Map p240 (34-38 Rua de Sao Roque; ⊙noon-7pm Tue-Fri, 3-7pm Sat & Sun; ☐7, 8, stop Social Welfare Bureau) Located in the Saint Lazarus district, this sexy subterranean cafe with hot pink walls belongs to Malaysian-Chinese fashion designer Venessa Cheah, who also lends her talent to the tasty and creative menu. The cocktails will give you a nice afternoon buzz. The cafe sells a small collection of knick-knacks such as jewellery, vintage postcards and handmade soaps.

 # ENTERTAINMENT

SUN NEVER LEFT – PUBLIC ART
PERFORMANCE FAIR

Map p240 (Rua de Sao Roque, St Lazarus District; admission free; ⊙3-6pm Sat & Sun; ☐7, 8) At the time of writing, a fair was being held by the **St Lazarus Church District Creative Industries Promotion Association** (☑2834 6626; www.cipa.org.mo) in the lovely St Lazarus District every weekend afternoon. There are stalls selling art and crafts, live music, food and drinks, and participants are mainly artists from the neighbourhood.

COMUNA DE PEDRA DANCE

Map p236 (石頭公社; ☑6628 0064; http://comunadepedra.blogspot.com) This edgy but elusive contemporary-dance company has performed in squares, parks, empty commercial buildings, factories, rooftops, the Ruins of the Church of St Paul and on stages in Macau, Hong Kong and overseas. Pinto Livros has information on its latest performances and tickets.

GRAND LISBOA CASINO CASINO

Map p236 (新葡京; ☑2838 2828; Avenida de Lisboa, Macau Peninsula; ☐3, 10) Connected to its little sister (Lisboa Casino) by a footbridge is the plush Grand Lisboa, with its glowing golden-bulb exterior and a truly kitsch flaming-torch-shaped towering structure that has become the landmark by which people navigate the peninsula streets. The **Crazy Paris Cabaret** (巴黎瘋狂豔舞團; ⊙4.30pm-12.30am) is also held here.

WYNN MACAU CASINO CASINO

Map p236 (永利娛樂場; ☑2888 9966; Wynn Macau, Rua Cidade de Sintra, NAPE, Macau Peninsula; ☐8, 10A) The Vegas-style Wynn Macau Casino is arguably the most upmarket and classy of the lot, with every game imagina-

---

BRIGHT LIGHTS, SIN CITY

Macau's seafront has turned into King Kong's playground, a space inhabited by gargantuan monuments in all forms of postmodern kitsch. Casinos are no stranger to a city known as the 'Vegas of the East', but while there was only one landmark house of cards in the past, now the sky's the limit. The change began when casino mogul Stanley Ho's monopoly ended in 2002 and Las Vegas operators set up shop in competition. There are now around 30 casinos in Macau, all with hotels attached.

Given the excess of it, the first glance inside a Macau casino may be startling. It's – by Vegas standards – quiet. First you'll hardly hear any whooping and clunking because slot machines make up only 5% of total casino winnings (versus Vegas' 60%). Here table games are the staple, mostly baccarat, then roulette and a dice game called *dai sai* ('big small'). Second, drunks are hard to come by. Chinese players believe that booze dulls their skill (even when none is required).

Over 80% of gamblers and 95% of high rollers come from mainland China. The latter play inside members-only rooms where the total amount wagered on any given day can exceed a country's GDP, and where money allows you to do things like smash a chandelier with an ashtray and not pay for it.

For recreational players, your closest brush with a casino's seedy side will probably be harassment by tip hustlers – scam artists who hang around tables acting like your new best friend. They can steal your chips, nag you for a cut and/or try to drag you off to a casino that'll tip them for bringing clients.

Casinos are open 24 hours. To enter, you must be 18 years or older and properly dressed.

ble (up to $2500 minimum bet) and original Matisse and Renoir paintings on the premises.

SHOPPING

TOP CHOICE MERCEARIA PORTUGUESA
FOOD, JEWELLERY

Map p236 (☑2856 2708; www.merceariaportuguesa.com; 8 Calcada da Igreja de Sao Lazaro; ◷noon-8pm; ◻7, 8) The charming Portuguese corner shop opened by a film director and actress has a small but well-curated selection of provisions, such as canned food, jams and honeys, soaps and chinaware, gold jewellery, wooden toys and bath products from Portugal, gorgeously packaged and reasonably priced.

OLD CITY
ANTIQUES, SOUVENIRS

Browsing through the shops in the old city, specifically on crumbly Rua dos Ervanários and Rua de Nossa Senhora do Amparo (Map p240) near the Ruins of St Paul, can be a great experience. There are shops selling stamps, jade, incense and goldfish. In the afternoon flea-market vendors spread their wares on the ground.

You can also look for antiques or replicas at shops on or near Rua de São Paulo, Rua das Estalagens and Rua de São António. Rua de Madeira and Rua dos Mercadores, which lead up to Rua da Tercena and its flea market (Map p240) have stores selling mah-jong tiles and birdcages. With their humble, one- or two-storey houses dating from agricultural times, these are lovely streets to walk around in, even if you don't buy anything. Stores selling pork jerky, egg rolls and almond cookies are scattered all over town. Standards are pretty much the same, so just hop into the nearest one.

TOP CHOICE MACAU CREATIONS
CLOTHING, HOMEWARES

Map p240 (澳門佳作; ☑2835 2954; www.macaucreations.com; 5a Rua da Ressurreicao; ◷10am-10pm; ◻3, 6, 26) Excellent Macau-themed clothes, stationery and memorabilia designed by 30 artists living in the city, including Russian Konstantin Bessmertny and Macanese Carlos Marreiros.

G17 GALLERY
CERAMICS

Map p240 (陶藝館; ☑2834 6626; 17a Rua de Sao Miguel; ◷10am-7pm Mon-Sat, 2-6pm Sun; ◻7, 8) A small, new gallery that displays and sells ceramics and pottery by Macau's artists.

MOD DESIGN STORE
CLOTHING, ACCESSORIES

Map p240 (www.mod-store.com; B1, Macau Tourism & Cultural Activity Centre, Ruins of St Paul & Companhia de Jesus Sq; ◷9am-7pm; ◻3, 6, 26) The newly opened Mod shop next to the Ruins of the Church of St Paul sells souvenirs from Portugal and T-shirts designed by Macau's designers.

PINTO LIVROS
BOOKS

Map p240 (邊度有書; http://blog.roodo.com/pintolivros; 1a Veng Heng Bldg, 31 Largo do Senado; ◷11.30am-11pm; ◻3, 6, 26A) This upstairs reading room overlooking Largo do Senado has a decent selection of titles in art and culture, a few esoteric CDs and two resident cats.

LINES LAB
CLOTHING

Map p240 (www.lineslab.com; Shop A3, 8 Calçada da Igreja de São Lazaro; ◷1-8pm, closed Mon; ◻7, 8) Two Lisbon-trained designers opened this boutique in the Old Ladies' House art space and created edgy Macau-inspired clothes and bags for it.

SPORTS & ACTIVITIES

CANIDROME
SPECTATOR SPORT

Map p236 (逸園賽狗場; ☑2822 1199, racing information hotline 2833 3399, Hong Kong hotline 800 932 199; www.macauyydog.com; Avenida do General Castelo Branco; admission MOP$10; ◻1, 3, 25) Macau's Canidrome, in the northern part of the Macau Peninsula, is the only facility for greyhound racing in Asia. Greyhound races are held on Monday, Thursday, Saturday and Sunday at 7.30pm. There are 16 races per night, with six to eight dogs chasing a mechanical rabbit around the 455m oval track at speeds of up to 60km/h.

AJ HACKETT
ADVENTURE

Map p236 (☑8988 8875; http://macau.ajhackett.com) New Zealand–based AJ Hackett organises all kinds of adventure climbs up and around the Macau Tower.

MANFRED GOTTSCHALK /GETTY IMAGES ©

MANFRED GOTTSCHALK /GETTY IMAGES ©

3

LONELY PLANET /GETTY IMAGES ©

1. Grand Lisboa Casino (p250)

The golden dome-shaped exterior of the plush Grand Lisboa has become a landmark.

2. A-Ma Temple (p257)

Pre-dating the Portuguese, this temple is dedicated to A-Ma, goddess of the sea.

3. Portuguese Sausage & Rice

Many Macanese menus blend Chinese, South Asian and Portuguese dishes and flavours.

4. Chapel of St Francis Xavier (p257)

Built in 1928, this chapel contains paintings of the infant Christ with a Chinese Madonna.

MACAU'S BLADESMAN

Want a really special memento of your trip? One of Macau's top designers, Antonio Conceição Junior (aka Antonio Cejunior) custom-designs swords (www.arscives. com/bladesign) inspired by Macau, ancient cultures, mythology and the modern world.

The charismatic artist has designed Eastern blades such as katana, tanto and dhakris, Western sabres, hand-and-a-halves and cutlasses, as well as hybrids featuring, say, a Western-style blade with a sword guard inspired by the Harley Davidson wheel. Sleek, precise and original, they're works of contemporary art, rather than imitations of 'real' weaponry.

After he finishes the design, Antonio will recommend bladesmiths in North America who will deal directly with the customers and ship them the finished products. Interested parties should start by emailing him at antonio.cejunior@ gmail.com. Expect about one to two weeks for the design and a design fee of about US$3000.

Formerly a director of the Museum of Macau, Antonio is a versatile artist with a large repertoire spanning fashion, jewellery, medallions and book covers. His website (www.arscives.com) includes a section called 'How to Work with a Designer'. Yes, Antonio's a meticulous guy.

GRAND PRIX
SPECTATOR SPORT

(☑2855 5555; www.macau.grandprix.gov.mo) The biggest sporting event of the year is the Macau Formula 3 Grand Prix, held in the third week of November. The 6.2km Guia circuit starts near the Casino Lisboa and follows the shoreline along Avenida da Amizade, going around the reservoir and back through the city.

HIKING
HIKING

There are two trails on Guia Hill in central Macau Peninsula which are good for a stroll or jog. The Walk of 33 Curves (1.7km) circles the hill; inside this loop is the shorter Fitness Circuit Walk, with 20 exercise stations. You can access these by the Guia Cable Car.

The Islands: Taipa & Coloane

Explore

Jump on a bus to sleepy Coloane Village and take an easy two-hour stroll around here, taking in the ambience, the harbour and making stops at the Chapel of St Francis Xavier and the Tam Kong Temple. Then bus it to the Cotai Strip to check out the mega casino resorts. You can play the tables, catch a free show or have a drink. Then cab it or bus it to Taipa. Wander through Taipa Village to Avenida da Praia and spend an hour or so inside the three-part Taipa House Museum. If you're feeling peckish, Rua De Cunha is the place to go for a nice Macanese dinner or some homemade dessert. If not, check out Taipa's assortment of Chinese temples, before hitting the restaurants.

The Best...

➡ **Sight** Taipa House Museum (p255)
➡ **Place to eat** António (p258)
➡ **Place to drink** Macallan Whisky Bar & Lounge (p258)

Top Tip

The small **Taipa Flea Market** (Map p255; www.iacm.gov.mo; Bombeiros Sq, Rua do Regedor & Rua das Gaivotas; ☺11am-8pm), organised on Sunday for most parts of the year, is a good place to shop for toys and souvenirs.

Getting There & Away

Bus (between the Peninsula and Taipa) 11, 22, 28A, 30, 33, AP1; (between the Peninsula and Coloane via Taipa) 21, 21A, 2521, 21A, 25, 26, 26A.

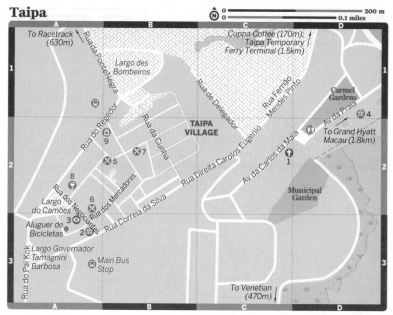

Taipa

⊙ SIGHTS

⊙ Taipa

TAIPA VILLAGE   VILLAGE

(🚌22, 26, 33) The historical part of Taipa is best preserved in this village in the south of the island. With a tidy sprawl of traditional Chinese shops and some excellent restaurants, the village is punctuated by grand colonial villas, churches and ancient temples. Avenida da Praia, a tree-lined esplanade with wrought-iron benches, is perfect for a leisurely stroll.

You can rent bicycles in Taipa Village from **Aluguer de Bicicletas** (Map p255; 📱2882 7975; 36 Largo Governador Tamagini Barbosa); there's no English sign but it's next to the Don Quixote restaurant.

TAIPA HOUSE MUSEUM   MUSEUM

Map p255 (龍環葡韻住宅式博物館; Casa Museum da Taipa; Avenida da Praia; adult/student MOP$5/3, Tue free; ⊙10am-6pm Tue-Sun; 🚌22, 28A, 26) The restored villas here were the summer residences of wealthy Macanese. The House of the Regions of Portugal showcases Portuguese traditions. The House of the Islands looks at the history of Taipa and Coloane, with displays on traditional indus-

tries, such as fishing and the manufacture of fireworks. The Macanese House offers a snapshot of life in the early 20th century.

MUSEUM OF TAIPA & COLOANE HISTORY   MUSEUM

Map p255 (路氹歷史館; Museu da História da Taipa e Coloane; Rua Correia da Silva; adult/student & senior MOP$5/2, Tue free; ⊙10am-6pm Tue-Sun; 🚌22, 28A, 26) This museum has a display of excavated relics and other artefacts on the 1st floor, while the 2nd floor

Coloane

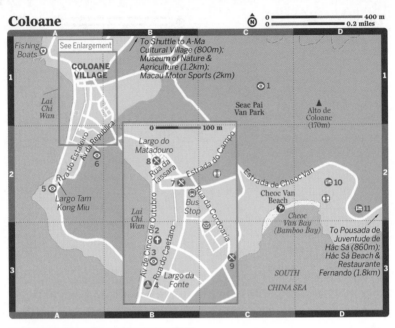

Coloane

◎ Sights   (p257)
1 A-Ma Statue & Temple........................C1
2 Chapel of St Francis Xavier B3
3 Coloane Library.................................B3
4 Kun Iam Temple.................................B3
5 Tam Kong Temple A2
6 Tin Hau Temple..................................A2

✖ Eating   (p258)
7 Café Nga Tim......................................B2
8 Lord Stow's Cafe................................B2
9 Lord Stow's Garden Café....................C3

◎ Sleeping   (p262)
10 Pousada de Coloane...........................D2
11 Pousada de Juventude de
   Cheoc Van......................................D2

contains religious objects, handicrafts and
architectural models.

CHURCH OF OUR LADY OF CARMEL CHURCH
Map p255 (Igreja de Nossa Senhora de Carmo;
Rue da Restauração; ☐22, 28A, 26) Built in
1885, this pretty church stands on a hill
overlooking the harbour, scenic Taipa Village and the pastel-coloured villas built in
1921 that now constitute the Taipa House
Museum.

PAK TAI TEMPLE TEMPLE
Map p255 (北帝廟; Templo Pak Tai; Rua do Regedor) Pak Tai Temple sits quietly in a breezy
square framed by old trees. It is dedicated
to a martial deity – the Taoist God (Tai) of
the North (Pak) – who defeated the Demon
King who was terrorising the universe. A
pair of Chinese lions guards the entrance
to the temple. On the third day of the third
lunar month each year, there are Cantonese opera performances at the temple.

POU TAI TEMPLE TEMPLE
(菩提禪院; Pou Tai Un; 5 Estrada Lou Lim Ieok;
⊙9am-6pm; ☐25, 33) This is the largest
temple complex on the islands. The main
hall, dedicated to the Three Precious Buddhas, contains an enormous bronze statue
of Lord Gautama, and there are prayer pavilions and orchid greenhouses scattered
around the complex. There's also a popular
vegetarian restaurant.

FOUR-FACED BUDDHA SHRINE SHRINE
(四面佛; O Buda de Quatro Faces; cnr Estrada
Governador Albano de Oliveira & Rua de Fat San;
☐11, 22, 26) Northeast of the Macau Jockey
Club racetrack's main entrance is this
Buddhist shrine guarded by four stone
elephants and festooned with gold leaf and
Thai-style floral bouquets. It's a popular

place to pray and make offerings before race meetings.

⊙ Coloane

CHAPEL OF ST FRANCIS XAVIER CHURCH

Map p256 (聖方濟各教堂; Capela de São Francisco Xavier; Avenida de Cinco de Outubro; ⊙10am-8pm; ☐21, 25, 26A) The highlight of Coloane village, this chapel was built in 1928 and contains paintings of the infant Christ with a Chinese Madonna, and other reminders of Christianity and colonialism in Asia. It's a quirky little place painted in yellow and embellished with red lanterns. In front of the chapel are a monument and fountain surrounded by four cannonballs that commemorate the successful – and final – routing of pirates in 1910.

COLOANE LIBRARY LIBRARY

Map p256 (路環圖書館; Rua de Cinco de Outubro, Coloane; ⊙1-7pm Mon-Sat; @; ☐21A, 25, 26A) This mini Grecian temple, built in 1917, still functions as a public library.

TEMPLES TEMPLE

(☐21A, 25, 26A) Southeast of the Chapel of St Francis Xavier, between Travessa de Caetano and Travessa de Pagode, is a small Kun Iam Temple (觀音廟), just an altar inside a little walled compound. If you walk a bit further to the southeast, you'll find a Tin Hau Temple (天后廟) up in Largo Tin Hau Miu.

At the south end of Avenida de Cinco de Outubro in Largo Tam Kong Miu, **Tam Kong Temple** (Map p256; 譚公廟; ⊙8.30am-6pm) is dedicated to a Taoist god of seafarers. To the right of the main altar is a long whale bone carved into a model of a dragon boat. To the left of the main altar is a path leading to the roof, which has views of the village and waterfront.

HÁC SÁ BEACH BEACH

off Map p256 (黑沙海灘; ☐21A, 25, 26A) Hác Sá (Black Sand) is the most popular beach in Macau. The sand is indeed a grey to blackish colour and makes the water look somewhat dirty (especially at the tide line), but it's perfectly clean. Lifeguards are on duty from 10am to 6pm Monday to Saturday and from 9am to 6pm Sunday May to October.

A-MA STATUE & TEMPLE MEMORIAL, TEMPLE

Map p256 (媽祖像及媽閣廟; Estátua da Deusa A-Ma; Estrada do Alto de Coloane) Atop Alto de Coloane (176m), this 20m-high white jade statue of the goddess who gave Macau its name was erected in 1998. Below it is **Tian Hou Temple** (天后廟; ⊙8am-7.30pm), which, together with the statue, form the core of A-Ma Cultural Village (媽祖文化村), a religious complex with a museum, retreat, medical centres and a vegetarian restaurant.

A free bus runs from the A-Ma ornamental entrance gate (媽祖文化村石牌坊) on Estrada de Seac Pai Van (bus 21A, 25, 50) half-hourly from 8am to 6pm. You can also reach both by following the Coloane Trail (Trilho de Coloane) from Seac Pai Van Park.

CHEOC VAN BEACH BEACH

Map p256 (竹灣海灘; Estrada de Cheoc Van; ☐21A, 25, 26A) About 1.5km down Estrada de Cheoc Van, which runs east and then southeast from Coloane Village, is the beach at Cheoc Van (Bamboo Bay). There are changing rooms and toilets and, in season, lifeguards on duty (from 10am to 6pm Monday to Saturday, from 9am to 6pm Sunday May to October).

FREE SEAC PAI VAN PARK PARK

Map p256 (石排灣郊野公園; Estrada de Seac Pai Van; ⊙9am-6pm Tue-Sun; ☐21A, 26A, 50) At the end of Cotai, this 20-hectare park, built in the wooded hills on the western side of the island, has somewhat unkempt gardens sprouting species of plants and trees from around the world, a children's zoo, a lake with swans and other waterfowl, and a walk-through **aviary** (小鳥天堂; ⊙9am-5pm Tue-Sun), which contains rare birds. The **Museum of Nature & Agriculture** (土地暨自然博物館; Museu Natural e Agrário; ☏2882 7277; admission free; ⊙10am-6pm Tue-Sun) has traditional farming equipment, dioramas of Coloane's ecosystem and displays cataloguing a wide range of the island's fauna and flora.

✕ EATING

✕ Taipa

TOP CHOICE BANZA PORTUGUESE $$$

(百姓餐廳; ☏2882 1519; G&H, Block 5, Edificio Nam San Garden, 154a&b, Avenida de Kwong Tung,

Taipa; meals MOP$200-500; ⊙lunch & dinner; 🚌11, 16, 28A) This welcoming place is run by a Portuguese former lawyer and gourmand who's said to have owned an amazing seafood restaurant in Boracay before opening this place. The Portuguese classics here are well executed and if you'd like, Banza could recommend a bottle from his interesting selection of Portuguese wines.

TOP CHOICE ANTÓNIO PORTUGUESE $$$

Map p255 (安東尼奧餐廳; ☎2899 9998; www.antoniomacau.com; 3 Rua dos Negociantes, Taipa; meals MOP250-1200; ⊙lunch & dinner Mon-Fri, noon-10.30pm Sat & Sun; 🚌22, 26) It's hard not to fall in love with António. The cosy mahogany-framed dining room, the meticulously thought-out menu and the entertaining and celebrated chef António Coelho all make this the place to go for all of your traditional Portuguese favourites. If you can only try one Portuguese restaurant in Macau, make it this one.

A PETISQUEIRA PORTUGUESE $$

Map p255 (葡國美食天地; ☎2882 5354; 15 Rua de São João; meals MOP$175-430; ⊙lunch & dinner; 🚌22, 28A) 'The Snackery' is an amicable place with myriad Portuguese choices set in a little alley that is easy to overlook. It serves its own *queijo fresca da casa* (homemade cheese). Try the baked seafood with rice.

O SANTOS MACANESE $$

Map p255 (☎2882 7508; 20 Rua da Cunha, Taipa; meals MOP$150-250; ⊙lunch & dinner; 🚌22, 26) Despite its location on the touristy Rua da Cunha, charming O Santos keeps its standards up. Patrons have been coming back for the chicken and rice in blood and friendly banter with the owner (a former naval chef) for 20 years.

BEIJING KITCHEN NORTHERN CHINESE $$

(滿堂彩; ☎8868 1234; 1st fl, City of Dreams, Estrada do Istmo, Cotai, Coloane-Taipa; meals from MOP$300; ⊙lunch & dinner; 🚌50, 35) This upscale restaurant does a very rare (for Hong Kong and Macau) Peking duck (MOP$320 duck, four ways, reserve when booking) that's roasted with fruit-wood, and it's excellent. The wood imparts a fragrance to the skin (crisp with a hint of melted fat), the meat (tender and flavourful), even the bones (which can be fried and served if you like). A side of (heavenly) vegetables dumplings would do very well to cleanse your palate after the duck.

POU TAI TEMPLE RESTAURANT CHINESE, VEGETARIAN $

(5 Estrada Lou Lim Ieok; dishes MOP$40-60; ⊙11am-8pm Mon-Sat, 9am-9pm Sun; 🖉) This strictly vegetarian restaurant, set in a Buddhist temple in northern Taipa, is a great find for the health conscious.

🍴 Coloane

RESTAURANTE FERNANDO PORTUGUESE $$

off Map p256 (法蘭度餐廳; ☎2888 2264; 9 Hác Sá beach; meals MOP$150-270; ⊙noon-9.30pm; 🚌21A, 25, 26A) Fernando is probably the most famous restaurant in Coloane. It has a devoted clientele and is famed for its seafood. The easy-breezy atmosphere makes it perfect for a protracted lunch by the sea. The bar stays open till midnight.

CAFÉ NGA TIM MACANESE $

Map p256 (雅憩花園餐廳; Rua Caetano, Coloane; mains MOP$70-200; ⊙noon-1am; 🚌21A, 25, 26A) We love the Chinese-Portuguese food, the small-town atmosphere, the view of the Chapel of St Francis Xavier, the prices and the owner – a guitar- and *erhu*-strumming ex-cop named Feeling.

LORD STOW'S CAFÉ CAFE $

Map p256 (安德魯咖啡店; 9 Largo do Matadouro; pastries from MOP$15, sandwiches from MOP$38; ⊙10.30am-7pm; 🚌21A, 25, 26A) Though the celebrated English baker Andrew Stow passed away, **Lord Stow's Bakery** (澳門安德魯餅店; 1 Rua da Tassara; ⊙7am-10pm Thu-Tue, to 7pm Wed) keeps his memory alive by serving his renowned *pastéis de nata*. **Lord Stow's Garden Café** (安德魯花園咖啡; 105 Rua da Cordoaria; ⊙10.30am-7pm) near the Coloane bus stop has a relaxing patio.

DRINKING

TOP CHOICE MACALLAN WHISKY BAR & LOUNGE BAR

(203, 2nd fl, Galaxy Hotel; 🚌25, 25X) Arguably the best of the new watering-holes in Macau, this handsome whisky bar features lots of oak panels, Jacobean rugs and a real fireplace. The 400-plus whisky labels include representatives from Ireland, France, Sweden and India, and a 1963 Glemorangie, besides the usual suspects. It opens at 5pm.

CLUB CUBIC
CLUB, DJ

(www.cubic-cod.com; 2105-02, City of Dreams, Estrada do Istmo, Cotai; 🚌50, 35) Spanning some 2700 sq metres, the flashy, two-level Club Cubic at the Hard Rock Hotel features themed rooms, a champagne bar and a large 'disco' ball that can hold up to four people. There are DJs mixing a variety of tunes, including hip hop, techno and Korean pop, that are pumped out of the club's top-notch sound system.

MCSORLEY'S ALE HOUSE
PUB

(麥時利愛爾蘭酒吧; Shop 1038, Venetian Macao Resort Hotel, Estrada da Baía de Nossa Senhora da Esperança, Taipa; 🚌25, 25X) This cosy tavern-style watering hole in the Venetian is a genial spot that attracts rugby and soccer fanatics watching footy on the telly with its live-satellite broadcasts of European matches. The selection of imported beers and pub grub is extensive and reasonably priced.

OLD TAIPA TAVERN
PUB

Map p255 (好客鄉村餐廳; 21 Rua dos Negociantes, Taipa; 🚌22, 28A, 26; 🕿) Known as 'OTT', its location near the Pak Tai Temple at Taipa Village makes this delightful bar a sublime spot to watch the comings and goings in the centre of the village. Local bands perform on Mondays from 8pm to midnight.

CUPPA COFFEE
CAFE

off Map p255 (104 Rua Fernão Mendes Pinto, Taipa; ⊙8am-8pm; 🕿; 🚌25, 26;) A laid-back cafe favoured by hipsters and travellers, this place serves (besides a decent cuppa) freshly baked bread, yummy sandwiches and a variety of healthy and great-tasting smoothies.

 ## ENTERTAINMENT

GALAXY MACAU CASINO
CASINO

(澳門銀河綜合渡假城; 🚌25,25X) The latest addition to Macau's gaming firmament is Hong Kong-owned Galaxy. The massive 'palace-inspired' complex has soaring ambitions targeted at China's mass market, and it's obvious. The casino is dripping with metaphors for wealth and auspiciousness, and it has announced plans to double its size, with a new wing that will house two new hotels, 500 more gambling tables and more retail outlets. Galaxy is within walking distance of the Venetian and City of Dreams.

🏃 SPORTS & ACTIVITIES

🚶 Taipa

HORSE RACING
HORSE RACING

Regular flat racing takes place at the **Taipa racetrack** (Hipodromo da Taipa; 🚌11, 22, 25) of the **Macau Jockey Club** (澳門賽馬會; Jockey Clube de Macau; ☎ 2882 1188, racing information hotline 2882 0868; www.macauhorse.com; Estrada Governador Albano de Oliveira; admission MOP$20; 🚌11, 15, 22) throughout the year, usually on Saturday or Sunday from 2pm, and midweek (generally Tuesday or Wednesday) from 5pm. Summer recess lasts from late August to mid-September.

CYCLING
CYCLING

There are two cycling trails in Taipa. The longer Taipa Grande trail (bus 21A, 26, 28A) can be accessed via a paved road off the Estrada Colonel Nicolau de Mesquita, near the United Chinese Cemetery; whereas the Taipa Pequena Trail (bus 21A, 33, 35) is reachable by way of Estrada Lou Lim Ieok, behind the Regency Hotel. Bicycles can be rented from a kiosk near the bus stop adjacent to the Museum of Taipa and Coloane History in Taipa Village. Cycling across the Macau–Taipa bridges is prohibited.

HIKING
HIKING

The Little Taipa Trail (Trilho de Taipa Pequena) is a 2km-long circuit around a hill (111m) of that name in northwestern Taipa, reachable via Estrada Lou Lim Ieok. The 2.2km-long Big Taipa Trail (Trilho de Taipa Grande) rings Taipa Grande, a 160m-high hill at the eastern end of the island. You can access the trail via a short paved road off Estrada Colonel Nicolau de Mesquita.

🚶 Coloane

WATERSPORTS EQUIPMENT STANDS
WATER SPORTS

(水上運動器材出租處) There are watersports equipment stands, where you can hire windsurfing boards, jet skis and water scooters, at either end of Hác Sá beach.

COLOANE TRAIL
HIKING

Coloane's and Macau's longest trail, the 8100m Coloane Trail (Trilho de Coloane),

MACAU THE ISLANDS: TAIPA & COLOANE

NEED TO KNOW

Rates

Most large hotels add a 10% service charge and 5% government tax to the bill. Rates shoot up on Friday or Saturday, while during the week you can find incredible deals at travel agencies and the following:

Macau.com (www.macau.com)

Agoda (www.agoda.com)

Shun Tak Centre (200 Connaught Rd, Sheung Wan, Hong Kong)

Macau Ferry Terminal Check for information in the arrival hall.

Shuttle Buses

Most midrange and top-end hotels have shuttle buses to/from the ferry terminal and, for those on the Cotai Strip, also to/from the peninsula.

begins in the mid-section of Estrada do Alto de Coloane (bus 21A, stop Estrata Do Campo, enter Estrata Militar across the road, after 600m, turn right) and winds around the island. You can make a detour to Alto de Coloane (170m) to see the A-Ma Statue.

The shorter Northeast Coloane Trail (Trilho Nordeste de Coloane), near Ká Hó, runs for about 3km. Other trails that offer good hiking include the 1.5km-long Altinho de Ká Hó Trail and the 1.5km-long Hác Sá Reservoir Circuit (Circuito da Barragem de Hác Sá), which both loop around the reservoir to the northwest of Hác Sá beach.

MACAU MOTOR SPORTS CLUB GO-KARTING

off Map p256 (☑2888 2126; Estrada de Seac Pai Van, Coloane; per 10/20min MOP$100/180; ☽11:30am-7pm Mon-Fri, 11am-8pm Sat & Sun; ☐21A, 25) This club runs a kartodrome (小型賽車場) which has a picturesque 1.2km professional go-karting circuit at the southern end of the Cotai Strip.

MACAU GOLF & COUNTRY CLUB GOLF

(澳門高爾夫球鄉村俱樂部; ☑2887 1188; www.macaugolfandcountryclub.com; 1918 Estrada de Hác Sá; ☐15) The 18-hole, par-71 course at Macau Golf & Country Club, connected to the Westin Resort Macau on Coloane by walkway on the 9th floor, is open to foreigners through the hotel. Green fees are MOP$1550/2880 on weekdays/weekends, and you must have a handicap certificate to tee off. There's also a **driving range** (☑2887 1111; per 40 balls MOP$45), from where you drive balls into the ocean.

🛏 SLEEPING

The vast majority of new hotels in Macau are aimed at the moneyed rather than budget travellers, so you have to look hard for good budget sleeping options. But for those with the cash, there are world-class choices.

Macau Peninsula has the greatest range of accommodation that is close to the major sights. Lodging on the islands comprise big casino hotels or reasonably priced options that are a little out of the way.

All rooms have air-conditioning and a bathroom unless otherwise stated. Prices listed here are the rack rates quoted to walk-in customers.

🛏 Macau Peninsula

TOP CHOICE **POUSADA DE MONG HÁ** INN $$

Map p236 (澳門望廈迎賓館; ☑2851 5222; www.ift.edu.mo; Colina de Mong Há; r MOP$600-1200, ste from MOP$1200; ☀@🛜; ☐5, 22, 25) Sitting atop Mong Há Hill near the ruins of a fort built in 1849 is this Portuguese-style inn run by students at the Instituto de Formação Turística (Institute for Tourism Studies). Rooms are well appointed (some

ACCOMMODATION PRICES

Breakfast is usually included with hotels marked $$ and $$$.

$	under MOP$700
$$	MOP$700–MOP$2000
$$$	over MOP$2000

equipped with computers) and service attentive. Rates include breakfast. Discounts of 25% to 40% midweek and off season.

TOP CHOICE MANDARIN ORIENTAL LUXURY HOTEL $$$

Map p236 (☑8805 8888; www.mandarin oriental.com/macau; Avenida Dr Sun Yat Sen, NAPE; r MOP$3500-4500, ste MOP$6200-7000; ☺@☎☒) A great high-end option, the new Mandarin has everything associated with the brand – elegance, superlative service, comfortable rooms and excellent facilities. Though not big in size, it's a refreshing contrast to the glossy casino hotels.

POUSADA DE SÃO TIAGO HISTORIC HOTEL $$$

Map p236 (☑2837 8111; www.saotiago.com.mo; Fortaleza de São Tiago da Barra, Avenida de República; ste MOP$3000-4200; ☺@☒; ☐6, 9, 28B) Built into the ruins of the 17th-century Barra Fort, the landmark São Tiago is the most romantic place to stay in Macau. No other hotels in Macau can boast such a rich history. All 12 rooms have been renovated and upgraded to elegantly furnished suites, and it still has an old-world grandeur. Discounts of up to 35% off season.

MGM GRAND MACAU CASINO HOTEL $$$

Map p236 (☑8802 1888; www.mgmgrand macau.com; Avenida Dr Sun Yat Sen, NAPE; r from MOP$3200, ste from MOP$7800; ☺@☒; ☐8, 3A, 12) This casino hotel has a youthful vibe and contemporary architecture featuring a baroque-inspired wave motif that's repeated inside the stylish rooms. Choose the seaside rooms for the sweeping harbour views. Other reasons for staying here are the optically fantastic spa and the classy drinking places. Discounts of 35% to 50% off season.

HOTEL SINTRA HOTEL $$

Map p236 (澳門新麗華酒店; ☑2871 0111; www.hotelsintra.com; Avenida de Do João IV; r MOP$1250-1900, ste from MOP$2360; ☐3, 11, 22) This centrally located three-star hotel is great value. The rooms are spotless and the staff polite. Our only complaint is the slow lift. Oh, and rooms facing the Grand Emperor Hotel may find the big LED screen disturbing. Discounts of up to 50% midweek.

ROCKS HOTEL BOUTIQUE HOTEL $$$

Map p236 (☑2295 6528; www.rockshotel.com.mo; Macau Fisherman's Wharf; r MOP$1880-2980, ste from MOP$4080; ☺☎; ☐3A, 5, 23;) This elegant Victorian-style boutique hotel is set amid a tribal-hut African restaurant and casino. All rooms feature a balcony, most with a view of the bay. And unlike most hotels in Macau, Rocks doesn't come with a casino.

SOFITEL MACAU AT PONTE 16 CASINO HOTEL $$$

Map p240 (澳門十六浦索菲特大酒店; ☑8861 0016; www.sofitel.com; Rua do Visconde Paço de Arcos; r MOP$1420-2220, ste from MOP$4220; ☎; ☐1, 3, 4;) This reasonably priced luxury hotel from a high-end chain offers some atmospheric views of the sleepy Inner Harbour and the ruins of São Paulo on the other side. Rooms are modern and large, and the beds are inviting.

RIVIERA HOTEL MACAU HOTEL $$

Map p236 (濠璟酒店; ☑2833 9955; www.rivi erahotel.com.mo; 11-13 Rua do Comendador Kou Ho Neng; r MOP$1080-1180, ste from MOP$2080; ☐9, 16, 28B) If you prefer somewhere more secluded, head to this hotel near the legendary Bela Vista. Most rooms have wonderful views of the historic Avenida da República and Sai Van Lake from the balconies.

OLE LONDON HOTEL INN $

Map p240 (澳萊英京酒店; ☑2893 7761; http:// olelondonhotel.com; 4-6 Praça de Ponte e Horta; d MOP$390-480; @☎; ☐2, 7, 10A) This inn near the Inner Harbour has smart, spotless rooms. They are small, but given its location and rates you can't really complain. Bigger discounts if you book via www. macau.com.

NEW NAM PAN HOTEL GUESTHOUSE $

Map p240 (新南濱賓館; ☑2848 2842; www. cnMacauHotel.com; 2nd fl, 8 Avenida de D Joao IV; s/d/tr/q MOP$380/580/780/880, with increases on weekends of MOP$100-200; ☎; ☐3, 5, 10) Central location, a rustic vibe and eight spotless rooms make New Nan Pan a good budget option.

VILA UNIVERSAL GUESTHOUSE $

Map p240 (大利迎賓館; ☑2857 3247, 2857 5602; Cheng Peng Bldg, 73 Rua Felicidade; s/d from MOP$280/350; ☎; ☐3, 6, 26) Fish tanks, seashell displays and yellow sofas in the lobby impart a homely atmosphere, but the 32 rooms, though clean and decent, are more impersonal. Expect to pay MOP$50 to MOP$80 more on weekends

SAN VA HOSPEDARIA　　GUESTHOUSE $

Map p240 (新華大旅店; ☑2857 3701; www.san vahotel.com; 65-67 Rua de Felicidade; d/tw with shared bathroon MOP$150-270; ☒3, 6, 26A) Built in 1873, San Va is about the cheapest and most atmospheric lodging in town (Wong Kar-wai filmed parts of *2046* here). It's also very basic, with tiny rooms and shared bathrooms. At the time of writing, the air-conditioned rooms, rooms with private showers and access to the patio are closed until after 2012.

AUGUSTERS LODGE　　GUESTHOUSE $

Map p240 (☑2871 3242, 6664 5026; www.au gusters.de; Flat 3j, Block 4, Kam Loi Bldg, 24 Rua do Dr Pedro Jose Lobo; dm from MOP$130/person; ☎; ☒6, 11, 19) Something of a backpackers' hub, this tiny, friendly guesthouse has basic but clean rooms with shared bathrooms and a kitchen. It's above the CTM shop and it's always full. You get 15% off if you book in advance.

MACAU MASTERS HOTEL　　HOTEL $$

Map p240 (萬事發酒店; ☑2893 7572; www.mas tershotel-macau.com; 162 Rua das Lorchas; s/d from MOP$680/980; ☉☎; ☒1, 2, 10) A shabby exterior hides a smartly maintained hotel with small, well-equipped, if somewhat outmoded, rooms. Electricity supply is sometimes unstable and the lift is slow.

🛏 The Islands

⭐TOP CHOICE POUSADA DE COLOANE　　HOTEL $$

Map p256 (路環竹灣酒店; ☑2882 2143; www. hotelpcoloane.com.mo; Estrada de Cheoc Van, Coloane; r from MOP$750; ☒21A, 25; @✉) This 30-room hotel with its Portuguese-style rooms (all with balconies and sea views) is great value, though some rooms are better maintained than others. And the location above Cheoc Van beach is about as chilled as you'll find. Rates drop considerably during midweek. Discounts of 20% to 40% off season.

POUSADA DE JUVENTUDE DE CHEOC VAN　　HOSTEL $

Map p256 (☑2888 2024; www.dsej.gov.mo; Rua de António Francisco, Coloane; dm/tw/q from $100/160/120; ☒21A, 25, 26A) This beachside hostel under the government's Education and Youth Affairs Bureau is excellent value, but you need to book three months in advance and show an International Youth Card or International Youth Hostel Card upon check-in. Men and women are separated. Other conditions apply. See website for details.

POUSADA DE JUVENTUDE DE HÁC SÁ　　HOSTEL $

off Map p256 (☑2888 2024; Rua de Hác Sá Long Chao Kok, Coloane) Same beachside deal as Pousada de Juventude de Cheoc Van, but slightly different location.

GRAND HYATT MACAU　　CASINO HOTEL $$$

off Map p255 (☑8868 1234; http://macau.grand. hyatt.com; City of Dreams, Estrada do Istmo, Cotai; r MOP$1300-3200, ste from MOP$2300; ☉@☎✉; ☒35, 50;) The most tasteful of the casino hotels on the Cotai Strip, the Grand Hyatt is part of the City of Dreams casino-shopping-performance complex. The massive rooms come with glass-and-marble showering areas and a full battery of technology.

BANYAN TREE LUXURY HOTEL　　LUXURY HOTEL $$$

(☑8883 8833; www.banyantree.com/en/macau; Galaxy, Avenida Marginal Flor de Lotus, Cotai; ste MOP$2880-63,800, villas MOP$23,600-35,100; ☒25, 25X) One of two hotels at the new Galaxy Macau, this extravagant resort recreates tropical-style luxury in Macau. All 10 villas come with private gardens and swimming pools, while the suites have huge baths set by the window. If you need more pampering, there's a spa with state-of-the-art facilities. Slightly more affordable than Banyan Tree is the other hotel at the Galaxy, **Okura** (www.hotelokuramacau.com; r MOP$2200-5600, ste MOP$3000-20,000), which offers luxury with a Japanese twist.

Sleeping

In a city where real estate is the price of gold, money makes all the difference when you're seeking accommodation. If you have cash, you'll be spoiled for choice, so wide is the range of luxurious places. The midrange options are less inspiring but adequate, while further down, the pickings get thinner – the defining feature here is hostels with tiny rooms.

New Trends

Since the easing of cross-border travel restrictions by China in 2003, mainland visitors have become the single largest market for Hong Kong. As most of them are middle class and are here to shop, they seek out midrange lodging in central locations. This has led to a proliferation of hotels and serviced apartments falling in the middle of the price spectrum that cater to these tourists as well as trade-fair regulars.

To keep their edge, more and more hotels, including upmarket ones, are offering long-stay deals and low-season discounts.

It's worth noting that during peak seasons, the rates at some of the new midrange hotels, especially those in Wan Chai, Yau Ma Tei and Tsim Sha Tsui, can be up to five times the low-season rates. This discrepancy is not as marked in top-end hotels (some have even reduced prices to stay competitive) or the cheapest places.

Keep in mind that whatever your budget, accommodation costs are generally higher in Hong Kong than in most other Asian cities, but cheaper than in Europe and the US.

Top-End Hotels

Hong Kong's luxury hotels are locked in an arms race for the dollars of affluent travellers. Their weapons are superstar restaurants, lavish spa complexes and smooth service catering to your most footling whims. It doesn't come cheaply though. Prices for top-of-the-range hotels start from about $1600 per room. A few of them offer comfort, amenities and service that compete with or surpass that of the world's finest five-star hotels.

Midrange Hotels

While midrange hotels used to be generic business and/or leisure establishments with little to distinguish one from another, many new places have sprung up that are uniquely cool to look at and easy on the pocket, with room rates hovering in the high hundreds and dipping to budget range in the low season. Rooms at these places tend to be small and come with limited cable TV, wireless broadband connection and room service.

Guesthouses

Dominating the lower end of the accommodation market are guesthouses, usually a block of tiny rooms squeezed into a converted apartment or two. Often several guesthouses operate out of the same building. Your options are greater if there are two of you; find a double room in a clean guesthouse for $200 to $250 and your accommodation costs will fall sharply. Some offer dormitory accommodation for those on tight budgets.

Though rooms are small, the places listed here are clean and cheerily shabby or neat and austere, rather than grim and grimy. All have air-con and most have TVs, phones and private bathrooms. Anything under $600 should be considered budget.

Depending on the season, try to negotiate a better deal, as a lot of places will be eager to fill empty rooms. Most guesthouses offer some sort of internet access, from a communal PC to free in-room wi-fi.

Serviced Apartments

Those staying in Hong Kong for over a month may be interested in serviced apartments. These range in size from studios to three-bedroomers, and usually come with a kitchen, cooking and eating utensils, maid service and laundry facilities. Plusher ones may even have DVD players, a pool and gym.

Hostels & Campsites

The **Hong Kong Youth Hostels Association** (香港青年旅舍協會; HKYHA; ☎2788 1638; www.yha.org.hk; Shop 118, 1st fl, Fu Cheong Shopping Centre, Shum Mong Rd, Sham Shui Po; Ⓜ Nam Cheong, exit A) maintains eight hostels affiliated with Hostelling International (HI). It also sells HKYHA and HI cards. If you haven't applied for membership in your own country, visit the HKYHA office or the hostels to do so. Be sure to take along a visa-sized photo and ID.

All HKYHA hostels have separate toilets and showers for men and women, and cooking facilities. They provide blankets, pillows and sheet bags. Most have lockers available.

Prices for a bed in a dormitory range from $45 to $110 a night, depending on the hostel and whether you are a junior (under 18 years of age) or senior member.

The **Country & Marine Parks Authority** (☎1823; www.afcd.gov.hk) maintains 40 basic campsites in the New Territories and Outlying Islands that are intended for walkers and hikers.

Low-Season Discounts

Don't be shocked by the rack rates! Many hotels slash prices by up to 70% for nightly stays outside the peak season.

➡ Garden View (p267)
➡ Metropark (p270)
➡ Harbour View (p270)
➡ Wifi Boutique Hotel (p270)
➡ City Garden Hotel (p272)
➡ BP International (p274)
➡ Stanford Hillview Hotel (p275)
➡ Kowloon Hotel (p274)
➡ Knutsford Hotel (p275)

➡ Hotel Panorama (p276)
➡ Eaton Smart (p278)

Packages

As well as the serviced apartments listed here, many of the hotels and guesthouses reviewed offer long-term deals and/or packages for stays of a week or more; some are available only with advanced booking. Remember to inquire when you reserve a room.

➡ Garden View (p267)
➡ Harbour View (p270)
➡ Mingle Place by the Park (p270)
➡ Ying King Apartment (p271)
➡ Cosmopolitan Hotel (p271)
➡ Chung Kiu Inn (p272)
➡ City Garden Hotel Hong Kong (p272)
➡ Butterfly on Prat (p275)
➡ Eaton Smart (p278)
➡ Anne Black YWCA (p279)

Facilities

Unless specified otherwise, all rooms listed here have private bathrooms and air-conditioning, and all but the cheapest will have cable TV in English. Almost all midrange to top-end hotels, and most guesthouses, offer broadband and/or wi-fi access, as well as computers for guests' use. All hotels midrange and above, and some budget places have nonsmoking floors, or are nonsmoking.

Accommodation Websites

Lonely Planet (hotels.lonelyplanet.com) Has listings of hostels, B&Bs and hotels, and online booking service.

Hong Kong Hotels Association (www.hkha.org) For the booking of hotels under the association.

Traveller Services (香港旅遊; www.travel ler.com.hk) For accommodation in Hong Kong, Macau and Shēnzhèn.

Phoenix Services Agency (峯寧旅運社; www.statravel.hk) Online booking of relatively affordable accommodation.

Hong Kong Tourism Board (www.discover hongkong.com) Lets you search some 200 licensed hotels and guesthouses in Hong Kong.

Lonely Planet's Top Choice

Peninsula Hong Kong (p274) World-class luxury and colonial elegance at the harbour end of Tsim Sha Tsui.

Upper House (p269) A Zen-like atmosphere, yoga on the lawn and warm service overlooking the hills in Admiralty.

Hyatt Regency Tsim Sha Tsui (p273) This self-assured veteran offers well-appointed rooms and smooth service from a prime location.

T Hotel (p272) A hidden gem in Pok Fu Lam run by the charming students of the hospitality institute.

Hotel Icon (p273) Professionals and students of hotel management deliver pristine service in cool, contemporary surroundings.

Best by Budget

$
Helena May (p269)
Y-Loft Square Youth Hostel (p272)
Salisbury (p274)
Hop Inn (p276)

$$
Hotel LKF (p268)
Harbour View (p270)
Madera (p276)
Hotel LBP (p268)
Fleming (p271)

$$$
Mandarin Oriental (p267)
Four Seasons (p267)
Landmark Oriental (p267)
Hyatt Regency Tsim Sha Tsui (p273)

Best for Children

InterContinental Hong Kong (p275)
Burlington II (p270)
Salisbury (p274)
Island Shangri-la (p269)
BP International (p274)
Boat Moksha (p273)

Best for Clubbing

Lan Kwai Fong Hotel (p268)
Metropark (p270)
Knutsford Hotel (p275)
Stanford Hillview Hotel (p275)
Empire Kowloon (p275)
Minden (p276)

Best for Scenery

Pilgrim's Hall (p190)
Bradbury Jockey Club Youth Hostel (p190)
Ritz-Carlton (p276)
Garden View (p267)
Hyatt Regency Sha Tin (p190)

Best for Design

Hotel Icon (p273)
Lanson Place (p271)
Landmark Oriental (p267)
Putman (p267)
Nic & Trig's (p280)

Best Retro Vibe

Nic & Trig's (p280)
Mariner's Club (p273)
Mei Ho House Youth Hostel (p276)

Best for Quirkiness

Boat Moksha (p273)
Mingle Place by the Park (p270)
Dragon Inn (p277)
Cosmopolitan (p271)

NEED TO KNOW

Price Ranges
Nightly rates for a double room:
→ **$** Up to $900
→ **$$** $900–$1500
→ **$$$** Over $1500

Monthly rates for a one-bedroom apartment:
→ **$** Up to $15,000
→ **$$** $15,000–$25,000
→ **$$$** Over $25,000

High Season
When big trade fairs come to town, accommodation in Wan Chai (and areas with easy access to Wan Chai, such as Tsim Sha Tsui) is very tight and prices rocket. Check exact dates at www.discoverhongkong.com.
→ January, March to early May (trade-fair season)
→ October–November
→ Chinese New Year (late January or February)

Reservations
Booking a room is not essential outside peak periods, but during the shoulder and low seasons, you can get discounts of up to 50% off rack rates if you book online, through a travel agent or with the **Hong Kong Hotels Association** (香港酒店業協會; HKHA; ☏2383 8380; www.hkha.org), which has reservation centres on level 5 of the airport.

Taxes
Most midrange and top-end hotels and a small number of budget places add 10% service and 3% government tax to your bill.

SLEEPING

Where to Stay

Neighbourhood	For	Against
Hong Kong Island: Central	Close to the Star Ferry pier, famous skyscrapers and luxury malls; within walking distance of bars and eats; good transport links.	The nearest eats, sleeps, bars and shops are pricey; gets quiet after office hours.
Hong Kong Island: the Peak & the Northwest	In the thick of the nightlife and dining action; close to the Peak and the historic sites in Sheung Wan.	Sloping topography, hence more trips up- and downhill; districts further west are quiet and away from the action.
Hong Kong Island: Wan Chai & the Northeast	Good for Hong Kong Park, Happy Valley Racecourse and shopping; abundant eating and drinking options; great transport links.	Wan Chai and Causeway Bay are traffic-choked and crowded; districts further east are a little worn and far away.
Hong Kong Island: Aberdeen & the South	Great for Aberdeen Typhoon Shelter, Stanley Market, Horizon Plaza, swimming and hiking around Repulse Bay and Shek O.	Not central, frequent traffic jams near Aberdeen Tunnel, limited sleeps, eats, bars and shops.
Kowloon	Convenient for Museum of Art and of History, best views of the harbour; great for shopping, eating, even 'slumming'; cool mix of old and new, high-brow and low-heel; great transport links.	Crowded and traffic-choked around Nathan Rd; some areas can be touristy and/or a little seedy.
New Territories	Fewer crowds, fresher air; handy for outdoor sports, nature tours, walled villages; prices generally lower.	Far from the action; fewer eats, sleeps, bars and shops; little to do at night.
Outlying Islands	Laid-back vibe, nice setting, good for seafood on Lamma, windsurfing on Cheung Chau, hiking the Lantau Trail and loads of beaches.	Longer time spent commuting; fewer eats, sleeps, bars and shops; activities dependent on weather.

🛏 Hong Kong Island: Central

The lion's share of Hong Kong Island's luxury hotels is in Central, catering predominantly to moneyed leisure travellers and busy, corporate types. The service and facilities you'll find here are the best in town. Whether it's child-minding service, dinner reservations or combating jetlag you need, it will be done with efficiency, and possibly a smile.

FOUR SEASONS LUXURY HOTEL **$$$**

Map p362 (四季酒店; ☎3196 8888; www.fourseasons.com/hongkong; 8 Finance St, Central; r $4500-6500, ste $9300-63,000; @☎⚡; ⓜHong Kong, exit F) The Four Seasons arguably edges into top place on the island for its amazing views and its location close to the Star Ferry, Hong Kong station, the inland and Sheung Wan. It also features palatial rooms and a glorious pool and spa complex. Its restaurants, Lung King Heen and Caprice, both have three Michelin stars. Service is pristine and personable.

MANDARIN ORIENTAL LUXURY HOTEL **$$$**

Map p362 (文華東方酒店; ☎2522 0111; www.mandarinoriental.com/hong kong/; 5 Connaught Rd, Central; r $3800-6000, ste from $6500-45,000, Landmark Oriental d from $5200, ste $9300; @☎⚡; ⓜ Central, exit J3) The venerable Mandarin has historically set the standard in Asia (it was named one of world's top 11 hotels), and continues to be a contender for the top spot, despite competition from the likes of the Four Seasons. The styling, service, food and atmosphere are stellar throughout and there's a sense of gracious, old-world charm. It's also home to a great restaurant, Pierre. The sleek **Landmark Oriental** (Map p362; ☎2132 0088; 15 Queen's Rd Central; r $3500-6800, ste $9300-45,000; @☎⚡), just across the way, offers modern luxury, but with a business vibe throughout, including at its restaurant Amber.

GARDEN VIEW HOTEL **$$**

Map p370 (女青年會園景軒; ☎2877 3737; http://the-garden-view-ywca.hotel-rn.com; 1 MacDonnell Rd, Central; r/ste low season $880/1760, high season $2500/2900, weekly per day from $1500, per month from $19,500; @⚡; ⓠgreen minibus 1A) Straddling the border of Central and the Mid-Levels, the YWCA-run Garden View is favoured by families and professionals with a smaller expense account. Its 133 rooms overlook the Zoological & Botanical Gardens, and are very close to a large supermarket and the restaurants in Admiralty, including Pure Veggie House. Accommodation here is plain but quiet and functional, and comes with an outdoor swimming pool. No free wi-fi. Daily rates drop substantially in the low season.

🛏 Hong Kong Island: the Peak & the Northwest

PUTMAN SERVICED APARTMENTS **$$**

Map p368 (☎2233 2233; www.theputman.com; 202-206 Queen's Rd Central; studios $1000-1200, flats $2400, studios/flats per month from $23,000/48,000; @☎; ⓜSheung Wan, exit A or E) Behind the art deco-inspired glass facade, this designer outfit has three cool-toned studios for shorter stays and 25 one-bedroom flats for long-term rental. Each flat occupies an entire storey and the floor-to-ceiling windows allow a lot of natural light. You also get space (the flats are 120 sq metres and the studios are 30 sq metres to 40 sq metres) and impeccable taste here. The kitchens come with designer cooking utensils, crockery, stemware and laundry facilities. Prices include membership to a gym nearby.

BAUHINIA SERVICED APARTMENTS **$**

Map p368 (寶軒酒店; ☎2156 3000; www.apartments.com.hk; 119-121 Connaught Rd Central; 1-bed flats per month $15,500-19,000, 2-bed flats per month $20,000-28,000, r $2500-2900; ⓜSheung Wan, exit A1) Bauhinia now has 42 rooms for daily rental in addition to its original serviced apartments. Rooms are small but spotless and you can't complain about the location, which is right next to the MTR station. Staff are friendly and service efficient. Enter from Man Wah Lane.

BISHOP LEI INTERNATIONAL HOUSE HOTEL **$**

Map p368 (宏基國際賓館; ☎2868 0828; www.bishopleihtl.com.hk; 4 Robinson Rd, the Mid-Levels; s/d/ste from $650/700/1250; @⚡; ⓠ23 or 40) This hotel in residential Mid-Levels, though out of the way, provides a lot of bang for your buck. It boasts good service, a swimming pool, a gym and proximity to the Zoological & Botanical Gardens. The standard single and double rooms are small. It's worth paying a little more for the larger, harbour-facing rooms, which offer good views of the skyline and the cathedral from high up. Buses to Central and Wan Chai stop in front of the hotel.

HOTEL LBP
BUSINESS HOTEL $$$

Map p368 (西關酒店; ☎2681 9388; www.hotel lbp.com.hk; 77-91 Queen's Rd W; r $1100-1820, monthly packages from $17,000; @🛜; Ⓜ Sheung Wan) Just 600m west of Sheung Wan MTR station, this new kid on the block is a good-value choice. Each of the 46 rooms has at least 21 sq metres, a reasonable size by Hong Kong standards. The decor won't wow you, but you'll feel comfy and clean enough. Rooms facing south offer views of Hollywood Rd Park.

COURTYARD BY
MARRIOTT HONG KONG
BUSINESS HOTEL $$$

(香港萬怡酒店; ☎3717 8888; www.marriott. com/hotel-search/china/; 167 Connaught Rd W; r $1560-2440, ste $3450; @🛜; 🚌5 or 5B from Central) This hotel juggles luxury with limited space and it works. Most rooms offer harbour views and are smartly decorated with modern furnishings. The plump beds and high-thread-count sheets guarantee you a good night's sleep. Service is impeccable. There's an Airbus stop across the street.

DORSETT REGENCY HOTEL
HONG KONG
HOTEL $$$

(香港帝盛酒店; ☎2655 5333; www.dorsett regency.com; 18 Davis Street, Kennedy Town; r $1200-2500, ste $4200; @🛜🏊; 🚌5B or 5X from Central) Tucked away in Kennedy Town, the west end of Hong Kong Island, this boutique hotel has 209 well-lit rooms with modern design. The rooms are moderately sized and all have free wi-fi. It's worth the extra buck for the larger, harbour-view room. There are enough buses linking Kennedy Town to Central, and the complimentary shuttle service (hourly departure) to Sheung Wan, Hong Kong station and Wan Chai is there in case you feel a little isolated.

YWCA BUILDING
SERVICED APARTMENTS $$

Map p368 (女青大廈; ☎2915 2345; www.ywca. org.hk; 38c Bonham Rd, the Mid-Levels; studios per month from $9500, 1-bedroom apt $18,800; 🚌23, 40 or 40M) This YWCA has 99 studios and apartments, open to men and women. It's out of the way, but accessible by bus from Admiralty and Central. All rooms require a minimum stay of seven nights.

HOTEL LKF
HOTEL $$$

Map p366 (隆堡蘭桂坊酒店; ☎3518 9688; www.hotel-lkf.com.hk; 33 Wyndham St, Central; r from $3500, ste from $5000; @🛜; Ⓜ Central, exit D2) Located on the upper, flatter section of Wydham St, Hotel LKF is arguably the best gateway to the Lan Kwai Fong action, but is far enough above it not to be disturbed by it. It has high-tech rooms in muted tones and they brim with all the trimmings you'll need: fluffy bathrobes, espresso machines and free bedtime milk and cookies. There's a plush spa and yoga studio in the building.

LAN KWAI FONG HOTEL
BOUTIQUE HOTEL $$$

Map p368 (蘭桂坊酒店@九如坊; ☎3650 0000; www.lankwaifonghotel.com.hk; 3 Kau U Fong, Central; r/ste from $1480/2880; @🛜; Ⓜ Sheung Wan, exit E2) This well-located hotel (not to be confused with Hotel LKF) is closer to SOHO than Lan Kwai Fong. The Chinese decor with a contemporary twist adds an aesthetic touch to the reasonably spacious digs. The service is top-notch.

BUTTERFLY ON
WELLINGTON
BOUTIQUE HOTEL $$$

Map p368 (晉逸精品酒店中環; ☎3962 1688; www.butterflyhk.com; 122 Wellington St, Central; r $2800-3600, ste $5000; @🛜; Ⓜ Sheung Wan, exit D2) Sitting in the heart of Soho, the Butterfly is just a stone's throw from the Central Escalators. The market and shops on Wellington St are closed in the evening, so having a good sleep is not a problem. The rooms are fresh-looking and tastefully appointed with an oriental touch. Hefty discounts (as low as $900) are offered in quiet months. Its branch **Butterfly on Hollywood** (晉逸好萊塢精品酒店; Map p368; ☎3962 8357; www.butterflyhk.com; 263 Hollywood Rd; r $1850-2500, ste $4500; @🛜; Ⓜ Central, exit E2) has rooms with a modern design and offers more discounts.

IBIS
HOTEL $$

Map p368 (上環宜必思酒店; ☎2252 2929; www.ibishotel.com; 18-30 Des Voeux Rd W; @; 🚌5B from Central) Scheduled to open in late 2012, the 550-room Ibis will provide a more affordable option in this expensive part of town.

HANLUN HABITATS
SERVICED APARTMENTS $$$

Map p366 (☎2868 0168; www.hanlunhabitats. com; 21st fl, Winway Bldg, 50 Wellington St, Central; Ⓜ Central, exit D2) This agency has three properties with serviced and furnished flats within striking distance of each other in the Mid-Levels and they can be easily accessed, via the Central Escalator, from Central and Soho. **Orchid** (Map p368; 22 Mosque St, the Mid-Levels; ☎; Ⓜ Central, exit D1) has one-bedroom flats measuring about 44 sq metres from $22,000 a month. **Peach Blossom** (Map p368; 15 Mosque St, the Mid-Levels; ☎; Ⓜ Central, exit D1) has one-bedroom flats of about 52 sq metres for $28,000. **Lily Court** (Map p368; 28 Robinson Rd, the Mid-Levels; ☎; 🚌 26) has one-bedroom flats of about 48 sq metres for around $26,000.

JOCKEY CLUB MOUNT DAVIS HOSTEL
HOSTEL $

(賽馬會摩星嶺青年旅舍; ☎ 2817 5715; www.yha.org.hk; Mt Davis Path, Kennedy Town; dm members under/over 18yr $75/110, 2-/4-/6-bed r members $300/460/680; @☎; 🚌 5, green minibus 54) This hostel was under renovation at the time of writing, so expect to see improved facilities when you check in. It's on a prime spot atop Mt Davis, so great views of Victoria Harbour are guaranteed. It's far away from everything though. To get there, board the free shuttle bus from **Shun Tak Centre** (信德中心; 200 Connaught Rd Central, Sheung Wan); check the HKYHA website for the schedule. Alternatively, catch bus 5 from Admiralty MTR station and alight at Felix Villas. Then walk back 100m and follow Mt Davis Path (not Mt Davis Rd). The walk is about 2km. A taxi from Central costs about $60.

🛏 Hong Kong Island: Wan Chai & the Northeast

Admiralty, with easy access to Hong Kong Park, the Pacific Place mall and the Asia Society Hong Kong Centre, has a handful of high-end hotels. Wan Chai, favoured by trade-fair regulars and mainland tourists, has midrange lodging, with a sprinkling of cheaper guesthouses and some high-end options near the Convention & Exhibition Centre. In addition to good-value midrange options, Causeway Bay is relatively well served by inexpensive guesthouses, especially on or around Paterson St. During the low season guesthouses often struggle to fill beds and rooms; most will offer discounts to anyone staying longer than a few nights.

HELENA MAY
HOSTEL $

Map p370 (梅夫人婦女會主樓; ☎ 2522 6766; www.helenamay.com; 35 Garden Rd, Central; s/d $400/580, monthly $9900/13,100, studios minimum stay 1 month $13,860-18,060) If you like the peninsula's colonial setting but not its price tag, this grand dame could be your cup of tea. Founded in 1916 as a social club for single European women in the territory, the Helena May is now a private club for women of all nationalities (p107) and a hostel with 43 smallish but decent rooms. Rooms in the main building are women's-only with shared bathrooms, while the studio flats in an adjacent building are also open to men. You have to be 18 or above to live there. The building is a stone's throw from the Peak Tram Terminus and the Zoological & Botanical Gardens.

UPPER HOUSE
BOUTIQUE HOTEL $$$

Map p370 (☎ 2918 1838; www.upperhouse.com; 88 Queensway, Pacific Pl, Admiralty; r/ste from $4000/9000; @☎; Ⓜ Admiralty, exit F) Every corner of this boutique hotel spells zen-like serenity – the understated lobby, the sleek eco-minded rooms, the elegant sculptures, the warm and discreet service and the manicured lawn where guests can join free yoga classes. Other pluses include a free and 'bottomless' minibar, and easy access to the Admiralty MTR station. Guests can pay to use the pool facilities of nearby hotels. A superb alternative to luxury options in Central and Admiralty, if you don't mind fewer luxuries.

ISLAND SHANGRI-LA HONG KONG
LUXURY HOTEL $$$

Map p370 (港島香格里拉大酒店; ☎ 2877 3838; www.shangri-la.com; Pacific Pl, Supreme Court Rd, Admiralty; r/ste from $3700/8900; @☎🏊; Ⓜ Admiralty, exit F, via Pacific Pl Mall) This monolithic hotel offers plush sophistication with an early '90s vibe. The rooms are not brand spanking new but still lovely, and they're matched by a good gym, a swimming pool and excellent service. Take a quick ride up the bubble lift that links the 39th and 56th floors; you'll catch a glance of the hotel's signature 60m-high painting, a mountainous Chinese landscape that's quite impressive.

REGAL ICLUB HOTEL
BUSINESS HOTEL $$

Map p372 (☎ 3669 8668; www.regalhotel.com; 211 Johnston Rd, Wan Chai; d $800-1100, ste

$1900; @☎; MWan Chai, exit A3) This modern 99-room hotel in the heart of Wan Chai is a good choice if functionality and location are more important to you than large rooms, clockwork service and a lavish breakfast. The smallest rooms are tiny, but feel larger thanks to the use of glass, mirrors and white furniture.

BURLINGTON II   SERVICED APARTMENTS $$$

Map p372 (☑leasing/customer service 3653 9888/3421 2968; www.burlington-hk.com; 55-57 Hennessy Rd; per day $1000-1600, studio monthly from $19,000, 1-bedroom apt from $27,000; @☎; MWan Chai, exit B1) The 84 serviced apartments at this centrally located address are available for short-term lease of three days minimum. The crisp, young-looking units, ranging from 28 sq metres to 60 sq metres, come with very basic cooking and eating utensils, and views of the Hennessy Rd tram tracks. Huge discounts are available outside the high seasons.

GRAND HYATT HOTEL   LUXURY HOTEL $$$

Map p372 (君悅酒店; ☑2588 1234; www.hongkong.grand.hyatt.com; 1 Harbour Rd, Wan Chai; r $2900-5600, ste $8500-55,000; @☎☒; ☐18, MWan Chai, exit A5) Vast and unrestrained luxury in the public and private areas is the defining characteristic here. Subtle it is not. The rooms are huge and sport desks bristling with technology, marble-clad bathrooms and some great views. Its Champagne Bar is classy and its Italian restaurant Grissini offers one of the best Sunday brunches in town. The stunning Plateau, a 7500-sq-metre spa complex with every treatment imaginable, is an oasis on the 11th floor with its own residential rooms.

METROPARK HOTEL   HOTEL $$$

Map p372 (香港銅鑼灣維景酒店; ☑2863 7330; www.metroparkhotelwanchai.com; 41-49 Hennessy Rd, Wan Chai; r/f/ste from $2500/3800/6000, low season r from $770; @☎; MWan Chai, exit B) Metropark is a good-value option in Wan Chai, within walking distance of Admiralty and Causeway Bay and very close to the bars and the computer centre. Staff are helpful and courteous. Some of the rooms have a damp musty smell, so you may want to double-check before moving in. At the time of writing, there's limited wi-fi but the hotel has plans to expand coverage.

HARBOUR VIEW   HOTEL $$$

Map p372 (香港灣景國際; ☑2802 0111; www.theharbourview.com.hk; 4 Harbour Rd, Wan Chai; r $2000, fortnightly/monthly packages from $10,500/21,000; @☎; ☐18, MWan Chai, exit A5) Right next door to the Hong Kong Arts Centre and a mere stroll to the Hong Kong Convention & Exhibition Centre and Wan Chai ferry terminal, this 320-room, YMCA-run hotel is excellent value. It offers simply furnished but adequate rooms, and exceptionally friendly staff. Some rooms overlook a dark courtyard which can be a bit creepy; ask for a room facing the street. Room prices drop by 45% in low season; these discounts are not available during trade-fair periods.

JJ HOTEL   HOTEL $$

Map p372 (君俊商務酒店; ☑2904 7300; www.jjhotel.com.hk; 9th fl, Lucky Centre, 165-171 Wan Chai Rd, Wan Chai; r $1200-1400, f $2700; @☎; MWan Chai, exit A3) This place has 40 clean, basic rooms occupying four floors. Don't expect over-the-top trimmings, but your needs will be taken care of. There's a free left-luggage service for up to 15 days. Rooms are reasonably sized for this price and for Hong Kong. No breakfast is served but there are plenty of eating options nearby. Malaysian-Chinese restaurant Old Bazaar is on the same road.

WIFI BOUTIQUE HOTEL   BUSINESS HOTEL $$

off Map p372 (☑2558 8939; www.wifihotel.com.hk; 366 Lockhart Rd, Wan Chai; r/ste from $1288/2000; ☎; MCauseway Bay, exit C) A favourite of mainland shoppers, this two-year-old hotel between Wan Chai and Causeway Bay has 52 small but clean and nonsmoking rooms with free wi-fi. Rates can drop dramatically outside the peak seasons.

MINGLE PLACE BY THE PARK   HOTEL $$

Map p372 (☑2838 1109; www.mingleplace.com; 143 Wan Chai Rd; r $1100-2000, monthly packages $1500-24,000; @☎; MWan Chai, exit A3) The most interesting hotel in the Mingle Place chain, this five-storey hotel is housed in a restored 1960s tenement building with a balcony and a lovely terrazzo staircase. Rooms are thoughtfully decorated with quirky '60s paraphernalia. Some rooms, including the cubicle-sized 'lite' rooms, have tiny balconies.

YING KING APARTMENT GUESTHOUSE $

Map p372 (英京迎賓館; ☑2573 2049; 9th fl, Mei Wah Mansion, 172-176 Johnston Rd, Wan Chai; r from $350, monthly package per day from $300; @; Ⓜ Wan Chai, exit A3) Marooned somewhat across from the business end of Wan Chai, this little place trims its prices accordingly. The rooms are squeaky clean, with air-con and bathrooms, and there is internet access in the lobby. No nonsmoking area.

FLEMING BUSINESS HOTEL $$$

Map p372 (芬名酒店; ☑3607 2288; www.the fleming.com; 41 Fleming Rd, Causeway Bay; r $1200-3680; Ⓜ Wan Chai, exit A2; @🛜) This stylish, smallish hotel in Wan Chai is great value for money. Located on a quiet road set back from all the nighttime madness, the rooms strike a good balance between smart minimalism and cosy homeliness. Executive rooms come complete with a home office, kitchenette and yoga mats, and there's also a secure, women-only floor. Staff are polite and friendly. There's free wine in the lobby during cocktail hour.

J PLUS BOUTIQUE HOTEL $$$

Map p374 (☑3196 9000; www.jiahongkong.com; 1-5 Irving St, Causeway Bay; r $1500-2800, ste $1900-6000; @🛜; Ⓜ Causeway Bay, exit F) Formerly named Jia, this boutique hotel occupies a prime location in Causeway Bay within walking distance of bus, tram and MTR stations. The Philippe Starck-inspired rooms are small and some are starting to show their age (humidity is bad for light-coloured furniture). Some taxi drivers may not know it, so tell them you're going to the Regal hotel which is right across the street.

PARK LANE HONG KONG HOTEL $$$

Map p374 (柏寧酒店; ☑2293 8888; www.park lane.com.hk; 310 Gloucester Rd, Causeway Bay; r/ste from $2800/8000; @🛜; Ⓜ Causeway Bay, exit E) With restful views of Victoria Park to the east and busy Causeway Bay to the west, the Park Lane is a good choice for those who want to be both in and out of the action. Try to get one of the renovated rooms above the 10th floor; they're much better. Park Lane is favoured by tourists who are here to shop, so the lobby and the entrance area can get noisy and crowded. There's also a large gym.

LANSON PLACE HOTEL $$$

Map p374 (☑3477 6888; www.lansonplace.com; 133 Leighton Rd; r $270-3800, ste from $5800;

@🛜; Ⓜ Causeway Bay, exit F) This plush hotel is an oasis of calm and class amid the Causeway Bay din. The spacious rooms blend classic style with modern fittings and feature lavish bathrooms. There's plenty of public lounging space and a concierge service. If you get one of the corner rooms, there are windows overlooking two different streets.

SHAMA SERVICED APARTMENTS $$

Map p374 (☑2202 5555; www.shama.com; 7th fl, 8 Russell St, Causeway Bay; r from $1350, min 2 nights, studios per month from $26,200, 1-/2-bedroom apt from $36,300/63,000; @🛜; Ⓜ Causeway Bay, exit A) These are among the most attractive serviced apartments in town, in a block opposite Times Square shopping mall. Ranging from fairly spacious studio flats to two-bedroom apartments, they're all tastefully furnished and exceedingly comfortable. Features and extras include wi-fi, daily maid service, DVD equipment, laundry facilities and membership to gyms. Studios and one-bedroom apartments are now available for short-term lease. There are also branches in five other locations in town. Contact the **Shama main office** (☑2522 3082; www.shama.com; 8th fl, Shama Pl, 30 Hollywood Rd, Central) for details.

COSMOPOLITAN HOTEL HOTEL $$

(香港麗都酒店; ☑3552 1111; www.cosmopoli tanhotel.com.hk; 387-397 Queen's Rd E; r/ste from $900/1800; Ⓜ Causeway Bay, exit A; @🛜) The views here are unusual – Hong Kong Cemetery to the south and the Happy Valley Racecourse to the east. If tombstones spook you out, request a room with frosted windows; that said, rooms facing the racecourse are supposed to have better feng shui. All rooms are decent and come with 11 pillow choices! Cosmopolitan is actually closer to Queen's Rd East in Wan Chai than to Causeway Bay, but there's a shuttle service to the latter. There are 20% to 30% discounts offered on longer stays, depending on the season.

METROPARK HOTEL HOTEL $$$

Map p374 (維景酒店; ☑2600 1000; www. metroparkhotel.com; 148 Tung Lo Wan Rd, Causeway Bay; s/d $1200/2500, ste from $6800; @🛜🏊; Ⓜ Causeway Bay, exit E) This flashy tower overlooking Victoria Park makes the most of its easterly location, with 70% of its 243 rooms boasting sweeping city-harbour views through floor-to-ceiling windows.

Rooms are bright but the basic ones don't have bathtubs. Like the Wan Chai branch, this hotel is working on expanding wi-fi coverage. Check the website for discounts and packages.

CITY GARDEN HOTEL
HONG KONG
HOTEL $$$

off Map p374 (城市花園酒店; ☑2887 2888; www.citygarden.com.hk; 9 City Garden Rd, North Point; r $900-2850, ste from $3000, fortnightly/monthly from $8200/13,800; @; MFortress Hill, exit A) Only five minutes' walk from Fortress Hill MTR station, this exceptionally well-turned-out hotel also boasts large rooms (by local standards), good service, free and fast wi-fi and a generous discounting policy. Enter from the corner of Electric Rd and Power St.

ALISAN GUEST HOUSE
GUESTHOUSE $

Map p374 (☑2838 0762; http://home.hkstar.com/~alisangh; Flat A, 5th fl, Hoito Ct, 23 Cannon St, Causeway Bay; s/d/tr $320/440/660, 10% increase during high season; @☎; MCauseway Bay, exit D1) Spread through several apartments, the rooms in this small family-run place are clean, the welcome warm and the advice good. There are 21 spotless rooms with air-con, bathrooms and free internet. The multilingual owners are helpful and can organise China visas. There's a computer, a communal fridge and microwave oven in the tiny kitchen. Enter from 23 Cannon St.

CHUNG KIU INN
HOSTEL $

Map p374 (中僑賓館; ☑2895 3304; www.chungkiuinn.com.hk; Flat P, 15th fl, Hong Kong Mansion, 1 Yee Wo St; s $250-350, d & tw $350-450, tr $400-500, q $500-600, monthly s/d $5000/6000, s without bathroom $4500; MCauseway Bay, exit E; @☎) This hostel, with three-dozen rooms spread over the 9th and 15th floors of the same building, is tidy but the rooms are small and basic. Cheaper rooms with shared bathrooms are available. Communication might be difficult, as the owner speaks no English.

TOP CHOICE CAUSEWAY CORNER
SERVICED APARTMENTS $$

Map p374 (銅鑼閣; ☑2838 3211; www.causewaycorner.com; 18 Percival St, Causeway Bay; nightly $1000-1700, monthly $15,000-23,000; @☎; MCauseway Bay, exit C) A welcome addition to the range of Hong Kong serviced apartments, Japanese-owned Causeway Corner has 105 units that come with showers, micro-wave oven, fridge, eating utensils and twice-a-week maid service. But what we love most is the communal Japanese bath, complete with a shared shower area and an onsen! The compact rooms are neat and pleasantly furnished. A minimum consecutive stay of three nights applies. Stays of at least 14 days go down to about $1000 a day.

EAST HONG KONG
BUSINESS HOTEL $$

(☑3968 3808; www.east-hongkong.com; 29 Taikoo Shing Rd, Taikoo Shing, Quarry Bay; r/ste from $1388/3500; MTai Koo, exit D1; @☎☒) This 345-room hotel on the eastern part of the island has clean lines and lots of natural light, which is quite uplifting for a business hotel. Corner harbour-view rooms, commanding good views, cost more than rooms on the lower floors which look on to buildings nearby. The bar, Sugar, is great for sunset cocktails. There's a 24-hour gym and for an extra $160, you'll get breakfast. A 20% discount applies if you're staying 10 to 20 nights.

TOP CHOICE Y-LOFT YOUTH SQUARE HOSTEL
HOSTEL $$

(☑3721 8989; http://youthsquare.hk; 238 Chai Wan Rd, Chai Wan; tw/tr low season $600/900, high season $1200/1800, ste $3000; @☎; MChai Wan, exit A) If you don't mind trading 20 extra minutes on the MTR for an excellent budget option, you'll be rewarded with large, clean and cheerful rooms in Chai Wan (not Wan Chai!) The beaches and bazaar of Stanley are only 15 minutes away by bus from the 16X bus stop opposite the MTR station. To reach the hostel from exit A, go straight through the mall to the footbridge and take the first exit on your right. Reception's on the 12th floor. Staff are very friendly.

Hong Kong Island: Aberdeen & the South

TOP CHOICE THE T HOTEL
HOTEL $$

(T酒店; ☑3717 7388; www.vtc.edu.hk/thotel/; 6/F, VTC Pokfulam Complex, 145 Pokfulam Rd, Pok Fu Lam; r/ste $1030/1880; @☎☒; ☐7 or 91 from Central, 973 from Tsim Sha Tsui) Ah, we almost don't want to tell you about this gem on the island! The 30-room T, perched high in the serene neighbourhood of Po Fu Lam, is entirely run by students of the local hospitality training institute. The young trainees are attentive, cheerful and very eager to hone their skills, especially at the check-in desk. Rooms are sparkling new and spacious, and offer ocean or mountain views. The food and beverage outlets, run by the famous culinary school in the complex, provide excellent Chinese and Western meals.

BOAT MOKSHA
HOUSEBOAT $

Map p376 (☑6935 9091; www.airbnb.com/rooms/65117; Shum Wan Rd, Wong Chuk Hang, Aberdeen; r $760-1000; @🅰🕙; ☐72A from Causeway Bay or 75 from Central, below Exchange Sq) Finally, there's a nonterrestrial lodging option in this archipelago of 260 plus islands. This cosy houseboat moored on the eastern side of Aberdeen is a floating B&B that offers 360-degree sea views, modern facilities and very comfy beds. The front deck room is reasonably sized so you don't need to squeeze. Upstairs, the suite room is an affordable luxury. The friendly owners Saral and Sweety also live on the boat and have lots of local tips for you. Booking in advance is a must. To get there, take bus 72A or 75 towards Aberdeen and alight at the terminus. Water taxis ($7) will take you to the boat from the dock opposite the bus terminus.

🛏 Kowloon

Splendour rubs shoulders with squalor in Kowloon. There is a huge range of hotels and guesthouses, catering to all budgets, between the two extremes. Tsim Sha Tsui has a number of top-end hotels, some glamorous, some anonymous. Things start getting cheaper as you go north. Yau Ma tei has several midrange options, plus cheap, basic hotels and a good assortment of guesthouses.

TOP CHOICE HYATT REGENCY TSIM SHA TSUI
LUXURY HOTEL $$$

Map p380 (尖沙咀凱悅酒店; ☑2311 1234; http://hongkong.tsimshatsui.hyatt.com; 18 Hanoi Rd, Tsim Sha Tsui; r $1800-2900, ste from $3500; @🅰🕙; Ⓜ Tsim Sha Tsui, exit D2) Top marks to this Tsim Sha Tsui classic, which has reopened at a new address next to the K11 shopping mall. Though not superfluously opulent, it exudes understated elegance and the composure of a true classic. Staff are warm, helpful and knowledgeable. The well-appointed rooms are relatively spacious with those on the upper floors commanding views over the city. We loved the photos of Tsim Sha Tsui by a local photographer, which add a thoughtful touch to the decor.

TOP CHOICE MARINER'S CLUB
HOTEL $

Map p380 (☑2368 8261; www.marinersclub.org.hk; 11 Middle Rd; s/d without bathroom $330/$480, s/d with bathroom $600-810, ste $1000, prices for shipping companies are about $80 less for each category; @🅰🕙; Ⓜ East Tsim Sha Tsu, exit K) A great budget choice if you're a seafarer or attached to a shipping company. Opened in 1967 for visiting 'China coasters', this 12-storey club overlooking the Middle Road Children's Playground has a lazy, old-world charm about it. There are 100 rooms including 30 new ones on the 4th and 5th floors (the only ones offering wi-fi). The 70 old rooms are basic with retro furniture and red-and-black vinyl flooring. They have a certain austerity about them. There's also a first-rate swimming pool, restaurants that are open to the public and a chapel with Anglican and Catholic services. Anyone can book, but they'll ask to see your mariner's ID or proof of shipping-company employment at check-in. That said, we've had reports they're not that strict about this, especially when business is quiet.

HOTEL ICON
LUXURY HOTEL $$$

Map p380 (唯港薈; ☑3400 1000; www.hotel-icon.com; r $2200-4100, ste $3000-5100; 17 Science Museum Rd, Tsim Sha Tsui; 🕙🕙; Ⓜ East Tsim Sha Tsui, exit P1) The rooms at this teaching hotel of a university are clean, modern and spacious, and the service is excellent. Icon is a 10-minute walk from the MTR station, and there's a shuttle service to the more central parts of Tsim Sha Tsui. Not all rooms have harbour views and children are not allowed into the terrace lounge, but overall, it's great value for money. It's within walking distance of the Science Museum, the History Museum and the northern section of the Tsim Sha Tsui East Promenade.

PINNACLE APARTMENT
SERVICED APARTMENTS $$

Map p380 (豪居; ☑2734 8288; www.pinnacleapartment.com; 8 Minden Ave, Tsim Sha Tsui; 1-bedroom apt per month $24,000-38,000, 2-bedroom $34,000-49,000; @🅰🕙; Ⓜ Tsim Sha Tsui, exit G) This elegant block of serviced apartments belonging to the Miramar Hotel has one- to three-bedroom apartments with or without a study. Ranging in size from 47 sq metres to 90 sq metres, with some enjoying harbour views, they come with kitchen facilities, once-a-week maid service, and complimentary use of the pool, gym and jacuzzi. The staff are pleasant. Pinnacle is close to the Middle Road Children's Playground.

PENINSULA HONG KONG   LUXURY HOTEL $$$

Map p378 (香港半島酒店; ☏2920 2888; www. peninsula.com; Salisbury Rd, Tsim Sha Tsui; r $5000-7000, ste from $8200; @ 🖿 🕿 ; Ⓜ Tsim Sha Tsui, exit E) Lording it over the southern tip of Kowloon, Hong Kong's finest hotel evokes colonial elegance. Your main dilemma will be how to get here: landing on the rooftop helipad or arriving in one of the hotel's 14-strong fleet of Rolls Royce Phantoms. Some 300 classic European-style rooms boast wi-fi, CD and DVD players, as well as marble bathrooms. Many rooms in the Pen's 20-storey annexe offer spectacular harbour views; in the original building you'll have to make do with the glorious interiors. There's a top-notch spa and swimming pool. Gaddi's is one of the best French restaurants in town.

MIRA   LUXURY HOTEL $$$

Map p378 (☏2368 1111; www.themirahotel. com; 118-130 Nathan Rd; r $3200-4500, ste from $5000; Ⓜ Tsim Sha Tsui, exit B1; @ 🖿 🕿) Mira tries to impress with colour-themed rooms, designer chairs and a darkened entrance so cool you'd expect to see a bouncer. Techies will drool over the gadgets, which include a mobile phone for local calls, an iPod dock and a flat-screen TV. And the staff are generally helpful. However, the standard rooms are small with low ceilings and the walls are thin. The Mira is a stone's throw from Kowloon Park.

LANGHAM   LUXURY HOTEL $$$

Map p378 (香港朗廷酒店; ☏2375 1133; www. langhamhotels.com/langham/hongkong; 8 Peking Rd, Tsim Sha Tsui; r/ste from $2550/3000; @ 🖿 ; MTR Tsim Sha Tsui, exit E 🕿) There's an opulent feel about the Langham with its chandeliers and classic rooms that were renovated not too long ago. The 24-hour gym is small and a little rundown, but this is made up for by the inviting open-air pool. Another of its strengths is the restaurants. Besides Michelin-starred T'ang Court, there's the Bostonian with its good-value Sunday lunch semibuffet, and Main Street

Deli with its great sandwiches and cool art deco setting.

KOWLOON HOTEL HONG KONG   HOTEL $$$

Map p378 (九龍酒店; ☏2929 2888; www.the kowloonhotel.com; 19-21 Nathan Rd; s from $2000, d $2100, ste from $3900; @ 🛜 ; Ⓜ Tsim Sha Tsui, exit E) The Kowloon Hotel has a dated feel about it, with its 1990s techno aesthetic and a lobby that resembles an airport lounge. Nevertheless, the hotel is popular for its unflappable service, central location and decent if rather small rooms. Rates drop dramatically in the low season.

BP INTERNATIONAL HOTEL   HOTEL $$

Map p378 (龍堡國際酒店; ☏2376 1111; www. bpih.com.hk; 8 Austin Rd; r/ste from $1450/5200; @ 🛜 ; Ⓜ Jordan, exit C) This enormous hotel overlooks Kowloon Park and is relatively convenient to most places of interest in Tsim Sha Tsui. The rooms are of a reasonable standard and some of the more expensive ones have good harbour views. There are family rooms with bunk beds available, making this a good option if you're travelling with kids. Haggle before you book: depending on the season and day of the week, prices are often reduced by 50%.

SALISBURY   HOTEL $$

Map p378 (香港基督教青年會; ☏2268 7888; www.ymcahk.org.hk; 41 Salisbury Rd, Tsim Sha Tsui; dm $260, s/d/ste from $850/950/1600; @ 🖿 🕿 ; Ⓜ Tsim Sha Tsui, exit E) If you can manage to book a room at this fabulously located hostel/hotel, you'll be rewarded with professional service and excellent exercise facilities, including a swimming pool, a fitness centre and a climbing wall. The rooms and suites are comfortable but simple, so keep your eyes on the harbour: that view would cost you five times as much at the Peninsula next door. The four-bed dormitory rooms are a bonus, but restrictions apply: check-in is at 2pm, no one can stay more than seven consecutive nights, and walk-in guests aren't accepted if they've been in Hong Kong for more than seven days. The 7th floor is the smoking floor.

SEALAND HOUSE   GUESTHOUSE $

Map p378 (海怡賓館; ☏2368 9522; www.seal andhouse.com.hk; Flat D, 8th fl, Majestic House, 80 Nathan Rd, Tsim Sha Tsui; s $320-380, d $350-420, tr $350-480; @ 🛜 ; Ⓜ Tsim Sha Tsui, exit B2) This eight-room place, towering above Nathan Rd, is small and outmoded, but clean and very bright. Wi-fi is included in the rates. Rooms without private bathrooms are a bit cheaper. The building is old, so water pressure can be unstable. Enter from Cameron Rd.

INTERCONTINENTAL HONG KONG
LUXURY HOTEL $$$

Map p380 (香港洲際酒店; ☎2721 1211; www.intercontinental.com; 18 Salisbury Rd; r $5100, ste from $9900; @🛜🏊; Ⓜ Tsim Sha Tsui, exit F) Occupying arguably the finest waterfront position in the territory, the InterContinental tilts at modernity while bowing to colonial traditions, such as a fleet of navy-blue Rolls Royces, doormen liveried in white and incessant brass polishing. The emphasis on service ensures a lot of return customers, from rock stars to business VIPs. Restaurants such as the Steak House, Nobu and Spoon are top class. The InterContinental Lobby Lounge bar has the best views in Hong Kong.

CHELSEA HOTEL
HOTEL $

Map p380 (☎2311 9511; www.chelseahotel.hk; 8a Hanoi Rd, Tsim Sha Tsui; r from $600, up to double peak season; 🛜; Ⓜ Tsim Sha Tsui, exit D2) The rooms at this centrally located hotel are tiny and basic but adequate, as is the service. Some rooms on the 15th and 16th floors have glimpses of the harbour. Reception is on the 1st floor.

KNUTSFORD HOTEL
HOTEL $$

Map p380 (樂仕酒店; ☎2377 1180; www.acesitehotel.com; 8 Observatory Ct, Tsim Sha Tsui; s $1000, d $1200-1800; 🛜; Ⓜ Tsim Sha Tsui, exit B1) The 28 coffin-sized rooms here feel quite airy, thanks to savvy use of glass and whites. The service, by contrast, can be nonchalant. The hotel is in a quiet corner of Tsim Sha Tsui's old residential quarter, yet close to the watering holes of Knutsford Tce. Tall people would find the beds cramped.

KOWLOON SHANGRI-LA
LUXURY HOTEL $$$

Map p380 (九龍香格里拉酒店; ☎2721 2111; www.shangri-la.com; 64 Mody Rd, Tsim Sha Tsui East; r $2000-4000, ste from $3980; @🛜🏊; Ⓜ East Tsim Sha Tsui, exit P1) The views, the bars and restaurants here, including Tapas Bar, are excellent. It's almost as swish as its sister hotel, the Island Shangri-La Hong Kong. We love the enormous murals of imperial Chinese scenes in the lobby.

ROYAL GARDEN
LUXURY HOTEL $$$

Map p380 (帝苑酒店; ☎2721 5215; www.rghk.com.hk; 69 Mody Rd, Tsim Sha Tsui; r $3400-3800, ste from $16,100; @🛜🏊; 🚌5C or 8, Ⓜ East Tsim Sha Tsui, exit P1) Despite its '80s-style aesthetics, the 422-room Royal Garden is still going strong as one of the best options in the eastern part of Tsim Sha Tsui. From the blonde-wood and chrome lobby and atrium to the rooftop sports complex (25m pool, putting green and tennis court with million-dollar views), the Royal Garden ticks all the boxes. The rooms are highly specced with plasma screens and large, comfortable beds. You should be able to secure large discounts off the quoted rates. Sabatini on the 3rd floor serves sumptuous northern Italian food.

BUTTERFLY ON PRAT
HOTEL $$$

Map p380 (☎3962 8888; www.butterflyhk.com; 21 Prat Av, Tsim Sha Tsui; low season/peak season r $900/4000, ste $1900-5000; @🛜; Ⓜ Tsim Sha Tsui, exit A2) Its nouveau baroque lobby may look a little flighty, but don't be put off. All 22 rooms are presentable, with matching fabrics, glass partitions, queen-sized beds and a host of conveniences, including microwave ovens, broadband and TVs with 30 channels. Staff are attentive and guests get discounts at eateries nearby. There is a 10% to 15% discount for stays of over three or 14 days. Music from the clubs nearby can be in heard in some of the rooms. Inquire before you book.

STANFORD HILLVIEW HOTEL
HOTEL $$

Map p380 (仕德福山景酒店; ☎2722 7822; www.stanfordhillview.com; 13-17 Observatory Rd, Tsim Sha Tsui; r $1480-2680, ste from $3180; 🛜; Ⓜ Tsim Sha Tsui, exit B1) At the eastern end of Knutsford Tce, the Stanford is a decent choice if you value location over new rooms and top-notch service. Sitting on a quiet hill at the backdoor of the Hong Kong Observatory, Stanford is just seconds away from the bars on Knutsford Tce and a downhill stroll from the old residential quarter of Tsim Sha Tsui. Huge discounts are available during the low season.

EMPIRE KOWLOON
HOTEL $$$

Map p380 (尖沙咀皇悅酒店; ☎3692 2222; www.empirehotel.com.hk; 62 Kimberley Rd; r/ste from $1600/3200; @🛜🏊; Ⓜ Tsim Sha Tsui, exit B2) This hotel offers decent rooms and an excellent indoor atrium swimming pool and spa. It's in the old residential quarter of Tsim Sha Tsui. Check the website for promotions.

HOP INN
HOSTEL $

Map p378 (☑2881 7331; www.hopinn.hk; Flat A, 2nd fl, Hanyee Bldg, 19-21 Hankow Rd, Tsim Sha Tsui; @🛜; MTsim Sha Tsui, exit A1; s $410-510, d & tw $520-740, tr $650-930) This nonsmoking guesthouse has a youthful vibe and nine spotless but tiny rooms, each featuring illustrations by a different Hong Kong artist. Some have no windows but they're quieter than the ones that do. The new branch **Hop Inn on Carnarvon** (9th fl, James S Lee Mansion, 33-35 Carnarvon Rd) has brand-new rooms. We particularly liked the one designed by local artist Sim Chan. Both branches have free in-room wi-fi and will help to organise China visas.

MINDEN
HOTEL $$

Map p380 (棉登酒店; ☑2739 7777; www.theminden.com; 7 Minden Ave, Tsim Sha Tsui; r $1300-1800, ste $3000; @; MTsim Sha Tsui, exit G) This almost-boutique 64-room hotel, tucked away on relatively quiet Minden Ave, is well located for both Tsim Sha Tsui and East Tsim Sha Tsui stations, and very reasonable value. The lobby is packed with an eclectic mix of Asian and Western curios and furnishings, while the rooms are serene and comfortable, with all the amenities you'd expect included in the rates.

YHA MEI HO HOUSE YOUTH HOSTEL
HOSTEL $

Map p382 (☑2788 1638; www.meihohouse.hk; Block 41, Shek Kip Mei Estate, Sham Shui Po; MSham Shui Po, exit D2; 🚍A21) This 50-year-old public housing estate block should have reopened its doors as a YHA youth hostel by the time you read this, with all 129 rooms converted from public housing units. Great promise for a really cool budget choice.

HOTEL PANORAMA
HOTEL $$$

Map p380 (麗景酒店; ☑3550 0388; www.hotelpanorama.com.hk; 8a Hart Ave; r/ste from $3000/8000; @🛜; MEast Tsim Sha Tsui, exit N) As its name suggests, you'll find panoramic views at this hotel – but only above the 17th floor. The lower rooms overlook old buildings nearby, which not everyone likes. That said, all rooms are tastefully furnished, and the breezy Sky Garden on the 40th floor offers great vistas of Tsim Sha Tsui. The tourist desk helps to organise China

visas. Low-season discounts are offered and there's wi-fi in the lobby.

STAR GUEST HOUSE
GUESTHOUSE $

Map p380 (星華旅店; ☑2723 8951; www.starguesthouse.com.hk; Flat B, 6th fl, 21 Cameron Rd; s & d without bathroom $300, s/d with bathroom $400/500, tw & tr $650; @🛜; MTsim Sha Tsui, exit B2) This excellent guesthouse and its sister property just up the road, the **Lee Garden Guest House** (麗園旅店; Map p380; ☑2367 2284; charliechan@iname.com; 8th fl, D Block, 36 Cameron Rd), with a total of 45 rooms, are owned by the charismatic Charlie Chan, who can arrange most things for you, including China visas. Long-term stayers get good discounts. The rooms at the Star have satellite TV, while Lee Garden has a computer for guests' use.

W HONG KONG
LUXURY HOTEL $$$

Map p382 (☑3717 2222; www.whotels.com; 1 Austin Rd West; r from $2500, ste $8000; @🛜🏊; MKowloon, exit C1) W features uberstylish interiors created by an Australian and a Japanese designer, with rooms named 'wonderful', 'spectacular', 'fantastic'...which are in fact, quite wonderful and spectacular, especially with the views from the 36th floor and up. This is *the* go-to hotel if you're after designer furniture. We were also impressed by the spacious gym with harbour views, and the 'highest pool in the city' (72nd floor). W attracts a crowd of young professionals who like to hang out at its bar and pool lounge. W is right on top of the Airport Express Kowloon Station and the Elements Mall.

RITZ-CARLTON HONG KONG
LUXURY HOTEL $$$

Map p382 (麗思卡爾頓酒店; www.ritzcarlton.com; 1 Austin Rd West, Jordan; r $6000-7800, ste from $8000; 🛜🏊) Sitting atop the Airport Express Kowloon Station, this out-of-the-way luxury hotel is the tallest hotel on earth at the time of writing (the lobby's on the 103rd floor). The over-the-top decor features heavy furniture and a superfluity of shiny services that's supposedly favoured by mainland travellers. That said, the service is pristine, Tin Lung Heen serves superb Chinese food, and the views are stunning on clear days.

MADERA HONG KONG
HOTEL $$

(www.hotelmadera.com.hk; 1-9 Cheong Lok St, Yau Ma Tei; d/tw/ste $1400/1800/2800; MJordan, exit B1) A spirited addition to Kowloon's

BUDGET BLOCKS IN TSIM SHA TSUI

Chungking Mansions

Say 'budget accommodation' and 'Hong Kong' in one breath and everyone thinks of **Chungking Mansions** (重慶大廈; Map p378; 36-44 Nathan Rd, Tsim Sha Tsui; M Tsim Sha Tsui, exit F). Built in 1961, CKM is a labyrinth of homes, guesthouses, Indian restaurants, souvenir stalls and foreign-exchange shops spread over five 17-storey blocks in the heart of Tsim Sha Tsui. According to anthropologist Gordon Mathews, it has a resident population of about 4000 and an estimated 10,000 daily visitors. Over 120 different nationalities – predominantly South Asian and African – pass through its doors in a single year.

Though standards vary significantly, most of the guesthouses at CKM – including the ones recommended here – are clean and quite comfortable. It's worth bearing in mind, however, that rooms are usually the size of cupboards and you have to shower right next to the toilet. The rooms typically come with air-con and TV and, sometimes, a phone. Many guesthouses can get you a Chinese visa quickly, most have internet access and some have wi-fi and laundry service.

Bargaining for a bed or room is always possible, though you won't get very far in the high season. You can often negotiate a cheaper price if you stay more than, say, a week, but never try that on the first night – stay one night and find out how you like it before handing over more rent. Once you pay, there are usually no refunds.

Dragon Inn (龍匯賓館; Map p378; ☎2368 2007; dragoinn@netvigator.com; Flat B5, 3rd fl, B Block; s $320-490, d $380-680, 'honeymoon rooms' $550-670, tr $530-620, q $560-680) It's owned by the chairperson of the Incorporated Owners of CKM – a shrewd and helpful matron with the political correctness of a Ming emperor and a taste for florals. It has squeaky clean rooms with private bathrooms, drinking water and a hairdryer; there are discounts for students, seniors and repeat customers. (And, yes, the spelling of its email address really is 'dragoinn'.)

Holiday Guesthouse (Map p378; ☎2316 7152, 9121 8072; fax 2316 7181; Flat E1, 6th fl, E Block; s $250-600, d $350-700; @ 🛜) An upmarket Nepali-run place with 23 pleasant rooms.

Yan Yan Guest House (欣欣賓館; Map p378; ☎2366 8930, 9489 3891; fax 2721 0840; Flat E1, 8th fl, E Block; s $130-180, d $160-200; 🛜) This is one of the last of the Chinese-owned guesthouses in the overwhelmingly subcontinental E Block. Wi-fi reception is better in the front rooms. **New Yan Yan Guesthouse** (新欣賓館; ☎2723 5671; Flat E5, 12th fl, E Block; 🛜), in the same block, is managed by the same people.

Park Guesthouse (百樂賓館; Map p378; ☎2368 1689; fax 2367 7889; Flat A1, 15th fl, A Block; s/d $200/400, without bathroom $200; 🛜) A basic but welcoming 45-room guesthouse that comes recommended by readers.

Mirador Mansion

Above an arcade between Mody and Carnarvon Rds sits 54-year-old **Mirador Mansion** (Map p378; 54-64 Nathan Rd; M Tsim Sha Tsui, exit D2). It was here – and not Chungking Mansions – where Wong Kar-wai filmed most of *Chungking Express* (1994).

Cosmic Guest House (宇宙賓館; Map p378; ☎2369 6669; www.cosmicguesthouse.com; Flats A1-A2, Block F1 [reception], 12th fl; d/tw $180/350, tr $330-390, q $380-520, f from $500; @ 🛜) With some 80 beds, this is one of the largest guesthouses in town. It's clean and quiet with big and bright rooms (well, those with windows) and a very helpful owner. There's internet access in every room. Some even have rain showers… wedged into 1-metre-sq bathrooms!

Mei Lam Guest House (美林賓館; Map p378; ☎2721 5278, 9095 1379; fax 2723 6168; Flat D1, 5th fl; s/d from $200, d $250-350; 🛜) This excellent place has modern rooms packed with extras, including internet access.

midrange options, Madera is close to the Temple Street Night Market and the Jordan MTR station, and a brisk 20-minute walk from the Star Ferry. The decent-sized rooms come in neutral tones with bright, happy accents. There's also a ladies' floor and a hypo-allergenic floor. The gym is tiny but adequate.

EATON SMART HOTEL $$$
Map p382 (香港逸東「智」酒店; ☎2782 1818; www.hongkong.eatonhotels.com; 380 Nathan Rd, Yau Ma Tei; r $2350-3200, ste from $3250; @☒;

Ⓜ Jordan, exit B1) Leave the chaos of Nathan Rd behind as you step into the Eaton's grand lobby. The rooms are relatively large and most, except some of the 'superior' rooms, are well maintained. Staff are courteous and there's a rooftop pool. Booking on the internet can halve the quoted rates and there are 'linger longer for less' rates. Enter from Pak Hoi St.

CITYVIEW HOTEL $$$
Map p382 (城景國際; ☎2771 9111; www.thecityview.com.hk; 23 Waterloo Rd, Yau Ma Tei; r $1880,

---

STANDBY HOTELS

At busy times, the best hotels can get booked out. The following are some standby, midrange alternatives that should have rooms available and will do if you get stuck without a bed for the night.

Hong Kong Island

Luk Kwok Hotel (六國酒店; Map p372; ☎2866 2166; www.gloucesterlukkwok.com.hk/; 72 Gloucester Rd, Wan Chai; r/ste from $2100/4000; @☒; ☐18) Few frills but an attentive staff and you're close to the convention centre and the bustle (and hustle) of Wan Chai. Low-season prices drop by half.

Newton Hotel Hong Kong (香港麗東酒店; Map p374; ☎2807 2333; www.newtonhk.com; 218 Electric Rd; r $1600-2800, ste $3500; @; ⒨Fortress Hill, exit A) A great little hotel – it's just a shame it's in less-than-sexy North Point. Fortress Hill metro station is just opposite. Causeway Bay is a pleasant walk away through Victoria Park.

Holiday Inn Express (香港銅鑼灣快捷假日酒店; Map p374; ☎3558 6688; www.hiexpress.com/hotels/us/en/hong-kong/hkgcw/hoteldetail; 33 Sharp St E; r $1480-1980; @; ⒨Causeway Bay, exit A) Delivers what it promises: consistent and affordable accommodation, and it's right next to the Times Square shopping mall.

Regal Hongkong Hotel (富豪香港酒店; Map p374; ☎2890 6633; www.regalhongkong.com; 88 Yee Wo St, Causeway Bay; r $2000-5000, ste from $6000; @☒; ⒨Causeway Bay, exit F) This Sino-baroque palace drips with gilt and has a rooftop Roman-style *piscina* (pool). Over the top in the nicest possible way. The new floors (31st to 33rd) offer more privacy. Deals are available if you book two or three weeks in advance.

Walden Hotel (華登酒店; ☎8200 3308; www.walden-hotel.com; 353 Hennessy Rd; r from $2100; @; ⒨Causeway Bay, exit C) You may not like the corporate feel or the dim bathrooms, but you'll admit the location is very competitive. Inquire about deals and long-stay packages. Don't be scared by the rates, 70% low-season discounts are offered.

Kowloon

Harbour Plaza North Point (北角海逸酒店; ☎2187 8888; www.harbour-plaza.com; 665 King's Rd, Quarry Bay; s/d from $1900/2150; @☒; ⒨Quarry Bay, exit C) A business hotel that's in Quarry Bay rather than North Point. Rooms are adequate and the outdoor pool is a nice surprise.

Royal Pacific Hotel & Towers (皇家太平洋酒店; Map p378; ☎2736 1188; www.royalpacific.com.hk; China Hong Kong City, 33 Canton Rd, Tsim Sha Tsui; r from $1500; @; ⒨Tsim Sha Tsui, exit E) An easy stroll to Kowloon Park and the China and Macau ferry terminal. Reception is on the 3rd floor; service can be both slow and harried at times.

Dorsett Seaview Hotel (Map p382; ☎2782 0882; www.dorsettseaview.com.hk; 268 Shanghai St, Yau Ma Tei; r $580-1900; ☎; ⒨Yau Ma Tei, exit C) A clean, basic, well-located standby. Book online for the best rates.

tr $2280, ste from $3080; @🛜🚊; Ⓜ Yau Ma Tei, exit A2;) All 413 rooms at this YMCA-affiliated hotel are clean and smart and feature mellow tones and stylish fabrics. The service is also excellent. The hotel occupies a quiet corner between Yau Ma Tei and Mong Kok. It's a short stroll from the Yau Ma Tei Theatre and the Yau Ma Tei Wholesale Fruit Market.

NOVOTEL
HOTEL $$

Map p382 (📞3965 8888; www.novotel.com; 348 Nathan Rd, Yau Ma Tei; r $1200-3000; @🛜; Ⓜ Jordan, exit B2) Although it claims to be on the 'golden mile' of Tsim Sha Tsui, Novotel's actual address is nowhere near the harbour; rather, it's at the doorstep of Yau Ma Tei. It's also accessed via Saigon St, not Nathan Rd. Despite the misleading address, Novotel is a bright, contemporary hotel with a spacious lobby and 400 pleasant rooms that were renovated in 2008. They're the same size, but the more costly rooms have better views and nicer decor.

NATHAN HOTEL
HOTEL $$$

Map p382 (彌敦酒店; 📞2388 5141; www.nathanhotel.com; 378 Nathan Rd, Yau Ma Tei; r/ste from $2180/4280; @🛜; Ⓜ Jordan, exit B1) All 166 rooms are spacious and decent, but try to avoid lower-floor rooms facing Nathan Rd, because they can be noisy. It's in a good location, right near the Jordan MTR station and Temple St, and we like the turbaned doorman. Enter from Pak Hoi St.

CARITAS BIANCHI LODGE
GUESTHOUSE $$

Map p382 (明愛白英奇賓館; 📞2388 1111; www.caritas-chs.org.hk/eng/bianchi_lodge.asp; 4 Cliff Rd; s/d & tw/f incl breakfast from $750/870/1080; Ⓜ Yau Ma Tei, exit D) This 90-room hotel/guesthouse is run by a Catholic NGO. Though it's just off Nathan Rd (and a goalie's throw from Yau Ma Tei MTR station), the rear rooms are quiet and some have views of King's Park. All rooms are clean with private bathrooms is included. The wait for lifts can be long, especially at night.

CASA HOTEL
HOTEL $$$

Map p382 (📞3758 7777; www.casahotel.com.hk; 487-489 Nathan Rd; s/d/f $1080/1580/2680; @🛜; Ⓜ Yau Ma Tei, exit C) A favourite of mainland tourists, Casa is pretty sleek for this price and this part of town. The rooms are clean but be prepared to shower right next to the toilet. Rooms ending in 04 or 09 between the 3rd and 8th floors are larger, but

there's no wi-fi on the 7th floor. The lobby is always full of people waiting to check in and guests here can be noisy, as can the traffic from Nathan Rd.

BOOTH LODGE
GUESTHOUSE $$

Map p382 (卜維廉賓館; 📞2771 9266; http://boothlodge.salvation.org.hk; 11 Wing Sing La, Yau Ma Tei; r incl breakfast $620-1500; @🛜; Ⓜ Yau Ma Tei, exit D) Run by the Salvation Army, this 53-room place is spartan but clean and comfortable. Promotional rates for rooms can drop to $500. Reception is on the 7th floor.

GOLDEN ISLAND GUESTHOUSE
GUESTHOUSE $

Map p382 (金島賓館; 📞9583 5051, 2783 7952; www.gig.com.hk; Flat 1-2, 7th fl, Alhambra Bldg, 385 Nathan Rd, Yau Ma Tei; s $180-220, d $220-360, tr $250-350, q $320-450; @🛜; Ⓜ Yau Ma Tei, exit C) This 30-room guesthouse with an affiliated tour agency offers the best deal in the Alhambra Building. All rooms come with private bathrooms, toiletries, TV, phone and free wi-fi; some are locked with key-cards. Staff can help you make ticket and day-tour arrangements. Jessie Fu, the young owner, is amiable and speaks good English. You can make reservations on its website.

HAKKA'S GUEST HOUSE
GUESTHOUSE $

Map p382 (嘉應賓館; 📞2771 3656; www.hakkas.hostel.com; Flat L, 3rd fl, New Lucky House, 300-306 Nathan Rd, Yau Ma Tei; d/tw/tr/f from $250/300/350/400; @; Ⓜ Jordan, exit B1) This is the most decent guesthouse in New Lucky House and each of the nine ultra-clean guestrooms has a phone, TV and shower. The affable owner, Kevin Koo, is a keen hiker and he'll invite guests out with him for country walks on Sunday. Mr Koo sometimes sends spillovers to **Ying Pin** (📞2771 0888; 2nd fl, New Lucky House) downstairs, which offers basic accommodation. Hakka Guest House is between Jordan and Yau Ma Tei.

ANNE BLACK YWCA
GUESTHOUSE $$

Map p383 (女青柏顏露斯; 📞2713 9211; www.ywca.org.hk; 5 Man Fuk Rd, Yau Ma Tei; r with bathroom $1100-1300, without bathroom $750, monthly packages from $6000; @🛜; Ⓜ Yau Ma Tei, exit D) This YWCA-run guesthouse, which accommodates both women and men, is near Pui Ching and Waterloo Rds in Mong Kok, behind and uphill from a petrol station. There are laundry facilities and a decent restaurant. Conveniently, almost half of the rooms are singles.

CARITAS LODGE
GUESTHOUSE $

Map p383 (明愛賓館; ☎2339 3777; www.caritas-chs.org.hk; 134 Boundary St, Mong Kok; s/d incl breakfast from $550/600; @⊗; ⓂMong Kok East, exit C or D) With just 40 rooms, this place is as nice as its sister guesthouse, Caritas Bianchi Lodge, but the rooms are smaller and it's further afield. Still, you couldn't get much closer to the bird market, and the New Territories is (officially) just across the road.

LANGHAM PLACE HOTEL
HOTEL $$$

Map p383 (朗豪酒店; ☎3552 3388; http://hongkong.langhamplacehotels.com/; 555 Shanghai St; r/ste from $3000/5200; @⊗⊠; ⓂMong Kok, exit C3) Peering out from one of the rooms of this colossal tower hotel, you'd never suspect for a moment that you were in Mong Kok. It's a triumph for the district. The special guest-room features include multifunction IP phones, DVD players, marble bathrooms and room safes that can fit (and recharge) a laptop. Reception is on the 4th floor and the hotel is linked to the Langham Place Mall. The 20m rooftop pool, gym and spa all command great views over Kowloon.

ROYAL PLAZA HOTEL
HOTEL $$$

Map p383 (帝京酒店; ☎2928 8822; www.royalplaza.com.hk; 193 Prince Edward Rd W, Mong Kok; s $2600-4100, d $3000-4500, ste from $5800; @⊗⊠; ⓂMong Kok East Rail) The plushness is a bit overdone, but the 671-room Royal Plaza is comfortable and central; the bird and flower markets are on the other side of Prince Edward Rd. The rooms are well equipped, with heated no-steam bathroom mirrors, and some have kitchenettes and wi-fi. The outdoor pool with underwater music is a lounge-lizard's nirvana. The Mong Kok KCR station is accessible through the adjoining Grand Century Place shopping centre, making this a handy spot if you've business in the New Territories or mainland China.

SUNNY DAY HOTEL
HOTEL $$

Map p383 (新天地酒店; ☎3760 8888; www.sunnydayhotel.cn; 419 Reclamation St, Mong Kok; s/d $900/1300, low season s from $680; ⊗; ⓂMong Kok, exit C4) This 39-room hotel has small rooms overlooking Reclamation St and Langham Pl. The warm russet walls in the lift lobbies are a nice touch, but the litter outside the windows is a reminder that this is Mong Kok. The staff are quite helpful.

NIC & TRIG'S
GUESTHOUSE $

Map p383 (☎6333 5352; rooms@nostalgic.org; 705 Shanghai St, Mong Kok; r from $400; ⊗; ⓂPrince Edward, exit C1) Run by a cool hipster couple, this place inside a 'walk-up' tenement building (c 1957) has three rooms. They were inspired respectively by the '60s (think Wong Kar-wai's *In the Mood for Love*), the '70s with Bruce Lee posters, and the Cantopop era featuring vinyl records and pop-style furniture. Toilet and shower areas are shared; provisions are basic. If you need anything, just ask. The owners are very nice, and won't hesitate to give you recommendations on where to eat and visit. Email and they will tell you how to get there.

Understand Hong Kong

Hong Kong Today

The election in March 2012 of Leung Chun-ying as Hong Kong's fourth post-1997 Chief Executive has taken the territory into uncharted political waters. For many, a malaise has set in, what with global economic uncertainties, spiralling living costs and an increasingly tricky relationship with the city's great neighbour – and master – to the north. But one certainty is that this indefatigable city will always find a way to win through.

Best on Film

In the Mood for Love (2000) Wong Kar-wai's masterpiece of smouldering love in 1960s Hong Kong.

Little Cheung (1999) A gritty take on the realities of post-1997 Hong Kong.

Love in a Puff (2010) A chain-smoking tribute to contemporary Hong Kong life.

My Life as McDull (2001) A heart-warming animation about an indigenous pig character.

Comrades: Almost a Love Story (1996) Two mainland migrants take a reality check in this maddening city.

Best in Print

Hong Kong State of Mind (Jason Ng; 2011) A crash course on the city's idiosyncrasies.

The Hungry Ghosts (Anne Berry; 2009) Restless spirits haunt this expertly crafted tale.

Gweilo: Memories of a Hong Kong Childhood (Martin Booth; 2004) A much-acclaimed memoir of life in 1950s Hong Kong.

Hong Kong: A Cultural History (Michael Ingham; 2007) The definitive title in this category.

Triad (Derek Lambert; 1991) A gripping (though violent) British police superintendent v Chinese underworld yarn.

The State of Play

Hong Kong has witnessed much political strife and public discontent with the government since the turn of the decade. Public grievances have centred on a long list of increasingly intractable issues, from slow democratic reforms and perceived collusion between the government and big business, to stifling property prices and the drain on public resources of mainland immigrants. The interference of Běijīng's Hong Kong–based proxies around Leung Chun-ying's ascent to the top post in town marks a definitive dynamics shift in the local political landscape, and serves as an ominous forewarning of what's to come as the 'One Country, Two Systems' principle increasingly comes under threat.

While many hope that Leung can turn his populist overtures into action by, for instance, providing more social housing, the realities of Hong Kong's peculiar political system are such that, even with the introduction of a more representative legislature for the 2012–17 period, the balance of power will always tilt in the landed elite's favour.

Basic Economics

Inflation hit a 16-year high in 2011 and, while it may have slowed down since, the truth is that for many, Hong Kong has become a depressingly expensive place to live. The costs of utilities, public transport, food and, crucially, housing, are racing ahead of people's spending power, and one now has to pay double for the luxury to dream about winning the lottery after the price of a Mark Six ticket went up to HK$10 in 2010. Despite the reasonable economic growth rates of the past few years, a widening income gap has appeared. Hong Kong has more billionaires than most countries, but many more people struggle to meet fairly basic levels of subsistence.

A New Era

There's a prevailing mood in Hong Kong society today that the city has passed its heyday. Once savvy and confident, it wouldn't be unfair to suggest that Hong Kong people are today resigned to the fact that their city is increasingly like the mainland. Walk down any street and you'll hear and see more putonghua and simplified Chinese characters (as opposed to the local use of Cantonese and the traditional Chinese script) than at any time since the handover. The Chinese national anthem plays on TV at 6pm every day. Even the Sha Tin horseracing on Saturday afternoon – a weekly ritual for tens of thousands stretching back to the late 1970s – has been switched to Sunday to, at least in part, accommodate the high rollers from across the border, thus depriving many working-class men of the one family day they have.

But despite the general mood of anxiety, all is not doom and gloom. If anything, the multiple challenges that are confronting the city are stirring a strong spirit among the people to defend Hong Kong's core values (namely, the rule of law and civil liberties), and to actively define who they are in the face of Běijīng's homogenisation.

New Waves

Protest marches, often feisty and carnival-esque, take place just about every other Sunday in Hong Kong. Young people are increasingly coming to the forefront of resistance, such as when they spearheaded tens of thousands of people, including parents, to take to the streets in July 2012 to protest the introduction in schools of 'national education' classes that they fear will lead to political brainwashing.

At the same time, Hong Kong is still the only place in the whole of China where the crackdown on the Tiān'ānmén pro-democracy uprising of 4 June 1989 can be openly commemorated. The city's unique status has allowed it to continue to be a force of change for the rest of China. As Běijīng desperately searches for a formula of soft power to project on the international stage, the answers they need may well lie in the rebellious tendencies of their semi-autonomous territory in the south.

Part of the city's growing assertion of its own distinctive identity is an increasing awareness among the young population to preserve Hong Kong's social heritage. Funky collectives have flowered in the past few years to document the social history of storied neighbourhoods caught in the tide of urban redevelopment, such as Wan Chai and Yau Ma Tei. The perennial tussle for space in the city has also seen the growth of alternative music venues and urban farms in old factory buildings. As always, there's more than meets the eye in this pulsating metropolis, which has time and again shown an extraordinary ability to rebound, adapt and excel.

population per sq km

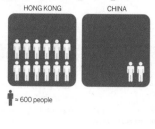

HONG KONG   CHINA

= 600 people

occupations
(% of population)

41.4 — Wholesale & Retail Trade, Restaurants & Hotels

16.8 — Community & Social Services

12.5 — Financing, Insurance & Real Estate

6.7 — Manufacturing & Construction

6.3 — Transport & Communications

16.3 — Other

if Hong Kong were 100 people

93 would be Chinese
2 would be Indonesian
2 would be Filipino
3 would be Other

History

The name Hong Kong came from the Cantonese *heung gawng* ('fragrant harbour' or 'incense harbour'), which was inspired by the scent of sandalwood incense piled at what is now Aberdeen, on the western edge of the island. In the very long scale of history, Hong Kong as we know it today has existed for a mere blink of an eye. But there was a lot going on in the region before that wintry morning in 1841 when a contingent of British marines clambered ashore and planted the Union Jack on the western part of Hong Kong Island, claiming it for the British Crown.

EARLY INHABITANTS

Hong Kong has supported human life since at least the Middle Neolithic Period (c 4000–2500 BC). Artefacts uncovered at almost 100 archaeological sites in the territory suggest that the inhabitants of these settlements shared similar cultural characteristics to the people who lived in the Pearl River Delta. The remnants of Bronze Age habitations (c 1500–220 BC) unearthed on Lamma and Lantau Islands, among other places – as well as the eight extant geometric rock carvings along Hong Kong's coastline – also indicate that these early peoples practised some form of folk religion involving animal worship.

THE FIVE GREAT CLANS

The first of Hong Kong's mighty 'Five Clans' – Han Chinese, whose descendants hold political and economic clout to this day – began settling the area around the 11th century. The first and most powerful of the arrivals was the Tang, who initially settled around Yuen Long (the walled village of Kat Hing Wai is part of this cluster).

The Tang clan was followed by the Hau and the Pang, who spread around present-day Sheung Shui and Fanling. These three clans were followed by the Liu in the 14th century and the Man a century later.

The Cantonese-speaking newcomers called themselves *bun day* (Punti), meaning 'indigenous' or 'local' – something they clearly were not. They

> Archaeologists say Hong Kong's Stone Age inhabitants enjoyed a relatively nutritious diet of iron-rich vegetables, small mammals, shellfish and fish harvested far offshore. Early Chinese historical records call the diverse maritime peoples along China's southeastern coasts the 'Hundred Yue' tribes, which potentially included some of Hong Kong's prehistoric inhabitants.

TIMELINE

4000–1500 BC	214 BC	1000–1400 AD
Small groups of Neolithic hunter-gatherers and fisherfolk settle in coastal areas; a handful of tools, pottery and other artefacts are the only remnants left by these nomads.	Chinese emperor Qin Shi Huang conquers present-day Guǎngxī, Guǎngdōng and Fújiàn after a long period of war. Hong Kong comes under greater cultural influence from the north.	Hong Kong's Five Clans –Tang, Hau, Pang, Liu and Man – settle in what is now the New Territories and build walled villages in the fertile plains and valleys.

looked down on the original inhabitants, the Tanka, many of whom had been shunted off the land and had moved onto the sea to live on boats.

AN IMPERIAL OUTPOST

Clinging to the southern edge of the Chinese province of Canton (now Guǎngdōng), the peninsula and islands that became the territory of Hong Kong counted only as a remote pocket in a neglected corner of the Chinese empire.

The Punti flourished until the struggle that saw the moribund Ming dynasty (1368–1644) overthrown. The victorious Qing (1644–1911), angered by the resistance put up by southerners loyal to the ancien régime, ordered in the 1660s a forced evacuation inland of all the inhabitants of China's southeastern coastal area, including Hong Kong.

More than four generations passed before the population was able to recover to its mid-17th-century level, boosted in part by the influx of the Hakka (Cantonese for 'guest people'), who moved here in the 18th century and up to the mid-19th century. A few vestiges of their language, songs, folklore and cooking survive, most visibly in the wide-brimmed, black-fringed bamboo hats sported by Hakka women in the New Territories.

ARRIVAL OF THE OUTER BARBARIANS

For centuries the Pearl River estuary had been an important trading artery centred on the port of Canton (now Guǎngzhōu). Some of the first foreign traders (or 'outer barbarians') were Arab traders who entered – and sacked – the settlement as early as the 8th century AD. Similarly, the Ming emperors regarded their subjects to the south as an utterly uncivilised bunch. It was therefore fitting that the Cantonese should trade with the 'outer barbarians'.

Regular trade between China and Europe began in 1557 when Portuguese navigators set up a base in Macau, 65km west of Hong Kong. Dutch traders came in the wake of the Portuguese, followed by the French. British ships appeared as early as 1683 from the East India Company concessions along the coast of India, and by 1711 the company had established offices and warehouses in Guǎngzhōu to trade for tea, silk and porcelain.

THE FIRST OPIUM WAR & BRITISH HONG KONG

China did not reciprocate Europe's voracious demand for its products, for the most part shunning foreign manufactured goods. The

The discovery of coins and pottery from the Eastern Han dynasty (AD 25–220) on Lantau and at several important digs, including a tomb at Lei Cheng Uk in central Kowloon, attests to a growing Han influence in Hong Kong at the start of the first millennium.

In 1276 the boy emperor Duan Zong and his younger brother, Bing, were forced to flee to Hong Kong as the Mongols swept aside the remaining army of the Song dynasty (AD 960–1279). After Mongol ships defeated the tattered remnants of the imperial fleet in a battle on the Pearl River, the Song dynasty was definitively ended.

1557	1644	1683	1757
Portuguese navigators set up a base in Macau, and are followed by Dutch and then French traders. Regular trade begins between China and Europe.	The Ming dynasty (1368–1644) is overthrown by the Qing dynasty, which reigns until 1911.	British East India Company ships begin to arrive, and by 1711 the company has established offices and warehouses in Guǎngzhōu, to trade for tea, silk and porcelain.	An imperial edict restricts European trade to the cohong (local merchants guild) in Guǎngzhōu; growing discontent with the trading system sets the stage for the First Opium War.

foreigners' ensuing trade deficit was soon reversed, however, after the British discovered a commodity that the Chinese did want: opium.

The British, with a virtually inexhaustible supply of the drug from the poppy fields of India, developed the trade aggressively. Consequently, opium addiction spread out of control in China, and the country's silver reserves became perilously drained.

In late 1838 Emperor Dao Guang (r 1820–50) appointed Lin Zexu, governor of Húnán and Húběi and a Mandarin of great integrity, to stamp out the opium trade. His rather successful campaign would ultimately lead to the First Opium War (or First Anglo-Chinese War) of 1839–42.

In January 1841 a naval landing party hoisted the British flag at Possession Point (now Possession St) on Hong Kong Island. Subsequently, the Treaty of Nanking abolished the monopoly system of trade, opened five 'treaty ports' to British residents and foreign trade, exempted British nationals from all Chinese laws and ceded the strategically useful island of Hong Kong to the British 'in perpetuity'.

Hong Kong, with its deep, well-sheltered harbour, formally became a British possession on 26 June 1843, and its first governor, Sir Henry Pottinger, took charge. A primitive, chaotic and lawless settlement soon sprang up.

> Today's Triads still recite an oath of allegiance to the Ming, but their loyalty these days is to the dollar rather than the vanquished Son of Heaven.

THE TRIADS

Hong Kong's Triads, which continue to run the territory's drug, prostitution, people-smuggling, gambling and loan-sharking rackets, weren't always the gangster operations they are today.

They were founded as secret and patriotic societies that opposed the corrupt and brutal Qing (Manchu) dynasty and aided the revolution that eventually toppled it in 1911. The fact that these organisations had adopted Kwan Tai (or Kwan Yu), the god of war and upholder of righteousness, integrity and loyalty, as their patron, lent them further respectability. The Triads descended into crime and vice during the Chinese Civil War (1945–49), and came in droves to Hong Kong after the communists came to power in 1949. Today they are the Chinese equivalent of the Mafia.

The communists smashed the Triad-controlled drug racket in Shànghǎi after the 1949 revolution. Having long memories and fearing a repeat could occur with the looming 1997 handover, many Hong Kong–based hoods moved their operations to ethnic-Chinese communities in countries such as Thailand, the Philippines, Australia, Canada and the US. Since 1997, however, many Triads have moved back into Hong Kong and have even expanded their operations onto the mainland.

The definitive work on the Triads is *Triad Societies in Hong Kong* by WP Morgan, a former subinspector with the Royal Hong Kong Police.

1773	1799	1841
Opium smuggling to China skyrockets after the British East India Company monopolises production and export of Indian opium.	China's silver reserves drain rapidly as opium addiction sweeps through China. The Qing emperor issues an edict banning opium trade in the country.	British marines plant the Union flag on the western part of Hong Kong Island, claiming the land for the British Crown.

GROWING PAINS

What would later be called the Second Opium War (or Second Anglo-Chinese War) broke out in October 1856. The victorious British forced the Chinese to sign the Convention of Peking in 1860, which ceded Kowloon Peninsula and Stonecutters Island to Britain. Britain was now in complete control of Victoria Harbour and its approaches.

As the Qing dynasty slid into major chaos towards the end of the 19th century, the British government petitioned China to extend the colony into the New Territories. The June 1898 Convention of Peking handed Britain a larger-than-expected slice of territory that included 235 islands and ran north to the Shumchun (Shēnzhèn) River, increasing the colony's size by 90%.

A SLEEPY BACKWATER

While Hong Kong's major trading houses, including Jardine Matheson and Swire, prospered from their trade with China, the colony hardly thrived in its first few decades. Fever, bubonic plague and typhoons threatened life and property, and at first the colony attracted a fair number of criminals and vice merchants.

Gradually Hong Kong began to shape itself into a more substantial community. Nonetheless, from the late 19th century right up to WWII, Hong Kong lived in the shadow of the treaty port of Shànghǎi, which had become Asia's premier trade and financial centre – not to mention its style capital.

The colony's population continued to grow thanks to the waves of immigrants fleeing the Chinese Revolution of 1911, which ousted the decaying Qing dynasty and ushered in several decades of strife, rampaging warlords and famine. The Japanese invasion of China in 1937 sparked another major exodus to these shores.

Hong Kong's status as a British colony would offer the refugees only a temporary haven. The day after Japan attacked the US naval base at Pearl Harbor on 7 December 1941, its military machine swept down from Guǎngzhōu and into Hong Kong.

Conditions under Japanese rule were harsh, with indiscriminate killings of mostly Chinese civilians; Western civilians were incarcerated at Stanley Prison on Hong Kong Island. Many Hong Kong Chinese fled to Macau, administered by neutral Portugal.

HISTORY GROWING PAINS

Alarmed by the spread of addiction and the silver draining from the country to pay for opium, the Qing emperor issued an edict in 1799 banning the trade of opium in China. The ban had little effect and the lucrative trade continued.

'Albert is so amused at my having got the island of Hong Kong', wrote Queen Victoria to King Leopold of Belgium in 1841. At the time, Hong Kong was little more than a backwater of about 20 villages and hamlets.

1842	1860	1894	1895
China cedes Hong Kong Island to Britain. The British foreign secretary at the time calls Hong Kong 'a barren island with hardly a house upon it!'.	Under the Convention of Peking, China cedes Kowloon Peninsula and Stonecutters Island to Britain, giving Britain complete control of Victoria Harbour and its approaches.	Bubonic plague breaks out for the first time in Hong Kong, killing 2500 of mainly local Chinese; trade suffers badly as ships avoid the plague-infested port.	Future Chinese national hero Sun Yatsen plots an insurrection in southern China from his base in Hong Kong; it fails and the British ban Sun from the territory.

THE ROAD TO BOOMTOWN

After Japan's withdrawal from Hong Kong, and subsequent surrender in August 1945, the colony looked set to resume its hibernation. But events both at home and on the mainland forced the colony in a new direction.

The Chinese Civil War (1945–49) and the subsequent Communist takeover of China unleashed a torrent of refugees – both rich and poor – into Hong Kong. The refugees brought along capital and cheap labour which would prove vital to Hong Kong's economic takeoff. On a paltry, war-torn foundation, local and foreign businesses built a huge manufacturing (notably textiles and garments) and financial services centre that transformed Hong Kong into one of the world's great economic miracles.

Hong Kong's stability received a hard battering at the height of the Cultural Revolution in 1967, as local procommunist groups instigated a series of anticolonial demonstrations, strikes and riots. The violence soon mushroomed into bombings and arson attacks, and the colony's economy was paralysed for months. The riot came to an end in December 1967, when Chinese Premier Zhou Enlai ordered the procommunist groups to stop.

In the early years of British Hong Kong, opium dens, gambling clubs and brothels proliferated; just a year after Britain took possession, an estimated 450 prostitutes worked out of two-dozen brothels, including a fair number of foreign prostitutes clustered in Lyndhurst Tce, which today is home to a hip bar scene.

A SOCIETY IN TRANSITION

After the 1967 crisis the colonial government initiated a series of reforms to alleviate social discontent and to foster a sense of belonging to Hong Kong. In the next decade the government introduced more labour laws, and invested heavily in public housing, medical service, education and recreational activities for youth.

Although Hong Kong's stock market collapsed in 1973, its economy resumed its upward trend later in the decade. The 'Open Door' policy of Deng Xiaoping, who took control of China in the confusion after Mao Zedong's death in 1976, revived Hong Kong's role as the gateway to the mainland and it boomed. By the end of the 1980s, Hong Kong was one of the richest places in Asia, second only to Japan in terms of GDP per capita.

THE 1997 QUESTION

Few people gave much thought to Hong Kong's future until 1979, when the governor of Hong Kong, Murray MacLehose, raised the issue with Deng Xiaoping on his first official visit to Běijīng. Britain was legally

1898	1911	1937	1941
China hands the New Territories to Britain in a 99-year lease, which begins on 1 July 1898 and ends at midnight on 30 June 1997.	The colony's population expands as waves of immigrants flee the Chinese Revolution on the mainland.	Pouncing on a country weakened by a bloody civil war, Japan invades China; as many as 750,000 mainlanders seek shelter in Hong Kong over the next three years.	British forces surrender to Japanese forces on Christmas Day; the population in Hong Kong is more than halved during almost four years of Japanese occupation.

bound to hand back only the New Territories – not Hong Kong Island and Kowloon, which had been ceded to it forever. However, the fact that nearly half of Hong Kong's population lived in the New Territories by that time made it an untenable division.

It was Deng Xiaoping who decided that the time was ripe to recover Hong Kong, forcing the British to the negotiating table. The views of Hong Kong people were not sought whatsoever. The inevitable conclusion laid to rest the political jitters and commercial concerns that had in 1983 seen the Hong Kong dollar collapse – and subsequently be pegged to the US dollar.

Despite soothing words from the Chinese, British and Hong Kong governments, over the next 13 years the population of Hong Kong were to suffer considerable anxiety at the possible political and economic consequences of the handover.

ONE COUNTRY, TWO SYSTEMS

Under the *Sino-British Joint Declaration on the Question of Hong Kong of December 1984,* Hong Kong would be reborn as a Special Administrative Region (SAR) of China. This meant its capitalist system would be permitted to continue, while across the border China's version of socialism would continue. The Chinese catchphrase for this was 'One Country, Two Systems'.

The *Basic Law for Hong Kong,* the future SAR's constitution, preserved Hong Kong's English common-law judicial system and guaranteed the right of property and ownership, as well as other key civil liberties. The SAR would enjoy a high degree of autonomy with the exception of foreign affairs and matters of defence.

Despite these assurances, many families and individuals had little faith in a future Hong Kong under Chinese rule, and a so-called brain drain ensued when tens of thousands left the colony for the United States, Canada, Australia and New Zealand towards the end of the 1980s.

TIĀN'ĀNMÉN & ITS AFTERMATH

The concern of many Hong Kong people over their future turned to out-and-out fear on 4 June 1989, when the Chinese army killed pro-democracy demonstrators in Bĕijīng 's Tiān'ānmén Square.

Tiān'ānmén was a watershed for Hong Kong. Sino-British relations deteriorated, the stock market fell 22% in one day and a great deal of capital left the territory for destinations overseas.

HISTORY ONE COUNTRY, TWO SYSTEMS

In the early 1970s, the construction of the first three 'New Towns' (Sha Tin, Tsuen Wan and Tuen Mun) commenced, marking the start of a massive and unprecedented public-housing program that would, and still does, house millions of Hong Kong people.

NEW TOWNS

1962	1967	1971	
The great famine caused by the Great Leap Forward in China drives 70,000 people to flee into Hong Kong in less than three months.	Riots and bombings by procommunist groups rock Hong Kong; armed Chinese militia cross the border, killing five policemen and penetrating 3km into the New Territories before pulling back.	A former child actor called Bruce Lee lands his first adult leading role in the kung fu film *The Big Boss;* it becomes a smash around the world.	

Bruce Lee statue (p138)

GAVIN HELLIER/GETTY IMAGES ©

The Hong Kong government sought to rebuild confidence by announcing plans for a new airport and shipping port in what was the world's most expensive (HK$160 billion or US$20.6 billion) infrastructure project of the day.

The Tiān'ānmén protests had strengthened the resolve of those people who either could not or would not leave, giving rise to the territory's first official political parties. In a bid to restore credibility, the government introduced a Bill of Rights in 1990 and the following year gave Hong Kong citizens the right to choose 18 of the 60 members of the Legislative Council (LegCo), which until then had essentially been a rubber-stamp body chosen by the government and special-interest groups.

DEMOCRACY & THE LAST GOVERNOR

One of the first parties to emerge was the United Democrats of Hong Kong, led by outspoken democrats Martin Lee and Szeto Wah. The pair, initially courted by China for their anticolonial positions and appointed to the committee that drafted the Basic Law, subsequently infuriated Běijīng by publicly burning copies of the proto-constitution in protest over Tiān'ānmén. Predictably, China denounced them as subversives.

In the aftermath of the Tiān'ānmén Square protests of 1989, an underground smuggling operation, code-named Yellow Bird, was set up in Hong Kong to spirit many activists to safety overseas. Meanwhile Hong Kong–based Chinese officials who had criticised the killings were either yanked from their posts or sought asylum in the West.

Chris Patten, Hong Kong's 28th – and last – British governor, arrived in 1992, pledging to sceptical citizens that democracy reforms would be sped up. China reacted badly, first levelling daily verbal attacks at him, then threatening the post-1997 careers of any pro-democracy politicians or officials. When these tactics failed, China targeted Hong Kong's economy. Talks on certain business contracts and infrastructure projects straddling 1997 suddenly came to a halt, including the new airport program.

Sensing that it had alienated even its supporters in Hong Kong, China backed down and in 1994 gave its blessing to the new airport at Chek Lap Kok. It remained hostile to direct elections, however, and vowed to disband the democratically elected legislature after 1997. It eventually did what it said by installing an interim rubber-stamp body which would serve until June 1998.

As for the executive branch of power, China organised an 'election' in December 1996 to select Hong Kong's first postcolonial leader. But Tung Chee Hwa (1937–), the Shànghǎi-born shipping magnate hand-picked to be the SAR's first chief executive, won approval by retaining Patten's right-hand woman, Anson Chan, as his chief secretary and Donald Tsang as financial secretary.

1976	**1982**	**1984**
Deng Xiaoping takes control of China after Mao Zedong's death, and revives Hong Kong's role as the gateway to the mainland.	British PM Margaret Thatcher visits Běijīng to begin talks on Hong Kong's future. Two years of closed-door wrangling between the Chinese and British ensues.	Hong Kong's future is sealed in the *Sino-British Joint Declaration on the Question of Hong Kong*; the city's capitalist system will continue after 1997.

AFP/GETTY IMAGES ©

Deng Xiaoping

On the night of 30 June 1997, the handover celebrations held in the purpose-built extension of the Hong Kong Convention & Exhibition Centre in Wan Chai were watched by millions of people around the world. Chris Patten shed a tear while Chinese President Jiang Zemin beamed and Prince Charles was outwardly stoic (but privately scathing, describing the Chinese leaders in a diary leaked years later to the British tabloids as 'appalling old waxworks').

So the curtain fell on a century and a half of British rule, and the new chief executive Tung summed up Chinese feelings about the handover with the words: 'Now we are masters of our own house'.

HONG KONG POST-1997

Almost as soon as the euphoria of the 1997 handover faded, things started going badly in Hong Kong. The financial crisis that had rocked other parts of Asia began to be felt in Hong Kong at the end of 1997. A strain of deadly avian flu saw the city slaughter more than one million chickens.

The credibility of the SAR administration was severely damaged in 1999 when the government challenged a High Court ruling that upheld

CHINA'S HONG KONG INVASION PLAN

The peaceful agreement that eventually settled the status of Hong Kong was by no means a foregone conclusion in the decades leading up to it. The key negotiators have since revealed just how touchy China felt about Hong Kong and how close it came to retaking the territory by force.

Margaret Thatcher, the British prime minister who negotiated the deal, said later that Deng Xiaoping, then China's leader, told her he 'could walk in and take the whole lot this afternoon'.

She replied that China would lose everything if it did. 'There is nothing I could do to stop you,' she said, 'but the eyes of the world would now know what China is like.'

Lu Ping, the top Chinese negotiator, recently confirmed that this was no bluff on Deng's part. Deng feared that announcing the date for the 1997 handover would provoke serious unrest in Hong Kong, and China would be compelled to invade as a result.

According to Lu, China had also been hours away from invading during 1967, at the height of the chaotic Cultural Revolution, when a radical faction of the People's Liberation Army (PLA) was poised to invade the British colony during procommunist riots. The invasion was called off only by a late-night order from Premier Zhou Enlai to the local army commander, Huang Yongsheng, a radical Maoist who had been itching to invade.

1989	1990	1997	2001
More than a million Hong Kong people march in support of the pro-democracy movement in Běijīng; Chinese troops kill protesting students in and around Tiān'ānmén Square.	The government introduces a Bill of Rights and in 1991 gives Hong Kong citizens the right to choose 18 of the 60 members of the Legislative Council (LegCo).	The rain falls, Chris Patten cries and Hong Kong returns to Chinese sovereignty; avian flu breaks out, six people die and more than a million chickens are culled.	Tung Chee Hwa follows his Běijīng masters in labelling the Falun Gong political/ spiritual group a 'vicious cult' and limits their activities in Hong Kong.

EMIGRANTS

residency rights for China-born offspring of Hong Kong citizens, regardless of the parents' residency status at the time of the child's birth. The ruling was based on certain clauses of the Basic Law, and the government calculated that it would potentially make 1.67 million people from the mainland eligible for right of abode in the territory. The SAR administration appealed to the standing committee of the NPC, China's rubber-stamp parliament, to reinterpret these clauses. The NPC complied, and ruled that at least one parent must already have acquired permanent residency status at the time of the birth.

As a result, the mainland stands accused of interfering in Hong Kong's judicial independence via intrusion into the city's legal system, and the apparent withholding of universal suffrage from Hong Kong citizens. Clearly the mainland government wields huge influence, but in the first few years after the handover (at least up until the historic 500,000-strong antigovernment protests of 1 July 2003, which changed Běijīng's stance on Hong Kong), it largely chose to tread lightly, honouring the spirit of the handover agreement to a great extent.

THE CLAMOUR FOR DEMOCRACY

In the wake of the Tiān'ānmén Square killings, local Hong Kong people with money and skills made a mad dash to emigrate to any country that would take them. During the worst period more than 1000 people were leaving each week, especially for Canada and Australia.

Tung Chee Hwa's first term is remembered as much for his confusing housing policy, which many blamed for a sustained fall in property prices, as for such vacuous infrastructure proposals as a Chinese medicine port. Despite his poor standing in the polls, Tung was returned for a second five-year term in March 2002.

Controversy continued to dog his time in office, however, most notably in March 2003, with the government's failure to contain the Severe Acute Respiratory Syndrome (SARS) epidemic at an early stage, provoking a torrent of blame. The outbreak killed 299 people, infected 1755 and all but closed Hong Kong down for weeks.

In July 2003 the government incensed the public yet further when it tried to turn Article 23 of the Basic Law into legislation; the National Security Bill raised fears that Hong Kong's press freedom and civil liberties would be undermined. In the face of massive public protests – of 500,000 people or more – the government shelved the bill indefinitely.

In March 2005 Tung announced his resignation as chief executive. His replacement was the bow-tie-wearing chief secretary Sir Donald Tsang, who had continuously served as Hong Kong's financial secretary since before the handover through 2001, when he became the city's number-two public official.

Compared to Tung, Tsang was a welcome replacement for both the Běijīng powerbrokers and the Hong Kong public. In 2007 Tsang was

2003	2006	2009	2009
SARS all but shuts down Hong Kong for weeks. The Closer Economic Partnership Agreement with the mainland government provides favourable business opportunities.	Heavily pregnant women are banned from entering the territory after a flood of mainland Chinese women enter Hong Kong to give birth and claim citizenship for their children.	Hong Kong's population exceeds seven million and the unemployment rate grows to almost 5% in the face of the world's worst economic crisis since the Great Depression.	Some 150,000 people attend the 20th anniversary candlelight vigil held in Victoria Park to mark the 4 June 1989 Tiān'ānmén Square killings.

easily re-elected with Běijīng's blessing. However, he soon suffered an erosion of public confidence when he was seen to renege on a series of promises, including delaying a highly anticipated consultation on reforming the electoral process for the chief executive and legislature to make the 2012 polls more democratic.

The clamour for democracy reached a crescendo in 2010 as two landmark political events took place in successive months. In May five pro-democracy lawmakers were re-elected to LegCo after they collectively resigned four months earlier in the hope that the resulting by-elections would serve as a de facto referendum on universal suffrage. The pro-Běijīng parties boycotted the contests, however, and the quintet's campaign came unstuck, even though they could claim to have been returned to the chamber by a respectable vote.

The pro-democracy parties had in fact been divided over the political strategy behind the forced by-elections, and the long-running differences among the key players imploded the following month when the biggest of them all, the Democratic Party, sided with the government in a new political reform package that would see LegCo earn a slightly increased percentage of popularly elected seats at the expense of delayed universal suffrage for the entire legislature and for the election of Hong Kong's chief executive.

The calls for democracy have continued since, most notably around the election – by a 1200-member body of predominantly pro-Běijīng notables – of the SAR's fourth chief executive in March 2012. Leung Chun-ying, a stalwart in Hong Kong politics with impeccably close links to Běijīng, defeated the long-time hopeful and former civil-service chief Henry Tang in a race that would be remembered as much for the carnival of scandals it served up as for the less-than-delicate meddling by Běijīng behind the scenes.

A CHANGED CITY?

Visitors returning to Hong Kong since July 1997 would see and feel little material difference walking around the city today. Perhaps the most striking thing for returning visitors from the West is the influx of a new breed of visitor: mainland Chinese, who now make up nearly 70% of the territory's visitor numbers.

In many ways Hong Kong has benefited from closer ties with the mainland. The growth in Hong Kong's tourism would have been impossible without the influx of mainland tourists, and the Closer Economic Partnership Agreement signed with the mainland government in 2003

Hong Kong is the only place under Chinese rule that still mourns those killed in 1989. Every year on 4 June, tens of thousands of people gather at Victoria Park to attend a candle-light vigil held in commemoration of those who lost their lives.

A measure of just how successful the handover had generally been came in a 2007 BBC interview with Margaret Thatcher. Marking the 10th anniversary of the handover of Hong Kong from Britain to China, Thatcher, to her own surprise, deemed China's overall performance a success.

Candlelit vigil, anniversary of Tiān'ānmén Square killings

IMAGESTATE MEDIA PARTNERS LIMITED – IMPACT PHOTOS/ALAMY ©

2010
LegCo approves $66.9 billion for the Hong Kong portion of the highly controversial Guǎngzhōu–Hong Kong high-speed rail link, following 25 hours of heated debate.

2010
The pro-democracy camp splits over a government reform package which ensures a slightly more representative LegCo but gives no definitive date on universal suffrage in all elections.

provided favourable business opportunities to Hong Kong's investors and industries.

However, the seemingly headlong rush for the Chinese tourist dollar, with the attendant proliferation of luxury stores in areas such as Causeway Bay and Canton Rd in Tsim Sha Tsui, has pushed up shop rentals across the board, fuelling inflation and taking many small traders off Hong Kong's once accommodating streetscape. Similarly, the property market, flush with cash from mainland speculators, has become prohibitively expensive for ordinary folk. Of most concern to Hong Kong people are the tens of thousands of mainland Chinese migrants and pregnant women who have poured into the city in the past decade or so (any child born in Hong Kong, even to noncitizens, has a right of abode). Worries abound that the influx is putting an ever-increasing strain on Hong Kong's public services, and the cultural – and material wealth – differences between locals and 'mainlanders' look set to provide more fodder for both sensationalist and sobering news headlines in the years to come.

While closer ties with the mainland have often been met with uneasy feelings, might history one day identify an equal and opposite reaction going on? Hong Kong's dazzling success and core values arguably exert 'soft' power that influences thinking on the mainland. It might be hard to measure, but in the enclave that sheltered and inspired the fathers of powerful mainland movements (Sun Yatsen and Zhou Enlai), it should not be dismissed.

What is certain is that, more than 15 years on from the handover, Hong Kong people are asking questions about their identity more intensely than ever as Hong Kong and mainland China, for better or worse, increasingly intertwine.

In September 2008 melamine-tainted milk products imported from the mainland were found in Hong Kong, further souring the opinion of many regarding the city's increasing integration with the mainland in many aspects of day-to-day life.

2011	2011	2012	2012
A minimum wage of $28 takes effect, and inflation hits a 16-year high; the Government gives a $6000 cash handout to every adult permanent resident in a budget U-turn.	Public hospitals stop accepting reservations from pregnant mainland women through year's end; immigration officials block 1930 heavily pregnant women from crossing the border.	Property surveyor Leung Chun-ying begins a five-year term as the fourth Hong Kong SAR chief executive after beating former civil-service head Henry Tang in a scandal-plagued election.	Tens of thousands take to the streets to protest a new national education curriculum that they fear will brainwash students with Chinese Communist Party propaganda.

Arts

Hong Kong's arts scene is more vibrant than its reputation suggests. There are musical ensembles of all persuasions, an assortment of theatre groups, Chinese and modern dance troupes, and numerous art organisations. A number of new venues, such as the Jockey Club Creative Arts Centre in New Kowloon and the high-profile White Cube and Gagosian Gallery in Central, have emerged in recent years. Government funds allow organisers to bring in top international performers, and the number of international arts festivals hosted here seems to grow each year. Chinese opera performances can be seen in both formal settings and on the street.

ART

Hong Kong is one of the three most important art auction centres in the world, along with New York and London. Theoretically, it can only get stronger, given that China has already surpassed the US as the world's largest market for art and antiques. Despite some industry concern about the ability of the Chinese market to promote stable, long-term growth, Hong Kong will continue to ride the bull wave nimbly – and with gusto – for as long as the overheated market keeps its lid on.

That said, more could be done to nurture local art. The protracted uncertainty over the direction of the West Kowloon Cultural District has frustrated many local artists, but it is hoped that the proposed establishment in 2013 of a new government department to specifically cater for arts and culture will have the necessary powers to develop and implement culture-related policies for the city.

Contemporary Hong Kong art tends not to bother too much with grandiose narratives about nationhood and religion, preferring to take an introverted view of the world and expressing visions of Chinese-ness outside of the national frame.

The best sources for up-to-date information on Hong Kong and Asian art are *Asian Art News* (www.asianartnews.com), the free monthly *Art Map* (www.artmap.com.hk), the **Asia Art Archive** (Map p368; ☑2815 1112; www.aaa. org.hk; 11th fl, Hollywood Centre, 233 Hollywood Rd, Sheung Wan; ◷10am-6pm Mon-Sat) and the **Hong Kong International Association of Art Critics** (www.aic-ahk.org), which has online reviews of exhibitions in the city.

Roots

In general, Chinese painters of the past were interested in traditional forms and painting processes – not necessarily composition and colour. Brush strokes and the utensils used to produce them are of vital importance and interest. In traditional Chinese art, change for the sake of change was never the philosophy or the trend; Chinese artists would compare their work with that of the master and judge it accordingly.

The influential Lingnan School of Painting, founded by the watercolourist Chao Shao-an (1905–98) in the 1930s and relocated to Hong Kong in 1948, attempted to move away from this tradition. It combined

Top Museums for Hong Kong Art

Hong Kong Museum of Art (Tsim Sha Tsui)

Hong Kong Arts Centre (Wan Chai)

Hong Kong Visual Arts Centre (Wan Chai)

ART SPACES & GALLERIES

Nonprofit exhibition spaces in Hong Kong include **Para/Site Artspace** (藝術空間; Map p368; 2517 4620; www.para-site.org.hk; 4 Po Yan St, Sheung Wan; noon-7pm Wed-Sun), the most consistent and promising of the local artists' cooperatives; **Fotan Art Studios** (伙炭藝術工作室; www.fotanian.com), a labyrinth of artists' lofts in vacated factory buildings set against the rolling hills of Fo Tan; the nine-storey Jockey Club Creative Arts Centre (p147), which was converted from an industrial building and houses artists' studios; and Cattle Depot Artist Village (p149), a one-time slaughterhouse that is home to a colony of local artists. The best time to visit Fotan Art Studios and the JC-CAC is during their open studios (see their websites for the dates).

The following commercial galleries do not charge an admission fee.

➡ **10 Chancery Lane Gallery** (Map p366; 2810 0065; www.10chancerylanegallery.com; Ground fl, 10 Chancery Lane, Central; 10am-6pm Mon-Sat) Specialises in contemporary works by local, regional and international artists.

➡ **Amelia Johnson Contemporary** (Map p368; 2548 2286; www.ameliajohnsoncontemporary.com; Ground fl, 6-10 Shin Hing St, Central; 11am-7pm Tue-Sat) Shows the works of emerging and established artists from Hong Kong and overseas in a range of media. It also runs an annual exhibition of works by promising young artists.

➡ **Blindspot Gallery** (Map p366; 2517 6238; www.blindspotgallery.com; 24-26a, Aberdeen St, Central; 11am-7pm Tue-Sat) An up-and-coming gallery specialising in contemporary photography mainly from Hong Kong and other parts of Asia.

➡ **Grotto Fine Art** (嘉圖; Map p366; 2121 2270; www.grottofineart.com; 2nd fl, 31c-d Wyndham St, Central; 11am-7pm Mon-Sat) The only gallery that represents exclusively Hong Kong artists. It features modern and contemporary works, from painting and sculpture to installation pieces.

➡ **Hanart TZ Gallery** (漢雅軒; Map p362; 2526 9019; www.hanart.com; 407 Pedder Bldg, 12 Pedder St, Central; 10am-6.30pm Mon-Sat) Hanart is la crème de la crème of art galleries in Hong Kong and was instrumental in introducing contemporary Chinese art to the world.

➡ **Osage Gallery** (2793 4817; www.osagegallery.com; 5th fl, Kian Dai Industrial Bldg, 73-75 Hung To Rd; 10am-7pm Mon-Sun) With an enormous warehouse-style exhibition space in Kwun Tong, this gallery specialises in Hong Kong, Chinese and Asian art.

➡ **Schoeni Art Gallery** (Map p366; 2869 8802; www.schoeni.com.hk; 21-31 Old Bailey St, Soho; 10.30am-6.30pm Mon-Sat) Well-established gallery specialising in neo-realist and postmodern mainland Chinese art. It has three branches, with the main one on Old Bailey St.

➡ **Sin Sin Fine Art** (Map p368; 2858 5072; www.sinsin.com.hk; 53-54 Sai St, Sheung Wan; 9.30am-6.30pm Mon-Sat, 2-6pm Sun) Eclectic gallery owned and run by a local fashion designer and showing Hong Kong, mainland Chinese and Southeast Asian art.

➡ **Input/Output Gallery** (Map p368; 3105 1127; http://inputoutput.tv; 28 Tai Ping Shan St, Sheung Wan; 11am-7pm Tue-Sat, noon-5pm Sun) The only gallery in Hong Kong that focuses on new media arts.

traditional Chinese, Japanese and Western artistic methods to produce a rather decorative style, and dominated the small art market in Hong Kong for the next two decades.

The most distinct group of painters and sculptors to appear in Hong Kong were the proponents of the New Ink Painting movement who came to prominence in the late 1960s. Most had strong links to China or its cultural heritage. The movement aimed at reconciling Chinese and Western ideas by steering traditional Chinese ink painting towards abstract expressionism. Lui Shou-kwan (1919–75), who arrived in Hong Kong in 1948, was the earliest and the best known of the New Ink Painting artists. Lui worked for the Yau Ma Tei ferry as a pier inspector and taught in his spare time. Speaking no English, his only experience of the West was through pictures and books borrowed from the British Council library. Many of the artists who became associated with the movement were his students.

The only major artist to break free of the dominant style of the era was Luis Chan (1905–95). Born in Panama, Chan came to Hong Kong at the age of five, where he learnt to paint from art magazines and a correspondence course. Stylistically, Chan was a loner with no apparent allegiance to any painting tradition. He was also a genius who, particularly in his post-'60s works, transformed Hong Kong into a fantastical realm of dreams and hallucinations. His 1976 painting *Ping Chau* is a bizarre interpretation of the somnolent outlying island which is at once puzzling and endearing.

Avant-Garde

The 1980s and '90s saw the coming of age of artists born after WWII, many of whom had received their training abroad. Less burdened by the need to reconcile East and West, they devoted their efforts to defining avant-garde art, often through Western mediums. They were also politically engaged. Wong Yan-kwai, a painter educated in France, was arguably the most influential artist of that period and is still one of the most accomplished today. His powerful paintings in vibrant colours are free of any social or historical context. Wong's mural graces Club 71 in Central.

London-trained Antonio Mak (1951–94) is Hong Kong's most famous contemporary sculptor and is known for his figurative pieces in cast bronze. He focused on the human figure as well as on animals important in Chinese legend and mythology (eg horses and tigers), and was greatly influenced by Rodin.

Salisbury Gardens, leading to the entrance of the Hong Kong Museum of Art in Tsim Sha Tsui, is lined with modern sculptures by contemporary Hong Kong sculptors. Dotted among the greenery of Kowloon Park is Sculpture Walk (Map p378), with 30 marble, bronze and other weather-resistant works by both local and overseas artists, including a bronze by Mak called *Torso* and one by Britain's late Sir Eduardo Paolozzi (1924–2005) called *Concept of Newton*.

Antonio Mak's work employs much visual 'punning'. In his *Bible from Happy Valley* (1992), a racehorse is portrayed with a winglike book made of lead across its back. The word 'book' in Cantonese has the same sound as 'to lose (at gambling)'.

Contemporary

Compared to their predecessors, Hong Kong's young artists – those born in the '70s and '80s – take a more internalised view of the world. They are overwhelmingly unfussed with orthodox Chinese culture and older generations' attempts to amalgamate East and West. Instead, they're often looking for – or perhaps, trying to retrieve – something that is uniquely Hong Kong. Nonetheless, their works show eloquence in a host of mediums, from Wilson Shieh's cheeky urban paintings using Chinese *gōngbǐ* (fine-brush) techniques to Jaffa Lam's sculpture installations.

Chow Chun-fai's background across a wide spectrum of media has seen him work between different art forms, such as photographs from classical paintings, or paintings from films. Adrian Wong's playful works involve his family connections to prominent names in the local entertainment industry, and indigenous superstitions. Kacey Wong's exciting installations can usually move about and invariably involve some kind of Hong Kong theme or common household treasure recast in a jovial light. His *Sleepwalker* (2011) contraption imbues the bunk bed – an indispensable fixture in Hong Kong's tight living spaces – with life and speaks to a mass aspiration, or doomed desperation, for a more humane habitat.

ANTONIO MAK

TSANG TSOU-CHOI

Photography

Hong Kong is endowed with internationally competitive photographers, and some of their works can be seen in the Hong Kong Heritage Museum (p182).

Working in black and white, documentary photographer Yau Leung (1941–97) captured some of the most stunning and iconic images of 1960s Hong Kong, while art photographer So Hing-keung focuses on the shadows, figurative and literal, of the city in creations known for their psychological depth. Hong Kong–born, London-based visual artist Kurt Tong explores his multilayered identity, family heritage and memories through thoughtful documentary photography. *In Case it Rains in Heaven* (2010), his best-known project, is presented like a high-end shopping catalogue of stylised portraits of paper-made objects burnt as offerings for the deceased. The combustible items honoured by Tong run the gamut of modern human desires in Chinese societies.

Street Art & Other Arts

Street graffiti was almost nonexistent or largely unrecognised in Hong Kong until the passing in 2007 of the self-proclaimed 'King of Kowloon' (aka Tsang Tsou-choi), who for decades had smothered the city with his trademark rambling, childlike calligraphy that cursed the Queen of England for 'usurping' his rightful land. His irrepressible daily reveries and inimitable visual style eventually inspired many artists and designers, and won him exhibitions both at home and abroad.

Street art has noticeably grown in Hong Kong since, perhaps with the King's benediction. This trend in part stems from a new-found confidence among a younger generation of artists to express their dissatisfaction with the social problems of the day using means that are more open and combative. After the April 2011 arrest in mainland China of the prominent artist and activist Ai Weiwei, a number of artists in Hong Kong came forth with a dose of creative surprises to raise public attention of his case and to rally for his release. Most memorably, Ai-inspired graffiti stencils appeared on pavements, overpasses and walls for five nights straight around the city, thanks to a lone operator known only as 'Tangerine'.

There are only about four Tsang Tsou-choi works left on Hong Kong's streets today (with three subject to the mercy of the elements), but you won't miss the concrete pillar that bears his imperial treatise at the Star Ferry pier in Tsim Sha Tsui.

ART VERSUS INVISIBILITY: LEUNG PING-KWAN

Why is food one of your favourite metaphors? When Hong Kong was returned to China in 1997, the West says, 'Poor you!', and China tells us, 'You should be happy!' But the reality is neither... We carry on loving and eating. So instead of heroic tragedies, I write about the wear and tear of daily life, about history, about our emotional complexities through food and romance.

What are some of the features of Hong Kong literature? A mature urban sensibility. It was exploring the individual's psychology when mainland Chinese literature focused on collective values, experimenting with modernism when the latter was writing realist narratives about the building of a nation. Today the best mainland fiction is that depicting the lives of peasants – rural problems are the concern of contemporary China; but portrayals of urban life or foreign cultures tend to be melodramatic and clichéd. By contrast, Hong Kong literature talks about both with much greater sophistication.

Why is Hong Kong literature so 'invisible'? We don't have our own literary museum; our government does not promote literature through international cultural exchange. Our society and its representative media are commercially oriented and lack cultural vision. Hong Kong literature has evolved for the most part under colonial rule.

An interview with Hong Kong poet Leung Ping-kwan, aka 'Ya Si' (1948–).

Equally unorthodox in its use of public space is Street Art Movement, a new group that stages seemingly impromptu gallery shows in the most ordinary of common spaces. In March 2012 the group organised an art ride along the Tsuen Wan line on the MTR, sketching and clipping their finished drawings onto laundry lines that they strung up inside the train carriages as fresh interest poured in at every station.

Contemporary ceramics is another field in which Hong Kong artists enjoy an edge beyond the city's borders. Fiona Wong, one of the city's best-known ceramic artists, makes life-sized sculptural works of clothing, shoes and other familiar items.

MUSIC

Western Classical

Western classical music is very popular in Hong Kong. The territory boasts the Hong Kong Philharmonic Orchestra, the Hong Kong Sinfonietta and the City Chamber Orchestra of Hong Kong. Opportunities to see big-name soloists and major orchestras abound throughout the year, especially during the Hong Kong Arts Festival in February/March. The **Hong Kong International Piano Competition** (http://chshk.brinkster.net), with its star-studded jury, is held every three years in October/November. The **Hong Kong Academy for Performing Arts** (Map p372; www.hkapa.edu) has free concerts almost daily.

> The Leisure and Cultural Services Department (www.lcsd.gov.hk) regularly stages free arts and entertainment shows at its venues throughout the territory.

Jazz

The best times to experience world-class jazz in the city are during the **Hong Kong International Jazz Festival** (www.hkijf.com), which takes place in the final quarter of the year, and the Hong Kong Arts Festival in February/March. Hong Kong also has a small but zealous circle of local musicians, including the 17-piece **Saturday Night Jazz Orchestra** (www.saturdaynight-jazz.com), which plays big-band sounds every month. Other names to watch out for include guitarist Eugene Pao, the first local jazz artist to sign with an international label, and pianist Ted Lo, who has played with Astrud Gilberto and Herbie Hancock.

Traditional Chinese

You won't hear much traditional Chinese music on the streets of Hong Kong, except perhaps the sound of the doleful *dī-daa,* a clarinet-like instrument played in funeral processions; the hollow-sounding *gǔ* (drums) and crashing *luó* (gongs) and *bat* (cymbals) at lion dances; the *èrhú,* a two-stringed fiddle favoured by beggars for its plaintive sound; or strains of Cantonese opera wafting from the radio of a minibus driver. You can sample this kind of music, albeit in a form adapted to a symphony-orchestra model, at concerts given by the **Hong Kong Chinese Orchestra** (www.hkco.org). For more authentic fare, catch a Chinese opera or check out the Temple Street Night Market, where street performers deliver operatic excerpts.

Canto-Pop

Hong Kong's home-grown popular-music scene is dominated by 'Canto-pop' – compositions that often blend Western rock, pop and R&B with Chinese melodies and lyrics. Rarely radical, the songs invariably deal with such teenage concerns as unrequited love and loneliness; to many they sound like the American pop songs of the 1950s. The music is slick and eminently singable – thus the explosion of karaoke bars throughout the territory. Attending a Canto-pop concert is to see the city at its sweetest and most over the top, with screaming, silly dancing, Day-Glo wigs and enough floral tributes to set up a flower market.

Canto-pop scaled new heights from the mid-1980s to mid-1990s and turned singers like Anita Mui, Leslie Cheung, Alan Tam, Priscilla Chan and Danny Chan into household names in Hong Kong and among Chinese communities around the world. The peak of this Canto-pop golden age came with the advent of the so-called Four Kings: thespian/singer Andy Lau, Mr Nice Guy Jacky Cheung, dancer-turned-crooner Aaron Kwok and teen heart-throb Leon Lai.

It never quite reached that altitude again. Subsequent arrivals such as Beijing waif Faye Wong, Sammi Cheung, Kelly Chen and protohunk Nicholas Tse took their turns on the throne for a time. But today most stars are a packaged phenomenon. Singers from the mainland and Taiwan – singer/songwriter Jay Chou is one example – are competing with local stars and gaining new fans here, and the strongest influences on local music are now coming from Japan and Korea. There are also acts making their marks from the edge of the mainstream, such as Ellen Lo and Eman Lam, two 'urban folk' singer-songwriters, and My Little Airport, a dapper act whose irreverent multilingual lyrics are often speckled with cute Chinglish.

Originally designed for sports events, the Hong Kong Coliseum in Hung Hom is the prime venue for Canto-pop concerts. In the past, only the superstars could perform here, but now practically anyone with a bit of fame in the local entertainment industry can come and throw a bash.

THEATRE

Much, though not all, theatre in Hong Kong is Western in form, if not content. Traditional Chinese theatre can still be experienced, but Western theatre has been very influential. Most productions are staged in Cantonese, and a large number are new plays by Hong Kong writers. The fully professional **Hong Kong Repertory Theatre** (www.hkrep.com) and **Chung Ying Theatre Company** (www.chungying.com) put on Cantonese productions, very often with English titles. **Theatre**

RICHARD I'ANSON/GETTY IMAGES ©

Chinese opera at Sunbeam Theatre (p123)

du Pif (www.thtdupif.com), formed by a professional Scottish-Chinese couple, puts on innovative works incorporating text, movement and visuals, in English and/or Cantonese. **Hong Kong Players** (www.hong kongplayers.com), consisting of expatriate amateurs, mounts classical and modern productions in English, while **Zuni Icosahedron** (www. zuni.org.hk) creates conceptual multimedia works known for their experimental format.

Among the more popular venues are the Fringe Club theatres in Central. The Hong Kong Cultural Centre, Hong Kong Academy for the Performing Arts, Hong Kong City Hall and the Hong Kong Arts Centre all host foreign productions, ranging from large-scale Western musicals to minimalist Japanese theatre.

ARTS THEATRE

The Cantonese opera Sunbeam Theatre seems to face a closure crisis every few years when its lease expires. The most recent crisis, in February 2012, was averted only when a group of private benefactors intervened at the last minute.

Chinese Opera

Chinese opera *(hei kuk)*, one of the three oldest dramatic art forms in the world, is a colourful, cacophonous spectacle featuring music, singing, martial arts, acrobatics and acting. Admittedly, it can take some getting used to. Female characters, whether played by men or women, sing in falsetto. The instrumental accompaniment often takes the form of drumming, gonging and other nonmelodic punctuation. And the whole affair can last four to six hours. But the costumes are splendid and the plots are adapted from legends and historical tales with universal themes. If you happen to attend a performance by a leading Cantonese opera troupe such as Chor Fung Ming, you'll experience some of the best moments of Chinese opera.

Cantonese opera *(yuet-kek)* is a regional variety of Chinese opera that flourished in Hong Kong, particularly in the 1950s when opera virtuosi fleeing China composed and performed a spate of original works in the territory. But eventually the limelight shifted to the sleek, leather-clad kid on the block – cinema – and things have been going downhill for Cantonese opera since. A shortage of performance venues is a problem. At present there are only two venues, Sunbeam Theatre (p123) in North Point and the recently restored Yau Ma Tei Theatre (p146), that are dedicated to the promotion and development of Chinese opera.

The best way to experience Cantonese opera is by attending a 'performance for the gods' *(sun kung hei)* in a temporary theatre. During major Chinese festivals, such as the Lunar New Year, Mid-Autumn Festival and Tin Hau Festival, rural communities invite troupes to perform. The performances usually take place on a makeshift stage set up in a temple or a bamboo shed, and it is a jovial, laid-back event for the whole family that lasts several days.

For a more formal experience, try the Hong Kong Arts Festival in February/March. **Ko Shan Theatre** (www.lcsd.gov.hk/CE/CulturalService/KST) also has Cantonese opera offerings. But the most reliable venue for opera performances year-round is Sunbeam Theatre, while Yau Ma Tei Theatre is expected to also develop an active show calendar on the other side of the harbour. At other times, you might stumble upon a performance at the Temple Street Night Market nearby.

Liu Yichang (1918–), Hong Kong's most respected senior writer, is the author of the stream of consciousness novella *Tête-bêche* which inspired Wong Kar-wai's *In the Mood for Love*.

You can also check out the enlightening Cantonese-opera display at the Hong Kong Heritage Museum, where the Hong Kong Tourist Board (HKTB) offers a Chinese-opera appreciation course every Saturday from 2.30pm to 3.45pm.

Other varieties of Chinese opera being performed in Hong Kong by local and/or visiting troupes include Peking opera, a highly refined form that uses almost no scenery but different kinds of traditional props; and Kun opera, the oldest form and one designated a Masterpiece of the Oral and Intangible Heritage of Humanity by Unesco.

TRANSLATED HONG KONG FICTION

The Cockroach and Other Stories (1995) by Liu Yichang Liu Yichang (1918–), Hong Kong's most respected senior writer, is believed to have written the first stream-of-consciousness novel in Chinese literature. 'The Cockroach' is a Kafkaesque exploration of psychology and philosophy. In 'Indecision', a woman is torn between staying in Hong Kong and returning to her mad husband in Shànghǎi.

Islands and Continents: Short Stories (2007) by Leung Ping-kwan Anti-heroes enter the limelight against the background of Hong Kong history. In 'Postcolonial Affairs of Food and the Heart', a man devours the culinary and erotic delights of other cultures in a bid to find his identity. Leung has also published the bilingual *Travelling with a Bitter Melon: Selected Poems (1973–1998)*.

Love in a Fallen City: And Other Stories by Eileen Chang Chang (1920–95) is considered by some to be the best modern Chinese writer. In the title story set during WWII, a divorcée pursues a liaison with a playboy from Shànghǎi to Hong Kong. Director Ann Hui made it into a film starring Chow Yun-fat. Chang also wrote *Lust, Caution*, a tale of love and espionage, which was adapted for film by Ang Lee.

My City: A Hong Kong Story (1993) by Xi Xi This novel offers a personal vision of Hong Kong in the '60s and '70s through the lives of a telephone repairman, his family, friends and, come to think of it, pineapples and stationery. *Asia Weekly* ranked it one of the top 100 works of 20th-century Chinese fiction.

Renditions Nos 47 & 48: Hong Kong Nineties (1997) Two writers to watch in this collection of 1990s Hong Kong fiction are Wong Bik-wan (1961–) and Dung Kai-cheung (1969–). Wong, a flamenco dancer, writes with a violent passion. 'Plenty and Sorrow' is a tale about Shànghǎi, with a chunk of cannibalism thrown in. Dung recreates the legend of the Father of Chinese Agriculture in 'The Young Shen Nong'.

LITERATURE

Hong Kong has long suffered from the misconception that it does not have a literature of its own, but, in fact, the city has seen a thriving microclimate in the vast landscape of Chinese literature, where the same sun shining on other parts of China has spawned distinct smells, textures and voices.

The website www. renditions.org has excellent info on Chinese literature published in English. Hong Kong University Press (www.hk upress.org) also publishes works by local Chinese writers.

From the 1920s to the 1940s, Hong Kong was a haven for Chinese writers on the run. These émigrés continued their writing here, their influence lasting until the 1970s when the first generation of writers born and/or raised locally came into their own. The relative creative freedom offered by the city has spawned works in a variety of genres and subjects, from prose poems to experimental novels, from swordplay romance to life as a make-up artist for the dead.

Hong Kong Collage: Contemporary Stories and Writing (ed Martha PY Cheung; 1998) is an important collection of fiction and essays by 15 contemporary local writers. *To Pierce the Material Screen: an Anthology of Twentieth Century Hong Kong Literature* (ed Eva Hung; *Renditions;* 2008) is a two-volume anthology featuring established figures, younger names and emerging voices, and spans 75 years. In *From the Bluest Part of the Harbour: Poems from Hong Kong* (ed Andrew Parkin; 1996), 12 modern poets reveal the emotions of Hong Kong people in the run-up to 1997. For critical articles on Hong Kong literature, check out the special Hong Kong issue (winter 2008) of the *Journal of Modern Literature in Chinese* (Lingnan University of Hong Kong).

The major literary festival in the city is the **Hong Kong Literary Festival** (www.festival.org.hk), which seems to be held in a different month every year.

Cinema

Once known as the 'Hollywood of the Far East', Hong Kong was for decades the third-largest motion-picture industry in the world (after Mumbai and Hollywood) and the second-largest exporter. Now it produces a few dozen films each year, down from well over 200 in the early 1990s. Yet Hong Kong film continues to play an important role on the world cinema stage as it searches for a new identity in the Greater China market.

The One-Armed Swordsman (1967), directed by Chang Cheh, was one of the first of a new style of martial-arts films featuring male heroes and serious bloodletting.

MARTIAL ARTS

Hong Kong cinema became known to the West when a former child actor appeared as a sinewy hero in a kung fu film. But before Bruce Lee unleashed his high-pitched war cry in *The Big Boss* (1971), the kung fu genre was alive and kicking. The *Wong Fei-hung* series, featuring the adventures of a folk hero, has been named by the *Guinness Book of Records* as the longest-running cinema serial dedicated to one man, with roughly a hundred episodes made from 1949 to 1970 alone. The works of the signature directors of the period – Chang Cheh, whose macho aesthetics seduced Quentin Tarantino, and King Hu, who favoured a more refined style of combat – continue to influence films today.

The decade after Lee's death saw the leap to stardom of two martial artists: Jackie Chan and Jet Li. Chan's blend of slapstick and action, as seen in *Snake in the Eagle's Shadow* (1978), a collaboration with action choreographer Yuen Wo-ping (who choreographed the action on *Crouching Tiger, Hidden Dragon* and *The Matrix*), became an instant hit. He later added stunts to the formula, resulting in the hits *Police Story* and the *Rush Hour* series. Li garnered international acclaim when he teamed up with director Tsui Hark in *Once Upon a Time in China* (1991). Despite his reputation for tampering with a print just hours before its premiere, Tsui introduced sophisticated visuals and rhythmic editing into the martial arts genre, most notably in Hong Kong's first special-effects extravaganza, *Zu: Warriors from the Magic Mountain* (1983). As a producer, he helped to create John Woo's gangster classic *A Better Tomorrow* (1986).

The 1970s saw the start of another trend spearheaded by actor-director-screenwriter Michael Hui, who produced comedies satirising the realities and dreams of Hong Kong people. *Games Gamblers Play* (1974) was the highest grossing film of its time, even surpassing the movies of Bruce Lee.

Fast forward to the 21st century, when a Bruce Lee craze briefly returned on the 35th anniversary of his death with the release of *Ip Man* (2008), a fawning semi-speculative biopic of Lee's mentor. A sequel, *Ip Man 2* (2011), was more chop socky and less solemn, though the nationalist hero treatment still applied, with a Sinophobic British pugilist in postwar Hong Kong replacing Japanese soldiers as the enemy. Also cashing in on Lee's revived legend is *Bruce Lee, My Brother* (2010), a coming-of-age comedy based on a published recollection of childhood memories that the master's siblings shared of their famous brother. Similarly nostalgic is *Gallants* (2010), a retro comedy in which various kung fu stars of yesteryear paid a feisty homage to an old genre. The low-budget film won Best Picture at the 2011 Hong Kong Film Awards. *Ashes of Time Redux* (2008) is a shorter cut of Wong Kar Wai's haunting 'non-action action movie' of the same name from 1994.

NEW WAVE

Tsui Hark belonged to the New Wave, a group of filmmakers of the late 1970s and '80s who grew up in Hong Kong, and were trained at film schools overseas as well as in local TV. Their works had a more contemporary sensibility, unlike those of their émigré predecessors, and were more artistically adventurous.

Ann Hui, Asia's top female director, is a New Waver who has won awards both locally and overseas. *Song of the Exile* (1990), a tale about the marriage between a Japanese woman and a Chinese man just after the Sino-Japanese War, won Best Film at both the Asian Pacific Film Festival and the Rimini Film Festival in Italy.

Once Upon a Time in China (1991) is the first of Tsui Hark's five-part epic that follows folk hero Wong Fei-hung (Jet Li) as he battles government officials, gangsters and foreign entrepreneurs to protect his martial-arts school in 19th-century China.

INTERNATIONAL ACCLAIM

The 1990s saw Hong Kong gaining unprecedented respect on the global film-festival circuit. Besides Ann Hui, Wong Kar Wai received Best Director at the Cannes Film Festival for *Happy Together* in 1997. Auteur of the cult favourite *Chungking Express* (1994), Wong is famous almost as much for his elliptical mood pieces as for his disregard of shooting deadlines. In the same year, Fruit Chan bagged the Special Jury Prize at the Locarno International Film Festival with *Made in Hong Kong,* an edgy number shot on film stock Chan had scraped together while working on other projects.

TOUGH TIMES & NEW DIRECTION

Due to changes in the market, in the 1990s the Hong Kong film industry sank into a gloom from which it has not recovered. The return to China also presented problems related to censorship or, more often, self-censorship. But there have been sunny patches, too. *Infernal Affairs*

GETTY IMAGES ©

Jet Li

(2002), directed by Andrew Lau and Alan Mak, made such an impact on its release that it was heralded as a box-office miracle, though it suffered some loss in translation in Martin Scorsese's remake, *The Departed*. *Election* (2005) and *Election 2* (2006), by master of Hong Kong noir Johnnie To, also enjoyed immense critical and box-office success.

Echoes of the Rainbow (2010), a rather maudlin tale about the battling spirit of Hong Kong people in the turbulent 1960s, won a Crystal Bear at the Berlin Film Festival. Meanwhile, veteran thespian Deanie Ip won the Best Actress award at the Venice Film Festival for her role as a traditional housemaid in Ann Hui's *A Simple Life* (2011), an elegant drama about aging and loneliness.

The past few years have also seen a string of big-budget Hong Kong–China collaborations, most notably the *Ip Man* series and *Bodyguards and Assassins* (2009), a story of anti-Qing intrigue set in 1905 Hong Kong. The trend of growing cooperation with the wealthy – and lucrative – Chinese market looks set to take hold as local filmmakers seek new ways to finance their celluloid (or digital) fantasies.

The Warlords (2007), directed by Peter Chan, is a period war film about sworn brothers forced to betray one another by the realities of war – and showing it's possible to please both Hong Kong and mainland audiences.

FILM FESTIVALS & AWARDS

The Hong Kong International Film Festival (every March/April), now in its third decade, is the best in Asia and boasts a laudable if precarious balance of art-house choices and titles offering red-carpet opportunities. The Hong Kong Film Awards is also among the most respected in this part of the world. The Hong Kong Film Archive (p113) is a treasure trove of Hong Kong films and resources on them.

Days of Being Wild (1990), set in the 1960s, is a star-studded piece directed by Wong Kar Wai and steered along by the characters' accounts of seemingly mundane events. It won Best Picture at the 1991 Hong Kong Film Awards.

HONG KONG IN FILM

Hong Kong has been the setting of many Western-made films, including: *Love is a Many-Splendored Thing* (1955), starring William Holden, and Jennifer Jones as his Eurasian doctor paramour, with great shots on and from Victoria Peak; *The World of Suzie Wong* (1960), with Holden again and Nancy Kwan as the pouting bar girl from Wan Chai; and *The Man with the Golden Gun* (1974), with Roger Moore as James Bond and filmed partly in a Tsim Sha Tsui topless bar. More recently, in *The Dark Knight* (2008), Christian Bale's Batman performed one of his trademark escapes from Two International Finance Centre (although a planned scene in which the superhero would drop from a plane into the harbour was axed after the film's producers found the water quality could pose a potential health danger). An excellent source for spotting familiar locations is the two-part freebie *Hong Kong Movie Odyssey Guide* from the Hong Kong Tourist Board (HKTB).

Architecture

Welcome to the most dazzling skyline in the world. We defy you not to be awed as you stand for the first time at the harbour's edge in Tsim Sha Tsui and see Hong Kong Island's majestic panorama of skyscrapers march up those steep, jungle-clad hills. This spectacle has been created because in Hong Kong buildings are knocked down and replaced with taller, shinier versions almost while your back is turned. The scarcity of land, the strains of a growing population and the rapacity of developers – as well as the opportunism of the common speculator – drive this relentless cycle of destruction and construction.

HERITAGE PRESERVATION

The government's risible record in preserving architecturally important buildings went almost entirely unregretted by most until very recently. The destruction of the iconic Star Ferry Terminal in Central marked a surprising reversal in public apathy. Heartfelt protests greeted the wrecking balls in late 2006, but to no avail (see boxed text, p321).

Anxious to avoid another faux pas, the government announced that the Streamline Moderne–style Wan Chai Market would be partially preserved (a luxury apartment tower will have risen over it by the time you read this book).

Meanwhile the nearby Pawn, a flashy drinking hole converted from four old tenements and a century-old pawn shop, is a running sore with heritage activists who argue that the Urban Renewal Authority has shortchanged the public by refusing to list the building's rooftop terrace as an unrestricted public space. Similarly, the former Marine Police Headquarters in Tsim Sha Tsui, now yet another hotel-cum-shopping centre, has disappointed many after the original landscape was razed.

There have been some bright spots, however, most notably when the government stopped the demolition of the magnificent King Yin Lei (1937; see boxed text, p89), a private, Chinese Renaissance-style mansion on Stubbs Rd over Happy Valley. Even more significantly, the government launched in 2008 a scheme for the 'revitalisation' of historic monuments, which allows NGOs to pitch for the use of these buildings. The nascent program has already seen the restoration of the Old Tai O Police Station (see p202) and the distinctive pre-WWII shophouse **Lui Seng Chun** (Map p383).

Despite these positive examples of heritage preservation, the reality remains that the imperatives of the property market, in the name of urban redevelopment, continue to dictate the city's future and its connection with the past. The deep, protracted uncertainty over the fate of the West Wing of the former Government Secretariat in Central – a fine model of understated elegance and a vital place of contact between the former colonial administration and the people – shows that no building in Hong Kong, no matter how valued its architectural and historical heritage, is truly safe from the bulldozers.

TRADITIONAL CHINESE ARCHITECTURE

About the only examples of 19th-century Chinese architecture left in urban Hong Kong are the popular Tin Hau temples, including those at Tin Hau near Causeway Bay, Aberdeen, Stanley and Yau Ma Tei. Museums in Chai Wan and Tsuen Wan have preserved a few 18th-century Hakka village structures. More substantial physical reminders of the past lie in the New Territories and the Outlying Islands, where walled villages, fortresses and even a 15th-century pagoda can still be seen.

EAST-MET-WEST ARCHITECTURE

Architectural cross-play had already been in vogue long before soy sauce Western (p37) appeared in colonial Hong Kong. Largely the preserve of the wealthy and the religious, local examples of fusion architecture have not earned the same level of public recognition as has been accorded to some outright, nostalgia-jerking colonial landmarks.

The abandoned Shek Lo Mansion in Fanling (1925; p174) resembles a Kaiping *diāolóu* (a fortified tower that blends Chinese and Western architectural elements) across the border in Guǎngdōng. The ostensibly Chinese Tai Fu Tai Mansion (1865; p174) in Yuen Long hides a mandarin's love of rococo stuccowork, stained-glass geometry and baroque arched doorways behind brick walls.

The Anglican **St Mary's Church** (Map p374), at 2a Tai Hang Rd in Causeway Bay, is a somewhat comical orientalist exercise from 1937 while a subtle Eurasian interior graces the cathedral-like Buddhist temple at the contemporaneous Tung Lin Kok Yuen, at 15 Shan Kwong Rd in Happy Valley.

Tai Hang's Lin Fa Kung (p111) is a small Kwun Yum temple with a unique octagonal design and side entrances reminiscent of a medieval Catholic chapel.

COLONIAL ARCHITECTURE

Most of the colonial architecture left in the city is on Hong Kong Island, especially in Central, such as the former Legislative Council building (1912; p71) and Government House, residence of all British governors from 1855 to 1997. In Sheung Wan there is Western Market (1906; p86), and in the Mid-Levels the Edwardian-style Old Pathological Institute, now the Hong Kong Museum of Medical Sciences (1905; p87). The Old Stanley Police Station (1859; p131) and nearby Murray House (1848; p130) are important colonial structures on the southern part of Hong Kong Island.

The interesting **Hong Kong Antiquities & Monuments Office** (Map p378; ☎2721 2326; www.amo.gov.hk; 136 Nathan Rd, Tsim Sha Tsui; ☉9am-5pm Mon-Sat), located in a British schoolhouse that dates from 1902, has information and exhibits on current preservation efforts.

CONTEMPORARY ARCHITECTURE

Hong Kong's verticality was born out of necessity – the scarcity of land and the sloping terrain have always put property at a premium in this densely populated place. Some buildings, such as Central Plaza and International Commercial Centre, have seized height at all costs; a privileged few, such as the Hong Kong Convention & Exhibition Centre

---

Victorian & Edwardian Buildings

Central Police Station (Soho)

Nam Koo Terrace (Wan Chai)

Kam Tong Hall (The Mid-Levels)

Western Market (Sheung Wan)

Neo-Classical Buildings

Former Legislative Council Building (Central)

Hung Hing Ying Building, University of Hong Kong (The Mid-Levels)

ARCHITECTURE TRADITIONAL CHINESE ARCHITECTURE

(p107) and the windowless Hong Kong Cultural Centre (p142), have pulled off audacious moves to go horizontal.

Internationally celebrated modern architecture in the city includes the Hong Kong & Shanghai Bank building in Central and the Hong Kong International Airport in Chep Lap Kok (opened in 1998) – both by English architect Norman Foster, in Late Modern high-tech style – as well as IM Pei's soaring symphony of triangular geometry that is the Bank of China Tower (p70).

For more on Hong Kong's contemporary architecture, pick up a copy of the illustrated pocket guide *Skylines Hong Kong,* by Peter Moss, or the more specialist *Hong Kong: A Guide to Recent Architecture,* by Andrew Yeoh and Juanita Cheung.

Modern Trends

Bank of China Buildings (Central)

International Finance Centre (Central)

Hongkong & Shanghai Bank Building (Central)

Hong Kong International Airport (Lantau)

DISTINCTIVELY URBAN VISTAS

For thrill-seekers, a seemingly ordinary tram ride across the northern shore of Hong Kong Island often feels more like an impossible hurtle through an endless canyon of high-rises. Indeed, similar psychogeography can be experienced in much of urban Hong Kong. While the bulk of the buildings here may be uninspired office and apartment blocks sprouting cheek by jowl throughout the territory, there are perverse spectacles to be found as various forms of the built environment routinely challenge conventional notions of scale and proportion to achieve their purpose.

A classic example is the tumbledown Oceanic Mansion (1010-1030 King's Rd), a forbidding cliff of pulverised dwellings that soars above a tight, sloping bend in the shadows of a country park in Quarry Bay. Near the western end of the tramline in Kennedy Town, Hill Rd Flyover (off Map p376) is a towering urban racetrack that lures traffic from the rarefied heights of Pok Fu Lam to the siren call of Central, *Blade Runner*–like.

RODNEY HYETT/GETTY IMAGES©

Interior of the HSBC Building (p68)

The same sense of space or freedom can rarely be manufactured by the many luxury real-estate projects you will see in Hong Kong, however, even if they've been romantically christened with names like Sorrento, Leguna Verde or Cullinan. Tiny living spaces remain the norm in this city.

Those interested in the future of the city's urban landscape can visit the **Hong Kong Planning & Infrastructure Exhibition Gallery** (Map p362; ☎3102 1242; www.infrastructuregallery.gov.hk; Ground fl, Murray Rd Multi-storey Car Park Bldg, 2 Murray Rd, Central; ⊙10am-6pm Wed-Mon).

Macau's History & Culture

HISTORY

Ou Mun, Macau's Chinese name (Aomén in Mandarin), means Gateway of the Bay. This is what the Portuguese were after when they arrived in the 16th century – a trading gateway in the Far East. Trade did prosper for some time, and Macau's colonial buildings live to tell of its former glory. But the decline of Portugal as a colonial power, and Hong Kong's rise as the dominant trading post, changed the course of history for Macau.

Colonial Portuguese architecture survives throughout Macau, infused with Chinese features and the styles of Portugal's trading partners and former colonies. (In Hong Kong, by contrast, the Western model was transplanted with far fewer adaptations.)

Arrival of the Portuguese

The first Portuguese contingent, led by Jorge Álvares, set foot on Chinese soil in 1513 at a place they called Tamaõ, about 80km southwest of the mouth of the Pearl River. However, the exposed anchorage there forced the Portuguese traders to search for a better port.

At the time, Macau was inhabited by a small number of mostly Cantonese-speaking farmers and fisherfolk from Fújiàn. In 1557 officials at Guǎngzhōu let the Portuguese build temporary shelters on the peninsula in exchange for customs dues and rent. The Portuguese also agreed to rid the area of the pirates that were endemic at the time. Neither side expected that for the next 400 years, the Portuguese would dominate Macau's history.

A Trading Powerhouse

Macau grew rapidly as a trading centre. Acting as agents for the Chinese merchants, who were forbidden to leave the country by imperial decree, Portuguese traders took Chinese goods to Goa and exchanged them for cotton and textiles. The cloth was then taken to Malacca, where it was traded for spices and sandalwood. The Portuguese would then carry on to Nagasaki in Japan, where the cargo from Malacca was exchanged for Japanese silver, swords, lacquerware and fans that would in turn be traded in Macau for more Chinese goods.

GANG VIOLENCE

The years 1996 to 1998 were a grim showdown for Macau and its all-important tourism industry – an escalating number of gangland killings took place. Some 40 people were killed as senior Triad leaders jostled for control of lucrative gambling rackets, and one international hotel was raked with AK-47 gunfire.

As the handover approached, China put pressure on Portugal to clean up its act. The government issued a new anti-Triad law calling for a lengthy prison term for anyone found to be a senior leader. Wan Kwok Koi, a prominent Triad leader, was arrested and sentenced to 15 years; many other Triad members fled overseas. The violence was calmed, though Triad activity in Macau was by no means stamped out.

During the late 16th century, the Portuguese in Macau were at the forefront of all international commerce between China and Japan. In 1586 Macau was conferred the status of a city by the Portuguese Crown: Cidade de Nome de Deus (City of the Name of God).

By the beginning of the 17th century, Macau was home to several thousand permanent residents, including about 900 Portuguese, Christian converts from Malacca and Japan, and a large number of slaves from colonial outposts in Africa, India and the Malay Peninsula. Many Chinese moved to Macau from across the border, working as traders, craftspeople, hawkers, labourers and coolies; by the close of the century, their numbers reached 40,000.

Besides trading, Macau had also become a centre of Christianity in Asia. Among the earliest missionaries was Francis Xavier of the Jesuit order, who was later canonised.

The Portuguese in Macau, along with their Macanese descendants, created a home away from home, with luxurious villas overlooking the Praia Grande and splendid baroque churches, paid for with the wealth generated by their monopoly on trade between China and Japan.

Portuguese Decline

In 1580 Spanish armies occupied Portugal and, for more than 60 years, three Spanish kings ruled over the country and its empire. In the early years of the 17th century, the Dutch moved to seize the rich Portuguese enclaves of Macau, Nagasaki and Malacca. In June 1622 some 13 Dutch warships carrying 1300 men attacked Macau, but retreated when a shell fired by a Jesuit priest from one of the cannons on Monte Fort hit a stock of gunpowder and blew the Hollanders out of the water.

The Portuguese felt that they should follow the footsteps of the British and push China for sovereignty over Macau, a territory they had occupied for three centuries. Negotiations began in 1862, although it was not until 1887 that a treaty was signed in which China effectively recognised Portuguese sovereignty over Macau in perpetuity.

With the advent of the steamship, however, there were fewer trans-shipments from Chinese ports going through Macau. The enclave's future economy was greatly assisted by the legalisation of gambling in the 1850s, but by the close of the 19th century the ascent of the British colony and the decline of the Portuguese territory had become irreversible.

Macau in the 20th Century

By the turn of the 20th century, Macau was little more than a haven for Chinese refugees fleeing war, famine and political oppression. Among them was Sun Yatsen, founder of the Republic of China, who lived in Macau before the 1911 revolution.

MACAU'S HISTORY & CULTURE HISTORY

TIMELINE

4000 BC
Archaeological finds from Hác Sá and Ká Hó bays on Coloane island suggest that Macau is inhabited in Neolithic times.

AD 500
Macau serves as a stop in the Maritime Silk Road for merchant ships travelling between Southeast Asia and Guǎngzhōu.

1277
Mongols invade China during the Southern Song dynasty; some 50,000 people seek refuge in Macau.

1513
The Portuguese, under Jorge Álvares, land in the Pearl River Delta of China.

1557
The Ming court leases Macau to Portugal for tribute paid to Běijīng; the Portuguese build the first walled village in Macau.

1560–80
Jesuits and Dominicans arrive in Macau, turning it into a Catholic missionary hub.

1601
The Dutch attack Macau. Further raids culminate in a full-scale – but ultimately unsuccessful – invasion in 1622, prompting construction of the Guia Fortress.

1680
Lisbon appoints the first Portuguese governor of Macau. Macau's role as a major trading port is in decline.

In the mid-1920s large numbers of Chinese immigrants arrived, fleeing civil strife in China. Then, during WWII, people from Hong Kong and China, as well as Asian-based Europeans, took refuge in Macau, a neutral port. By 1943 the population had increased to 500,000. There was another influx of Chinese refugees in 1949 when the communists took power in China.

In 1974 the new left-wing government in Portugal began to divest Portugal of the last remnants of its empire. Lisbon tried to return Macau to China, but the word from Běijīng was that China wished Macau to remain as it was – at least for the time being.

In 1986 China and Portugal began negotiations on returning Macau to China, and an agreement was signed the following April. Under the so-called Sino-Portuguese Pact, Macau would become a Special Administrative Region of China. On 20 December 1999, 442 years of Portuguese rule officially ended. Like Hong Kong, the Macau SAR is supposed to enjoy a 'high degree of autonomy' for 50 years in all matters except defence and foreign affairs, under the slogan 'one country, two systems'.

Macau has directly elected some of the members of its Legislative Assembly since the assembly's founding in 1976 but, unlike Hong Kong, it did not rush through last-minute proposals to widen the franchise or speed up democratisation. The existing legislature continued to serve throughout the handover, unlike in the British territory.

Macau After 1999

The most significant change for Macau since 1999 has been the liberalisation of casino licences in 2001. This led to an influx of mostly American casinos, and in 2006 Macau supplanted Las Vegas as the world's gambling capital, bringing about a drastic socio-economic shift. While the casino industry has become the primary driver of economic growth, it has also increased Macau's dependence on gambling as well as income inequality. The ever-expanding industry has also caused a labour shortage, as its high-paying jobs requiring little or no professional skills have lured many young people into giving up their studies. The labour shortage also led to an influx of illegal migrant workers and has become a rallying cause of labour protests in Macau.

CULTURE

While traditional culture among the Chinese of Macau is similar to that of Hong Kong, the Macanese community – a tiny community of the descendents of intermarriages between Portuguese and Asians – has a vastly different culture that has evolved through the centuries. It is very distinct and exists almost solely in Macau. The Macanese have a unique cuisine, festivals and traditions, and even their own dialect called Patuá, a Creole language derived mainly from Malay, Sinhalese,

CONFUCIANISM VERSUS CATHOLICISM

As the Portuguese lost ground to the Dutch and English in trade, religious infighting weakened the status of Macau as a Christian centre. In what came to be known as the Rites Controversy, the Jesuits maintained that central aspects of Chinese belief – such as ancestor worship and Confucianism – were not incompatible with the Christian faith. The Dominicans and Franciscans, equally well represented in Macau, disagreed. It took an edict by Pope Clement XI in 1715 condemning the rites as idolatrous to settle the matter and this stopped further missionary expansion into China.

Cantonese and Portuguese. José dos Santos Ferreira (1919–93), aka Adé, was a poet who wrote in Patuá.

Macau has far greater linguistic complexity than its postcolonial neighbour, Hong Kong. Cantonese, English, Portuguese, Mandarin and Patuá are all spoken in Macau, not to mention the minorities speaking Thai, Tetun, Indonesian, Filipino, Burmese and languages from the Indian subcontinent.

Today, however, English is used and understood more widely than Portuguese. Some Macau residents are worried that the growing influence of English and Mandarin will dilute the Mediterrasian character of Macau, to the detriment of its culture.

For the vast majority of Macau Chinese people, Taoism and Buddhism are the dominant religions. That said, the Roman Catholic Church is still going strong with an estimated 30,000 believers (about 6% of the population). Macau consists of a single diocese, directly responsible to Rome.

Architecture

Macau has a unique heritage consisting of both Portuguese and Chinese architecture. What often appears at a glance to be 'Portuguese' architecture is actually a complex fusion of Portuguese and Chinese building styles, techniques and materials, with influences from other parts of Asia such as Goa, the Philippines and Malacca, and contributions from the Italian and Spanish missioners who infused it with their sensibilities and traditions. Generally the only buildings in the city that are wholly Chinese or Portuguese are temples and fortresses.

Fusion

Examples of Mediterrasian architecture abound, including the Ruins of the Church of St Paul (p233), and 'Portuguese' churches.

Even Chinese residences sport a mix of influences. The Mandarin's House (p239) has Western-style arches and window panels inlaid with mother-of-pearl, a technique of ornamentation practised in India, the Philippines and other parts of Asia. Inside another residence, Lou Kau Mansion (p239), neoclassical balustrades and stained-glass windows embellish a Chinese maze behind a grey facade.

Modernism

Macau has a strong heritage of modernism. As well as the modernist villas on Bishop Hill, the 'Red Market', Pier 8 and the East Asia Hotel are fine examples of Chinese art deco (see p244).

Agricultural

The 'old city' – around Rua das Estalagens, Rua de Madeira and Rua dos Mercadores, and Rua da Tercena and also Rua de Felicidade (Street of Happiness) – has clan-related structures comprising an alley and a

1851
Taking advantage of China's weakness during the Opium War, Portugal occupies Taipa and later takes control of Coloane in 1864.

1865
The Portuguese turn Macau into a major point on the 'coolie' slave-trade circuit. *Dea del Mar* sets sail from Macau with 550 slaves from southern China; only 162 survive the journey to Tahiti.

1937–45
Macau enjoys a brief period of prosperity as a neutral port during WWII.

1949
Communists take over China and declare the Protocol of Lisbon an 'unequal treaty'.

1966
Violent riots break out in Macau. The government proposes that Portugal leave but, fearing the economic shock to Hong Kong, the Chinese refuse the offer.

1974
The new left-wing government in Portugal decides to relinquish all its colonies, including those in Africa and the Indonesian archipelago.

1999
Macau returns to China on 20 December as a Special Administrative Region (SAR), ending almost 450 years of Portuguese rule.

2001
The casino licence is opened up, leading to an economic boom that further polarises Macau society.

CHRONICLER OF MACAU

George Chinnery was an English painter renowned as a chronicler of colonial Macau. Taipans and mandarins in the early 19th century liked to commission portraits of themselves and their loved ones, and Chinnery was the master of the genre. But today he is perhaps best known for his Macau landscapes and fragmentary sketches of everyday life.

Chinnery was born in London in 1774 and set sail for India in 1802. He spent the next 23 years in Madras and Calcutta, as a popular portrait painter to British colonial society. He fled to Macau in 1825 to escape spiralling debt and his wife ('the ugliest woman I ever saw in my life'), and took up residence at 8 Rua de Inácio Baptista, just south of the Church of St Lawrence, where he lived until his death in 1852.

communal altar, as well as humble, one- or two-storey Chinese houses from agricultural times (see p251).

Literature

The most active literary organisation in Macau is the nonprofit Association of Stories in Macao (ASM), which promotes, through publishing, the poetry and fiction of Macau-based authors. The founder of ASM is Christopher (Kit) Kelen, an Australian poet and critic, who has lived in Hong Kong and Macau for more than 10 years.

Kelen has been bringing together the different writers in Macau (and sometimes even Hong Kong) who write in Chinese, English and Portuguese. His efforts have given rise to two solid anthologies of Macau poetry: *I Roll the Dice: Contemporary Macao Poetry* (2008) and *Portuguese Poets of Macau* (2010). The first features the works of contemporary Chinese-speaking poets in Macau, as well as poetry by Portuguese- or English-speaking residents of Macau. The second contains the works of some 40 poets, rendered into English. Contributors include contemporary poets and early writers who have left their mark on Macau, such as Portugal's national poet, Luís de Camões (1524–80), and the symbolist poet Camilio de Almeida Pessanha (1867–1926) who was buried in the Cemetery of St Michael the Archangel.

Other works by or about Macau's writers include:

As from the Living Page: One Hundred Poems for Yao Feng Christopher Kelen
Republic of the East John Mateer
Glitter on the Sketch Agnes Vong
Antologia de Poetas de Macau Jorge Arrimar & Yao Jingming
Nam Wan Henrique de Senna Fernandes

Painting

Macau can lay claim to having spawned or influenced a number of artists, some born in the territory and some from Guǎngdōng Province. Their work is on display in the Macau Museum of Art, while some of Macau's best contemporary art can be seen at AFA Macau.

The most important Western artist to have lived in Macau was George Chinnery (1774–1852). Other influential European painters who spent time in Macau include the Scottish physician Thomas Watson (1815–60), Chinnery's pupil Frenchman Auguste Borget (1808–77), and watercolourist Marciano António Baptista (1856–1930), who was born in Macau.

Guan Qiaochang (1825–60), another of Chinnery's pupils, was a Chinese artist who painted in the Western style and worked under the name Lamqua.

Survival Guide

Hong Kong Transport

GETTING TO HONG KONG

Most international travellers arrive and depart via Hong Kong International Airport. Travellers to and from mainland China can use ferry, road or rail links to Guǎngdōng and points beyond. Hong Kong is accessible from Macau via ferry or helicopter.

More than 100 airlines operate between Hong Kong International Airport and some 160 destinations around the world. Flights include from New York (16 hours), Los Angeles (15 hours), Sydney (9½ hours), London (12 hours) and Běijīng (3½ hours). There are regular buses connecting Hong Kong with major destinations in neighbouring Guǎngdōng province. Twelve trains run between Hong Kong and Guǎngzhōu (two hours), and to Běijīng (23½ hours) and Shànghǎi (18½ hours) on alternate days. Visas are required to cross the border to the mainland.

Regularly scheduled ferries link the China Ferry Terminal in Kowloon and/or the Macau Ferry Terminal on Hong Kong Island with a string of towns and cities on the Pearl River Delta, including Macau. Trips take two to three hours.

Flights, tours and rail tickets can be booked online at lonelyplanet.com/bookings.

Check any of these websites for good deals on airline tickets:

Cheap flights (www.cheap flights.com)

ebookers (www.ebookers. com)

Expedia (www.expedia.com)

Last Minute (www.lastminute. com)

Opodo (www.opodo.com)

Skyscanner (www.skyscan ner.net)

For details on travel agencies in Hong Kong, see p335.

Air

There are flights between Hong Kong and around 40 cities in mainland China. Destinations and sample adult return fares are Běijīng ($3000 to $4500), Chéngdū ($2500 to $3700), Kūnmíng ($2500 to $4000) and Shànghǎi ($2500 to $4500). One-way fares are a bit more than half the return price.

Major airlines flying between Hong Kong and mainland cities:

Cathay Pacific Airways (CX; ☎2747 1888; www.cathay pacific.com) Hong Kong's major international airline has flights to 15 cities in mainland China.

Dragonair (KA; ☎3193 3888; www.dragonair.com) Owned by Cathay Pacific, Dragonair specialises in regional flights and flies to 18 cities in mainland China.

Hong Kong Airlines (HX; ☎3151 1888; www.hongkong airlines.com) Cheaper airline

that specialises in regional routes, including 13 cities in mainland China.

Hong Kong International Airport

Designed by British architect Sir Norman Foster, the **Hong Kong International Airport** (☎2181 8888; www.hkairport. com) is on Chek Lap Kok, a largely reclaimed area off Lantau's northern coast. Highways, bridges (including the 2.2km-long Tsing Ma Bridge, one of the world's longest suspension bridges) and a fast train link the airport with Kowloon and Hong Kong Island.

The two terminals have a wide range of shops, restaurants, cafes, ATMs and moneychangers. Useful counters for visitors:

Hong Kong Tourism Board (HKTB; ☎2508 1234; www.dis coverhongkong.com) Maintains information centres in Buffer Halls A and B located after Customs in Terminal 1.

Hong Kong Hotels Association (HKHA; ☎2383 8380, 2769 8822; www.hkha.org; ☺7am-midnight) Counters are located inside the Buffer Halls. HKHA deals with midrange and top-end hotels only and does not handle hostels, guesthouses or other budget accommodation.

China Travel Service (中國旅行社; CTS; ☎2261 2472; www.ctshk.com; ☺7am-10pm) Has four counters in the termi-

CLIMATE CHANGE & TRAVEL

Every form of transport that relies on carbon-based fuel generates CO_2, the main cause of human-induced climate change. Modern travel is dependent on aeroplanes, which might use less fuel per kilometre per person than most cars but travel much greater distances. The altitude at which aircraft emit gases (including CO_2) and particles also contributes to their climate change impact. Many websites offer 'carbon calculators' that allow people to estimate the carbon emissions generated by their journey and, for those who wish to do so, to offset the impact of the greenhouse gases emitted with contributions to portfolios of climate-friendly initiatives throughout the world. Lonely Planet offsets the carbon footprint of all staff and author travel.

nals, including one in Arrival Hall A which issues China visas (normally takes five to six hours).

AIRPORT EXPRESS

The **Airport Express line** (☑2881 8888; www.mtr.com. hk) of the Mass Transit Railway (MTR) is the fastest (and most expensive) way to get to and from Hong Kong International Airport. It departs every 10 to 12 minutes from 6am to 1am daily to Hong Kong station ($100) in Central, calling at Kowloon station ($90) in Jordan and at Tsing Yi island ($60) en route; the full trip takes 24 minutes. Adult return fares, valid for a month, are $180/160/110. Children three to 11 years pay half-fare.

Vending machines dispense tickets at the airport and train stations en route. You can also buy an Airport Express Travel Pass, which allows three days of unlimited travel on the MTR and Light Rail and one/two trips on the Airport Express ($220/300).

Airport Express has two shuttle buses on Hong Kong Island (H1 and H2) and five in Kowloon (K1 to K5), with free transfers for passengers between Hong Kong and Kowloon stations and major hotels. The buses run every 12 to 20 minutes between 6.12am and 11.12pm. Schedules and routes are available at Airport Express and MTR stations and on the Airport Express website.

If you are booked on a scheduled flight and taking the Airport Express to the airport, most airlines allow you to check in your bags and receive your boarding pass from 90 minutes to one day before your flight at Hong Kong or Kowloon Airport Express stations (open 5.30am to 12.30am).

BUS

There are also good bus links to/from the airport. Major hotel and guesthouse areas on Hong Kong Island are served by the A11 ($40) and A12 ($45) buses; the A21 ($33) covers similar areas in Kowloon. Buses run every 10 to 30 minutes from about 6am to between midnight and 1am. There are also quite a few night buses (designated 'N'). Buy your ticket at the booth near the airport bus stand.

These buses have plenty of room for luggage, and announcements are usually made in English, Cantonese and Mandarin notifying passengers of hotels at each stop.

Bus drivers in Hong Kong do not give change, but it is available at the ground transportation centre at the airport, as are Octopus cards (p319). Normal returns are double the one-way fare. Unless otherwise stated, children aged between three and 11 years and seniors over 65 pay half-fare.

For more details on the routes, check the 'Transport' section at www.hkairport. com.

TAXI

In addition to the fares listed, passengers have to pay $5 for every piece of baggage that is carried inside the baggage compartment.

There are limousine service counters in the arrivals hall and at the ground transportation centre, including **Parklane Limousine Service** (☑2730 0662; www.hongkonglimo.com) and **Intercontinental Hire Cars** (☑3193 9333; www. trans-island.com.hk). In a car

TAXI FARES

DESTINATION	FARE ($)
Central, Admiralty, Wan Chai, Causeway Bay (Hong Kong Island)	280-300
Tsim Sha Tsui, Jordan, Yau Ma Tei, Mong Kok, Hung Hom (Kowloon)	220-230
Sha Tin (New Territories)	260
Tsuen Wan (New Territories)	195
Tung Chung (Lantau)	40-50

seating up to four people, expect to pay $650 to $810 to destinations in Hong Kong Island and urban Kowloon and from $600 to $1000 to the New Territories.

Train

One-way and return tickets for Guǎngzhōu, Běijīng and Shànghǎi can be booked 60 days in advance at MTR stations in Hung Hom, Mong Kok, Kowloon Tong and Sha Tin, and at MTR Travel at Admiralty station. Tickets to Guǎngzhōu can also be booked with a credit card on the MTR website (www.it3. mtr.com.hk) or via the **Tele-Ticketing Hotline** (☑2947 7888).

Shēnzhèn

Reaching Shēnzhèn is a breeze. Just board the MTR East Rail and ride it to Lo Wu or Lok Ma Chau; the mainland is 200m away. The first train to Lo Wu/Lok Ma Chau leaves Hung Hom station at 5.30/5.35am, the last at 11.07/9.35pm, and the trip takes about 43/48 minutes. The border crossing at Lo Wu opens at 6.30am and closes at midnight. The crossing at Lok Ma Chau is open around the clock.

Guǎngzhōu

High-speed intercity trains leave Hung Hom station for Guǎngzhōu East train station 12 times a day between 7.25am and 7.24pm, returning from that station the same number of times from 8.19am to 9.32pm. The trip takes approximately 1¾ hours. One-way tickets cost $230/190 in 1st/2nd class for adults and $115/95 for children aged five to nine. A cheaper but less convenient option is to take the MTR East Rail train to Lo Wu, cross through immigration into Shēnzhèn and catch a local train from there to Guǎngzhōu. There are fre-

quent high-speed trains (¥75 to ¥95, 52 minutes to 1¼ hours) that run throughout the day.

Běijīng & Shànghǎi

There are direct rail links between Hung Hom and both Shànghǎi and Běijīng. Trains to Běijīng West train station (hard/soft/deluxe sleeper from $574/934/1191) depart on alternate days at 3.15pm, arriving at 2.51pm the following day. Trains to Shànghǎi (hard/soft/deluxe sleeper from $508/825/1039) also depart on alternate days at 3.15pm, arriving at 10am the following day.

Bus

Several transport companies in Hong Kong offer bus services to Guǎngzhōu, Shēnzhèn airport and other destinations in the Pearl River Delta:

China Travel Tours Transportation Services (CTS; ☑2764 9803; http://ctsbus.hkcts.com)

Trans-Island Limousine Service (☑3193 9333; www.trans-island.com.hk) Mainland destinations and one-way fares from Hong Kong include Dōngguǎn ($100), Fóshān ($100), Guǎngzhōu ($110), Huìzhōu ($80), Kāipíng ($160), Shàntóu ($120 to $200), Shēnzhèn's Bǎoān airport ($120), Xiàmén ($310 to $348) and Zhōngshān ($100). Schedules vary enormously according to carrier and place, but buses leave throughout the day and departures are frequent.

In addition, at Hong Kong International Airport buses run by CTS and Trans-Island link Hong Kong International Airport with many points in southern China.

Ferry

Chu Kong Passenger Transportation Company (☑2858 3876; www.cksp.com. hk) provides regularly scheduled ferries that link the **China Ferry Terminal** (中港碼頭; Map p378; 33 Canton Rd, Tsim Sha Tsui) in Kowloon and/or the **Hong Kong–Macau Ferry Terminal** (Map p368; 200 Connaught Rd, Sheung Wan) on Hong Kong Island with a string of towns and cities on the Pearl River Delta – but not central Guǎngzhōu or Shēnzhèn.

Mainland destinations and one-way minimum fares from Hong Kong include:

Zhūhǎi $190, 70 minutes

Zhōngshān $210, 1½ hours

Shùndé $228, two hours

Zhàoqìng $220, four hours

Kāipíng $180, four hours

Shékǒu $110, one hour

A fast ferry service called the **Skypier** (☑2215 3232) links Hong Kong airport with seven Pearl River Delta destinations: Shékǒu near Shēnzhèn, Shēnzhèn Fúyǒng, Dōngguǎn, Zhōngshān, Zhūhǎi, Nánshā and Macau. The service enables travellers to board ferries directly without clearing Hong Kong customs and immigration. Book a ticket prior to boarding from the ticketing desks located in the transfer area on Arrivals level 5 close to the immigration counters. An air-side bus then takes you to the ferry terminal.

Visas

Everyone except Hong Kong Chinese residents must have a visa to enter mainland China. Visas can be arranged by **China Travel Service** (CTS; ☑2998 7888; www.ctshk. com), the mainland-affiliated agency; a good many hostels and guesthouses; and most Hong Kong travel agents.

GETTING AROUND HONG KONG

Hong Kong is small and crowded, and public transport is the only practical way to move people. The ultramodern Mass Transit Railway (MTR) is the quickest way to get to most urban destinations. The bus system is extensive and as efficient as the traffic allows, but it can be bewildering for short-term travellers. Ferries are fast and economical and throw in spectacular harbour views at no extra cost. Trams are really just for fun.

MTR

The **Mass Transit Railway** (MTR; ☎2881 8888; www.mtr.com.hk) is the name for Hong Kong's rail system comprising underground, overland and light rail (slower tram-style) services. Universally known as the 'MTR', it is clean, fast and safe and transports around four million people daily.

Though it costs more than bus travel, the MTR is the quickest way to get to most destinations in Hong Kong.

Train

There are 82 stations on nine underground and overland lines, and a Light Rail network that covers the northwest New Territories. Trains run every two to 14 minutes from around 6am to sometime between midnight and 1am.

Tickets cost $4 to $25, but trips to stations bordering mainland China (Lo Wu and Lok Ma Chau) can cost up to $50. Children aged between three and 11 years and seniors over 65 pay half-fare. Ticket machines accept notes and coins and dispense change.

Once you've passed through the turnstile to begin a journey you have 90 minutes to complete it before the ticket becomes invalid. If you have underpaid (by mistake or otherwise), you can make up the difference at an MTR service counter next to the turnstile.

If possible, it's best to avoid the rush hours: 7.30am to 9.30am and 5pm to 7pm weekdays. Smoking, eating and drinking are not permitted in MTR stations or on the trains, and violators are subject to a fine of $5000. There are no toilets in any of the MTR stations.

MTR exit signs use an alphanumeric system and there can be as many as a dozen to choose from. We give the correct exit for sights and destinations wherever possible, but you may find yourself studying the exit table from time to time and scratching your head. There are always maps of the local area at each exit.

Light Rail Lines

The MTR's Light Rail system is rather like a modern, air-conditioned version of the trams in Hong Kong, but it's much faster. It runs in the northwest New Territories and operates from about 5.30am to between 12.15am and 1am. Trams run every four to 12 minutes, depending on the line and time of day.

Fares are $4 to $5.80, depending on the number of zones (from one to five) travelled; children and seniors over 65 pay from $2 to $2.90. If you don't have an Octopus card, you can buy single-journey tickets from vending machines on the platforms. There are no gates or turnstiles and customers are trusted to validate their ticket or Octopus card when they board and exit.

Travel & Tourist Passes

The **Octopus card** (☎2266 2222; www.octopuscards.com) is a rechargeable 'smart card' valid on the MTR and most forms of public transport in Hong Kong.

It also allows you to make purchases at retail outlets across the territory (such as convenience stores and supermarkets).

The card costs $150 ($70 for children and seniors), which includes a $50 refundable deposit and $100 worth of travel. Octopus fares are about 5% cheaper than ordinary ones on the MTR. You can buy one and recharge at any MTR stations.

For shorter stays:

Airport Express Travel Pass ($220/300 one/two trips on the Airport Express) Also allows three consecutive days of unlimited travel on the MTR.

MTR Tourist Day Pass ($55 for adult, $25 for children aged three to 11) Valid on the MTR for 24 hours after the first use.

Tourist Cross-boundary Travel Pass ($85/120 one/two days consecutive travel) Allows unlimited travel on the MTR and two single journeys to/from Lo Wu or Lok Ma Chau stations.

Bus

Hong Kong's extensive bus system will take you just about anywhere in the territory. Since Kowloon and the northern side of Hong Kong Island are so well served by the MTR, most visitors use the buses primarily to explore the southern side of Hong Kong Island, the New Territories and Lantau Island.

Most buses run from 5.30am or 6am until midnight or 12.30am, though there are smaller numbers of night buses that run from 12.45am to 5am or later. Bus fares cost $2.50 to $52, depending on the destination. Fares for night buses cost from $6 to $32. You will need exact change or an Octopus card.

On Hong Kong Island the most important bus stations are the bus terminus below Exchange Sq (Map p362) in Central and the one at

Admiralty. From these stations you can catch buses to Aberdeen, Repulse Bay, Stanley and other destinations on the southern side of Hong Kong Island. In Kowloon the Star Ferry bus terminal (Map p378) has buses heading up Nathan Rd and to the Hung Hom train station.

Figuring out which bus you want can be difficult, but **City Bus** (✆2873 0818) and **First Bus** (✆2136 8888; www.nwstbus.com.hk), owned by the same company, and **Kowloon Motor Bus** (KMB; ✆2745 4466; www.kmb.hk) provides a user-friendly route search on its websites. KMB also has a route app for smartphones.

Most parts of Lantau Island are served by the **New Lantao Bus** (✆2984 9848; www.newlantaobus.com). Major bus stations are located in Mui Wo ferry terminal and Tung Chung MTR station.

Minibus

Minibuses are vans with no more than 16 seats. They come in two varieties: red and green.

The red minibuses ($2 to $22) are cream-coloured with a red roof or stripe, and they pick up and discharge passengers wherever they are hailed or asked to stop along fixed routes. The destination and price are displayed on a card propped up on the windscreen, but these are often only written in Chinese. You usually hand the driver the fare when you get off, and change is given. You can use your Octopus card on certain routes.

Maxicabs ($2.50 to $24), commonly known as 'green minibuses', are also cream-coloured but with a green roof or stripe, and they make designated stops. You must put the exact fare in the cash box when you get in or you can use your Octopus card. Two popular routes are the

6 ($4.70) from Hankow Rd in Tsim Sha Tsui to Tsim Sha Tsui East and Hung Hom station in Kowloon, and the 1 ($8.40) to Victoria Peak from next to Hong Kong station.

Boat

Despite Hong Kong's comprehensive road and rail public-transport system, the territory still relies very much on ferries to get across the harbour and to reach the Outlying Islands. Cross-harbour Star Ferry is faster and cheaper than buses and the MTR. They're also great fun and afford stunning views. While Lantau can be reached by MTR and bus, for the other Outlying Islands ferries remain the only game in town.

Star Ferry

You can't say you've 'done' Hong Kong until you've taken a ride on a **Star Ferry** (✆2367 7065; www.starferry. com.hk), that wonderful fleet of electric-diesel vessels with names like *Morning Star, Celestial Star* and *Twinkling Star*.

There are two Star Ferry routes, but by far the most popular is the one running between Central (Pier 7) and Tsim Sha Tsui ($2 to $3, every six to 12 minutes from 6.30am to 11.30pm). Quite frankly, there's no other trip like it in the world. Try to take a trip on a clear night from Kowloon to Central. It's not half as dramatic in the opposite direction.

Star Ferry also links Wan Chai with Tsim Sha Tsui ($2.50 to $3, every eight to 20 minutes from 7.20am to 11pm). The coin-operated turnstiles do not give change, but you can get change from the ticket window or use an Octopus card.

Outlying Islands Ferries

Regular ferry services link the main Outlying Islands to Hong Kong. Fares are reasonable and the ferries are comfortable and usually air-conditioned. They have toilets, and some have a basic bar that serves snacks and cold drinks. The ferries can get very crowded on Saturday afternoon and all day Sunday, especially in the warmer months.

There are two types of ferries: the large 'ordinary ferries' that, with the exception of those to Lamma, offer ordinary and deluxe classes; and the smaller 'fast ferries' that cut travel time by between 10 and 20 minutes, but cost between 50% and 100% more.

Prices are higher on Sunday and public holidays. Unless stated otherwise, children aged three to 11 years, seniors over 65 years and people with disabilities pay half-fare on both types of ferries and in both classes. Return is double the single fare.

Tickets are available from booths at the ferry piers, but avoid queuing at busy times by using an Octopus card or putting the exact change into the turnstile as you enter. Ferry timetables are prominently displayed at all ferry piers, or you can read them on the ferry companies' websites.

Three separate ferry companies operate services to the outlying islands from the ferry terminal in Central (map p368):

Discovery Bay Transportation Service (✆2987 7351; www.hkri.com) Provides fast-speed regular ferry between Central (Pier 3) and Discovery Bay on Lantau Island.

Hong Kong & Kowloon Ferry Co (HKKF; ✆2815 6063; www.hkkf.com.hk) Serves destinations on Lamma only.

New World First Ferry
(NWFF; ☎2131 8181; www.nwff.com.hk) NWFF boats sail to/from Cheung Chau, Peng Chau and Lantau, and connect all three via an interisland service ($11.10 for all sectors, every 1¾ hours from 6am to 10.50pm).

Listed below are some of the more popular routes:

Central (Pier 6)–Mui Wo on Lantau Island Adult ordinary/deluxe class/fast ferry $14.50/24.10/28.40 ($21.40/35.30/40.80 on Sunday and public holidays); 50 to 55 minutes with large ferry and 31 minutes with fast ferry; departures around every half-hour from 6.10am (from 7am Sunday and public holidays). The last ferry from Mui Wo to Central departs at 11.30pm.

Central (Pier 4)–Yung Shue Wan on Lamma Island Adult $16.10 ($22.30 on Sunday and public holidays); 30 to 35 minutes; departures approximately every half-hour to an hour. The last boat to Central from Yung Shue Wan departs at 11.30pm.

Central (Pier 4)–Sok Kwu Wan on Lamma Island Adult $19.80 ($28 on Sunday and public holidays); 40 minutes; departures every 1½ hours or so from 7.20am to 11.30pm. The last ferry to Central from Sok Kwu Wan is at 10.40pm.

Central (Pier 5)–Cheung Chau (ordinary ferry) Adult ordinary/deluxe class/fast ferry $12.60/19.20/24.60 ($18.40/28.70/35.30 on Sunday and public holidays); 55 to 60 minutes with large ferry and 35 minutes with fast ferry; departures approximately every half-hour from 6.10am. The last boat to Central from Cheung Chau departs at 11.45pm.

Ferry services to less-visited but scenic spots:

Tsui Wah Ferry Service
(☎2527 2513, 2272 2022;

www.traway.com.hk) Has slower ferries from Ma Liu Shui (15 minutes' walk from the University MTR station) to Tap Mun Chau and Sai Kung Peninsula (twice daily); Ma Liu Shui to Tung Ping Chau (only on weekend and public holidays); from Aberdeen to Po Toi Island (on Tuesday, Thursday, Saturday and Sunday).

Tram

Hong Kong's venerable old trams, operated by **Hongkong Tramways Ltd** (☎2548 7102; www.hktramways.com), are tall and narrow double-decker streetcars. They are slow, but they're cheap and a great way to explore the city. Try to get a seat at the front window on the upper deck for a first-class view while rattling through the crowded streets.

For a flat fare of $2.50 (dropped in a box beside the driver as you disembark) you can rattle along as far as you like over 16km of track, 3km of which wends its way into Happy Valley. Trams operate from 6am to midnight and arrive every couple of minutes. There are six routes but they all move on the same tracks along the northern coast of Hong Kong Island. The longest run (Kennedy Town–Shau Kei Wan, with a change at Western Market) takes about 1½ hours.

Peak Tram

The **Peak Tram** (☎2522 0922; www.thepeak.com.hk; 1 way/return adult $28/40, seniors over 65 & child 3-11yr $11/18) is not really a tram but a cable-hauled funicular railway that has been scaling the 396m ascent to the highest point on Hong Kong Island since 1888. It is thus the oldest form of public transport in the territory. It's such a steep ride that the floor is angled to help standing passengers stay upright.

The Peak Tram runs every 10 to 15 minutes from 7am to midnight. The lower terminus is behind the St John's Building (Map p370). The upper tram terminus is in the Peak Tower. Avoid going on Sunday and public holidays when there are usually long queues. Octopus cards can be used.

Between 10am and 11.40pm, open-deck (or air-conditioned) bus 15C ($4.20, every 15 to 20 minutes) takes passengers between the bus terminus near Central Ferry Pier 7 and the lower tram terminus.

Taxi

Hong Kong taxis are a bargain compared with those in other world-class cities. With more than 18,000 cruising the streets of the territory, they're easy to flag down, except during rush hour, when it rains or during the driver shift-change period (around 4pm daily).

'Urban taxis' – those in Kowloon and on Hong Kong Island – are red with silver roofs and they can go anywhere except in Lantau. New Territories taxis are green with white tops, and Lantau taxis are blue. You need to take a red taxi in New Territories if your destination is in Hong Kong, Kowloon or city centres of the new towns in New Territories.

When a taxi is available, there should be a red 'For Hire' sign illuminated on the meter that's visible through the windscreen. At night the 'Taxi' sign on the roof will be lit up as well. Taxis will not stop at bus stops or in restricted zones where a yellow line is painted next to the kerb.

Some taxi drivers speak English well; others don't know a word of English. It's never a bad idea to have your destination written down in Chinese.

The law requires that everyone in a vehicle wears a seat belt. Both driver and passenger(s) will be fined if stopped by the police and not wearing a seat belt, and most drivers will gently remind you to buckle up before proceeding.

There is a luggage fee of $4 to $5 per bag, but (depending on the size) not all drivers insist on this payment. It costs an extra $4 to $5 to book a taxi by telephone. Try to carry smaller bills and coins; most drivers are hesitant to make change for anything over $100. There are no extra late-night charges and no extra passenger charges. You can tip up to 10%, but most Hong Kong people just leave the little brown coins and a dollar or two.

Passengers must pay the toll if a taxi goes through the many Hong Kong harbour or mountain tunnels or uses the Lantau Link to Tung Chung or the airport. Though the Cross-Harbour Tunnel costs only $10, you'll have to pay $20 if, say, you take a Hong Kong taxi from Hong Kong Island to Kowloon. If you manage to find a Kowloon taxi returning 'home', you'll pay only $10. (It works the other way round as well, of course.) If you cross the harbour via the Western Harbour Tunnel, you must pay the $40 toll plus $15 for the return unless you can find a taxi heading for its base. Similarly, if you use the Eastern Harbour Crossing, you may have to pay the $25 toll plus $15. There's no way of avoiding the whopping toll of $30 in both directions when a taxi uses the Lantau Link.

There is no double charge for the other roads and tunnels: Aberdeen ($5), Lion Rock ($8), Shing Mun ($5), Tate's Cairn ($14), Tai Lam ($30) and Tseung Kwan O ($3).

Though most Hong Kong taxi drivers are scrupulously honest, if you feel you've been ripped off, take down the taxi or driver's licence number (usually displayed on the sun visor in front) and call the **Transport Complaints Unit hotline** (☎2889 9999) or the **Transport Department hotline** (☎2804 2600) to lodge a complaint. Be sure to have all the relevant details: when, where and how much. If you leave something behind in a taxi, ring the **Road Co-op Lost & Found hotline** (☎187 2920); most drivers turn in lost property.

TAXI SYSTEM

TYPE OF TAXI	FIRST 2KM	EVERY ADDITIONAL 200M & MINUTE OF WAITING
Urban taxi (red)	$20	$1.50 ($1 if fare exceeds $72.50)
New Territories taxi (green)	$16.50	$1.30 ($1 if fare exceeds $55)
Lantau taxi (blue)	$15	$1.30 ($1.20 if fare exceeds $132)

Car & Motorcycle

Hong Kong's maze of one-way streets and dizzying expressways isn't for the faint-hearted. Traffic is heavy and finding a parking space is difficult and very expensive. If you are determined to see Hong Kong under your own steam, do yourself a favour and rent a car with a driver.

Vehicles drive on the left-hand side of the road in Hong Kong, as in the UK, Australia and Macau, but *not* in mainland China. Seat belts must be worn by the driver and all passengers, in both the front and back seats. Police are strict and give out traffic tickets at the drop of a hat.

Hong Kong allows most foreigners over the age of 18 to drive for up to 12 months with a valid licence from home. It's still a good idea to carry an International Driving Permit (IDP) as well. Car-hire firms accept IDPs or driving licences from your home country. Drivers must usually be at least 25 years of age.

Ace Hire Car (☑2572 7663, 2893 0541; www.acehirecar. com.hk) Hires chauffeur-driven Mercedes Benz for $250 per hour (minimum two to five hours, depending on location).

Avis (☑2890 6988; www. avis.com.hk) Hires a Toyota Corolla or Honda Civic for a day/weekend/week for $930/1980/3700. The same car with chauffeur costs $350 per hour, with a minimum of three hours.

Bicycle

Cycling in urbanised Kowloon or Hong Kong Island would be suicide, but in the quiet areas of the islands (including southern Hong Kong Island) and the New Territories, a bike can be a lovely way to get around. It's more recreational than a form of transport, though – the hilly terrain will slow you down (unless you're mountain biking). Be advised that bicycle-hire shops and kiosks tend to run out of bikes early on weekends if the weather is good.

TOURS

Despite its size, Hong Kong has a profusion of organised tours. There are tours available to just about anywhere in the territory and they can make good a option if you only have a short time in Hong Kong or don't want to deal with public transport. Some tours are standard excursions covering major sights on Hong Kong Island, such as the Peak and Hollywood Rd, while other tours take you on harbour cruises, out to the islands or through the New Territories.

Some of the best tours are offered by the **Hong Kong Tourism Board** (HKTB; ☑2508 1234; www.discover hongkong.com), and tours run by individual companies can usually be booked at any HKTB branch.

Harbour Tours

The easiest way to see the full extent of Victoria Harbour from sea level is to join a circular **Star Ferry Harbour Tour** (☑2118 6201; www.starferry.com.hk/tour), of which there are a number of different options. Most of the tours depart from the Star Ferry Pier in Tsim Sha Tsui, but there are also departures from the piers at Central and Wan Chai; see the website for details.

Single daytime round trip Departs hourly between 2.05pm and 7.05pm daily; costs $70/63 adult/concession (children aged three to 12 years and seniors over 65).

Full-/half-day hopping pass Available from 11.05am to 10.05pm/6.05pm respectively; costs $200/95 adult, $180/86 concession.

Night two-hour round trip Includes watching a multimedia show over the harbour; departs at 7.05pm and is $170/153 adult/concession.

Single night ride Taken between 7.05pm (6.05pm in winter) and 10.05pm; costs $140/126.

If you opt for fancier harbour tours, you can check the following tour operators which offer harbour tours with drinks, food and even buffet!

Hong Kong Ferry Group (☑2802 2886; www.cruise. com.hk) Offers two harbour cruises in a large boat with buffet dinner and live band performance; costs $300 ($210 for children) for sunset cruise and $400 ($260 for children) for Symphony of Lights cruise.

Water Tours (☑2926 3868; www.watertours.com.hk) Six different tours of the harbour, as well as dinner and cocktail cruises, are available. Prices range from $230 ($135 for children aged two to 12 years) for the Morning Harbour & Noon Day Gun Firing Cruise, to $310 ($220 for children) for the Harbour Lights and $450 ($420 for children) for the Lei Yue Mun Seafood Village Dinner Cruise.

Nature Tours

Eco Travel (☑3105 0767; www.ecotravel.hk) Its north-east New Territories geopark tour is a charming seven-hour trip that takes you to see the sedimentary rock formations of Yan Chau Tong Marine Park (Double Haven) and stops at the Hakka walled village in Lai Chi Wo where you will see the best-preserved feng shui trees in Hong Kong. The final stop is Ap Chau (Duck Island), which is famous for its breccia, sea cliff and other wave-cut landforms. Some tours include traditional Hakka lunch. Departs at 9am from MTR University station ($580 per person).

Hong Kong Dolphinwatch (☑2984 1414; www.hkdolphin watch.com) As well as offering a scenic dolphin-spotting expedition, the four-hour tour (adult/child $380/190) off Lantau includes information on the plight of the endangered Chinese white dolphin, of which between 100 and 200 inhabit Hong Kong's coastal waters. Departs 8.50am from the Kowloon Hotel in Tsim Sha Tsui every Wednesday, Friday and Sunday.

Kayak and Hike (☑9300 5197; www.kayak-and-hike. com) The seven-hour Sai Kung geopark kayak tour provides an exciting option for exploring the beauty of Sai Kung. It takes you to a kayak base at nearby Bluff Island in a junk, from where you paddle to a beach to enjoy swimming and snorkelling. Departs 8.45am at Sai Kung old pier ($700 per person). You need to pack your lunch.

Splendid Tours & Travel (☑2316 2151; www.splendid. hk) Runs the Sai Kung coastal tour, a six-hour cruise that explores the beautiful coastline, peaceful waters and diverse geological formations of Sai Kung, the 'back garden of Hong Kong'. It includes a stop at the Unesco Heritage Site, Hung Shing Temple, on Kau Sai Chau. Departs at 8.20am at the Excelsior Hotel in Causeway Bay ($680 per person).

Walk Hong Kong (☑9187 8641; www.walkhongkong. com) Offers a range of hiking

tours to some of most beautiful places in Hong Kong, eg deserted beaches in Sai Kung ($800 per person, 8½ hours), Dragon's Back in Shek O ($500 per person, four hours), hexagonal volcanic column wall in Sai Kung ($800, 8½ hours).

City Tours

Big Bus Company (☑2723 2108; www.bigbustours.com; adult/child 24hr $350/250, night tour $200) A good way to get your bearings in the city is on the hop-on, hop-off, open-topped double-deckers. Three tours are available: the Kowloon Route takes in much of the Tsim Sha Tsui and Hung Hom waterfront; the Hong Kong Island Route explores Central, Admiralty, Wan Chai and Causeway Bay; and the Green Tour goes to Stanley Market and Aberdeen.

Gray Line (☑2368 7111; www.grayline.com.hk; per adult/child 3-11yr from $560/460) Has a one-day tour taking in Man Mo Temple, Victoria Peak, Aberdeen and Stanley Market.

Heliservices (☑2802 0200; www.heliservices. com.hk) If you hanker to see Hong Kong from on high (and hang the expense), Heliservices has chartered Aerospatiale Squirrels for up to five passengers available for $5200/13,000/19,500 for 12-/30-/45-minute periods.

Splendid Tours & Travel (☑2316 2151; www.splendid tours.com) Runs some inter-

esting half- and one-day tours. Cost ranges from $420/320 per adult/child aged three to 12 years to $800/680.

Culture Tours

Gray Line (☑2368 7111; www.grayline.com.hk) The ever-popular five-hour Heritage Tour ($380/330 per person/ child under 16 years) takes in New Territories sights such as Man Mo Temple in Tai Po, the Tang Chung Ling Ancestral Hall in Leung Yeuk Tau village and the walled settlement of Lo Wai.

Sky Bird Tours (☑2736 2282; www.skybird.com.hk) Traditional lifestyle tour. Learn all about taichi, feng shui and Chinese tea with a four-hour tour ($298 per person). Tours depart 7.30am from the Excelsior Hong Kong Hotel in Causeway Bay and 7.45am from the Salisbury YMCA in Tsim Sha Tsui on Monday, Wednesday and Friday.

Splendid Tours & Travel (☑2316 2151; www.splen didtours.com) The Come Horseracing tour is available during the racing season (September to early July). Includes admission to the Visitors' Box of the Hong Kong Jockey Club Members' Enclosures and buffet with drinks. Tours scheduled at night (Wednesday) last about 5½ hours, while daytime tours (Saturday or Sunday) are about seven hours. Costs $770 per person.

Macau Transport

GETTING TO MACAU

Most travellers arrive in Macau by ferry from Hong Kong. If you are coming from mainland China, you can use ferry or buses from Guǎngdōng, or fly from selected cities in mainland China.

Macau International Airport is connected to limited destinations in Asia. If you are coming from outside Asia and destined for Macau, your best option is to fly to Hong Kong International Airport (see p316) and take a ferry to Macau without going through Hong Kong customs.

Nationals of Australia, Canada, the EU, New Zealand and most other countries (but not US citizens) can purchase their China visas at the border with Zhūhǎi, but it will ultimately save you time if you get one in advance. These are available in Hong Kong (see p318) or in Macau from **China Travel Service** (中國旅行社; CTS; Map p236; ☑2870 0888; www.cts.com.mo; 207 Avenida do Dr Rodrigo Rodrigues, Nam Kwong Bldg; ⊘9am-6pm), usually in one day.

Sea

Ferry and catamaran tickets can be booked in advance at the ferry terminals, many travel agencies or online. You can also simply buy tickets on the spot, though advance booking is recommended if you travel on weekends or public holidays. There is a standby queue for passengers wanting to travel before their ticketed sailing. You need to arrive at the pier at least 15 minutes before departure, but you should allow 30 minutes because of occasional long queues at immigration.

You are limited to 10kg of carry-on luggage in economy class, but oversized or overweight bags can be checked.

To/From Hong Kong

The vast majority of travellers make their way from Hong Kong to Macau by ferry. The journey takes just an hour and there are frequent departures throughout the day, with reduced service between midnight and 7am.

Most ferries depart from **Hong Kong–Macau Ferry Terminal** (Map p368; 200 Connaught Rd, Shun Tak Centre, Sheung Wan) on Hong Kong Island or the **China Ferry Terminal** (中港碼頭; Map p378; 33 Canton Rd, Tsim Sha Tsui) in Kowloon, and arrive at Macau Maritime Ferry Terminal (in the outer harbour) or Taipa Temporary Ferry Terminal.

TurboJet (☑800 3628 3628, in Hong Kong information 2859 3333, toll free bookings 800 1628 1628; www. turbojet.com.hk) has regular departures from Hong Kong–Macau Ferry Terminal (every 15 minutes) and China Ferry Terminal (every 30 minutes) to Macau from 7am to midnight, and less frequent service after midnight. Fares are HK$151/291 (economy/ superclass), and it costs about 10% more for weekends and 20% more for night service (6.15pm to 6.30am).

CotaiJet (☑2885 0595, in Hong Kong 2359 9990; www.co taijet.com.mo) has high-speed catamarans connecting Hong Kong–Macau Ferry Terminal and **Taipa Temporary Ferry Terminal** (off Map p255; ☑2885 0595) every half-hour between 6.30am and midnight. Fares are HK$151/201 (Cotai class/Cotai first) and it costs about 10% more for weekends and 20% more for night service (after 6pm). Free shuttles at the ferry terminal in Taipa will take you to destinations along the Cotai Strip.

To/From Mainland China

TurboJet has 10 departures from the Macau Maritime Ferry Terminal daily to the port of Shékǒu in Shēnzhèn between 9.45am and 8.45pm. The journey takes 60 minutes and costs MOP$210/330 (economy/super class). Ten ferries return from Shékǒu between 8.15am and 7.30pm. TurboJet also has five departures to Shēnzhèn airport (MOP$210/355, one hour) from 11.30am to 7.30pm and two departures to Nánshā in Guǎngzhōu (MOP$180/280) at 10.45am and 4.15pm.

Yuet Tung Shipping Co (☑2893 9944; www.ytmacau. com) has ferries connecting

Macau (Taipa Temporary Ferry Terminal) with Shékǒu (MOP$155). The boat departs from Macau at 11am, 2pm and 7pm and takes 1½ hours. There is a boat that leaves from Taipa for Jiāngmén (MOP$50) daily at 3.15pm. The journey takes 70 minutes. Ferries also leave from Macau Maritime Ferry Terminal for Wānzǎi in Zhūhǎi (MOP$12). Departures are every half-hour between 8am and 4.15pm, returning a half-hour later.

Land

Macau is an easy gateway by land into China. Simply take bus 3, 5 or 9 to the **border gate** (關閘; Portas do Cerco; ☉7am-midnight) and walk across. A second – and much less busy crossing – is the **Cotai Frontier Post** (☉9am-8pm) on the causeway linking Taipa and Coloane, which allows visitors to cross over the Lotus Flower Bridge by shuttle bus (MOP$4) to Héngqín in Zhūhǎi. Buses 15, 21 and 26 will drop you off at the crossing.

If you want to travel further afield in China, buses run by **Kee Kwan Motor Road Co** (歧關車路有限公司; ☎2893 3888; ☉7.15am-9pm) leave the bus station on Rua das Lorchas. Buses for Guǎngzhōu (MOP$77, 2½ hours) depart about every 15 minutes, and for Zhōngshān (MOP$40, one hour) every 20 minutes between 8am and 6.30pm. There are many buses to Guǎngzhōu (MOP$150) and Dōngguǎn (MOP$150) from Macau International Airport.

Air

There are regular flights between Macau and Běijīng, Hángzhōu, Nánjīng, Níngbō, Shànghǎi and Xiàmén and less frequent flights to Chéngdū, Chóngqìng, Fúzhōu, Héféi, Nánníng,

Tàiyuán, Wǔhàn and Wúxī. Check www.macau-airport.com for timetable and airlines.

Macau International Airport

Located on Taipa Island, **Macau International Airport** (☎2886 1111; www.macau-airport.com) is only 20 minutes from the city centre. It has frequent services to destinations including Bangkok, Chiang Mai, Kaohsiung, Kuala Lumpur, Manila, Osaka, Seoul, Singapore, Taipei and Tokyo.

If you are flying into Macau, check with your hotel if there is pick-up service. A taxi from the airport to the town centre should cost about MOP$50, plus a surcharge of MOP$5. Large bags cost an extra MOP$3.

Airport bus AP1 (MOP$4.20) leaves the airport and zips around Taipa before heading to the Macau Maritime Ferry Terminal and the border gate. The bus stops at a number of major hotels en route and departs every five to 12 minutes from 6.30am to midnight. Other services run to Praça de Ferreira do Amaral (MT1 and MT2) and Coloane (bus 26).

FERRY

Macau is linked directly to Hong Kong International Airport by TurboJet, which has eight ferries operating between 10am and 10pm. It costs MOP$233/178/126 per adult/child/infant and takes 45 minutes. However, please note that this ferry service is for transit passengers only. It is not applicable to passengers originating in Hong Kong.

Helicopter

Travel to Macau by helicopter is a viable option and is becoming increasingly popular for residents and visitors alike. **Sky Shuttle** (☎in Hong Kong 2108 9898; www.skyshuttlehk.com) runs a 15-minute helicopter shuttle

service between Macau and Hong Kong (HK$3700, tax included) with up to 27 daily flights leaving between 9am and 11pm. Flights arrive and depart in Macau from the roof of the ferry terminal. In Hong Kong, departures are from the helipad atop the ferry pier that is linked to the **Shun Tak Centre** (信德中心; Map p368; 200 Connaught Rd Central) in Sheung Wan.

Sky Shuttle also has a helicopter shuttle linking Macau with Shēnzhèn six times a day from 10.15am to 7.45pm (11.45am to 8.30pm from Shēnzhèn) for HK$4800. The trip takes 15 minutes.

GETTING AROUND MACAU

Public Transport

Public buses and minibuses run by **TCM** (☎2885 0060; www.tcm.com.mo), **Transmac** (☎2827 1122; www.transmac.com.mo) and **Reolian** (☎2877 7888; www.reolian.com.mo) operate from 6am until shortly after midnight. Fares – MOP$3.20 on the peninsula, MOP$4.20 to Taipa Village, MOP$5 to Coloane Village and MOP$6.40 to Hác Sá beach – are dropped into a box upon entry (exact change needed), or you can pay with a Macau Pass, which can be purchased in numerous supermarkets and convenience stores. The card costs MOP$130 at first purchase, which includes a refundable deposit of MOP$30. A minimum of MOP$50 is required to add money to the card each time. Expect buses to be very crowded.

The *Macau Tourist Map* has a full list of bus companies' routes and it's worth picking one up from Macau Government Tourist Office (MGTO) outlets; you check the routes online. The two most useful buses on the peninsula are buses 3 and 3A, which run between the ferry terminal and the city centre, near the post office. Both continue up to the border crossing with the mainland, as does bus 5, which can be boarded along Avenida Almeida Ribeiro. Bus 12 runs from the ferry terminal, past the Lisboa Hotel and then up to Lou Lim loc Garden and Kun Iam Temple. The best services to Taipa and Coloane are buses 21A, 25 and 26A. Buses to the airport are AP1, 26, MT1 and MT2.

Taxi

Flag fall is MOP$13 for the first 1.6km and MOP$1.50 for each additional 230m. There is a MOP$5 surcharge to go to Coloane; travelling between Taipa and Coloane is MOP$2 extra. For yellow radio taxis call ☎2851 9519 or ☎2893 9939.

Car & Motorcycle

The streets of Macau Peninsula are a gridlock of cars and mopeds that will cut you off at every turn.

Avis Rent A Car (☎2872 6571; www.avis.com.mo; Room 1022, Ground fl, Macau Maritime Ferry Terminal; ⊙10am-1pm & 2-4pm) Hires out cars from MOP$700 to MOP$1400 per day (20% more expensive on weekends). Chauffeur-driven services start from MOP$300 per hour. Also has an office at the Grand Lapa Hotel car park (open 8am to 10pm).

Burgeon Rent A Car (☎2828 3399; www.burgeon rentacar.com; Shop O, P & Q, Block 2, La Baie Du Noble, Avenida Do Nordeste) Hires Kia cars with the cheapest model starting from MOP$190/270/390 for six/11/24 hours. The cheapest car with chauffeur costs MOP$160 per hour, with a minimum of two hours.

Hong Kong Directory A–Z

Business Hours

The following list summarises standard opening hours. Reviews in this book won't list opening hours unless they differ significantly from these.

Banks 9am to 4.30pm or 5.30pm Monday to Friday, 9am to 12.30pm Saturday

Offices 9am to 5.30pm or 6pm Monday to Friday (lunch hour 1pm to 2pm)

Museums 10am to between 5pm and 9pm; closed Monday, Tuesday or Thursday

Restaurants 11am to 3pm and 6pm to 11pm

Shops Usually 10am to 8pm

Customs Regulations

➡ The duty-free allowance for visitors arriving in Hong Kong (including those coming from Macau and mainland China) is 19 cigarettes (or one cigar or 25g of tobacco) and 1L of spirits.

➡ There are few other import taxes, and you can bring in reasonable quantities of almost anything.

Discount Cards

Hong Kong Museums Pass

This pass allows multiple entries to six of Hong Kong's museums: Hong Kong Museum of Coastal Defence on Hong Kong Island; the Hong Kong Science Museum, Hong Kong Museum of History, Hong Kong Museum of Art and Hong Kong Space Museum (excluding Space Theatre) in Kowloon; and the Hong Kong Heritage Museum in the New Territories. Passes valid for seven consecutive days cost $30. Passes are available from Hong Kong Tourism Board (HKTB) outlets and participating museums. Note that these six museums are all free on Wednesdays.

Hostel Card

A Hostelling International (HI) card, or the equivalent, is of relatively limited use in Hong Kong, as there are only seven HI-affiliated hostels here, and most are in remote locations in the New Territories. If you arrive without a card and want to stay in one of these hostels, you can apply for one from the **Hong Kong Youth Hostels Association** (HKYHA; ☎2788 1638; www.yha.org.hk; Shop 118, 1/F, Fu Cheong Shopping Centre, Sham Mong Rd, Sham Shui Po, Kowloon; HI card under/over 18yr $50/130) or upon arrival at the hostel.

Seniors Card

Many attractions in Hong Kong offer discounts for people aged over 60 or 65. Most of Hong Kong's museums are either free or half-price for those over 60, and most forms of public transport offer a 50% discount to anyone over 65. A passport or ID with a photo should be sufficient proof of age.

Student, Youth & Teacher Cards

The International Student Identity Card (ISIC), a plastic ID-style card with your photograph, provides discounts on some forms of transport and cheaper admission to museums and other sights. If you're aged under 26 but not a student, you can apply for an International Youth Travel Card (IYTC) issued by the Federation of International Youth Travel Organisations (FIYTO), which gives much the same discounts and benefits. Teachers can apply for the International Teacher Identity Card (ITIC).

Hong Kong Student Travel, based at **Sincerity Travel** (永安旅遊; Map p378; ☎2730 2800; Room 833-834, Star House, 3 Salisbury Rd, Tsim Sha Tsui; ◷9.30am-8pm Mon-Sat, noon-6pm Sun), can issue you any of these cards instantly for $100. Make sure you bring your student ID or other credentials along with you.

Electricity

220V/50Hz

The standard is 220V, 50Hz AC, and the power plugs used are British three square pins.

Emergency

Police, Fire & Ambulance (☏999)

Gay & Lesbian Travellers

Those travelling to Hong Kong will find a small but vibrant and growing gay-and-lesbian scene in the Special Administrative Region (SAR). It may not compete with the likes of London or Sydney, but Hong Kong has come a long way all the same.

In 1991 the Crimes (Amendment) Ordinance removed criminal penalties for homosexual acts between consenting adults over the age of 18. Since then gay groups have been lobbying for legislation to address the issue of discrimination on the grounds of sexual orientation. Despite these changes, however, Hong Kong Chinese society remains fairly conservative, and it can still be risky for gays and lesbians to come out to family members or their employers.

Check out the latest events in Hong Kong's first free gay lifestyle magazine, *DS Magazine*.

Health

The occasional avian- or swine-flu outbreak notwithstanding, health conditions in the region are good. Travellers have a low risk of contracting infectious diseases, apart from travellers' diarrhoea, which is common throughout Asia. The health system is generally excellent. There is currently no vaccination requirement for travellers visiting Hong Kong. However, observe good personal and food hygiene and take antimosquito measures to prevent infectious diseases.

Diseases

DENGUE FEVER

Dengue is a viral disease transmitted by mosquitoes, and there are occasional outbreaks in Hong Kong. Unlike the malaria mosquito, the *Aedes aegypti* mosquito, which transmits the dengue virus, is most active during the day, and is found mainly in urban areas, in and around human dwellings. Signs and symptoms of dengue fever include a sudden onset of high fever, headache, joint and muscle pains (hence its old name, 'breakbone fever'), and nausea and vomiting. A rash of small red spots sometimes appears three to four days after the onset of fever.

You should seek medical attention as soon as possible if you think you may be infected. A blood test can exclude malaria and indicate the possibility of dengue fever. There is no specific treatment for dengue. Aspirin should be avoided, as it increases the risk of haemorrhaging. The best prevention is to avoid mosquito bites at all times by covering up, and using insect repellents containing th... and mos...

GIARDIA

This is a [...] jumps on [...] have diar[...]es a mor[...] with inter[...] loose sto[...] and some nausea. There may be a metallic taste in the mouth. Avoiding potentially contaminated foods and always washing your hands can help prevent giardia.

HEPATITIS A

Hepatitis A is a virus common in Hong Kong and Macau, and is transmitted through contaminated water and shellfish.

HEPATITIS B

While this is common in the area, it can only be transmitted by unprotected sex, sharing needles, treading on a discarded needle, or receiving contaminated blood in very remote areas of China.

INFLUENZA

Hong Kong has a bad flu season over the winter months from December to March. Symptoms include a cold (runny nose etc) with a high fever and aches and pains. You should wash your hands frequently, avoid anybody you know who has the flu and consider getting a flu shot before you travel.

TRAVELLERS' DIARRHOEA

To prevent diarrhoea, avoid tap water unless it has been boiled, filtered or chemically disinfected (eg with iodine tablets); only eat fresh fruits and vegetables if they're cooked or peeled; be wary of dairy products that might contain unpasteurised milk; and be highly selective when eating food from street vendors.

If you develop diarrhoea, be sure to drink plenty of fluids, preferably an oral rehydration solution containing lots of salt and sugar. A few loose stools doesn't mean you require treatment, but if

encing more
...ive stools a day,
...d start taking an an-
...(usually a quinolone
...) and an anti-diarrhoeal
...ent (such as loperamide).
...f diarrhoea is bloody, or per-
sists for more than 72 hours,
or is accompanied by fever,
shaking, chills or severe
abdominal pain, you should
seek medical attention.

Environmental Hazards

INSECTS
Mosquitoes are prevalent
in Hong Kong. You should
always use insect repel-
lent during warm and hot
weather and if you're bitten,
use hydrocortisone cream
to reduce swelling. Lamma
Island is home to large red
centipedes, which have a
poisonous bite that causes
swelling and discomfort in
most cases, but can be more
dangerous (and supposedly
in very rare cases deadly) for
young children.

MAMMALS
Wild boars and aggressive
dogs are a minor hazard in
some of the more remote
parts of the New Territories.
Wild boars are shy and
retiring most of the time
but are dangerous when
they feel threatened, so give
them a wide berth and avoid
disturbing thick areas of
undergrowth.

SNAKES
There are many snakes
in Hong Kong, and some
are deadly, but you are
unlikely to encounter any.
Still, always take care when
bushwalking, particularly on
Lamma and Lantau Islands.
Go straight to a public hospital if bitten; private doctors
do not stock antivenene.

WATER
Avoid drinking the tap water. Bottled water is a safer
option, or you can boil tap
water for three minutes.

Recommended Immunisations

There are no required vac-
cinations for entry into Hong

Kong or Macau unless you will
be travelling to the mainland
or elsewhere in the region.

If your health insurance
doesn't cover you for medical expenses abroad, consider supplemental insurance
(check out www.lonelyplanet
.com/bookings/insurance.
do for more information).

Internet Access

Long since fully cabled with
broadband, getting online
in Hong Kong should be a
breeze.

Free wi-fi is increasingly
available in hotels and public
areas, including the airport,
public libraries, key cultural
and recreational centres,
large parks, major MTR stations (eg Central and Causeway Bay), shopping malls
and an increasing number of
cafes and bars. You can also
get a free 60-minute PCCW
Wi-Fi pass, available at HKTB
visitor centres.

You can also purchase
a PCCW account online or
at convenience stores and
PCCW stores and access the
internet via any of PCCW's
7000 plus wi-fi hot spots
in Hong Kong. Buy a 3G
rechargeable SIM card from
the shops of **PCCW** (www2.
pccwmobile.com), **SmarTone**
(www.smartone.com) and
other service providers. Card
price is similar and can be as
cheap as $48. PCCW charg-
es $3/MK and SmarTone
charges $8/hour.

If you don't have a computer, try the following:

Central Library (Map p374;
☑3150 1234; www.hkpl.gov.
hk; 66 Causeway Rd, Causeway
Bay; ☺10am-9pm Thu-Tue,
1-9pm Wed) Free access.

Pacific Coffee Company
(Map p378; ☑25371688; www.
pacificcoffee.com; G/F, The
Workstation, 43 Lyndhurst
Tce, Central; ☺7am-11pm
Mon-Wed, 7am-1am Thu-Sat,
8am-11pm Sun) Free access
with purchase; one of scores of
branches in Hong Kong.

Left Luggage

➡ Left-luggage lockers are in
major MTR train stations, including the Hung Hom station; the
West Tower of the Shun Tak Centre in Sheung Wan, from where
the Macau ferry departs; and the
China ferry terminal in Tsim Sha
Tsui. Luggage costs between
$20 and $30 for each hour
(depending on the locker size).

➡ Hong Kong Airport Express
station has a left-luggage office
open from 5.30am to 1.30am on
Level 3 of **Terminal 2** (☑2261
0110; ☺5.30am-1.30am).
Storage here costs $10 for
each hour and $120 for each
day. Generally the machines
don't use keys but spit out a
numbered ticket when you
have deposited your money
and closed the door. You have
to punch in this number when
you retrieve your bag, so keep
it somewhere safe or write the
number down. Most hotels and
even some guesthouses and
hostels have left-luggage rooms
and will let you leave your gear
behind, even if you've already
checked out and won't be staying on your return. There is
usually a charge for this service,
so be sure to inquire first.

Legal Matters

➡ Carry your passport all the
time. As a visitor, you are required to show your identification if the police require it.

➡ *All* forms of narcotics are
illegal in Hong Kong. Whether
it's heroin, opium, 'ice', ecstasy
or marijuana, the law makes no
distinction. If police or customs
officials find dope or even
smoking equipment in your
possession, you can expect to
be arrested immediately.

➡ If you run into legal trouble,
contact the **Legal Aid Department** (☑2537 7677;
☺24hr hotline), which provides
residents and visitors with rep-

resentation, subject to a means and merits test.

Maps

Most popular trails have maps at the starting point and bilingual signs along the trails. If you're heading for any of Hong Kong's four major trails, you can get a copy of the trail map produced by the Country & Marine Parks Authority, which is available at the Map Publication Centres:

North Point branch

(☑2231 3187; 23rd fl, North Point Government Offices, 333 Java Rd; ⊙8.45am-5.30pm Mon-Fri)

Yau Ma Tei branch

(☑2780 0981; 382 Nathan Rd; ⊙8.45am-5.30pm Mon-Fri)

Medical Services

The standard of medical care in Hong Kong is generally excellent but expensive. Always take out travel insurance before you travel. Healthcare is divided into public and private, and there is no interaction between the two.

Clinics

There are many English-speaking general practitioners, specialists and dentists in Hong Kong, who can be found through your consulate, a private hospital or the *Yellow Pages*. If money is tight, take yourself to the nearest public-hospital emergency room and be prepared to wait. The general inquiry number for hospitals is ☑2300 6555.

Hospitals & Emergency Rooms

In the case of an emergency, all ambulances (☑999) will take you to a government-run public hospital where, as a visitor, you will be required to pay a hefty fee for using emergency treatment. Treatment is guaranteed in any case; people who cannot pay

immediately will be billed later. While the emergency care is excellent, you may wish to transfer to a private hospital once you are stable.

Public and private hospitals with 24-hour accident and emergency departments are listed below.

HONG KONG ISLAND

Hong Kong Central Hospital (港中醫院; Map p366; ☑2522 3141; 1 Lower Albert Rd, Central) Private.

Matilda International Hospital (明德國際醫院; ☑2849 0111; 41 Mt Kellett Rd, the Peak) Private.

Queen Mary Hospital (瑪麗醫院; ☑2255 3838; 102 Pok Fu Lam Rd, Pok Fu Lam) Public.

KOWLOON

Hong Kong Baptist Hospital (瑪嘉烈醫院; ☑2339 8888; 222 Waterloo Rd, Kowloon Tong) Private.

Princess Margaret Hospital (☑2990 1111; 2-10 Princess Margaret Hospital Rd, Lai Chi Kok) Public.

Queen Elizabeth Hospital (伊利沙伯醫院; ☑2958 8888; 30 Gascoigne Rd, Yau Ma Tei) Public.

NEW TERRITORIES

Prince of Wales Hospital (威爾斯親王醫院; ☑2632 2211; 30-32 Ngan Shing St, Sha Tin) Public.

Pharmacies

➡ Pharmacies are abundant; they bear a red-and-white cross outside and there should be a registered pharmacist available inside.

➡ In Hong Kong many medications can be bought over the counter without a prescription, but always check it is a known brand and that the expiry date is valid.

➡ Birth-control pills, pads, tampons and condoms are available over the counter in pharmacies,

as well as in stores such as Watson's and Mannings.

Money

The local currency is the Hong Kong dollar ($), which is divided into 100 cents. Bills are issued in denominations of $10, $20, $50, $100, $500 and $1000. There are little copper coins worth 10¢, 20¢ and 50¢, silver-coloured $1, $2 and $5 coins, and a nickel and bronze $10 coin.

Three local banks issue notes: HSBC (formerly the Hong Kong & Shanghai Bank), the Standard Chartered Bank and the Bank of China (all but the $10 bill).

ATMs

Automated Teller Machines (ATMs) can be found almost everywhere in Hong Kong and are almost always linked up to international money systems such as Cirrus, Maestro, Plus and Visa Electron. Some HSBC so-called Electronic Money machines offer cash withdrawal facilities for Visa and MasterCard holders; American Express (Amex) cardholders have access to Jetco ATMs and can withdraw local currency and travellers cheques at Express Cash ATMs in town.

Changing Money

Hong Kong has no currency controls; locals and foreigners can bring, send in or take out as much money as they like.

Banks in Hong Kong generally offer the best rates, though two of the biggest ones (Standard Chartered Bank and Hang Seng Bank) levy a $50 commission for each transaction for those who don't hold accounts. Avoid HSBC, where this charge is $100. If you're changing the equivalent of several hundred US dollars or more, the exchange rate improves, which usually makes up for the fee.

Licensed moneychangers, such as Chequepoint,

abound in touristed areas, including Tsim Sha Tsui. While they are convenient (usually open on Sundays, holidays and late into the evenings) and take no commission per se, the less-than-attractive exchange rates offered are equivalent to a 5% commission. These rates are clearly posted, though if you're changing several hundred US dollars or more you might be able to bargain for a better rate. Before the actual exchange is made, the moneychanger is required by law to give you a form to sign that clearly shows the amount due to you, the exchange rate and any service charges. Try to avoid the exchange counters at the airport or in hotels, which offer some of the worst rates in Hong Kong.

No foreign-currency black market exists in Hong Kong. If anyone on the street does approach you to change money, assume it's a scam.

Credit Cards

The most widely accepted credit cards in Hong Kong are Visa, MasterCard, Amex, Diners Club and JCB – and pretty much in that order. It may be an idea to carry two, just in case.

Some shops in Hong Kong add a surcharge to offset the commission charged by credit companies, which can range from 2.5% to 7%. In theory, this is prohibited by the credit companies, but to get around this many shops will offer a 5% discount if you pay with cash.

If a card is lost or stolen, you must inform both the **police** (☎2527 7177) and the issuing company as soon as possible; otherwise, you may have to pay for the purchases that have been racked up on your card. Some 24-hour numbers for cancelling cards:

American Express (☎2811 6122)

Diners Club (☎2860 1888)

MasterCard (☎800 966 677)

Visa (☎800 900 782) Might be able to help you should you lose your Visa card, but in general you must deal with the issuing bank in the case of an emergency.

Tipping

➧ Hong Kong isn't particularly conscious of tipping and there is no obligation to tip, say, taxi drivers; just round the fare up, or you can throw in a dollar or two more.

➧ It's almost mandatory to tip hotel porters $10 to $20, and for porters at the airport, $2 to $5 a suitcase is normally expected. The porters putting your bags on a push cart at Hong Kong or Kowloon Airport Express station do not expect a gratuity, though; it's all part of the service.

➧ Most hotels and many restaurants add a 10% service charge to the bill. Check for hidden extras before you tip.

Travellers Cheques & Cards

Travellers cheques and their modern equivalent, ATM-style cards that can be credited with cash in advance, offer protection from theft but are becoming less common due to the preponderance of ATMs. Most banks will cash travellers cheques, and they all charge a fee, often irrespective of whether you are an account holder or not.

If any cheques are lost or stolen, contact the issuing office or the nearest branch of the issuing agency immediately. **American Express** (☎3002 1276) can usually arrange replacement cheques within 24 hours.

Newspapers & Magazines

➧ The main English-language newspaper in the city is the daily broadsheet *South China Morning Post* (www.scmp. com), which has always toed the government line, both before and after the handover. It has the largest circulation and is read by more Hong Kong Chinese than expatriates.

➧ The livelier and slightly punchier tabloid *Hong Kong Standard* (www.thestandard. com.hk), published Monday to Saturday (weekend edition), is harder to find.

➧ The Běijīng mouthpiece *China Daily* (www.chinadaily.com.cn) also prints a Hong Kong English-language edition of its paper.

➧ Hong Kong has its share of English-language periodicals, including a slew of homegrown (and Asian-focused) business-related magazines. *Time, Newsweek* and the *Economist* are all available in their current editions.

Post

Hong Kong Post (☎2921 2222; www.hongkongpost.com) is generally excellent; local letters are often delivered the same day they are sent and there is Saturday delivery. The staff at most post offices speak English, and the lavender-coloured mail boxes with lime-green posts are clearly marked in English.

Receiving Mail

If a letter is addressed c/o Poste Restante, GPO Hong Kong, it will go to the GPO on Hong Kong Island. Pick it up at counter No 29 from 8am to 6pm Monday to Saturday only. If you want your letters to go to Kowloon, have them addressed as follows: c/o Poste Restante, Tsim Sha Tsui Post Office, 10 Middle Rd, Tsim Sha Tsui, Kowloon. Overseas mail is normally held for two months and local mail for two weeks.

Sending Mail

On Hong Kong Island, the **General Post Office** (中央

郵政局; Map p362; 2 Connaught Pl, Central; ⊙8am-6pm Mon-Sat, 9am-5pm Sun) is just east of the Hong Kong station. In Kowloon, the **Tsim Sha Tsui Post Office** (尖沙咀郵局; Ground fl, Hermes House, 10 Middle Rd, Tsim Sha Tsui; ⊙9am-6pm Mon-Sat, to 2pm Sun) is just east of the southern end of Nathan Rd. Post office branches elsewhere keep shorter hours and usually don't open on Sunday.

You should allow five days for delivery of letters, postcards and aerogrammes to the UK, Continental Europe and Australia, and five to six days to the USA.

COURIER SERVICES
Private companies offering courier delivery service include the following:
DHL International (☎2400 3388)
Federal Express (☎2730 3333)
UPS (☎2735 3535)

All three have pick-up points around the territory. Many MTR stations have DHL outlets, including the **MTR Central branch** (☎2877 2848) next to exit H, and the **MTR Admiralty branch** (☎2529 5778) next to exit E.

POSTAL RATES
Local mail is $1.40 for up to 30g. Airmail letters and postcards for the first 20/30g are $2.40/4.50 to Asia (excluding Japan) and $3/5.30 elsewhere, and $120/130 respectively per kilogram. Aerogrammes are $2.30.

SPEEDPOST
Letters and small parcels sent via Hong Kong Post's **Speedpost** (☎2921 2288; www.hongkongpost.com/speedpost) should reach any of 210 destinations worldwide within two days and are automatically registered. Speedpost rates vary enormously according to destination; every post office has a schedule of fees and a timetable.

Public Holidays

Western and Chinese culture combine to create an interesting mix – and number – of public holidays in Hong Kong and Macau. Determining the exact date of some of them is tricky, as there are traditionally two calendars in use: the Gregorian solar (or Western) calendar and the Chinese lunar calendar.

New Year's Day 1 January

Chinese New Year 11 to 13 February 2013, 31 January to 2 February 2014

Easter 29 March to 1 April 2013, 18 to 21 April 2014

Ching Ming 4 April

Labour Day 1 May

Buddha's Birthday 17 May 2013, 6 May 2014

Dragon Boat (Tuen Ng) Festival 12 June 2013, 2 June 2014

Hong Kong SAR Establishment Day 1 July

Mid-Autumn Festival 20 September 2013, 9 September 2014

China National Day 1 October

Chung Yeung 14 October 2013, 2 October 2014

Christmas Day 25 December

Boxing Day 26 December

Radio

The following are Hong Kong's most popular English-language radio stations:

AM 864 Hit parade; 864AM.

Metro Plus News; 1044AM.

RTHK Radio 3 Current affairs and talkback; 567AM, 1584AM, 97.9FM and 106.8FM.

RTHK Radio 4 Classical music; 97.6–98.9FM.

RTHK Radio 6 BBC World Service relays; 675AM.

The *South China Morning Post* publishes a daily schedule of radio programs.

Safe Travel

Hong Kong is generally a very safe place, but as everywhere, things can go awry. Although it is safe to walk around just about anywhere in the territory after dark, it's best to stick to well-lit areas. Tourist districts, such as Tsim Sha Tsui, are heavily patrolled by the police. In the event of an emergency, ring ☎999.

Hong Kong has its share of local pickpockets and thieves. Carry as little cash and as few valuables as possible, and if you put a bag down, keep an eye on it. This also applies to restaurants and pubs, particularly in touristy areas such as the Peak Tram. If your bag doesn't accompany you to the toilet, don't expect to find it when you return.

If you are robbed, you can obtain a loss report for insurance purposes at the police station in the area in which the crime occurred. For locations and contact details of police stations in Hong Kong, visit www.police.gov.hk and click on 'e-Report Room'.

Taxes & Refunds

There is no sales tax in Hong Kong.

Telephone
International Calls & Rates

Hong Kong's 'country' code is ☎852. To call someone outside Hong Kong, dial ☎001, then the country code, then the local area code (you usually drop the initial zero if there is one) and the number.

Remember that phone rates in Hong Kong are cheaper from 9pm to 8am on weekdays and throughout the weekend. If the phone you're using has the facility, dial ☎0060 first and then the number; rates will be cheaper at any time.

You can make International Direct Dial (IDD) calls to

almost anywhere in the world from most public telephones in Hong Kong, but you'll need a phonecard, available from most public service providers, such as PCCW's Hello card. You can buy phonecards at any PCCW branch, at 7-Eleven and Circle K convenience stores, Mannings pharmacies or Vango supermarkets.

PCCW (☎2888 2888; www.pccw.com) has retail outlets throughout the territory, where you can buy phonecards, mobile phones and accessories. The most convenient shop for travellers is the **Central branch** (Ground fl, 113 Des Voeux Rd Central; ☉10am-8.30pm Mon-Sat, 11am-8pm Sun). There's also a **Causeway Bay branch** (G3, Ground fl, McDonald's Bldg, 46-54 Yee Wo St; ☉10am-10pm Mon-Sun).

Local Calls & Rates

All calls made from private phones in Hong Kong are local calls and therefore free. From public payphones calls cost $1 for five minutes. Pay phones accept $1, $2, $5 and $10 coins. Hotels charge from $3 to $5 for local calls.

All landline numbers in the territory have eight digits (except ☎800 toll-free numbers and specific hotlines).

Mobile Phones

Hong Kong locals are addicted to their mobile telephones, which work everywhere, including in the harbour tunnels and on the MTR. Any GSM-compatible phone can be used here.

PCCW and other service providers have mobile phones and accessories along with rechargeable SIM cards for sale from $48. Local calls work out to cost between 6¢ and 12¢ a minute (calls to the mainland are about $1.80/minute).

Useful Numbers

The following are some important telephone numbers and codes. Both the tele-

phone directory and the *Yellow Pages* can be consulted online at www.yp.com.hk.

International dialling code (☎001)

International directory inquiries (☎10015)

Local directory inquiries (☎1081)

Reverse-charge/collect calls (☎10010)

Time & temperature (☎18501)

Weather (☎187 8200)

Time

Hong Kong does not have daylight-saving time. Hong Kong time is eight hours ahead of GMT and London; 13 hours ahead of New York; 16 hours ahead of San Francisco; the same time as Singapore, Manila and Perth; and two hours behind Sydney.

Toilets

Hong Kong has never had as many public toilets as other world-class cities, but that is changing rapidly, with new ones being built and old ones refurbished and reopened. They are always free to use. Almost all public toilets have access for people with disabilities, and baby-changing shelves in both men's and women's rooms. Equip yourself with tissues, though; public toilets in Hong Kong are often out of toilet paper.

Tourist Information

The enterprising and energetic **Hong Kong Tourism Board** (HKTB; www.discoverhongkong.com) is one of the most helpful and useful tourist organisations in the world. Staff are welcoming and have reams of information. Most of its literature is free,

though it also sells a few useful publications and books, as well as postcards, T-shirts and souvenirs.

While on the ground in Hong Kong, phone the **HKTB Visitor Hotline** (☎2508 1234; ☉9am-6pm) if you have a query or problem, or you're lost. Staff are eager to help.

HKTB Visitor Information & Service Centres can be found on Hong Kong Island, in Kowloon, at Hong Kong International Airport on Lantau Island, and in Lo Wu, which is on the border with the mainland. Outside these centres and at several other places in the territory you'll be able to find iCyberlink screens, from which you can conveniently access the HKTB website and database 24 hours a day.

Hong Kong International Airport HKTB Centres (Chek Lap Kok; ☉7am-11pm) There are centres in Halls A and B on the arrivals level in Terminal 1 and the E2 transfer area.

Hong Kong Island HKTB Centre (港島旅客諮詢及服務中心; Peak Piazza; ☉9am-9pm)

Kowloon HKTB Centre (香港旅遊發展局; Map p378; Star Ferry Concourse, Tsim Sha Tsui; ☉8am-8pm)

Lo Wu HKTB Centre (羅湖旅客諮詢及服務中心; 2nd fl, Arrival Hall, Lo Wu Terminal Bldg; ☉8am-6pm)

Travel Agencies

You'll find travel agencies everywhere in Hong Kong, but the following are among the most reliable and offer the best deals on air tickets:

Concorde Travel (Map p366; ☎2526 3391; www.concorde-travel.com; 1st fl, Galuxe Bldg, 8-10 On Lan St, Central; ☉9am-5.30pm Mon-Fri, to 1pm Sat) This is a long-established and highly dependable agency owned and operated by Aussie expats.

Natori Travel (樂途旅遊 有限公司; Map p366; ☑2810 1681; www.natoritvl.com; Room 2207, Melbourne Plaza, 33 Queen's Rd Central; ⊘9am-7pm Mon-Fri, to 4pm Sat) Readers have long used and recommended this place.

Phoenix Services Agency (峯寧旅運社; Map p380; ☑2722 7378; Room 1404, 14th fl, Austin Tower, 22-26 Austin Ave, Tsim Sha Tsui; ⊘9am-6pm Mon-Fri, to 4pm Sat) Phoenix is one of the best places in Hong Kong to buy air tickets, get China visas and seek travel advice. It is also the Hong Kong agent for the student and discount-travel company STA Travel.

Traveller Services (Map p378; ☑2375 2222; www.take traveller.com; 1813 Miramar Tower, 132 Nathan Rd, Tsim Sha Tsui; ⊘9am-6pm Mon-Fri, to 1pm Sat) Very reliable for good-value air tickets.

Travellers with Disabilities

People with disabilities have to cope with substantial obstacles in Hong Kong, including the stairs at many MTR stations, as well as pedestrian overpasses, narrow and crowded footpaths, and steep hills. On the other hand, some buses are accessible by wheelchair, taxis are never hard to find, most buildings have lifts (many with Braille panels) and MTR stations have Braille maps with recorded information. Wheelchairs can negotiate the lower decks of most ferries.

For further information about facilities and services in Hong Kong for travellers with disabilities:

Easy Access Travel (☑2772 7301; www.travpulse.

com; Ground fl, HKSR Lam Tin Complex, 7 Rehab Path, Lam Tin, Kowloon) Offers tours and accessible transport services.

Hong Kong Society for Rehabilitation (香港復康 會; ☑3143 2800; www.access guide.hk) The website carries practical information for travellers with disabilities.

Transport Department (www.td.gov.hk) Provides guides to public transportation, parking and pedestrian crossing for people with disabilities.

Visas & Passports

A passport is essential for visiting Hong Kong, and it needs to be valid for at least one month after the period of your stay in Hong Kong. Carry your passport at all times as this is the only form of identification acceptable to the Hong Kong police.

The vast majority of travellers, including citizens of Australia, Canada, the EU, Israel, Japan, New Zealand and the USA, are allowed to enter the Hong Kong Special Administrative Region (SAR) without a visa and stay for 90 days. Holders of British passports can stay up to 180 days without a visa, but British Dependent Territories and British Overseas citizens not holding a visa are only allowed to remain 90 days. Holders of many African (including South African), South American and Middle Eastern passports do not require visas for visits of 30 days or less. You can check visa requirements on www.immd.gov.hk/ehtml/hk visas_4.htm.

Anyone wishing to stay longer than the visa-free period must apply for a visa before travelling to Hong Kong.

If you do require a visa, you must apply beforehand at the nearest Chinese consulate or embassy; for addresses and contact information, consult the website www.fmprc.gov.cn/eng/wjb/zwjg/.

If you plan on visiting mainland China, you must have a visa, and US citizens must apply for their visas prior to crossing the border; for further details: www.fmprc.gov.cn.

Visa Extensions

You have to apply for visa extensions in person at the **Hong Kong Immigration Department** (Map p372; ☑2824 6111; www.immd.gov.hk; 2nd fl, Immigration Tower, 7 Gloucester Rd, Wan Chai; ⊘8.45am-4.30pm Mon-Fri, 9-11.30am Sat) seven days from visa expiry. Check www.immd.gov.hk/ehtml/hkvisas_4.htm for more details.

Weights & Measures

Although the international metric system is in official use in Hong Kong, traditional Chinese weights and measures are still common. At local markets, meat, fish and produce are sold by the *léung,* equivalent to 37.8g, and the *gàn* (catty), which is equivalent to about 600g. There are 16 *léung* to the *gàn.* Gold and silver are sold by the *tael,* which is exactly the same as a *léung.*

Women Travellers

Hong Kong is a safe city for women, though commonsense caution should be observed, especially at night. Few women – visitors or residents – complain of bad treatment, intimidation or aggression. Having said that, some Chinese men regard Western women as 'easy'. If you are sexually assaulted, call the **Rape Crisis Centre Hotline** (☑2375 5322).

Macau Directory A–Z

Much of the advice given for Hong Kong (see p328) also applies to Macau.

Business Hours

Banks Open from 9am to 5pm weekdays and to 1pm on Saturday.

Government offices Usually open from 9am to 1pm and 2.30pm to 5.30pm (or 5.45pm) on weekdays.

Customs Regulations

➡ Customs formalities are few.
➡ The duty-free quota for visitors is 100 cigarettes and 1L of spirits.

Discount Cards

The Macau Museums Pass allows entry to the Grand Prix Museum, the Maritime Museum, Lin Zexu Memorial Hall in Lin Fung Temple, the Macau Museum of Art and the Macau Museum, and is valid for five days. It costs MOP$25/12 adult/concession, and is available from the Macau Government Tourist Office (MGTO; see p338) or any participating museum.

Electricity

220V/50Hz

➡ Electricity in Macau is at 220V, 50Hz.
➡ Power plugs are the three-pin, square-shaped or round-shaped type.

Emergency

Police, Fire & Ambulance (☑999)
24-hour Tourists' Emergency Hotline (☑112)

Health

See Health, p329, much of which also applies to Macau.

Internet Access

Free Wi-fi

You can access free public wi-fi in touristy and busy areas daily from 8am to 1am the following day. User name and password are 'wifigo'. Each session lasts 45 minutes but you can reconnect again.

Paid Wi-fi

You can buy prepaid phone-cards from CTM (p338), ranging from MOP$50 to MOP$130, which allow you to enjoy mobile broadband; or buy a mobile broadband pass which allows you unlimited internet access for either one day (MOP$120) or five days (MOP$220).

Macau has few internet cafes, but most major hotels have internet facilities. You can get online at the following places:

MGTO Information Counter at Largo do Senado (旅遊諮詢處; Map p240; ☑8397 1120; ☺9am-6pm)

Multimedia Library in Macau Museum of Art (Map p236; Macau Cultural Centre, Avenida Xian Xing Hai; ☺2-7pm Tue-Fri, 11am-7pm Sat & Sun)

Public libraries Visit the following websites for locations and opening hours: www.library.gov.mo and library.iacm.gov.mo.

Left Luggage

➜ There are electronic lockers on both the arrivals and departure levels of the Macau ferry terminal. They cost MOP$20 or MOP$25, depending on the size, for the first two hours and MOP$25/30 for each additional 12-hour period.

➜ There is also a left-luggage counter on the departures level at the Macau International Airport that's open 24 hours. It charges MOP$10 hourly and MOP$80 daily.

Legal Matters

➜ The legal age for gambling in Macau is 18 for tourists.

➜ Possession of any kind of illicit drugs can lead to imprisonment.

Maps

The MGTO distributes the excellent (and free) *Macau Tourist Map*, with major tourist sights and streets labelled in English, Portuguese and Chinese, small insert maps of Taipa and Coloane, and bus routes marked.

Medical Services

Macau's two hospitals both have 24-hour emergency services.

Centro Hospitalar Conde Saõ Januário (山頂醫院; Map p236; ☑2831 3731; Estrada do Visconde de São Januário) Southwest of Guia Fort.

Hospital Kiang Wu (鏡湖醫院; Map p236; ☑2837 1333; Rua de Coelho do Amaral) Northeast of the ruins of the Church of St Paul.

Money

Macau's currency is the pataca (MOP$), which is divided up into 100 avos. Bills are issued in denominations of MOP$10, MOP$20, MOP$50, MOP$100, MOP$500 and MOP$1000. There are little copper coins worth 10, 20 and 50 avos, and silver-coloured MOP$1, MOP$2, MOP$5 and MOP$10 coins.

The pataca is pegged to the Hong Kong dollar at the rate of MOP$103.20 to HK$100. As a result, exchange rates for the pataca are virtually the same as for the Hong Kong dollar. Hong Kong bills and coins (except the $10 coins) are accepted everywhere in Macau. When you spend Hong Kong dollars in big hotels, restaurants and department stores, usually your change will be returned in that currency. Try to use up all your patacas before leaving Macau.

Most ATMs allow you to choose between patacas and Hong Kong dollars, and credit cards are readily accepted at Macau's hotels, larger restaurants and casinos. You can also change cash and travellers cheques at the banks lining Avenida da Praia Grande and Avenida de Almeida Ribeiro, as well as at major hotels.

Tipping is not a must, but is expected. MOP$10 or MOP$20 will do for hotel porters, and tip around 10% of the restaurant bill.

Post

Correios de Macau, Macau's postal system, is efficient and inexpensive.

The **main post office** (郵政總局; Map p240; ☑2832 3666; 126 Avenida de Almeida Ribeiro; ◷9am-6pm Mon-Fri, 9am-1pm Sat) faces Largo do Senado; pick up poste restante from counter 1 or 2. There are other post offices in Macau Peninsula, including a **Macau ferry terminal branch** (☑2872 8079; ◷10am-7pm Mon-Sat).

Domestic letters cost MOP$1.50/2 for up to 20/50g, while those to Hong Kong are MOP$2.50/4. For international mail, Macau divides the world into zones: zone 1 (MOP$4/5 for up to 10/20g) is East, South and Southeast Asia; zone 2 (MOP$5/6.50) is everywhere else except for the mainland, which is MOP$3.50/4.50.

EMS Speedpost (☑2859 6688) is available at the main post office. The following companies can also arrange express forwarding:

DHL (☑2837 2828)

Federal Express (☑2870 3333)

UPS (☑2875 1616)

Public Holidays

New Year's Day 1 January

Chinese New Year 11 to 13 February 2013, 31 January to 2 February 2014

Easter 29 to 30 March 2013, 18 to 19 April 2014

Ching Ming 4 April

Labour Day 1 May

Buddha's Birthday 17 May 2013, 6 May 2014

Dragon Boat (Tuen Ng) Festival 12 June 2013, 2 June 2014

Mid-Autumn Festival 20 September 2013, 9 September 2014

China National Day 1 October

Chung Yeung 14 October 2013, 2 October 2014

All Souls' Day 2 November

Feast of the Immaculate Conception 8 December

Winter Solstice 9 December 2013, 29 December 2014

Macau SAR Establishment Day 20 December

Christmas Eve 24 December

Christmas Day 25 December

Safe Travel

➜ Violent crime against visitors in Macau is low but pickpocketing and other street crime can occur in some areas.

➜ Take extra caution of passports and valuables in crowded areas and when visiting casinos late at night.

Telephone

Macau's telephone service provider is **Companhia de Telecomunicações de Macau** (澳門電訊; CTM; ☎inquiry hotline 1000; www. ctm.net). Convenient CTM branches in Macau include the following:

Leal Senado Shop (Map p240; 21 Largo do Senado; ☉10.30am-7.30pm)

Pedro Coutinho Shop (澳門電訊總店; 25 Rua Pedro Coutinho; ☉10.30am-7.30pm) Two blocks northeast of the Lou Lim Ioc Garden.

Local calls are free from private telephones; at a public payphone they cost MOP$1 for five minutes. Most hotels will charge you MOP$3.

Phone Codes

The international access code for every country, except Hong Kong, is ☎00. If you want to phone Hong Kong, dial ☎01 first, then the number you want; you do not need to dial Hong Kong's country code (☎852). To call Macau from abroad – including Hong Kong – the country code is ☎853.

Phonecards

All pay phones permit International Direct Dialling (IDD) using an Easy Call phonecard available to purchase from CTM for MOP$10/50/90/100. Rates are cheaper from 9pm to 8am on weekdays and all day Saturday and Sunday. Prepaid SIM cards are available from CTM for MOP$50/130 (for local calls) and MOP$50/100/130 (with IDD and international roaming), which allow internet access through mobile broadband.

Useful Numbers

International directory assistance (☎101)

Local directory assistance (☎181)

Tourist Information

The **Macau Government Tourist Office** (澳門旅遊局; MGTO; Map p362; ☎2831 5566; www.macautourism.gov. mo) is a well-organised and helpful source of information. Its dispenses information and a large selection of free literature, including pamphlets on everything from Chinese temples and Catholic churches to fortresses, gardens and walks. It has a half-dozen outlets scattered around town, including at:

Guia Lighthouse (Map p236; ☎2856 9808; ☉9am-1pm & 2.15-5.30pm)

Largo do Senado (Map p240; ☎8397 1120; ☉9am-6pm)

Macau ferry terminal (Map p236; ☎2872 6416; ☉9am-10pm)

Macau International Airport (☎2886 1418; ☉10am-7pm) Mezzanine Level.

The MGTO also runs a **24-hour Tourism Hotline** (☎2833 3000) to provide advice and assistance. If you run into trouble, you can call the **24-hour Tourists' Emergency Hotline** (☎112).

MGTO also has a **Hong Kong branch** (☎2857 2287; 336-337 Shun Tak Center, 200 Connaught Rd, Central; ☉9am-10pm).

Travellers with Disabilities

Macau is not exactly friendly to travellers with disabilities. The historical part of Macau sits on hilly landscape and pavement is often uneven. The newer parts, eg around the Cotai Strip, are flat and have wider streets.

Macau law requires accessible facilities in public buildings (usually in the form of a ramp) and handicapped parking in public parking lots. Cross walks generally have audible signals for the hearing-impaired.

Public transport, including taxis, is not equipped to accommodate the physically disabled. The airport is quite accessible, but accessing the ferries from Hong Kong to Macau would require assistance from the staff.

Visas

Most travellers, including citizens of the EU, Australia, New Zealand, the USA, Canada and South Africa, can enter Macau with just their passports for between 30 and 90 days.

Travellers who do require them can get visas valid for 30 days on arrival in Macau. They cost MOP$100/50/200 for adult/child under 12 years/family.

You can get a single one-month extension from the Macau **Immigration Department** (澳門入境處; Map p236; ☎2872 5488; Ground fl, Travessa da Amizade; ☉9am-5pm Mon-Fri).

Websites

Useful Macau websites:

Cityguide (www.cityguide. gov.mo) A good source of practical information, such as transport routes.

Macau Cultural Institute (www.icm.gov.mo) Macau's cultural offerings month by month.

Macau Government Information (www.macau.gov. mo) The number-one source for nontourism information about Macau.

Macau Government Tourist Office (www.macau tourism.gov.mo) The best source of information for visiting Macau.

Macau Yellow Pages (www.yp.com.mo) Telephone directory with maps.

Language

Cantonese is the most popular Chinese dialect in Hong Kong, Guǎngzhōu and the surrounding area. Cantonese speakers can read Chinese characters, but will pronounce many characters differently from a Mandarin speaker.

Several systems of Romanisation for Cantonese script exist, and no single one has emerged as an official standard. In this chapter we use Lonely Planet's pronunciation guide designed for maximum accuracy with minimum complexity.

Pronunciation

Vowels

a	as the 'u' in 'but'
ai	as in 'aisle' (short sound)
au	as the 'ou' in 'out'
ay	as in 'pay'
eu	as the 'er' in 'fern'
eui	as in French *feuille* (eu with i)
ew	as in 'blew' (short and pronounced with tightened lips)
i	as the 'ee' in 'deep'
iu	as the 'yu' in 'yuletide'
o	as in 'go'
oy	as in 'boy'
u	as in 'put'
ui	as in French *oui*

Consonants

In Cantonese, the ng sound can appear at the start of a word. Practise by saying 'sing along' slowly and then do away with the 'si'.

WANT MORE?

For in-depth language information and handy phrases, check out Lonely Planet's *China phrasebook*. You'll find it at **shop.lonelyplanet.com**, or you can buy Lonely Planet's iPhone phrasebooks at the Apple App Store.

Note that words ending with the consonant sounds p, t, and k must be clipped in Cantonese. You can hear this in English as well – say 'pit' and 'tip' and listen to how much shorter the 'p' sound is in 'tip'.

Many Cantonese speakers, particularly young people, replace an 'n' sound with an 'l' if a word begins with it – náy (you), is often heard as láy. Where relevant, this change is reflected in our pronunciation guides.

Tones

Cantonese is a language with a large number of words with the same pronunciation but a different meaning, eg gwàt (dig up) and gwàt (bones). What distinguishes these homophones is their 'tonal' quality – the raising and the lowering of pitch on certain syllables. Tones in Cantonese fall on vowels (a, e, i, o, u) and on the consonant n.

To give you a taste of how these tones work, we've included them in our red pronunciation guides in this chapter – they show six tones, divided into high and low pitch groups. High-pitch tones involve tightening the vocal muscles to get a higher note, whereas low-pitch tones are made by relaxing the vocal chords to get a lower note. The tones are indicated with the following accent marks:

à	high
á	high rising
a	level
à̲	low falling
á̲	low rising
a̲	low

Basics

Hello.	哈佬。	hàa·ló
Goodbye.	再見。	joy·gin
How are you?	你幾好啊嗎？	láy gáy hó à maa
Fine.	幾好。	gáy hó

Excuse me. (to get attention)	對唔住 。	deui·ǹg·jew
Excuse me. (to get past)	唔該借借 。	ǹg·gòy je·je
Sorry.	對唔住 。	deui·ǹg·jew
Yes.	係 。	hai
No.	不係 。	ǹg·hai
Please ...	唔該……	ǹg·gòy ...
Thank you.	多謝 。	dàw·je
You're welcome.	唔駛客氣 。	ǹg·sái haak·hay

What's your name?
你叫乜嘢名 ? láy giu màt·yé méng aa

My name is ...
我叫…… ngáw giu ...

Do you speak English?
你識唔識講 英文啊 ? láy sik·ǹg·sik gáwng yìng·mán aa

I don't understand.
我唔明 。 ngáw ǹg mìng

Accommodation

campsite	營地	yìng·day
guesthouse	賓館	bàn·gún
hostel	招待所	jiù·doy·sáw
hotel	酒店	jáu·dim
Do you have a ... room?	有冇…… 房 ?	yáu·mó ... fáwng
single	單人	dàan·yàn
double	雙人	sèung·yàn
How much is it per ...?	一……幾多 錢 ?	yàt ... gáy·dàw chín
night	晚	máan
person	個人	gaw yàn
air-con	空調	hùng·tiù
bathroom	沖涼房	chùng·lèung· fáwng
bed	床	chàwng
cot	BB床	bi·bi chàwng
window	窗	chèung

Directions

Where's ...?
……喺邊度? ... hái bìn·do

What's the address?
地址係 ? day·jí hai

KEY PATTERNS

To get by in Cantonese, mix and match these simple patterns with words of your choice:

When's (the next tour)?
(下個旅遊團) 係幾時 ? (haa·gaw léui·yàu·tèwn hai) gáy·sì

Where's (the station)?
(車站)喺邊度 ? (chè·jaam) hái·bìn·do

Where can I (buy a padlock)?
邊度可以 (買倒鎖) ? bìn·do háw·yí (mái dó sáw)

Do you have (a map)?
有冇 (地圖) ? yáu·mó (day·tò)

I need (a mechanic).
我要 (個整車 師傅) 。 ngáw yiu (gaw jíng·chè sì·fú)

I'd like (a taxi).
我想 (坐的士) 。 ngáw séung (cháw dìk·sí)

Can I (get a stand-by ticket)?
可唔可以 (買 張後補飛)呀 ? háw·ǹg·háw·yí (mái jèung hau·bó fày) aa

Could you please (write it down)?
唔該你 (寫落嚟)? ng·gòy láy (sé lawk lài)

Do I need (to book)?
駛唔駛 (定飛 先)呀 ? sái·ǹg·sái (deng·fày sin) aa

I have (a reservation).
我 (預定)咗 。 ngáw (yew·deng) jáw

behind	後面	hau·min
left	左邊	jáw·bìn
near ...	……附近	... fu·gan
next to ...	……旁邊	... pàwng·bin
on the corner	十字路口	sap·ji·lo·háu
opposite	對面	deui·min
right	右邊	yau·bìn
straight ahead	前面	chìn·min
traffic lights	紅綠燈	hùng·luk·dàng

Eating & Drinking

What would you recommend?
有乜嘢好介紹 ? yáu màt·yé hó gaai·siu

What's in that dish?
呢道菜有啲乜嘢 ? lày do choy yáu dì màt·yé

That was delicious.
真好味 。 jàn hó·may

Cheers!
乾杯 ! gàwn·bui

I'd like the bill, please.
唔該我要埋單 。 ǹg·gòy ngáw yiu màai·dàan

I'd like to book a table for ...	我想 訂張檯， ……嘅 。	ngáw séung deng jèung tóy ... ge
(eight) o'clock	(八) 點鐘	(bàat) dím·jùng
(two) people	(兩)位	(léung) wái

I don't eat ...	我唔吃……	ngáw ǹg sik ...
fish	魚	yéw
nuts	果仁	gwáw·yàn
poultry	雞鴨鵝	gài ngaap ngàw
red meat	牛羊肉	ngàu yèung yuk

Key Words

appetisers	涼盤	lèung·pún
baby food	嬰兒食品	yìng·yì sik·bán
bar	酒吧	jáu·bàa
bottle	樽	jèun
bowl	碗	wún
breakfast	早餐	jó·chàan
cafe	咖啡屋	gaa·fè·ngùk
children's menu	個小童菜單	gaw siú·tung choy·dàan
(too) cold	(太)凍	(taai) dung
dinner	晚飯	máan·faan
food	食物	sik·mat
fork	叉	chàa
glass	杯	bùi
halal	清真	chìng·jàn
high chair	高凳	gò·dang
hot (warm)	熱	yit
knife	刀	dò
kosher	猶太	yàu·tàai
local specialities	地方小食	day·fàwng siú·sik
lunch	午餐	ńg·chàan
market	街市	gàai·sí
main courses	主菜	jéw·choy
menu (in English)	(英文)菜單	(yìng·màn) choy·dàan
plate	碟	díp
restaurant	酒樓	jáu·làu
(too) spicy	(太)辣	(taai) laat
spoon	羹	gàng
supermarket	超市	chiù·sí
vegetarian food	齋食品	jàai sik·bán

Meat & Fish

beef	牛肉	ngàu·yuk
chicken	雞肉	gài·yuk
duck	鴨	ngaap
fish	魚	yéw
lamb	羊肉	yèung·yuk
pork	豬肉	jèw·yuk
seafood	海鮮	hóy·sìn

Fruit & Vegetables

apple	蘋果	pìng·gwáw
banana	香蕉	hèung·jiù
cabbage	白菜	baak·choy
carrot	紅蘿蔔	hùng·làw·baak
celery	芹菜	kàn·choy
cucumber	青瓜	chèng·gwàa
fruit	水果	séui·gwáw
grapes	葡提子	pò·tài·jí
green beans	扁荳	bín·dau
lemon	檸檬	lìng·mùng
lettuce	生菜	sàang·choy
mushroom	蘑菇	màw·gù
onion(s)	洋蔥	yèung·chùng
orange	橙	cháang
peach	桃	tó
pear	梨	láy
pineapple	菠蘿	bàw·làw
plum	梅	mùi
potato	薯仔	sèw·jái
spinach	菠菜	bàw·choy
tomato	番茄	fàan·ké
vegetable	蔬菜	sàw·choy

Other

bread	麵包	min·bàau
egg	蛋	dáan
herbs/spices	香料	hèung·liú
pepper	胡椒粉	wù·jiù·fán
rice	白飯	baak·faan
salt	鹽	yìm
soy sauce	豉油	si·yàu
sugar	砂糖	sàa·tàwng
vegetable oil	菜油	choy·yàu
vinegar	醋	cho

Signs

入口	Entrance
出口	Exit
廁所	Toilets
男	Men
女	Women

Drinks

beer	啤酒	bè·jáu
coffee	咖啡	gaa·fè
juice	果汁	gwáw·jàp
milk	牛奶	ngàu·láai
mineral water	礦泉水	kawng·chèwn·séui
red wine	紅葡萄酒	hùng·pò·tò·jáu
tea	茶	chàa
white wine	白葡萄酒	baak·pò·tò·jáu

Emergencies

Help!	救命！	gau·mèng
Go away!	走開！	jáu·hòy
I'm lost.	我蕩失路 。	ngáw dawng·sàk·lo
I'm sick.	我病咗 。	ngáw bẹng·jáw

Call a doctor!
快啲叫醫生！ faai·dì giu yì·sàng

Call the police!
快啲叫警察！ faai·dì giu gíng·chaat

Where are the toilets?
廁所喺邊度？ chi·sáw hái bìn·dọ

I'm allergic to ...
我對……過敏 。 ngáw deui ... gaw·mán

Shopping & Services

I'd like to buy ...
我想買…… ngáw séung máai ...

I'm just looking.
睇下 。 tái hạa

Can I look at it?
我可唔可以睇下？ ngáw háw·ǹg·háw·yí tái hạa

How much is it?
幾多錢？ gáy·dàw chín

That's too expensive.
太貴啦 。 taai gwai laa

Can you lower the price?
可唔可以平啲呀？ háw·ǹg·háw·yí pèng dì aa

There's a mistake in the bill.
帳單錯咗 。 jeung·dàan chaw jáw

Question Words

How?	點樣？	dím·yéung
What?	乜嘢？	màt·yé
When?	幾時？	gáy·sị̀
Where?	邊度？	bìn·dọ
Who?	邊個？	bìnz·gaw
Why?	點解？	dím·gáai

ATM	自動 提款機	jị·dụng tài·fún·gày
credit card	信用卡	seun·yụng·kàat
internet cafe	網吧	máwng·bàa
post office	郵局	yàu·gúk
tourist office	旅行社	léui·hàng·sé

Time & Dates

What time is it?	而家 幾點鐘？	yì·gàa gáy·dím·jùng
It's (10) o'clock.	(十)點鐘 。	(sạp)·dím·jùng
Half past (10).	(十)點半 。	(sạp)·dím bun

morning	朝早	jiù·jó
afternoon	下晝	hạa·jau
evening	夜晚	ye·máan
yesterday	寢日	kàm·yạt
today	今日	gàm·yạt
tomorrow	听日	tìng·yạt

Monday	星期一	sìng·kạy·yàt
Tuesday	星期二	sìng·kạy·yi
Wednesday	星期三	sìng·kạy·sàam
Thursday	星期四	sìng·kạy·say
Friday	星期五	sìng·kạy·ńg
Saturday	星期六	sìng·kạy·lụk
Sunday	星期日	sìng·kạy·yạt

January	一月	yàt·yẹwt
February	二月	yi·yẹwt
March	三月	sàam·yẹwt
April	四月	say·yẹwt
May	五月	ńg·yẹwt
June	六月	lụk·yẹwt
July	七月	chàt·yẹwt
August	八月	baat·yẹwt
September	九月	gáu·yẹwt
October	十月	sạp·yẹwt
November	十一月	sạp·yàt·yẹwt
December	十二月	sạp·yi·yẹwt

Transport

Public Transport

boat	船	sèwn
bus	巴士	bàa·sí
plane	飛機	fày·gày

Numbers

1	一	yàt
2	二	yi
3	三	sàam
4	四	say
5	五	ńg
6	六	luk
7	七	chàt
8	八	baat
9	九	gáu
10	十	sap
20	二十	yi·sap
30	三十	sàam·sap
40	四十	say·sap
50	五十	ńg·sap
60	六十	luk·sap
70	七十	chàt·sap
80	八十	baat·sap
90	九十	gáu·sap
100	一百	yàt·baak
1000	一千	yàt·chìn

taxi	的士	dìk·sí
train	火車	fáw·chè
tram	電車	din·chè

When's the ... (bus)?	……(巴士) 幾點開?	... (bàa·sí) gáy dím hòy
first	頭班	tàu·bàan
last	尾班	máy·bàan
next	下一班	haa·yàt·bàan

A ... ticket to (Panyu).	一張去 (番禺)嘅 ……飛。	yàt jèung heui (pùn·yèw) ge ... fày
1st-class	頭等	tàu·dáng
2nd-class	二等	yi·dáng
one-way	單程	dàan·chìng
return	雙程	sèung·chìng

What time does it leave?
幾點鐘出發? gáy·dím jùng chèut·faa

Does it stop at ...?
會唔會喺 ……停呀? wuí·ńg·wuí hái ... tìng aa

What time does it get to ...?
幾點鐘到……? gáy·dím jùng do ...

What's the next stop?
下個站 叫乜名? haa·gaw jaam giu màt méng

I'd like to get off at ...
我要喺…… 落車。 ngáw yiu hái ... lawk·chè

Please tell me when we get to ...
到……嘅時候, 唔該叫聲我。 do ... ge si·hau ng·gòy giu sèng ngáw

Please stop here.
唔該落車。 ng·gòy lawk·chè

aisle	路邊	lo·bìn
cancelled	取消	chéui·siù
delayed	押後	ngaat·hau
platform	月台	yéwt·tòy
ticket window	售票處	sau·piu·chew
timetable	時間表	si·gaan·biú
train station	火車站	fó·chè·jaam
window	窗口	chèung·háu

Driving & Cycling

I'd like to hire a ...	我想租 架……	ngáw séung jò gaa ...
4WD	4WD	fàw·wiù·jàai·fù
bicycle	單車	dàan·chè
car	車	chè
motorcycle	電單車	din·dàan·chè

baby seat	BB座	bi·bì jaw
diesel	柴油	chàai·yàu
helmet	頭盔	tàu·kwài
mechanic	修車師傅	sàu·chè si·fú
petrol	汽油	hay·yàu
service station	加油站	gàa·yàu·jàam

Is this the road to ...?
呢條路係唔係去 ……㗎? lày tiu lo hai·ng·hai heui ... gaa

Can I park here?
呢度泊唔泊得 車㗎? lày·do paak·ng·paak·dàk chè gaa

How long can I park here?
我喺呢度可以 停幾耐? ngáw hái lày·do háw·yí tìng gáy·loy

Where's the bicycle parking lot?
喺邊度停單車? háy·bìn·do tìng dàan·chè

The car/motorbike has broken down at ...
架車/電單車 係……壞咗。 gaa chè/din·dàan·chè hái ... waai jáw

I have a flat tyre.
我爆咗肽。 ngáw baau·jáw tàai

I've run out of petrol.
我冇晒油。 ngáw mó saai yáu

I'd like my bicycle repaired.
我想修呢架車。 ngáw séung sàu lày gaa chè

GLOSSARY

arhat – Buddhist disciple freed from the cycle of birth and death

bodhisattva – Buddhist striving towards enlightenment

cha chaan tang – local tea cafe serving Western-style beverages and snacks and/or Chinese dishes

cheongsam – a fashionable, tight-fitting Chinese dress with a slit up the side (*qípáo* in Mandarin)

dai pai dong – open-air eating stall, especially popular at night, but fast disappearing in Hong Kong

dim sum – literally 'touch the heart'; a Cantonese meal of various tidbits eaten as breakfast, brunch or lunch and offered from wheeled steam carts in restaurants; see also yum cha

dragon boat – long, narrow skiff in the shape of a dragon, used in races during the Dragon Boat Festival

feng shui – Mandarin spelling for the Cantonese *fung sui* meaning 'wind water'; the Chinese art of geomancy that manipulates or judges the environment to produce good fortune

Hakka – a Chinese ethnic group who speak a different Chinese language than the Cantonese; some Hakka people still lead traditional lives as farmers in the New Territories

hell money – fake-currency money burned as an offering to the spirits of the departed

HKTB – Hong Kong Tourism Board

junk – originally Chinese fishing boats or war vessels with square sails; diesel-powered, wooden pleasure yachts, which can be seen on Victoria Harbour

kaido – small- to medium-sized ferry that makes short runs on the open sea, usually used for nonscheduled services between small islands and fishing villages; sometimes spelled kaito

kung fu – the basis of many Asian martial arts

mah-jong – popular Chinese game played among four persons using tiles engraved with Chinese characters

MTR – Mass Transit Railway

nullah – uniquely Hong Kong word referring to a gutter or drain and occasionally used in place names

Punti – the first Cantonese-speaking settlers in Hong Kong

sampan – motorised launch that can only accommodate a few people and is too small to go on the open sea; mainly used for interharbour transport

SAR – Special Administrative Region of China; both Hong Kong and Macau are now SARs

SARS – Severe Acute Respiratory Syndrome

si yau sai chaan – 'soy sauce Western'; a cuisine that emerged in the 1950s featuring Western dishes of various origins prepared in a Chinese style

taichi – slow-motion shadow-boxing and form of exercise; also spelt tai chi or t'ai chi

tai tai – any married woman but especially the leisured wife of a businessman

Tanka – Chinese ethnic group that traditionally lives on boats

Triad – Chinese secret society originally founded as patriotic associations to protect Chinese culture from the influence of usurping Manchus, but today Hong Kong's equivalent of the Mafia

wan – bay

wet market – an outdoor market selling fruit, vegetables, fish and meat

yum cha – literally 'drink tea'; common Cantonese term for dim sum

MENU DECODER

Fish & Shellfish

baau·yew	鮑魚	abalone
daai·haa	大蝦	prawn
haa	蝦	shrimp
ho	蠔	oyster
lung haa	龍蝦	rock lobster
yau·yew	魷魚	squid
yew	魚	fish
yew chi	魚翅	shark's fin
yew daan	魚蛋	fish balls, usually made from pike

Meat & Poultry

gai	雞	chicken
jew sau	豬手	pork knuckle
jew·yuk	豬肉	pork
ngaap	鴨	duck
ngau yuk	牛肉	beef
ngaw	鵝	goose
paai guat	排骨	pork spareribs
yew jew	乳豬	suckling pig

Pastries

bo lo baau	菠蘿包	pineapple bun
gai mei baau	雞尾包	cocktail bun

Rice & Noodle Dishes

baak·faan	白飯	steamed white rice
chaau·faan	炒飯	fried rice
chaau·min	炒麵	fried noodles
faan	飯	rice
fan·si	粉絲	cellophane noodles or bean threads
haw·fan	河粉	wide, white, flat rice noodles that are usually pan-fried
juk	粥	congee
min	麵	noodles
sin·haa haa wan·tan	鮮蝦餛飩	wontons made with prawns
wan·tan min	餛飩麵	wonton noodle soup
yau·jaa·gwai	油炸鬼	'devils' tails'; dough rolled and fried in hot oil

Sauces

gaai laat	芥辣	hot mustard
ho yau	蠔油	oyster sauce
laat jiu jeung	辣椒醬	chilli sauce
si yau	豉油	soy sauce

Soups

aai yuk suk mai gang	蟹肉粟米羹	crab and sweet corn soup
baak·choy tawng	白菜湯	Chinese cabbage soup
daan faa·tawng	蛋花湯	'egg flower' (or drop) soup; light stock into which a raw egg is dropped
dung·gwaa tawng	冬瓜湯	winter-melon soup
wan·tan tawng	餛飩湯	wonton soup
yew·chi tawng	魚翅湯	shark's-fin soup
yin waw gang	燕窩羹	bird's-nest soup

Vegetarian Dishes

chun gewn	春卷	vegetarian spring rolls
gai lo may	雞滷味	mock chicken, barbecued pork or roast duck
gam gu sun jim	金菇筍尖	braised bamboo shoots and black mushrooms
law hon jaai	羅漢齋	braised mixed vegetables
law hon jaai yi min	羅漢齋伊麵	fried noodles with braised vegetables

Cantonese Dishes

baak cheuk haa	白灼蝦	poached prawns served with dipping sauces
chaa siu	叉燒	roast pork
ching chaau gaai laan	清炒芥蘭	stir-fried Chinese broccoli
ching jing yew	清蒸魚	whole steamed fish served with spring onions, ginger and soy sauce
geung chung chaau haai	薑蔥炒蟹	sautéed crab with ginger and spring onions
haai yuk paa dau miu	蟹肉扒豆苗	sautéed pea shoots with crab meat
ho yau choi sam	蠔油菜心	*choisum* with oyster sauce
ho yau ngau yuk	蠔油牛肉	deep-fried spare ribs served with coarse salt and pepper
jaa ji gai	炸子雞	crispy-skin chicken
jiu yim yau·yew	椒鹽魷魚	squid, dry-fried with salt and pepper
mui choi kau yuk	霉菜扣肉	twice-cooked pork with pickled cabbage
sai laan faa daai ji	西蘭花帶子	stir-fried broccoli with scallops
siu ngaap	燒鴨	roast duck
siu yew gaap	燒乳鴿	roast pigeon
siu yew jew	燒乳豬	roast suckling pig
yìm guk gai	鹽焗雞	salt-baked chicken, Hakka-style

Dim Sum

chaa siu baau	叉燒包	steamed barbecued-pork buns
cheung fan	腸粉	steamed rice-flour rolls with shrimp, beef or pork
ching chaau si choi	清炒時菜	fried green vegetable of the day
chiu·jau fan gwaw	潮州粉果	steamed dumpling with pork, peanuts and coriander
chun gewn	春卷	fried spring rolls
fan gwaw	粉果	steamed dumplings with shrimp and bamboo shoots
fu pay gewn	腐皮卷	crispy tofu rolls
fung jaau	鳳爪	fried chicken feet
haa gaau	蝦餃	steamed shrimp dumplings
law mai gai	糯米雞	sticky rice wrapped in a lotus leaf
paai gwat	排骨	small braised spare ribs with black beans
saan juk ngau yuk	山竹牛肉	steamed minced-beef balls
siu maai	燒賣	steamed pork and shrimp dumplings

Chiu Chow Dishes

bing faa gwun yin	冰花官燕	cold, sweet bird's-nest soup served as a dessert
chiu·jau lo seui ngaw	潮州滷水鵝	Chiu Chow braised goose
chiu·jau yew tong	潮州魚湯	aromatic fish soup
chiu·jau yi min	潮州伊麵	pan-fried egg noodles served with chives
dung jing haai	凍蒸蟹	cold steamed crab
jin ho beng	煎蠔餅	oyster omelette
sek lau gai	石榴雞	steamed egg-white pouches filled with minced chicken
tim·sewn hung·siu haa/ haai kau	甜酸紅燒蝦/蟹球	prawn or crab balls with sweet, sticky dipping sauce

Northern Dishes

bak·ging tin ngaap	北京填鴨	Peking duck
chong baau yeung yuk	蔥爆羊肉	sliced lamb with onions served on sizzling platter
gaau·ji	餃子	dumplings
gon chaau	乾炒牛肉絲	dried shredded beef with chilli sauce
ngau yuk si		
haau yeung·yuk	烤羊肉	roast lamb
sewn laat tong	酸辣湯	hot-and-sour soup with shredded pork (and sometimes congealed pig's blood)

Shanghainese Dishes

baat bo faan	八寶飯	steamed or pan-fried glutinous rice with 'eight treasures', eaten as a dessert
chong yau beng	蔥油餅	pan-fried spring onion cakes
chung·ji wong yew	松子黃魚	sweet-and-sour yellow croaker with pine nuts
daai jaap haai	大閘蟹	hairy crab (an autumn and winter dish)
fu gwai gai/ hat yi gai	富貴雞/ 乞丐雞	'beggar's chicken'; partially deboned chicken stuffed with pork, Chinese pickled cabbage, onions, mushrooms, ginger and other seasonings, wrapped in lotus leaves, sealed in wet clay or pastry and

		baked for several hours in hot ash
gon jin say gwai dau	乾煎四季豆	pan-fried spicy string beans
hung·siu si·ji·tau	紅燒獅子頭	Braised 'lion's head meatballs' – over sized pork meatballs
jeui gai	醉雞	drunken chicken
lung jeng haa jan	龍井蝦仁	shrimps with 'dragon-well' tea leaves
seung·hoi cho chaau	上海粗炒	fried Shànghǎi-style (thick) noodles with pork and cabbage
siu lung baau	小籠包	steamed minced-pork dumplings

Sichuan Dishes

ching jiu ngau yok si	青椒牛肉絲	sautéed shredded beef and green pepper
daam daam min	擔擔麵	noodles in savoury sauce
gong baau gai ding	宮爆雞丁	sautéed diced chicken and peanuts in sweet chilli sauce
jeung chaa haau ngaap	樟茶烤鴨	duck smoked in camphor wood
maa ngai seung sew	螞蟻上樹	'ants climbing trees'; cellophane noodles braised with seasoned minced pork
maa paw dau fu	麻婆豆腐	stewed tofu with minced pork and chilli
say·chewn ming haa	四川明蝦	Sichuan chilli prawns
wui gwaw yuk	回鍋肉	slices of braised pork with chillies
yew heung ke ji	魚香茄子	sautéed eggplant in a savoury, spicy sauce

Behind the Scenes

SEND US YOUR FEEDBACK

We love to hear from travellers – your comments keep us on our toes and help make our books better. Our well-travelled team reads every word on what you loved or loathed about this book. Although we cannot reply individually to postal submissions, we always guarantee that your feedback goes straight to the appropriate authors, in time for the next edition. Each person who sends us information is thanked in the next edition – the most useful submissions are rewarded with a selection of digital PDF chapters.

Visit **lonelyplanet.com/contact** to submit your updates and suggestions or to ask for help. Our award-winning website also features inspirational travel stories, news and discussions.

Note: We may edit, reproduce and incorporate your comments in Lonely Planet products such as guidebooks, websites and digital products, so let us know if you don't want your comments reproduced or your name acknowledged. For a copy of our privacy policy visit lonelyplanet.com/privacy.

OUR READERS

Many thanks to the travellers who used the last edition and wrote to us with helpful hints, useful advice and interesting anecdotes:

Ian Boyce, Kevin Burgess, Astrid Chan, Leslie Chiand, Rupert Cox, Anne & Philippe Croquet-Zouridakis, Dirk Dillinger, Nancy Engelaberg, Monica Fernandez, Mick Garton, Igor Golovko, Jana Green, Paul Gurn, David Harris, Adrian Ineichen, Diogenes Jesus, Renja Kinnunen, Ambrose Lee, Holger Lichau, Cecilia Litchfield, Ingeborg Moa, Delia Pereira, Eileen Synnott, Peter Tolman, Fransiska Weckesser.

AUTHOR THANKS

Piera Chen

Thanks to Ernesto Corpus, Yuen Ching-sum, Herman Lee, Teddy Lui, Janine Cheung and Madeleine Slavick for their generous assistance. A big thank you also to the kind souls from Macau and Guǎngzhōu, Venessa Cheah, Jeremy Chan, Luo Man Hua and Wen Zhaofang. To the angels and muses in my life, kisses. And to my husband Sze Pang-cheung, the deepest gratitude for his patience, understanding and wonderful support.

Chung Wah Chow

Massive thanks to Rebecca Kwok, Carol Leung, Lam Yee Yi, Wong Ka Man, Trey and Hera Menefee, and Tse Woon Cheung for their good company which made my research trips to the far-flung reaches of Hong Kong so much fun. Three cheers for Walter Ng and Mark Mak, for their encyclopedic knowledge of the New Territories. Big hugs to my soul mate and travel companion Haider Kikabhoy, for his sharp insights, love and bountiful support throughout.

ACKNOWLEDGMENTS

Cover photograph: Stanley Market, Hong Kong Island, Hong Kong; Huw Jones/Lonely Planet Images©.

THIS BOOK

This 15th edition of Lonely Planet's *Hong Kong* was researched and written by Piera Chen and Chung Wah Chow, both of whom wrote the previous edition along with Andrew Stone. This guidebook was commissioned in Lonely Planet's Melbourne office, and produced by the following:

Commissioning Editor Emily K Wolman

Coordinating Editors Kate Mathews, Erin Richards

Coordinating Cartographer Rachel Imeson

Coordinating Layout Designer Carol Jackson

Managing Editors Barbara Delissen, Brigitte Ellemor, Bruce Evans

Senior Editor Susan Paterson

Managing Cartographers Shahara Ahmed, Anita Banh, Mark Griffiths

Managing Layout Designer Chris Girdler

Assisting Editors Anne Mulvaney, Charlotte Orr, Helen Yeates

Assisting Cartographer Mick Garrett

Cover Research Naomi Parker

Internal Image Research Aude Vauconsant

Language Content Branislava Vladisavljevic

Thanks to Barbara Di Castro, Ryan Evans, Jane Hart, Anna Lorincz, Annelies Mertens, Kathleen Munnelly, Chung Charn Or, Trent Paton, Raphael Richards, Alison Ridgway, Gerard Walker

See also separate subindexes for:
EATING P354
DRINKING & NIGHTLIFE P356
ENTERTAINMENT P357
SHOPPING P357
SPORTS & ACTIVITIES P358
SLEEPING P358

Index

Sights 000
Map Pages **000**
Photo Pages **000**

INDEX EATING

Southorn Playground 108
spas 60
Splendid China (Shēnzhèn) 219
sports 57-61
St Andrew's Anglican Church 144
St John's Cathedral 71
St Joseph's Seminary Church (Macau) 239
St Lazarus Church District (Macau) 242
St Stephen's Beach 131
St Stephen's College's Heritage Trail 130
Stanley **377**
 food 133
 sights 130-1
Stanley Military Cemetery 130
Star Ferry 7, 29, 69, 71, 321, **7**
Statue Square 70
street art 298
Street of Happiness (Macau) 242
Sun Yat Sen Memorial House (Macau) 246
supermarkets 38-9
swords 254

T
Tai Fu Tai Mansion 174
Tai Fung Tong Art House (Macau) 242
Tai Hang 112
Tai Long Wan 186-7
Tai Long Wan Hiking Trail 186-7
Tai Miu Temple 190
Tai Mo Shan 169
Tai O 202-3
Tai Ping Shan Street 87
Tai Po 174-7, **176**
Tai Po Kau Nature Reserve 181
Tai Po Market 175
Taipa 254-260, **255**
 accommodation 262
 drinking & nightlife 258-9
 entertainment 259
 food 257-8
 sights 255-7
 sports & activities 259
 transport 254

Sights 000
Map Pages **000**
Photo Pages **000**

Taipa House Museum (Macau) 255
Taipa Racetrack (Macau) 259
Taipa Village (Macau) 255
Tam Kong Temple (Macau) 257
Tam Shui Hang Village 175
Tamar Park 107
Taoism 149
Tap Mun Chau 186
Tap Seac Square (Macau) 242-3
taxes 333
taxis 322
 fare structure 317, 322
 Macau 327
tea cafes 44, **31**
telephone services 18, 334
 Macau 338
Temple of the Six Banyan Trees (Guǎngzhōu) 224
Temple Street Night Market 10, 139, **10**
temples & shrines, see also individual temples
 Aberdeen 129-30
 Stanley 131
theatre 48, 50, 300-1
Tian Hou Temple (Macau) 257
Tian Tan Buddha 12, 193, **13, 206**
Tiān'ānmén Square 289-90
Tiānhé Computer Markets (Guǎngzhōu) 231
time 18, 334
Tin Hau 191
Tin Hau Temple 111, 146, 213
tipping 332
toilets 334
tourist information 18, 334-5
 Macau 338
tours 323-4
traditional culture 24
train travel
 to/from Hong Kong 318
 within Hong Kong 319
tram travel 12, 29, 321-2
Trappist Monastery 204-5
travel agencies 335
travel to/from Hong Kong 19, 316-18
travel to/from Macau 325-6
travel within Hong Kong 19, 319-23
travel within Macau 326-7
Triads 286, 310

Tsim Sha Tsui **138, 378**
 accommodation 277
 drinking & nightlife 157-8
 food 149-54
 shopping 159-60
 sights 142-6
 walks 145, **145**
Tsim Sha Tsui East Promenade 14, 138, **14, 152**
Tsing Ma Bridge 156
Tsing Shan Monastery 170
Tsing Yi 156
Tsuen Wan 167-9, **168**
Tsui Sing Lau 166
Tuen Mun 169-71
Tung Chung 205-8
Tung Lung Chau 214
Tung O Wan 197
Tung Wan Beach 211, **207**

U
ultimate frisbee 60
University Museum & Art Gallery 87
University of Hong Kong 87
Upper Cheung Sha 204

V
Victoria Park 109
Victoria Peak 7, 64-5, 84, **7**
views 22
visas 18, 318, 335-6
 Macau 338

W
wakeboarding 60
walks
 Central 73, **73**
 Kowloon 148, **148**
 pub crawl 100, **100**
 Tsim Sha Tsui 145, **145**
 Wan Chai 110, **110**
 wholesale district 88, **88**
walled villages 16, **16**
Wan Chai 65, 104-26, **372**
 accommodation 269
 dining 9
 drinking & nightlife 105, 121-2
 food 105, 114-16
 highlights 104-5
 markets 125, **119**
 shopping 105
 sights 107-9
 transport 105
 walks 110, **110**
weather 19, 25-7

websites 18, 40, 264
 Macau 338
Western Districts
 drinking & nightlife 98-9
 food 92-6
 sights 87
Western Market 86
Western Monastery 167
Whampoa Military Academy (Guǎngzhōu) 225
Wholesale Fruit Market 146
Window of the World (Shēnzhèn) 219
windsurfing 60
women travellers 335
Wong Shek 186-7
World Wide House 72

X
Xīnhài Revolution Museum (Guǎngzhōu) 225

Y
Yau Ma Tei **382**
 drinking & nightlife 158
 food 154-5
 shopping 160-2
 sights 146
Yau Ma Tei Theatre 17, 146
yoga 58
Yuen Long 171-3
Yuen Po Street Bird Garden & Flower Market 147, **152**
Yuen Yuen Institute 167, **179**
Yuèxiù Park (Guǎngzhōu) 224
Yung Shue Wan 195, **207**

 EATING
家嫂 151

A
A Lorcha (Macau) 248
A Petisqueira (Macau) 258
Aberdeen Fish Market Canteen 132
Al Molo 151
Alfonso III (Macau) 248
Ali Oli Bakery Cafe 189
Amber 75
AMMO 114
António (Macau) 258
Ap Lei Chau Market Cooked Food Centre 132
Assaf 92

Sights 000
Map Pages 000
Photo Pages **000**

🏃 **SPORTS & ACTIVITIES**

🛏 **SLEEPING**

Hong Kong Maps

Map Legend

Sights
- Beach
- Buddhist
- Castle
- Christian
- Hindu
- Islamic
- Jewish
- Monument
- Museum/Gallery
- Ruin
- Winery/Vineyard
- Zoo
- Other Sight

Eating
- Eating

Drinking & Nightlife
- Drinking & Nightlife
- Cafe

Entertainment
- Entertainment

Shopping
- Shopping

Sleeping
- Sleeping
- Camping

Sports & Activities
- Diving/Snorkelling
- Canoeing/Kayaking
- Skiing
- Surfing
- Swimming/Pool
- Walking
- Windsurfing
- Other Sports & Activities

Information
- Post Office
- Tourist Information

Transport
- Airport
- Border Crossing
- Bus
- Cable Car/Funicular
- Cycling
- Ferry
- Monorail
- Parking
- S-Bahn
- Taxi
- Train/Railway
- Tram
- Tube Station
- U-Bahn
- Underground Train Station
- Other Transport

Routes
- Tollway
- Freeway
- Primary
- Secondary
- Tertiary
- Lane
- Unsealed Road
- Plaza/Mall
- Steps
- Tunnel
- Pedestrian Overpass
- Walking Tour
- Walking Tour Detour
- Path

Boundaries
- International
- State/Province
- Disputed
- Regional/Suburb
- Marine Park
- Cliff
- Wall

Geographic
- Hut/Shelter
- Lighthouse
- Lookout
- Mountain/Volcano
- Oasis
- Park
- Pass
- Picnic Area
- Waterfall

Hydrography
- River/Creek
- Intermittent River
- Swamp/Mangrove
- Reef
- Canal
- Water
- Dry/Salt/Intermittent Lake
- Glacier

Areas
- Beach/Desert
- Cemetery (Christian)
- Cemetery (Other)
- Park/Forest
- Sportsground
- Sight (Building)
- Top Sight (Building)

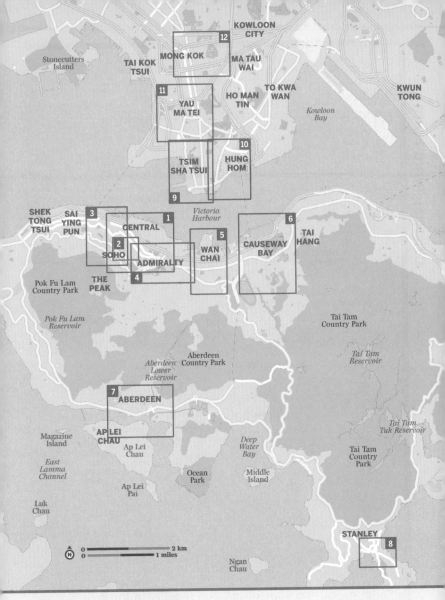

MAP INDEX

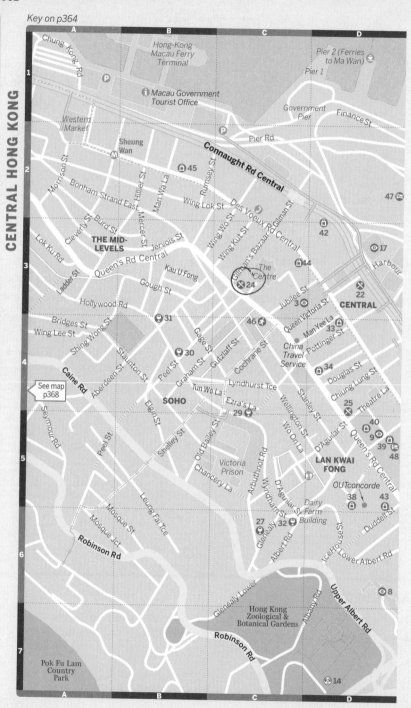

CENTRAL HONG KONG

Chung Kong Rd

Hong-Kong Macau Ferry Terminal

ⓘ Macau Government Tourist Office

Pier 2 (Ferries to Ma Wan)
Pier 1

Government Pier
Finance St

Western Market

Sheung Wan

45

Pier Rd

Connaught Rd Central

47

Morrison St

Bonham Strand East

Hillier St
Man Wa La

Mercer St

Rumsey St
Wing Lok St

Des Voeux Rd Central

Gilman St

42

Lok Ku Rd

Cleverly St

Burd St

Jervois St

Wing Wo St
Wing Kut St

Gilman's Bazaar

44

17

Harbour

THE MID-LEVELS

Queen's Rd Central

Kau U Fong

The Centre

24

Ladder St

Gough St

Jubilee St

22

CENTRAL

Bridges St

Hollywood Rd

31

Queen Victoria St

3

Man Yee La
33

Wing Lee St

Shing Wong St

46

China Travel Service

Pottinger St

34

Staunton St

Peel St

Gage St
Gutzlaff St

Cochrane St

Douglas St

Chiung Lung St

Theatre La

See map p368

Caine Rd

Aberdeen St

Graham St

Lyndhurst Tce

Stanley St

Wellington St

25

40

Elgin St

SOHO

Tun Wo La

Ezra's La

Wo On La

9
39

Seymour Rd

Peel St

Shelley St

Old Bailey St

29

D'Aguilar St

Queen's Rd Central

48

Chancery La

Victoria Prison

Arbuthnot Rd

LAN KWAI FONG

Mosque St

Leung Fai Tce

Wyndham St

D'Aguilar St

OUTconcorde

38

43

Duddell St

Mosque Jct

Robinson Rd

27
32

Glenealy

Albert Rd

Dairy Farm Building

Ice House St

Lower Albert Rd

Glenealy Lower

Hong Kong Zoological & Botanical Gardens

Albany Rd

Upper Albert Rd

8

Pok Fu Lam Country Park

Robinson Rd

14

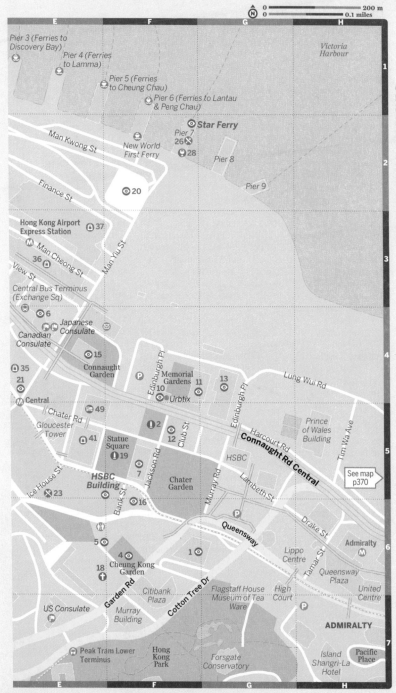

Pier 3 (Ferries to Discovery Bay)

Pier 4 (Ferries to Lamma)

Pier 5 (Ferries to Cheung Chau)

Pier 6 (Ferries to Lantau & Peng Chau)

Victoria Harbour

Man Kwong St

New World First Ferry

Star Ferry

Pier 7
26
28

Pier 8

Pier 9

Finance St

20

Hong Kong Airport Express Station

Man Cheong St

View St

Man Yiu St

Central Bus Terminus (Exchange Sq)

37

36

6

Japanese Consulate

Canadian Consulate

15

Connaught Garden

35

21

Central

Chater Rd

Gloucester Tower

49

Edinburgh Pl

Memorial Gardens

10

Urbtix

11

13

Lung Wui Rd

Harcourt Rd

Prince of Wales Building

Tim Wa Ave

41

Statue Square

19

2

12

Club St

Connaught Rd Central

HSBC

See map p370

Ice House St

23

HSBC Building

5

Bank St

Jackson Rd

7

16

Chater Garden

Murray Rd

Lambeth St

Drake St

Admiralty

Queensway

4

Cheung Kong Garden

18

1

Lippo Centre

Tamar St

Queensway Plaza

United Centre

US Consulate

Garden Rd

Citibank Plaza

Murray Building

Cotton Tree Dr

Flagstaff House Museum of Tea Ware

High Court

ADMIRALTY

Peak Tram Lower Terminus

Hong Kong Park

Forsgate Conservatory

Island Shangri-La Hotel

Pacific Place

0   200 m
0   0.1 miles

CENTRAL HONG KONG

CENTRAL HONG KONG *Map on p362*

LAN KWAI FONG & SOHO *Map on p366*

Key on p365

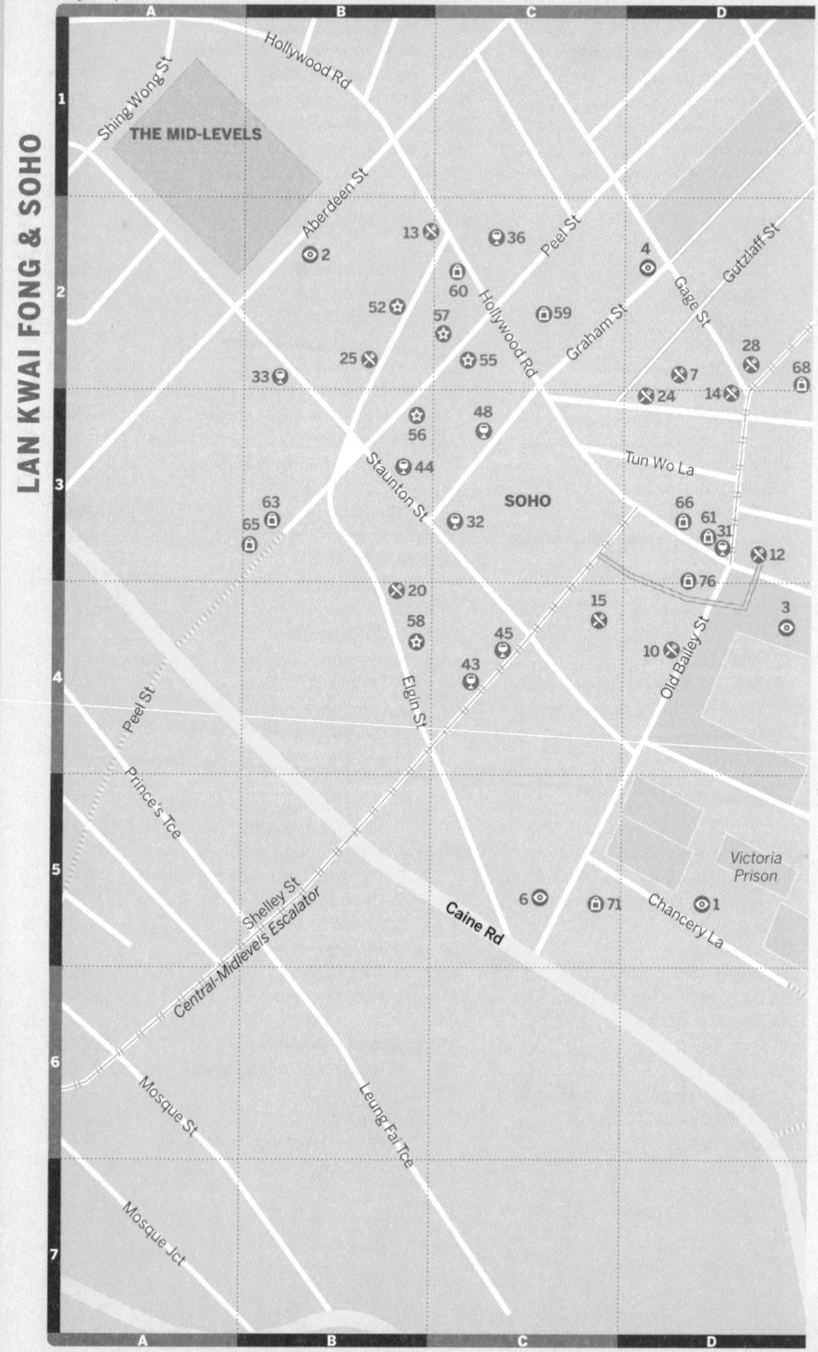

LAN KWAI FONG & SOHO

THE MID-LEVELS

Shing Wong St

Hollywood Rd

Aberdeen St

13

36

2

Peel St

52

57

60

Hollywood Rd

59

4

Graham St

Gage St

Gutzlaff St

25

55

33

7

28

68

24

14

48

56

44

Staunton St

SOHO

66

61

31

Tun Wo La

63

65

32

76

12

3

20

58

15

45

10

43

Elgin St

Old Bailey St

Peel St

Prince's Tce

Shelley St

Central-Mid-levels Escalator

Caine Rd

6

71

Chancery La

1

Victoria
Prison

Mosque St

Leung Fai Tce

Mosque Jct

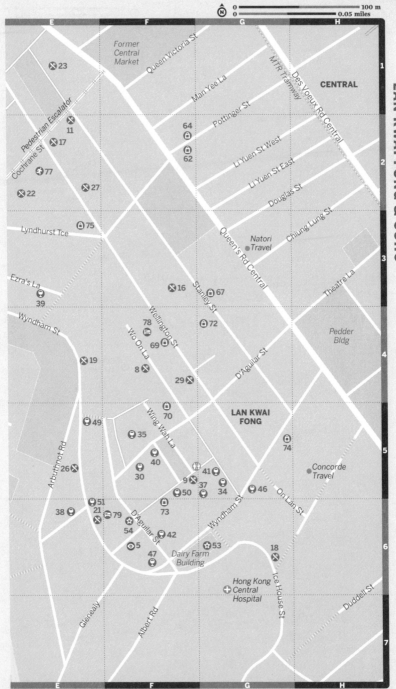

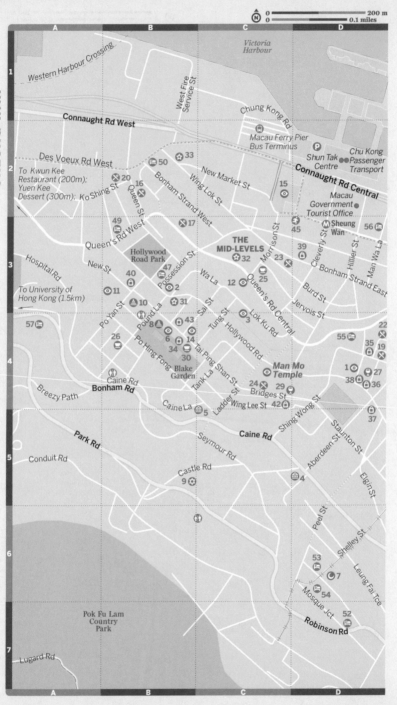

SHEUNG WAN

◉ Macau Ferry Pier

Hong Kong-
Macau Ferry
Terminal

Pier Rd Ⓟ

Ⓐ 44

Des Voeux Rd Central

Wing Lok St

18 ✖

Wing Wo St

Wing Kut St

Wellington St

51 ✖
21 ✖
Ⓐ 41

Gage St

Peel St
Gutzlaff St
Cochrane St

48 ⬤

Lyndhurst Tce

SOHO

See map p366

Old Bailey St

Chancery La

Caine Rd

Gilman's Bazaar

28 ⬤

Victoria Prison

✟ 13

⬤ 46

Glenealy Lower

E

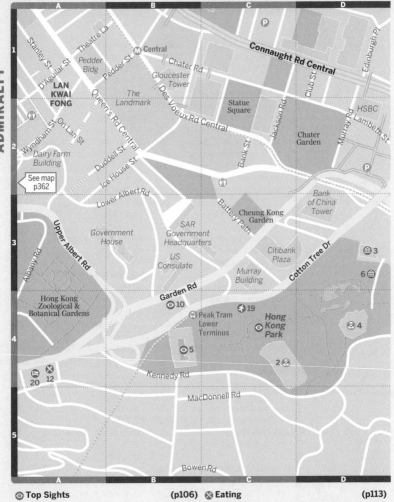

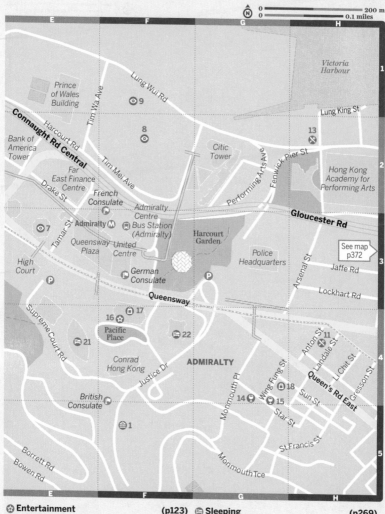

WAN CHAI

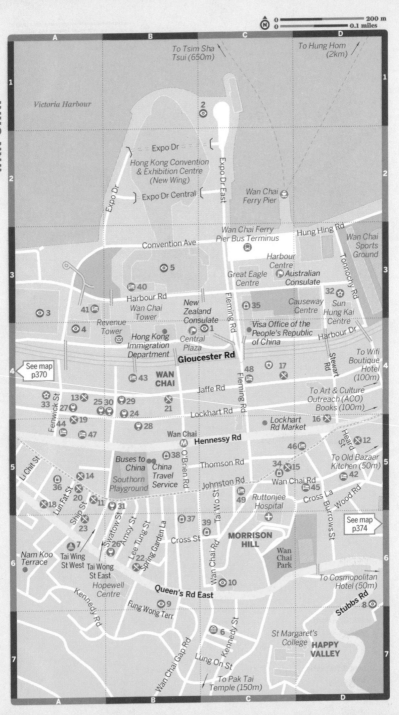

0   200 m
0   0.1 miles

A

Victoria Harbour

Expo Dr

Hong Kong Convention & Exhibition Centre (New Wing)

Expo Dr Central

Expo Dr East

2

Wan Chai Ferry Pier

Convention Ave

Wan Chai Ferry Pier Bus Terminus

Hung Hing Rd

Wan Chai Sports Ground

Tonnochy Rd

Harbour Centre

Great Eagle Centre

Australian Consulate

5

40

Harbour Rd

Wan Chai Tower

New Zealand Consulate

Fleming Rd

Causeway Centre

32 Sun Hung Kai Centre

41

3

Revenue Tower

4

Hong Kong Immigration Department

Central Plaza

1

Visa Office of the People's Republic of China

35

Harbour Dr

Stewart Rd

To Wifi Boutique Hotel (100m)

See map p370

43

WAN CHAI

Gloucester Rd

Jaffe Rd

Fleming Rd

48

17

To Art & Culture Outreach (ACO) Books (100m)

33 27

13

25 30

29

Lockhart Rd

16

Heard St

12

Fenwick St

44 19

47

24

21

28

Wan Chai

Hennessy Rd

Lockhart Rd Market

46

To Old Bazaar Kitchen (50m)

42

Li Chit St

36

14

Buses to China

China Travel Service

38

O'Brien Rd

Thomson Rd

34 15

Wan Chai Rd

45

Cross La

Heard St

Wood Rd

Lun Fat St

18

20

23

11

31

Southorn Playground

Ship St

Swatow St

Amoy St

Lee Tung St

Johnston Rd

49

Ruttonjee Hospital

Tai Wo St

Wan Chai Rd

See map p374

Nam Koo Terrace

7

Tai Wing St West

26

22

Spring Garden La

37

39

Cross St

MORRISON HILL

Wan Chai Park

To Cosmopolitan Hotel (50m)

Tai Wong St East

Hopewell Centre

Kennedy Rd

Fung Wong Terr

9

Queen's Rd East

10

Stubbs Rd

8

Burrows St

Wan Chai Gap Rd

6

Kennedy St

Lung On St

To Pak Tai Temple (150m)

St Margaret's College

HAPPY VALLEY

WAN CHAI

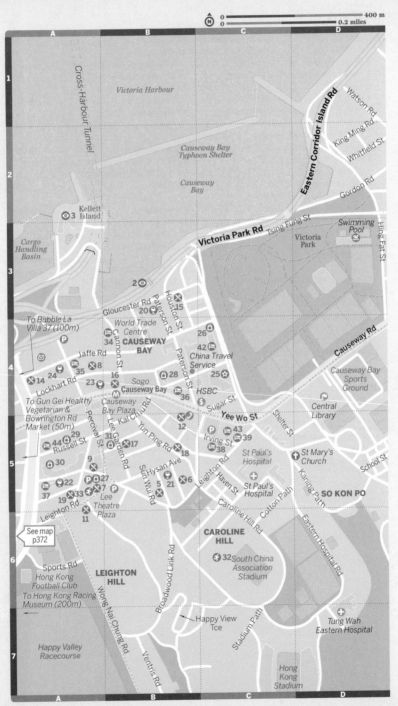

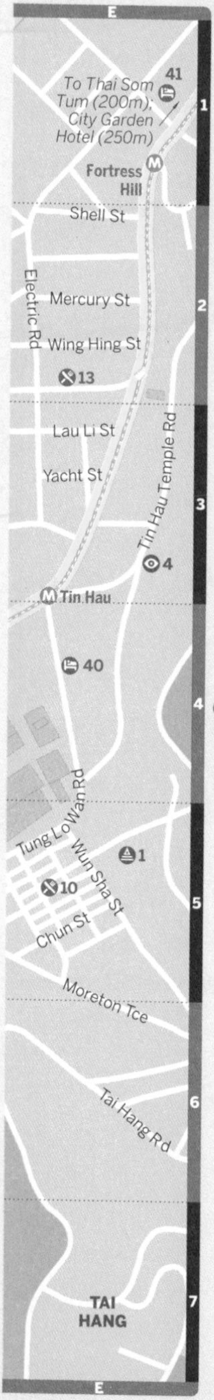

E
To Thai Som Tum (200m); City Garden Hotel (250m)
41
Fortress Hill
Shell St
Electric Rd
Mercury St
Wing Hing St
13
Lau Li St
Yacht St
Tin Hau Temple Rd
4
Tin Hau
40
Tung Lo Wan Rd
Wun Sha St
1
10
Chun St
Moreton Tce
Tai Hang Rd
TAI HANG
1
2
3
4
5
6
7
E

Sights (p109)

1 Lin Fa Temple........................E5
2 Noonday Gun........................B3
3 Royal Hong Kong Yacht Club..................................A2
4 Tin Hau Temple....................E3

Eating (p116)

5 Bella Vita...............................B5
Citysuper....................(see 30)
6 Farm House..........................B5
7 Fiat Caffe.............................A5
8 Forum...................................A4
9 Ho Hung Kee.........................A5
10 Hong Kee Congee Shop.......E5
11 IR 1968..................................A5
12 Iroha.....................................B5
Irori..............................(see 22)
13 Kin's Kitchen.........................E2
14 Manor Seafood Restaurant.........................A4
15 Pumpernickel.......................B3
16 Sushi Fuku-suke.................B4
17 Tai Ping Koon.......................B5
18 West Villa.............................B5
19 Yu..A5

Drinking & Nightlife (p122)

20 Dickens Bar..........................B3
21 East End Brewery & Inn Side Out...........................B5
22 Executive Bar.......................A5
Explode........................(see 12)
23 Oriental Sake Bar Yu-Zen....A4
24 Virus......................................A4

Entertainment (p123)

25 Windsor Cinema..................C4

Shopping (p123)

Citysuper....................(see 30)
26 D-Mop...................................C4
27 G.O.D.....................................A5
In Square....................(see 25)
28 Island Beverley....................B4
Lane Crawford...........(see 30)
29 Peoples' Recreation Community.......................A5
30 Times Square......................A5
31 Yiu Fung Store.....................B5

Sports & Activities (p126)

32 South China Athletic Association.......................C6
33 Towngas Cooking Centre....A5

Sleeping (p269)

34 Alisan Guest House.............B4
35 Causeway Corner................A4
36 Chung Kiu Inn.......................B4
37 Holiday Inn Express.............A5
38 J Plus....................................C5
39 Lanson Place.......................C5
40 Metropark Hotel..................E4
41 Newton Hotel Hong Kong.....E1
42 Park Lane Hong Kong..........C4
43 Regal Hongkong Hotel.........C5
44 Shama...................................A5

ABERDEEN

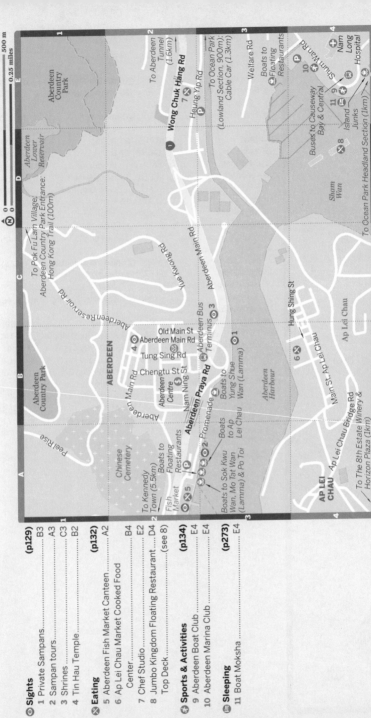

STANLEY

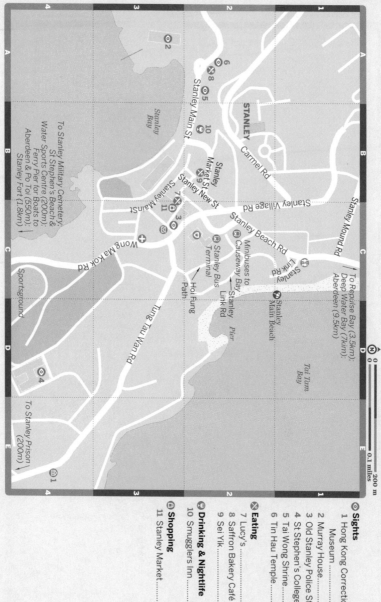

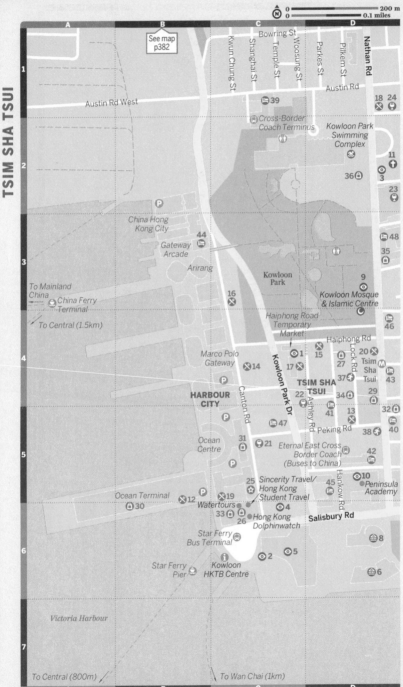

See map p382

0   200 m
0   0.1 miles

Bowring St
Kwun Chung St
Shanghai St
Temple St
Woosung St
Parkes St
Pilkem St
Nathan Rd

Austin Rd
Austin Rd West

39

Cross-Border
Coach Terminus

Kowloon Park
Swimming
Complex

18 24

11

36
3

23

48
35

China Hong
Kong City

44
Gateway
Arcade

Arirang

Kowloon
Park

9

To Mainland
China
China Ferry
Terminal

To Central (1.5km)

16

Kowloon Mosque
& Islamic Centre

46

Haiphong Road
Temporary
Market

Haiphong Rd

Marco Polo
Gateway

14

1
17
15

27
20

Lock Rd

Tsim
Sha
Tsui

37

HARBOUR
CITY

Canton Rd

Kowloon Park Dr

TSIM SHA
TSUI

22

34

43

29

47

Ashley Rd

41

13

32

38
40

Ocean
Centre

31
21

Eternal East Cross
Border Coach
(Buses to China)

42

25
Sincerity Travel/
Hong Kong
Student Travel

45

Hankow Rd

10
Peninsula
Academy

Ocean Terminal

12
30

19
Watertours
33
26

4

Hong Kong
Dolphinwatch

Salisbury Rd

Star Ferry
Bus Terminal

Star Ferry
Pier

Kowloon
HKTB Centre

2

5

8

6

Victoria Harbour

To Central (800m)

To Wan Chai (1km)

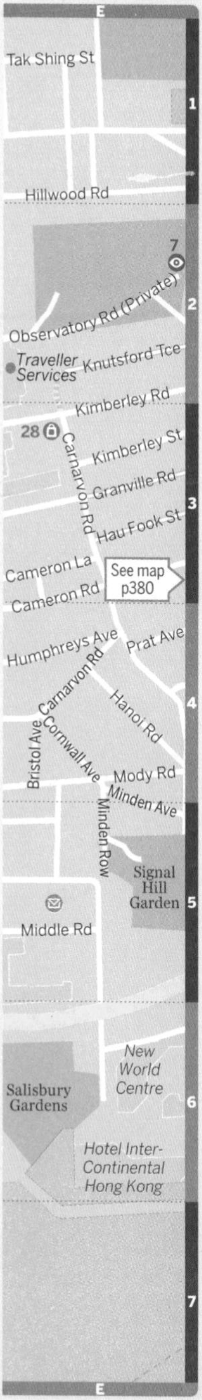
E
Tak Shing St
1
Hillwood Rd
7
2
Observatory Rd (Private)
Traveller Services
Knutsford Tce
Kimberley Rd
28
Carnarvon Rd
Kimberley St
Granville Rd
3
Hau Fook St
Cameron La
See map p380
Cameron Rd
Humphreys Ave
Prat Ave
Carnarvon Rd
Hanoi Rd
4
Bristol Ave
Cornwall Ave
Mody Rd
Minden Ave
Minden Row
Signal Hill Garden
5
Middle Rd
New World Centre
Salisbury Gardens
6
Hotel Inter-Continental Hong Kong
7
E

Sights (p142)

1 Fook Tak Ancient Temple C4
2 Former KCR Clock Tower C6
3 Former Kowloon British School D2
4 Former Marine Police Headquarters C6
Hong Kong Antiquities & Monuments Office ..... (see 3)
5 Hong Kong Cultural Centre C6
6 Hong Kong Museum of Art D6
7 Hong Kong Observatory E2
8 Hong Kong Space Museum & Theatre D6
9 Kung Fu Corner D3
10 Peninsula Hong Kong D5
11 St Andrew's Anglican Church D2

Eating (p149)

12 Al Molo B5
13 Branto D5
14 Din Tai Fung C4
Gaddi's ..... (see 10)
Golden Bull ..... (see 30)
15 Paramita Vegetarian House D4
Stables Grill ..... (see 4)
16 Sweet Dynasty C3
17 Tak Fat Beef Ball C4
T'ang Court ..... (see 47)
18 Typhoon Shelter Hing Kee Restaurant D1
19 Yé Shanghai C5
20 Ziafat D4

Drinking & Nightlife (p157)

21 Aqua Spirit C5
22 Ned Kelly's Last Stand C4
23 Pacific Coffee Company D2
24 Utopia D1
Vibes ..... (see 48)

Entertainment (p168)

25 Grand Ocean Cinema C5
Hong Kong Cultural Centre ..... (see 5)
The One Broadway Cinema ..... (see 35)
UA iSquare ..... (see 29)

Shopping (p159)

26 Chinese Arts & Crafts C6
27 Curio Alley D4
28 David Chan Photo Shop E3
I.T. ..... (see 14)
29 iSquare D4
30 Lane Crawford B6
31 Page One C5
32 Premier Jewellery D5
Star Computer City ..... (see 26)
33 Star House C6
34 Swindon Books D4
35 The One D3
Venilla Suite ..... (see 35)
36 Yue Hwa Chinese Products Emporium D2

Sports & Activities (p163)

37 Ocean Sky Divers D4
38 Wing Chun Yip Man Martial Arts Athletic Association D5

Sleeping (p273)

39 BP International Hotel C1
40 Chungking Mansions D5
Cosmic Guest House ..... (see 43)
Dragon Inn ..... (see 40)
Holiday Guesthouse ..... (see 40)
41 Hop Inn D5
42 Kowloon Hotel Hong Kong D5
Mei Lam Guesthouse ..... (see 43)
43 Mirador Mansion D4
New Yan Yan Guesthouse ..... (see 40)
Park Guesthouse ..... (see 40)
Peninsula Hong Kong ..... (see 10)
44 Royal Pacific Hotel & Towers B3
45 Salisbury D5
46 Sealand House D4
47 The Langham C5
48 The Mira D3
Yan Yan Guest House ..... (see 40)

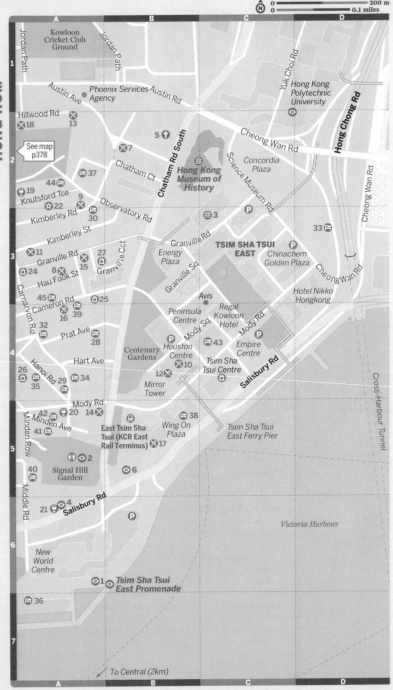

N
0 — 200 m
0 — 0.1 miles

Kowloon
Cricket Club
Ground

Jordan Path

Jordan Path

Austin Ave

Phoenix Services Austin Rd
Agency

Yuk Choi Rd

Hong Kong
Polytechnic
University

Hong Chong Rd

Hillwood Rd
18   13

See map
p378

7

5

Chatham Rd South

Cheong Wan Rd

Chatham Ct

37

Hong Kong
Museum of
History

Science Museum Rd

Concordia
Plaza

Cheong Wan Rd

44

19

Knutsford Tce

9

22

Kimberley Rd

30

Observatory Rd

3

TSIM SHA TSUI
EAST

Chinachem
Golden Plaza

33

Cheong Wan Rd

Kimberley St

Granville Rd

Energy
Plaza

Granville Sq

11

Granville Rd

27

24   8

15

Hau Fook St

Granville Ile Cct

Hotel Nikko
Hongkong

45

Cameron Rd

25

Avis

Peninsula
Centre

Regal
Kowloon
Hotel

Mody Rd

Carnarvon Rd

32

16   39

Prat Ave

28

Mody Sq

Empire
Centre

43

Salisbury Rd

Centenary
Gardens

Houston
Centre

10

Tsim Sha
Tsui Centre

Hart Ave

26

Hanoi Rd

29   34

35

12

Mirror
Tower

Mody Rd

42   20   14

Minden Ave

38

East Tsim Sha
Tsui (KCR East
Rail Terminus)

17

Wing On
Plaza

Tsim Sha Tsui
East Ferry Pier

Minden Row

41

40

Signal Hill
Garden

2

6

Middle Rd

21   4

Salisbury Rd

Cross-Harbour Tunnel

Victoria Harbour

New
World
Centre

1

Tsim Sha Tsui
East Promenade

36

To Central (2km)

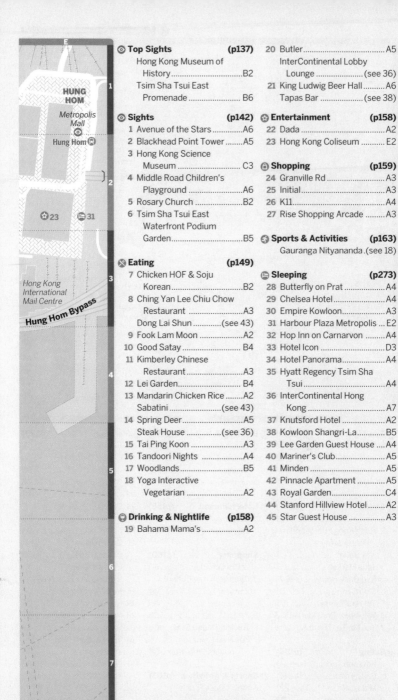

HUNG
HOM

*Metropolis
Mall*

Hung Hom

☼23   🚇31

*Hong Kong
International
Mail Centre*

Hung Hom Bypass

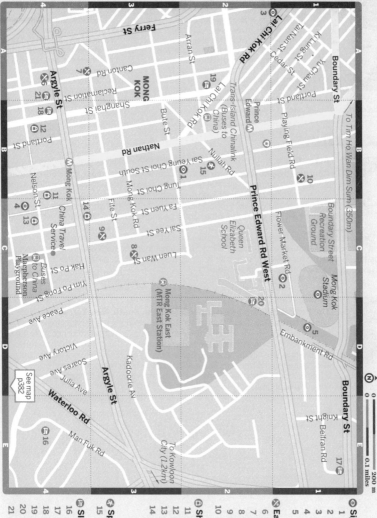

MONG KOK

To Tim Ho Wan Dim Sum (350m)

Our Story

A beat-up old car, a few dollars in the pocket and a sense of adventure. In 1972 that's all Tony and Maureen Wheeler needed for the trip of a lifetime – across Europe and Asia overland to Australia. It took several months, and at the end – broke but inspired – they sat at their kitchen table writing and stapling together their first travel guide, *Across Asia on the Cheap*. Within a week they'd sold 1500 copies. Lonely Planet was born.

Today, Lonely Planet has offices in Melbourne, London and Oakland, with more than 600 staff and writers. We share Tony's belief that 'a great guidebook should do three things: inform, educate and amuse'.

Our Writers

Piera Chen

Coordinating Author, Central, Wan Chai & the Northeast, Kowloon, Macau
Born to a Shanghainese father and a Pekingese mother in Hong Kong, Piera is a writer, editor and translator who divides her time between Hong Kong, Běijīng, Vancouver and various exotic holiday destinations, real and imagined. She is an avid traveller, a devoted mother and a passionate collector of life experiences. Piera coauthored the previous edition of this book, as well as Lonely Planet's *Hong Kong Encounter* and *China* guidebooks. While researching for this edition, one of her greatest joys was constantly challenging herself to see familiar landscapes with borrowed eyes. Besides the chapters listed above, she also wrote Macau's History & Culture and the Survival Guide, and cowrote the Plan Your Trip section.

Read more about Piera Chen at:
lonelyplanet.com/members/PieraChen

Chung Wah Chow

The Peak & the Northwest, Aberdeen & the South, New Territories, Outlying Islands, Day Trips Chung Wah enjoys exploring every nook and cranny both in her hometown of Hong Kong and elsewhere. With an advanced degree in translation studies, an insatiable travel lust and an affinity with obscure words and sounds, Chung Wah merged her talents by becoming a travel writer. She contributed to the previous two editions of this book and coauthored Lonely Planet's *China*. For this edition of *Hong Kong*, she also wrote the Understand chapters and cowrote the Plan Your Trip section.

Read more about Chung Wah Chow at:
lonelyplanet.com/members/cwchow

Published by Lonely Planet Publications Pty Ltd
ABN 36 005 607 983
15th edition – Jan 2013
ISBN 978 1 74179 850 0
© Lonely Planet 2013   Photographs © as indicated 2013
10 9 8 7 6 5 4 3 2 1
Printed in China

Although the authors and Lonely Planet have taken all reasonable care in preparing this book, we make no warranty about the accuracy or completeness of its content and, to the maximum extent permitted, disclaim all liability arising from its use.